JOHN MACKAY is one of Scotland's best known broadcasters. He is the face of the country's most watched news programme, the STV *News at Six,* and the current affairs programme *Scotland Tonight.* His career spans from the last days of the old newspaper era to the instant news of social media. MacKay was born in Glasgow, but his Hebridean heritage inspired him to write four successful novels, all based on the Isle of Lewis: *The Road Dance, Heartland, Last of the Line* and *Home.* An award-winning film adaptation of *The Road Dance* was released to critical acclaim in 2021.

By the same author

Fiction
The Road Dance, Luath Press, 2002
Heartland, Luath Press, 2004
Last of the Line, Luath Press, 2006
Home, Luath Press, 2021

Non-Fiction
Notes of a Newsman, Luath Press, 2015

Scotland Today... and Yesterday

Witness to a changing nation

JOHN MacKAY

Luath Press Limited
EDINBURGH
www.luath.co.uk

First published 2015
New updated and extended edition 2024

ISBN: 978-1-80425-189-8

The author's right to be identified as author
of this work under the Copyright, Designs
and Patents Act 1988 has been asserted.

Printed and bound by
CPI Antony Rowe Ltd., Chippenham

© John MacKay 2015, 2024

*For Jo, Kenny & Ross
who've heard it all before.*

Contents

Acknowledgements 13
Preface 15
Introduction 17

1986 19
Hercules the Bear
Women get legal right to claim housekeeping
Concerns over Chernobyl explosion
Gartcosh closure

1987 19
Barlinnie riot
General Election 1987
AIDS threat
Demolition of Apollo Theatre
Sunday opening of shops

1988 26
Orkney tales
Refugee concerns
Glasgow Garden Festival
Piper Alpha
Jim Sillars wins Govan by-election
David Murray buys Rangers
Lockerbie bombing

1989 35
NHS restructuring proposals
Bellgrove train crash
Annual Scotland England football rivalry under threat
Rangers sign first Catholic
House of Commons televised
Channel Tunnel concerns for Scotland

1990 40
Eastwood helicopter crash
Rangers invited to join European Super League
Ten die in plane crash on Harris
Neil Kinnock – Scottish Assembly free to raise taxes
Genetic fingerprinting
Offside rule changed

1991 43
First Gulf War
Downing Street mortar attack
Orkney child abuse allegations
Council Tax replaces Poll Tax
Newton rail crash

1992 46
Ravenscraig closure
General Election 1992
Scottish Super League
Changes to goalkeeper passback rules
Barcelona Olympics
ERM crisis

1993   52

Braer disaster

'Not Proven' campaign

Rangers in new Champions League

British football's most expensive signing

Nelson Mandela in Glasgow

1994   57

Celtic takeover by Fergus McCann

Frederick West's Scottish victims

John Smith's death

Trident submarines on the Clyde

Gordon Brown steps aside for Tony Blair

First T-in-the-Park

Girl Guide bus crash

National Lottery launch

Catholic Church sex abuse scandal

1995   63

Ecstasy deaths

M77 motorway

Local Government reorganisation

Death of Davie Cooper

Rising poverty

Skin cancer increasing

Braveheart premiere

Quebec Referendum

Big freeze

1996   69

Killer asbestos

Rising drug deaths

Dunblane

Last Polaris submarine

Greenock torture trial

Oasis at Loch Lomond

Labour propose referendum on devolution

Glasgow sick city of Europe

First commercial windfarm

E-coli outbreak

1997   81

General Election 1997

Conservative wipeout in Scotland

Death of Princess Diana

Devolution Referendum

Hamilton curfew

1998   91

Housing shortage

World Cup 1998

Edinburgh tram proposal

Scottish Six ruled out

1999   98

First Scottish Parliament election

Donald Dewar becomes Scotland's first First Minister

Opening of Scottish Parliament

Glasgow Airport crash

Scotland v England European Championship qualifiers

2000   105

Clause 28 row

Fuel crisis

Donald Dewar's death

Henry McLeish becomes First Minister

First Minister meets the Pope

Madonna's wedding

2001   113

Lockerbie Bomber conviction

Foot and Mouth outbreak

Resignation of First Minister Henry McLeish

Jack McConnell becomes First Minister

2002   117

Lockerbie Bomber's appeal

Champions League Final in Glasgow

French school bus crash

Firefighters' strike

Cowgate blaze

Catholic schools row

2003   122

Iraq War

Scottish Parliament elections 2003

Celtic in UEFA Cup Final

Holyrood building fiasco

2004   127

Rosepark Care Home fire

Alex Salmond returns as SNP leader

Holyrood Inquiry

Opening of new Scottish Parliament building

2005   131

Auschwitz anniversary

Make Poverty History march

G8 Summit at Gleneagles

Civil Partnerships

2006   136

Smoking ban

Bird Flu scare

East European immigration

2007   140

Scottish Parliament election 2007

Madeleine McCann disappears

Alex Salmond becomes First Minister

Gordon Brown becomes Prime Minister

Glasgow chosen to host Commonwealth Games

2008   147

Death Row Scot returns home

Rangers in UEFA Cup Final

Wendy Alexander resigns as Scottish Labour leader

Banking crisis

2009   150

RBS post worst losses in UK financial history

North Sea helicopter crash

Lockerbie Bomber freed

Peter Tobin sentenced to life

2010   154

General Election 2010

Coalition Government

Pope Benedict visits Scotland

Ed Miliband new Labour leader in UK Big Freeze

Tommy Sheridan convicted

2011   159

Scottish Parliament elections 2011

SNP majority Scottish Government

Launch of Scotland Tonight

Hurricane Bawbag

2012   165

Scottish Independence debate

Rangers go bust

Death of Lockerbie Bomber

Olympic Torch in Scotland

Andy Murray wins first Grand Slam

Olympic Homecoming parade

Kevin Bridges interview

Oscar Pistorius interview

Andy Murray interview

2013   177

Death of Margaret Thatcher

STV Independence debates

Andy Murray wins Wimbledon

Scottish Government white paper on Independence

Clutha tragedy

Death of Nelson Mandela

2014   186

Commonwealth Games in Glasgow

Scottish Independence Referendum

Johann Lamont resigns as Scottish Labour Leader

Nicola Sturgeon becomes First Minister

George Square tragedy

2015   214

General Election 2015

Conservative majority government

SNP landslide in Scotland

Death of Charles Kennedy

Debate on more powers for Scotland

2016   229

Work starts on two new ferries

Richard Gere interview

Scottish Election 2016

Brexit Vote

100th Anniversary of the Somme

Chilcot Inquiry

Andy Murray's second Wimbledon win

Theresa May wins Conservative Leadership

Theresa May becomes Prime Minister

Oil rig runs aground on Western Isles

Mark Millar interview

Donald Trump wins US Presidential Election

2017 238

Theresa May says, 'Now is not the time' for second Independence Referendum

Theresa May indicates a Hard Brexit

Inauguration of President Trump

David Tennant interview

First Minister rules out Independence Referendum in 2017

Scottish Parliament vote on second Independence Referendum

Prime Minister triggers Article 50 to withdraw from EU

Theresa May calls snap election for 8th June

Manchester Arena Bombing

General Election 2017

Opening of Queensferry Crossing

Kezia Dugdale resigns as Scottish Labour Leader

Kenny Dalglish interview

2018 252

Beast from the East

Michael Sheen interview

Archie Macpherson interview

Glasgow School of Art second fire

Donald Trump in Scotland

Runrig's last concert

Police investigate Alex Salmond

Kelly-Ann Woodland becomes co-presenter

Closure of Michelin tyre factory

Centenary of First World War Armistice

Theresa May's Brexit Deal

2019 259

Alex Salmond arrested and charged

Prime Minister Theresa May loses second 'Meaningful' vote on Brexit Deal

EU leaders agree to delay Brexit

Theresa May announces resignation

Danny MacAskill interview

Boris Johnson wins Conservative leadership contest

Boris Johnson becomes Prime Minister

Boris Johnson announces the proroguing of Parliament

Martina Navratilova interview

New Edinburgh children's hospital delayed

Court of Session rules proroguing of Parliament illegal

Man charged in 40-year-old Renee MacRae murder

Republican marches in Glasgow banned this weekend

Peter Howson interview

General Election 2019

2020   272

UK formally leaves the EU

First Covid case in Scotland

Billy Connolly

First Coronavirus death in Scotland

Alex Salmond trial

Prime Minister in intensive care

Aberdeen train crash

Announcement of vaccine

Agreement on Brexit Deal

2021   286

Death of the Duke of Edinburgh

Scottish Election 2021

Scotland's first game in an international tournament in 23 years

COP 26

2022   297

Russia invades Ukraine

Rangers in Europa League Final

Queen's Platinum Jubilee celebrations

Boris Johnson resigns

Liz Truss becomes Prime Minister

Death of Queen Elizabeth

Kwasi Kwarteng's mini-budget

Liz Truss resigns

Rishi Sunak becomes Prime Minister

UK Supreme Court rules against Independence Referendum

2023   311

Nicola Sturgeon resigns as First Minister

Nicola Sturgeon's final address to the Scottish Parliament

Humza Yousaf becomes new First Minister

King Charles III crowned

Nicola Sturgeon arrested

2024   323

UK Covid Inquiry in Scotland

Val McDermid interview

Humza Yousaf resigns as First Minister

John Swinney becomes SNP leader for a second time

Infected Blood Inquiry Report

Scotland in Euros 2024

General Election 2024

Death of Alex Salmond

Endnote   333

Acknowledgements

My thanks to:

Phil Taylor, Eddie Mair, Alison Walker, Dougie McGuire, Michael Crow, Sharon Frew, Howard Simpson, David Cowan, Mike Farrell, Pete Smith, Karen Greenshields and Ewan Petrie for their contributions.

Bernard Ponsonby, whose on-air analysis is such a key element of this history. Also, Colin Mackay who takes on that role later.

STV for the use of their archive.

Excerpts from BBC Scotland News, courtesy of the BBC.

Katie O'Donnell for providing transcripts of many interviews.

The STV Library team for delving into the recesses often and without complaint.

My many co-presenters, in particular Shereen Nanjiani, Raman Bhardwaj, Rona Dougall and Kelly-Ann Woodland for all that we have shared.

Too many colleagues past and present to thank individually.

www.euanandersonphotography.com for the author photo.

Particular thanks to Kenny MacKay and Stephen Townsend for their feedback.

Preface

It is ten years since the Scottish Independence Referendum. The anniversary of that result also marks 30 years since I joined STV News.

Scotland has changed dramatically over that time and yet much has remained the same. As a reporter and a news presenter, I have had the privilege of witnessing many of these changes at close hand.

Using contemporary reports, interview transcripts, personal diaries and recollections, this is the story of one of the most tumultuous periods in Scotland's peacetime history.

It is a re-edited and updated version of *Notes of a Newsman*, which was published in 2015. So much more has happened since then. In addition to the stories of the last ten years, I have uncovered more news archives to provide a fuller picture of the beginning of Scotland's transformation.

This book lays no claim to being the inside story. Quite the opposite. It is the story of a changing Scotland as it was heard and seen by the people at the time.

Introduction

As well as charting Scotland's story over the last four decades, this book reflects my developing career as a journalist. The stories covered in the first few years are not of national significance, but they are a glimpse of Scotland at that time. As my career moved on, so did the importance of the stories I reported. By the time of the creation of the Scottish Parliament I was presenting the STV News and most of the major stories are front and centre.

In the summer of 1986 I was preparing to go to London.

I didn't want to leave Scotland, but my ambition of working on the *Evening Times* in Glasgow would have to wait because they didn't take on trainees. Radio Clyde rejected me because they said I didn't have a voice for broadcasting.

My years as a paperboy, my £10 Letter of the Week to *SHOOT!* magazine, my degree, my editorship of the *Glasgow University Guardian* and wearing my trench coat to cold call at every paper I knew had all delivered nothing.

So, I was off to London and a postgraduate journalism course at City University. There is every chance that's where I would have remained. All roads led to London. I heard that then and I've heard it ever since.

Maybe it was the trench coat, I don't know, but *The Sunday Post* had seen something in me when I called and belatedly asked me back for an interview.

DC Thomson were good enough to give me a job as a trainee reporter and that was it. I was embarking on a career as a journalist in Scotland at the beginning of one of the most significant periods in the country's peacetime history.

1986

Thursday 31 July 1986

DIARY: I've got a job as a journalist! I went into *The Sunday Post* office in Port Dundas Road and the Glasgow Editor Robert Miller said, 'Well it looks like we've come to the end of the road and we're prepared to offer you a job as a trainee reporter at £90 a week.' I have my foot in the door and hopefully I'm embarking on an eventful and successful career.

The Sunday Post was a hugely popular newspaper with a circulation of around a million during the 1980s. It was a fascinating throwback to a different Scotland. Like a scene out of the old black and white movies, it was a place suited to a trench coat. There were wooden-framed telephone cubicles at the far end of the office for talking privately to contacts. One of the office girls would summon you if a call came in. It was a throwback in other ways. It was non-union, non-sensational and by-lines were rare, but DC Thomson had a deserved reputation for giving a start to young journalists and many familiar names in Scottish journalism got their first break there.

HERCULES THE BEAR

One of my early jobs was to meet Hercules the Bear. Everyone knew Hercules. He was the 'Big Softy' who starred in the popular Kleenex adverts. He lived with his owners Andy and Maggie Robin in a big house on the road to Perth. I can't recall what the story was, but Hercules was a star so that was reason enough. When I arrived there was no sign of him, but I seem to remember an ominously open cage. As I sat in the Robins' lovely lounge, he suddenly sauntered in paying me no mind. I paid him plenty. I didn't take my eyes off him as he padded around amiably. But Andy wanted me to see Hercules perform. This grizzly could act. He could wrestle. So, Andy started to playfully slap him. The bear pawed back, rearing up as he did so. Oh, but he was big. I mean really big. My student journalism had been limited mostly to the blathering of student politicians. This was the danger of front line reporting. From a lounge. In Perthshire. Wearing a trench coat. The truth is Hercules was so placid I think he'd have put a paw around my shoulder to show me out. He never got the chance. I was gone.

Sunday 31 August 1986
The Sunday Post

Some husbands may be in for a shock when the new Family Law (Scotland) Act 1985 comes into force tomorrow. For the first time, if a husband keeps his wife short on housekeeping, she can go to court and be awarded a fair amount. Previously, she'd have to leave him before she could get a court order. Children living at home can also take their parents to court for their keep. 'Revolutionary' is how some solicitors see the new laws.

Revolutionary indeed.

Sunday 14 September 1986

DIARY: Good feeling that the *Post*, the paper I've read for so long, had some of my work in it.

Some of my early *Sunday Post* stories.

A GHOST AT THE WEDDING IN LOCHBOISDALE

THREE CHEERS FOR THE FRIENDLY FIREMEN FROM STRANRAER

Sunday 5 October 1986
The Sunday Post

KIEV HERE WE COME

Celtic fans are already making plans to travel to Kiev to watch their team play – despite the Chernobyl threat. The city is only 65 miles away from the nuclear plant where there was a massive explosion earlier this year. Danny McCarron of the *Celtic View*, the club newspaper, insisted the club would not advise supporters to travel. 'Apart from the nuclear scare and the political situation, the difficulty in obtaining visas will discourage most people,' he said. A spokesman for the Scotland–USSR Society said, 'Official reports indicate the area is now safe.'

Celtic lost 3–1 to Dynamo Kiev.

Friday 10 October 1986
DIARY: Sent out on a story on last night's big fire at the McLellan Galleries. The wedding shop next to it was thought to have a number of dresses for brides on Saturday ruined. I had to check this. No there aren't. End of story.

As I was writing this it was announced that the McLellan Galleries were to be reopened after many years closed. The report included archive footage of the Galleries from the time of the fire. There in a shop window were the unharmed wedding dresses in all their pristine glory.

Sunday 2 November 1986
The Sunday Post

FIREWORKS TURNED TO TERROR FOR THOMAS

Playtime turned to terror for 11-year-old Thomas Reilly when an older youth stuffed a lighted banger into his pocket.

GEORGE IS SCOTLAND'S CHAMPION WHISTLER

78-year-old George Cruickshank from Falkirk was well known among locals for his whistling.

'The Road to the Isles' and 'The Northern Lights of Old Aberdeen' are among his favourites, though he's also been known to whistle the odd bit of opera.

This was a typical example of the Post's heartwarming stories in the middle pages. I had a lot of these early on.

Saturday 8 November 1986
A regular Saturday night routine was driving round the city police stations with early editions of the paper. You were more likely to get a tip from speaking to the desk sergeant face-to-face than you would from a telephone call.

Sunday 21 December 1986
The Sunday Post

AMID THE GLOOM

In the shadow of the closed steel works, Gartcosh village was a place of laughter yesterday. Despite the loss of 550 jobs earlier this year, the children were treated to their annual Christmas party as usual… Only a small number of the redundant workforce have found new employment. The rest are on training schemes or have nothing.

The closure of heavy, nationalised industries and the fallout from that was a feature of the Thatcher era.

Sunday 28 December 1986
The Sunday Post

MYSTERY OF MISSING LAWYER

The disappearance of a Scottish lawyer, only hours after he left to visit clients has left police in England and Scotland baffled.

This was my first front page, co-written as I recall. Tragically, the lawyer had died by suicide.

1987

Sunday 4 January 1987
The Sunday Post

NEW ROW OVER COLD PAYMENTS

Braemar, Scotland's coldest village, shivered in temperatures of 16 degrees below freezing on Friday with underfoot temperatures even lower at 19.3 degrees below. But the freezing conditions haven't been enough for OAPs in the village to qualify for extra heating allowances under the Government's new Severe Weather Payments Scheme.

DIARY: Spoke to SNP Chairman Gordon Wilson. Pleasant and well prepared. His comment was more of a dictation eg 'stop, new sentence.'

BARLINNIE RIOT

A riot erupted at Barlinnie Jail on Monday 5 January 1987. One hall was trashed and some prison officers were taken hostage. Prisoners took to the roof of the jail. Banners were hung alleging brutality and slates were thrown.

Saturday 10 January 1987

DIARY: Stood around in freezing conditions waiting for a statement following the end of the Barlinnie siege this morning. When the Scottish Office spokeswoman finally came out, I put my tape recorder out and taped the statement... Only problem was the pause button was on, so I never got anything! Fortunately, the statement was also printed. In the end we waited around for hours for very little.

Tape recorders – strictly speaking cassette recorders – were only beginning to appear at news conferences. The spokeswoman had looked at me askance as I thrust it in front of her. Maybe it was because the pause button was still on.

Thursday 22 January 1987
The Sunday Post

IT'S NOT EASY SITTING BESIDE A MINISTER AT IBROX

DIARY: Afternoon working on a story about a Rangers fan who pays a minister some cash each week so that he can shout abuse at games. Would like to do more news.

Sunday 25 January 1987
The Sunday Post

Livingston MP Robin Cook plans to meet senior management of Golden Wonder to discuss the threatened closure of their plant at Broxburn with the loss of 340 jobs. The crisps and snacks company announced the closure in an effort to streamline their operations, but Mr Cook claims that supermarkets ask that their brand name crisps be produced at the Broxburn plant because of its high quality produce.

DIARY: Also rewrote story of the Queen's fury over the leaking of the Duke of Edinburgh's letter to the Marines over Prince Edward's resignation. So, five articles in this week's issue.

Friday 30 January 1987

DIARY: Got total of £27.40 in expenses, so that'll keep me going until my salary is in the bank – what there is of it. The editor signing my expense sheet says, 'you sport boys eat well.' I'm news.

Saturday 31 January 1987

DIARY: Was down in the case room for a while watching how they put a page together. It certainly is an art, but a dying one. It seemed very fiddly to me and the new processes should speed it up.

The paper was changing, as most did in that period, from the old method of hot metal type to new, cheaper computerised technology.

Saturday 14 February 1987

DIARY: Went to a wedding in Milngavie. The story never existed (all to do with nine brothers wearing the same suits).

This was a typical experience. Every reporter has gone out with a heavy heart knowing that what will meet them will bear little resemblance to what was promised, but knowing, too, that they need to bring something back for the newsdesk.

Sunday 22 February 1987
The Sunday Post

ROLLS ROYCE PROTEST

Almost 2,000 workers at the Rolls Royce overhaul plant in East Kilbride will stage a two-hour walk out tomorrow in protest at privatisation plans.

Industrial unrest over privatisation was standard fare during the Thatcher years. This one had a personal connection because my Faither and brother worked in that plant.

Friday 27 February 1987

DIARY: Out at a special AIDS press conference at Glasgow Uni. Prof Jarrett at the forefront of the race to find a vaccine said, 'The permissive society is dead.'

The AIDS scare was reaching its peak in 1987. A Government-funded campaign told us, 'There is now a danger that has become a threat to us all. It is a deadly disease and there is no known cure.' This was emphasised by a gravestone with AIDS chiselled on it and the slogan 'Don't die of ignorance.' It's questionable that it was ever really a threat to us all, but the advances in treatments for HIV mean that people can now live long, healthy lives with the virus. And it's probably fair to say the permissive society is still alive.

Thursday 19 March 1987

DIARY: Frustrating day. In work I was landed with a couple of shitty jobs, including collecting quiz questions. That after we'd had an informal meeting about making the news harder.

I've seen this time and again from young people starting in newsrooms. There is a natural desire to get on, but it is easy to forget that you have to serve your time. That includes doing basic jobs.

GENERAL ELECTION 1987

As a junior reporter on a Sunday newspaper I had little involvement in covering the 1987 General Election. The following report, to which I contributed these vox pops, looked at first-time voters ahead of the election.

Sunday 22 March 1987
The Sunday Post

YOUNG SCOTS SAY 'NO' TO MRS THATCHER

Every party recognises that first-time voters are going to be a crucial factor in the next election. Since the last General Election in June 1983, 2.1 million voters have had their names added to the electoral register. They now account for almost five per cent of the total electorate of 43.4 million. Their votes could swing the result in many marginal constituencies and affect the overall result if it is a close call.

GILLIAN FISHER: There is no way I would vote for Margaret Thatcher and I have no confidence in Neil Kinnock. The Alliance will get my vote.

JAMES SMITH: The Labour Party is biased against Catholics, so I won't be voting for them. The Alliance just don't appeal to me and there's no way I would vote Tory. It seems the SNP is all that's left.

ANDREW WITHERSPOON: I don't have to think twice. My parents have always voted Conservative. Coming from a private school, which Labour want to abolish, I think I'll stick with that philosophy.

In June 1987 Margaret Thatcher won an historic third term with a significant parliamentary majority across the UK. That picture was not reflected in Scotland. Labour won 50 seats, the Conservatives dropped from 21 seats to ten, the SDP Liberal Alliance got nine seats, the SNP won three, an increase of one.

Sunday 17 May 1987
The Sunday Post

Princess Anne yesterday praised the people of Inverclyde for their record-breaking fundraising efforts. In her role as President of Save the Children, the Princess told a massed crowd at a charity fete in Greenock that they had renewed her faith in hospitality and generosity. Dressed in a red, woollen, two-piece suit, the Princess was treated to a series of displays, including a performance by a wheelchair dancing troupe.

DIARY: Down in Greenock... From 11.00am to 4.00pm and it was dull. I reckon we could have left after the Princess arrived at 12.15pm. Not much of a story. Felt sorry for her if she has to visit these affairs so often, meeting dull dignitaries and watching the same displays. Having said that, the fetes are great for locals – the whole town seemed to be out.

Sunday 12 July 1987
The Sunday Post

A plan to have an open-air Christmas market in Glasgow's George Square has caused a storm of protest. The proposed market would have 72 stalls, four chalets and an entertainment stage in the Square during the festive period. Now, a petition opposing the plan has been launched by stallholders at the all-year-round at Barrowland. They claim the George Square stalls would threaten their livelihoods and other markets might be forced to close.

Sunday 12 July 1987
The Sunday Post

The Glasgow Garden Festival is already proving to be a success nearly a year before it begins. Sales of the first batch of season tickets (at £15 a head) have been in excess of 70,000, smashing the organisers' estimates of 25,000... Orders for the season tickets have come mostly from the Glasgow area. But 15 per cent have come from around the world, including Canada, the US and Australia.

Sunday 19 July 1987
The Sunday Post

Thousands of Scottish would-be holidaymakers were caught in a nightmare yesterday as their Glasgow Fair Fortnight got underway. Bus, plane and weather problems combined to cause chaos and misery and ruin expensive holiday plans. The Scottish Bus Group strike led to angry scenes at bus stations in Edinburgh and Glasgow when passengers expecting to leave for resorts such as Blackpool, Scarborough and further south were told most services had been wiped out.

The Glasgow Fair, Blackpool and Scarborough are evocative of a different age of holidays.

During that summer I saw an advert for news trainees at BBC Radio Scotland. I ignored it initially because I didn't think broadcasting was for me. A combination of curiosity and youthful optimism made me submit an application late on, but with no real expectation of being selected from the thousands of others who applied.

Friday 18 September 1987

DIARY: Big day as regards the Radio Scotland job. Final interview and voice test. Given a selection of news items which had to be whittled down to two minutes. Taken to conference room with another six Radio Scotland officials – News Ed, Current Affairs Ed etc. Grilled me solidly for about 45 minutes. Mostly about news with a Scottish flavour – what Scottish stories should be given more exposure, most important Scottish stories of the week etc.

Thursday 24 September 1987

DIARY: I am going to work for the BBC! Got the phone call this evening. A two-year contract at £8,280 (+£634 shift allowance). A great opportunity. Ironic that earlier Flash (Bill Anderson – *The Sunday Post* editor) was down from Dundee. He pulled me into the TV room on my own... turned out to be a pep talk. I mentioned not being satisfied with my news contribution, but he said he was perfectly happy and I was scoring well throughout the paper.

Sunday 27 September 1987
The Sunday Post

The demolition of the Apollo Theatre in Glasgow this weekend has taken local traders by surprise and brought their takings tumbling down. Neighbouring businesses say they were not notified of the operation...The building is being demolished in the interests of public safety and a proposed 14-screen cinema costing £7 million is to be built on the site.

Glasgow's famous Apollo Theatre was demolished following its closure two years previously. The Apollo had hosted most of the major rock acts of the '70s and '80s and still holds a special place in the hearts of the city's music fans.

I'll always be grateful to *The Sunday Post*. I got my start on the paper and my colleagues took me under their wing. Many of them went on to success elsewhere. Others established themselves as significant figures in the DC Thomson operation.

I started at BBC Radio Scotland in November 1987. My initial training was on the news desk preparing the news bulletins. It was a different culture entirely with hourly deadlines. Central to the news output was a bank of telex machines. Every hour at 20 to the hour, they would start chuntering out three minutes' worth of news material from London, covering UK and international stories. This was called the 'rip-n-read' because that is exactly what you did with it – the stories were printed on a long sheet of telex paper and, using the edge of a ruler, you tore out the ones you wanted, stapled them onto a sheet of A5 paper and arranged them into the running order. In addition, a news voicer might be sent, which had to be recorded onto a cartridge. This was all complemented by Scottish stories and voicers from our own reporters and copy from local correspondents. You then descended two floors to where the newsreaders had their small continuity studios. That was how it was supposed to work, but news never does. The rip-n-read was frequently late, or there was a problem with the audio or there was a breaking story. Too often I would burst through as the pips were marking the final seconds towards the hour. I loved it. This was news as it was happening, or as close as it could be for the time.

Tuesday 17 November 1987
BBC Radio Scotland

A demonstration organised by the National Union of Students marched through Glasgow city centre this afternoon to protest against Government plans for education. Students from the 32 affiliated colleges in the West of Scotland took part in the protest. John MacKay reports...

This was my first BBC report.

Monday 7 December 1987
BBC Radio Scotland

Police in Glasgow are investigating the possibility that a batch of bad drugs have been responsible for three deaths over the weekend. The bodies of three men were found each with a hypodermic syringe beside them.

Drug deaths have remained a consistent story throughout the subsequent decades.

Tuesday 15 December 1987
BBC Radio Scotland

The bridge that leads to nowhere at last seems to be going somewhere. Developers have submitted a plan to Glasgow District Council which will transform the concrete eyesore into part of an £18 million office development, linking with a new office complex to be built at the bottom of Bath Street.

The bridge had been constructed in 1972 as part of the city's inner ring road. It was supposed to be part of a pedestrian walkway above the motorway, but that didn't happen and it was considered too costly to demolish. The office development is the distinctive brown office block, Tay House, sitting over the M8 motorway at Charing Cross. In 2024 plans for the redevelopment of the area included the demolition of the offices.

Undated news report 1987
BBC Radio Scotland

The Prime Minister has been urged to drop plans to retain Prestwick Airport's status as Scotland's sole transatlantic gateway airport. In a letter to Mrs Thatcher, the Chief Executive of the Glasgow Chamber of Commerce said that the building of road and rail links to Prestwick looks like an expensive way to buy votes in Ayrshire, Edinburgh West and Bearsden.

Until 1990 transatlantic flights from Scotland could only fly from Prestwick Airport.

Undated news report 1987
BBC Radio Scotland

Over two-thirds of Scottish people see no need for shops to open on a Sunday, according to organisers of a new movement – the Scottish Keep Sunday Special Campaign. They claim that Scottish society does not want or need Sunday trading. And they are backed by traders and trade unions.

There was no legal restriction on shops being open on a Sunday, but it was the custom. Town and city centres would be dead on a Sunday. That began to change rapidly in the 1990s.

Undated news report 1987
BBC Radio Scotland

Teaching schoolchildren in remote parts of the country could be revolutionised by new technology. Education officials from the Northern Isles and Highlands have been in Aberdeen to see demonstrations of the new equipment... The proposed scheme would allow schoolchildren to remain in their own communities. Videos, fax machines and computers would link pupils to teachers, who may be miles away, without the child having to leave their home area.

Undated news report 1987
BBC Radio Scotland

Later this morning Strathclyde Regional Council are expected to refuse planning permission for a £150 million leisure and shopping development for the 200-acre site at Shieldhall. There are 90 applications for developing similar sites in the region and it's expected that most of them will be rejected. The council's policy is one of urban renewal, rather than out-of-town developments. Another group opposed to the development of big hyper-markets are small businessmen... The Port Authority say the new scheme would create an estimated 3,500 jobs... and the proposals are part of their efforts to develop the Clyde now that traditional industries are waning.

The Braehead Shopping Centre was opened in 1999.

1988

Thursday 7 January 1988

BBC Radio Scotland trainees were sent to 'out-stations' around the country to gain intensive practical experience. I was assigned to BBC Radio Orkney under the guidance of station manager John Fergusson.

DIARY: Sent out on a 'jolly' today to the island of Sanday to the north-east. The flight was on a Loganair Islander. Ten seats, including pilot and co-pilot. A ten-minute flight from Kirkwall and when we came in to land I was amazed to find that we were coming down on a field with sheep scattering beneath us.

I knew there wouldn't be airports, but I thought the planes would land on the roads. City boy ignorance.

Monday 11 January 1988

DIARY: Committed the cardinal sin this morning. I had arranged to be in the studio with John again this morning – and I slept in. I'd set my alarm for 6.30am last night, but I hadn't switched it on. So, when I finally awoke at 8.30am the programme had already gone out. Fortunately, John took it in good part, but it can't happen again.

Tuesday 12 January 1988
BBC Radio Orkney

On the island of Shapinsay, two farmers with very different sizes of farms are both practising a very different type of care for their sheep. In Orkney it's unusual for farmers to take their sheep in for the winter but, as John MacKay has been finding out, that could very well change.

DIARY: On a boat for half an hour to sail to Shapinsay. Met by shepherd – Jim Foubister – who took me to his home where his wife Ina gave me dinner *(lunch actually, but I wasn't so sophisticated then)*. Did an interview with him about wintering sheep and then he took me to see another bloke about the same. Finally, he took me to the local laird's son who is breeding ducks for wild shoots. Crammed all that into a two-hour stay before the ship returned. If it hadn't been for Jim I'd never have made it. I can't get over how welcoming and helpful the islanders are.

Thursday 21 January 1988

DIARY: I had the continuity announcement at lunchtime sprung onto me. I was quite nervous as I flicked open my microphone for my first ever 'live' broadcast. I stumbled a couple of times and crashed into Robbie Shepherd's programme a bit early. It was the old dry throat, thumping heart syndrome. But John reckoned I'd done okay and it didn't sound as bad as I thought it had. I'm glad to get it out of the way because I'm presenting my first breakfast programme tomorrow.

Friday 22 January 1988
BBC Radio Orkney

Good morning. You're listening to BBC Radio Orkney. I'm John MacKay and over the next half hour we'll be hearing about privatisation plans in the health service, an Orkney student who's on his way to Japan and we hear from the Vice-President of the Scottish National Farmers' Union. All that and more to come. But first, the weather...

DIARY: Presented my first live show this morning and it went well. It helped to have got yesterday's out of the way. As soon as I opened the mic I was away and relaxed very quickly.

Starting with the weather forecast emphasised how important it was in the islands. I learned very quickly on radio how people relied on the forecast, not just in Orkney. On the national radio there was an hourly three-minute bulletin and there would be complaints if the 15 seconds of weather wasn't included.

Tuesday 26 January 1988

DIARY: Caught the 5.05pm flight to Shetland. I went to see the 'Up Helly Aa' procession – which was spectacular – with up to a thousand men marching with flaming torches. The burning of the traditional galley was quite a sight.

Tuesday 2 February 1988

DIARY: Big mistake this morning. We have market reports from two different Marts – one is the Kirkwall Auction Mart, the other is the West Mainland Mart and I spoke about them as if they're one and the same.

The islanders were very welcoming, but it must have pained them at times to hear a 'sooth-moother' like me make such basic errors. Pronouncing the island of Foula (Foola) wrongly was another one. It might seem trivial, but it matters. If you can't get the basics right, how can people be sure your other facts aren't as sloppy?

DIARY CONT: At a council meeting. I found it dull, uninspiring and full of old farmers and prim maids with starched drawers. Dry stuff.
Ah, the cliched arrogance of youth. This was local democracy in action.

Thursday 4 February 1988

The first Comic Relief Red Nose Day was held in February 1988. I had interviewed some children from Stromness who were going to school in their pyjamas to raise money. The interview ran the following day.

DIARY: Just before the final item finished I ran downstairs to check with Mairi *(Mairi Fotheringham – station assistant)* whether the weather summary had arrived on the telex machine. I ran back upstairs and ended up breathless.

What this entry doesn't detail, probably because of overwhelming embarrassment, is that the final item was the piece about the Stromness children. The very last clip was a young girl describing the night clothes she was wearing. I arrived back at the sound desk to fade up the mic just as she finished speaking. Having just run upstairs I was panting like a pervert and I knew it. In these situations there is no short remedy, you just have to wait until you get your breath back. It took a few of the longest seconds of my life.

Wednesday 10 February 1988
BBC Radio Orkney

The Celtic Supporters' Club held a successful annual dance last night and they entertained two very special guests. Celtic manager Billy McNeill and his wife are paying their first visit to Orkney.

BILLY MCNEILL, Celtic Manager: The supporters of Celtic have never really surprised me for a long time now, simply because of the fact that I've been used to them popping up everywhere... But it delights me, to be quite frank with you, that I've been invited to a place like Orkney, where, obviously, Celtic supporters here can only see the team on very few occasions and obviously keep in touch by radio and by newspapers and, perhaps, by telephone calls to friends on the mainland. So, it delights me to come here and share a night with them.

JM: Any prospect of the likes of a young Orkney footballer making it with Celtic?

BM: It's difficult, I think, just simply because of the environment. I'm not just speaking of Orkney, in particular, but any island round about Scotland, or indeed any other country. I think it's possibly the lack of any true competition which would always hold them back. That, plus the fact that there's always the difficulty of taking kids away from their parents at a very, very young age to provide the necessary competition. But we're always on the lookout for players from wherever.

DIARY: Interviewed the Celtic manager Billy McNeill today. Very impressed by him – genuine, warm and articulate. I'd half expected the big shot from the big city syndrome, but no. I liked him a lot.

Saturday 27 February 1988

DIARY: I had an interview to do on North Ronaldsay and we travelled in the wee Loganair Islander. Unfortunately, there was a blizzard on the way and it was a turbulent flight. I only had five minutes to get my interview, but I'd arranged to meet the guy at the airfield. On the way back it was just as bad and on the approach to the runway the pilot had real problems holding the plane level.

There was a big storm coming in and the pilot told me if I wasn't back in five minutes he would have to leave. I ran out to a small outbuilding, met my interviewee, recorded the interview and ran back to the plane, unknowingly stepping in cow dung as I did so. As we flew quickly back from North Ronaldsay the plane heated up and as the heat spread so did the pungent stench of shit emanating from my seat. There was evident suspicion among my fellow passengers that the turbulent flight had been too much for me.

Friday 4 March 1988

DIARY: Got a real scare on the flight home. We'd just taken off from Inverness *(the Orkney flight to Glasgow went via Inverness)* and reached our cruising altitude when the plane suddenly turned sharply and seemed to dive through the clouds. The pilot said we had to return because of a technical fault, but we had fire tenders on the runway and it was all very rushed. I now know the meaning of the term 'shaken'.

As we descended rapidly below the clouds all I could see was flashing blue emergency lights along the runway. The cabin was suddenly full of anxious chatter when previously it had been almost silent. Across from me were an elderly woman and a younger man. They didn't know each other, but she grasped his hand. The plane landed safely (the cause of the alarm had been a flashing warning light in the cockpit). In the arrivals lounge there were two coin-operated phones on the wall. I ran to one to alert my newsdesk. I could hear the other phone was being used by another reporter (a freelance). Meanwhile, the rest of the passengers lined up behind us waiting to phone their loved ones to tell them the drama behind their delay.

Thursday 10 March 1988
BBC Radio Orkney

Several residents from the north isles of Orkney are being sent on a special mission to the United States of America to help out with scientific research over there. The residents are not some of the human population, but local mice. Two consignments set off from Kirkwall Airport yesterday destined for Washington. For a number of years Professor Sam Berry has been carrying out detailed studies on the special characteristics of our mice here in Orkney.

PROFESSOR SAM BERRY, University College London: What will be looked at is their DNA, which is the actual chemistry of the genes. What the Americans are interested in – and this is indirectly related to AIDS research, because this is one of the things that everybody is interested in at the moment – the Americans are interested in viruses, which infect the mice and then they get absorbed into the actual genes of the mice and replicate when the cells divide. Which is not what happens to a normal virus, of course, but the AIDS virus does something rather in the same way. Now, the viruses in the mice are, of course, nothing to do with AIDS, nothing whatsoever to do with it, but it could be we might learn something about AIDS through looking at the mice.

I left Orkney with some reluctance at the end of my attachment in March 1988 and returned to the BBC Radio Scotland Newsroom in Glasgow.

Tuesday 19 April 1988

DIARY: Had to do a piece on a report which claims that Scotland isn't doing enough for refugees. But the organisers couldn't even line up a refugee family.

This is still a regular complaint by reporters. There is no point in sending out a news release to broadcasters if the main figures are away on holiday, unavailable for interview, don't want to speak etc. If you want good coverage for your story, provide an example who is willing to talk about their experience and a specialist who can give it authority. That's what the best PR people do. Time is often against reporters and the more you can set up, the better the coverage of your story will be. A reputation for providing tea and bacon rolls is a big plus, too.

Wednesday 20 April 1988
BBC Radio Scotland

RIKKI FULTON

Scottish Opera have announced details for their new season and there is one, rather surprising, introduction. Rikki Fulton – better known for more light-hearted roles – is playing the Lord Chancellor in Gilbert and Sullivan's *Iolanthe*.

RIKKI FULTON: I suppose a performer who's spent as long as I have doing so many characters, I don't think I've, perhaps, got anything new in terms of characterisation to offer. So, maybe this'll be a sort of amalgam of one or two. But I sincerely hope they won't be particularly recognisable.

JM: Do you see yourself as a new Pavarotti, or something like that?

RF: I do not. My voice is certainly not trained, even if it's clean about the house.

DIARY: First time I've felt the pressure of a deadline. Rikki Fulton – the popular comic actor – was there and I had to get an interview with him and the Opera's Managing Director. I couldn't interview them until midday, although the conference started at 11.00am. I had two snatches of interview on just after 12.45pm, so I was pleased.

In the pre-digital era, I would return from my story with the material recorded onto quarter inch tape. It was edited by marking the tape with a white chinagraph pencil and literally cutting it using a razor blade on an editing block. The edits were joined with sticky tape. Finally, a length of yellow, quarter inch lead-in tape was required to mark the start and red tape to mark the end of the piece.

THE GLASGOW GARDEN FESTIVAL

The Garden Festival was a huge success for Glasgow. Created on the site where STV and BBC Scotland are now, it converted a rundown dockland area into a garden wonderland with theme parks. Millions visited between April and September and it is remembered fondly. Many wondered why it could not be maintained permanently, especially when the housing which was supposed to be developed on the site never happened.

Thursday 28 April 1988
DIARY: The first day of the much heralded Glasgow Garden Festival. It's a credit to the city and while some parts seem to be bustling, the gardens are quiet and serene.

Monday 6 June 1988
DIARY: Down to Dalmuir to do a piece on asbestos burial and for the first time I used the cellnet phone to file copy.

My News Editor Robin Wyllie had handed me a heavy black box with a telephone receiver on top to try out. The contraption was so big it came in its own briefcase and clamped to the roof of the car. It was many years before the use of mobile phones became widespread.

Friday 10 June 1988
BBC Radio Scotland

Simple Minds are among the good and great on the bill at Wembley tomorrow in a concert to mark the 24th anniversary of Nelson Mandela being sentenced to life imprisonment. On Sunday the Minds' main man, Jim Kerr, will be among the speakers at a rally in Glasgow, which looks set to be the biggest ever anti-apartheid demonstration in Scotland.

JIM KERR, Simple Minds: I just manage to see the world going further than the end of my street. I hate injustice of any sort and in our songs we write about these ideals, maybe ideas. We have dreams of freedom, universal peace. And they seem dreams, but the only way of making dreams into a reality is by doing something physical, by making a stand.

JM: Is that the role of the rock star?

JK: I think it's the role of the individual. I will say that my favourite music has always been music that both entertained me and also passed on a message. And I think when that happens rock music becomes a lot more credible.

JM: On the day after the concert the Nelson Mandela Freedom March will start with a demonstration in Glasgow. The March will then cover 600 miles in five weeks, arriving in London on the 17th of July, the eve of Nelson Mandela's 70th birthday.

ISAMIL AYOB, Nelson Mandela's lawyer: Glasgow is the most important city in the UK as far as we are concerned because it was the very first city which made him a Freeman of the city and Winnie Mandela is the Rector of your university. Your Lord Provost also organised a worldwide campaign when 5,000 mayors, throughout the world, signed a petition for the release of Mandela. And all of that started in Glasgow.

PIPER ALPHA

On the night of 6 July 1988 the North Sea oil rig Piper Alpha exploded killing 167 men. It was caused by a gas leak during maintenance work and remains Britain's worst-ever oil disaster. The blaze took three weeks to extinguish.

Thursday 7 July 1988

DIARY: Today's news dominated by a tragedy in the North Sea. An oil rig – Piper Alpha – blew up and there are believed to be some 160 people lost. Apparently, flames were reaching up to 400 feet and some TV pictures of it were dramatic. There were also pictures of relatives severely distressed, screaming in the street. I think that is intrusive. Amazing how these stories develop. Peter Aitchison *(BBC colleague)* joined us in the bar last night from the newsroom after his shift. 'There's a fire on a North Sea rig, but it doesn't seem to be much,' he said. Then I woke up to hear that. A real shock.

The subsequent inquiry was covered extensively in our news bulletins for months afterwards, much of it very technical. The word 'flange' (a metal disc to seal the end of a pipe) became one of the most commonly used words in news reports.

I was temporarily off news at this time. BBC Radio Scotland decided it needed to reach out to a more youthful audience. As one of the youngest people in the station, I was, very reluctantly, part of the team which developed and produced the *No the Archie Macpherson Show*. The Executive Producer introduced a new comic writer who wrote sketches and a weekly soap. I thought him a pleasant guy, but I didn't connect with his humour. At production meetings I would argue that this or that sketch just wasn't funny. Armando Iannucci went on to have a hugely successful career as a comedy writer in the UK and Hollywood. I never produced another non-news programme again.

Saturday 10 September 1988

DIARY: My first football report today. No Premier League games on because of the forthcoming World Cup qualifier against Norway midweek. So, the focus was on the First Division. I was at Broomfield for Airdrie versus Kilmarnock. Must have been one of the first there. Settled in time for my tee-up piece just after 2.00pm – and from then until half-time I was doing a series of short pieces. Only one in the second half and a final summing up at full time. Also got Airdrie manager Gordon McQueen to do a telephone interview.

Airdrie won 5–1. Their first goal was scored by full back Tom Black who had a thick black moustache. I dialled the studio to update them and as presenter Tom Ferrie threw to me, my note with Tom Black's name on it blew over. There was a momentary panic as I announced the goalscorer was '...the man with the moustache...'

Everything was still done using a dial-up telephone. Far from the open mics now, you had to dial in if anything happened and hope the studio number wasn't engaged.

Friday 4 November 1988

DIARY: My last *Good Morning Scotland* as a producer – for quite a while at least. I've enjoyed the producing, but I'm not sure I'll miss it.

Producing GMS involved a long working day, a short sleep and then back in to put the programme out between 6.30am and 9.00am. It was two-and-a-half hours of live radio, reacting to stories that could be international or local. Taped reports would be commissioned, live interviewees set up, presenters briefed. It was challenging, but enjoyable.

Such was the status of the BBC, there was some incredulity in my family that I was working there. When a friend told my mother that she'd heard my name as producer in the credits for Good Morning Scotland, my mother had said, 'I don't think that would be our John.'

Undated report November 1988
BBC News

All police interviews with suspects in Strathclyde will soon be tape recorded. The Strathclyde Police Force are introducing a £1.3 million programme which will start with Maryhill Division next month. Other divisions will be included in the New Year.

This is now standard procedure for serious crimes.

Friday 11 November 1988

DIARY: Jim Sillars won the Govan by-election – turning a 19,000 Labour majority into a 3,000 SNP one. It's caused massive reverberations and what is clear is that the Tories are doing nothing for Scotland and Labour's 50 Scottish MPs are ineffectual.

One of the candidates in this by-election was an impressive young man called Bernard Ponsonby. He plays a very significant role later in this book.

Wednesday 23 November 1988

DIARY: Rangers have been bought by Scots businessman David Murray.

Rangers had begun their transformation two years previously under the chairmanship of David Holmes. His hiring of Graeme Souness as the new player manager and then an influx of top English players had transformed Rangers and Scottish football. Murray took Rangers to another level and invested huge sums trying to achieve success in Europe. It all came to a crashing end more than 20 years later.

David Murray would readily take direct calls from reporters which was great from our point of view, but also gave him a degree of manipulation. He liked to mess with reporters too. During a series of media interviews I went in after the BBC's highly regarded Alan Mackay. As my cameraman was setting up, Murray spoke of how good Alan was and what an interview he'd just done. I was followed by a former colleague Alison Douglas. She told me afterwards that he'd said the same about me. All of it just to put the reporter facing him a little on edge.

Monday 5 December 1988

DIARY: A press conference at police HQ. There's some nutter loose in the city.

Ah, Glasgow.

Wednesday 21 December 1988

LOCKERBIE BOMBING

A Pan Am jet flying from London to JFK Airport in New York exploded over the Scottish town of Lockerbie.

The BBC Radio Scotland newsroom had deserted quickly that evening, many to a Christmas party being held elsewhere in Broadcasting House. I had brought a book in anticipation of a quiet shift.

DIARY: Answered two very important calls just after 7.20pm. One said there was an explosion in the town of Lockerbie. A minute later the AA called – a patrolman had seen a plane come down on a housing estate. Quickly established that it was a Pan Am 747 flying from London to New York and all 259 on board were dead, plus 11 on the ground. As the night wore on the full scale of the disaster became clear and we broadcast through the night.

One of the first questions was where was Lockerbie? It was one of those names we were vaguely familiar with because we'd passed it driving south, but I don't think anyone could have said precisely where it was. It quickly became apparent it was not a military, but a passenger jet. We immediately thought it must be the London to Glasgow shuttle. Calls to air traffic control and airlines soon established that the plane missing was a Pan Am 747 flying from London to New York.

Duty News Editor Phil Taylor bashed out a script and told me to go to a studio and record it for transmission on Radio 4 at 8.00pm. In the days before 24-hour rolling news the first much of the UK would have heard about the tragedy was my young Scottish voice reading that script.

BBC Radio 4 News

Police in Dumfries say that 'many bodies' have been recovered from the wreckage in Lockerbie town centre where a Pan American Airlines Boeing 747 crashed in flames earlier this evening. The injured are being treated in hospitals throughout Dumfriesshire and Carlisle. Doctors and medical staff are being called in from a wide area. Police say that any members of the public offering blood should contact Dumfries Infirmary. The plane, flying from London to John F Kennedy Airport had 258 passengers on board. It's reported to have struck a petrol station, exploding and setting alight nearby houses. An eyewitness spoke of a 300-foot fire ball shooting into the sky. Police believe there are a 'huge number' of casualties. They have appealed to motorists travelling north or South to avoid the main A74 Glasgow to Carlisle road for the next few hours.

Kenny Macintyre – a reporter who worked off his wits – went straight to the phone book, looked up the number for the post office in Lockerbie and called. That quick reaction got one of the first eyewitness accounts of what people in the town were experiencing.

Phil Taylor, BBC Radio Scotland News Editor

Like all the truly memorable/remarkable/terrible stories of a life in journalism, the Lockerbie Bombing from a personal standpoint was one of those lurches from the mundane to the extraordinary and chaotic. Our sub-editor hung up the phone, paused, and then turned round to the newsdesk and said, 'It appears a plane has come down in Lockerbie.'

Within minutes of that conversation, we were getting calls from BBC Scotland journalists down in the south-west. Kenny Macintyre, being the genius journalist that he was, was also bashing the phones, trying all the contacts he could think of, including – no doubt – members of Mrs Thatcher's Cabinet. The next stab at what was really going on was a rumour that an RAF jet fighter, on a low-level training flight had crashed on to a petrol station. All these years later, writing this prompts me to go to Google Earth and to gaze down at the A74 as it passes the ill-fated Sherwood Crescent where a wing section from Pan Am Flight 103 created a crater 150 feet long, killing 11 people. Where did the petrol station rumour come from, I wonder? The nearest services are at Annandale 8.2 miles to the north. I guess the grim answer is: how else do you explain sheets of flame rising hundreds of feet from the side of a motorway on a chill December evening?

Over the next hours, our newsroom did what newsrooms have always done at such times of drama; we drafted in every member of staff we could reach. We despatched reporters – including a young Eddie Mair – producers, TV crews. Staff from BBC Scotland's Dumfries office became the point men and women, getting to the scene first, or as near the multiple sites of destruction as the emergency services could allow. The calls began flooding in from all around the world. Could we put one of our staff on the line to tell the story? Very quickly it started to emerge that 35 of the passengers were young students from Syracuse University in New York. They were returning home for Christmas. We began calling the University for reaction – and New York radio stations were calling us.

Eddie Mair, BBC Radio Scotland Reporter

I was despatched to get a colleague, David, out of the Christmas party and drive us both down to the scene. With my usual nose for news, I recall telling my editor it was probably nothing and why were we driving all that way?

En route, we turned on the radio news to hear for the first time reports of a passenger plane being lost. It was shocking to us both. We arrived somewhere close to Lockerbie to find the A74 closed and jammed with traffic, blocking our way. We were stuck some distance from where we needed to be. In a fit of inspiration/stupidity, I drove the car onto the central reservation and followed emergency service vehicles down the bumpy grass. That at least is my memory though I wonder whether it's false. The road has been upgraded and now there is no grassy division between carriageways. Did I really do that?

A deeply inexperienced 'reporter', I recall walking around the deserted streets of Lockerbie where front doors stood open, and Christmas lights twinkled. I recall seeing a woman's body in a garden, but that sight made no sense to me. Where were all the people? I found them in a pub on one of the main streets, crowded into the bar, watching the *Nine O'Clock News*: a slightly surreal moment interviewing traumatised witnesses about what had happened while they watched news from London which seemed to know more than they did.

BBC Radio 4 News

The airline says it appears certain that all those on board – believed to be more than 250 – have been killed. And in the last hour, there are reports of motorists who were travelling on the A74 just after seven o'clock this evening having been killed. A few minutes ago a local hotelier told us he'd seen several cars on fire. *(In fact, no motorists were killed. All 11 fatalities on the ground were in the town's Sherwood Crescent.)* In Lockerbie itself, the situation is still unclear although it's known that two residential areas have been flattened. Some houses were set on fire when the plane crashed into a petrol station and exploded. Eyewitnesses spoke of a fire ball... at least two explosions before the plane hit the town and a sense of the area being struck by an earthquake. Helicopters have been ferrying the dead and injured to local hospitals. It's known that three babies and a number of American military personnel and students were on board the plane. Police have sealed off part of Lockerbie and warned motorists that they must stay away from the A74 to allow the rescue operations to proceed.

The phone calls started coming in, from stations elsewhere in the UK and then from abroad. I reported to several American, Canadian and Australian stations. Some extracts from my reports reveal how the story changed as the evening moved on.

KSRO, Santa Rosa California, USA 'Live Line' with Larry Chiaroni

JM: The two nearest hospitals that have been dealing with casualties have been told to stand down. Everyone on board is understood to have been killed. There are no casualties coming in. At the moment, though, we do not know how many people on the ground have been killed, if indeed there have been any.

The plane was on fire when it hit the ground... It may have hit another plane. Or there were a number of American servicemen on board, so there are rumours that it may have been a bomb, but I stress that is purely speculation at the moment and we have no way of knowing as of yet.

There are large craters in the town centre. These craters are up to 30 feet deep. A number of houses have been destroyed, there are burned out cars on the roads. The police have imposed a two-mile exclusion zone around about the area where the plane came down.

The plane left London Heathrow at 6.00pm in the evening and it disappeared from radar screens at 7.19pm.

XTRA, San Diego, California, USA News Talk Hotline – Mark Williams

MARK WILLIAMS: John, we are getting reports here that it is apparently certain that this jet liner was blown out of the sky. What's being said there?

JM: That is certainly the speculation at the moment. There was no Mayday call and the plane just disappeared from radar screens without any panic coming from the pilots. It seems that whatever happened, happened very quickly and that would suggest it was a bomb. We're also led to believe that a warning went out to staff at a number of American embassies a few days ago informing that a threat to place a bomb on board a Pan Am flight from Frankfurt to the United States had been made, although the warning did not specify what flight would be affected.

MW: Are we getting any information on who was on board the aircraft?

JM: It's believed that were a number of students on board. Perhaps more significantly, is the fact that there were the servicemen on board who were returning from Frankfurt in Germany.

MW: Is there any speculation as to – if a bomb was planted on this aircraft – where it was planted, in Frankfurt or in London?

JM: The flight was Pan Am 103 and that originally left Frankfurt via London. It's believed that the plane that left Frankfurt is not the same plane that left London. Although it was the same flight number it may have been a different plane *(it wasn't)*. But that is purely speculation. We can't be certain on that.

MW: Do we have a count of how many people are dead?

JM: We understand that there were 260 people on board the Pan Am Boeing 747. They are all dead. At the moment we do not know how many people have been killed on the ground, but certainly we're talking in terms of at least 300 people in total, probably more *(the death toll was 270)*.

MW: Have they recovered the black box?

JM: There were two black boxes. They have been recovered and are being investigated.

Phil Taylor, BBC Radio Scotland News Editor

Most of us, I think, worked through the night. One of the things that does stand in my mind is the absence in those days – of course – of any 24-hour, rolling news capability in the UK. However, CNN had launched in the US eight years earlier and by 1988, was available in some BBC newsrooms including ours. Ironically, the first images of fire and smoke in the night sky of Lockerbie that I watched was on that CNN feed.

By the morning, we were beginning to see more of those dreadful scenes on our domestic TV services. The most terrible of all, surely, was the surreal image of the nose cone of the *Clipper Maid of the Seas*, lying on her side in a field at Tundergarth Church, just outside Lockerbie. What does hindsight tell me? Not much; just how terrible it is to think of all those lives lost and other lives changed forever in the blink of an eye at a few minutes after 7.00pm on the night of Wednesday 21 December 1988.

The tragedy of Lockerbie has been a vein running through my career. Thirty years later, while working on an extended STV News report, what emerges so strikingly is just how unfortunate the 11 victims on the ground were. The iconic image of the disaster is the nose cone of Pan Am Flight 103 lying in a field across the road from Tundergarth Church. Driving four miles west from there you emerge from the countryside onto a brae, the town spread out beneath. Behind you are fields. Before you is a field. Beyond the railway line and the motorway are more fields. Nestled in the folds of these fields is Lockerbie. To the south, like a tail to the body of the town, are the final few houses. This is where Sherwood Crescent lies. This is where people had settled down in their homes that Wednesday evening. And it is where they died without chance or warning. There is some debate over whether the flight was delayed in leaving Heathrow, giving rise to the theory that the bomb was timed to explode over the Atlantic, leaving no evidence. What is not in doubt is that when the bomb did explode at two minutes past seven, it tore the plane apart more than 30,000 feet above. A second or two later and the wreckage would probably have come down in the fields. With a bomb on board, the 259 souls on the plane were always doomed. But for those who died on the ground – beneath a flight scheduled to last hours – in an area surrounded by miles of farmland – mere seconds and feet determined their fate.

1989

Wednesday 4 January 1989
BBC Radio Scotland

Leaked details of the proposed restructuring of the National Health Service include plans to allow hospitals to opt-out of the system. The proposals were contained in a draft White Paper which has been considered by the Prime Minister.

Proposed changes to the NHS have always been and remain a fixture of any news bulletin.

Thursday 5 January 1989

DIARY: A TV crew was in the newsroom covering our day as part of a programme to let the public see what we do. They covered the morning meeting and were then assigned to follow me as the reporter. I was covering a dull story on a Loch Lomond development. They filmed me setting the story up, doing my interviews and editing the story together. It was very interesting and I was pleased to be part of it. Got a bit of slagging in the office about being a 'star'.

I got an even bigger slagging because I got lost on the way to the interview and managed to lose the film crew.

Monday 9 January 1989
BBC Radio Scotland

Scottish Ballet have attracted one of the world's foremost artistic directors to choreograph a new production in the spring. Oleg Vinogradov of the Kirov Ballet will work on an original version of *Petrushka*.

DIARY: Obviously, he's quite a big fish in that world. No English, so done through interpreter. Good interview, but had a bit of difficulty putting it together with his Russian dipping under the translator's voice.

'...quite a big fish in that world' did not do Oleg Vinogradov quite the justice he deserved as a choreographer of international renown.

BELLGROVE TRAIN CRASH
Monday 6 March 1989

Two people died and more than 50 were injured when two passenger trains collided near Bellgrove Station in Glasgow. An inquiry later found the cause of the accident was one of the drivers going through a danger signal.

The scene wasn't one of devastation, both trains were still on the track. They had collided head on and the front of one had risen up on top of the other one. I picked up as much as I could and headed back to the BBC. I did a rushed live two-way into the PM programme on Radio 4 with Valerie Singleton, whom I used to watch on Blue Peter. It was a surreal moment.

Undated report March 1989
BBC Radio Scotland

A Scottish Member of the European Parliament has claimed that many Scottish football clubs face financial ruin with the introduction of the European Market in 1992. Strathclyde West MEP Hugh McMahon says the proposals for the free movement of workers could mean financial doom for clubs which rely on transfer fees to survive.

This was pre-Bosman ruling. A player could not move to another club unless his current club agreed and they would have to be paid a transfer fee. These transfer fees helped sustain many clubs in an era before big television money.

Undated report 1989
BBC Radio Scotland

Strathclyde Police have introduced a new video car to the roads of the region in an effort to combat bad driving. The unmarked car has been fitted with video equipment which can film a driver's errors and even be used in evidence in a court action.

This is now standard practice.

Sunday 28 May 1989
BBC Radio Scotland

The President of the Scottish Football league says the future of the Scotland–England international should be reconsidered following the violence before and after yesterday's game in Glasgow. His remarks came after more than 250 fans were arrested during a day of street fighting in the city.

Scotland lost 2–0. This was the last of the annual Auld Enemy clashes.

June 1989
BBC Radio Scotland

The managing director of Caledonian MacBrayne, Colin Paterson, has told a public inquiry in North Uist that the company went ahead with a Sunday ferry service because it was certain there was demand. But earlier, a Western Isles councillor claimed the island would be 'loved to death' by visitors if Sunday sailings went ahead.

The Sunday ferry service to North Uist had begun in May 1989.

June 1989
BBC Radio Scotland

The annual rate of inflation has reached its highest level in seven years. Last month's figure of 8.3 per cent was lower than analysts had predicted, but it was still the 16th in a row which has seen a rise. The main causes of the increase were the rise in mortgage rates and the price rises for petrol and food.

RANGERS SIGN THEIR FIRST CATHOLIC PLAYER

1989 was the year when the Berlin Wall came down and Eastern bloc countries revolted against Communist rule. Rangers signing a Catholic footballer hardly stands comparison, but for many in Scotland it was just as seismic.

Monday 10 July 1989

I came in for a late shift, having followed Rangers' signing of Maurice Johnston throughout that morning. A young English colleague was preparing the 2.00pm bulletin and sought my opinion on whether Rangers' new signing was still worthy of being lead. It illustrated how localised this story was. Someone from elsewhere in the UK, understandably, couldn't quite grasp that such exclusion would have still been going on.

MAURICE JOHNSTON: I've come to a really big club, possibly one of the biggest in Europe.

GRAEME SOUNESS, Rangers Manager: Obviously, there were a lot of considerations we had to take into account – the main one being that he's an out and out quality player.

REPORTER: Are you troubled at all by the pressures that will be on him as the first Catholic to play here?

GS: There'll be pressures on all my players next year because we have a big squad, there's no one going to be an automatic choice and that includes Maurice. There's pressures playing at Rangers. You have to accept these things when you come here.

Some scarves were set on fire outside Ibrox and a significant number of the gathered fans were unhappy.

Fans' Vox Pops at Ibrox

They should keep to their own.

It's just unbelievable. I can't get over it. I'll maybe wake up in the morning and it'll not be true.

Everything is away now, isn't it? Religion and everything.

Johnston was at Rangers for more than two seasons and was generally considered to be a success. Celtic fans have never forgiven him. Rangers signing a Catholic is no longer news.

Some ten years later the *Daily Record* did a feature on Rangers' Italian captain Lorenzo Amoruso, including a photo of his mother at home in Florence. Side by side on her mantelpiece were a photo of the Rangers captain – her son – and the Pope. It was as vivid a statement as any that times had moved on.

Alison Walker, BBC Radio Sports Reporter

I was relatively new to the world of football journalism – a rookie reporter in sport. I'd done my share of interviews with managers and new players and been to a few press conferences. The newsroom generally wasn't interested in these – but on that day in July 1989 when Rangers called a press conference to announce the signing of a new player, I was told I wouldn't be going on my own. The seasoned newshound Kenny Macintyre would be going with me. There had been talk of Rangers signing their first Catholic player and this was potentially a major story.

I remember reading the *Scottish Sun* that morning. They'd run an exclusive, saying it would be Mo Johnston, yet most of us didn't believe it. We thought they'd taken a flyer because, after all, it wasn't in the 'Daily Souness', or the 'Daily Ranger' as we used to call the *Daily Record*.

We headed for the Blue Room at Ibrox. I remember it felt quite tense. There were loads of newspaper journalists in that room, every seat occupied and some standing. They kept us waiting. I wonder now if that was on purpose. The door at the end of the Blue Room opened, and as the assembled group walked in, there was a collective gasp of air from the audience. It was quite surreal. There was Maurice Johnston grinning widely, almost as widely as Graeme Souness and David Murray. One or two journalists rushed out, falling over themselves and each other. There weren't any mobile phones in those days, so this really was news to spread as quickly as possible. The announcement was made. The top table spoke and then there was a barrage of questions.

I am not sure I really understood the significance or magnitude of this signing until the moment when Mo walked into the room. I remember thinking, 'What is life going to be like for him now? Is he brave or stupid?'

As it turned out, he ended up being a huge footballing success at Rangers, but it can't have been easy for him. Thank goodness times have changed. I won't forget that day in July 1989. It was, for sure, one of those 'were you there?' moments.

Tuesday 25 July 1989
BBC Radio Scotland

A television programme claiming that alleged Nazi war criminals are living in Britain was suddenly halted in mid-transmission last night. Scottish Television say transmission was stopped after a late-night court order was granted in Edinburgh.

The interdict was granted to Anton Gecas. He was a Lithuanian who had fought with the Nazis after they had invaded during the Second World War. He had come to Scotland soon after the war. A judge later ruled that there was clear evidence Gecas had taken part in killing innocent civilians, including Jews in particular. He died in 2001.

Monday 25 September 1989
BBC Radio Scotland

Nearly a quarter of a million council house tenants applied to buy their homes between the introduction of the legislation allowing them to do so in 1980 and the end of 1988. According to figures published by the Scottish Development Department, over 138,000 dwellings were sold to sitting tenants in the same period.

The sale of council houses to their tenants was one of the principal policies which brought Margaret Thatcher to power in 1979. It came to an end in Scotland in 2016.

Tuesday 17 October 1989
DIARY: Drove through to Perth for the official opening of St Johnstone's McDiarmid Park against Manchester United. I was doing a piece for GMS *(Good Morning Scotland)*. Interviewed Alex Totten, Alex Ferguson, the team chairman and even the tea lady. Very pleased with it. Driving back I listened to the two tapes of material. One of them was blank! I was really pissed off. Very frustrating.

As well as Alex Ferguson, I had got United captain Bryan Robson and star forward Mark Hughes. They were all relaxed and had given good interviews. I had my report already prepared in my head, I knew the clips I wanted and how it would all fit together. The GMS producer Peter Aitchison had set aside a good few minutes of his programme for the piece I had promised him. All reporters have been there in one form or another – that futile pressing of buttons on the tape recorder, play, stop, rewind, play, stop, rewind further. Nothing. Of course, it's always because of faulty equipment...

Sunday 29 October 1989
DIARY: On an early shift and I was still drunk when I arrived *(following a stag night)*. So as the morning wore on I could feel myself sobering up. At about 10.00am I was sitting in the chair with the sun streaming onto my face and not a sound. I drifted into a blissful doze.

That blissful doze caused me to miss the 11.00am bulletin, forcing the news reader to use the 10.00am again. It was only his anxious call as we approached the midday bulletin that woke me up. Never again.

Thursday 2 November 1989
Sometimes the detail thrown up by the insignificant stories from local agency copy is wonderful. The following still makes me smile.

BBC Radio Scotland
A supervisor in a fish factory who was sacked for hitting a teenage girl in the face with a fish has won his claim for unfair dismissal. The incident arose from a row over the size of fish he was giving filleters at a seafood factory in Peterhead. This report from John MacKay.

An industrial tribunal in Aberdeen heard that the size of the fish had a direct bearing on the earnings of the filleters. When they complained to their supervisor, Mr P *(I think it's only fair to use initials here)*, that the fish were too big, he became involved in an argument with Miss M. Mr P pulled a fish from one of the boxes and hit her on the side of the face with it. Miss M told the tribunal that she was upset and the side of her face was covered with fish slime. Mr P accepted that he had been arguing with Miss M, but claimed that he had accidentally struck her with the fish. The tribunal said they had taken into account Miss M hadn't complained herself and that she was known to be cheeky. The tribunal awarded Mr P £1,290 in compensation, but said he was 20 per cent to blame.

Thursday 2 November 1989

DIARY: Eddie's *(Eddie Mair)* leaving for television where he'll be part of the *Reporting Scotland* team. I've thought of television myself and I think ultimately I'll find myself doing that. But what I enjoy about radio is the independence. If I want to do a story myself, I grab a Uher *(tape recorder)* and that's it. TV is much more complicated and a lot slower. But that is where the future of broadcasting lies and I suppose I'll have to try and get in some time.

Tuesday 21 November 1989

DIARY: Parliamentary and broadcasting history were made this afternoon when the House of Commons was televised live for the first time. Watched it and it wasn't particularly dramatic. Debates on the Queen's Speech. It'll get better when we get into *Prime Minister's Question Time.*

Coverage of parliamentary proceedings only began on radio in 1978. Throughout the 1980s any TV coverage of events in Parliament was audio-only covered by a photograph of the Commons chamber and an inset photograph of the politician speaking.

Tuesday 28 November 1989
BBC Radio Scotland

Scotland will be left in an economic backwater when the Channel Tunnel is opened unless there is a major investment in the railway network. The warning came from the General Secretary of the Scottish TUC, Campbell Christie, who was speaking prior to the special conference on railway investment which is being held in Glasgow today.

Monday 4 December 1989

DIARY: Eddie Mair made his debut as a presenter on *Reporting Scotland*. Didn't see it, but I'm sure he did well. Would maybe like to do something like that myself in the future.

Maybe...

Undated report December 1989
BBC Radio Scotland

The High Court in Glasgow has been hearing how sectarian violence flared when two neighbouring households watched this year's Rangers–Celtic Scottish Cup Final on television. A woman draped in an Irish tricolour ran from her house shouting insults at the family across the road. They in turn brandished a Union Jack and street battles broke out ending in the death of a man.

Undated report 1989
BBC Radio Scotland

Waste disposal methods in Scotland to be radically improved or the country could be awash with waste early next century. And the threat has led to a call for a national waste disposal authority.

1990

Wednesday 24 January 1990

DIARY: Just before 3.00pm we got a call saying a helicopter had crashed into a block of flats at Eastwood Toll. I was despatched in miserable weather. Traffic jams meant I had to abandon the car and walk the last mile, which was very unpleasant. I just missed a press statement by a police officer, but I got a couple of good eyewitnesses.

A policeman on board was killed.

Tuesday 13 February 1990
BBC Radio Scotland

As police in Glasgow continue the hunt for the killer of ten-year-old Christine Lee, her family have appealed for anyone with information to come forward and help the inquiry. Her body was found late last night in the Castlemilk area of the city, five hours after she'd gone missing.

DIARY: I covered the story throughout the day. I attended a police press conference, interviewed the man leading the hunt and packaged for 1.00pm. Also voiced for lunchtime and London (Radio 4). Then I went out to Castlemilk and spoke to the dead girl's uncle. Normally, I hate doorstepping, but this guy was willing enough and gave me a good interview. Also spoke to some young mothers in a nearby community centre. Packaged for *Good Evening Scotland* and for Radio 4, voiced for our 5.00pm and 6.00pm and also London's 6.00pm. I was extremely busy and didn't have a moment, but when you get into such a story you thrive under the pressure.

The devastation of the victim's family was rather overlooked by the enthusiastic young reporter caught up in the rush of a strong news story. Nineteen-year-old John Dowling was jailed for the rape and murder of Christine.

Saturday 17 February 1990
BBC Radio Scotland

It's been confirmed that Rangers have been approached to take part in a new European Super League. Only three British teams have been invited to take part and Rangers will be joined by Liverpool and Arsenal if the ban on English teams taking part in European competitions is lifted. Celtic have not been included.

JM: The new competition, which will replace the existing UEFA Cup, will feature the elite of European football, including AC Milan and Real Madrid. The league games will be played on Wednesday evenings and will begin in November next year. It's understood that fans will not be encouraged to travel to away games and, instead, visiting teams' supporters will see the game via satellite television. Rangers say they will continue to play in the Premier League. A provisional fixture list has been drawn up for the first Super League season in 1991–92, with plans for a grand final at Wembley in February 1992. The news will come as a shock to Celtic and Manchester United who are being left out because they are considered to lack the necessary business expertise and all-seater grounds.

This was the beginnings of what became the Champions League.

Friday 27 April 1990
BBC Radio Scotland

Scotland's Stephen Hendry is on course to become the youngest ever snooker World Champion. He beat the number two seed John Parrott in fine style last night and meets Jimmy White in the final, which starts today. White knocked out the defending champion, Steve Davis, in a close contest to set up a final between two of the most exciting players in the game.

Stephen Hendry won 18–12 and went on to win six more World Titles.

Monday 30 April 1990
BBC Radio Scotland

Ten people have been killed after a plane crashed into a hillside in Harris in the Outer Hebrides. The plane, a Shackleton, was taking part in an RAF exercise when it came down in low cloud. The Shackleton, a maritime reconnaissance aircraft, was based at RAF Lossiemouth.

Saturday 26 May 1990
BBC Radio Scotland

The Labour Leader, Neil Kinnock, says that under a Labour Government a future Scottish Assembly would be free to raise taxes without cash limits set by Westminster. In an interview in the *Observer*, Mr Kinnock claims that is what the country wants and that's what it will get.

JM: In the interview Mr Kinnock says there is a huge majority support for a form of Scottish Government with tax-raising powers. He pledges that a Labour Government would create such an assembly and it would be up to it what taxes could be levied. zMr Kinnock says the members of such an assembly would be conscious of not hoisting taxes too high. Not only would this inflict a burden on the Scottish people, he says, but it would deter inward investment.

Tuesday 26 June 1990
BBC Radio Scotland

The mother of a four-year-old girl has failed in her attempt to order a man to undergo genetic fingerprinting to prove whether he is the father of her child. At the Court of Session, three appeal judges ruled that under existing law the court had no power to order the test.

Tuesday 17 July 1990
BBC Radio Scotland

The offside rule in football is to be changed. The rule, which has probably caused more arguments in the game than any other, is to be adapted so that an attacker can now be in line with the defender instead of behind him. FIFA hope the change will lead to teams playing a more attacking game, and more goals. The change will come into force at the end of this month.

The offside law remains one of the most controversial in the game and has become ever more complex with further changes. The introduction of the Video Assistant Referee has made it even more complicated. However, this change established the principle of the advantage being given to the attacking player.

Friday 24 August 1990
BBC Radio Scotland

The Scottish football league programme starts tomorrow and as it does so the national coach, Andy Roxburgh, has warned that the success of Rangers could pose long-term problems for the international side... Andy Roxburgh said the influence of Rangers was now being felt throughout the Premier Division. He said Rangers' policy of buying the best players available had set a trend which other teams were following. Scottish football, Roxburgh said, was now peppered with a number of very good players from abroad. And while he acknowledged that this had raised the standard of football in Scotland, the national coach warned that it could stifle the development of young players.

After 1998 it took Scotland 20 years before they qualified for another tournament.

Thursday 22 November 1990

Margaret Thatcher resigned as Prime Minister after 11 years in power. The unpopularity of the Poll Tax, party divisions over Europe and, ultimately, the resignation of her Deputy Prime Minister, Sir Geoffrey Howe, brought her down. She had won a leadership ballot against Michael Heseltine, but not by enough to prevent a second ballot. When members of her Cabinet refused to back her in a second vote, she resigned. This was truly the end of an era that had transformed the UK. For good or bad Mrs Thatcher is, even now, a contentious issue, especially in Scotland.

Wednesday 28 November 1990

John Major became the new Prime Minister, defeating Michael Heseltine and Douglas Hurd in a ballot of MPs. At 47 he represented a new generation, although many considered him to be Mrs Thatcher's chosen successor. Unfortunately, on that day, your correspondent was focused on a job interview at the BBC and recorded nothing of the momentous event of the day. Of more concern appeared to be changing from a suit back into less formal wear so my colleagues wouldn't know I'd been for an interview. Of course, they did.

1991

During the early part of 1991 I was working mostly as a Duty Editor producing the main bulletins on BBC Radio Scotland. This meant I wasn't an on-mic reporter, so much of this year is recorded through diary entries.

Wednesday 9 January 1991

DIARY: Work dominated by late news that American–Iraq talks to avert a Gulf War had failed. The UN deadline is Tuesday and no sign of Iraq pulling out of Kuwait. War seems likely. We won't really be affected, but people will die.

Wednesday 16 January 1991

DIARY: War has begun in the Gulf. Allied planes have attacked various targets throughout Iraq and Kuwait. I had covered the *Six O'Clock* and the *Ten O'Clock* tonight pointing at the last hours before war. One of my headlines was 'More than a million troops now poised for war in the Gulf.'

The attacks began at midnight.

DIARY: Much of *(the coverage)* was given over to the American TV network CNN. Two of their reporters were giving a live commentary from a hotel in Baghdad, describing the explosions and the tracers in the sky. Sad though it is, I think the allied response was justified. I expect it will be quick and there's no question we'll win. But what follows could be nasty – terrorism.

Thursday 17 January 1991

DIARY: I produced the *Six O'Clock* and the *Ten O'Clock* news, dominated by the outbreak of the war in the Gulf. There was some great material. A British Tornado jet has crashed and the race is on to rescue the two-man crew who ejected. At midnight word came through that Iraq had fired missiles at Israel. In the event the Scud missiles caused little damage and minor injuries, but it's a whole new aspect to the war.

Tuesday 22 January 1991

DIARY: Had to completely redo the *Ten O'Clock* because Iraq had again launched Scud missiles at Israel. Three dead. How long can Israel stay out now?

Thursday 7 February 1991

DIARY: It was looking like being a quiet morning when news broke of a mortar bomb attack on Downing Street at about 10.10am. We didn't start getting material on it until nearer half past, but we got a news flash on and had an extended bulletin at 11.00am news. It was an education to watch Robin *(Robin Wyllie – News Editor)* in action.

Saturday 9 February 1991

DIARY: I was covering the second division game between Queen's Park and Dumbarton at Hampden – my first visit to the press box of the national stadium. The Radio Scotland point is a room on its own on top of the stand at the end of the press box. And bloody cold it was too. Was provided with a cup of tea, cake and a biscuit at half-time, which was very civilised. Game ended 1–1.

Queen's Park were an amateur side playing in the senior leagues up until 2019 when they finally turned professional.

Wednesday 27 February 1991

DIARY: The Allied advances in the Gulf continue to be remarkable – and the retreating Iraqi forces have been surrounded in Kuwait. One tragic incident, however, nine British soldiers, three of them Scottish, died when American planes accidentally bombed their trucks. We've lost more men through accidents and 'friendly fire' than we have from the Iraqis.

Tuesday 5 March 1991

DIARY: Major story in Scotland just now is about allegations of child abuse in Orkney – children taken from home by social workers etc. It's a legal minefield.

Thursday 4 April 1991

DIARY: News dominated by the Orkney case being thrown out by a sheriff far earlier than expected. The children arrived home in the islands this evening, so I managed an extended voice and clips from Orkney. It came late and was very long. I was editing it with two minutes before going on air. Tight, but worth it.

Friday 19 April 1991

DIARY: Hectic 1:00pm. Rangers due to announce new manager – Walter Smith – at 1:00pm. I had three people there with the Radio Car and had three contingency plans. What I hadn't counted on was a fire alarm delaying the announcement and while I had enough material to fill, just, I was anxious to get it. Well, Derek Rae came on at 1:24pm (we're off air at 1:28pm) and the line wouldn't work properly. I was snapping instructions all over and the adrenalin was pumping. We got him on the telephone with two minutes to spare. All hectic, but we got it.

Tuesday 23 April 1991

DIARY: Government has announced a new Council Tax to replace the Poll Tax – a u-turn if ever there was one.

The Poll Tax for funding local government was introduced in Scotland in 1989, a year before the rest of the UK. It was hugely unpopular and opponents argued that it meant the less well off were having to pay more while the better off paid less. There were widespread protests and a mass non-payment campaign. It was key to the downfall of Margaret Thatcher as Prime Minister the previous year.

Saturday 27 April 1991

DIARY: Onto Ibrox for a press conference announcing new assistant Archie Knox. Bit of hassle when they said it should only be for the Sundays. However, I got my interviews in the end with chairman David Murray, manager Walter Smith and Archie Knox. I asked in usual fashion if

Smith would identify himself on the tape to establish level and he must have assumed I wasn't sure who he was. The conversation went, 'Would you mind identifying yourself for the tape?' 'You must be fucking joking!' It was done with humour. I think.

Monday 22 July 1991

DIARY: Stroll in at the back of 5.00am, see a TV sub *(junior producer)*. 'How are you doing?' 'Been here all night.' Immediately alarm bells ring. 'Don't you know? A train crash, four dead.' Alarm bells ring, lights flash and off running. Fortunately, the late sub and reporter had it all under control.

Four people died in the Newton Rail Crash, including both drivers. Being oblivious to breaking stories could happen in the days before constant news on mobile phones.

Saturday 10 August 1991

DIARY: A new football season and it makes Saturdays feel more like they should. Covering the Morton 2–1 Partick Thistle game from Division One.

A new season always felt vibrant with new grass, new strips and new hope.

I thoroughly enjoyed radio, but there was no question it was the poor relation to television. I wanted to expand my experience and applied successfully for an attachment to the TV newsroom.

Monday 30 September 1991

DIARY: The start of my television attachment today and a whole new world. Watching *Reporting Scotland* going out from the gallery was fascinating. I don't like the thought that all the elements – studio, VT, graphics – come from different parts of the building.

Wednesday 2 October 1991
Reporting Scotland

The search for fisherman missing in the North Atlantic is continuing despite deteriorating weather conditions. The operation centred on the area near Rockall, some 250 miles west of the Outer Hebrides. Two RAF Nimrods have been searching throughout the day along with a merchant vessel.

DIARY: Got my first piece on *Reporting Scotland* tonight. It was just my voice under shots of Stornoway coastguard station with two interview clips included. All to do with a search for 16 Spanish fishermen. I didn't find it that difficult to do, although I did have to rewrite my first draft because it told the straightforward story radio style and altered it slightly to match the pictures when we got them later.

Thursday 3 October 1991

DIARY: Prepared my own bulletins this morning. It seems straightforward enough once you get into the way of it, but there really is not the same reaction time. Added to that, there's only 1:15 to fill and with weather it isn't much.

Thursday 24 October 1991
BBC Reporting Scotland

A Fatal Accident Inquiry has been hearing how a toddler died when the car she was in was overwhelmed by a river in spate. The inquiry in Haddington heard how the little girl's mother struggled to free her two children as water poured into the car. And there was a warning that the tragedy could happen again.

DIARY: Made my first camera appearance on *Reporting Scotland* tonight. It was a fairly quiet day all in, but I voiced a story on an FAI into a toddler who drowned when her mother tried to cross a swollen river in her car. By the afternoon we had some more on it, including pictures from the original tragedy. There weren't a lot of them, so I decided to do a piece to camera. It was three sentences and I did them from memory. I did it in one take. However, the sound man wanted another one to be sure and it took me about five more after that.

I was a young reporter making his on-screen debut and focused on doing a good job, but

the detachment from the tragic details of the story sounds rather callous now.

Saturday 26 October 1991

DIARY: Airdrie were playing Dundee United. Not a great game, United won 3–1, so there was plenty to say. Jim McLean, United's manager, wouldn't allow any interviews because of the SFA's policy of clobbering anybody who says anything controversial. He wants 'freedom of speech'.

I don't think I ever did interview Jim McLean, who delivered Dundee United to the brink of European glory. He was forever in dispute with the football authorities.

Thursday 28 November 1991
BBC Reporting Scotland

The Government is being asked to pay compensation to people who contracted the HIV virus from contaminated blood during medical treatment. The Edinburgh Labour MP, Gavin Strang, is urging the Government to reconsider its refusal to compensate victims.

DAVIE, victim: I had leukaemia and I had various treatments, chemotherapy and radiotherapy. And then I had a bone marrow transplant. And during that period, I was given quite a lot of blood products and it was discovered after I'd actually came through the transplant and got rid of the leukaemia that I was given infected platelets.

The infected blood scandal has been described as the worst treatment disaster in the history of the NHS. Thousands died after being infected by contaminated blood products in the 1970s and '80s. A damning inquiry report was published in 2024.

Tuesday 17 December 1991
BBC Reporting Scotland

The Western Isles Council is again appealing to the Government to bail it out of the crisis caused by its losses in BCCI. The move comes hours after two senior officials were sacked for their part in the £20 million investment. They've announced tonight they're to appeal. But councillors have postponed £3 million of cuts which could have seen schools and social work centres closed, and even bus services curtailed.

The closure of the BCCI Bank in July 1991 led to severe losses for local councils, most notably the Western Isles Council.

1992

1992 was a transitional year for me, working between radio and TV and then as a sports correspondent. Much of the coverage of this year is dominated by sport.

Wednesday 8 January 1992

DIARY: Today's main story being the closure of Ravenscraig two years earlier than expected and all that entails in terms of job losses and the effect on the Lanarkshire economy.

Many of the news bulletins I produced in the late 1980s included stories about the demise of these big nationalised industries. Ravenscraig was the last of them. The explosive demolition of the Ravenscraig towers was an iconic image of the time.

Monday 13 January 1992

DIARY: I have to remember that my news values are sometimes affected by what pictures are available. I still work along the lines of the story on its own merits and while that is ideally the best method, it can lead to dull TV with straight reads.

Tuesday 21 January 1992

DIARY: Dull shift in the TV Newsroom – at one point Eddie and I were playing Hangman!

Monday 27 January 1992

DIARY: Presented my first ever programme on national radio today, when I co-presented *Newsdrive* with Clare English. My familiarity with live broadcasting through my sports stuff helped. The programme went very smoothly.

One of the stories in the programme was very prescient of societal priorities 30 years later.

BBC Radio Scotland

Weather maps from the dinosaur era could hold the key to global warming. Next week scientists will meet in Edinburgh to debate the issue. Computers are helping produce charts showing what the earth's weather was like as far back as 150 million years ago.

DR STUART MONRO, British Geological Survey: Compared with the dinosaurs, man is having much more of an influence on his environment. The dinosaurs didn't put half as much toxic gas into the atmosphere as we do. Though, perhaps, some people say that their eating large quantities of vegetation and grass did cause a certain amount of fairly noxious vapours to go up into the upper atmosphere.

DOUGLAS MACLEOD, reporter: We're only beginning to understand that the weather, or at least climate, is very complicated. Are we absolutely sure that it's the changes we're making? I believe, for example, there was a mini-Ice Age in the 17th century. Could that now be affecting us?

SM: Indeed, and this is part of the problem of why we have to look back over the geological past. We have had a number of hiccups or glitches, peaks and troughs in the climatological record. We've got to look at that pattern and look at the pattern that's being established at the present day against that backdrop... At the present time we're very concerned about the ill that we're doing to our environment. We're trying to get in there to understand the science behind it first, so that we can try and put forward some remedial action for the future.

Wednesday 26 February 1992

DIARY: Presented midweek *Sportsound* tonight as a taster before fully presenting Saturday's programme. We were featuring a number of Scottish Cup ties, but principally the St Johnstone–Inverness Caley tie. Bob Crampsey joined me in the studio and he is very good – he's so knowledgeable about sport and you can throw a question to him and know he can fill the time. Also interviewed John Beattie about rugby and he too is a good speaker. I thought I did reasonably well, without clearly being a born presenter.

I noted that 'I doubt I could ever do presentation as my prime work, but it is a good sideline to have.'

Saturday 29 February 1992
BBC Radio Sport

ANNOUNCER: Now at just after two o'clock, John MacKay is your host for four hours of top-class sporting action. In *Sportsound*.

DIARY: Today was the big one – presenting *Sportsound*. I was undoubtedly helped by the fact that I'd been in the studio last week and presented the programme on Wednesday. Went in early and trawled through the wires for pieces which might be useful to me. Soaked in as much information as I could before lunch. Again, I was fortunate in not being too nervous beforehand. We went on air at 2.00pm and I was anchoring for the next four hours – and doing so with hardly anything in the way of scripts. I have a running order and that is my guide. I wrote plenty of notes on it, cues to reporters etc, but the more I force myself to adlib the better I'll become. Bob Crampsey wasn't in the studio, instead he was at a ground – Hearts v Celtic – but he was still the man I was having the discussions with. The first hour and a half and the last hour are the times when I had to be on my toes. Football, snooker, racing – we had it all. When I came out my head was absolutely thumping. Again, I felt I had done okay, but I could do a lot better.

Friday 3 April 1992

DIARY: This afternoon I had a training session on the autocue. I'd expected a small-scale attempt in the continuity cubicle, but News Editor Gordon Macmillan had organised a full-scale rehearsal from Studio A with the works – lighting, director, VT etc. Even had to go via make-up. I'd been wanting to play it so low-key that I left my suit jacket in the car. I did it immediately after the 3.55pm bulletin. We actually did it twice – the first one being a rehearsal. I didn't stumble and I followed the directions without a problem. My timings were fine too, so I was pleased. Dropped my jacket back in the car, washed off the make-up and returned low-key to the newsroom. Walked in and they all applauded me! It had been put through the internal system and they'd all seen it. So much for low-key.

The applause was not to mark my performance, but to let me know that everyone had seen it. Screen tests are never done on the quiet. Never.

The screen test was during the election campaign and included this story.

BBC Reporting Scotland

In an attack on the SNP, Labour's John Smith has described independent economic power for Scotland as 'an illusion'. But the nationalists insist independence is coming.

JOHN SMITH, Labour Leader: I don't think it would be realistically financially viable because we would still be so much part of the United Kingdom economy that any sort of independence would, I think, be illusory. I think it would make much more sense for us to establish a Scottish Parliament within the United Kingdom.

ALEX SALMOND, SNP leader: We're the Tory busters in Scottish politics because we are going to end Tory rule in Scotland, not just for one election, but we're going to end Tory rule in Scotland for good.

GENERAL ELECTION 1992
Thursday 9 April 1992

DIARY: Election Day, which has been getting built up so much since everyone began predicting the election would have been last summer. Also, there has been great interest in the Scottish Nationalists – who've been high profile. My own sense has been that while it may be causing great interest in the media and among the pundits, independence is just not the burning talking point among the voters. Labour's star has been rising and it's being seen as a close-run thing, possibly a hung Parliament.

I worked in the VT area logging and delivering

tapes. It was a frustrating experience because it felt detached from the action.

DIARY CONT: The first of the crucial seats to be called, Basildon, went to the Tories and it was instantly clear that the Labour breakthrough wasn't going to happen. So it was, the Tory majority slashed, but still 20 or so and an improvement against all predictions in Scotland. SNP down one – Jim Sillars out.

Friday 10 April 1992

DIARY: The atmosphere was one of after-the-party. Subdued and reflective, although amazement at the poor showing of the SNP. One or two people were actually very angry at the return of the Tories. The day's programme was dominated by reaction to the result. The Tories are cock-a-hoop with Scottish Secretary Ian Lang making the most of it. Who can blame him?

I returned to radio as the Sports Correspondent at the end of my TV attachment.

Friday 22 May 1992
BBC Radio Scotland

Twenty-five years ago today 11 Scottish footballers walked onto a pitch in Lisbon to play for the premier trophy in European club football. They faced the might of the legendary Italian side, Inter Milan. Celtic won by two goals to one. That match, the most famous victory in Scottish football, is now part of the game's folklore. John MacKay looks back...

I was quite daunted by interviewing these legends. They'd gathered in their green blazers for a celebratory event and had such an evidently strong bond. They were great, full of fun and happy to oblige my interview requests. Unfortunately, I have no record of what they said.

Friday 19 June 1992
BBC Radio Scotland

Scotland return home from the European Championships today. You could probably have written the script beforehand. Scotland unlucky to go down in the first two games, then finishing with a flourishing performance. That's what happened – they beat the CIS 3–0.

The CIS was a transitional football team of former Soviet states. It existed only for the 1992 European Championships.

DIARY: I went down with the radio van to meet them at Glasgow Airport. Hundreds of supporters were there and there was a real media scrum to get clips.

Friday 26 June 1992
BBC Radio Scotland

Scottish football is set for the biggest shake-up in its history with the announcement that the country's main five clubs intend to resign from the Scottish League. The chairmen of the clubs sent letters to the league tonight giving notice of their intention to breakaway. They are to set up their own league, the Scottish Super League.

Thursday 16 July 1992

DIARY: On to the SFA news conference on the changes to the laws of the game. The pass-back to the goalkeeper will now be punished with a free kick if the keeper picks it up. Fine in principle, but it'll just see the ball getting humped into the crowd. Personally, I think if they really want to improve football, they should radically alter the offside law.

This was part of the continued and generally successful attempt to make the game more attractive. Passing the ball back to the goalkeeper who could pick it up was a notorious time-wasting tactic and an easy way out for defenders under pressure. An ability to play the ball is now an essential skill for goalkeepers.

Tuesday 28 July 1992

DIARY: Plenty of Olympic material, although it has to be said the Games have still to come alive. The track and field events should be spread out more to maintain interest. Personally, I think the number of sports should be reduced (basketball and tennis, for example, have no place at the Olympics). For me, indeed for most, I think the Olympic Games are about track and field. I can see why swimming, gymnastics, cycling etc are included, but much of the rest should be ditched.

Friday 31 July 1992

DIARY: Used phrases like 'The Olympic flame will burn more fiercely today with the beginning of the athletics.' A bit colourful perhaps, but interest in the Games will really start now. I'd also done a package on Yvonne Murray, Tom McKean and Liz McColgan – the Scots who'll be running this weekend.

Later I completed a package on why a country like Denmark can produce good international sides *(they'd won the 1992 European Championships)*, but Scotland with a similar population can't.

Another of those issues that comes round and round again with consistent regularity, especially with regard to football. Listening to the shouts from the sidelines at children's football on a Saturday morning is a real insight into why we consistently fail to match our footballing aspirations.

Thursday 6 August 1992
BBC Radio Scotland

The Scottish Super League will be going ahead as planned, says its organisers, despite the refusal of the Scottish Football League to accept the resignations of the rebel clubs. And the Super League will be expanded from the original eight clubs to ten, with Motherwell being introduced as a new member today. As our Sports News Correspondent John MacKay reports, the clubs insist they mean business.

DIARY: A news conference by the organisers of the Scottish Super League at the Royal Scot Hotel on the outskirts of Edinburgh. Asked to take two Romanian journalists who are on work experience. Interesting observation from the two Romanians that, although Wallace Mercer *(chairman of the Super League)* is the mouthpiece of the Super League, both recognised that Rangers' David Murray was the main man, despite not saying much.

Friday 28 August 1992

DIARY: I've found while I've done this sports correspondent job that most people are helpful and friendly. But football, particularly the higher you go, and particularly the administrators, are for the most part difficult and pompous. Given what an arse they have made of the national game and given its current state (too many games and no European threat) they hardly have reason to be.

Wednesday 16 September 1992

DIARY: Major disruptions in the financial world with the pound's value plummeting. In a response that smacked of panic, the Government raised interest rates twice in the day, first by 2 per cent, then a further 3 per cent this afternoon. Everyone worried about the impact on mortgage payments, although building societies said they'd bide their time. Later still, the pound was suspended from the ERM *(Exchange Rate Mechanism)* and interest rates were cut again. All this caused quite a commotion in the newsroom and it's good having that sort of buzz. It'll be interesting to see whether the Chancellor *(Norman Lamont)* keeps his post. I'm not sure that it meant very much to people. If mortgage rates go up then obviously it will, but for the moment it all seems to be about invisible dealings by the city cats.

Wednesday 14 October 1992

DIARY: Scotland v Portugal World Cup qualifying tie at Ibrox. (Scotland lucky to get a 0–0 draw). I was doing the trackside interviews and I grabbed a couple of players when they came out to check the pitch (Craig Levein & Derek Whyte). I also interviewed Ian Durrant. My introduction to him said he was going to be a substitute and then I asked him, 'What will your role be tonight?'

Monday 26 October 1992

DIARY: I was doing the *One O'Clock News* and *Newsdrive*. Big issue now is Prime Minister John Major threatening Tory rebels with a General Election if they don't support him on Maastricht. Major has gone from Mr Nice Guy to Mr Incompetent in public perception.

The Maastricht Treaty introduced closer European co-operation.

The treaty was signed by 12 countries in the Dutch city of Maastricht in 1992 and went into effect in 1993. The agreement established greater co-operation between member states through economic, social, and legal channels. The Maastricht Treaty established the European Union's single currency system for the euro.

Friday 30 October 1992
BBC Radio Scotland

Today the contractors move in to begin the reconstruction of Hampden Park. No major matches will be played at the stadium for the next year. And when the fans return, gone will be the terraces that stir the images of the great crowds of the past.

DIARY: A football fan's dream today – I stood on the centre spot at Hampden Park and Lisbon Lion Billy McNeill bought me a pint. I'd arranged to meet football oracle, Bob Crampsey, there to hear some Hampden history. We were allowed to go on the pitch. What struck me was how short the pitch appeared to be, although it is certainly wide. A thrill ran through me as I stood on the turf looking to the terraces. Later called at Billy McNeill's pub to hear some of his memories and he bought me a pint while there. I've always liked McNeill whenever I've met him.

Thursday 5 November 1992

Rangers defeated Leeds United 2–1 in Champions League with goals from Mark Hateley and Ally McCoist to win 4–2 on aggregate.

DIARY: As much as anything else I'm pleased about the fact that the English media have been put in their place – the way in which they dismissed Rangers over the past few days has been irritating. Out to Ibrox later with the radio van to interview Walter Smith, the Rangers manager. He seemed to think he should only have been doing the newspapers, but eventually agreed to do radio and TV together. The whole newspaper/broadcast split in football is incredible and must be the only area in the reporting world which continues in that vein.

Football news conferences were heavily slanted in favour of the written press. There was quite a division between the two, however well you may get on with individual reporters personally. We would all gather, the 'electronic' media would ask our questions and then have to leave. Newspaper sports reporters wouldn't ask questions while radio and TV were there. The idea was to keep stories for the following day's papers. It didn't apply to any other area – politics, crime, etc – so why sport? Indeed, the Sunday newspapers often had an entire press conference to themselves. It seemed antiquated to me at the time and I couldn't see why football managers indulged it. They still do.

Thursday 10 December 1992

DIARY: A train to Edinburgh for the launch of a new venture to build a national stadium – this time in Lanarkshire. Bad day to launch it as all the European heads of state were arriving in Edinburgh ahead of the summit *(a European Council meeting)*. They did their presentation – outnumbering the four media bods by three to one – and quite impressive it was too.

The proposal was for a futuristic stadium next to the M8 motorway. Looking towards the new century it made sense to take the stadium out of an urban area with transport and parking limitations to a location where all that could be easily addressed. Even as I reported on it I knew it didn't have a chance. I'm sure the cost played a part, but lack of vision wouldn't have helped.

Saturday 12 December 1992

DIARY: Bad morning. Playing football before work. During the 3–1 defeat by Spatz in Coatbridge, I got an elbow in the mouth which split my lip badly and has chipped three of my front teeth. The lip, though badly gashed, will heal, but the teeth will need dental treatment. Added to that the team played poorly. I was doing the Airdrie–Motherwell game for TV and since I was playing in Coatbridge it seemed pointless to go home, so I went to my brother's to clean up my wound. I should have gone to hospital, but decided to wait. No problems at the game – bottom of the table clash which Motherwell won 2–0.

I did my match reports and interviews and then returned to my car to come home. As I checked the rear-view mirror, I saw a tracks of dried blood from the corner of my mouth to my chin. No one had said a word all afternoon. Obviously, not unusual in these parts of Lanarkshire.

Undated 1992
BBC Radio Scotland

Scotland throughout its history has been subject to wave upon wave of conquerors who've left their mark or, on occasions, settlers. But the most recent immigrants are the Asians and the story of their progress since they arrived in Scotland is told in a book which is nearing completion. And it'll surprise some people to know that the earliest of them came in 1505.

JM: The Scots thought they were Egyptians, these people that King James IV had given letters of recommendation to in 1505. They were known as 'gypsies', which is what caused the confusion with Egypt. But they originated from India and were Scotland's first Asian immigrants.

BASHIR MAAN, author, *The New Scots*: We only found out in the 19th century. And it was also a Scot, and he was in India, and he realised that a lot of words in the gypsies' language were akin to certain languages in India. He did the research on this subject and found out that the gypsies were actually a section of a tribe who still lives in India... (*Significant 20th-century Asian immigration began in 1918 with lascars being paid off from their jobs as seamen. Many became peddlers and brought over family and friends. They spread from Glasgow to other cities during the 1930s. The most significant immigration was in the 1950s following the partition of India*) Their contacts widened. I'm talking about those people who had relatives here or had been in Scotland... and more and more people got to know that you can go to Scotland and make a living... They are being absorbed now in the mainstream of life in Scotland. The first generation was the entrepreneurs, y'know, starting businesses, getting there by the hard way. But the children now do not want to continue, in many cases, in the same lines of business their parents are. They are going to universities, getting highly educated, going into professions like doctors, engineers, solicitors and all that.

Bashir Maan came to Scotland from Pakistan in 1953 and went on to become the first Muslim elected to public office in the UK as a Labour Councillor in Glasgow. In 2024 the First Minister of Scotland and leader of Scottish Labour were both of South Asian heritage.

1993

Friday 8 January 1993

DIARY: Celtic's announcement that they have effectively withdrawn from the Scottish Super League. We were told last night that the chairman would speak after 7.00am – he hung up on me. So, I phoned straight back and after some discussion he agreed to do me later, but refused an early live. Yet another PR disaster for Celtic, who're stumbling from one fiasco to another.

The story of the week has been the grounding of an oil tanker off the south coast of Shetland and the consequent pollution. I'm enjoying sport, but I wonder whether I'm losing touch with news.

The *Braer* ran aground off Shetland spilling more than 80,000 tonnes of crude oil and causing widespread damage.

Tuesday 26 January 1993

DIARY: Football legend Bobby Charlton was doing a promo for one of his soccer classes. For a man who was/is such a well-known figure, and in footballing terms 'legend' isn't too strong a description, I was impressed by what a genuinely nice man he was.

Thursday 11 February 1993

DIARY: I did another screen test for television. I did one last year and they said they were happy with it, but they've not needed any newsreaders since. The News Editor Gordon Macmillan said he wanted me to do another one today with the new set. I felt quite relaxed about it and perhaps last year's experience was a help.

Friday 12 February 1993

DIARY: I've to do my first television bulletin at the end of this month. They seem to have been happy with yesterday's screen test and I'll be doing the 9.28pm on 26 February. It could be the beginning of a new avenue in my career or I could make an arse of myself.

Opinions on this have varied ever since.

Saturday 13 February 1993
BBC Radio & TV Sport

PARTICK THISTLE 0–4 DUNDEE UNITED

Duncan Ferguson was the man everyone thought would be the star of the show, but in fact it was Paddy Connolly who caught the eye. Two goals, in actual fact three goals, but one the ref didn't see, and a performance which mesmerised Thistle. Just before half-time Connolly had the ball in the net, but it came off the back stanchion inside the goal and while Utd celebrated Thistle played on. The referee clearly didn't think the ball had gone in.

The ball rebounded from the stanchion inside the net and one of the Thistle players caught it in disgust. As the United players celebrated, the Thistle players walked back to position for the restart when it became apparent the ref was waving play on. There was incredulity on the pitch, around the ground and in the press box. It's the most bizarre refereeing decision I've ever seen in years of watching football.

Friday 26 February 1993

DIARY: I made my live television debut tonight, presenting BBC Scotland's 9:28pm news bulletin. It went smoothly enough, with no glaring errors and only one minor stumble. The lead story – strike at Yarrow's, then a court case about two youths killing a woman by rolling a car down steps, the financial problems at Monktonhall Colliery. Straightforward, although perhaps more reading than usual. Problem before we went on air when I couldn't hear talk-back. Technician sorted it out, but it left time for only one rehearsal. Shortly after that was it, I was on air. Happy and relieved when it was all over, although I felt quite comfortable doing it.

I'm not sure I looked comfortable, certainly not at the start. My face was flushed and there is a hint of perspiration on my forehead. The mouth was going like a washing machine to make sure I got the words out properly. Still, I began to present bulletins regularly so it couldn't have been so bad.

Monday 8 March 1993
BBC TV News

A nationwide campaign to abolish the criminal verdict of not proven has been launched. The verdict is used when a jury is unsure about the guilt or innocence of the accused. 36,000 people have already signed a petition calling for a change in the law.

KATE DUFFY, mother of murder victim Amanda Duffy: There are a lot of families out there who have gone through similar circumstances to ourselves and at the end of a trial, with a not proven verdict, you come out of that trial feeling that you have a life sentence.

Despite such campaigns and continued public disquiet, the not proven verdict, famously described by Sir Walter Scott as 'that bastard verdict', remains. Its abolition was part of a bill going through the Scottish Parliament in 2024.

Saturday 20 March 1993

DIARY: A new job reading the results on *Afternoon Sportscene*. I remember as a young boy I used to lie in front of the TV writing down the results in the paper for Faither as they were read out. And here was I reading them out! The guy whom I used to hear still does it from London and I had him coming through my cans *(headphones)* and tried to keep pace with him. It was an education sitting beside Dougie Donnelly as he presented – no scripts and little guidance – and he held the programme together seamlessly.

The graphics were generated from London, so you had to keep up with their announcer. I had listened to the results for as long as I remember, so I knew how to do the classic delivery – a high score up, a low score down.

Wednesday 7 April 1993
BBC Radio Scotland

Rangers play one of the most important games in their history tonight when they meet Marseille in the European Champions League. Victory would almost certainly assure either side a place in the European Cup *(first Champions League)* Final. The teams drew two-all at Ibrox in the first match in the section.

The match ended 1–1 and because of other results Rangers failed to make the final.

Thursday 29 April 1993
BBC Radio Scotland

It had to happen. Scotland were due a football humiliation after several years of respectable, if unspectacular results. Humiliated we were, thrashed 5–0 by Portugal in Lisbon. It means that Scotland will not be competing in the World Cup Finals in the United States next year, the first time we've failed to qualify since 1970. The national coach Andy Roxburgh said he was shattered.

This was my final report as sports correspondent. I enjoyed sport, but I felt detached from news and I didn't want that. It took me some time to be able to watch a football match for its own sake without composing a quick update in my head every ten minutes.

Monday 3 May 1993

DIARY: I presented my first ever *Good Morning Scotland* today along with Alan Douglas. He's a nice fellow and it was a fairly easy introduction to our flagship programme. Bosnia, riots in Moscow, political dispute in the UK over Maastricht. A busy morning.

Tuesday 4 May 1993

DIARY: Officially back on the reporters' rota today. No longer a trainee, a sub, a CNA – I'm a BBC reporter.

Becoming a reporter had been my ambition since I joined the corporation. I had enjoyed all my roles, the newsdesk especially, but to be a reporter on the BBC – that was beyond anything I could have hoped when I started in journalism.

Friday 7 May 1993
BBC Radio Scotland

A newborn baby girl found abandoned in Kilmarnock early this morning is making a good recovery in hospital. Police are appealing for her mother to come forward and want to hear from a mystery caller who alerted them to the baby's plight... Baby Susanne – as she's been christened by nursing staff – was found in the early hours of the morning. She had been born only three or four hours before. Doctors believe she was a full-term pregnancy and she weighs a healthy six pounds 14 ounces.

DIARY: She was only hours old and it made me sad to think of the child's start in life. And pity the mother, she must be frightened and confused. In the office at 5.22pm and I was the 5.30pm lead.

Wednesday 19 May 1993

DIARY: A call came through about a shooting incident in Cambuslang and I was sent out in the radio van. I didn't think I'd make it in time for the *Six O'Clock News* (left at 5:40pm), but I did – moving at a fair rate and even following a police van at one stage. The incident was on the town's Main Street and I parked on the main junction and put up the mast. Quickly spoke to a CID officer and a couple of witnesses – the first confirmed three injured, but said nothing more, the others spoke of a shopkeeper, woman and policeman being hit. Did an unscripted piece into the *Six O'Clock*. The police trapped the gunman in a house and there was a siege situation for a couple of hours before he was taken out.

Friday 21 May 1993
BBC Radio Scotland

The shopkeeper who was shot in the head during an armed raid in Cambuslang on Wednesday has died. Earlier today a man appeared in court in Glasgow accused of shooting the shopkeeper, a woman and a policeman.

Wednesday 9 June 1993

DIARY: Another TV bulletin tonight. It was a warm, close day and by evening, despite heavy showers, it was very humid. When I went into the studio and turned on the lights, the sweat just poured out because of the heat. It meant that every time we cut pictures I was having to wipe my face with a hanky. When I saw the tape later there was a sweat globule sitting on my jaw throughout – looked like a big plook.

Thursday 24 June 1993

DIARY: Everything overshadowed by announcement that Rosyth Dockyard has failed to win the refitting contract for nuclear subs, despite Government promises. Blanket coverage – political outrage, workers' despair.

Thursday 1 July 1993

DIARY: The Director General of the BBC, John Birt, was in viewing our operation. I don't like what he's doing to the organisation, putting marketplace management in place of quality and making news so analytical that the national bulletins are getting dull.

Tuesday 6 July 1993
BBC Radio Scotland

The husband of the Scottish aid worker shot dead by a sniper in Sarajevo has arrived home in Edinburgh. 63-year-old Alan Whitcutt described his wife's final moments and defended their decision to go to Bosnia. And he's urged volunteers to continue with their humanitarian work.

Thursday 15 July 1993
BBC Radio Scotland

The Scottish international footballer Duncan Ferguson has signed for Rangers in a deal which is the biggest in the history of British football. Rangers will pay Dundee United a fee which will eventually total £4 million. It ends months of speculation about the player's future.

JM: So was announced the biggest deal in the history of British football. A deal for a Scottish internationalist between two Scottish clubs. The Rangers chairman, David Murray, says it demonstrates Rangers' ambition to compete with the best in Europe.

DAVID MURRAY, Rangers Chairman: What I've repeatedly said is it's no use reducing your overdraft and making healthy profits if the dividends are not on the park. Our shareholders, I believe, and our supporters want dividends on the park and it's only by bringing in players like Duncan Ferguson we shall continue to do so. There's no point in having no borrowings and no trophies. Rangers is about having a bit of debt, which I'm prepared to continue doing, bringing it down gradually, and attracting the best talent to Rangers.

DUNCAN FERGUSON, Rangers: It's been my boyhood dream to come and play for the Rangers and it's just starting to sink in.

Duncan Ferguson's time at Rangers was short-lived. It's best remembered for his being charged with assault for head-butting John McStay of Raith Rovers during a game at Ibrox – a charge that ultimately led to him serving a short prison sentence. He established a more successful career in England after being sold to Everton.

Thursday 22 July 1993

DIARY: The news day dominated by Commons votes on the Maastricht Treaty towards closer European integration. The Government defeated a Labour amendment through the Speaker's casting vote, but lost another vote. It means the treaty can't be ratified... John Major has called for a vote of confidence tomorrow. The rebels will, doubtless, not risk bringing the Government down and they'll be able to push Maastricht through.

BBC Radio Scotland

Scottish football clubs have been warned that they'll be taken to court if they demand a transfer fee for players who they are no longer paying. The Players' Union say it's a gross injustice for a club to seek a fee from another club if the player is out of contract.

Friday 23 July 1993
BBC Radio Scotland

There has been a decrease in the number of births and deaths in Scotland, according to the latest statistics. The figures show there have been fewer infant deaths, but more homicides. More people have been getting married and divorced, and suicides have increased. The statistics are featured in the Registrar General's report for Scotland for the year 1992.

Undated report August 1993
BBC Radio Scotland

Football clubs in Britain have been accused of cashing in on the loyalty of their young fans by changing their strips too frequently. A consumer magazine has criticised clubs for bringing out a new kit too often and charging too much for it. The magazine highlights Manchester United, who brought out four new strips in just over a year. It's a lucrative business, of course, the replica shirts of some of the top clubs sell by the tens of thousands and the clubs benefit by millions of pounds.

SUE HARVEY, Editor, *Check It Out* magazine: Almost all of the clubs were changing either their home strips or their away strip every season. And the prices do seem to us excessively high. You can pay up to £51 as a top of the range price for a junior strip, and that is what Celtic are charging. And £64 for an adult strip. That does seem to us to be an awful lot of money.

UNKNOWN, Marketing Director, Umbro International: Our view is, and certainly it's one backed up by our research, is that parents are quite happy to pay £30 if something is lasting the child two years, insofar as it's something the kiddie wants to wear, rather than being forced to wear something which – they have to wear a top of some description – that they, perhaps, don't want to wear and it's costing £20.

BILL WILSON, Commercial Director SFA: As recently as five years ago football came into High Street fashion. In the past strips were used for playing football at whatever level…Nowadays that's not the case. It's a fashion garment. Companies like Umbro, like Adidas, design a strip that goes with jeans or shell bottoms or track bottoms and then football teams wear it. This is 100 per cent turnaround from what it used to be when we started. If you go into Marks & Spencer's they change their range, probably, about four times a year with the season. That's who the kit companies are competing with now… People demand a change. For example, we haven't changed the Scotland jersey for three years. We will be changing next year. And the sales of the Scotland jersey are almost at zero level because it's been on the market too long and people want to change.

Saturday 9 October 1993
BBC Scotland News

NELSON MANDELA IN GLASGOW

Nelson Mandela today said Scotland had been a source of great strength to him and his comrades during their struggle against apartheid in South Africa. He was speaking in Glasgow where he received the freedom of nine British cities and districts at a special ceremony. John MacKay was there…

NELSON MANDELA, (*speech excerpt from inside Glasgow City Chambers*): It is a special privilege to be a guest of this great City of Glasgow. It will always enjoy a distinguished place in the records of the international campaign against apartheid. The people of Glasgow were the first in the world to confer on me the Freedom of the City at a time when I and my comrades in the ANC were imprisoned on Robben Island serving life sentences, which in apartheid South Africa then meant imprisonment until death. Whilst we were physically denied our freedom in the country of our birth, a city, 6,000 miles away, and as removed as Glasgow, refused to accept the legitimacy of the apartheid system, and declared us to be free.

Sunday 10 October 1993
BBC Radio Scotland

Two Libyans accused of carrying out the Lockerbie Bombing will not be coming to Scotland to stand trial – at least not in the immediate future. The lawyers representing them have advised their clients not to surrender to the Scottish authorities. The two Scottish members of the international defence team have already arrived home.

Wednesday 20 October 1993
BBC Radio Scotland

Regional councils in Scotland have been dismissing claims by the campaign group 'Scottish Watch' that they will disrupt council business. The group is alarmed at the influence of English white settlers in rural Scotland… the group – with a membership of little more than a hundred – is opposed to what it claims is the 'Englishing' of Scottish culture. In particular, they want to deal with problems they say are caused by mass English immigration into Scottish rural areas. They insist they are not racists and are confident, despite general condemnation throughout the media and political world, their support will grow significantly.

Friday 3 December 1993
BBC Radio Scotland

Some of Scotland's wealthier church congregations are finding it increasingly difficult to provide financial support to aid other congregations. One minister has warned that some churches are so pressurised that 'the pips are squeaking'. It's another sign of the growing financial problems confronting the Kirk.

At the end of the year I made my debut presenting Reporting Scotland. I was a regular presenter on news bulletins and the sports

desks, so in one sense it wasn't a huge leap. But it was the station's flagship news programme and to anchor it was a big step up in prestige.

1994

Wednesday 2 February 1994
BBC Radio Scotland

An Irish student who gave away her child at birth to an Edinburgh couple has failed in a court attempt to get him back. She was appealing against a sheriff's ruling that an adoption order should be made in favour of the couple. Today, her appeal was overruled by three judges at the Court of Session.

The 25-year-old Irish woman had kept her pregnancy secret from her family and decided to put the baby up for adoption. She came to Edinburgh and stayed with a couple who proposed adopting the child. After the baby was born the mother returned to Ireland without him. Some time later she phoned the couple to say she wanted the baby back. They refused. The court ruled that the bond formed between the child and the adoptive parents could not be broken without detriment to the child.

Wednesday 2 March 1994
BBC Radio Scotland

CELTIC TAKEOVER

Celtic may have won 1–0 last night in a Premier League game against Kilmarnock, but the result has probably been lost in the furore surrounding the club's off-the-field activities. The relationship between the board and the club's supporters reached its nadir last night when the lowest crowd for nine years attended Parkhead. A boycott organised by the Celts For Change group and the Supporters' Association resulted in a crowd of just under 11 thousand going to the game, barely a fifth of the ground's capacity. Our reporter John MacKay spent the evening with the Celtic fans and reports now on their increasing frustrations.

JM: This is Baird's Bar in Glasgow's Gallowgate. It's a Celtic pub with memorabilia covering the walls. It's the night of a Celtic game and the place is half empty.

Vox Pops

Usually it's choc-a-bloc in here and the past two or three home games, you can see yourself. Usually, you can't move. It's a reflection of what's going on up the road.

I don't want to boycott Celtic, I love Celtic. I want to go out and shout my team on. But if me stopping going and the people like me stopping going gets rid of that shower up there, then I'll do it.

JM: The match kicks off with a Parkhead that isn't as empty as might have been anticipated. The traditional Celtic end is not full, but there is a fair covering of supporters. The away end of the ground is almost totally empty. And the traditional 'Jungle' is perhaps a third full.

It's the only thing left for the Celtic supporters now, to stay away. I think in the long run they'll go, the board. They've got to go.

JM: These are difficult times at Parkhead. The future direction of the club is unclear and the team on the park is having little success, although tonight they did win 1–0 against Kilmarnock. A last-minute goal from John Collins. It was a surreal atmosphere at Celtic Park which turned into the bizarre when, apart from Collins's goal, the highlight of the match was the sight of a fox running the full length of the pitch.

Celtic came within minutes of financial collapse. Their saviour was the Scottish-born, Celtic-supporting Canadian businessman Fergus McCann.

There was a major media presence as McCann arrived at Glasgow Airport. This drew its own crowd of onlookers, intrigued by the big name who was clearly expected. When he walked through international arrivals – a low-key figure with a moustache and bunnet – there was an explosion of light. You could see the bewilderment of the onlookers wondering who he was.

Saturday 5 March 1994
BBC Radio Scotland

Fergus McCann the man who's taken over Celtic says he wants the Bank of Scotland – the club's bankers – to explain why they permitted the club to get so close to receivership. He intends meeting bank officials over the next few days. Mr McCann was given a hero's welcome by the Celtic supporters before Celtic's game against St Johnstone in Perth this afternoon.

JM: Mr McCann said his priority now was to stabilise Celtic's financial position, develop a top-class stadium and provide money to build a competitive team.

Fergus McCann sold up after five years, having achieved exactly what he said he would do.

Saturday 2 April 1994
BBC Radio Scotland

The cause of a crash which killed five people, including three children, is unlikely to be known for several weeks. The dead were all travelling in an estate car which collided in a head-on smash with an articulated lorry on the notorious A96 road in Grampian. One of the victims was the son of a police officer called to the scene.

Thursday 14 April 1994
BBC Radio Scotland

Frederick West, the Gloucester builder who is already facing nine murder charges, has been charged with a tenth, that of his Scottish wife Rena Costello. It follows the discovery of a woman's body in a field at the weekend. Rena Costello, who was originally from Lanarkshire, has been missing for 20 years.

JM: Rena Costello... married Frederick West in the 1960s. Relatives spoke of their sadness. Her cousin Anne Graham said it was a terrible way for her to die. Rena had two daughters by Frederick West. One, Charmaine, has not been seen for several years. Detectives are anxious to trace her.

Eight-year-old Charmaine's remains were found the following month in the Wests' former home in Gloucester.

Thursday 12 May 1994

The Labour Leader John Smith died suddenly aged only 55. He was assumed to be the Prime Minister in waiting. I heard the news on the radio while on holiday.

Saturday 21 May 1994
BBC Reporting Scotland

Labour Party leaders in Scotland are considering the possibility that the Scottish Assembly building – the former Royal High School in Edinburgh – be renamed after John Smith. The party has pledged that's where a Scottish Parliament would sit if Labour gained power.

Wednesday 23 May 1994
BBC Radio Scotland

Two demonstrators have been arrested following the arrival of Britain's second Trident nuclear submarine on the Clyde. They were among a group of protesters opposed to the arrival of *Victorious* – which is the very latest in Britain's defence firepower. Costing £400 million and with the capacity to carry 16 Trident missiles, the new submarine will be based at Faslane.

Friday 27 May 1994
BBC Radio Scotland

Tonight, two pilots leave a Scottish airport at the beginning of a unique flight. Flying microlight aircraft, they will attempt to fly across the North Sea – the first time this has ever been attempted. If they succeed they will then fly their tiny planes around Europe.

JM, commentary from flight: Engines at full blast. We're now going along the runway and that's us up in the air. Very quickly. And going up to some height very quickly as well. You certainly don't get the surge that you might expect from a regular aircraft... We're now turning back towards the airport. A very steep turn... Again the craft holding quite steady, very much a surprise to me... Dropping now gently towards the runway. Speed still about 45 miles per hour. We're coming down. Just about to drop onto the tarmac. There we go!

My apparent calmness was betrayed by my final line, 'We're now back on sweet Mother Earth.'
The attempt to cross the North Sea was successful.

Wednesday 1 June 1994
BBC Radio Scotland

The Shadow Chancellor, Gordon Brown, has put an end to some of the speculation about the Labour leadership by announcing that he won't be standing. He said he would be supporting his friend Tony Blair, who's widely tipped as the most likely successor to John Smith. Some of Mr Brown's colleagues have praised his decision, describing it as being in the best interest of the party. But others have expressed disappointment.

JM: Gordon Brown said he had taken the decision in the interests of party unity. It now increases the likelihood of his friend and fellow moderniser, Tony Blair, inheriting the mantle of the late John Smith. Mr Brown has been praised for his decision, but not everyone is happy. There was dismay from a fellow Scot, Jimmy Wray, who is the chair of the Scottish Labour backbenchers.

Gordon Brown's stepping aside for Tony Blair became a running sore for Labour. It has been widely recorded how the tension between the two and their supporters undermined what a three-term Labour Government might have been able to achieve.

Monday 6 June 1994
BBC Radio Scotland

The popular television series *Taggart* will continue despite the death this morning of its star Mark McManus. Mr McManus died in his sleep while being treated for pneumonia in Glasgow's Victoria Infirmary. Tributes have been paid to the man who was the epitome of the hard Glasgow detective.

Mark McManus's classic line in the very first Taggart in 1983 – or 'Killer' as it was first known – 'We don't have ligatures in Maryhill' – marked it out as something special. STV did continue the series after his death until 2010.

Wednesday 15 June 1994
BBC Radio Scotland

The strike by signalling workers over pay has brought most of the country's railway system to a standstill. However, the impact on commuters in Scotland has not been as bad as expected. Railtrack, which is responsible for track and signals, has again insisted that an offer of almost 6 per cent to the RMT Union was a mistake, while Downing Street has denied that the Government intervened to block the higher offer.

Saturday 2 July 1994
BBC Radio Scotland

The Prince of Wales has been attacked as 'increasingly unsuitable to occupy the throne'. The leader of the Orange movement in Scotland has accused the Prince of wilful misunderstanding of the constitution of the realm. The claims follow the Prince's revelation that he wished to be head of more than just the Protestant churches.

Monday 4 July 1994
DIARY: Met Lorraine Davidson *(STV reporter and former BBC colleague)* on a job today and she repeated that Scottish TV wanted me. Finally phoned their head man, Scott Ferguson. Not in. Thought that was it, but he phoned back soon after and suggested meeting for a beer 'in the way these things are done.'

I was perfectly happy at the BBC and had never really considered moving, but I was intrigued by what STV might say.

Tuesday 5 July 1994
DIARY: The Head of Radio Scotland, James Boyle, is showing great interest in my proposed series *Dance Called America*. Called me at home and said he sees it as a big production effort with transmission in the spring. I'm excited about the idea, but the STV approach has thrown that into confusion.

I had pitched the idea of radio series based on Dr James Hunter's book Dance Called America on the Scottish diaspora in the US and Canada. It's a subject that has long fascinated me and the prospect of travelling round North America in the footsteps of the early Scottish settlers thrilled me. It was a real issue for me in deciding whether to move to STV. The series was eventually made by Radio 4.

Thursday 7 July 1994
DIARY: Met Scott Ferguson of STV. They want me as a reporter/presenter. I'd start off reporting, then do some breakfast bulletins and finally a stand-in presenter on *Scotland Today*, but reporting would be the mainstay.

Friday 8 July 1994
DIARY: I'm more convinced than ever that I'm going to move to Scottish Television. The BBC's Ken Cargill, despite telling me to see him on Friday, was tied up in meetings. When he finally called he said he hadn't really had a chance to think about it and didn't want to make promises he couldn't keep – spoke of attachments, but problems with Equal Opportunities. That's a cop-out. No question who wants me more.

This was classic BBC management fudge. My decision was made for me. I was happy at the BBC. My only request was to work more in the television newsroom. I had been trained by the BBC and had successfully filled just about every frontline role in the news operation. However, it's a move I have never regretted.

Saturday 23 July 1994
DIARY: Usual round of killings and car crashes, but little else. That would all be

very different were it someone I knew, but we only get the name and report it. The aftermath is of no interest. It's a sad reality.

There were three staples of weekend bulletins in the early part of my career: fatal car accidents involving teenagers – usually in rural areas – middle-aged motorcyclists crashing or murders in Northern Ireland. Sadly, the first two continue to occur with tragic frequency.

Saturday 30 July 1994

DIARY: Covered the first mass outdoor pop/rock festival in Scotland for more than 15 years, 'T-in-the-Park' at Strathclyde Park – named after the sponsor Tennent's. A relaxed atmosphere. Apart from looking a bit out of place wearing a suit and tie, I enjoyed it.

T-in-the-Park became a major part of Scotland's festival calendar and a rite of passage for many Scottish teenagers. It moved from Strathclyde Park to Ballado in 1997, expanded to a three-day event attracting tens of thousands each year. The last event was in Strathallan in Perthshire in 2016. It was replaced by the TRNSMT festival on Glasgow Green.

Monday 19 September 1994

DIARY: My first day at Scottish Television. I was thrown in at the deep end – which suits me – doing a piece on why a fatal bus crash happened and how it could be prevented. There is none of the fannying about that you have at the BBC as regards editing and getting a crew. It is obviously a smaller, busier operation.

Four people, including two girl guides, were killed when a double-decker bus hit a low bridge in Glasgow city centre.

STV News

This was an accident that could easily have been prevented. The police won't say why the driver went the way he did or why he didn't see the low bridge warning signs. But if a simple, electronic warning system had been in place four people could still be alive tonight. John MacKay reports.

I hadn't even had time to get started on the STV computer system. My first scripts were scribbled on bits of paper.

Tuesday 20 September 1994
STV News

A man who claimed to be Hannibal the Cannibal after biting two people has been jailed for six years at the High Court in Edinburgh.

DIARY: A piece on a guy who's been jailed for six years after being found guilty of biting off part of a woman's ear. Out to Feegie Park *(Ferguslie Park)* in Paisley. Managed to get a neighbour who'd found the woman to speak to me. It's the sort of story the BBC wouldn't touch, but which fascinates people.

The neighbour took a bit of persuasion, but finally invited us into his home. A newspaper photographer tried to follow our cameraman in and the guy said to him, 'No, no photographs.' TV can have that effect on people.

Friday 23 September 1994
STV News

The people of Drumchapel have been mourning the loss of the two girl guides killed in Sunday's horrific bus crash. Hundreds turned out for the funeral of Catherine McKnight and Margaret Riddick, who were both only ten years old. The minister at the funerals praised the community for the support they had been giving to the grieving families.

DIARY: Not a pleasant day's work... You never get used to white coffins.

Wednesday 28 September 1994

DIARY: Had to be back for 4.00pm to do a studio test for *Scotland Today*. Co-presented with Aasmah Mir. I was relaxed enough. Once I'm more in the style of the programme that'll help.

Tuesday 4 October 1994
STV News

One of Scotland's biggest ever public inquiries has begun in Ayr. It will recommend whether a 40-mile-long line of electricity pylons should be built across the heart of South Ayrshire. For months Scottish Power have argued that the power line will be a huge economic boost. The STOP campaigners say it will do irreparable damage to the landscape and local economy. The public lobbying is now over as both sides faced each other at the inquiry.

DIARY: Did my first live television link today into lunchtime *Scotland Today*. I had to supply track and rushes *(pictures and voice over)* for a lunchtime package plus cue it live on site, and then do a two-way with Shereen. My radio experience was invaluable there.

The pylons were built.

Wednesday 5 October 1994
STV News

Good evening. I'm Viv Lumsden.

I'm John MacKay and this is *Scotland Today* at 6.30pm.

DIARY: Presented *Scotland Today* this evening which came as rather a surprise. Spent the morning at a fatal accident inquiry in Linlithgow. When it adjourned for lunch I called in and they told me to come in because I was presenting! It went very well – co-presenter Viv Lumsden was great, as were all the technical staff.

Scott Ferguson (Head of News) said I'd done well, but then told me I'd need to wear a better shirt and tie the next time.

Friday 7 October 1994
STV News

A new style of police officer will take to the streets of Glasgow tomorrow. Equipped with a new, extendable baton and rigid handcuffs, they are far removed from the traditional bobby, but better able to defend themselves from assault.

Monday 11 October 1994

DIARY: I was presenting the programme – this time with Shereen. It wasn't as smooth as the first one (the second never is) and a lot of chopping and changing. Apart from being caught momentarily at the wrong camera once, it went well enough. Also got my first fan letter requesting a signed photo. Fame!

The thrill of recognition fades rapidly, although people are almost always very pleasant and it's a part of the job. The requests for autographs scribbled on random bits of paper has been replaced by the selfie photograph.

Wednesday 26 October 1994

DIARY: Pulling together features on problems in rural areas. 'We don't get into the countryside enough.' Spent much of the day in the North Ayrshire village of Dunlop. Problems are low wages, little employment, lack of housing and poor transport. At first, I was talking to suits – that's what you get on the phone – and it wasn't really standing up. However, got into the streets and, as ever, when you can persuade locals to speak you get a different perspective.

Wednesday 9 November 1994
STV News

It was almost too good to be true and so it's proved. Thousands of new jobs were promised for Clydebank, but now just five months after opening, HCI has gone bust. The board of the controversial private hospital today called in the receivers.

JM, live at HCI Hospital: The staff have been instructed not to say anything, but naturally they're all devastated. The overall impression of the hospital here is one of emptiness and that's really been the problem right from the start. A 260-bed hospital that never had more than 20 patients, an estimated 2,000 jobs that never came to more than 400.

DIARY: Out to HCI in Clydebank – the controversial private hospital which today called in the receivers. Did a live link into the programme, one of the lights blowing a minute before going on. We got it sorted with less than ten seconds to go. Big political brouhaha over the story because £30 million of public money pumped into it.

The hospital was brought into the NHS in 2002 and now serves the whole country as the Golden Jubilee Hospital.

Saturday 19 November 1994

DIARY: The National Lottery, which was launched with much fanfare this week, climaxed tonight. I bought two tickets, but I think only one number came up. There is much soul-searching from the usual sources about it being extra taxation and immoral etc. Personally, I see no harm – good causes benefit and nobody is forced to play.

The National Lottery continues to be a feature of national life.

Saturday 10 December 1994
STV News

The Catholic Church is embroiled in another child sex abuse scandal. It follows Scottish Television's revelations about young boys being abused at a Catholic college. Now it's emerged that another priest has been removed from his parish on the outskirts of Glasgow after admitting he'd interfered with young boys.

DIARY: Another priest exposed as a child abuser. He had been at Milton of Campsie, so up there. I was thoroughly drenched – with the water dripping from my coat into my shoes.

I chapped on one door which was answered by an elderly woman. It was clear she had no idea of the accusations against the priest. When I explained she gasped in shock and slammed the door on me. I was concerned for her wellbeing, but could hardly knock the door again.

1995

Thursday 2 February 1995
STV News

A political storm has blown up over claims that the Labour Party is to consider dropping its commitment to a Scottish Parliament having tax-raising powers. Other political parties have reacted strongly. Labour denies there is any change in its position.

JM: The storm has been whipped up by an amendment tabled for the party's conference in Inverness next month. The original motion backed 'the rights of the Scottish Parliament to vary levels of taxation within agreed parameters'. The amendment is not so unequivocal. While accepting the right of the Scottish Parliament to have tax-raising powers, it recognises there might be constraints. The whole episode underlines Labour's anxiety about not being seen as the party of high taxation. It's held that was the issue above any other which lost the last election for them. And that is why the party is so anxious to dampen any confusion over its policies on tax, either at Westminster or in a Scottish Parliament.

Thursday 9 February 1995
STV News

The campaign against the planned M77 motorway took on a different emphasis today. Until now the thrust of the campaign has been claims about the detrimental effect the road would have on the environment. Today, the concerns of the community were put to the fore. Locals fear having 53 thousand vehicles a day passing, almost literally, their back doorstep.

The motorway was constructed and opened in 1997.

Friday 10 February 1995
STV News

A fatal accident inquiry has heard a medical expert say that taking ecstasy tablets was like playing Russian roulette – it was not the harmless drug its users believe it to be. The inquiry into the deaths of three youths at the Hanger Thirteen club in Ayr also heard the manager admit that he couldn't ensure that drugs were not taken into the venue.

Monday 27 February 1995
STV News

Politics in Scotland is about to be thrown into turmoil and yet the signs are that most people don't know or don't care. The reorganisation of local government ending the system of two-tier councils which has lasted for 20 years will begin in five weeks when the elections for the new single-tier authorities take place. The changes will affect us all.

JM: Until now district councils have looked after services like housing, cleansing and recreation, parks and sports halls. The regional council has dealt with the larger concerns – the police, education, much of the roads and social work. As a rough guide the district council is the one to call if you have a problem in your house or on your pathway. As soon as you step into the street, any repairs need to be done by the region. Now, though, all these services will be merged under the one council. Only water and the children's reporter system will not be included. The council map of Scotland will be transformed. Only the three island councils will remain untouched. The existing 53 district and nine regional councils will be replaced by 29 single authorities. Council names like Strathclyde, Lothian and Monklands will disappear. New names like North Ayrshire and North Lanarkshire emerge. The estimated cost of all this ranges from between £100 to £500 million... This is one of the biggest pieces of legislation to affect Scotland. It will be a period of upheaval and change – and will have profound implications for the way in which Scotland is run.

Monday 6 March 1995
STV News

A mother and her three-year-old child have had a lucky escape from a blaze in a block of high-rise flats in Glasgow. The fire broke out on the second top floor of the Red Road flats, the highest block in Europe. Other residents were also taken to hospital.

DIARY: The blaze was on the 29th floor of the 30-floor flats. Fortunately, the woman and her toddler son escaped, but the flat was gutted. The fire brigade let us in to film and it was quite shocking, everything blackened. They were lucky.

Thursday 23 March 1995
STV News

The main news tonight. Football star Davie Cooper loses his fight for life aged only 39. Tributes have been made throughout the day in honour of the man who ranked among the best of Scotland's footballing sons. The former Rangers and Scotland star had been on a life-support machine in Glasgow's Southern General Hospital after suffering a brain haemorrhage. He'd collapsed during the filming of a soccer skills series for Scottish Television in Cumbernauld yesterday. Family and friends kept an all-night vigil at his bedside. Early this morning consultants switched off his ventilator after he'd been declared brain dead.

DIARY: I was presenting tonight's programme with Kirsty *(Kirsty Young)* and was the lead reader. I was very conscious of the fact that there would be hundreds of thousands of people watching the programme to see what we said and hear the tributes. Of any programme I've presented it's probably the one story I've felt most affected by. I never met the man, but in the late '70s and '80s he was one of my favourite players. He was a delight to watch. It feels as if a friend has died.

Thursday 6 April 1995

DIARY: Presenting the programme and that was hectic – possibly the most difficult I've done yet. Stories chopped and changed repeatedly, often at the last moment, there was pandemonium in the gallery, I was having to sight read stories, read off autocue and pad out. All part of the job, but rarely so much at once. On with Kirsty and we were both glad to get out of the studio.

DIARY CONT: Heading out to St Ninian's school in Eastwood for the count for the new East Renfrewshire authority in the local government elections. This one was important because it had been clearly gerrymandered to ensure a Tory authority. However, early on the word was they'd failed to keep control and the late results confirmed that. We did well – we got the interviewees that mattered, we called the result early and were confirmed correct.

Tuesday 18 April 1995
STV News

The Port Glasgow shipyard at the centre of a takeover battle launched its biggest ever vessel to date. The £16 million ferry, *Isle of Lewis*, will be the pride of the Caledonian MacBrayne fleet, and the largest ship sailing among the Western Isles. At the launch ceremony all thoughts of takeovers and buy-outs were forgotten.

My report described Ferguson's as one of the few recent success stories of the Clyde. Twenty-five years later it was at the centre of an enduring farce that plagued the Scottish Government.

Monday 1 May 1995
STV News

The poor are getting poorer and the rich are getting richer in Scotland's biggest region, according to a new report. A study of social trends in Strathclyde says the disparity between the well off and those struggling to make ends meet is growing wider. It paints a gloomy picture of long-term unemployment, increased homelessness and greater reliance on drugs and alcohol.

This issue never goes away. I have been reporting this story for decades and nothing, it seems, has changed.

Wednesday 3 May 1995

DIARY: A beautiful day which was just as well because I spent most of it standing in a farm deep in Lanarkshire *(Dunsyre)*. The story surrounds a cheese, Lanark Blue, which is at the centre of a struggle between the producer and the local council, which says it's unfit to eat.

The producer of Lanark Blue won his case and it continues to be produced today.

Wednesday 17 May 1995
STV News

An initiative to save the economy of Dunoon from collapse following the departure of the US Navy has been hailed a great success. An independent report released today says that three years on almost all of the 800 jobs dependent upon the US base have been replaced.

DIARY: Lovely day in Dunoon. Most of it in pleasant sunshine, the piece came together easily and a lovely lunch. Can't complain. Okay it's not frontline reporting, but it's nice to get these wee jobs now and again. At one point I was doing a walking piece to camera up a grassy hill overlooking the town. Inevitably, I slipped. One for the Christmas tape I don't doubt.

The TV programme It'll Be Alright On The Night was a forerunner of YouTube and TikTok in showing clips of embarrassing moments and things going wrong. They paid £250 if something you did was used on the programme. There were even repeat fees. It was alleged that some reporters would deliberately mess up a take in the hope of it making its way onto the programme. A standard blooper would be a reporter's reaction if they were doing a piece to camera and a driver beeped their horn as they passed. When you're against a deadline, on the fourth attempt at a complicated piece to camera and some tosser still thinks pressing their horn is original and funny, the reaction in language and gesture is spontaneous and heartfelt.

Wednesday 14 June 1995
STV News

One of the biggest rock bands in the world paid an unscheduled visit to Glasgow today causing the city centre to almost grind to a halt. Thousands turned out to see Bon Jovi play. Many of them travelled from across Scotland and waited for hours to see their heroes.

The event was at Tower Records in Argyle Street. The PR woman instructed us that they were not to be approached and only selected media were to ask questions. The moment they appeared she was swamped by a surge of reporters and crews like a scene from a comedy. The band were fine. At one point I had cameraman Alan Denniston sitting on my shoulders to get a better shot. Good fun.

Wednesday 21 June 1995
STV News

A West Lothian woman has scooped the biggest ever pools win in Scotland. Audrey Grieve from Linlithgow was presented with a cheque for more than £2 million by comedienne Ruby Wax at a ceremony in Glasgow. Mrs Grieve said she hadn't even checked her numbers when the official appeared at her door with the good news.

DIARY: The pools companies are losing out to the National Lottery, so they made a big effort for this.

The pools are still played online in a variety of forms, but on a far smaller scale than before the Lottery.

Wednesday 5 July 1995
STV News

The sunshine may have gone away, but many people are still making every effort to cultivate that glamorous tanned look on sunbeds. They do so as some of the world's top skin specialists gather for a conference in Glasgow, and one of their main themes is that sunbeds can cause skin cancer.

Skin cancer continues to be one of the most common cancers.

Thursday 13 July 1995
STV News

Hundreds of holidaymakers have changed their travelling plans to avoid the 24-hour strike by train drivers which starts at midnight tonight. The dispute over pay will completely shut down the rail network at the beginning of one of the busiest weekends of the year. Bus companies expect a bonanza.

DIARY: I was doing the same story last year.

Thursday 20 July 1995
STV News

The role of the social services in Glasgow has been called into question after the body of an elderly man lay undiscovered in his city flat for nine months. Police found 75-year-old Malcolm Boyes after breaking through the door of his home. Today, shocked locals have spoken of their disbelief that such a tragedy could have happened in their midst.

A sad, familiar story.

Monday 14 August 1995
STV News

Throughout the country this week veterans of the Far East campaign against the Japanese will be commemorating the 50th anniversary of VJ Day in mass gatherings. These will be the last. The passage of time has succeeded where the barbarity of the Japanese failed...

JM: The hair may be white or gone, the bearing a little more stooped than it was all those years ago. But the pride still burns fiercely in these men. And the memories. Visions which even now they cannot put words to. This weekend's gathering of the Burma Star will be the last. Caged in cases in the Royal Scots Museum *(a Japanese sword and flag)*, these relics of the Japanese war seem almost stately. For the men who saw them in more gruesome circumstances they were the very symbols of evil. But no matter the images created, only those who were there can know of man's inhumanity. And while some of these prisoners of war can enjoy their peaceful surroundings, they can never escape from the past.

JOHN TOMLINSON, Prisoner of War on the Burma Railway: He was carrying a basket of earth and all of a sudden he dropped. The Japanese guard came along and he said, 'Dead.' There was no such thing as taking him away and burying him, just throw the dirt over the top of him... I never knew there was such a thing as VJ Day because I was that happy with being in hospital and being released and away from the barbarians, you understand? It never even dawned on me that people were celebrating the war had finished or we'd dropped a bomb on Hiroshima. I just thought I'm free.

TOM SCOTT, Japanese Prisoner of War: I had so many beatings-up that it tells a tale on you. I've got a spinal complaint, so you suffer at times with that.

JOE HENRY, Japanese Prisoner of War: I had a lot of that, bad dreams and what not, waking up with shudders. And that went on for quite a while. And it still happens. The likes of maybe today we're talking about it. Maybe tonight I'll have a wee setback... It always comes back. It was a bad, bad time. But that's my real thought – mates that I lost *(falls to silence)*.

These old boys – all gone now – remain among the most memorable interviewees I have ever met.

Monday 4 September 1995
STV News

After all the hype, the historical arguments and the Hollywood hullabaloo, it's finally happened. The European premiere of *Braveheart*. Stirling was brought to a standstill last night. Thousands of fans flooded into the town for the gala night screening of Mel Gibson's latest movie. But the premiere attracted more than the usual collection of film critics. Scotland's politicians were also out in force, fighting over William Wallace's historical legacy.

MEL GIBSON, Director and star: I'm not Scottish and I didn't make the film for those purposes, to be used as some kind of political tool for political gain or loss. I think that whatever happens, the Scottish people will make it happen.

ALEX SALMOND, SNP Leader: I think the most important thing is the message. The message that comes out of this film is very clear indeed and, hopefully, that's got some relevance to modern day Scotland.

The film was a huge hit and won Oscars for Best Picture and Best Director. It is often cited as being a factor in the resurgence of Scottish nationalism.

Sunday 15 October 1995
STV News

The Scottish boxer James Murray has died. His fight for life ended early this morning. But the calls for banning the sport have already been rejected by both the Government and the boxing establishment.

Jim Murray was fighting for the British Bantamweight title on Friday 13 October. He had been winning on points when knocked down in the last round.

Wednesday 25 October 1995

DIARY: Did a story on a block of flats in Paisley which could have been used to house people, but instead are to be demolished. Got the cameraman to shoot it with the sky in the background until a flash of lightning appeared *(there had been several)*. So, my opening line was 'This is the building at the centre of the storm *(upsound of thunder over lightning flash)*.' Very hammy, but livened up the piece.

Monday 30 October 1995
STV News

A new nation could be born tonight when the outcome of the Independence Referendum in Quebec is known. Quebecers have been going to the polls to decide whether the French-speaking province should break away from the Canadian Federation. As John MacKay reports, it's an issue which has clear parallels with Scotland...

JM: The results of the Canadian referendum will be known in the early hours of the morning. Pundits are saying it's too close to call. The Québécois are seeking what many Scottish nationalists seek – independence for a nation perceived to be smothered by a dominant neighbour and the right to make decisions for themselves. The fabric of the argument presented by Canadian federalists is that the economy would suffer as people fearful of the future took their investment elsewhere, jobs would be lost as industry pulls out to relocate and taxes would increase to pay for independence. Quebec, it's claimed, earns more from Canada than it puts in. The result is so close that even if it is no to independence, the issue will not go away.

The parallels with the Scottish Independence Referendum nearly 20 years later were very apparent. Quebec voted against independence by the narrowest of margins.

Thursday 2 November 1995
STV News

For most of us the question of where we are going to live when we get older is one we put to the back of our minds. But it's an issue which we are increasingly going to have to confront as residential care for the elderly goes through an upheaval. The key question is funding. This week the Church of Scotland announced that it is closing four of its homes for the elderly because of lack of money.

JM: As people live longer, so the cost of matching their needs grows. With a proportionally smaller working population, the costs of matching those needs are harder to meet.

Thirty years later, people living longer, a smaller supporting workforce and care for the elderly is an even more pressing issue.

Friday 3 November 1995
STV News

Scottish children aged as young as seven are suffering from alcoholism. But a conference in Glasgow has been hearing that such problems are being overlooked in the fight to battle drugs. Researchers have been arguing that the political focus is on combatting drug misuse, while the wider issue of underage drinking is being ignored.

Monday 6 November 1995
STV News

For the first time in Scotland, detectives are carrying out genetic fingerprinting of the entire male population of an area in an attempt to track down a vicious attacker. All men in the Vale of Leven area are being asked to submit DNA samples in an effort to close the net on a man who carried out an indecent assault of an old lady in her home. But the methods have been called into question by opponents of DNA testing.

Wednesday 15 November 1995
STV News

The rave scene in Scotland is to be subject to a Government clampdown. Strict legislation is to be introduced which will force rave organisers to comply with safety standards. Those who don't will not be allowed to operate. But on the day of the announcement a row has erupted over the decision by Scotland's biggest venue to cancel a rave scheduled for later this month.

The cancelled event was at the SECC.

Friday 15 December 1995
DIARY: Final day of camera training. Did some filming in the St Enoch Centre. I've enjoyed the experience, but I hope it's never necessary to use the camera professionally.

This was one of the various attempts to introduce VJs (video journalists), reporters who film their own material. The development of smaller cameras and smartphones

has made VJS or MMJ (multi-media journalists) a common feature in TV newsrooms now, but dedicated craft camera operators are still essential.

Thursday 28 December 1995
STV News

The freeze has claimed its first homeless victim. Fifty-four-year-old John Murphy died in Bathgate after falling. Police say a postmortem has still to be carried out, but say there is no question that the sub-zero temperatures were a key factor. The tragedy has caused outrage among homeless charities and tonight other homeless have been speaking about their fears for their lives.

DIARY: Temperatures hitting record lows – approaching minus 20C. When you're walking you don't feel it straight away, but eventually your cheeks begin to pinch and your face feels really frozen.

Some time later a former primary school teacher of mine, Irene Crawford, told me she had seen this report. She had taught both me and one of the homeless people I'd interviewed and it struck her how life can turn out so differently for people. A sobering thought.

1996

KILLER ASBESTOS
Tuesday 9 January 1996
DIARY: Travelled through to Edinburgh to speak to a woman who'd contracted the asbestos condition through cleaning her father's work boots as a child. She's 49 and knows she could die if it advances – just one of the hundreds of lives ruined by asbestos producers.

Thursday 11 January 1996
DIARY: A full day in Leeds. We were going to interview June Hancock – whose compensation victory in the English courts is the basis of our documentary. She grew up beside an asbestos factory, but never worked in it. She's now dying from mesothelioma. It was well worth the journey because she was an excellent interviewee and I couldn't have scripted her answers better. Did some pieces to camera in the Armley district where she grew up – it was real *Coronation Street*-style. While it's better to have more space you can appreciate how these places had a close community spirit.

June Hancock died in 1997. A research fund was established in her name.

The report wasn't broadcast until two months later in March 1996.

Tuesday 12 March 1996
STV News

A *Scottish Reporters* programme tonight will reveal how doctors are misdiagnosing a disease which will kill hundreds of Scots over the next 30 years. Experts say that mesothelioma, which is contracted from exposure to asbestos, is a health timebomb. Many of its victims have never worked with asbestos and do not know they have the condition. The fact that their doctors fail to diagnose it also means that they cannot pursue claims for compensation.

Wednesday 21 February 1996

DIARY: Big story was the closure of the Cummins Engineering plant in Shotts with the loss of 700 jobs. A profit-making plant where the workers met all their productivity targets. I went out at lunchtime to vox pop the workers. There they were talking about being 'devastated' and what the future held *(nothing)* and still with mortgages to pay. Not for the first time I feel intrusive – drive in, get the soundbite and away without any real understanding of what these men are going through.

Wednesday 6 March 1996
STV News

Glasgow is to be the focus for a series of initiatives to tackle the city's drug problem. The rate of deaths this year is already matching that of last year when two hundred drug users died. A strategic plan – the first of its kind in Scotland – has been launched to reduce the level of drug abuse.

JM: The strategic plan outlines how the various drug agencies can be coordinated to better tackle the city's drug problem. But not all are agreed on the best way forward.

REV RODERICK CAMPBELL, Greater Glasgow Drug Action Team: There are a lot of strongly and sincerely held views in the drugs world. The role of the DAT is not to favour one or the other, but to try to see the development of both to monitor and evaluate the success of the methodology and try to encourage development.

MICHAEL FORSYTH, Scottish Secretary: This is a daunting task. Drugs misuse is an enormous and complex problem. There are no easy solutions, although some people seem to think there is and that they have a simple solution. It's vital to be clear about priorities and the aims of services at a local level.

JIM DOHERTY, Gallowgate Family Support Group: As far as we can find out it's salaried employees of the health board who's speaking for us parents. We don't need them to speak for us, we can speak for ourselves.

One of the many drugs initiatives over the years. Most involved would concur with Michael Forsyth's observation that drug misuse is an 'enormous and complex' problem. A regular complaint through the years has been that projects would have their funding cut or weren't followed through. The figures are even worse now.

THE DUNBLANE SHOOTINGS

Wednesday 13 March 1996

PA Copy – Central Scotland News Agency – Tim Bugler

Reports are coming in of a shooting at Dunblane Primary School, Perthshire. The Scottish Ambulance Service said 12 children are believed dead and eight or nine injured. Police have been called from throughout the area and all five doctors from Dunblane Surgery are reported to have been called to the school.

DIARY: Today I worked on what must rank as the most appalling story I've ever been involved in – including Lockerbie. A gunman walked into the gymnasium of Dunblane Primary School and massacred 16 Primary One children and their teacher. He used four handguns and must have picked them off individually. It is incomprehensible why anyone should do this, how they would be capable of it. It seems the killer Thomas Hamilton was rumoured locally as a pervert. Whatever, how could any human being do this? During a quiet moment I cried and wanted to hold my own children.

First word came at the back of 10.00am. I drove up to Dunblane with cameraman Mike Haggerty, holding that PA copy and not convinced it was correct. How could it be? Dunblane? No way. I was fully expecting the car phone to ring and be told to return to base because it was a false alarm. It was only when Mike undertook a police car and it didn't react that I began to realise the truth of the awfulness that lay ahead of us. I will never forget running up to the school amid desperate parents arriving to find out what had happened to their children.

DIARY CONT: We never saw the full horror, but what we did see was heart-rending.

Parents filled with panic and tears swarming to the school to find out if their child was safe. One spoke of the overwhelming relief of finding hers, immediately followed by the guilt that she felt that way. One father described to me how the parents of those in the class were taken into a room and the wailing coming from it forced him to look away.

Dougie Mcguire, STV News Reporter

The morning of the shootings at Dunblane I started a round of calls – something most reporters do as a routine part of a shift. I got through to the Duty Room at Central Scotland Police, and asked if there was anything doing, frankly expecting the usual 'No, all quiet', but this morning was different. I shouted across the newsroom to Jon Keane *(News Editor)* that there had been a shooting at a school in Dunblane, there were casualties but no details. He looked stunned. Dave Smith, my cameraman, appeared and we scrambled out into the Cowcaddens car park, heading for one of the distinctive STV Volvos shouting at the desk that we were going to Dunblane. I was on the phone, trying to find out what had happened. With nothing sensible coming out of the calls I was making to the police, I called Ambulance Control, hoping they would be able to help. I can still picture the inside of the car, my tweed jacket sleeve and the notepad on my knee when the girl on the phone said the most devastating words.

'Ambulance are in attendance at Dunblane Primary School. There are 16 children dead, and two adults,' she told me.

'Sorry, did you say 16 children?'

'Yes, it's awful.'

She wasn't wrong.

Most journalists will admit, I think, that there is a rush of adrenalin and excitement when a story like this breaks, and however appalling it seems now, I was in that state when we got to the school.

Several police cars came out of the school as we were setting up, the officers inside them cradling their sub-machine guns and looking blank. Ambulances were moving about, heading in and out of the playground, and then the screaming hit me. I could actually hear people – parents obviously – crying, from where we were standing outside the school grounds. When I heard that haunting sound that was the moment this story got real for me, the adrenalin started to fade, and the awful nature of what we, the first TV crew on the scene, were witnessing started to become clear. There were terribly distressed people – mothers mostly – running past our camera, sobbing hysterically, with other parents reaching for them and trying to slow them down.

Everything was confused and we could feel the raw emotion flooding the street. The beat cops who were around looked utterly desolate. We snatched what we could and sent off our first tape via a motorbike courier. Soon the Strathclyde Police media team arrived and read out the horrible details of what had happened to a small scrum of reporters and camera crews which had assembled. There was an audible gasp from the media when he said, 'Sixteen, one-six children and their teacher are dead.' Soon hundreds of crews from across the world would descend on this 'quiet Scottish market town' as Dunblane came to be known.

In all the confusion and with people coming and going I ended up working with Mike Haggerty and it was his memorable vision of the bullet holes in the gym window which led off our coverage for the evening programme, followed by Dave's terribly distressing footage from when we had first arrived.

DIARY CONT: Eventually you become numb to the overwhelming grief around. This evening from our OB position you could see into the gym, although only the policemen/forensics moving around. What horrors they must have seen.

STV News

It's being called 'The Slaughter of the Innocents'. Sixteen small children and their teacher murdered by a gunman in a Dunblane Primary School. The killer later shot himself. Tonight, 13 other children still lie injured in hospital as the sheer scale of the horror unfolds. It happened just after 9.30am this morning as the five- and six-year-olds played in the school gymnasium. A man burst in and massacred them with four automatic weapons. We have an hour-long programme to report the story that the Prime Minister has called beyond belief. Tonight, the town of Dunblane is struggling to comprehend a tragedy beyond words. Sixteen children went happily to school this morning. Tonight, they have not come home, their young lives cut short in a moment of appalling brutality.

I had written these words as my opening link for the hour-long news special we had prepared. Standing at our position on a hill above the school, I was told that we had technical problems and the programme may have to come from the studio in Glasgow. That was confirmed in the final moments before we went live and I heard Shereen beginning to read my words.

DIARY CONT: The programme was a disaster because we couldn't get our live links to work. Whatever my annoyance at our poor performance it matters not. Tonight, I can't help but think of the horrors of that gymnasium and the misery in the homes of the dead children.

Dougie Mcguire, STV News Reporter

I don't remember a lot more about those days, other than having a persistent headache from constant mobile phone use, the cold weather, and an increasing desire to distance myself from the story. I have always thought it is a disgrace when reporters chase bereaved families who have just lost their beloved son or daughter, but it seemed a tackier and more obviously nasty thing to do in this case and I wanted nothing to do with it. Something about Dunblane affected me far more than Lockerbie, the only other major disaster I had been intimately involved with, and a desire never to do more reporting of that kind helped steer me towards the world of PR a few months later. I also remember being embarrassed by the tabloid media (STV included) endlessly repeating film of the piles of flowers which people placed outside the school, and the over-written reports about the 'Angels of Dunblane' – a theme generated by one particular wreath. It might seem odd to be making these points, but I feel that with an event as awful as this, there is little need to overdo the tone of the reporting. The dreadful facts speak eloquently enough for themselves. I think in some ways the journalists who sweep into town and make themselves the story must add further pain to the unimaginable grief that the victims' families are feeling. But just try telling that to the desk...

Thursday 14 March 1996
STV News

It's become clear that Thomas Hamilton wasn't acting on any spur-of-the-moment impulse. This morning *Scotland Today* received a package from him. It contained letters that he had sent to senior public figures, including the Queen. And it provides a chilling insight into his state of mind.

JM: It seems now that Thomas Hamilton's massacre of the children of Dunblane Primary was not a moment of madness, but planned to the last detail. Before going to the school to carry out his slaughter, he posted copies of letters about his grievances to a number of outlets. These are the letters he sent to the *Scotland Today* newsdesk. The date on the postmark is yesterday and he used two second-class stamps. They include letters to various senior figures, including the Queen. Some are written on a computer, others in small, neat handwriting.

DIARY: Original intention was that I should return to Dunblane today, but when I arrived in the office we had just received a package of photocopied letters written by killer Thomas Hamilton and I was put to work on those. We quickly established as best we could that they were genuine (checking with recipients), but it also became apparent from checking the writing that Hamilton had sent them to us himself. This made his act all the more appalling because he had clearly planned what he was going to do – it wasn't simply a few moments of madness. It was a sobering thought to realise that the letters in my hands had been photocopied and folded into the envelope by Hamilton, he put stamps on it and sent it to us before setting out to commit the most indescribable outrage. The letters charted a growing grievance spread over the last five or so years. They described how his work with children and his whole life was being undermined by rumours of him being a pervert. He mentions Dunblane Primary School where teachers were spreading this 'poison'. By this evening I had put together a four minute 30 second report which is one of the best I've done, but you could hardly fail with the material. I still struggle to comprehend the sheer horror of what happened and what the parents are going through.

Tuesday 9 April 1996
STV News

A tobacco company has failed in its attempt to force a widow to put up a £2 million bond before attempting to sue them. Imperial Tobacco wanted Margaret McTear to put up the money as security to cover their legal costs if her claim against them failed. Mrs McTear is pursuing a test case action begun by her late husband alleging that the tobacco company should have warned him of the health risks when he began smoking as a teenager. The company's petition was rejected by the Court of Session.

Margaret McTear ultimately failed to win the case against Imperial Tobacco.

Tuesday 16 April 1996
STV News

Two hundred and fifty years ago today the last battle to be fought on British soil ended with the Highland army of Bonnie Prince Charlie being crushed by Government troops on a moor at Culloden. It brought to an end the Jacobite rebellion and the dreams of many who'd wanted a Catholic Stuart back on the British throne. Thousands of modern day clansmen from around the world have today gathered at the battle site near Inverness to commemorate the event.

DIARY: The story of the uprising stirs the blood and mists the eyes, if you gloss over the realities.

Tuesday 23 April 1996
STV News

A disused railway bridge which links the north and south banks of the River Clyde should be torn down, according to locals stunned by the drowning of a young boy. People in the Carmyle area of Glasgow say that the bridge encourages youths from both sides of the river to provoke each other. Twelve-year-old Hugh Burns fell into the river and was swept away as he tried to escape from a gang of youths chasing him.

DIARY: Returned to the area, Carmyle, later, to get a new line. At one point I was in the house of one of the boy's companions, who'd survived. The father was upset and complaining that his son had to go to stay elsewhere because of harassment, including staking out their house and chasing the boy over fences to get a photo. I don't think that's acceptable and it makes me uncomfortable about my profession. The guy said I'd been courteous and fine, but others had acted like scum. We spoke for 20 minutes, but he didn't want to go on camera and that was that. Usually I persuade them, this time I didn't, but I would not have been comfortable adopting the tabloid tactics. Different if it's a crook, but not a victim.

Thursday 25 April 1996
STV News

A new survey has shown that children get more stressed about their school exams than anything else. Four-fifths of teenagers told the charity Childline that facing final exams was their main worry. One school in Paisley has taken a lead in helping its pupils to come to terms with the stress of it all.

JM: The Childline survey showed that 79 per cent worried more about exams than anything else. 66 per cent were concerned for their future. Others feared being attacked and 44 per cent cited problems at home.

Perhaps contrary to the prevailing view, less than a fifth worried about the environment.

The mental health of young people is much more to the fore now, especially following the pandemic. Concern for the environment is now a much greater issue for them.

Your reporter was not so sympathetic at the time. I described myself as that day's 'heap-of-mince' correspondent.

Tuesday 7 May 1996
STV News

A high-profile campaign to combat drug use has been launched by the leaders of the four main political parties. The MPs put their differences aside to join a 'battle bus' which is taking the anti-drugs message through the country's major cities. It's in Edinburgh this lunchtime after leaving Aberdeen this morning. Sports stars, the business community and media personalities have also joined the project. But... some critics say the message being put across will miss its target.

The much-mocked photo call in which Michael Forsyth, George Robertson, Alex Salmond and Jim Wallace danced very self-consciously in sweatshirts with teenagers in a club. The intention was sincere, but it was always going to be open to ridicule.

Monday 13 May 1996
STV News

Britain's last Polaris submarine sailed back into the Firth of Clyde today at the end of its final patrol. The nuclear submarines, first used in the 1960s, have become obsolete with the introduction of Trident. For some it was a sad day, for others a case of good riddance.

DIARY: It's the sort of story you can't really fail – good story, great pictures. Polaris is being replaced by the bigger, even more destructive Trident. It begs the question how much destructive power do you need? What better uses could the money be put to? However, history teaches that you never should leave yourself totally exposed. My own feeling is that the threat to world peace now is more likely to come from China, or even more likely, the fundamental Muslims *(the phrase now would be Islamists).*

Tuesday 14 May 1996
STV News

An appeal by a charity hospice to be allowed to care for the woman at the centre of Scotland's right-to-die' case has been rejected. The priest who runs the charity had asked that Janet Johnston be kept alive and transferred to the hospice in Liverpool to be looked after. However, both Mrs Johnston's family and Law Hospital, where she has been in a coma for the past four years, have rejected the appeal. The procedures to remove her feeding tubes are expected to begin later this week.

Scotland's first right-to-die case. Janet Johnston died on 31 May, 15 days after her feeding tubes were withdrawn.

Thursday 16 May 1996
STV News

Barbaric, disgusting and abhorrent. The words of a judge after four teenage girls and a 21-year-old man were all found guilty of torturing another woman in a flat in Greenock. A fifth girl had earlier pleaded guilty to lesser charges. There were angry scenes in the High Court in Glasgow as sentences totalling 50 years were handed out. John MacKay reports on today's verdicts and the events surrounding the prolonged attack on the group's victim.

DIARY: A highly pressurised day. The Greenock Torture trial which I've been working on, on and off for the past week or so, ended late and I got my piece finished with less than a minute to go, it was that tight. The fascination of seeing people who face serious charges sitting in the dock and the whole tension of waiting for the jury's verdict and then the sentence is intense. The reaction from the accused as they were given sentences ranging from 16 to three and a half years was of much sobbing as their families wailed in the public gallery. Five of them were teenage girls. However, the savagery of the acts meant that you could feel no sympathy.

The public gallery erupted when the sentences were handed down as the families of some of the convicted shouted at each other. Outside people hammered on the prison van as it took the prisoners off to jail, which my cameraman managed to film. I thought the drama in the courtroom was more spectacular as the court officers tried to restore order, so I led my report with that. I had no images of it, though, because there was no camera in the courtroom and so I had to cover it with dull shots of the exterior of the court. My first shots should have been the banging on the prison van because that would immediately draw in the viewer, even although it was not perhaps the strongest line. It was a basic lesson in TV reporting.

Monday 20 May 1996
STV News

Top pop group Oasis are at the centre of a row over their summer concerts on Loch Lomondside. Eighty thousand tickets have been sold for the two-day event in August, but people in the local town of Balloch say the tickets have been sold without proper planning permission being granted and without them having been consulted. The town, they claim, will be unable to cope.

JM: Both concerts sold out as soon as the tickets went on sale. Thousands will be spending the night in the makeshift camping areas which, given that Balloch is a one-toilet town, could cause problems.

Balloch had one public toilet that I could see, so I couldn't resist that line. I ended my report saying that the townsfolk hoped they 'Don't Look Back in Anger' at the event. There's nothing I can say now in mitigation.

Thursday 23 May 1996
STV News

The largest ever exhibition of the work of Charles Rennie Mackintosh opens tonight in Glasgow. The 350 exhibits will span his entire career and include a reconstruction of one of his celebrated tearooms. There has been no celebration of Mackintosh quite like it and... there never will be again.

DIARY: I was very pleased with my piece – nice shots, atmospheric music and a minimum of voice. However, I neglected to say where it's being held, so we had a lot of calls saying lovely story, but where is it? Basic.

It was at the McLellan Galleries in Glasgow.

THE DUNBLANE INQUIRY
Wednesday 29 May 1996
STV News

The opening day of the Dunblane Inquiry has heard harrowing accounts of the moment Thomas Hamilton opened fire on a Primary One class. Part-time PE teacher Eileen Harrild, who survived the attack, described how she could not comprehend what was happening as the gunman began shooting. Lord Cullen was told that Hamilton had fired 105 shots from one gun before turning a second on himself. Police officers and medical staff have also been describing the scene on their arrival at the school.

JM: The 43-year-old PE teacher described how she was about to start lessons when she became aware of the gym doors opening suddenly. A man in a woolly hat and earmuffs came in, his arms extended, and started firing. She was the first hit, wounded in the arms and chest. She stumbled towards a storeroom in the gym followed by four or five children and another teacher. All had been injured. The shooting continued rapidly as Hamilton moved round the gym. There was a brief lull before the shooting started again. Then Mrs Harrild said there was silence. The shooting and the screaming had stopped. The other teacher to hide in the storeroom gave a written statement. Children were screaming so loudly she said it was as if the noise was inside her head. One child repeatedly said, 'What a bad man.' She tried to pull a mat over them for protection, but she couldn't because of wounds to her head and legs. I thought it was the end, she said. The inquiry heard experts describe how Hamilton had fired 105 bullets in the four minutes of shooting. All came from a Smith and Wesson revolver. He used one bullet from a Browning pistol to shoot himself.

Jack Beattie, one of the first doctors on the scene, described how he had gone from victim to victim checking who could be saved and who was dead. Senior police officer Detective Chief Superintendent John Ogg described how investigations had revealed that Hamilton had worked his way round the gym, left through a fire exit and shot into other classes before returning. He described how difficult it had been to identify some victims. The label on one child's clothes didn't match any of the names on the register. The one person who knew them all so well, Gwen Mayor, was herself dead.

DIARY: Eileen Harrild's testimony, delivered with little emotion, was gripping and harrowing. The hall was absolutely silent as she spoke. Two images she described were heartbreaking – first of all she said the Primary One children had lined up outside the gym, already in their gym clothes and very excited. Later she said, '…then there was silence. The shooting and the screaming had stopped.' There could have been no more than ten minutes in between these contrasting images.

To this day the evidence given on the first day of the Cullen Inquiry, and in particular the first eyewitness account by Eileen Harrild, remains the most compelling experience I've ever had as a reporter.

Thursday 30 May 1996
STV News

'It was a scene of unimaginable carnage.' That was head teacher Ron Taylor's description of the moment he entered Dunblane School's gymnasium after Thomas Hamilton had shot dead 16 children and their teacher. Mr Taylor was giving evidence on the second day of Lord Cullen's inquiry into the shootings. Later, he said he couldn't understand why anyone should want to keep a weapon at home. He could only imagine they had never seen the effects of a gun – he had.

JM: Today head teacher Ron Taylor relived events which he described as 'one's worst nightmare'. In remarkably composed testimony, he betrayed little emotion except when asked about when he tended the injured children.

Mr Taylor first became aware that something was seriously wrong when a teacher came into his room and told him, 'There's a man in the school with a gun. Get down.' He ran to the gym and as he burst through the door he saw a scene which he described as 'unimaginable carnage'. The air was thick with blue smoke and there was a strong smell of cordite. Some children were crying, but looked to be less injured. Mr Taylor had other teachers remove them. He moved through the gymnasium to establish what had happened. Thomas Hamilton was lying on the floor at the top of the hall. He seemed to be still moving. The school janitor kicked a gun away from him. Asked if he tended to injured children, Mr Taylor replied in a soft voice, 'Yes.'

Another witness, Agnes Awlson, the school's deputy head, said when she had entered the gym she had tried to attend to some children. The janitor told her, 'You can't help them Mrs Awlson, they're gone.'

Later the inquiry heard from 64-year-old Agnes Watt, the mother of Thomas Hamilton, although he had been adopted by his grandparents. She said she saw her son twice a week and he phoned her every night. The day before the killings he had spent the afternoon with her. He'd had a bath and a meal and they talked. Nothing was out of the ordinary, she said. She only found out about what he'd done when she phoned his house and the police answered. The man she considered to be a caring son was the same man who killed the children.

DIARY: It was torrential rain for much of the day which wasn't much fun for poor Mike Haggerty *(cameraman)* – who has to wait outside *(to get shots of departing witnesses)*. Strong testimony again today from head teacher Ron Taylor and later Hamilton's mother. You couldn't help but feel sorry for her – she was just like any wifie of 60-odd years and was trying to keep some dignity in spite of knowing what her son had become. She was a sympathetic figure.

Friday 31 May 1996
STV News

The Dunblane Inquiry has heard that Thomas Hamilton may have been planning his attack on the school for two years. In written evidence to the inquiry, a member of one of Hamilton's boys' clubs said he was asked to describe the layout of the school and the times that youngsters would be together for assembly.

Hamilton carried enough ammunition to wipe out the entire school. It is believed he had intended shooting them at assembly.

Wednesday 12 June 1996
STV News

Two police officers have told the Cullen Inquiry that they had bad feelings about killer Thomas Hamilton when they met him. The officers, who were involved in processing his firearms certificate, said that despite their misgivings, his application was passed because there were no convictions against him.

Thursday 27 June 1996
STV News

In a total reversal of previous policy, Labour have confirmed they're to hold a referendum on their plans for the Scottish Parliament. Shadow Scottish Secretary George Robertson today admitted he'd got it wrong in the past and he claimed consulting voters before a bill went through Westminster would strengthen the case for Devolution. Mr Blair may have some convincing to do. The reaction from within his party has ranged from muted to unfavourable. Outside the party, the proposal has upset Labour's constitutional convention partners. Indeed, the only people showing any satisfaction are Labour's political opponents.

JM: Until today Labour activists believed the party's position to be clear. As they promised at the last election, Labour would win at Westminster and within a year provide a Scottish Parliament with tax-raising powers. Now that isn't so clear and many of the faithful feel aggrieved that they haven't been consulted over such a major change in policy.

ARCHIE GRAHAM, former Executive member: What we are seeing is yet another example of a move towards a democratic centralist system where we elect a leader and then the leader and his office decide everything and then hand down policy to the rest of us.

CAMPBELL CHRISTIE, Scottish TUC: I have no doubt that when people vote in the General Election in the next few months and they vote Labour, they will be clear that they are voting Labour who will establish a Scottish Parliament with tax varying powers. Having got that mandate I see no reason for a further mandate to be achieved.

ALEX SALMOND, SNP Leader: It's a delaying device, it's a wrecking tactic as indeed it was in 1979. The only difference is that then the referendum device was played by Labour's backbenchers, now it's the Labour leadership at the highest level who are deploying this wrecking device and delaying tactic.

MICHAEL FORSYTH, Scottish Secretary: They will have to introduce a bill for a referendum and that will have to be closely argued in Parliament. People will want to know what the questions are, all of which is going to take a year. So, how can they say they're going to have a referendum to find out what the policy is, and they're going to introduce the policy all within a year? It can't be done.

JM: To discuss today's changes I'm joined by Labour's Chief Whip Donald Dewar. Mr Dewar, hasn't Michael Heseltine got it right *(comments in the House of Commons)*, this is more about appeasing Middle England and selling out Scotland?

DONALD DEWAR, Labour Chief Whip: No. I thought that was tremendous pantomime, but not serious politics. This is a confident move by a confident party. We are constantly told by the carping and criticising Conservatives that we don't have the consent of Scotland, that there's no support for what we're going to do and what we're saying is we'll call your bluff.

JM: They've been saying that for ages. What has changed?

DD: We've looked at the need to have certainty, we've looked at the way we can implement this. There's absolutely no retreat on the commitment to Devolution or the Devolution policy, but what we have decided is that the way in which we can build it on sure foundations is to go to Parliament with the impetus and the moral authority that comes from a direct endorsement by the people of Scotland.

Wednesday 3 July 1996

DIARY: I sat in on Scottish Questions in the Commons chamber, above the PM John Major as he announced the return of the Stone of Destiny to Scotland. Just before he spoke he tapped his thumbs on his notes – a very human act. The Employment Secretary Gillian Shepherd sat on the hallowed green benches, shoes off, feet up, absently picking her toes... it was like a big club and there is little doubt the real business of government does not happen in there.

Thursday 4 July 1996
STV News

Whatever the competing claims from Scone and Arbroath, Edinburgh looks the favourite for the Stone's final resting place. But the debate may be academic. Some are sticking to the claims that the Stone of Destiny is already in Scotland and the one resting in Westminster is a fake.

The Stone was displayed at Edinburgh Castle, but in 2024 it was relocated to Perth Museum.

Tuesday 9 July 1996
STV News

The parents of some of the children killed in the Dunblane shooting have been speaking publicly for the first time. They told a news conference that the right of their children to live far outweighs anyone's right to own a gun. They want all guns banned. Facing the cameras for the first time, they spoke of their anger at how Thomas Hamilton was legally entitled to carry a gun and the distress caused by the delay in being told their children had been killed.

DIARY: Their basic message was ban all guns, and certainly in the case of handguns who can argue? They were just such normal people. What else would they be? One read a statement. 'We will never get over it. There will always be a hole in our lives,' she said.

Wednesday 10 July 1996
STV News

It took only a few minutes for Thomas Hamilton to kill the children of Primary One. It has taken six weeks for the inquiry to hear why. It'll take Lord Cullen many weeks more to make recommendations to prevent such a tragedy ever happening again.

DIARY: The final day of the Dunblane Inquiry – it wasn't quite the mad rush I was anticipating. I was beginning to weary of it towards the end. But as the Crown QC said in his closing address, 'We must never lose sight of these little shattered bodies. That is what brought us here.' I doubt I will ever have to work on a more harrowing story in my career. I hope not.

Tuesday 16 July 1996
STV News

The town of Ayr, for centuries the main fishing port on the Ayrshire coast, has finally lost its market to nearby Troon. The old market in Ayr is to be closed and moved five miles up the coast. It has caused a clash between traditionalists and progressives.

Friday 26 July 1996
DIARY: To Kilmarnock to knock off an interview with the Labour Deputy Leader John Prescott. Very funny – he stumbled over one question three times, ending by stamping his foot and saying, 'Fuck!' Didn't take to him – brusque and rude.

Monday 19 August 1996
STV News

As Edinburgh considers prolonging the closure of the Royal Mile and sanctioning an extension of outdoor drinking, Glasgow has gone ahead with its controversial ban on the consumption of alcohol in the open air. The new by-law came into force at midnight. The police have adopted a low-key approach and there have been no fines issued on the first day.

WILLIAM MCKENZIE: We just sit here and have a drink, have a good time, then go home. Other people are sitting up there and shout at people who pass. So, I can understand why this is being done.

WILLIAM BLACK: See a public house in Sauchiehall Street, they've got tables outside. They're not going to stop them from drinking, but they're still drinking in public. So why are they going to stop us from drinking and not stop them from drinking?

FIONA HALL: When people are drinking in public places and are disorderly I'd say no. But if people are out for picnics and have a bottle of wine, I don't see that as a problem as long as it's not to excess.

JAMES COLEMAN, Glasgow City Councillor: Where you usually saw groups of youths hanging around drinking or a procession of people outside football grounds standing drinking. I'd expect to see that disappear.

Tuesday 20 August 1996
STV News

Glasgow's image as the 'sick city' of Europe is slowly changing. Fewer people are suffering heart attacks and the cancer rate is falling. But in its local health strategy document the city's health board says more work needs to be done. This is Greater Glasgow Health Board's second strategy plan for improving the city's health into the next millennium.

HARRY BURNS, Director of Public Health; We've made great strides in Glasgow in improving health. Over the past 20 years the risk of premature death from strokes, heart disease and cancer has decreased substantially. There are other areas that we have not seen such significant improvements. What we're trying to do is point out to the public the initiatives that we feel necessary to bring about these improvements.

Glasgow continues to labour under the 'sick city' label. One in four men in Glasgow won't reach their 65th birthday.

Thursday 29 August 1996
STV News

Scotland's first commercially run wind farm began generating electricity onto the national grid for the first time today. It's one of the first to get through all the planning stages which have prevented similar projects happening in the past. Unlike many similar projects this has had the full backing of the local community.

JM: Hagshaw Hill above Douglas in South Lanarkshire. Twenty-six wind turbines producing enough electricity for 17,000 homes. In the new millennium it may be that thousands more will have their power produced by this technology and wind farms will be a common sight.

DIARY: It's the sort of story that on first sight seems dull, but which in actual fact, I found fascinating. We had a rush to get something sent away for lunchtime, but we could then spend more time at the site getting good pictures. It was a surreal experience, standing on top of this hill with great views over Lanarkshire, surrounded by these vast turbines swishing through the breeze. Very peculiar and a damn sight better than being stuck in the office.

Windfarms are now a common and often controversial feature across the landscape.

Thursday 5 September 1996

DIARY: An intriguing opportunity has been offered to me. Sky Scottish – a new channel funded by Sky and ourselves will involve a half hour news programme – not dissimilar to *Scotland Today*, but pan-Scottish. Scott (Scott Ferguson – STV Head of News) wants me to front it with Andrea Brymer, who's a rising star at STV. He says Andrea is exotic looking, but when she opens her mouth she's a Brechin butcher's daughter. We are 'nineties', he says. The programme would go on satellite and cable an hour later.

Monday 7 October 1996
STV News

Thousands of benefit staff have been striking across Scotland on the day the Government introduces the controversial Job Seekers' Allowance. Unions say they fear for their members' safety because of the resentment from people who are having their benefits cut.

Wednesday 9 October 1996
STV News

Seventeen candles burned in Dunblane Cathedral today. Each one in remembrance of the victims of the Dunblane shootings. They were lit during a memorial service attended by the Prince of Wales. In a moving service during which the parents of each dead child lit a candle with their name on it, the message was 'out of darkness into light'.

DIARY: We weren't allowed inside – the BBC providing live coverage and pool pictures – so we watched it from the links van. It was very moving. At one point the parents of each child lit a candle for their child as a piper played 'Lament for the Children'. I would have wept if I was on my own.

Friday 18 October 1996
STV News

Scotland needs a nationwide strategy to tackle widespread poverty. The Scottish Anti-Poverty Network has based that claim on what's said to have been the widest consultation on poverty ever undertaken in Scotland. Latest figures show that nearly a fifth of Scottish families are dependent on income support. But the Government says it's spending billions to relieve the problem.

DIARY: Pulled together a piece on an anti-poverty campaign. It's the sort of worthy piece that has to be done on a quiet day and I could almost do it with my eyes shut.

The cynicism comes from the story having been covered so often with, it seems, little change.

Friday 1 November 1996

DIARY: Sky Scottish was launched today and it all seems to have gone smoothly. I welcomed viewers to the first *Scotland Today* on Sky Scottish and then on we went with the news – about the Government's gun control bill. It went very well except in the first intro I'd read my piece and as Andrea was reading hers there was a panic that the taped report wasn't at the start. Fortunately, it made it, but credit to Andrea for holding her nerve on what was such a big occasion for her. There was more hassle in production terms today than any of the dry runs (changing ITN pictures to Sky, that sort of thing).

I would regularly present Scotland Today on STV and then essentially the same programme again on Sky Scottish.

Wednesday 27 November 1996
STV News

It's now Britain's worst-ever outbreak of the deadly E-coli bug. Six people are dead, more than 100 are being treated and health officials say there could be more deaths to come. Today's toll included three Lanarkshire pensioners and the first suspected case outside the Wishaw area. After a three-day delay, environmental health experts have revealed 30 outlets across the whole of Central Scotland were supplied by the butcher at the centre of the food poisoning outbreak. Local MPs are now demanding to know why action wasn't taken earlier to trace meat which may have been contaminated.

Twenty-one people died in the outbreak.

1997

Friday 17 January 1997

DIARY: Interviewed the Defence Secretary Michael Portillo in Renfrew. He is, some predict, a future leader of the Conservative Party and a possible Prime Minister. He came into the news conference and shook hands with everyone. The only other person I've ever seen do that is the Scottish Office Minister, Lord James Douglas Hamilton. When he does it there is a sense that he is a very nice man – which he is. But with Portillo there was a smarminess which was unappealing.

Michael Portillo never did become the leader of the Conservatives. His defeat in his constituency of Enfield Southgate became one of the defining images of the 1997 election. He has built a new career as a TV presenter and author and comes across as a better fellow for it.

Tuesday 21 January 1997
STV News

There's growing pressure on the Leader of the SNP, Alex Salmond, to reveal how his party would vote on any Devolution Referendum introduced by a Labour Government. An opinion poll for STV shows that almost four-fifths of the electorate think the SNP should explain their intentions. The poll also showed that a large majority of SNP supporters think they should campaign for a 'Yes' vote in the referendum.

JM: Since Labour revealed their plans to hold a two-question referendum on Devolution if they win the election, the SNP have consistently refused to say how they would urge supporters to vote. The party's view is that, yes they support the idea of a referendum, but not the questions proposed by Labour.

JAMES MITCHELL, political analyst: I think the fact that a higher proportion of the SNP's supporters want the SNP to play a full part in the referendum and campaign for a 'Yes' vote – a higher proportion than the public at large – is vitally important.

IAN LAWSON, SNP activist: You can't trust the Labour Party. I've witnessed betrayal after betrayal... Basically, if they can convince me that they've got the support for their own proposals from within the Labour Party in England, then will be the time for the SNP to make their judgement.'

The SNP did campaign for a Yes-Yes vote in the Devolution Referendum.

Thursday 6 March 1997

DIARY: The day's main stories – local authority budget cuts and council tax increases, prison officers' association warning of dangerous overcrowding and tonight's Old Firm tie being the game of the season. Laughed with one of my colleagues that this could have been any day over the past few years – the same stories coming round.

GENERAL ELECTION 1997

Wednesday 2 April 1997
STV News

The opposition parties have been quick to dismiss the Scottish Conservative manifesto. Launching their election campaign, the Scottish National Party described it as an anti-Scottish document wrapped up in a tartan ribbon.

ALEX SALMOND, SNP leader: If the Tories are going down south of the border – and that's what it looks like just now – when people in Scotland have that realisation, then I think it'll free up the vote for Scotland, to vote in Scotland's interest.

JM: For the Scottish National Party to make an impact, they must break through into the urban areas of the Central Belt. Failure to break into Labour's heartland means that, again, they could end up with just a handful of seats.

DIARY: The General Election campaign began properly for me today as I travelled through to Edinburgh for an SNP news conference. I'll be attached to the SNP for the duration. There seems, at this stage, little doubt that Labour will be triumphant.

Thursday 3 April 1997
STV News

Launching Labour's manifesto, Tony Blair unveiled plans to put Devolution on a parliamentary fast track. And he appealed to the public to trust New Labour. But his opponents have attacked the manifesto as a con.

DIARY: Saw Tony Blair, our likely PM, for the first time in the flesh today – surprisingly more tanned looking than one might have thought. He was visiting Stirling (the one really interesting seat in Scotland – will Michael Forsyth hold on or not?). He was mobbed and it was great to get in amongst it, totally ignoring the pool arrangements as Bobby Whitelaw *(cameraman)* and I leapt fences to get in with the crowd. A real adrenalin buzz, then a sprint to get the pictures sent back by satellite because he was late arriving. People say they can't trust him and on such a short exposure who can say? What did strike me was that he was uncomfortable in the crowd – he did not come across as a 'meet-the-people' kind of man in the way that John Major clearly relishes.

Friday 4 April 1997

DIARY: Big row today was over Tony Blair's visit to Scotland and comments he's made re a Scottish Parliament. It's all about detail and semantics and I think much of it is over the head of the electorate. He's been damaged, though, as people have either twisted what he said (eg if English parish councils can raise tax why not a Scottish Parliament, is not comparing one with the other). His talk of sovereignty remaining with him as an English MP was misjudged. This is where you can get sucked into an election campaign when the Big Picture gets bogged down in a morass of detail.

Monday 7 April 1997
STV News

Promising a sovereign Parliament for a sovereign people, the Scottish National Party have launched their manifesto. They say they'll set up a powerhouse Parliament to create jobs, cut taxes for the low paid and spend more on the health service. But the opposition parties have been scathing in their attacks on the Nationalist's plans, describing the manifesto as a Disney World alternative based on polo mint economics.

JM: The Scottish National Party's campaign in 1997 is, they say, based on realism. Grand predictions made by the politicians and pundits in 1992 failed to materialise. Slogans like 'Free by 93' have embarrassed the party ever since. They hope that the pledges made in their manifesto will show that the SNP is both sensible and electable.

DIARY: I suspect it could be a disappointing election for the SNP, although up to seven to eight seats will please them.

Tuesday 8 April 1997

DIARY: SNP were in Glasgow, but hardly anyone appeared so it was short and sweet. So far, I haven't really been asking questions at the news conferences – the sooner they are over the sooner I can do the one-to-ones *(interviews)*. Onto a church news conference where the church is basically saying none of the parties was offering anything for the poor. To illustrate it I went to a shopping arcade in Drumchapel – all boarded up and graffiti covered. Almost everyone I vox popped was apathetic and while traditionally they would have been Labour, it's clear that Tony Blair holds nothing for them.

STV News Vox Pops

I think they're a' in it for themselves.

The Tories have been in for most of my life, so maybe see what the others can do. Gie them a chance.

JM: You're not convinced they'd make a difference?

Naw, no' really.

As Billy Connolly says, don't vote for them, you're only encouraging them. Honestly.

JM: You think they're all the same?

Aye.

I don't think anybody would make much difference. No' in a place like this, anyway.

Tuesday 22 April 1997
STV News

There were rowdy scenes when a council meeting in Paisley was disrupted by protesting parents today. The uproar was caused by a council decision to increase nursery school charges by £5 a week. Some children have been excluded from their nurseries after their parents refused to pay.

DIARY: Parent protests at Renfrewshire District Council over a £5 increase in nursery school charges... It turned out to be good stuff with the council meeting disrupted by the parents' protests. The leading Labour group would just not allow it to be discussed, which was stupid. Great pictures in the chamber.

Wednesday 30 April 1997
STV News

JM: A campaign to win hearts and minds. A powerhouse Parliament funded by billions of pounds worth of oil revenues making Scotland the eighth richest nation in the world. That's been the SNP campaign – aimed at overcoming the fear factor, those who doubt Scotland can go it alone. 'Yes we can' has been their cry.

ALEX SALMOND, SNP Leader: We won the economic argument. For the first time in a generation people in Scotland by a majority now believe that Scotland would be better off as an independent country. That's been a major victory for us in the campaign. But y'know, tomorrow is going to be about more than just economics. Tomorrow is about national pride, self respect, whether we are a real country or just some sort of English county as London parties, in varying degrees, seem to think we are.

JM: If the SNP end their campaign as the second party in Scotland in terms of parliamentary seats they will consider it a success. Their real chance for power though, would come in any future Scottish Parliament where the proposed PR voting system would give them a bigger say in Scotland's affairs.

Thursday 1 May 1997

DIARY: Election Day. By midnight it was clear Labour had won.

Friday 2 May 1997
STV News

Conservatives in Scotland are adjusting to electoral devastation... with not a single parliamentary seat left north of the border. The high national profile of big names like Michael Forsyth and Malcolm Rifkind didn't save them. They all fell to the Labour landslide. With all the results now in the nation's political map has been dramatically altered – the final pockets of blue north of the border brushed out. Labour have gone up six to 56 seats, the Liberal Democrats have lost one and gained three to give them a total of ten MPs, the SNP have doubled their number of seats to six and the Tories, of course, have none at all. By share of the vote Labour have 46 per cent, the Nationalists 22, Conservatives 17, Lib Dems 13 and other parties 2 per cent. John MacKay has the story of the night.

JM: They fell like skittles in a bowling alley. Ten seats from the north to the borders. Conservative after Conservative was toppled. Three men who were among the most powerful in the land yesterday are today out of a job.

MICHAEL FORSYTH: There has been a tidal wave against us which is very sad. People clearly wanted a change.

IAN LANG: Scotland is rapidly turning into a one-party state and that is bad for politics and very bad for Scotland's future.

MALCOLM RIFKIND: For my colleagues both north and south of the border this has been a very sad and very worrying evening.

JM: The attacks came from all sides. From the smallest majority in Ayr to the supposedly safe seat in Eastwood, the Scottish electorate hammered home their rejection. Across the political divide there was joy unconfined as others prepared for government.

GORDON BROWN, Labour MP: The Labour Party is now ready to rebuild the bond of trust between the British people and their government.

ALEX SALMOND, Leader, SNP: Now we've managed to increase our share of the vote further and double our parliamentary representation, I think we're entitled to a bit of the kudos this evening.

JM: Today Scotland stands as a Conservative free zone. The party controls no councils and it has no Members of Parliament.

DIARY: It's a landslide. Labour have stormed into Government on a massive majority. An historic night. As one of my colleagues observed, 'It's a sea change.' When they look back on politics, 1997 will be up there with the other great events. There are no Conservative MPs in Scotland anymore, all ten roundly thumped. It has taken everyone by surprise – even the Labour Party. The country has sent out the clearest message that quite simply it was time for change. The Conservatives have been in power too long and have run out of ideas, their government was pursuing issues out of dogma and not need eg bureaucratisation of the NHS. I do believe John Major was a decent man and I admire his rise from nothing. I am concerned about Labour's majority being so big and there being no effective opposition. Today was a new dawn for Britain, I wonder what sort of age it will be.

Friday 6 June 1997

DIARY: To Irvine to interview a couple whose premature daughter has been left to die because the doctor said that at 23 weeks she wasn't viable. Raised a number of issues – if the baby is battling to survive, shouldn't they at least try to help it, and if it's a mother's right to have a pregnancy terminated, why doesn't a mother have the right to insist the child be given every chance of survival? It all made a good piece with the tearful testimony from the mother.

Thursday 12 June 1997
STV News

A huge bonfire burned on the island of Eigg last night to mark the transfer of ownership of the island to the islanders themselves. Festivities have been going on all day as the islanders celebrate taking control of their own land from an absentee landlord. And the Government has said that it will help other communities in the Highlands to win ownership of the land on which they live.

JOHN CHESTER, islander: It's really more a sense of relief than anything else that this has finally come through. And even now, though we've known the island was going to be sold for two months now, I think most people are not really getting to grips with it even yet.

DIARY: I had good pictures to work with and it's the sort of piece I enjoy doing. My final line was 'As the Hebridean rain fell it was as if years of neglect was being washed away.' Perhaps a bit much, but the piece lent itself to some poetic licence.

Monday 14 July 1997
STV News

Prison officers say they're furious with the Government's decision to press ahead with the building of Scotland's first private jail. They're accusing ministers of following a Tory agenda of privatisation. The new prison is designed to help cope with overcrowding in Scotland's jails. It's to be built and run by private operators at a site near Kilmarnock.

The 500-capacity Kilmarnock prison was opened in 1999 and entered public ownership in 2024 when the 25-year contract ended.

Thursday 24 July 1997
STV News

More open, more accessible and more accountable government for the 21st century. That's Donald Dewar's claim for his Devolution plans, unveiled in the Commons this afternoon. The Scottish Secretary outlined a home rule scheme that involves a Parliament with tax-raising powers elected by a system of proportional representation. The White Paper has been welcomed by the SNP and the Liberal Democrats, but the Conservatives say the plans are dangerous, damaging and dishonest.

DONALD DEWAR, Scottish Secretary: The Government's target is for the Scottish Parliament to assume its full responsibilities in January in the Year 2000. That, indeed, will be a new Parliament for a new millennium... Like many others in this House and beyond, I have campaigned hard for a Scottish Parliament over the years. Few occasions in my long parliamentary career have given me as much pleasure as coming here today to present our firm proposals for that Scottish Parliament.

MICHAEL ANCRAM, Conservative Constitutional Spokesman: These proposals are not even half-baked. It is not too late for the Government to consider the damage which will result from constitutional reform, not just in the short term, but for generations to come.

FIONA ROSS, Political Correspondent: The Parliament will effectively take over the responsibilities of the Scottish Office with power to make laws in such areas as health, education, including further and higher education, the criminal justice system, local government and social work. The UK Parliament will retain power over foreign policy, defence, economic policy and social security.

DIARY: Devolution Day – the Government publishing its White Paper for a Scottish Parliament. Why are hardly any of Labour's 56 MPs going to stand for this Scottish Parliament? Because they know where the power will really be?

Monday 28 July 1997

DIARY: Paul *(Paul McKinney, News Editor)* revealed to me that a survey of viewers (this is a regular thing) showed that they regard my dress sense to be dull (how dare they!). I prefer dark clothes because they are more authoritative and I'm not allowed to wear blue.

I could not wear blue because we used a blue screen backdrop. If I wore anything blue, it would pick up what was projected behind me. No one ever mentioned it over the years we used this set. Quite a contrast later when I regularly wore blue to match the colours of a newer set – the Blue Tie MacKay myth of social networks.

Thursday 31 July 1997

DIARY: So, the last *Scotland Today* on Sky Scottish. We played it straight as we signed off, nothing over the top. It's a shame and I enjoyed doing it, but at least I've got my new programme starting on Sunday.

Sky Scottish had pockets of audiences all over the place. We got feedback from places like Marbella and Rome and we were particularly chuffed by that. And we were big in Bosnia – a line I enjoyed using – because of the presence of Scottish troops there.

Sunday 3 August 1997
The Scottish Review

Good evening and welcome to the first edition of *The Scottish Review* with me, John MacKay. During the next hour we'll be looking back at this week's main Scottish news stories. And we'll be discussing claims that the Government has gone soft on crime in Scotland by deciding not to implement controversial plans for an automatic life sentence for serious sex and violent offenders.

DIARY: The new programme, *The Scottish Review*, went out for the first time today. General feeling was that it was good for a first programme.

Wednesday 27 August 1997
STV News

While the Devolution campaigners have been appearing in front of cameras, it seems there's been only limited direct contact with the voters themselves. In the latest of our special series of reports on the referendum, John MacKay has visited two of the most fiercely contested seats at May's General Election where he found little evidence of any campaigning on Devolution.

JM: Stirling was one of the most keenly contested seats in Scotland during the General Election. It's a hot bed of political activity and the scene, three weeks before polling day, of a visit by the prospective Prime Minister. Two weeks before the referendum, which could lead to the biggest upheaval in the political history of the UK, this is the same street.

Vox Pops

During the election you were getting people coming to your door and to the office. You knew what was going on. This time there's been nothing.

You're the first to approach us.

There's been nothing here.

Absolutely disgraceful. There has been nothing.

I haven't seen any posters.

PAOLO VESTRI, Scotland Forward: The political parties and ourselves took a strategic decision that, rather than have a six-week campaign like the General Election and which people got fed up with, it'd be better to have an effective, snappy campaign.

BRIAN MONTEITH, Think Twice: This campaign has been rushed by the Government. There was no need to do that. People are on holiday etc. Both campaigns have suffered. However, over the next two weeks you'll see a far higher profile campaign.

DEATH OF PRINCESS DIANA
Sunday 31 August 1997
STV News

The people of Scotland have been paying tribute to Diana, Princess of Wales. Prayers have been said at services throughout the country. Campaigning in the Devolution Referendum has been suspended. Flowers have been laid by the public at Holyrood Palace and in Glasgow's George Square.

DIARY: Awoken at 6.35am by the phone going. It was Nicki *(Nicki McGowan, Sunday producer)* with the quite shocking news that Diana, Princess of Wales had been killed in a car crash in Paris. She was only 36. After the initial shock it struck me that there was an awful inevitability about the tragedy. She was the world's most photographed woman, an icon of our time. It has stunned most people and has been an event that united the nation. She was treated badly by the royal family, but she was also a manipulator who could not, to my mind, keep away from the headlines and front pages. Nonetheless, she will now become a tragic figure in history, more so than even Marilyn Monroe, the one figure with whom there are clear parallels. I fronted a special Scottish bulletin at 5.55pm for 20 minutes, with a black tie and much gravitas. The BBC and ITV had blanket coverage – too much by the end of the day I thought, but nonetheless you kept getting drawn back to it. Above all it can't be forgotten that while Diana has moved into legend, two young boys have lost their mother and you have to feel for them.

JM: Fiona, you mentioned the Devolution Referendum may have to be postponed, is this really feasible?

FIONA ROSS, Political Correspondent: It is feasible. It's not necessarily likely at the moment, a lot depends on the funeral arrangements. For example, it would not be feasible, obviously, to run a referendum campaign on the future of Scotland on the same day as Princess Diana's funeral. But, of course, politicians really don't want to get into this at the moment, apart from anything else, everybody is quite literally grief stricken. There are also very serious implications here, I mean it's not just as easy as putting a line through it and saying, och we'll hold it a week later. They actually have to recall Parliament to do this and re-legislate because it's in the Referendum Act that the referendum is held on the 11th of September. So, there is quite a serious problem potentially facing the Government here.

JM: So, if we stick with the current timetable how would that effect campaigning, do you think?

FR: Well, I don't think there'd be any. I mean there won't be any until after the Princess's funeral. Now, I think realistically the funeral isn't going to take place for at least a week. So, we may end up with just one or two days campaigning right up against the actual date. I really don't see anybody campaigning between now and the funeral.

Monday 1 September 1997

DIARY: The national mourning of the death of Diana continues unabated. Throughout the country people are laying flowers and signing books of condolence. Queues are stretching for literally hours. More details are emerging too. It's a horrendous story and an awful waste. The funeral will be on Saturday, so we've got almost a week more of this to go through. It is clearly something which has touched everyone, though. I don't buy into this image of the tragic, fairy tale princess who had finally found true love. Dodi al Fahyed was a playboy she'd been seeing for a couple of months. I suspect that too would have ended in tears. Still, a tragic, tragic story.

Saturday 6 September 1997

DIARY: A remarkable day dominated by the funeral of Diana, Princess of Wales. It seems incredible to be writing that of the woman whose image has probably been the one I've been most exposed to for my adult life. You could not fail to be stirred and moved by the theatre of it.

Wednesday 10 September 1997
STV News

The 100-hour campaign is almost over. The polls open in just over 12 hours. On the eve of Scotland's date with destiny, the politicians have been setting out their stall for the last time. Scotland Forward say go for it, urging a double Yes vote. The No-No campaign warned again on taxation and the break-up of the Union.

DIARY: Worked today on a look back over the Devolution Referendum campaign. Frankly, it's been lacklustre and uninspiring. Indeed, it's really only happened in the last 100 hours since Princess Diana's funeral. Plenty of television discussion and newspaper analysis, but nothing like the energy of the General Election campaign. That's probably the reason why it hasn't sparked, everyone used their energies in the election. And the result of the election meant that the referendum was a foregone conclusion.

THE DEVOLUTION REFERENDUM
Thursday 11 September 1997

DIARY: Referendum Day. The day Scotland decided whether it wanted to have its own devolved Parliament. By the early hours it was clear that it did. I was at the Clackmannanshire count, the smallest mainland authority and expected to provide the fastest result. It did at around 12.42am – a resounding 'Yes-Yes', not entirely unexpected. Finally stood down at 1.30am.

Friday 12 September 1997
STV News

After 300 years the Scottish people are tonight contemplating the prospect of a Parliament sitting once again in the capital city. The result was a landslide for the Yes campaigners with larger majorities on both referendum questions than many had dared to hope. Seventy-four per cent of voters backed a Scottish Parliament. Sixty-three per cent supported tax varying powers. Just over 60 per cent of the electorate went to the polls. The Prime Minister wasted no time in heading north to celebrate and congratulate. Alex Salmond and Jim Wallace were also buoyant after a campaign which saw unprecedented levels of co-operation between Labour, the SNP and the Liberal Democrats.

JM: Edinburgh. The day the settled will of the Scottish people became known. A good day for Scotland and a good day for the United Kingdom, said the Prime Minister Tony Blair. Scotland had shown the way forward. The politicians had trusted the people, he said, and now the people had shown they trusted themselves

TONY BLAIR, Prime Minister: Scotland does not need to choose and should not be forced to choose between separation and no change. There is a better, modern way forward. That way is Devolution and today Scotland has shown that's what it wants.

DONALD DEWAR, Scottish Secretary: The people of Scotland have delivered us their trust and we will deliver for them. The settled will of the Scottish people is there for all to see.

JM: Earlier he had shared a platform with the leaders of the other parties. The question now is how long that unity will continue?

ALEX SALMOND, SNP Leader: There's a job of opposition as well. The Labour Party in West Central Scotland suffer the same problems as the Tories at Westminster. They've got to be opposed and the SNP have a responsibility of opposition. That's a responsibility we intend to live up to.

JIM WALLACE, Scottish Liberal Democrats: It'll come as no surprise that we still believe there's a need to invest more in education. To do so we'd maybe wish to use a penny of the tax varying powers, but the important thing is there is a choice.

JM: An historic day. For most a euphoric day. Scotland has decided. The people have celebrated. Now the hard work begins.

DONALD DEWAR, Scottish Secretary: It was a smashing night, a smashing result. It exceeded my expectations and we outperformed the polls. The important thing is that it gives stability, it gives a tremendous platform for launching the bill. It gives impetus and moral authority and I think it has cut down the room for argument. The principle is established. Tony Blair was particularly anxious that we should have public endorsement. We took that head on and we have got a remarkable response.

JM: We've seen a great deal of harmony on the political platforms. Does this herald a new era of consensus politics perhaps?

DD: I don't know. I'm neither looking for confrontation, but I'd be cautious about consensus. Consensus is where there is agreement and on this there was agreement. What people were agreeing was that they wanted to come in behind the Labour Government policy, a devolved Parliament within the United Kingdom. And what we've got is evidence of the settled will of the Scottish people. They want that stronger voice, they want to remain within the United Kingdom and that's what we're going to deliver.

JM: And finally, are we looking at the man who could be Scotland's First Minister?

DD: *(chortling)* I don't know who'll be Scotland's First Minister. That's a little way away yet. We've got to elect the Parliament first and then they've got to decide who they want. I don't know, there's a lot of speculation, but my job is to complete the unfinished business. I've got the green light. I've got, I think, the moral authority and impetus from last night's tremendous victory and I'm determined to get that show on the road as quickly as I can.

DIARY: An historic day and a good one to be a journalist. Scotland has voted overwhelmingly for a Scottish Parliament. I had about four hours sleep at home before going back to work and through to Edinburgh where it was all happening. First up a photo call of Scottish party leaders in Edinburgh City Chambers. Then a sit-down interview with the Scottish Secretary Donald Dewar, something rather sprung on me because our people obviously had no idea it was happening. Then Tony Blair made a stage-managed visit to Parliament Square. I was coordinating three cameras, accessing pool material and fixing interviews. All the while I'm trying to report too. Nonetheless, I wouldn't have missed it – a real sense of occasion, of being a witness to history in the making.

Tuesday 16 September 1997
STV News

A Catholic priest in Ayrshire is at the centre of a police investigation into allegations of child abuse stretching back 20 years. Father Paul Moore has been removed from his parish in Prestwick and is understood to have been undergoing treatment. Detectives are interviewing some of his alleged victims.

DIARY: Back on the road with a vengeance today. Story of yet another child abusing priest – this time in Ayrshire. The church had already hidden him away in an abbey and the crimes stretched back to the '70s. In torrential rain I chapped doors in both his former parishes. No great surprise that no one would speak on camera, although I got some good background material to pad out the piece. Ended up being the lead story too.

Francis Moore – known as Father Paul – was finally jailed in 2018 after being convicted for historic sex crimes against three children and later a student priest. He was later defrocked by the Pope and died while still a prisoner.

Thursday 9 October 1997
STV News

The Prime Minister's office is refusing to become involved in the row over the proposed transfer of a Scottish murderer to the Maze prison in Belfast. Jason Campbell, who slit the throat of a teenager for wearing a Celtic top, could be moved within days. In Northern Ireland itself, the move has been widely condemned.

There was strong opposition to this in Northern Ireland, even among Loyalists.

They didn't want Campbell holding the same status as other Loyalist prisoners at the Maze. The leading Unionist newspaper, the Belfast News, had the headline, 'No place for the Scottish Butcher' and asked, 'Will someone in the Northern Ireland Office explain what legitimate political cause Campbell was purporting to represent in perpetrating such a heinous act?'

Wednesday 22 October 1997

DIARY: Did a story about a photographic exhibition in Ayr depicting photos of deformed babies in formaldehyde. It was shocking and tasteless. I can understand why science may need to preserve them, but not for public show. It's wrong.

Thursday 23 October 1997
STV News

Seven children were taken home to their parents in Hamilton last night at the start of a controversial curfew introduced by Strathclyde Police. They were all picked up by police foot patrols who took to the streets after dark.

DIARY: Police in Hamilton were setting up what to all intents and purposes was an after dark curfew on young children. Followed a patrol around and it was farcical with the kids regarding the TV cameras as a magnet. The idea of the media facility wasn't good. You have to ask what are their parents doing?

Monday 3 November 1997

DIARY: The one thing that always spoils your day as a journalist is when you're assigned to a story that involves local government finance. The gist of the story is that Glasgow City Council is being bailed out of a financial crisis by other, better off councils. At a COSLA news conference this afternoon to discuss all of this. Most of the points being made were cruising at altitude over my head. Then the desk decided it had to be the lead. I'd be surprised if the viewers understood any of it because I didn't.

Friday 14 November 1997
STV News

Primary school children are to be targeted in a national £1 million drugs awareness campaign. Scotland Against Drugs are leading the initiative with the backing of some of the country's largest businesses. The aim is to provide a uniform approach to drugs education across the country.

I wonder how much money has been spent on these campaigns and initiatives over the years and to what end?

DIARY: Paul McKinney *(Head of News)* suggested I could be a parliamentary corr at Westminster in place of Lorraine *(Lorraine Davidson who was leaving)*, but I said no.

Much like my time as sports correspondent, I didn't want to be cut off from daily news.

Monday 24 November 1997
STV News

Britain's new drugs Tsar has caused a storm of protest by backing a controversial treatment programme. Keith Hellawell, on his first visit to Scotland since being appointed to lead the fight against drugs, claims the methadone programme works and he wouldn't rule out people staying on it for life. But tonight, some drugs campaigners have criticised his comments, saying methadone kills more addicts than it cures.

Sunday 30 November 1997

DIARY: *Scottish Review...* Discussion was on what it meant to be Scottish. SNP parliamentary candidate Nicola Sturgeon was one of the debaters. She is very sharp.

Thursday 11 December 1997
STV News

One of the greats of Scottish football was cremated today. Billy Bremner, the former captain of Scotland and Leeds United died at the weekend, two days before his 55th birthday. The mourners at his funeral read like a who's who of the footballing heroes from the '60s and '70s.

JOE JORDAN, Ex-Leeds United and Scotland: To find words to describe him as a player is difficult, but as a friend it's easy because he was always there.

DIARY: I remember him well as a player and saw him play for Scotland. Later I found him to be a very pleasant man via telephone conversations I had with him when Radio Scotland's sports corr.

1998

Monday 9 February 1998
STV News

Glasgow was a city where dreams came true today. The World Cup has begun a tour of the countries competing in this summer's tournament. Scotland was first and everyone from Craig Brown to Govan grannies wanted to touch it.

DIARY: I held the World Cup today. The World Cup sponsors Coca Cola are taking it on tour and today it was in Glasgow at various locations. From Munich, Buenos Aires, Rome and LA to Ruchill! All the hacks and snappers were like kids getting their photos taken with it – me included. Five kilos of gold, but it was the prestige of it that mattered. In truth, I don't believe it was the genuine article whatever they say. Touching it takes away from its mystique and one fun shot we had of an elderly woman carting it along in her shopping trolley made a mockery of it. Still, it was nice to dream.

Friday 13 February 1998
STV News

An elderly man whose body lay undiscovered in his house for at least a month might have been saved, says his former care warden, if her post hadn't been axed by council cuts. Jimmy Mochan's remains were only discovered in his council flat after neighbours complained of the smell. Tonight, there are warnings it could happen again.

DIARY: The warden service at the flats had been withdrawn last year. I managed to get a hold of his former warden and she said it will happen again and again. We also had her speaking during a demo last year warning of the dangers of cuts to old folk. It gave us a great line and we wiped the floor with the BBC.

There is no intense rivalry on the ground between STV and BBC. Many of us have been colleagues at different times and, with one or two exceptions, will help each other out if possible, but it's good to beat them.

Tuesday 24 February 1998
STV News

More than 200,000 houses need to be built in Scotland in the next decade. The preference is to use brownfield sites within city boundaries. However, as John MacKay reports, in some places that option is not available and pressure continues to be exerted on the green belt.

Shortage of housing, particularly social housing, is another continuing issue.

Sunday 8 March 1998

DIARY: The debate – Old and New Labour – was lively. Stalwart Janey Buchan dismissing new, young Labour (Blair McDougall) as 'ambitious wee creeps'. Lively stuff.

Sky Scottish Review

JM: You said, Janey, it wasn't New Labour, it was right-wing Labour. *(to Blair McDougall)* Are you right-wing? Are you a Socialist?

BLAIR MCDOUGALL: I'm certainly a Socialist.

JM: *(to Janey Buchan)* Do you recognise him as a Socialist?

JANEY BUCHAN: Well, I don't know him.

JM: Do you recognise New Labour as Socialism?

JB: No, because they tell us they're not.

BM: That's simply not true. When Tony Blair reformed Clause 4...

JB: He didn't reform it. He banished it. There's a different thing. Reform, we'll all go for reform. But I do know the difference between reform and battering it out of existence.

JM: Blair, is that your feeling, it was battered out of existence?

BM: The old Clause 4 was poetic, but it didn't really mean anything to the average person in the street...We can't just appeal to the people in the party, we need to go out...

(The debate continues)

JM: Can you stay in the Labour Party as it is?

JB: Oh, of course. Where else am I gonnae go? Anyway, I'm no' gonnae shift out for a bunch of ambitious wee creeps.

JM: Blair, are you an ambitious wee creep? You and your type?

BM: I'm certainly ambitious. Whether I'm a wee creep is another matter altogether...

Monday 16 March 1998

DIARY: Young boy killed after climbing a tree underneath an electricity pylon. Quiet day, so out to try to make something of it, which in the end I did. Got some good local vox pops and spoke to a very articulate wee girl who'd been in the boy's class. I made something out of almost nothing and that's professionally satisfying. It reinforces to me one of the lessons of journalism, don't sit at the desk phoning, always go out to the scene – you get a better feel for the story.

Tuesday 17 March 1998

DIARY: Meeting today about the future of our newsroom ie desktop editing etc. I think it's quite exciting, but my concerns are that it's flawed to believe that all journalists will be able to edit well and that jobs will be lost, not so much in the newsroom, but on the technical side. Training is due to begin in the summer.

Desktop editing is now standard practice for reporters, although specialist craft editors are still an essential element in the newsroom.

Thursday 26 March 1998

DIARY: Today was the sort of day that makes you more inspired by your job – with the feeling that maybe you don't appreciate it enough. I went on a helicopter for the first time over to Kintyre. It was one of those hit the ground running and cram in as much as possible... I had a bit of fun with it.

STV News

The Lord Chancellor, Lord Irvine, could be in more trouble over DIY. After the row over the decoration of his London home, he's now facing an investigation of work at his holiday home in Kintyre. *Scotland Today* has discovered the local council is examining a complaint that work may have been carried out at the house without the proper building consent.

The row was over the decorating his parliamentary residence costing more than £650,000, including £60,000 for wallpaper.

LORD DERRY IRVINE, Lord Chancellor: *(Speaking in March 1998)* We're talking about quality materials which are capable of lasting 60 or 70 years. You're not talking about something down at the DIY store, which may collapse after a year or two.

JM: There's not quite the same choice in Kintyre.

CHRISTINE CUPPLES, local DIY supplier: *(unrolling wallpapers in the store)* He could have had this one at £3.50. Or if he wanted a more expensive one, here is one at £6.50.

DIARY: None of the local tradesmen, unsurprisingly, would say anything and it was a struggle to get local reaction. Anyway, finally got it in the can and away. Back at base much unnecessary caution from producer, delay getting into editing and not with the fastest editor, so I missed my hit time. That hurt professionally, but it was a good yarn.

The helicopter landed in a hotel car park and myself and the cameraman got out to collect a hire car. I could see all these faces in the hotel waiting expectantly to see who this very important person must be. Then bemusement as they clearly wondered, who the hell is that?

Monday 30 March 1998

DIARY: At a drugs conference this morning, a further strategy for the next few years – basically saying that once drug abusers are stable they need something meaningful to go on to – a job. The ex-addicts I spoke to, though, talked of wanting to work with other addicts. I'm not so sure how that moves them on – they are still part of that culture and it's not a complete break.

Another drugs strategy.

Friday 3 April 1998

DIARY: Diverted from my original job to a house fire in Kilwinning in which two children died. Looks as though the mother was attempting suicide. Tragic, but because there was no real sign of damage – it was all smoke – there was a strange air about the place. There was no great sense of emotion from bystanders.

Tuesday 28 April 1998

DIARY: Launch of a new sport strategy for Scotland. Set at the new Hampden Park which is rapidly taking shape. It looks very impressive, although they had space for a running track which they decided not to do – short-sighted SFA? Surely not. It's good to have such a national stadium, but frankly it should not have been built where it was – inner city stadia are of the 19th century. For the 21st century they should be built out of town with good access – not necessarily a greenfield site, but say somewhere like Ravenscraig. The problem is that would require vision and lack of self-interest.

Hampden had to be closed during and after the Commonwealth Games in 2014 to install and then remove a running track.

Sunday 3 May 1998
Seven Days

JM: I'm joined now by the Secretary of State for Scotland, Donald Dewar, celebrating – to the very day – the first anniversary of getting Scotland's top political post. A new opinion poll out this morning putting the SNP neck and neck with Labour in Scotland might, however, suggest 'celebrating' is an inappropriate word.

DONALD DEWAR, Scottish Secretary: I never had any doubt about going for the Scottish Parliament, personally. I wanted to do it and I want to see these major themes *(long-term unemployment, raise standards in education, make the health service patient friendly)* because that's what it's got to be about. It's about setting a new framework for people in Scotland and tackling the problems in a distinctively Scottish way. I don't want it to be dominated by another period of years of arguing about further constitutional change. Let's get on with the job and make it prove itself.

JM: At this point in time, looking ahead to it, it would appear that the consensus politics that delivered that Parliament might not exist in the Parliament and we may well, indeed, get bogged down. Is that something you fear?

DD: I hope not. I very much hope not. The nationalists, for a start, are saying that there must be an Independence Referendum. That's their demand. That must be met before they will have any discussions or co-operation on anything else. I mean, that's a shame because I think that we want, as I say, to make this Parliament work for Scotland and I think that we want a period of stability in terms of the arguments about whether we go further or don't go further. The important thing, I think, is the programmes that we can push through.

DIARY: The new programme *Seven Days* aired for the first time today – the best day of the year which won't do much for ratings. The final part was an 11-minute set-piece interview with the Scottish Secretary Donald Dewar. It was supposed to be relaxed and conversational and it was. I pushed him on the threat from the SNP and later I thought I should have pushed him more on the personality issue between him and Alex Salmond.

Monday 11 May 1998
STV News

A major part of Scotland's build-up to the World Cup began today – the filming of the video for the World Cup song – 'Don't Come Too Soon' by Del Amitri. The Tartan Army invaded Prestwick Airport to star behind potential Mel Gibsons like Colin Hendry and Gordon Durie.

DIARY: Sent out to Prestwick Airport because 'we think Del Amitri are filming their World Cup video there.' I was thoroughly pissed off, but as sometimes happens it turned out to be fine. Hung around for a while getting shots, vox pops, disappeared to the seafront for lunch and returned to get the players, Colin Hendry, the Scottish captain, and Justin Currie of Del Amitri.

DIARY *(cont)*: Big story was the resignation of the Celtic coach Wim Jansen over disputes with Fergus McCann and Jack Brown. Celtic have an incredible knack of creating a fiasco from success. The fans, understandably, are raging.

Monday 18 May 1998
STV News

And finally, as we're always told, the Scottish diet is terrible. Deep-fried Mars Bars plumbed our culinary depths. There have been attempts to expand our horizons – alligator burgers and frogs legs to name a couple. But something new could be about to save the nation's health.

DIARY: Today it was about a chippy in Dunblane selling ostrich haggis! It's a bit of a gimmick, but it seems to be selling and people who sampled it thought it was good. Ended up at the ostrich farm near Thornhill in Stirlingshire. The farmer took us into their enclosure and they were right up at my face, pecking my watch and shoes. They were young ones, apparently fully grown they can reach up to eight feet high and then I'd have been really uncomfortable. Got a good wee piece out of it and it passed a pleasant afternoon in the country.

Tuesday 9 June 1998

DIARY: The World Cup begins tomorrow with Scotland taking on World Champions Brazil in the opening match. For Scotland it doesn't come much better than that. The build-up has reached a crescendo now and it's what everyone is talking about – where are you watching it? What's your prediction? Everyone is up for it. I reported on the options available – pub, house, big tents in Glasgow Green and even churches.

Wednesday 10 June 1998
STV News

Scotland have lost the opening match of the World Cup Finals in France against Brazil 2–1. In a match full of tension, an early lead by Brazil was levelled by a penalty from John Collins. Then, after an impressive display by the Scots – and in one of the cruellest ironies – it was an own goal by Tom Boyd that sealed Scotland's fate.

The image of John Collins equalising from the penalty spot is now part of Scottish football's iconography.

Tuesday 23 June 1998
STV News

An entire nation will grind to a halt in about an hour from now when Scotland take on Morocco for a place in the next round of the World Cup finals. Roads have been jammed as people try to get home in time for the game and energy companies are expecting power surges during breaks. And the nation is confident – bookies say punters are pouring money onto a Scotland victory.

Scotland were gubbed 3–0 and went out of the World Cup in France.

Sunday 28 June 1998

DIARY: *Seven Days* is a good wee programme. We had a jazz guitarist Martin Taylor, of whom I'd never heard, but is a man of international stature based in Ayrshire. I don't like jazz, but I'm in awe of his virtuosity.

Tuesday 4 August 1998
STV News

A mother who killed her own twin children by poisoning their juice and then setting fire to their bedroom has been sent to Carstairs. The 31-year-old pleaded guilty to culpable homicide on the grounds of diminished responsibility. The High Court in Glasgow heard she'd tried to take her own life after taking those of her children. On being revived by doctors she told them, 'If I'd known I'd be alive I wouldn't have done it. I told them we'd be together.'

DIARY: Tragic story today following on from a story I covered on 3 April about a mother who killed her two children, but failed to kill herself. She's to remain in Carstairs. The details were awful, how she crushed tablets (painkillers) into their night-time juice. She'd tried it a couple of times before, but couldn't go through with it. Goodness knows what drives someone to kill her children.

Monday 10 August 1998

Reporting on a meeting of Glasgow social workers. There were a lot of politically motivated activists around and much ill-feeling towards the media.

DIARY: At one point myself and cameraman Ross Armstrong were in a circle surrounded by people, chanting 'Scum! Scum!' I can't say I felt intimidated, although it was uncomfortable for a few seconds. Dealt with it by ignoring them and getting on with the job.

Thursday 13 August 1998
STV News

NHS waiting lists in Scotland have fallen for the first time in two years. But nearly 90,000 Scots are still in the queue for treatment. And in some areas, including Glasgow, the number of people waiting for care is still increasing. The Government is welcoming the overall fall, but the opposition are accusing ministers of 'waffle failure'.

JM: The reduction of hospital waiting lists was a key pledge made by Labour when it came into Government last year. But despite cutting bureaucracy costs in its first year, it was unable to halt the seemingly relentless lengthening waiting lists – up almost 7,000 in two years – a source of huge embarrassment to the new Government. With more money being put into the health service, today the Government could finally announce the rise has been halted.

NHS waiting lists are another regular for the reporters. They were then and they still are. However, unlike some hardly annuals, people really do care about this. By 2024 the NHS waiting lists in Scotland were at 800,000.

Wednesday 26 August 1998

DIARY: Paul *(Paul McKinney, Head of News)* told me that he wanted me to co-anchor the 6.30pm with Shereen now that Viv is going. The slight downside is that he'd want me to do it five nights a week and give up *Seven Days*. My priority has always been to do the 6.30pm and if it came down to a choice there is no doubt what I'd do.

Monday 14 September 1998

DIARY: Celtic's AGM was expected to be a stormy affair and it was, but it never came near the disorder that some suggested might happen. Despite Celtic winning the Championship last year, the fans are angry that Wim Jansen left, are unconvinced by Dr Josef Venglos and that there have been no new signings. Reporters were allowed to be present and I have to say that Fergus McCann and Jock Brown (the two targets for the anger, especially the latter) handled it no problem. I was amazed at how poor so many of the questions were.

Wednesday 16 September 1998

DIARY: Tonight's programme was hectic. The first two stories didn't make their hit time, the satellite link failed, the autocue packed in, tapes were late starting and another one was spat out mid-story. It was pandemonium. It really was a case of not knowing what's coming next, but that's what we're paid for and the viewers would only have noticed the obvious eg a tape clock appearing at one point.

Thursday 17 September 1998

DIARY: Last day working exclusively as a reporter. Back on the caretakers' strike – lots of flats damaged because concierges were off duty. Some kids alleged to me that the caretakers had put them up to it, which gave me a strong line.

Monday 21 September 1998

DIARY: For now into the foreseeable future I'll be the main co-anchor on the 6.30pm – presentation will be my priority, not a reporter who fills in.

I had reservations about coming off the road as a reporter, but I enjoyed presentation and the buzz of live broadcasting. I also liked having an overview of the day's events. Before the instant alerts of social media, reporters would often be unaware of what was happening outside of their own story.

Tuesday 22 September 1998
STV News

Trams could soon be reintroduced to Edinburgh after a 40-year absence. A company in the capital is proposing to bring them back as a way of combatting traffic pollution and congestion in the city.

LIZ MONAGHAN, STV reporter: Running from Haymarket along the length of Princes Street, down Leith Walk to the docks, the company behind the project say commuters would benefit greatly.

This was the start of a long, expensive, tortuous episode for Edinburgh.

Tuesday 20 October 1998

DIARY: Started on Editstar *(desktop editing)* today and it looks fascinating. I'm a bit dubious about the principle of journalists doing the editing, because it leaves less time for actual reporting – which is what we're supposed to do. However, that concern aside, I think I'll enjoy it – it's closer to my time in radio when you had complete control over the work you did.

Tuesday 24 November 1998

DIARY: So, the new age has dawned – we began broadcasting using the new system. And it was a disaster! Camera shots were wrong, over-the-shoulders *(on-screen images)* covered my face, soengs *(taped reports)* were late. It was just an unacceptable mess. Most of it was caused not by human error, but by equipment just not doing what it's supposed to do.

Walking down Sauchiehall Street just after that, some wise guy came up to me with a newspaper held over his face and said, 'A'right big man!' There were a few similar episodes.

Monday 30 November 1998

DIARY: *Scotland Today* fell off the air – the first time that has happened to my knowledge. It was a humiliation – nothing less. We went on air knowing that there would be a problem with a live link to Fiona Ross, but otherwise no indication of the fiasco to follow. Supposed to start on a two-shot to camera three, but I was punched up on a single to cam one. The story wasn't on autocue either. Fiona couldn't hear us properly, but did manage to cue her own package. Then a two-way with her failed – she didn't hear. Next package had a sound problem, as did the next and other pieces seemed to have disappeared altogether. The gallery was pandemonium, but there's no director anymore so no one was really telling us what to do. All I could hear was swearing and 'We're going to crash off air!' said repeatedly. All the while Shereen and I are having to apologise for the problems – often with the cameras actually shifting while we were in shot. Had a breathing space in sport, most of which was on tape, which clarified the decision that we were going to have to come off. Had a final headline sequence which was also a fiasco and then I had to fill for a minute or so, apologising for the chaos and saying we'd fallen below our 'high standards'. In the great scheme of things it's not important, but it was professionally humiliating. There was a short meeting afterwards, but everyone too shattered to say much.

As fate would have it we were wearing sprigs of lucky white heather because it was St Andrew's Day. To fill the time left the station had put on an excerpt of a classic STV series Edge of the Land, which featured stunning views of Scotland's coastline from the air. The phones were lighting up as the shattered team returned to the newsroom. We answered them with some trepidation, apologies at the ready. So many of the calls, however, were to say that Edge of the Land was brilliant.

Thursday 3 December 1998

DIARY: I presented the inevitable fiasco in the 11.00am bulletin and was so pissed off that I went for a walk (soengs *(taped reports)* froze etc, stills *(photos)* flashed up at the wrong time). An elderly woman stopped me (turns out her name was MacKay too and recently widowed and she ends up kissing my hand). She told me she'd be thinking of me.

That stays with me. That poor, recently widowed woman saying she'd be thinking of me because a TV programme went wrong.

Thursday 10 December 1998

DIARY: The BBC Governors today ruled, mistakenly, that there could be no Scottish *Six O'Clock News* on the Beeb. I have long been convinced of the need for such a thing with the Scottish Parliament on the horizon. The London news is often irrelevant here. The focus has been on the BBC as the public broadcaster, but in a classic BBC fudge, Scotland is to be given an extra £10m to cover the Holyrood Parliament. There is also a persuasive argument that our strength is our local identity and it may be diluted by doing international, UK and local stuff. Interesting times.

Wednesday 23 December 1998

DIARY: During tonight's 6.30pm David Tanner mentioned Rangers would be signing new goalie Stefan Klos tomorrow and I made the crack about when we can expect to hear about his knee injury (which seems to affect every Rangers signing). Inevitably it lit up the phone lines with one caller calling me a 'snidey Fenian bastard.' Funny if it wasn't so sad.

1999

Friday 15 January 1999

DIARY: I had to take on a pre-arranged set-piece interview with Cardinal Thomas Winning – Scotland's leading RC. He's marking 50 years as a priest with a special mass on Sunday. Interview was good – he spoke of a permissive society that has 'gone sick' and the objective of 'one church' in Scotland in the next 50 years. He stands for something and does so unwaveringly. As a man he's pleasant enough, but you would never get too close to him.

TONY BLAIR ON POVERTY AND SOCIAL EXCLUSION
Friday 5 February 1999

DIARY: I interviewed the Prime Minister today – the first time I've done so. In this job you soon lose the thrill of meeting famous people, but there's no doubt that meeting the Prime Minister had more impact than most. He met me, shook my hand, did the interview, but there was no chit chat. He sat on a bed to pose for a photograph for a snapper and cracked a joke about checking what was behind him, but I could never say there was a glimpse of the real man. He certainly did not have any sort of aura, but he's good at what he does. He was up here to do some Nat bashing, but *Seven Days* got a last-minute chance to speak to him and asked me to interview him specifically on poverty and social exclusion.

TONY BLAIR, Prime Minister: The real purpose of the new social exclusion unit is to bring together the various bits of government so that money for the New Deal and for young people to get jobs, the extra money on housing and their education and health all comes together, so that we're trying to revitalise a whole area. But, of course, it takes a lot of time because we're dealing with some very deep-seated, deep-rooted problems.

JM: The Scottish National Party is making much of social exclusion. You're talking about time. There are 90 days until the elections to the Scottish Parliament. Are you concerned this is an area where the SNP can make inroads?

TB: The only party that has a policy for youth unemployment is us. The New Deal is the biggest youth unemployment scheme there's ever been. And the costs of independence in terms of taxes and jobs and industry will far outweigh anything they can put into issues like social exclusion, so people have got a choice about this. If you're going to put that extra money into schools and hospitals then that's one thing, but if Scotland really did decide that it wanted to go independent the costs of independence would far outweigh any of these investments.

Thursday 11 February 1999

DIARY: Doing some promos for the programme next week with a view to our moving time to 6.00pm in March. The theme is 'First in Scotland' because we'll now be on ahead of *Rep Scot*.

Monday 1 March 1999

DIARY: 1999 is the year everyone is ignoring and it's rattling by quickly.

Monday 8 March 1999

DIARY: So, we went on at the earlier time tonight – 6.00pm, with a little tinkering to the format of the show. It was a good programme – very pacy and completely clean. We were helped by having a good lead – the sacking of SFA Chief Executive Jim Farry. The half hour less didn't make much difference with people making their hit-times *(deadline)*.

Thursday 19 March 1999
STV News

The two men charged with the Lockerbie Bombing will be handed over for trial within three weeks. The Libyan leader Colonel Gaddafi agreed to the surrender of the two after talks with the South African President Nelson Mandela. He gave the Libyans guarantees about the men's future and they'll now be handed over to the United Nations.

Thursday 22 April 1999

DIARY: Polls showing the SNP vote in free fall. Much is being made of this election failing to come to life and I think that is true.

Friday 23 April 1999

DIARY: There was a fiasco over the appearance of SNP Leader Alex Salmond on our phone-in. Main problem was his shirt which was blue and keying against our blue background. I had to make the dash to the changing room to grab a selection of shirts. I then had to stand in a small room with an understandably irate Salmond trying to calm him down as he stripped off his shirt and tried on other ones. He was fuming.

SCOTTISH ELECTION 1999
Wednesday 5 May 1999

DIARY: A final frantic day of campaigning. Asked to go out to do what was effectively a public information piece on the ballot papers and what to do with them. Tomorrow is an historic day for Scotland and yet there is no sense of that.

Thursday 6 May 1999

DIARY: The historic day dawns. Scots vote for their own Parliament for the first time in nearly 300 years; ordinary Scots for the first time ever. Yet there has been no sense of history either in the build-up or today. I was at the Glasgow SECC. The big question was Glasgow Govan – could the SNP take it from Labour (they couldn't). Also, could Tommy Sheridan (Scottish Socialist) get in under the list system? Yes, he did. Frustrating night for me because of comms problems they couldn't pick us up at Glasgow for the first hour and a half, so all my preparation work was a waste of time. Got Gordon Jackson, Govan winner, first and Tommy Sheridan.

Friday 7 May 1999
STV News – live from Edinburgh with Shereen Nanjiani

The first Scottish Government for 300 years will be a Labour/Liberal Democrat coalition after the Scottish people refused to give any party enough seats to run the country on their own. Labour will be the single largest party in the new Parliament by some distance. With the final results now in, Labour have won 56 seats, their likely coalition partners, the Lib Dems, have won 17. The Conservatives won no first-past-the-post seats, but picked up 18 top-up seats. And the SNP become the official opposition with 35 seats. Independent Denis Canavan, Socialist leader Tommy Sheridan and Britain's first Green Party parliamentarian, Robin Harper, make up the 129-member parliament.

JM: We're joined now by the Leader of the SNP and now the leader of the official opposition in the new Parliament, Alex Salmond. Congratulations on becoming a member of the new Parliament.

ALEX SALMOND, SNP leader: Thank you very much.

JM: Are you disappointed you didn't make the 40 threshold?

AS: Well, that's your threshold. I mean this is the biggest parliamentary group in the SNP's history and the largest number of parliamentarians we've ever had before is 11. Now we're going to have 35 in this new Parliament, that's tremendously exciting. We're going to be a real opposition for Scotland's Parliament and that role as a vibrant, innovative opposition is in many ways just as important as the administration.

JM: You didn't make the breakthrough in the Central Belt that perhaps you would have hoped for, particularly in places like Glasgow Govan. That must surely be a disappointment?

AS: We had huge swings. I mean we had a 16 per cent swing in Glasgow Baillieston for example and right across Central Scotland, in areas where we used to be a mile behind Labour, we're breathing down their necks.

DIARY: A new day dawns on a new Scotland. So those of us involved would like to portray it. The truth is that there seems to be a remarkable indifference. The turnout was about 58 per cent – so not far off half the population didn't bother. By the end of the programme Edinburgh Castle was shrouded in mist. Alex Salmond seemed relatively okay and was certainly not bowing to suggestions that by failing to get what some regarded as a 40-seat threshold he would quit. Labour will be the dominant party, but they don't have an overall majority, so a Lib–Lab pact is likely. There has been much talk of a new style of politics. My suspicion is that it'll mirror Westminster. Give it time.

Wednesday 12 May 1999
STV News – live from the Assembly Hall on The Mound with Bernard Ponsonby

Today the Scottish Parliament met for the first time just through these doors. It's not been a day of high drama, rather one of procedure and getting down to business. Coalition talks between Labour and the Liberal Democrats to take the oath and elect a Presiding Officer, the equivalent of The Speaker in the House of Commons… At 9.31am this morning history was made.

PAUL GRICE, Parliament Chief Executive: Welcome to this, the first meeting of the Scottish Parliament established under the Scotland Act 1998.

WINNIE EWING, SNP MSP: The Scottish Parliament, adjourned on the 25th day of March in the year 1707, is hereby reconvened.

DIARY: I have to say that for the first time during the whole process since the referendum, I felt that I was witnessing history being made. There was a definite sense of occasion. The whole tone coming through was of a different, more relaxed Parliament, less constrained by tradition.

DONALD DEWAR BECOMES SCOTLAND'S FIRST FIRST MINISTER

Thursday 13 May 1999

STV News

Donald Dewar is Scotland's First Minister. He was finally voted into the post at a special session of the Edinburgh Parliament this afternoon. Within the last few minutes the Labour group in the Parliament has ratified a coalition deal with the Liberal Democrats.

DONALD DEWAR, FIRST MINISTER: Scotland's Parliament is no longer a political pamphlet, a campaign trail, a waving flag. It is here. It is real.

Donald Dewar's first TV interview as First Minister.

JM: We're joined live from Edinburgh by Scotland's First Minister Donald Dewar. First of all, congratulations on your appointment.

DONALD DEWAR, First Minister: Thank you very much indeed. I'm obviously very thrilled and very conscious of the responsibilities.

JM: You have come from a meeting where the Labour group has ratified the coalition deal. Can you tell us what the details are?

DD: No. I'm waiting, of course, for the outcome of the other meeting, which is with the Liberal Democrats. What I can say is that the essence of any good agreement is that both sides are satisfied with it and both sides see advantages, not just for themselves, but for good government in Scotland. It gives stability, it means we'll have an administration that can deliver priorities that Scotland voted for.

JM: Can you understand why people might see it as a stitch-up? They may see that this is something agreed in a back room and this is not the spirit of the new politics.

DD: All I can say to you is that there were long and detailed negotiations in which a large number of Liberal Democrats took part and we reached an agreement which both of us felt we could recommend to our parliamentary groups. And if you're talking about a willingness to look beyond narrow party bands in order to reach agreements that are in the interests of the people of Scotland, I would have thought there would be a widespread welcome for this flexibility and for the ability to put together two programmes to get the best possible deal for Scotland.

DIARY: The main issue was the coalition deal agreed between Labour and the Lib Dems. He was standing outside the Parliament hearing me on an earpiece, so it would have been unfair to keep interrupting him meaning that maybe it wasn't as hard an interview as I'd have liked.

Friday 14 May 1999

DONALD DEWAR, Scottish Labour Leader: We believe the decision is right for our respective parties. Much more importantly, it is right for the Parliament and for the wider community of Scotland. It will give government that can deliver on a programme that reflects Scotland's priorities and takes account of the way Scotland voted last week. Politicians should be capable of moving beyond party boundaries and acting for the common good. This agreement is such a move.

JIM WALLACE, Scottish Lib Dem leader: The spirit of the referendum places a significant obligation on the politicians of Scotland to make this Parliament work for Scotland. Through this partnership we will deliver better education, better health, in short, better government for Scotland…This historic agreement will ensure that Scotland's first Parliament for 300 years will make a difference for all of the people of Scotland.

DIARY: A deal between Labour and the Lib Dems to form a coalition government. The Lib Dems will be undermined by negotiating on their insistence on the abolition of tuition fees. 'Not negotiable,' they said. They'll be slaughtered for this and rightly so.

Friday 28 May 1999

DIARY: The programme went fine, although we had a light-hearted report on men crying, showing their true emotion. I, obviously jokingly, said 'bunch of sissies'. The phones were ringing by the time I got down to the newsroom. I think some people just sit waiting to be offended.

This has become even more apparent since the rise of social media. There are people who wait trembling in anticipation of being offended. This goes hand in hand with demands for apologies. That said, the line I used was of its time. I wouldn't even think of it now.

Monday 31 May 1999

DIARY: Very, very sad news this morning of the death of my former BBC colleague Kenny Macintyre. He died yesterday evening having suffered a heart attack while out running. His tie was still on his desk. Kenny was something of a professional father figure. He was also, unquestionably, the best reporter I've ever worked with. There were tributes from the Prime Minister, the First Minister etc which said something about the standing of the man. It is remarkable how many people regarded him as a confidant – me included. I'll miss him.

Kenny Macintyre was a phenomenon. He was Radio Scotland's political correspondent and his contacts were extraordinary. It seemed that absolutely anyone would take his calls. He worked all the hours of the week and would go home to Mull at the weekend. His drive to and from the ferry in Oban defied the basic laws of distance and time, but he always made it. There are more anecdotes about Kenny Macintyre than anyone else I've ever known and all of us who knew him will have one of our own. His death at 54 was a shock.

OPENING OF THE SCOTTISH PARLIAMENT

Thursday 1 July 1999

HM THE QUEEN, address to the Scottish Parliament: It is our solemn duty in this chamber with the eyes of the country upon us to mark the point when this new Parliament assumes its full powers in the service of the Scottish people. It is a moment, rare in the life of any nation, when we step across the threshold of a new constitutional age.

STV News – live from Edinburgh Castle with Shereen Nanjiani

1 July 1999. The day Edinburgh was able to call itself a capital again. A Scottish Parliament is opened after 300 years.

Good evening and welcome to Edinburgh. You join us from the castle, high above the city which today has truly witnessed history in the making.

We were told: There shall be a Scottish Parliament. Now there IS a Scottish Parliament. Opened by the Queen in a ceremony that mixed all the grandeur of a state occasion.

An emotional day too. The expectations are high. More than anyone else, the man charged with making a success of this Parliament is the First Minister Donald Dewar. I spoke to him and asked him for reflections on the day...

DONALD DEWAR, First Minister: I thought it was just a happy day. Everyone was enjoying themselves. There was a tremendous buzz, a real atmosphere. And the most outstanding heroes of the day was the crowd. They were there in enormous numbers, people from all over Scotland. It wasn't just Edinburgh, I met people from all different parts of Scotland and there was a genuine warmth and enthusiasm which I just found enormously encouraging.

JM: There has been criticism of the early days of the Parliament, MSPs working out salaries, working out hours. You've said the reason for that was the Parliament didn't have the powers to do anything more. It now does have, so what can we expect to see?

DD: Well, obviously there is a legislative programme we've got to get underway. We've got to start the hearings and the pre-legislative scrutiny, but, you know, the whole point of the six-week period was to get all these housekeeping matters behind us. But we also looked at, for example, freedom of information, very important, we also looked at tuition fees and higher education. We had an important statement about the way we're going to handle the Education Bill. Macintosh, which is going to affect really radically our whole local government system, was previewed and we're going to have some announcements tomorrow. There's a lot been happening. I mean, at the end of the day, the power of the press is to set the agenda. Now that has got to be a selective process, but the fact that they highlight certain things doesn't mean that there is not a lot of other things going on.

JM: The Queen said in her speech that it was your obligation to set lasting standards. Is this Parliament capable of that?

DD: Well, they are fallible human beings like everyone else and they're open to the pressures of public opinion. What we are doing is that we are setting high standards and we're setting out to try and hold to them.

JM: Finally, Mr Dewar, is this it, or do you think there is maybe a sense that what we've seen today might push the Scottish people to take that extra step towards independence?

DD: There is, I think, always an attraction about simple solutions, but the trouble about simple solutions is they usually leave the problems behind them and I think that what we've got to do is make sure that government serves Scotland, listens to Scotland and deals with the real priorities of Scotland. And if we do that, I think we can work effectively and happily and democratically within the partnership which is our United Kingdom. But that's a continuing argument. Let's get on in the meantime with actually dealing with the issues that are central to the everyday lives of the people in Scotland.

DIARY: Another of this year's historical days – the official opening of the Scottish Parliament by the Queen and the formal handover of powers from Westminster. Watched the ceremony on TV, but what really made it special for me was when Concorde and nine Red Arrows staged a fly past over Edinburgh Castle. *(Less than ten minutes later in the west I was in the car with my young son)* Concorde and the Red Arrows flew low directly over us. It was a wonderful moment. I must have been quite excited because after they passed he asked, 'Why were you shouting, Daddy?'

We did the programme from the western defences of the Castle and a wonderful location it was too, if a bit breezy. Interviewed Donald Dewar and told him, for what it was worth, that his speech hit the mark.

Friday 30 July 1999
STV News – live from Greenock

Good evening from Greenock where 200,000 visitors have already arrived to see the start of the Tall Ship extravaganza. Over the next four days half a million more will witness one of the great spectacles of the year. The atmosphere has been building all day with these magnificent vessels from 16 different countries arriving at the Tail o' the Bank.

DIARY: The weather was good, probably too good because there wasn't enough wind for the ships to use their sails which would have been very impressive. Still, it was impressive enough.

Friday 3 September 1999
STV News – live from Glasgow Airport

Eight people are dead and three are seriously injured in a plane crash near Glasgow Airport. The Cessna light aircraft was on an internal flight to Aberdeen when it appears to have lost power and come down in farmland. The plane, operated by Edinburgh Air Charter, had taken off from Glasgow Airport at 12.25pm. It made a normal ascent, but crashed in flames less than 12 minutes later at 12.37pm. The plane was carrying air crew from the Airtours company and full investigation into the tragedy is due to begin later this evening.

A Fatal Accident Inquiry concluded that an engine had malfunctioned and the pilot had

closed the wrong engine, his judgement possibly hampered by the fact that a bang had been heard from the good engine soon after take-off.

SCOTLAND v ENGLAND EUROPEAN CHAMPIONSHIP QUALIFIERS

Friday 12 November 1999

STV News – live from Hampden with Jane Lewis

Good evening from Hampden. In just under 20 hours the game we've all been waiting for will be under way. The atmosphere is already building here as the Scots get set to face the Auld Enemy for the first time in three years.

DIARY: I've been watching how people have been getting wound up for the match and I can't. I've been cutting packages of nostalgia all week, including the memorable '77 win at Wembley, when I remember being so excited and the '74 win at Hampden, which I attended. Great wallowing in it, but no expectation of achieving anything like it tomorrow. If we get a draw to make a game of it at Wembley that's all we can ask.

Scotland lost 2–0.

Wednesday 17 November 1999

STV News – live from Wembley with Kirstin Gove

Good evening. In two hours time Scotland will take to this field of dreams in the hope of overcoming the 2–0 deficit from Saturday's first match.

Here at Wembley the waiting is almost over. In the words of our national side's captain and talisman, Colin Hendry, Scotland need a ridiculously impressive performance to beat the English. If they're looking for inspiration for their mission impossible, we'll leave you tonight with some of the images from past glories and of the Tartan Army gathering in hope of a win against all the odds. From all of us here, good night and good luck Scotland.

DIARY: Scotland beat England 1–0 at Wembley. We still go out over two legs, but it was a close thing. Wembley was odd in that, trackside, the legendary large pitch wasn't so big, the tunnel wasn't so long and the terraces not so impressive, but later looking down from high up in the Olympic Gallery there was a sense of grandeur – it was greater than the sum of its parts. Scotland thoroughly deserved their win through a Don Hutchinson goal and almost got the vital second minutes from the end. Another heroic failure.

We were live behind the goal immediately in front of the tunnel and it all went to plan. We hung around after that, but it became quickly clear that we were going to get moved and any hope of hanging around trackside was not on *(there had been an oversight in getting us tickets to see the actual game)*. Ended up spending an hour going from pillar to post, finally blagging our way into the ITV area. Jane, Kirstin and I sitting among English fans and barely able to contain ourselves.

Scotland came so close to getting the second goal that would have extended the tie when a Christian Dailly header was wonderfully saved by David Seaman in the last ten minutes.

Monday 22 November 1999

DIARY: Annoyed with myself when I neglected to move a script that had been read and also drifted away. Next thing I found myself on camera, ignoring the autocue and reading from script, exactly what had been read before. I apologised and moved on, but it was sloppy.

Wednesday 22 December 1999

DIARY: Straight out to Lanarkshire on a tragic story. A family of four killed when their home was ripped apart by a gas explosion in the middle of the night. They had no chance. These tragic stories always seem to happen at this time of year. When I got there it was a shock to see how the house was literally flattened to rubble. A terrible tragedy.

2000

Monday 17 January 2000
STV News

The leader of Scotland's Roman Catholics is tonight under fire for speaking out against what he called 'the perversion of homosexuality'. Cardinal Winning made his controversial comments as he weighed into the debate over the proposed scrapping of Section 28. That's the legislation which prohibits local authorities from promoting the acceptability of homosexuality. The Cardinal told *Scotland Today* that the Scottish Executive should concentrate its efforts on issues of greater importance.

CARDINAL THOMAS WINNING: The Catholic Church doesn't have any concern about people who are homosexual. It's the homosexual acts that we object to very much. I hesitate to use the word perversion, but let's face up to the truth of this situation, that's what it is. Are we now being asked to say what was wrong before is now right and they can go ahead and do it?

TIM HOPKINS, Equality Network: I'm appalled by it. Cardinal Winning seems to be calling for a return to the old days when gay people were treated like burglars and locked up. It's appalling prejudice and I think that most people in Scotland will feel the same way.

WENDY ALEXANDER, Communities Minister: I think we're hoping that in the new Scotland we'll perhaps understand a little more and condemn a little less. The First Minister earlier today talked about a tolerance for a new century and for a new Scotland. I think that's the spirit of the Executive's proposals.

FIONA ROSS, Political Correspondent: Public opinion is difficult to judge. A survey of Scottish Television viewers last week showed that 82 per cent want Section 28 to stay. Brian Souter (the businessman who funded a private referendum on the issue and characterised his campaign with the quote, 'We didnae vote for it and we're no' havin' it.') may have touched a nerve. This was hailed as a great reforming, liberal measure heralding the dawn of a new Scotland. But it may just be that Scotland isn't quite as tolerant as some people would like to think.

I didn't flag this story up to the newsdesk as anything significant when I returned with the interview because, although it was hard hitting, I thought Cardinal Winning had said the same thing before. Apparently not in these words.

Tuesday 18 January 2000
STV News

Seven days after the sinking of the *Solway Harvester*, marine accident investigators are beginning an underwater examination of the wreckage to find out why the tragedy happened. All seven members of the Kirkcudbright-based ship were lost when it sank suddenly in bad weather off the Isle of Man. Investigators hope evidence from video cameras on a mini-submarine will show that the bodies are still on board and can be recovered.

Friday 25 February 2000

DIARY: Last programme under the old, blue 'chromakey' system. It will be no loss to see it go. It was a cold, dated set. The new set looks to be a significant improvement.

Monday 6 March 2000
STV News

Church leaders have been explaining why they're against the repeal of Section 28 – the controversial legislation that bans the promotion of homosexuality. Giving evidence to MSPS, representatives of several faiths claimed the Government's compromise proposals were unacceptable, arguing heterosexual family relationships must be upheld as the ideal.

Wednesday 8 March 2000
STV News

A new campaign has been launched calling for the repeal of the controversial Section 28.

MSPs and supporters of gay rights gathered in the shadow of the Scottish Parliament calling for the legislation to be scrapped. They say they want an end to a law which discriminates against gay people.

Thursday 16 March 2000

DIARY: Volunteered to go with a camera to film the departure of Romanian 'economic' refugees from houses in Sighthill. They've been begging and apparently shouldn't have been sent here in the first place. Got some good footage out of it and ended up with the lead piece. The women especially dressed so differently and gold teeth are prominent. I was struck, though, by the smell from them and their belongings – it's the smell of poverty, musty and stale.

Monday 8 May 2000
STV News

The First Minister Donald Dewar is said to be 'stable' in intensive care following a four-hour heart operation. Surgeons replaced a leaking heart valve in a major, but routine procedure in Glasgow Royal Infirmary. Mr Dewar was admitted to hospital yesterday and is expected to stay there for about ten days.

Thursday 11 May 2000

DIARY: All became hectic just before we went on air after a fairly routine day. The Government announced what is effectively a climb down on their plans to repeal the anti-homosexual Clause 28. I had a good interview with Education Minister Sam Galbraith, a wily politician, in which it was apparent that he couldn't admit the obvious.

STV News

A dramatic turn of events after months of campaigning between pro and anti-clause campaigners. The Government saying that they won't move on the issue. Well, to explain now why they have we're joined by the Education Minister Sam Galbraith. Mr Galbraith, nothing but a climbdown surely?

SAM GALBRAITH, Education Minister: Och now now, you shouldn't use that language. What we've done is, my Education Committee asked me to consider this question of some underpinning statutory guidance. We've been listening to the mums and dads and we've responded to that and that's what we've done today.

JM: Why didn't you listen to them months ago when they were all saying this?

SG: We've been listening to them for some time, so we have.

JM: So why did it take you so long to react?

SG: These are matters that need careful consideration. I think we've done the right thing, we have been listening to the mums and dads and we've responded to them. This is a listening Government and we've done the right thing by them.

Wednesday 21 June 2000
STV News

The law which bans the promotion of homosexuality in schools will be repealed within the next hour. Gay rights campaigners are hailing the Parliament's decision to scrap Section 28 *(also sometimes referred to as Clause 28)* as a victory, but Conservative MSPs have vowed to continue to fight to keep the clause.

MICHAEL CROW, Scottish Parliamentary Correspondent: The issue has rumbled on for the past nine months, dominating the new Parliament's agenda. But for some gay rights campaigners the fight to repeal Section 28 has lasted years, not months. The issue has caused the Executive no end of problems. Right up to the wire the politicians were still arguing.

Wednesday 28 June 2000

DIARY: Through to Edinburgh for the first anniversary of the Parliament (general opinion is that it could do more and has squandered time on issues like Clause 28).

The Scottish Parliament was based in the Church of Scotland's General Assembly Hall

on The Mound in Edinburgh for the first four years of its existence. Interviews with politicians and political reporters were conducted in a corridor in the main entrance floored with black and white tiles – the black and white corridor.

Monday 17 July 2000
STV News

The SNP leader, Alex Salmond, has resigned. After ten years in the job, he's decided to stand down, although he intends staying on as an MSP. Mr Salmond's announcement stunned colleagues and opponents alike. He said, 'after ten years it's time to hand on the torch.'

ALEX SALMOND, SNP Leader: I always said that ten years was the allotted span of an SNP leader. I'd always promised myself I'd take a serious look at this when the ten years was up.

BRIAN WILSON, Labour: I think Alex Salmond woke up after the Scottish elections and realised they hadn't won. Now he's facing another x years in opposition. In a way, it doesn't surprise me he's walked away from that.

FIONA ROSS, Political Correspondent: Ultimately, his hopes have been dashed. He leaves a party deeply split between those who want independence tomorrow and those who want to move gradually. A difficult job for anyone to take over.

Wednesday 2 August 2000

DIARY: A surprise announcement that the Chancellor Gordon Brown is marrying in Fife tomorrow. I pulled together a 50-second piece, but five minutes before going on air the studio reported that there was a serious sound problem. It was perfectly good on the computer, but there was a technical fault between there and the server. Anyway, I got them to play it mute while I read my script live. Pleased to pull it off – professional satisfaction.

In the earlier days of TV news this was standard practice for reporters.

Wednesday 6 September 2000

DIARY: Sitting in the Scottish Parliament chamber to watch the beginning of a debate on education – the political subject of the moment because of the exams fiasco. No consensus politics here – very much in the Westminster yah-boo style. Also, like Westminster, the chamber is much smaller than you'd expect.

FUEL STRIKE
Tuesday 12 September 2000
STV News

Scotland is facing the prospect of paralysis tonight as the fuel crisis hits home. More than half of the country's petrol stations closed today leaving many areas without supply. But significantly, public support still seems to be with the protesters, who have again brought chaos to the streets.

Hauliers and farmers were campaigning about the high taxation of fuel. The hauliers took convoys of hundreds into Edinburgh and Aberdeen, and crawled slowly through the streets to bring them to a halt. An STV phone poll showed 96 per cent backing for the truckers. At the time unleaded petrol was typically around 79p per litre and diesel was 81p per litre.

Vox Pops

I support the guys who are blockading. The price of petrol is outrageous.

The French have got it right, haven't they? *(French truckers had been successful in a similar campaign)* That's what's wrong here, we all give in too easily.

TONY BLAIR, Prime Minister: I do not in any way minimise the plight of some of the hauliers and farmers who are genuinely suffering, but the way to help them is not to harm the rest of the country. I regret deeply the inconvenience and difficulty caused to the public, but the consequences of giving in to this type of blockade would be infinitely worse. For that reason, let me assure the public that the action required to get the situation back to normal will be taken. It will take some time to get everything back working as it should be, but it will be done.'

TRUCKERS:

It cripples us standing at the side of the road, but it's at the stage that we've got to stand up and say, right we've got to do something. Everybody has to stand up and do something.

This Government will have to listen. That's all we're asking for – a reduction in the fuel cost.

DIARY: Fuel crisis is overwhelming everything. Some people are struggling with most petrol stations closed. Everyone is talking about it. Our programme tonight was almost entirely given over to it. It's been the first real test of Tony Blair's Government.

Wednesday 13 September 2000

DIARY: More fuel crisis – tankers not leaving refineries and now real fears of food shortages. What is so interesting is that people still widely support the protesters and that must be worrying for the Government. Tony Blair is coming out of it all very badly – the first time he's really been getting an all-round kicking. It seems that the Government is too arrogant. We've been performing well and the audience have been turning to us in huge numbers.

The blockades ended because the protesters did not want to lose public support, which might have happened if warnings about threats to essential services became a reality. They gave the Government a 60-day deadline to reduce fuel duty. The Chancellor Gordon Brown made some concessions in his pre-budget report in November.

Thursday 28 September 2000
STV News

The SNP's leader, John Swinney, made his debut in the Scottish Parliament this afternoon at First Minister Questions. He immediately launched into an attack on Labour's treatment of pensioners, claiming the party isn't listening to the people of Scotland.

John Swinney had been elected SNP leader five days before.

DEATH OF FIRST MINISTER DONALD DEWAR

Tuesday 10 October 2000
First news approx 5.45pm

PA SNAP: Scottish First Minister Donald Dewar has been taken to Edinburgh Royal Infirmary after a fall, a spokesman said tonight.

PA SNAP: Scottish First Minister Donald Dewar is 'seriously ill', a spokesman said tonight.

Wednesday 11 October 2000

DAVID WHITTON, First Minister's Spokesman: It's with deep sadness I have to report that Scotland's First Minister, Donald Dewar, has died... After discussion with his consultants, those treating him, the decision was taken to turn off his life-support system. The cause of the First Minister's death was a brain haemorrhage.

STV News

The First Minister is dead. Tonight, Scotland is a nation in mourning.

The man regarded as the 'Father of the Nation' passed away shortly after midday at Edinburgh's Western General Hospital, where he was being treated after suffering a brain haemorrhage.

MARTIN GEISSLER, Reporter: This afternoon at Edinburgh's Western General Hospital we learned what was, by then, the inevitable. Scotland's First Minister had lost his fight for life. Over the course of yesterday evening it became clear that Donald Dewar was very seriously ill. Today, Scotland lost a remarkable politician and an honest and decent man.

DAVID WHITTON, First Minister's Spokesman: Donald Dewar was a man of many parts. I would sum it up by saying he's the best First Minister Scotland could have had.

DIARY: We carried a report in last night's programme saying he had been taken to hospital as a precaution following a fall. That developed with a brain haemorrhage and although not officially declared dead until 12.18pm today, they knew last night there was no hope. It dominated today, of course, and we put out a good programme tonight, including tributes. It wasn't a frantic day because it was well planned and everything came together well. What was cause for more thought was getting the tone right. His death was sudden and unexpected (despite open heart surgery earlier this year) and it leaves a gaping hole in Scottish politics with no one capable of filling his shoes. He had always pursued a Scottish Parliament and it is fitting that he saw it happen. One can get carried away on sentiment – he was a ditherer – but his public persona was of a decent man who could not fully come to terms with the gloss of modern politics. For the little I know of him, I liked him. He had a sense of humour and that distinctive 'umm aah' delivery. Bernard Ponsonby, our reporter, said that in a hundred years when the history of this time in Scotland is written, Donald Dewar's name will stand out. I think that is true.

Thursday 12 October 2000
STV News

MSPs are returning to the Parliament this afternoon to pay their respects to the late First Minister. In a unique event, the leaders of the four main parties will each express the deep sense of loss and sadness felt at the death of Donald Dewar.

MICHAEL CROW, Scottish Parliamentary Correspondent: His seat in the centre of the chamber will be left empty as a mark of respect. Acting First Minister Jim Wallace and Labour's senior spokesman Henry McLeish will be on either side of the empty chair and they'll be opening and closing tributes. The SNP leader John Swinney will talk of how Donald Dewar put the good of Scotland before politics during 1997 referendum campaign and the Conservative leader David McLetchie will say how he set standards in the Scottish Parliament that few will be able to equal.

Wednesday 18 October 2000
STV News

A man you could trust. A man of vision and integrity. Gordon Brown summed up the feelings of the country this afternoon as Scotland said farewell to its First Minister. The funeral service was a fitting tribute to the man who devoted his life to the ideals of equality and social justice. The most powerful in the land were there, including most of the Cabinet and the Prince of Wales. But there were no divisions inside Glasgow's great Cathedral. Civic leaders sat beside shop workers and pensioners – all united in grief for the nation's lost leader.

GORDON BROWN, Chancellor: Donald Dewar would have been the last to acknowledge the true scale of his achievement. But the friend we lost only seven days ago was one of only a handful of people across the centuries of whom it could be said, he founded a new Parliament. What was special about Donald as a politician was that he consistently and tirelessly pushed the logic of his decency and worked for a more just and equal society.

Vox Pops

I just came because I just felt... I felt it was appropriate to come.

I respected the man. He was all for Scotland and so am I.

He was a great leader of the Scots. One of the true political heroes of the time. He's going to be missed a lot.

FIONA ROSS, political correspondent and close friend of Donald Dewar: Donald wasn't interested in clothes, he wasn't interested in how he looked, he walked about looking like a complete tip. It doesn't matter what you tried to do about it. I tried bullying, I tried threats, intimidation. None of it worked. D'you know, I bought him a tie once? He used it to wipe the windscreen of his car... Donald Dewar was many things to many people. He was a proud father, he was loyal to his party, he was loyal to his country. He was a true Scot. He loved the culture, the people, the history. Sadly, he's now part of Scotland's history.

DIARY: The funeral of First Minister Donald Dewar, the closest Scotland has had, or will have, to a 'State' funeral for many a year. We had built a proper studio in Cathedral Square looking onto the Cathedral doors. Our special programme began at 2.00pm and almost immediately I had to talk over the arrival of the Prime Minister. The great and the good were all there and perhaps the best part of it all was the applause from the watching crowd as Donald Dewar's cortege drove through the city. The playing of 'A Man's a Man' on the fiddle at the end was very moving.

HENRY McLEISH BECOMES FIRST MINISTER

Henry McLeish was elected by an internal vote of the Scottish Labour Party to become the second First Minister.

Friday 20 October 2000
STV News

HENRY MCLEISH, speech to Labour Party: Colleagues it's a very, very, very great privilege. Thanks for the honour. Let me say, I won't let you down.

He was formally appointed by the Scottish Parliament on Thursday 26 October.

Thursday 26 October 2000
STV News

HENRY MCLEISH, First Minister: I will speak up for Scotland on every occasion, for every part of Scotland and for everyone in this country.

Interview with Shereen Nanjiani:

It was a historic moment, it was a moment of high emotion for me. A great honour. Obviously great challenges and opportunities ahead and I very much welcome that. Nevertheless, today has been a consuming day and I was very, very proud indeed.

Friday 27 October 2000
STV News

Henry McLeish was officially installed as Scotland's new First Minister this afternoon. The Queen handed Mr McLeish a Royal Warrant of Appointment at Holyrood Palace in Edinburgh. He then took a series of oaths confirming his appointment at the Court of Session.

Tuesday 31 October 2000
STV News

The cost of building the new Scottish Parliament could be much more than the £195 million limit set by MSPs. According to the man responsible for the cost of the project, the budget set earlier this year is only a target and not set in stone. The admission is being described as astonishing by MSPs. Meanwhile, a report out today raises further doubts over whether Holyrood will be built to budget and on time.

The final cost of the Parliament was £414 million.

FIRST MINISTER IN ROME TO MEET THE POPE

Sunday 3 December 2000

DIARY: Tonight, I'm in Rome which was dark by the time we got there. A hire car had been arranged for us, which we'd both been dubious about – justifiably as it turned out. It took us three hours until we finally chanced upon the street we were looking for having previously driven so far north we were into the red light district and then suburbs. A most frustrating evening. Even asked for directions in 'MacKay's' Scottish theme pub, but they couldn't help.

We could not for the life of us find our hotel. When I saw 'MacKay's Pub' my spirits soared, but quickly sagged. When I shared my enthusiasm about having the same name as the bar, they could not have cared less. Later as our spirits flagged further, I told Fraser Cleland, the cameraman with me,

that we would stop at the very next person we saw. Sure enough, we saw a figure under a street light. As we coasted towards her, I was struck by her pose and the shortness of her skirt. It took a moment for my sluggish brain to interpret these signals. There followed frantic exhortations to Fraser to go on, go on! I don't think the '...asking for directions' defence would have worked.

Monday 4 December 2000
STV News

A chorus of 'Flower of Scotland' rang round the unlikely setting of the Vatican today after the First Minister had an historic meeting with the Pope. Henry McLeish is there along with other prominent Scots to celebrate the 400th anniversary of the founding of the college which trains Scottish priests.

JM: Here in Rome, the Eternal City, the leader of the historic Catholic Church meets the leader of the fledgling Scottish Parliament.

POPE JOHN PAUL II: A warm greeting to the Secretary of State for Scotland and the First Minister, as well as distinguished visitors and benefactors who are honouring this occasion with their presence.

HENRY MCLEISH, First Minister: It was wonderful to represent Scotland on your first trip abroad with a visit to the Vatican and an audience with His Holiness the Pope. But I think it is also significant for Scotland because I think it is absolutely vital that we have a very inclusive society, we have a very tolerant society and also a society that speaks to each other and listens to each other. So, all in all it's been a wonderful day.

CARDINAL THOMAS WINNING: The contrast between the Scotland of the 17th century and Scotland of the Year 2000 is quite extraordinary. The Scottish Parliament outlawed the Catholic Church in 1560. And today we have the First Minister of a new Parliament in Scotland *(in Rome)*, which for me and for the Catholic community is a very important presence.

DIARY: Today could not have gone any better, especially given our total lack of planning. The Vatican is beautiful. Apparently, Rome has been cleaned up significantly for this Millennium year. My worry was getting in to get shots of the First Minister actually meeting the Pope. We had two breaks – first a Scottish Television religious programme, *Eikon*, was being filmed by an independent production company who'd arranged passes some time ago. I knew some of them and had a promise that I could get whatever they shot. However, my former colleague Ronnie Convery was there with Cardinal Winning (he's his PR man) and his ability to speak Italian smoothed some corners. We chanced our arm and managed to blag our way right into the Vatican. We were in a gallery in the hall where the audience was taking place and I suspect that if Fraser had worn a tie we'd have got onto the dais itself. Anyway, with our own camera and *Eikon*'s close-ups I had every shot I needed. At the end the Scottish contingent sang 'Flower of Scotland' which gave me my closing line for my piece to camera. I'd already arranged to meet Henry McLeish outside and Cardinal Winning. It was fascinating being so close to the Pope. He's old – 80 now and clearly failing – but there is an aura. I sat yards from him and was struck by how weary he seemed to be.

It might have been a December, but Rome was still glorious. We wandered through the piazzas and Christmas markets and dined and drank wine under the stars at the Pantheon. It was seductively romantic, but for the fact I was looking at a hairy faced cameraman.

Friday 8 December 2000
STV News

Chaos. Shambles. Fiasco. Just some of the words used by MSPs to describe the summer's exams crisis as they revealed today there were very nearly no results at all this year. The Scottish Parliament's Education Committee made 56 recommendations in a damning report and warned there were no guarantees for next year's exams

A new exam system had been introduced in 2000. It was plagued with problems and the SQA (Scottish Qualifications Authority) had to admit that some students received incorrect exam results. Some didn't receive any.

MADONNA'S WEDDING
Thursday 21 December 2000

DIARY: Dornoch is a media village now. The area outside the cathedral was a forest of snappers' ladders. Wandered about getting a feel for things and speaking to some locals. They were all quite thrilled by it. Every other station had built platforms, but I was stuck on the ground and squashed by the crowd. It worked out rather well. We were part of the atmosphere. Tonight's event was the christening of Madonna's son Rocco – significant because it was likely to be the only photo opportunity we'd get. We were live as the cars began arriving with various celebrities and they kept throwing to me to describe what was going on. Unfortunately, Madonna didn't arrive until after we'd gone off air, but it was good stuff, nonetheless. It was a carnival atmosphere in Dornoch and enjoyable to be there.

I found myself spouting the following. It went against every professional instinct, talking with little knowledge of the subject and, worse, no confirmation. Having said that, it was great fun.

JM: We have seen Stella McCartney, the leading designer at the Chloé fashion group. She, of course was expected to design Madonna's wedding dress. Stories here that there are in fact going to be three wedding dresses. One is going to be worn at the actual ceremony, one is going to be worn at a dinner – that will be designed by Donatella Versace – and there is also going to be a gown in the evening, which is also going to be designed by Donatella Versace.

We've got a big Mercedes at the back. That may indeed be her. Yes, that's Madonna arriving. Arriving for the christening of her son Rocco. There's the car pulling up. She's sitting in the passenger seat at the back and we'll see her come out in a moment. *(Sting emerges)*. It's not, it's Trudie Tyler (actually Styler – Sting's wife). It's not Madonna. It's Sting and his wife Trudie Tyler *(still wrong)*, who, of course, brought the couple, Guy Ritchie and Madonna together *(I had to be up on my celebrity gossip for this sort of insight)*.

One photographer was arrested after hiding in the church organ in Dornoch Cathedral.

Friday 22 December 2000

DIARY: Today was a contrast to last night's fun. Scores of media crews etc standing outside the entrance to Skibo Castle waiting in vain for something to happen or to be confirmed. A couple of cars arrived later in the day and a couple of photographers were ejected. Apart from that there was nothing.

I spent my day doing two-ways into our programmes saying nothing was happening. My lunchtime stuff was very light-hearted and I had a couple of interviewees, including NBC's correspondent. In the evening I had the same light-heartedness, but made the point that it was another classic example of Madonna's manipulation of the media. I even did a two-way with *Canada AM* – Canada's national breakfast programme – and heard later that my sister-in-law and nephew had seen it.

The media lock out for the wedding was very effective. The following excerpts from some of my live reports show my failure to hide the tedium we were all feeling.

JM: Another Land Rover has just gone in, we've all got terribly excited, nobody in it. And that's been the story of the event so far. I was asked last night what Madonna was wearing and I said a yellow dress. Apparently, that doesn't suffice. So, my understanding is that it is a cream silk creation by Stella McCartney. Her £49,000 diamond bracelet has got 19 carats of diamonds and is designed to go with the Gothic dress she will be wearing. I thought I had to get that right. That's it. Now you know.

We know for sure that Gwyneth Paltrow

is here, we saw her at the christening last night. Rupert Everett is here. Sting and his wife Trudie Tyler *(still wrong)* are here, so we know these people are here for definite. Now as for the rest; Brad Pitt was apparently spotted buying a packet of fags down in Inverness and was pursued. Nobody has seen him since, so we don't know if he's going to be here either. Whether his girlfriend Jennifer Aniston is going to be with him or not, we don't know. Gwyneth Paltrow is Brad Pitt's ex and, of course, there might be a bit of tension there between her and Jennifer Aniston. The suspicion is, therefore, that Jennifer Aniston may not come. George Clooney apparently stayed very quietly in Bonar Bridge. Nobody recognised him until after he'd gone. Apparently, he was buying a packet of fags as well, so there's going to be a lot of smoking going on.

During all this, my infant son told his teacher that his daddy was at Madonna's wedding. Earlier in the month he'd told her I was away to see the Pope. The teacher, not knowing my job, remarked on the wee fellow's lively imagination. It's easy to forget what a privileged role journalists have.

2001

Wednesday 31 January 2001
STV News

A Libyan intelligence agent is tonight starting a life sentence for the Lockerbie Bombing. The decision by judges at the unique Scottish Court in the Netherlands to convict Abdelbaset Al-Megrahi and to free his co-accused is having a worldwide impact.

Martin Geissler's report said after nine years under suspicion and nine months on trial, Megrahi's conviction made him the biggest mass murderer in British criminal history.

DIARY: This morning one of the two Libyans accused of the Lockerbie Bombing – Megrahi – was found guilty. The other – Fahaima – not guilty. The verdict surprised most of us. The prosecution case was almost entirely circumstantial. It dominated all our news. Most of the work was done by David Cowan and Martin Geissler in the Netherlands.

Wednesday 28 February 2001

DIARY: *Scotland Today* is the best regional news programme in Britain – official. We won the award at tonight's Royal Television Society presentation and it is great news. Among the tributes paid to it was that it was 'well presented.' It's a real boost. We had an inkling that we might have won from the positioning of our table near the front. It was great when a shot of Sarah *(Sarah Heaney co-presenter)* and me was flashed up. When I watched later some of the war reporting and investigative reporting that were up for prizes it was a bit humbling. But this is a great achievement. The schmoozing that went on was a bit much for me, but otherwise an enjoyable night. Eventually crashed into my bed about 4.00am.

As we sat among the news media glitterati, I studied the award. When I leaned forward to put it back on the table it slipped from my hand and smashed some glasses very loudly. There was a momentary pause in the proceedings before it dawned on them that the breaking glass was just the Scots, so they carried on.

FOOT AND MOUTH OUTBREAK
Thursday 1 March 2001

DIARY: Home after only about four hours sleep. Went for a kip before returning to work. Woken by a phone call from Norman Corbett *(News Producer)* asking me to go down to Lockerbie to present the programme live from there because the foot and mouth outbreak has hit Scotland at a farm there. I thought he was taking the piss, but no.

STV News – live from Lockerbie

Good evening, live from Lockerbie where earlier today the first case of the foot and mouth outbreak in Scotland was confirmed. Tests at a farm at Canonbie, just 15 miles from here, later also proved positive. The news is devastating for Scotland's farmers and, indeed, for the industry as a whole. And tonight, with tests being carried out at a third farm, the entire country is beginning to feel the impact. Whole swathes of the countryside are being cut off from the public.

The foot and mouth outbreak resulted in the culling of millions of livestock. Many farmers left the industry. The National Audit Office estimated it cost the country £8 billion.

Tuesday 13 March 2001
STV News

Sixty years ago tonight was the first night of the Clydebank Blitz. Planes of the German Luftwaffe targeted the Clydeside town and dropped tonnes of high explosives. A thousand people died. Thousands more were injured and many more left homeless. Tonight, the town begins a series of commemorative events to remember that dreadful time.

DIARY: Some of the testimony was very moving, especially from a woman named Helen McNeil who very vividly recalled the devastation.

HELEN MCNEIL, eyewitness: They were blazing, there were stones in the road, there was fire, there was noise, everybody was screaming. (*I'd*) never seen that before as a six-year-old... There was hoses everywhere, firemen everywhere, people shouting. The smell of smoke. Big tenement buildings that had been very high up for a wee six-year-old were flat... Tramcars halved in two, buses broken down... a terrible scene... We got to Pattison Street, this was where her (*mother's*) two uncles had lived. We just turned round and the one close on that side of the road that the tenement was down was them. And my mother just ran up. It was blazing and smelly, the smoke was awful. You can still smell it. And the warden ran to my mother and I just heard the man saying to her, 'Nobody got out o' there, hen.'

The horror of the Second World War is disappearing from living memory now, but at this time there were still many who remembered its impact on the civilian population in Scotland. It's hard for us now to comprehend what that experience must have been like.

Tuesday 24 April 2001
STV News – live from Bathgate

It was the news that the workforce here had dreaded, yet expected. Motorola today confirmed the closure of this giant complex in West Lothian leaving more than 3,000 workers to face the dole. The problem is simple – not enough people want to buy the mobile phones that are made here. But the consequences for the workforce are devastating.

DIARY: The loss of 3,200 jobs at Motorola in Bathgate in West Lothian – the single biggest job announcement in at least a decade, possibly more. We did the programme live from there. I'm rather struck by the lack of as much gloom as one might expect – perhaps because there are other opportunities in the area. Still, a terrible blow.

CARDINAL THOMAS WINNING'S FUNERAL
Monday 25 June 2001
STV News

Good afternoon from St Andrew's Cathedral in the heart of Glasgow, where royalty, senior politicians, churchmen, family and ordinary folk have gathered for the funeral of Cardinal Thomas Winning.

FATHER PATRICK BURKE: I would say, although there is deep sadness, all of us who are Catholics and well beyond the Catholic Church, are deeply sad at the death of Cardinal Winning, I would say there is a spirit of joy, giving thanks to God for everything that he did, for all that he achieved and all that he did for many of us. And hope. Hope in the resurrection. We know that he's gone to meet the God he served.

Vox Pops

It was absolutely marvellous with all the community. It didn't matter what religion you were, he was very, very good.

He had a lovely twinkle in his eye, a lovely twinkle. He was always mischievous looking. He was lovely. A lot of lovely memories.

I remember him as a wonderful priest and someone it was a privilege to know, and I've known him a long time. And he'll be greatly missed and I feel he'll be irreplaceable.

DIARY: All the pomp and ceremony is impressive and although some would like to do away with it, for my part such spectacles are important and a connection with the past.

Friday 29 June 2001
STV News

Glasgow's multi-million-pound Science Centre will finally open for paying customers tomorrow, more than a week after it was embarrassingly forced to close. Last Friday it emerged the £75 million site's entertainment licence wasn't valid.

Tuesday 11 September 2001

Along with the rest of the world we watched in horror as the hijacked planes flew into the Twin Towers at the World Trade Centre in New York City.

DIARY: We were reduced to shorter bulletins and nobody had any issue with that. We focused on the Americans trapped here because of the air restrictions and Scots with family over there. It's really all we could do.

Friday 12 October 2001
STV News

A man described as 'a serial killer in the making' is tonight starting a life sentence for the murder of Kilmarnock teenager Barry Wallace. After the verdict it was revealed that William Beggs has killed before and has a history of horrifying violence against young men in England and Scotland. Barry Wallace's parents said this afternoon, 'We are glad this devil's trail of destruction has been halted.'

DIARY: It is a gruesome story involving Beggs picking up Wallace – who was trying to get home after a works night out – taking him to his flat, handcuffing him, raping him, killing him and then chopping up his body, later disposing of the pieces in Loch Lomond – the head being discovered on Troon beach. Horrifying. Much of the case was circumstantial and there was a real fear he might get off with it.

THE RESIGNATION OF HENRY McLEISH AS FIRST MINISTER
Friday 2 November 2001
STV News

Scotland's First Minister is facing the biggest crisis of his political career over the 'Officegate' affair. Henry McLeish has refused to answer questions on 11 years' worth of rent earned by sub-letting his Glenrothes constituency offices after paying back £9,000 to Westminster last week.

Henry McLeish had sublet part of his constituency office to a legal firm, which was against the rules. He had repaid the money he had received, but an admission that there had been further sublets since 1987 which he could not account for had created a political crisis.

Thursday 8 November 2001
STV News – live from The Mound in Edinburgh

Good evening from Edinburgh on a day of high drama that has sent shock waves through Scottish politics and reverberated across the nation. For the second time in little more than a year the country is looking for a new First Minister.

HENRY MCLEISH, statement to Parliament: What is important is that I take full, personal responsibility. Others who work with me and for me have been criticised, but the ultimate responsibility is mine and mine alone. I will continue with my duties as MSP for Central Fife, serving the people I know and grew up with. Sir David *(Sir David Steel, Presiding Officer)* that, in itself, is and remains an enormous privilege for me. Thank you, Sir David and colleagues for the courtesy.

JM: Bernard, it's not so much a case of what Henry McLeish did, but how he handled it.

BERNARD PONSONBY, Political Editor: It's how he handled it because there is a golden rule in politics for a major politician, if there are any questions over your probity or over your competence and managerial skills, what you have to do is that you have to get everything out in the open on day one. But he didn't do that. As a consequence he's been hounded, as a consequence information has been drip fed into the public domain and it's all created the impression that events were driving Henry McLeish rather than Henry McLeish taking control of events. And that's always suicide for a politician. And when it comes to questioning his competence, I think he realised that it had the consequences of destabilising the Executive and destabilising Labour ahead of the next elections in 2003.

JM – I'm joined here in Edinburgh by some of the main players in the events over the past few days.

DAVID MCLETCHIE, Scottish Conservative Leader: We said that Henry McLeish should resign because his conduct was unbecoming of the First Minister of Scotland. He has come to the same conclusion in tendering his resignation. He did so in a dignified manner this afternoon in the Scottish Parliament and now we have to draw a veil over that and move on.

JOHN SWINNEY, SNP Leader: It's obviously been a sad day for Henry McLeish personally and we all feel for that, but it was quite clear that this issue was not going away. The First Minister, by not coming clean about the issue a long time ago, had undermined the trust that has to exist between the public and the First Minister. Now what we've seen is the Scottish Parliament having to oversee a mess created at Westminster and it's been the Scottish Parliament's openness and transparency that's brought this to light and it demonstrates to everyone, particularly the Labour Party, that these things have got to be brought to the surface.

CATHY JAMIESON, Deputy Leader of Scottish Labour: I think it's important to recognise that the whole of the parliamentary Labour Party accepted Henry's resignation with some regret. We believe that he did a good job in the time that he was First Minister for Scotland, he had a clear commitment to the Parliament. And now what we want to do is to move on, to deliver our programme by having an election, open, transparent and above board with all sections of the party to ensure that we select a leader.

JM: Henry McLeish said it was time for others to lead in his resignation speech. The Officegate affair has now been played out, the next act begins. Who will be Scotland's new leader? Good night.

DIARY: It took everyone by surprise. Had he said right at the beginning, 'Here's what happened, I'm sorry,' it would have blown over. However, it was complete and utter incompetence and that is how his time in the post has come across. He wept when he was appointed First Minister and I was rather taken by the fact that it meant something to him, but he's been a disappointment.

Tuesday 6 November 2001
STV News

It's official, Pottermania is gripping the country. And in the capital it's reaching fever pitch. Following the star-studded premiere in London at the weekend, tonight it's Scotland's turn to celebrate the adventures of a boy wizard. The Scottish premiere of *Harry Potter* is taking place in Edinburgh

DIARY: Charity premiere of *Harry Potter and the Philosopher's Stone* at the Ocean Terminal in Leith. *Harry Potter* has been a publishing phenomenon for the past five years and the film is expected to be just as big.

It was and all the sequels thereafter.

JACK McCONNELL BECOMES FIRST MINISTER
Thursday 22 November 2001
STV News

Scotland tonight has a new First Minister. Jack McConnell was installed as the leader of the nation and promised, 'I'll listen to the people.' Mr McConnell pledges to deliver on public services and act on the priorities that matter to real people.

JACK MCCONNELL, First Minister in speech to Parliament: Politics and public service are about nothing if they're not based on principles, focused on improving lives and dedicated to a better world. We come from different places, those of us who are here serving in this Parliament. We've all been in different circumstances, but the greatest challenge that we all face is to leave a better world to those who follow us.

JMK: The First Minister joins us now live from Edinburgh. First of all, Mr McConnell, congratulations on your appointment.

JACK MCCONNELL: Thank you very much, John.

JMK: Hundreds of thousands of people are watching you just now. What difference are you going to make to their lives?

JMC: I want to do three things as First Minister. Firstly, I want to ensure that we are focused in that Scottish Parliament on the delivery of vital public services that really matter, the people's priorities – education, health, transport, jobs and crime. Secondly, I want to make sure that we build confidence in the Parliament by being open and transparent in all that we do. And thirdly, and by much the most important, I want to make sure that every child in Scotland has the sort of opportunities that I've had in life and that we close that opportunity gap, so that those who have the worst possible start in life do not then have the worst possible adulthood.

JMK – Your election has been described by some as a coronation, by others as a stitch-up, and you were Labour's only candidate for office. Does that undermine your authority?

JMC – I think it's great to have such confidence from my colleagues that they are prepared to support me in that way and I now want to make sure that we move quickly to make the sort of improvement in public services to deal with the issue of public confidence in the Parliament and to make sure that our budgets, our decisions and our actions are skewed in favour of new opportunities for those who need them most. And if we get the chance to do that over the next few weeks and months, I believe the year 2002 can see the hopes and ambitions of the people of Scotland for that Parliament now start to be realised.

2002

Monday 14 January 2002

DIARY: Produced my first programme at STV today – the lunchtime opt-out. Proved to be something of a baptism of fire with one piece not playing and having to be dropped down.

I enjoyed producing news programmes, but ultimately producing the evening news and presenting it was not practical. Trying to make production decisions while on air in the studio was fraught.

SCOTLAND WOMEN CURLING TEAM WIN GOLD AT THE WINTER OLYMPICS

Tuesday 26 February 2002

STV News – live from Glasgow Airport

Five days after their success Scotland's Golden Girls are home. Before the Winter Olympics few people would have known who they were. Now they're national heroines, their arrival today greeted by bagpipes, by well wishers and, of course, the usual media scrum.

RONA MARTIN, Team Skip: I can't quite take it in yet. We went away to play curling, we won the competition, came back, but all of this is a lot to take in.

DIARY: It's one of those good news stories that gives everyone a lift and they are nice people.

LOCKERBIE BOMBER'S APPEAL

Wednesday 13 March 2002

DIARY: To Camp Zeist. Steve *(Steve Kydd – cameraman)* and Craig *(Craig Millar – reporter)* had both been there before so they told me what to do – cars searched, everything searched. Our camera position is in the 'shooting gallery' specially built across from the special court. I'd managed to speak to lawyers from both sides and was prepared for my two-way into the 6.00pm.

Thursday 14 March 2002
STV News

'This is not a time for celebration or despair, but a time to think about how we prevent it ever happening again.' The words of Jim Swire, whose daughter died when Pan Am Flight 103 blew up over Lockerbie. Tonight, the man responsible for Britain's biggest mass murder is heading to Scotland to serve his life sentence after five judges rejected Abdelbaset Al-Megrahi's appeal at the Scottish Court in the Netherlands.

SARAH HEANEY: John MacKay is in Camp Zeist and was in court for today's verdict. John, can you describe first what it was like in the courtroom?

JM: Very dramatic, Sarah. In the moments just before Lord Cullen announced the judgement the tension was palpable. He was expected to speak for about ten to 15 minutes. In the end he spoke for a lot less than that and seemed to take people by surprise by how quickly he announced the appeal was not being upheld. It took a moment or two for that to sink in. When it did, Al-Megrahi's wife stood up wailing and started to run towards the back of the court. Relatives tried to hold her back. Al-Megrahi's brother put his hands to his face. Al-Megrahi himself looked forlornly at his wife, his face ashen. Just feet away the relatives of the victims hugged each other, applauding. Somebody shouted 'Yes!' A contrast of emotions. And in the midst of all of this, Al-Megrahi was taken away from the court almost unnoticed.

SH: John, where is Al-Megrahi and what happens now?

JM: He is in this compound behind me, in the jail where he has been for the last three years. He will be removed, we believe, this evening in a joint operation between Scottish Police, the Scottish Prison Service and Dutch authorities. He is a high security prisoner, so no details are being released at all about what his movements will be... An area is being prepared for what we believe will be a helicopter landing and at some point he will be taken off to his ultimate destination – Barlinnie Jail in Glasgow.

One lighter moment in a generally sombre day happened later in the afternoon when I went for a wander during a lull in proceedings. Camp Zeist was a former airbase for the Dutch military and included an outdoor aircraft museum. Although it was deserted, it occurred to me that there must be a toilet there and I could use the facilities. As I walked about I suddenly heard the screech and scrunch of a car skidding on the stones behind me. Startled, I looked round and saw one police officer behind the open car door with a drawn weapon and another walking towards me. He demanded to see my ID, which I fumbled to show him, all the time watching the guy with the gun. They quickly realised this was not some saboteur of the trial, but an eejit who'd meandered away from the right zone. Interestingly, the officer pronounced my surname correctly. The Netherlands is the only place that ever happens because my clan has historical ties with the Dutch. Anyway, I explained rather sheepishly that I'd been looking for a toilet. The officer, with some incredulity, swept his hand towards the thick forest that surrounded the entire base. 'The toilet is everywhere,' he said.

Monday 18 March 2002

The £17 million Millennium Wheel will carry its first boat between the Firth and Clyde and Union canals this week, marking the biggest ever revamp of the UK's waterways. The two canals meet at Falkirk where the massive structure will raise and lower boats the 25 metres between them. Its creators are confident the centrepiece of the now 68-mile link will be a success.

PROF GEORGE FLEMING, British Waterways Board: I think the Falkirk Wheel is a brilliant piece of engineering and it's British engineering, Scottish engineering at its best. And I believe it will be a great success. And it will be a great success for Scotland and a great success for Falkirk.

Thursday 21 March 2002
STV News

The Scottish skiing hero Alain Baxter has been stripped of his bronze medal and branded a drugs cheat by Olympic chiefs. Less than a month after his historic performance in Salt Lake City, the International Olympic Committee has demanded that he returns his medal after testing positive for the drug methamphetamine. At an emotional news conference, Baxter confirmed he'd unknowingly taken the banned substance by using a nasal inhaler which hadn't been cleared with the team doctors.

CRAIG REEDIE, Chairman, British Olympic Association: The BOA is convinced that in no way can Alain be described as a, and I quote, 'drugs cheat'. We believe the offence to be modest and the punishment severe.

DIARY: He's been harshly dealt with. He took a Vicks nasal spray in the US, not realising it was made up differently from the one in the UK that he's been taking since childhood. It seems very unfair – no one doubts him.

Tuesday 26 March 2002
STV News

The jobs of around 500 workers are under threat this evening after a huge flood at Scotland's last remaining deep mine. Around 17 million gallons of water cascaded through the Longannet pit in Fife at the weekend. Management say if it had happened 24 hours earlier many miners would have been killed.

CHAMPIONS LEAGUE FINAL

Wednesday 15 May 2002
STV News – live from Hampden Park with Jane Lewis

Tonight's the night. The arena is set. The prize is waiting to be claimed. The best in Europe compete before the eyes of the world. Glasgow is transformed into a carnival city. But can tonight's game match the glories of the past?

Good evening from Hampden Park for tonight's Champions League Final. The stage is set for a European showdown between Real Madrid and Bayer Leverkusen. With kick-off less than two hours away, fans are already pouring into the stadium and the atmosphere is building. Glasgow has been transformed into a festival city. Thousands of fans are creating a carnival atmosphere.

DIARY: It was some spectacle. The Real Madrid fans created a good atmosphere. It felt a privilege to be there. Real scored quickly through Raul. The Germans came back into it with an equaliser and really took a grip on the game before Zinedine Zidane scored a wonderful goal just before half-time – a volley from just inside the box. Normally a goal produces a mass exhalation – a roar – but this was a mass inhalation – a gasp – before the crowd went crazy. An incredible moment. Much comparison with the classic 1960 final beforehand, but it didn't come close. However, Zidane's goal will live on in the memory.

Thursday 27 June 2002

DIARY: Started the day as a producer in Glasgow and ended it in a motel outside Dijon in East Central France. The lead story was the news of a coach crash involving schoolchildren from Largs Academy. One 15-year-old girl died.

Friday 28 June 2002
STV News

The bus driver in the French coach crash tragedy has been charged with involuntary manslaughter after the death of Ayrshire schoolgirl, Katherine Fish. Prosecutors believe the driver swerved at the last minute after taking the wrong road as he drove a party from Largs Academy on a school trip to Barcelona.

DIARY: Basically, just got whatever we could, a couple of interviews etc, but mostly sitting around. Did two lives into the lunchtime programme and then had to do an 'as live' and a track and rushes *(voice track and unedited footage)* for the back of 3.00pm.

However, round about then some of the children were released from the hospital, some in ambulances, some in taxis. Got some good shots, a couple of snatched sound bites and an interview with the school headteacher. Had to dump everything I had prepared before. After that we heard the driver was being charged with involuntary manslaughter. In the 15 minutes before our feed time it was quite pressurised.

Much of the material we got was down to the sharpness of my cameraman Bobby Whitelaw, who spotted activity at the hospital as we hacks were shooting the breeze to pass the time. The reporter and camera operator have to work as a team and feed off each other. Bobby was one of the very best.

Thursday 18 July 2002
STV News

Scotland's first national park for Loch Lomond and the Trossachs, officially opens today as the new authority takes over the powers to shape the future of 700 square miles of natural heritage. The need to reconcile the interests of business and the environment will spark a huge debate in the coming months.

Wednesday 13 November 2002

DIARY: The start of a 48-hour strike by firefighters. They were walking out bang on 6.00pm just as we were going on air, so we decided to do the programme live from Cowcaddens fire station, just up the road. There were a lot of technical problems eg a camera failing and no communication between the satellite truck and the gallery. As we were into the on-air countdown my earpiece separated and I only got it sorted with less than ten seconds to go. All very hairy, but it's when the job is most enjoyable. The firefighters were actually walking out as I began speaking.

Friday 29 November 2002

DIARY: After work drinks. Conversed with young colleagues Ewan Petrie and Lesley

Colquhoun. Discussed how they would change the programme. Lesley thinks we should make it 'more cool' and I asked her how she would make me 'cooler'. She candidly said I wouldn't do it because I was 'too old.'

Lesley continues to be a colleague and we've never spoken of it again.

Monday 9 December 2002

DIARY: Spent all day through in Edinburgh. A huge fire – which was only finally damped down this evening – has gutted buildings in the Cowgate in the Old Town. I was to anchor there after lunchtime and this evening. Not much for me to do other than answer some questions, introduce packages etc and do a couple of interviews.

Wednesday 11 December 2002
STV News

Scotland's Catholic Bishops say they are dismayed and angered at attempts to link denominational schools and sectarianism. Critics claim separating pupils because of their faith reinforces divisions in the community and does nothing for religious tolerance.

FRED FORRESTER, Former Deputy General Secretary, EIS: Catholic schools are implicated in it and really ought to accept that fact. They are not the cause of it, I would concede that readily, but their existence is implicated in prolonging sectarianism.

MARIO CONTI, Archbishop of Glasgow: The suggestion that somehow or other these schools are the cause of, the origin of, or the continuation of sectarianism within the community is quite unfair and really quite offensive. It's almost as bad as saying, as was said in the '20s of the last century, we've got a problem here with sectarianism, we've got a problem of bigotry, let's send the Irish back to Ireland.

JM: But surely one way to tackle sectarianism is greater understanding and if children are brought up separately then that understanding isn't going to be there.

MC: You give that as an analysis, but I'm not sure that analysis is correct. To blame, first of all, religion for sectarianism, for the bigotry that is in the country, for the divisions which are in Glasgow, and then to pinpoint Catholic schools as somehow a contributory factor to it is an unfair analysis and is offensive to the Catholic community. I want to say that as strongly as possible at this point because I don't want anybody to be under the impression that somehow or other we're going to sit down, listen to all this and gradually see something that we think is important being whittled away or undermined.

The issue of state funded denominational schools continues to surface periodically.

DIARY CONT: An unfortunate first tonight. I couldn't remain in the studio until the end of the programme because I had to dash to the loo to be sick. It was very unpleasant. The only part I was missing for was the goodbye, but I was clearly missing. I'd begun to feel uncomfortable soon after we went on air, but it was only as we got onto the sport that I was having problems. In the end, there was only once choice I could make.

The programme ended with Shereen saying goodnight and the camera pulling out to reveal my empty chair.

2003

Friday 3 January 2003

DIARY: Saw the new set for the programme. We are making quite a radical departure away from sitting behind a desk to sitting on a 'news bench' (sofa). I had strong reservations, but it looks excellent on camera and the colours and lighting are good. We're provided with a variety of new shots and we move about the set more. The downside, the only one, is the theme tune which is insipid.

Monday 13 January 2003
STV News

'We must disarm Iraq.' That's the stark warning from the Prime Minister Tony Blair as he again stated that Saddam Hussein must be stripped of his weapons of mass destruction. It comes as anti-war protesters greeted the Royal Navy flagship *Ark Royal* as it sailed into Scotland this morning.

Thursday 16 January 2003
STV News

The Prime Minister is in Scotland this evening rallying support for possible military action against Iraq. His arrival comes as the Scottish Parliament debated the legitimacy of war with Saddam, Meanwhile, an exclusive poll for this channel... shows overwhelming opposition in Scotland to war without further UN backing.

Wednesday 29 January 2003
STV News

He posed as a loving husband and caring father, but tonight Nat Fraser is facing 25 years behind bars for murdering his wife. The jury convicted him without knowing that he'd already attempted to strangle her weeks before she disappeared. Arlene's body has never been found, but the trial heard claims that Fraser had dismembered and scattered her remains, leaving his own children without a mother. The judge said these children now need to be told what their father has done and there was only one word to describe it – evil.

The case ran for nearly five years and grabbed the nation's attention.

Friday 31 January 2003
STV News

The Prime Minister will meet President George Bush at the White House in the next few minutes for a crucial summit on military action in Iraq. It's being described as a council of war. The talks come as Scottish regiments in Germany make final preparations before leaving in the next few days for the Gulf.

Friday 7 February 2003
STV News

The RAF has announced that up to 2,000 personnel from its Scottish bases have been placed on standby for war on Iraq. Aircraft from Leuchars, Lossiemouth and Kinloss are being prepared to join the military build-up in the Gulf. It's estimated that more than 4,000 Scottish men and women could be deployed to the region over the coming weeks.

Monday 17 February 2003
STV News

Anti-war protesters say they're confident war can still be stopped after record turnouts for demonstrations at the weekend. An estimated 80,000 people took to the streets of Glasgow on Saturday to voice their opposition to war in Iraq. Organisers are keen to maintain the strong feeling and are calling for people to take part in civil disobedience if Tony Blair continues towards war.

Tuesday 18 February 2003
STV News

The Prime Minister has been setting out what he describes as the moral case for war against Saddam Hussein. Despite the massive anti-war campaign and his own plummeting support, Mr Blair insists military action on Iraq is the right course of action. His comments have come under fire from opposition parties and peace activists who claim the Prime Minister has no right to preach on morality.

TONY BLAIR, Prime Minister: The reason for doing so is not because the nature of the regime can in itself provide justification for war, but it can at least show that if we do have to take military action, we do so in the sure knowledge that we are removing one of the most barbarous and detestable regimes in modern political history.

Wednesday 19 February 2003
STV News

Divisions in the Labour Party in Scotland over a possible war in Iraq have been exposed today by a former Scottish Executive Minister. Susan Deacon has tabled a motion in the Scottish Parliament warning that any conflict would be illegal and unnecessary. The former Health Minister has been backed by a number of colleagues, despite party leader Jack McConnell calling for unity yesterday.

Monday 17 March 2003
STV News

Britain and America appear to be just hours away from going to war with Iraq as moves towards military action in the Gulf claimed the first high-profile political casualty. Robin Cook resigned as Leader of the Commons in protest after Tony Blair and George Bush abandoned diplomatic efforts to resolve the crisis through the United Nations. Today's events appear to signal that war is now inevitable. The UN failed to reach consensus on a new resolution authorising war. Following an emergency Cabinet meeting, the Foreign Secretary Jack Straw will address MPs in the next hour. And President Bush is to address the American people at 1.00am our time.

Thursday 20 March 2003
STV News

Thousands of Scottish servicemen and women are tonight steeling themselves to take part in an invasion of Iraq. Infantrymen and tank crews are waiting for orders in Kuwait. RAF Tornados from Scottish bases are on standby to join the aerial bombardment. At home their families are waiting for news from the front. Meanwhile, anti-war protests continued across the country

Friday 21 March 2003
STV News

Scottish soldiers are tonight reported to be advancing towards Basra, Iraq's second city. The Ministry of Defence says the Black Watch are taking part in a joint British and American offensive. Lead elements of the force are said to be on the outskirts of Basra, which is a key strategic objective of the allies.

Monday 14 April 2003

DIARY: The Scottish Parliament election campaign is well underway, although it's unlikely most people have noticed. We led with it for the first time tonight – a row over NHS waiting lists.

SCOTTISH ELECTION 2003
Thursday 1 May 2003

DIARY: Not a night of glory for me. I was to do the late bulletin and then dash off to Hamilton for the first result. It was always cutting it fine, but when I got lost it became impossible. I arrived as the winning candidate – Tom McCabe – made his acceptance speech. It wasn't actually that big a deal. We didn't have our own election programme and were really just doing inserts into the ITV News channel. I did an interview with McCabe and that was my night.

Friday 2nd May 2003

STV News – with Shereen Nanjiani

Tonight's top stories.

The Joy of Six. Voters shake up Scottish politics as the biggest winners are the smaller parties.

Jack's back for four more years and set for coalition talks.

Poor show as more than half the electorate don't vote.

Scotland's parliamentary elections have seen a night of stunning success for the underdogs. Labour may be returning to power, but with the narrowest of margins. Election 2003 will be remembered for the rise of the Greens, the Scottish Socialists and single issue candidates – the pensioner and the hospital campaigner who will take their seats alongside the established parties in the chamber.

So how does the chamber look? Labour on 50 seats, down five from the last Parliament. The Lib Dems on 17, that's up one. It brings the coalition partners two seats more than the decisive 65 seats needed for a majority. The SNP are on 27, down six, and the Tories are on 18, down one. And there are the big changes. The Greens on seven, the Scottish Socialist Party on six and the independents on four.

JACK MCCONNELL, Leader, Scottish Labour: Yesterday's votes gave Labour in Scotland the honour of being the largest party in the Scottish Parliament. I believe people across Scotland did that because Scottish Labour put forward the ideas and the policies to tackle directly the priorities the people of Scotland have.

JIM WALLACE, Leader, Scottish Liberal Democrats: We actually held our position whilst the Labour Party, which has been senior party in the coalition, actually fell back. That must strengthen our position, it changes the balance if there was to be a coalition, if we were to go into negotiation.

DAVID MCLETCHIE, Leader, Scottish Conservatives: If any of you wish to eat your words in private, take a wee serving of humble pie, we'll be available at the conclusion of this press conference.

JM: For the Scottish National Party it might have been a slick campaign, but it didn't translate into the breakthrough to government. For a time they were ahead in the polls, but finished up losing six MSPs. The party leader John Swinney joins us now live from Edinburgh. Mr Swinney, you said earlier on today that you had moved from being a party of protest, but were not yet accepted as a party of government. What do you do now?

JOHN SWINNEY, Leader SNP: Well, I think that's an inaccurate reflection of what happened last night. We were vulnerable on the regional list vote. We had most of our members elected by that system four years ago and obviously there were new faces, new parties came onto the scene this time round and it made us vulnerable. What I recognise is that the SNP in wanting to deliver Scottish independence has got to have leadership of the first-past-the-post constituencies in Scotland and that's what I'm equipping the party to do... What the election leaves us with is a necessity to make sure the SNP completes the transition that I've set it on of moving from being a party of protest vote into a party of government, of alternative government.

DIARY: Should make for a more interesting Parliament and it's no bad thing that the big parties have lost. It has been a singularly uninspiring election. Aside from how the politicians fared, the big story of the election is voter apathy with fewer than half of the electorate deciding to vote.

CELTIC IN THE UEFA CUP FINAL IN SEVILLE

Tuesday 20 May 2003

STV News – live from Seville with Jane Lewis

Good evening from Seville with just 24 hours to go until the big kick-off. The temperatures and the tension are high here in the build-up to tomorrow's UEFA Cup Final. Tens of thousands of Celtic fans are already here, desperate not to miss the biggest game for their club in a generation.

The heat was intense and as we prepared to go on air I was perspiring a lot. One effect of this, bizarrely, was the dye from the dark suede shoes I was wearing began to stain the trouser leg of my light chinos. As I was getting the countdown to going on air, one of the Celtic fans watching shouted, 'Haw big man, you've pished yersel'!' I uttered 'Good evening' with that alarming thought in my head.

DIARY: I travelled with the satellite to a nice setting on the waterfront of the Guadalquivir, with the Torro Del Oro *(Tower of Gold)* as our backdrop. Very picturesque. Took myself a walk up to the Cathedral, around which was the largest gathering of Celtic fans. Anchored the programme this evening from our location and it went well. Big day ahead tomorrow. Seville is a lovely city. It is very hot in the afternoon though, baking hot in the mid to high 30s.

Wednesday 21 May 2003

DIARY: Everything focused on today and it went very well until much later when I was hit on the head by a thrown bottle. Broadcasting for most of the day. At first, we were in a square near to the Cathedral that was heaving with Celtic fans, perhaps 15–20,000. I had to do the 11.00am bulletin standing on a camera box with them pushing on to me in fun, hitting me with a rubber mallet and draping Celtic scarves on me. By 12.50pm (1.50pm Seville time) the *Daily Record* bus arrived and I did much of the programme from on top of that with Celtic fans in the background. I anchored the 2.00pm from there, the first half with Jane and then a phone-in and texts with Jim Delahunt for the second half. The humour of the Celtic fans was very good. By this time (3.30pm local time) it was absolutely baking.

STV News – live from Seville with Jane Lewis

Good evening and welcome to Seville for this special edition of *Scotland Today*. With the kick-off approaching, the waiting is nearly over. It's more than 30 years since Celtic enjoyed European success and the 75,000 fans here and the hundreds of thousands of fans at home believe that that European dream could come true tonight. The excitement and tension have been building in this city throughout the day ahead of the UEFA Cup Final – and let's just give you a taste of that just now *(upsound of thousands of Celtic fans singing)*.

MARTIN O'NEILL, Celtic Manager: We have reached a final now and we've done it with some terrifically gifted players that people seem to forget. And we've done it with a terrific spirit, the sort of spirit that I think was typical of the 1967 team.

JOSÉ MOURINHO, Porto Coach: I have a lot of respect for Celtic. I have more than respect for Celtic, I respect football and to respect football is to understand that the big final is 50–50.

JM: Well, this is the Spanish city of Seville, but you wouldn't believe it *(upsound of Celtic fans cheering)*. Celtic fans often sing that if you know their history it's enough to make your heart go. Another chapter will be written in that history tonight and there's no doubt their hearts will be going. From *Scotland Today* in Seville, good night and good luck to Celtic.

DIARY: The bus and us moved to another site near the stadium for the evening. It was at one of the big screens available for fans without tickets. By now though, the *Daily Record* bus had been required to leave because of abuse from fans – who regard it as the Daily Ranger. Anyway, we got on to the *Scottish Sun* bus and Jane and I anchored the 6.00pm from there. No denying it was a triumph – all going smoothly and capturing the atmosphere perfectly. Back in Glasgow they were raving about it.

I remained on the bus to watch the match, but as time passed a handful of scumbags began to have a go – some resentment over *The Sun* this time. As the match progressed some missiles began to get thrown, glass tumblers, fags and I got spat on. Then Larsson equalised for a second time. Shortly after a bottle came out of the darkness and hit me towards the back of my head above the right ear. I just buckled and went down, although I never lost consciousness. I was very dizzy, though, and decided to go straight back to the hotel, fortunately getting a taxi quickly.

The Spanish police grabbed the morons responsible and gestured as if to ask what did I want done with them. I wanted them punished, but the thought of getting involved in a foreign legal system and perhaps having to attend a court hearing wasn't something I wanted to do, so I gestured to let them go. I've never understood what their problem was. The Celtic fans were in great form during our time in Seville. The incident happened immediately after Henrik Larsson had brought Celtic back into the game again. Rather than enjoy the moment, these clowns preferred to focus on some trivial grievance about a bus.

DIARY: I sat in my room watching Celtic lose 3-2 in extra time, but I remember little of it. When I did try to go to sleep, I couldn't. Every time I was about to fall over something in my system forced me awake. My colleagues Raman Bhardwaj and later Jim Delahunt called at different times to check on me and evidently weren't happy with what they saw. Jane Lewis got the hotel to order a doctor for me. In a mixture of broken English and sign language he diagnosed shock, I think. Anyway, he gave me a shot of something and only then did I sleep, after about 4.30am.

When my son was very young his gran had knitted him a superhero figure and he would ask me to take it wherever I went away and keep it on my bed. I continued to do so long after he'd grown out of it, almost as a tradition. I'd always be careful to put it in my case in the morning to avoid strange looks from the hotel maids. On the day of the game I had forgotten to do that and returned to see the figure placed prominently on top of my pillow. Later, when the doctor came to see me, he was accompanied by an assistant, a member of the hotel staff, Jane, Raman, Jim, my editor Paul McKinney and possibly a couple of others. They all left as the doctor prepared to give me a jag. The last thing I remember seeing before drifting off was the superhero figure still proudly on top of my pillow. They would all have seen it. I drifted into oblivion thinking, Nooooo! It has never been mentioned, but I know they know.

Monday 27 October 2003

STV News reported on the history of the Scottish Parliament project. Initially proposed at a budget of £40 million, in 1998 Donald Dewar had announced the new Scottish Parliament would be built on the site of an old brewery next to Holyrood Palace. The architect Enrique Miralles was chosen in part because his company had a track record of completing projects on time and on budget. By June 1999 the cost had risen to £109 million and MPs were calling for a review. By April 2000 it was £195 million and again assurances were given that it wouldn't cost any more. By December 2001 it had reached £260 million and a year later it was £325 million. The final bill was £414 million. And it was three years late.

Wednesday 19 November 2003

Holland v Scotland for a place in the Euro 2004 finals. Scotland had won the first leg in Glasgow 1-0.

STV News – live from the Amsterdam Arena with Jane Lewis

Scotland Today comes to you live from the spectacular Amsterdam Arena. Could this be where Bertie's Bravehearts become national heroes? The Tartan Army are, of course, over here and they're hoping for a night to remember. The roof of the Amsterdam Arena is open and the crowd is beginning to fill in to this spectacular stadium. Will it be another near miss for Scotland or will it be a night of glory? One thing is certain – an entire nation is behind them. From all of us at the Amsterdam Arena, it's goodnight and come on Scotland!

It wasn't a near miss, Scotland were hammered 6-0. My hotel was several miles out of Amsterdam because it was a late decision to send me. I had been dismayed that I would probably miss out on an after-match beer with my colleagues. When the time came, I was only too glad to slip away from the game early.

It was bad night all round. A misunderstanding with Dutch security at the stadium meant that later on they wouldn't let us return to the trackside where our camera was positioned. With less than ten minutes to on air I was reduced to saying to the armed security on the gate, 'I'm begging you.' It worked.

Wednesday 26 November 2003
STV News

The number of people stabbed to death in Scotland is at its highest level for a decade. Shocking figures released today also show that our country has the third highest murder rate in the European Union with Glasgow being one of the most dangerous cities in Britain. Ministers blame a blade and booze culture, but say they are confident they can change things.

Knife crime dropped significantly following a determined campaign, including the introduction of jail sentences for carrying a knife.

2004

Saturday 31 January 2004
STV News – live from Rosepark Care Home

Good evening from the Rosepark Care Home in Uddingston in Lanarkshire where today ten elderly residents died. Many of the pensioners are thought to have been overcome by smoke as they slept. The fire began at 4.40am this morning in a storage cupboard. The Queen has led messages of sympathy to the relatives of those who died. Tonight, three elderly people are still critically ill in hospital. Another four remain in hospital for further treatment.

JOAN COLLINS

Thursday 6 May 2004

I asked her for make-up advice for my colleagues.

STV News

JOAN COLLINS: Clean *(laughs)*. Always wear lipstick, but not on your teeth. And powder. I don't think shiny faces are very attractive. And be groomed.

MARYHILL FACTORY EXPLOSION

Tuesday 11 May 2004
STV News – live from Maryhill with Shereen Nanjiani

Several people remain trapped under the rubble of this Glasgow plastics factory. They've been there for six hours after the building collapsed like a house of cards. In the last few minutes it's been confirmed that three people have been killed, 24 are still being treated in hospital, 16 of them are in a serious condition. The emergency services have been working through the day here to rescue those under the rubble. It's understood firefighters have been talking to at least one of those trapped beneath the debris.

The final toll of the ICL Plastics Factory (sometimes known as Stockline) explosion

was nine dead and 33 injured. It was caused by gas leaking from corroded underground pipes.

Sharon Frew, STV Reporter
I admit I froze when I first saw all the debris and rubble, the woman sitting on the kerb with an oxygen mask on her face, the man lying on the road, who was being treated by a doctor. I later learned that he and his staff had run from a nearby GP surgery when they heard the blast. Another woman was being told to keep breathing into a paper bag by a nurse. Then I spotted a girl being helped from the wreckage, covered in dust. She was calling out for someone to help find her sister. My cameraman, Gary shouted at me, 'Come on' or something like that. His words made me snap back and focus. Medical staff were here helping the walking wounded. My job was to find out what had happened.

Nothing I had done before had prepared me for the major disaster now in front of me.

When I took the call from the newsdesk, all the producer told me was 'head to Grovepark Street, there's a report of an explosion at a factory.' We were minutes away from the scene. We arrived as the first emergency crews did, before any police cordon had been set up. We walked down the street with firefighters and paramedics running past us to the devastated building.

Filming as we went, I knew I had to find eyewitnesses, but I was surrounded by people who were unable to talk. Then I noticed a small crowd that had gathered. The men, wearing overalls, were covered in dust, one had a bandage on his head to stem the bleeding. Both were clearly in shock, but they agreed to speak to me and described how they'd been working in the factory when suddenly, there was a bang and everything went black. They crawled through the darkness to safety.

Even after ten more years' experience as a reporter, I'm not sure you're ever really prepared for what faces you when you first arrive at the scene of a major disaster. I've covered many more in the decade that followed. What I do know is that the news footage and interviews gathered in those first minutes are vital. These are images that could be shown, as with the Maryhill explosion, for years to come. It's important to try and get to the heart of what happened, to keep your eyes and ears open, to find eyewitnesses, but above all, report calmly and with care and compassion.

JOHN SWINNEY RESIGNS AS LEADER OF THE SNP

Tuesday 22 June 2004
STV News

John Swinney is giving up the leadership of the SNP, blaming back biting and constant criticism from within the party. His decision follows mounting pressure after poor results at the European elections.

JOHN SWINNEY, Leader, SNP: It has become clear to me over the last few days that the constant and relentless speculation over my position is obscuring and, crucially in my judgement, will continue to obscure the political objectives of the SNP... No member of the SNP should ever underestimate the damage that is caused to our movement by the loose and dangerous talk of the few.

I first remembered John Swinney coming into the BBC for interviews and was always struck by the evident decency of the man. I thought his party had treated him poorly.

Friday 3 September 2004
STV News

'It's good to be back.' The words of Alex Salmond as he secured the leadership of the SNP for the second time. The Banff and Buchan MP defeated Mike Russell and Roseanna Cunningham, winning more than 75 per cent of the vote. Mr Salmond's running mate Nicola Sturgeon was elected deputy leader.

HOLYROOD INQUIRY

Wednesday 15 September 2004
STV News – live from Holyrood

Good evening and welcome to the heart of the capital where tonight the eyes of the nation are on the building behind me and their thoughts are concentrated on the pronouncements of one man. Lord Fraser of Carmyllie was given the task of working out how our country's finest minds managed to make such an unholy mess of providing a building from which the Scottish Parliament could run the country. It's three years late and ten times over-budget and when you hear Lord Fraser's findings you might have trouble trusting some of those involved to run a raffle.

We'll be looking at who was blamed in Lord Fraser's report. In differing degrees; the civil servants who were managing the project, but withheld key information from ministers about costs and the risk to the tax payer; the politicians who were supposed to be in charge, but never seemed to get a grip; the Spanish architects who showed scant regard for costs. And the Father of Devolution himself, Donald Dewar, who didn't knowingly mislead Parliament, but who rushed the whole thing through and failed to spot how it was going so disastrously wrong.

LORD FRASER OF CARMYLLIE: I have a number of sharp criticisms and recommendations to make on matters which ought to have been better understood. Nevertheless, there is no single villain of the peace.

JM: It's worth noting that in all the months of this inquiry when the great and the good appeared before Lord Fraser, rarely, if ever, was there a word of apology. Indeed, Lord Fraser himself said that the walls of the Canongate echoed to the cries of, 'It wisnae me.' Some of these people will be uncomfortable tonight.

JM: We're joined now by Margo MacDonald MSP, a long-term critic of the project. You said you hoped this report would decide who would get MBEs and who would get P45s. Are you happy that's been achieved?

MARGO MACDONALD: Unfortunately, I think some of the latter have managed to escape to other jobs. But it's a very detailed report and I don't think that Peter Fraser has actually missed anybody and hit the wall… Everybody who trooped into the witness box to give evidence said, oh it wisnae me. And they were still at it today.

JM: The Scottish Parliament is now open for business and in full operation. The inquiry into the fiasco surrounding its construction is now complete. History will judge this building by what happens inside and that will depend on the people we elect to represent us there. Good night.

To my eye the Parliament building looks like an attempt to do up some 1960s new town council flats. The interior is impressive, but the exterior does not proclaim the building to be the seat of the Scottish Government.

Michael Crow, STV Political Correspondent

As Westminster Correspondent I reported on the referendum and subsequent Scotland Bill going through the Houses of Parliament. I then moved home to Scotland to cover the birth of the new Scottish Parliament. It was an exciting time to be a political journalist.

Donald Dewar, Alex Salmond, Jim Wallace and David McLetchie were the leaders of the main political parties – all big political beasts. The election of a Green MSP, Robin Harper, and Tommy Sheridan from the SSP, was hugely symbolic as it promised a new type of politics in the UK. The electoral arithmetic also led to a coalition government – something not seen in peacetime British politics since the 1930s. All the media coverage was of a new political dawn for Scotland.

For me Donald Dewar's brilliant speech at the opening of the Parliament best captured this historic time:

'Today, we look forward to the time when this moment will be seen as a turning point: the day when democracy was renewed in Scotland, when we revitalised our place in this our United Kingdom. This is about more than our politics and our laws. This is about who we are, how we carry ourselves.'

Unfortunately, the Parliament did not carry itself as well as people had hoped and, perhaps unsurprisingly, MSPs struggled to live up to the huge burden of expectation that had been placed upon them. Within a short period of time the positive coverage gave way to negative stories about commemorative medals, lobbying, pay and allowances.

And nothing epitomised the fall from grace as keenly as the building of the new Scottish Parliament. Huge cost overruns, a lack of accountability and a complete lack of sensitivity at how damaging the story could be, ensured it dominated political coverage for years. Westminster created the Scottish Parliament, but then delivered a hospital pass in the form of the Holyrood building contract. But as an institution the Parliament, for its part, failed its first real test in managing the fallout.

All this served to switch the focus of political coverage from Westminster to the Scottish Parliament. MPs, much to their annoyance, rarely got a look in to the stories of the day. MSPs were more accessible and more newsworthy and the political dynamic in Scotland was changed forever. While the Parliament may now be a permanent and constructive part of the Scottish political landscape, its early days promised much, but struggled to live up to the high expectations placed upon it. A new political dawn was ushered in – but perhaps not the one that people had anticipated.

OPENING OF THE NEW SCOTTISH PARLIAMENT

Saturday 9 October 2004
Opening ceremony

JACK MCCONNELL, First Minister: This chamber... at the heart of our new Scottish Parliament building. It is a heart that should beat with the pulse of the nation and resound with the passion of Scotland. This chamber – a triumph of design and engineering – is the place Scotland's Parliament can now call home... After five years our young Parliament can now take up occupation of this, the permanent address. This is a building to which we have come amid debate and controversy...

It is now accepted without dispute that this is the permanent home for the nation's final discussion on matters that affect the way we live and the way we shape the lives of future generations...

Five years ago Scotland found a new voice. Today we celebrate a new confidence. A permanent Parliament with which to announce our ambitions, encourage our enterprise and fight for fairness. We have a new building that will be the envy of many the world over. But today more than anything we have a Parliament that has come of age in a country whose time has come.

Thursday 4 November 2004
STV News

Three Black Watch soldiers have been killed in a bomb blast at their base near Baghdad. Reports are coming in that one interpreter has also been killed and there are eight others injured.

Monday 22 November 2004
STV News

It's been described as football's game of hate. The Old Firm showdown at the weekend was one of the most explosive in recent years. Today the First Minister slammed both Rangers and Celtic. Jack McConnell said the scenes were unacceptable and a step back in time.

Even by Old Firm standards this was an intense game, including sendings-off, incidents that should have resulted in more sendings-off, accusations of provocation by various players towards the crowd, police involvement and more.

2005

Thursday 20 January 2005
STV News

Tearful mourners today remembered the five members of the same family killed last week in the worst storms to hit Scotland in a decade. More than a thousand mourners turned out on Benbecula to say their farewells to Archie and Murdina MacPherson, their two children Andrew and Hanna and grandfather Calum Campbell. The family had only returned to South Uist two years ago to start a new life in a safer community.

Monday 24 January 2005

HOLOCAUST MEMORIAL

The concentration camps at Auschwitz Birkenau were liberated in January 1945. Of the six million who died in the Holocaust, one and a half million had perished there. To mark the 60th anniversary I travelled to Poland with producer Howard Simpson and cameraman Neil McLaren. Despite being very sunny, it was bitterly cold and the three of us were chilled to the bone. And to the soul. We produced three reports. The images Neil filmed, the survivors Howard had found and the melancholic music of Arvo Part's 'Spiegel im Speigel', all made my words superfluous.

STV News

This Thursday is Holocaust Memorial Day when the world remembers the millions who died in the Nazi extermination camps. This year also commemorates the 60th anniversary of the liberation of Auschwitz. More than any other death camp, Auschwitz symbolises the horror of the Holocaust.

DAY 1

JM: (*shot of Polish road sign with the name Oświęcim*) The southern Polish town of Oświęcim is rather nondescript. Houses, a railway and some factories. (*shot of sign saying Auschwitz*) But when it's given its German name it takes on a much greater significance.

ERNEST LEVY, Auschwitz Survivor: One simply did not want to believe it that things like that are happening, are possible. You don't want to believe it. Like my late father, who perished in Buchenwald, always said, 'It'll be alright, y'know. Just one more dance. We will move.' But we didn't move. We got caught in the tragedy.

TERESA WONTOR-CICHY, Auschwitz Historian: It's a cemetery. The biggest cemetery in the world.

JM: (*shots of museum displays*) This is human hair. Some pleats remain in place. It was used to make carpets and nets. There are shoes. Personal items. Other remains (*shot of children's clothes and toys*), like so much at Auschwitz, are beyond words.

MARIANNE GRANT, Auschwitz Survivor: Most of the children were taken away. Of course, the babies they took away right away. The children were gassed and for work only the adults were allowed to live.'

JM: (*at the gas chamber*) The dying was neither quick. Nor quiet.

ERNEST LEVY, Auschwitz Survivor: You couldn't breathe from the stench. It was lying on my chest the smell. The terrible, terrible stench. Och, it is indescribable.

JM: Some survivors found sanctuary in Scotland. We'll hear their stories tomorrow.

DAY 2

STV News

In this second report we hear from those who survived and found refuge here in Scotland.

JM: Sixty years ago the Third Reich was facing collapse and the Nazis had failed in their attempt to wipe out the Jews from Europe. In time many of these displaced people, who had lost everything, found sanctuary in the UK. For some, Scotland became home. They brought with them vivid testimony of the horrors of the death camps.

ERNEST LEVY, 40 years in Scotland: They didn't look at you, practically. Life and death, but for them it was absolutely nothing. Just, you go there, you go there. I looked reasonably well and young and so I was sent to the left. But there was no real thought in it, who is going to the right, who is going to live, who is going to die.

MARIANNE GRANT, 40 years in Scotland: When Mengele (*Josef Mengele, the notorious Nazi doctor at Auschwitz, known as the Angel of Death*) called you, well I tell you, I was trembling. And he said, 'You draw me this.' And I did that and I knew if I made a blob this was me finished. I actually painted for my life.

BOB KUTNER, Jewish Refugee and allied interrogator, 50 years in Scotland: He was a young man about 19. SS, I think he was an officer. But when I interrogated him – I had the documentation lying there – and I said that it said here that he'd killed nine Jews in a cellar. And he said, 'No I didn't, it was only eight.' He kept giving me an argument and then he said, 'Ah well, what's one Jew more or less?'

JM: Every victim had a story. One of particular resonance for Scotland was that of Stefan Jasieński, a Polish soldier who trained here before returning to aid the resistance.

TERESA WONTOR-CICHY, Auschwitz Historian: He was captured and brought here to Auschwitz and to different cells. But in one of them he stayed and he left some drawings. In January '45, so a few days before the liberation, Stefan Jasieński was executed here in Auschwitz.

JM: These are carvings that Stefan Jasieński made on his cell door here in Auschwitz. It's mostly biographical detail and happier moments from his life. For instance, here's his family crest. And here he is parachuting back into Poland. Of particular interest to us, though, is this one here – a greyhound dog from Glasgow. When Jasieński and his comrades were training in Scotland they enjoyed nothing more than going to the greyhound racing in Glasgow. And night after night they saw this dog, number four, coming in last. One evening Jasieński had a good feeling about the dog, bet on it and sure enough the dog won. It's rather moving to think that this greyhound from Glasgow brought some light to Jasieński in his last, dark, desperate hours here in Auschwitz.

JM: Why do you think you survived when so many others didn't?

ERNEST LEVY: In the back of your mind there is always a little hope left, a little hope. Maybe I'll survive and I will tell the world what happened. It's that incentive, you know? And that's always at the back of your mind, maybe I will survive. I will fight on. Fight on and fight on 'til the last moment. Don't give in.

DAY 3

JM: (*Walking through Auschwitz*) What's very disconcerting about Auschwitz is that it is not exactly as you expect it to appear. This apparent avenue, for example, is almost unthreatening. (*turning to reveal prison wire*) It's only when you see it from a different perspective and you see the barbed wire and the watchtower that you realise this was a place of horror. Block 11 was the Death Block and at the Death Wall literally thousands and thousands of men, women and children were executed.

MARIANNE GRANT, 40 years in Scotland: Anything can happen again, anywhere. You can see people are hating each other and killing each other all over the world today, which is horrendous. That's why we can't forget, we must never forget. We've got to bring it up again and again and again.

JM: This pond is a deep, gloomy, grey colour. That may be explained by the fact that it lies adjacent to what was once a gas chamber and crematorium here at Birkenau. The ashes of countless thousands of people were dumped in this water.

ERNEST LEVY, Auschwitz Survivor: We can't turn the clock back. We have to learn to co-exist. We have to learn from the past and it is a very important anniversary. Because here we are the last Mohicans who can tell you the first-hand experiences. There are very few left. And with every survivor who dies and every day that passes, to remember what happened to the world, becomes more and more important.

BOB KUTNER, Jewish Refugee: The evil of those days can be repeated and repeated and repeated if it isn't stopped. It's a bit late to stop it now, but it's not too late to teach on-coming generations what that evil was. And you can only hope that most young people will appreciate that what happened then was the most unbelievable blot on humanity.

JM: More visitors of all ages are coming here than ever before. Perhaps they recognise the pleas in the memorial here. 'Forever let this place be a cry of despair and a warning to humanity.'

Marianne Grant died in 2007 aged 86.

Ernest Levy died in 2009 aged 84.

Bob Kutner died in 2015 aged 91.

MAKE POVERTY HISTORY MARCH
Monday 6 June 2005
STV News

Sir Bob Geldof has urged his critics to calm down. He argues that Edinburgh can and will cope with an influx of protesters, but can't be sure that his target of a million will be met.

SIR BOB GELDOF, Live8 organiser: Are a million going to show up? I mean, I'd like it, but is it likely? I don't know. I'd like if we just went up to Edinburgh to celebrate this moment where we were able to change the world a little bit, totally peacefully, in great spirits, in a celebratory mood. And most important of all, utterly peacefully. Not the least for the reason that you must show absolute respect – **absolute** respect – to those people who can't even crawl as we walk our way there. So, that would be my view on it... Calm down, you guys. It'll be fine, it'll be a wonderful moment for Edinburgh to celebrate and, indeed, all of Scotland, who should just join in...

JM: Are you concerned, though, that certainly in a Scottish context, this whole row about a million people coming to Edinburgh will overshadow the actual message itself?

BG: No.

JM: You believe it will emphasise it?

BG: I think it's absolutely irrelevant to the message. I think that this interview is a bit silly, really, because you're not dealing with the great problem of – at this second as we speak – 50,000 children are dying today in Africa. I think that's really very important.

DIARY: I made the case that the message of poverty was being overshadowed by security concerns – precisely the points that were being made in the Scottish Parliament today. He was a strange interviewee, either monosyllabic or verbose, but not unpleasant.

Saturday 2 July 2005
STV News – live from The Meadows in Edinburgh

This is *Scotland Today* live from Edinburgh and one of the biggest demonstrations this country has ever seen. An estimated 225,000 people have marched through the streets of the capital and formed a human ring around the city centre. Their message to the world leaders arriving in Gleneagles next week is clear – Make Poverty History. They hope that message will be heard.

Vox Pops

I think all these amounts of people can make a difference, even if it's a small one.

If you don't do anything you won't get anything. Join in and make your voice heard.

I hope it'll make a difference. I'm not full of confidence, but I hope it will. Damn well should because there's an awful lot of people here saying what they think and I hope someone's listening.

JM: The build-up to this rally was, arguably almost as much about the possibility of trouble as it was about the actual message itself. Thankfully, despite the huge turnout, there were no arrests.

The rally has heard from very powerful

speakers with very powerful messages, among them comic and actor Eddie Izzard and *Lord of the Rings* star Billy Boyd. They both join us now.

JM: Billy Boyd from *Lord of the Rings*, you're a Scot, have you ever seen anything like this here?

BILLY BOYD: No, I don't think we have in Scotland. I mean this is huge. Someone was just saying it's over 200,000 people. I think at one point they were expecting 40–50,000 people, so it's huge. In fact, it's so huge that me and Eddie tried to get on the march at one point and we couldn't even get on. We had to do our own.

JM: That attitude is there, but do you think that in the reality it will happen, something will change?

EDDIE IZZARD: They've made political investment in this and if this week goes off and nothing happens they're going to feel rather foolish. And people do want to leave a legacy, there's egos involved here and so there is political agendas and whatever, but I think leaving a legacy of we made slavery history now let's make poverty history, it can be done.

JM: Today's rally here in Edinburgh, a huge rally, is the beginning of a series of events building up to and through the G8 Summit at Gleneagles. A very powerful message has been sent to world leaders. This time next week we will know if they have listened.

G8 SUMMIT AT GLENEAGLES
Wednesday 6 July 2005
STV News at Six – live from Gleneagles

Good evening, live from Gleneagles where behind us eight of the world's most powerful men over the next three days will hold talks aimed at ending poverty in Africa and tackling climate change. But for the second time this week there have been shocking scenes of violence. More than 100 demonstrators have been arrested and up to 30 police officers have been badly injured, some of them requiring hospital treatment..

JM: Bernard, again the politics of policing is going to be crucial today. What have you made of today's events?

BERNARD PONSONBY, Political Editor: I think we should state a number of things. First of all, there was trouble here today, John, because a number of people were hell bent on creating trouble, particularly those anarchists who were at that eco-camp based in Stirling. Now the police would make the point that at the end of the day the world leaders arrived at Prestwick, they were transported by helicopter onto the lawn just here behind us and they're safe and sound. But we also have to bear in mind a number of people have been injured. It took us three hours to get in, it took some of our colleagues four hours to get in and at one point we were held up when literally half a dozen people were dancing in the middle of the road. The police, it appeared, were quite happy to simply watch them dance.

JM: So, should the police have been more firm with the anarchists?

BP: That's one of the questions they're going to have to ask themselves overnight. Right from day one they have used this word 'proportionate', proportionate policing, but let's just look at a number of issues. A couple of thousand people who wanted to go to Auchterarder to that G8 alternative march couldn't get there because Gleneagles was cut off because of the activity of these anarchists. These were the people who were hell bent on all of the disruption. Their activities, which were by and large away from Gleneagles, they were not arrested, cut across the civil liberties of many people in Central Scotland who couldn't go to work. It cut across the civil liberties of those people who wanted to go to a legitimate protest and couldn't get there. That's a question which I think the police are going to have to reflect on this evening.

I remember returning to the impressive media village and having to go through security checkpoints, showing a special pass. One of the people ahead of me was the First Minister of Scotland, Jack McConnell. This was Scotland and national leaders and

their entourages were being flown right onto the hotel grounds, but Scotland's First Minister was obliged to go through the same security as the rest of us. I thought it was demeaning.

The G8 Summit was overtaken on its second day, 7 July, by the bombings in London. Word began to filter through in the morning to the media centre. At first it was reported as an electrical fault on the underground. When the true scale of the horror became apparent, the summit became secondary on the news agenda.

Friday 8 July 2005
STV News – Live from Gleneagles

Good evening from Gleneagles. Poverty has not been made history. The G8 Summit, so overshadowed by events in London yesterday, has now broken up with assurances from Tony Blair that big progress has been made on Africa. Now they have agreed to double aid to $50 billion, but some charities are saying tonight that the world's richest countries have turned their backs on the world's poor.

TONY BLAIR, Prime Minister: It's in the nature of politics that you do not achieve absolutely everything you want to achieve, but nonetheless I believe we have made very substantial progress indeed. As I said to you earlier today, we did not simply by this communique make poverty history, but we do show how it can be done.

SIR BOB GELDOF, Live8 organiser: Africa and the poor of that continent have got more out of the last three days than they have ever got in any previous summit, let's be clear. And they got that because three billion people demanded that it should be so.

The biggest entourage I saw at the whole event was that fussing around U2 singer Bono.

On the final afternoon of the summit I stood on my own at our position on the TV platform looking onto Gleneagles Hotel clarifying my thoughts for our *Six O'Clock News*. A big limousine purred away and the occupant in the rear seat waved as he passed by. It was only at the last moment I realised it was the Russian President Vladimir Putin. I looked around me and couldn't see anyone else. He must have been waving at the lone figure he saw watching him and I hadn't responded. I watched my back for a few days after that.

Thursday 22 September 2005
STV News

Mike Watson, the Labour Lord and former Glasgow MSP, is spending his first night in a prison cell after being sentenced to 16 months for starting a fire and endangering lives at an upmarket hotel. The sheriff said jail was the only option for the disgraced politician who'd admitted setting curtains alight after an awards dinner for the country's top politicians.

Monday 31 October 2005
STV News

The leader of the Scottish Conservatives, David McLetchie, has resigned over the row about the taxi expenses he charged to the Scottish Parliament. The circumstances of his departure are ironically similar to those which saw the departure of the former First Minister Henry McLeish. Mr McLetchie had led the attack at the time and now he himself has been brought down.

The row had been about the use of taxis for party political rather than parliamentary purposes, which is against the rules. Mr McLetchie said the claims had been made in good faith, but recognised the damage done to the Scottish Conservatives. Annabel Goldie took over as leader unopposed.

Tuesday 20 December 2005
STV News

Just as thousands of people do every year, they promised to love, honour and respect each other in sickness and in health, for richer, for poorer, for better, for worse. John Maguire and Laurence Scott-Mackay became the first couple in Scotland to exchange vows in what has been called a 'gay wedding', or to give it its official name, a civil partnership ceremony.

2006

Friday 27 January 2006
STV News

Fifty years ago this month the body of a young woman (*Anne Knielands*) was found in East Kilbride. Her murder was the first of a number of killings that would terrorise Glasgow and Lanarkshire. A mass murderer was on the loose, killing indiscriminately. Young women never returned home from nights out and families died in their beds. The terror ended only when Peter Manuel went to the gallows at Barlinnie Prison.

JM: Peter Manuel was a career criminal. A nocturnal creature who ranged across Lanarkshire and Glasgow from his family home in Birkenshaw. But the murder of Anne Knielands made him a killer, a killer who couldn't stop.

RONNIE BURGESS, photographer: He was talking to the police officer and I thought this is my opportunity to get a picture of him. Put the camera up, took his picture and he said, 'I'll get you for that.' And the policeman said, 'Are you threatening him?' He says, 'No,' he says, 'I'm promising him.' And then the next day he came into the newspaper office looking for me... I saw him next when I was sitting in the press box at the High Court in Glasgow when Lord Cameron passed his judgement on him – 'Hang by the neck until you are dead.' And that was Peter Manuel for me.

Wednesday 1 February 2006
STV News

Anti-war vigils are taking place across Scotland tonight protesting at the mounting human cost of Britain's engagement in Iraq. It follows the death yesterday of Gordon Pritchard, the 100th British soldier to die since the conflict began. It emerged today that the Edinburgh corporal met the Prime Minister during his service in Iraq. Tony Blair is coming under ever increasing pressure to bring the troops home.

Tuesday 7 February 2006
STV News

A former policewoman who was wrongly accused of leaving her fingerprints at a murder scene has won £750 thousand in compensation. The award marks the end of a nine-year battle for justice by Shirley McKie, who even contemplated suicide as she fought to clear her name.

SUZI MAIR, Reporter: Shirley McKie's ordeal began back in 1997 when she was working as a police officer for the Strathclyde force. She was accused of leaving a fingerprint at the scene of the murder of Kilmarnock spinster Marion Ross. She always insisted she had never been there, that the mark couldn't be hers. After testifying at the trial of the man accused of the murder, she was charged with perjury, but cleared after fingerprint experts from all over the world supported her story... But she'd lost her job and reputation.

SHIRLEY McKIE: I beat them... It shows it can be done.

Wednesday 15 February 2006

DIARY: Shereen, Jane and Sarah are all leaving the company, their voluntary redundancies accepted. Alan Saunby is another one going. Shereen is the most popular face and her loss will be a blow.

The STV audience adored Shereen. She had a warmth that came through the screen and everywhere I went people would ask where she was. We came through a lot together, presented many big programmes, laughed, squabbled and made a good team. She called herself my 'other, other half' and that just about sums it up. It was my pleasure to work with her. Her departure genuinely was the end of an era at STV.

Friday 17 March 2006
STV News

Thousands of people turned out today to pay their final respects to Jimmy Johnstone. The Celtic legend died on Monday after a long battle with motor neurone disease. His former Lisbon Lion teammates, current Old Firm managers and players, joined mourners to say goodbye to a football great.

JM: They came in their thousands for the last time to cheer Jimmy Johnstone at Parkhead. They paid tribute to a man whose footballing talent brings colour to the black and white footage of the time. And his teammates remembered too. Together they bestrode the football fields of Scotland and of Europe as Champions.

BILLY McNEILL, Lisbon Lion: The first time I laid eyes on Jimmy Johnstone was whilst playing in a first team game at Celtic Park as a young player and when the ball went behind the goals at the Rangers end at Celtic Park this wee ballboy with a mass of red curly hair used to get the ball and start flicking it up. He was flicking it up 20–30 times. The team wasn't particularly sparkling then, not as good as the team today. Wee Neilie Mauchin saw him and shouted, 'quick get that ball off that wee fella before he embarrasses us further!'

WILLIE HAUGHEY, family friend: Could I read a telegram that the family received this morning that would have meant so much to Jimmy? It's actually from his hero, it says 'On behalf of all the members of this club, our deepest condolences at the death of Jimmy Johnstone... from Alfredo Di Stefano and everyone at Real Madrid.'

JM: At Parkhead the wind twisted and tormented a flag. Just as Jimmy Johnstone had done to defenders throughout the years.

SMOKING BAN
Friday 24 March 2006
STV News – live from a Glasgow pub

A new page in Scotland's history will be written this Sunday, 26 March 2006, when it becomes illegal to smoke in indoor public places. Tonight is the last Friday night smokers will be able to light-up while enjoying a night out. The measures will be enforced with a determination to halt Scotland's unenviable health record. Some killer facts: 13,000 people die every year in Scotland from using tobacco. Around 1,000 Scots who have never smoked die every year from passive smoking. It's estimated this ban will prevent 219 deaths a year from lung cancer and heart disease, and up to 187 from stroke and respiratory diseases. Of course, not everyone is in favour of the ban. There are those who argue bars could be forced to close, jobs could go, and the ban will signal the end of social culture as we know it.

JACK MCCONNELL, First Minister: I think Scotland is a law-abiding country, I think we are law-abiding people, I think people understand the arguments. The reality is that more than two-thirds of Scots are not smokers, more than two-thirds of those who do smoke want to give up and I think we will see widespread compliance for the ban, enthusiastic support for it and eventually those are particularly unhappy realising that they need to go with the majority.

As I was broadcasting from the pub on a major change to the Scottish way of life, the regular activities of a Friday night pub continued behind me, including the deliveries of Chinese takeaways.

The ban was introduced without too many problems. It is now a common sight across the country to see people standing outside pubs and offices having a fag.

Tuesday 28 March 2006
STV News

Scotland's controversial new super-regiment has been officially launched with special re-badging ceremonies at bases across the world. This effectively marks the end of Scotland's six infantry regiments. By August they will officially be five battalions in one super-regiment, the Royal Regiment of Scotland. Despite fierce criticism from anti-merger campaigners, the commander of the Royal Regiment of Scotland says he's optimistic the new identity will eventually win over the critics.

Thursday 6 April 2006
STV News – live from Fife

The deadly H5N1 bird flu virus is here in Cellardyke in Fife. A dead swan found here in the harbour just at the slipway behind me has tested positive. That was confirmed this afternoon. Tonight, the Executive has announced sweeping measures to contain the virus, but already there are 14 other birds across the country being tested. A huge area from Fife, moving north through Perth to Dundee to Angus, has been declared a wild bird risk area. A quarter of a million birds need to be taken indoors to prevent the spread of the disease.

If contracted by humans, bird flu can be lethal. Under normal circumstances humans are unlikely to be infected, but the threat of a pandemic caused by a cross-species virus remains very real. No humans were infected in Scotland and the restrictions were lifted that same month.

I was despatched to Cellardyke at short notice without knowing much about bird flu. At the back of my mind there was a slight concern about travelling to the place where this virus was potentially lurking. As I walked down the picturesque, cobbled streets of the village, I was disconcerted to see two separate splashes of vomit. This was ramped up even further when a downy feather blew into my face as the street opened up to reveal the harbour. Then on the final countdown to going on air, I glanced down at my script as a prompt and saw streaks of blood on it. I managed to control the panic as I went live. Just.

It turned out the blood had come from a paper cut on my finger. One specialist later told me, you'd have had to boil that swan down into soup and drink it before you'd even have been at risk. I didn't know that at the time, though.

STV MOVES TO PACIFIC QUAY

In July 2006 STV moved from our old studios at Cowcaddens to new premises on the south bank of the River Clyde at Pacific

Quay. It was the start of a new era. A key part of that was the move to single presentation. We took an entirely new approach and changed the role from one of presenter to that of an anchor who was the focal point for live links to reporters/interviewees at other locations. The new era was a success on every level. The newer studio allowed us to make *Scotland Today* look so much better. Our audience climbed significantly and there was widespread critical praise. For me, STV *News* has never been better.

This was when the 'I'm John MacKay' took on a life of its own as a catchphrase. I had said it often enough before in programmes with other presenters, but maybe it stood out more when I was on my own. It is repeated back to me constantly. Indeed, I've been told more than once that a child's first words have been 'Ohn A-Kay.'

Tuesday 22 August 2006
STV News

One in ten immigrants who has come to the UK in the past two years from Europe, has settled in Scotland. The majority of the 32,000 people who've arrived here are working in the hospitality industry. Both Glasgow and Edinburgh already have large Polish communities, but other nationalities are now establishing their identities.

Monday 18 September 2006
STV News

Up until now it's been known as the Squinty Bridge, but today the new crossing over the River Clyde in Glasgow was formally opened to traffic and given its official name. The *(£20 million)* Clyde Arc, as it's now being called, is the first new road and pedestrian bridge to be built over the river in more than 30 years.

KELLY-ANN BISHOP, Reporter: The four-lane bridge, which can also be used by pedestrians, will be able to cope with the addition of a tram system in the future. But for now, it's hoped the new crossing will not only make travelling easier, but also, with its iconic image, reflect Glasgow's reputation as a city with style.

The four lanes have essentially been squeezed into two, with two, usually empty, bus-lanes. It is the cause of much frustration during the extended queues of cars attending concerts at the adjacent SEC campus.

Monday 2 October 2006
STV News

A police investigation is underway tonight into perjury allegations arising from the Tommy Sheridan defamation trial. It was just two months ago that Mr Sheridan won an action against the *News of the World*, which had printed sex claims about him. But yesterday the Sunday newspaper published video footage which allegedly show the MSP admitting a number of the claims.

Thursday 5 October 2006
STV News

The appointment of the first woman *(Eilish Angiolini)* to be Lord Advocate was overshadowed today by an unprecedented row over her legal experience...

JAMIE LIVINGSTONE, reporter: Annabel Goldie *(Scottish Conservative Leader)* questioned the depth of Eilish Angiolini's legal experience after she was nominated by the First Minister to become the new Lord Advocate... Mr McConnell made waves when he appointed the coalman's daughter from Glasgow as Solicitor General five years ago. She was the first non-advocate to hold the office. Today, Miss Angiolini branded that appointment a 'huge leap of faith' as she insisted that she will protect the weakest and worst in Scottish society in her new role.

Wednesday 1 November 2006
STV News

According to a new poll, more than half of the electorate now want an end to the Union. In the ICM poll, 51 per cent said they are for an independent Scotland, 39 per cent against and 10 per cent said they didn't know. The findings have also handed a boost to the SNP, as 32 per cent said they would vote Nationalist compared to 30 per cent for Labour on the constituency vote in next year's Scottish elections.

Wednesday 8 November 2006
STV News

'Savage and barbaric'. Three men are found guilty of the race-hate murder of 15-year-old Kriss Donald. The judge condemned the crime as a cold-blooded execution. The killers will serve a minimum of 70 years behind bars. A crime of appalling inhumanity. Kriss Donald was bundled into a car, subjected to nearly five hours of agonising torture, before being stabbed and burned alive. The reason? He was white. The three killers will now face life behind bars for the 15-year-old's murder and abduction.

Kriss Donald was picked at random. He was the wrong colour in the wrong place at the wrong time.

2007

Monday 8 January 2007
DIARY: The launch of our split news operation, where we split the programme mid-way through for five or six minutes and the east coast gets news more local to them and same for the west.

Tuesday 23 January 2007
STV News

The First Minister Jack McConnell says he's disappointed to have been dragged into the cash-for-peerages controversy. Scotland's Labour Leader was questioned by police on a nomination he made to the House of Lords as part of their ten-month-long inquiry into the alleged sale of honours for money by leading politicians.

The Cash for Honours scandal had begun the previous year after complaints by the SNP MP Angus MacNeil that wealthy donors to the Labour Party had been offered peerages. No one was charged after an investigation lasting more than a year. Tony Blair was the first serving Prime Minister to be interviewed (as a witness) during a police investigation.

Wednesday 24 January 2007
STV News

Over the last four years, thousands of youngsters have been taking part in one of the biggest ever studies into family life. Its initial findings reveal step-families will soon outnumber any other. Single parents now raise one in five children and grandparents play an even greater role in their upbringing.

Thursday 1 March 2007
STV News

The Royal Bank of Scotland has announced the biggest profit ever made by a Scottish company. Edinburgh-based RBS made £9.2

billion, 16 per cent more than the previous year. Thousands of its Scottish staff are to receive bonuses for the ninth year in a row.

SCOTTSH ELECTION 2007
Wednesday 2 May 2007
STV News

The campaigning is almost over. Early tomorrow morning the polling stations open for what is expected to be one of the most dramatic elections in recent history. The polls show the gap between the two leading parties is the closest in more than 30 years.

BERNARD PONSONBY, Political Editor: Since last year Labour have fought this election on the policy of their principal opponents – independence. Yes, they believe they have a responsibility to say to voters this will lead to chaos and you will end up paying. Jack McConnell admits it's negative. Is that negativity born out of desperation? Is it better ground than fighting on your record and defending a lame duck Prime Minister? Well, the polls are showing that Labour are clawing their way back – if they are to be the largest party on Friday the strategy will be vindicated. If not, perhaps recrimination and even resignation will be the order of the day. You simply can't lose and expect to lead. The stakes are high for Jack McConnell tomorrow. I think he personally has had a good campaign, but has he done enough to hold onto power and to his job? Over to the voters.

MICHAEL CROW, Political Correspondent: It is just too close to call. There are a number of important factors which could determine whether the SNP win this election. Firstly, have they done enough to attract the undecided voters? Secondly, will disaffected Labour voters switch to the SNP or stay at home? There is no doubt that the core SNP vote will turn out. They are enthused, they feel their time has come. The question is, has Alex Salmond done enough to persuade people who haven't voted SNP before to vote for him tomorrow? They've spent over a million pounds on the campaign. They are ahead in the polls. If they can't win this election then one wonders if their time will ever come.

Friday 4 May 2007
STV News – live from the Scottish Parliament with Andrea Brymer

Good evening from the capital and welcome to this 60-minute special, live from the Scottish Parliament. The Scottish National Party have won the Scottish elections, by the narrowest of margins. Within the last half hour, at the last count, of the last region to declare, the SNP secured victory by 47 seats to Labour's 46. But how, here at the heart of Scottish democracy, could things have gone so wrong? How were a hundred and 50,000 voters written off? How could so many ballot papers have been spoiled?

Just to confirm the total results – the SNP on 47 seats, Labour on 46, the Conservatives on 17, the Liberal Democrats on 16, the Greens on two and an independent, Margo MacDonald.

JM: So, the SNP have won the Election by one seat. Nicola Sturgeon of the party joins us now at the Scottish Parliament. Congratulations on your success.

NICOLA STURGEON, Deputy Leader, SNP: It's a tremendous achievement, John, the people of Scotland have today chosen a new political path. They've opted to put the SNP in the driving seat of Scotland's new Government. It's an enormous responsibility and it's one we're determined to discharge with humility, with imagination and with a great deal of passion.

JM: But it's not quite the margin you would have wished.

NS: We are in a PR system and, of course, narrow margins are to be expected, but we've not only won the largest number of seats, we're significantly ahead in terms of the popular vote. I think the SNP have resoundingly won this election. Labour have lost it. The people of Scotland want now a new political direction and it's for the SNP to lead them in that new direction.

JM: On this, the most controversial of elections, it was an extremely tense night at polling stations across the whole country. Every vote has been hard fought for in one the closest ever battles between Labour and the SNP.

MICHAEL CROW, Political Correspondent: It was meant to be the most exciting election for a generation. It has ended up being a national embarrassment and a democratic farce. Up to 150,000 people have had their votes rejected because of a catalogue of problems. Confusion over how to fill in the ballot papers has rendered many invalid. People have been putting crosses in the wrong place and numbers where they shouldn't have. This has led to problems with the new electronic counting system, delayed results and left democracy in chaos.

ALEX SALMOND, Leader, SNP: Scotland wants a change of government, they want the SNP to be given the opportunity to show what we can do. That's why we've been voted in as the largest party – by one seat in terms of seats, but by a very, very substantial vote in terms of the popular vote and we've got to fulfil that obligation and to approach people in that manner.

JACK MCCONNELL, Leader, Scottish Labour: Five days ago all of the pundits were writing us off and Labour has achieved the most significant turnaround in the final week of an election campaign in Scotland in living memory.

BERNARD PONSONBY, Political Editor: For the last 50 years Labour have been the dominant force in Scottish politics. 3 May 2007 will be the date when the historians will say, perhaps it has just come to an end. The SNP have won this election, there is no question of that, they have won the most seats and they've also won the popular vote... The Labour percentage share of the vote was only down slightly. What actually happened in this election was that the SNP managed to squeeze the minor parties.

Wednesday 9 May 2007
STV News

Scotland's 129 new MSPs were sworn in today at the Scottish Parliament, however they failed to elect a Presiding Officer and had to adjourn proceedings until Monday. Meanwhile, talks between the SNP and the Greens to set up an Executive are ongoing, but the Liberal Democrats are still refusing to negotiate.

One of the first acts of the new SNP administration was to change the title of the Scottish Executive to the Scottish Government.

STV News (cont)

Glasgow's Commonwealth Games Bid team have made their final pitch to host the competition in 2014. During a ceremony in London earlier they submitted their final plans for the Games with a display of traditional Scottish song and dance to convince the judges of their merits. Our reporter Debi Edward was there and joins us now from London, Debi, how did it go?

DEBI EDWARD, Reporter: I think the judges couldn't fail to be impressed with the bid team and a rousing rendition of 'Scotland the Brave'. As for the bid document itself, well I haven't quite had time to digest all of its 600 pages but it does give a comprehensive breakdown of the venues and costs of the Games. The team claim to have the £338 million bill covered and 90 per cent of the infrastructure already in place or due for completion within three to four years. This all made for a confident presentation this lunchtime.

Monday 14 May 2007
STV News

The days continue to pass, there are still few leads, but the McCann family's belief that their daughter, Madeleine, is safe and well is unwavering. Her father Gerry McCann said that until the family saw 'concrete evidence to the contrary' they continued to be convinced she is safe. His wife Kate, clinging to hope, said she could not even consider leaving Portugal without her daughter.

Madeleine McCann disappeared on holiday with her family in Portugal on the evening of 3 May 2007. The story circulated on 4 May, but because of the Scottish election result and the verdict in the first Peter Tobin trial, there was no space to carry it. At the time that didn't seem significant. The story has never gone away as her parents continue to hope that she will be found.

ALEX SALMOND BECOMES FIRST MINISTER

Wednesday 16 May 2007
STV News

Scotland has a new First Minister and, for the first time, he is a nationalist. The SNP Leader Alex Salmond was elected after winning a vote of all MSPs. He beat the Labour Leader Jack McConnell by the narrowest of margins. But with the Conservatives and the Lib Dems abstaining it was enough for history to be made.

BERNARD PONSONBY, Political Editor – at the Scottish Parliament: After so many false dawns they are finally in Government. Independence is closer but only really in a theoretical sense. Why? Because tomorrow the cold chill of realpolitik will hit Alex Salmond. He has no majority in this place. No majority on the bureau that decides the business and no majority on the committees. The next four years will be a long slog, but an exciting one nevertheless.

JM: Politicians from all parties have also been paying tribute to the outgoing First Minister, Jack McConnell. Today he said it had been a privilege and an honour to lead Scotland for the last five-and-a-half years and he hoped he had left the country in a better state than when he had come to power.

MICHAEL CROW, Political Correspondent: He defined Devolution by tackling hitherto taboos – the smoking ban, sectarianism, Labour's hold on local government. The legacy is one of steadying devolution.

GORDON BROWN BECOMES PRIME MINISTER

Wednesday 27 June 2007
STV News – live from Westminster

It has been a day of ceremony, a day of history here at Westminster – the day a Scot once again became the Prime Minister of the United Kingdom... 27 June 2007 a date Gordon Brown is unlikely to forget. As power was handed from Tony Blair to Number Ten's new incumbent, it marked the realisation of a lifelong dream for the boy from Kirkcaldy.

TONY BLAIR, Prime Minister – in the House of Commons: I wish everyone, friend or foe, well. And that is that. The end.

GORDON BROWN, Prime Minister – outside 10 Downing Street: I have just accepted the invitation from Her Majesty the Queen to form a government... I grew up in the town that I now represent in Parliament. I went to the local school. I wouldn't be standing here without the opportunities that I received there. And I want the best of chances for everyone. That is my mission.

JM: It's important to Scotland, obviously, that the relationship between the First Minister and the new Prime Minister is workable. Do you think you can achieve that?

ALEX SALMOND, First Minister: I'm quite certain I'll get on with Gordon Brown a lot better than I could get on with Tony Blair. Indeed, I'm certain I'll get on with Gordon Brown a lot better than Gordon Brown got on with Tony Blair. So, I'm looking at this very constructively and I want to work as best we can for the people of Scotland, as well as having legitimate disagreements about the constitutional future of our country.

JM: So, Gordon Brown is now the Prime Minister of the United Kingdom. The Blair era is over. The Brown era has begun.

Our programme from Westminster was a challenging one. I was standing beneath a pergola to protect me from the rain that had been pouring all afternoon. Minutes before going on air, the cameraman asked me to take a few paces back to catch more of the light. At that instant a gust of wind blew beneath the pergola, lifting up the roof and a pool of water that had gathered there. I was soaked and had no idea where it had come from. I thought someone had thrown something onto me. The only choice was to run the few hundred yards from our position on College Green back to the media centre at Millbank. An alert member of staff there had seen what happened and came running out with towels. The quickest of dry downs and then ready to go on air. What more could go wrong? I had pre-recorded our opening titles. As soon as they started playing all contact with the studio was lost (including mobile phones). I knew the titles were running and I tried to judge when I should start speaking. It wasn't entirely clean, but it could have been much worse. Bernard Ponsonby was at Downing Street and comms with him went down during our two-way. Bernard's input was a significant part of the programme, so he had to make his way quickly from Downing Street to our broadcast position on College Green. It is an abiding memory of Bernard running towards me with, in his own words, 'my three arses bouncing off the pavement.'

Tony Blair's premiership will be remembered as one that started with energy and hope in 1997, but was overtaken by spin and will be forever tainted by the Iraq War. How a man of Tony Blair's apparent political surefootedness could have got it so wrong will always be a mystery. We went to war in the pretext of Iraq having weapons of mass destruction ready to strike against us. They didn't and few people believed they did.

GLASGOW AIRPORT BOMBING

Saturday 30 June 2007
STV News

A blazing car has crashed into the main terminal building at Glasgow Airport. The incident happened around 3.15pm this afternoon. The airport has now been sealed off. Passengers have been evacuated as police try to piece together exactly what happened.

Two Islamist terrorists drove a jeep loaded with gas canisters into the entrance of Glasgow Airport. They had based themselves in a house in Houston in Renfrewshire as they prepared to explode two car bombs in London. When that plot failed and they knew the police were onto them, they tried to carry out a terror attack at Glasgow Airport. That failed also through a combination of their incompetence and the heroics of police and public at the scene. One of them died from burns a month later. The other – a doctor who'd been working in a Scottish hospital – was jailed for life.

I had gone on holiday that day and the Glasgow Airport attack must rank as the biggest story I missed.

BILLY CONNOLLY

Thursday 2 August 2007
STV News

Billy Connolly says the silent majority in Scotland should stand up to the minority of bigots who give the country a bad name. He has been named as patron of the Celtic Foundation, which has tackling sectarianism as one of its principle aims. Speaking to *Scotland Today*, the Scottish comic legend was frank in his condemnation.

BILLY CONNOLLY: I think the only way to prevent bigotry is by example – by children looking at you at a game, by looking at you standing up for yourself and saying how much you dislike this thing... It's not good saying something when the news is on. A sort of 'That'll be right' attitude when someone says something about Israel, about Protestants... It's a sharp intake of breath when someone says something, that's where it all begins. It starts at home. And then they start hanging out with people who feel the same way. I am not a bigot, I don't spend time with them. I know I can recognise them a mile away, the Celtic supporter with their weird tattoos. Guys approach me with them. I think it's getting better.

Billy Connolly was a comedy hero of mine and as we waited to do the interview he proved why. He didn't work a routine, he was just a naturally funny, funny man.

JACK McCONNELL RESIGNS AS SCOTTISH LABOUR LEADER

Wednesday 15 August 2007
STV News

The former First Minister Jack McConnell has resigned as Leader of the Scottish Labour Party. He had been under pressure to quit his job after losing power in the Holyrood elections back in May. He will remain an MSP, but will also carry out education work in Africa. Tonight, Wendy Alexander has emerged as the overwhelming favourite to take over as leader.

JACK McCONNELL: I was in no doubt when I took over that devolution was in trouble and I had to steady the ship. That was very much my view at the time. And I think we proved over the last four years that once you've steadied the ship and you've set a course, it is possible to make progress, and that happened in a whole range of areas.

ALEX SALMOND, First Minister: I think he once said – you would judge every First Minister by whether he left Scotland a better place than he found it. I think judged on that criteria he leaves a substantial contribution to Scottish public life and I wish him well.

NICOL STEPHEN, Leader, Scottish Liberal Democrats: He was always prepared to set aside narrow party dogma to work in coalition. Being First Minister when there are two parties in power is never easy.

WENDY ALEXANDER BECOMES NEW SCOTTISH LABOUR LEADER

Tuesday 21 August 2007
STV News

Wendy Alexander is the new Leader of the Scottish Labour Party. She was the sole candidate for the position when nominations closed today and she will be formally installed on 14 September.

WENDY ALEXANDER, Scottish Labour Leader: I think what happened today is that Labour signalled it's ready to move on. We need to reform the party, we need to review our policies and we need to reconnect with voters and that's what we're all united in doing... I think what Scotland is looking for from its politicians is change, there's no doubt about that. But I think the change they're really looking for is social and economic change. It is about schools and hospitals much more than they're looking for constitutional change and so the real question is, is Scotland interested in the people's priorities or in Alex Salmond's priorities? And that's the debate that we're going to take to him on behalf of the people.

Monday 8 October 2007
STV News

The Prime Minister has been defending his handling of the on/off election debacle. Gordon Brown did admit that he had considered calling a snap election, but denied he'd been put off by a Tory surge in the opinion polls

There was intense speculation, fuelled by Downing Street, that Gordon Brown would call a quick election soon after becoming Prime Minister to take advantage of favourable polls. His reputation was damaged when he decided not to, being accused of being a bottler and a ditherer.

Tuesday 23 October 2007

DIARY: Lucky enough to get a ticket for tonight's Rangers v Barcelona clash in the Champions League. It was a defensive siege for most of the game, but Rangers held out for a 0–0 draw in an enthralling game. The young Argentinian Messi is superb.

Reporters at Ibrox were served with scotch pies and bovrils at half-time. It was amusing to watch the Spanish journalists studying the pies in wonder, despite the reassurances from their Scottish counterparts. At the end of the game, almost to a man, they had

nibbled away at the crust of the pie, but the grey meat was left untouched.

Wednesday 31 October 2007

DIARY: The Chief Inspector of Prisons made yet another report from yet another prison highlighting overcrowding. We could have taken any report from any month over the past ten years and done the same thing.

Friday 9 November 2007
STV News

Good evening from Glasgow – tonight the heart of the Commonwealth. Over a quarter of the world's population – that's almost two billion people have chosen this city to host the 2014 Games.

DEBI EDWARD, Reporter in Sri Lanka: Yes, in seven years' time it's hoped the result which was dramatically delivered here in Sri Lanka will transform Scotland's biggest city, its people and its health.

JM: So, this is where the hard work begins. Glasgow has got seven years to get ready for 2014. A great deal of planning is already in place to make sure we have world-class facilities capable of hosting top-flight events.

Wednesday 14 November 2007
STV News

For 16 years the family of Scottish schoolgirl Vicky Hamilton have endured the agony of not knowing where she was. Tonight, that long wait is over. Her remains have been found in the garden of a house in Kent by police investigating the disappearance of another teenager. The house was previously occupied by Peter Tobin.

Sunday 30 December 2007
STV News

Tributes are being paid to Motherwell captain Phil O'Donnell, who died after collapsing during yesterday's match against Dundee United. The 35-year-old's club has described his death as an 'unspeakable tragedy' and fans have been laying flowers and other tributes at Fir Park.

2008

Wednesday 9 January 2008
STV News

Kenny Richey spent 20 years on death row, but tonight he is only moments away from a new life at home in Scotland. The 43-year-old was freed from prison in Ohio on Monday. On leaving jail he thanked all those supporters 'who believed in his innocence'. Tonight, he will have chance to thank them in person and will be coming through the terminal at Edinburgh Airport shortly.

Kenneth Richey, who had been raised in Scotland, had been sentenced to death 21 years previously for setting fire to an apartment in which a two-year-old girl died. He consistently denied guilt.

DIARY: The First Minister, Alex Salmond, was touring the building. When he came into the studio where I was waiting, we had a brief conversation about Hearts – his team. He seems relaxed and assured in his role.

Saturday 15 March 2008

DIARY: Down to London for the ITN News Awards which are not as prestigious as the RTS Awards. Quite a squad of us. The usual routine with these award ceremonies is that your seating indicates how you've done. We never anticipate much at the ITV awards because we're not formally part of ITV. Anyway, my seat was A1 with the others beside me. I assumed we must have done well. We hadn't. Only won 'Image of the Year' for the burning Cherokee at Glasgow Airport and that was actually taken by a viewer.

RANGERS IN THE UEFA CUP FINAL 2008

Wednesday 14 May 2008
STV News – live from Manchester

Good evening from Manchester on a night when a team from Glasgow are now on the brink of becoming European legends. Rangers play Zenit St Petersburg in the UEFA Cup Final. There will be a worldwide audience of half a billion people and STV is the only place to watch all the action live from seven o'clock. *(aerial shot)* Outside the stadium we can see some dramatic images from Manchester City centre. They were saying earlier that the sun was out, the sky was blue and the earth was blue, too.

STV News at 10.30pm – live from Manchester

Ranger's UEFA Cup dream has come to an end. In an enthralling cup final in Manchester, the Ibrox side lost 2–0.

DIARY: A big day and one that ended in predictable disappointment. Until mid-afternoon I was focused on the fanzone at Albert Square, presenting the morning and lunchtime bulletins from a bus there. I attempted to go in amongst the crowd to do my blog around 10.00am, but was mobbed and pulled almost to the ground and had beer sprayed on me, which made it pointless.

Even at that time some people were hammered and I sensed that the exuberance could spill over into trouble. In fairness, there were a lot of people just having a good time, but the usual scum let them down. The state of some fans in the streets was appalling. I was embarrassed. Mind you, at that stage the local Mancunians I spoke to seemed to be enjoying the atmosphere.

I went to the City of Manchester stadium for late afternoon passing so many pissed fans on the way. Our programme at 6.00pm felt like a good programme, all anchored from trackside.

Disappointing, but Rangers didn't deserve to win. I waited for the presentation of the trophy just about ten rows behind me and headed off to do the late bulletin outside the stadium. Credit to the fans inside the stadium who applauded Zenit as they took the trophy. The late bulletin was really very good, but already reports of trouble after a big screen failed at the Piccadilly fanzone. Got a lift back from cameraman Michael Hunter and others and the flotsam on the streets was a grim sight.

Thursday 15 May 2008
STV News

It started in high spirits, an invasion of Scottish football fans partying in the sun, excited by a UEFA Cup Final. But when a big screen failed, leaving thousands of fans unable to watch the game, the night turned into one of running battles and violence. Gordon Brown today said the minority of Rangers fans involved in the chaos in Manchester were a 'disgrace'

DIARY: The usual excuses will be trotted out about the failure of the screens and police over reaction. The fact is that unfortunately Scotland has a significant population of idiots who cannot control themselves with alcohol. There was the usual bottle throwing of course, which beggars belief. Who are they trying to hurt?

When we had travelled down to Manchester we saw banners stretched out on motorway footbridges and flyovers as far down as Liverpool wishing Rangers all the best. On the way home we saw only two as we came into Glasgow. One said, 'Welcome home losers.' It was funny.

Thursday 15 May 2008 *(cont)*
STV News

The man who many said put the Celtic back into Celtic, Tommy Burns, has died from cancer at the age of 51. The former Parkhead player and manager was loved and respected by fans across Glasgow's often bitter footballing divide. Hundreds of them have been paying tribute to him at Celtic Park since early this morning.

RESIGNATION OF WENDY ALEXANDER AS SCOTTISH LABOUR LEADER

Thursday 26 June 2008
STV News

It has been another traumatic day for the Scottish Labour Leader Wendy Alexander. The Scottish Parliament's Standards Committee has voted to suspend her from Parliament for a day for failing to register donations to her leadership campaign. Tonight, she insists she will remain as Labour Leader as she suffers the potential humiliation of being the first party chief to be banned from Parliament.

Wendy Alexander resigned as leader of Scottish Labour two days later. She maintained throughout that she had followed parliamentary advice on registering donations.

Saturday 13 September 2008
STV News

Iain Gray is the new Leader of the Scottish Labour Party. His margin of victory over Cathy Jamieson and Andy Kerr was more comfortable than expected. And he signalled he's ready to axe the council tax, back more powers for the Scottish Parliament and support prison sentences for carrying knives.

THE BANKING CRISIS

Monday 15 September 2008
STV News

Share prices at two of Scotland's largest banks, HBOS and RBS, have fallen sharply in response to news that America's fourth largest investment bank, Lehman Brothers, has filed for bankruptcy. HBOS saw its share price plummet by 30 per cent while RBS saw a drop of more than 12 per cent.

Tuesday 16 September 2008
STV News

The share price of one of Scotland's biggest companies took another pounding today as the fallout continued from the collapse of the American bank, Lehman Brothers. Halifax Bank of Scotland has seen its stock market value halved in just two days. There was more bad news for the economy when it was announced that inflation was now close to 5 per cent.

Thursday 18 September 2008
STV News

It has created Britain's biggest bank, but there are fears tonight the Lloyds TSB takeover of HBOS could cost thousands of Scottish jobs. The Edinburgh-based company has been swallowed up in a deal worth more than £12 billion. Union leaders say compulsory redundancies must be avoided.

Tuesday 30 September 2008

DIARY: Still concerns about the financial meltdown of the markets and threats of bank collapses. For most people, though, I think it is a bit removed. Maybe when the costs of loans increase, or if the economy begins to collapse and jobs are hit, then people will feel affected, but not yet.

Wednesday 8 October 2008
STV News

In the most dramatic day in the history of British banking, the Government have put together a multi-billion-pound rescue package aimed at restoring confidence in a battered system, protecting savers and homeowners and allaying fears about the security of deposits. The politicians have been united today. The markets have steadied. But tonight it's too early to say if the corner has been turned.

BERNARD PONSONBY, Political Editor: In 50 years' time economic historians will reflect that 8 October 2008 was the day when the state bailed out capitalist failure of quite breathtaking proportions. Normally, bankers rail against Government regulation and intervention. Yesterday, the suits held a corporate begging bowl out to the very taxpayers they have done so much to harm. Before the markets opened the Chancellor revealed details of the rescue plan. The Government would shore up banks by buying £25 billion in shares. A further £25 billion would be made available to improve liquidity, should it be needed. £200 billion for the Bank of England to protect banks from going bust. Almost immediately the stock market fell, but banking shares, hammered yesterday in a vortex of panic, rallied... For the man in the street, well, worries about savings should logically disappear. Greater lending by banks might kickstart the housing market with better mortgage deals.

Bernard was a model of impartiality, but his anger with what greedy, incompetent bankers had subjected us to is barely contained here.

LIVE BROADCAST FROM INSIDE BARLINNIE PRISON

Wednesday 12 November 2008
STV News – live from inside Barlinnie Prison

Good evening from behind the bars of E-hall in Glasgow's Barlinnie prison. Within these century-old walls 1,664 men. Among them fraudsters, drink drivers, gangsters, murderers, child abusers and rapists.

Scotland's biggest jail, currently at 40 per cent over-capacity is bursting at the seams with criminals. Rough justice – or just desserts – is what we're looking at tonight, as our reporters are granted unprecedented access to all areas. Over the next half hour – how the prison copes with such numbers. The scourge of drugs. The habitual criminal who continually reoffends. We'll also hear the victims of the inmates and how their lives have been ruined.

The highs and lows of drug dealing and drug abuse are what brings large numbers here. The habits don't end at the jail cell door. Barlinnie is the largest single supplier of methadone in Europe. A lot of hard work goes into rehabilitating addicts before release, but vital efforts are hampered by the smuggling of a steady flow of drugs into the prison.

DIARY: As we went on air I was only getting white noise through my earpiece, but I had to keep it in my ear or it would have been seen. I relied on a visual cue and that went smoothly. The prisoners started shouting and hammering doors when I made reference to 'murderers and rapists' being among them – which is true, although there aren't many there. That noise was maintained for much of the programme. It all seemed to pass very quickly. I could tell it had gone well. The prison guys were pleased as well, they thought it had been fair.

I was very taken by how comparatively relaxed the regime seemed to be, with prisoners and guards and us mingling. That doesn't change the fact that there are bad bastards in there. However, clearly there are people in there who shouldn't be and nothing is gained by society or them by their incarceration.

Tuesday 2 December 2008
STV News – live from Bathgate

Good evening from Bathgate in West Lothian, the town where convicted killer Peter Tobin lived. The town where Vicky Hamilton died. Seventeen years it took to bring Tobin to justice, a 17-year-long nightmare for Vicky's family. But at the High Court in Dundee finally justice, closure. And a life sentence for the Butcher of Bathgate.

2009

Wednesday 7 January 2009
STV News

The first seven days of 2009 have been dominated by the cash crisis across the globe, the effects on the UK economy and the very real impact on Scots facing a new year on the dole. Tonight, the car industry here is the latest to be hit by the worldwide economic tsunami. Figures from the Scottish Motor Trade Association show that car sales in Scotland fell by 15 per cent last year. There are now calls for the Treasury to step in and ensure banks release more finance to consumers.

Monday 19 January 2009
STV News

The Prime Minister today said he was angry with the Royal Bank of Scotland as it announced it faced the biggest loss in British corporate history. Gordon Brown spoke out as the Government announced its second multi-billion-pound bail out of Britain's banks. He said the Edinburgh-based bank had taken irresponsible risks with people's money.

Thursday 26 February 2009
STV News

As report cards go, it's the worst possible result. RBS – the Royal Bank of Scotland – once the world's fifth largest bank has posted the worst loss in UK financial history – £24 billion. The dire news comes as it emerged that the bank's former Chief Executive Sir Fred Goodwin, widely blamed for the bank's demise, is receiving a £650,000 a year pension. And there are reports tonight that Sir Fred has rejected calls to give up that pension.

STV News (cont)

He boasted about how well he got on with the boy, but behind the facade was a cold and calculating man who killed his girlfriend's son. Robert Cunningham dabbled with heroin and smoked cannabis every day. One afternoon last March, he lost his temper with Brandon Muir and stamped on the toddler hard enough to rupture the child's bowel. Today at the High Court in Glasgow a jury took just an hour and a half to convict him of killing him.

DIARY: An unremittingly grim case. His mother's scumbag 'lover' hit the child so hard that his intestines burst and then they didn't get him attention. The animal got off with culpable homicide because the child might have survived if he had received emergency treatment, which the bastard didn't get for him. Once again, the law is seen to be an ass. I cut my interview with the social workers. They were saying bureaucracy, lack of manpower and public support make their job very difficult.

Tuesday 10 March 2009

DIARY: A newsroom meeting this evening to discuss the new relaunch on 23 March. The bombshell dropped was that the name *Scotland Today* is being ditched – as is *North Tonight* – and we're all now '*STV News*'.

Wednesday 11 March 2009
STV News

Falling house prices, rising repossessions – the Scottish property market is in the grip of decline. The situation is blamed on a shortage of available credit with under-fire banks refusing to lend. Today, light at the end of the tunnel. Edinburgh-based RBS announced a massive cash injection in a move it's hoped will kick start Scotland's property market.

Thursday 2 April 2009
STV News – live from Aberdeen Harbour with Andrea Brymer

Good evening from the harbour at Aberdeen. Tonight, Scotland mourns 16 oil workers lost to the North Sea. Sixteen men who were just doing their job. Sixteen men who were just miles from home. In the hours since the tragedy happened the search for the men and the reasons for the tragedy go on. Tonight, the very latest on our country's worst offshore disaster since Piper Alpha.

DAVID MARSLAND, Reporter: Officially, this is still a search and rescue mission... But it was long ago conceded that there is no hope of the eight men still missing being found alive... Some wreckage has already been recovered. It's being examined for clues as to what caused a helicopter flying in perfect conditions to suddenly crash, apparently without warning.

The accident was caused by the failure of a gearbox.

Tuesday 5 May 2009
STV News

To snooker and after winning the World Championship for a third time, John Higgins says more titles will follow. The Scot's victory over Shaun Murphy has earned him a £250,000 payout. The triumph also sees the Wizard of Wishaw join an elite band of players.

Monday 25 May 2009
Sir Alex Ferguson Documentary

In 48 hours Sir Alex Ferguson is poised to become the greatest ever British manager. Victory in the Champions League Final in Rome will propel him to a realm never achieved before. Greater than Busby. Greater than Paisley. Greater than Clough. Greater, even, than Stein.

SIR ALEX FERGUSON *(speaking in 1993 on taking his Manchester United team on a tour of Govan)*: I took them down to my wee bakers in Shaw Street and I got ten dozen tattie scones, six dozen scones, cakes, biscuits, the lot. And the players are going off their heads waiting for me. And, of course, all the punters are congregating around the bus. The window opens about the third storey up. 'Haw Alex, come on up for a cup of tea.' I says, 'I can't, I've got the team.' She says, 'Bring them up!' *(laughs*

The documentary was to mark Sir Alex's attempt to win the Champions League for a third time with Manchester United. They lost 2–0 to Barcelona.

Thursday 20 August 2009
STV News

Hundreds have been celebrating the return of the Lockerbie Bomber in Tripoli after he was released on compassionate grounds – a decision US President Barack Obama has labelled a mistake. Terminally ill with cancer, Abdelbaset Al-Megrahi was shown mercy by Scotland's Justice Secretary. But the move has provoked anger from American relatives who described his release as disgusting.

KENNY MACASKILL, Scottish Justice Secretary: Mr Al-Megrahi did not show his victims any comfort or compassion. No compassion was shown by him to them. But that alone is not a reason for us to deny compassion to him and his family in his final days. Our justice system demands that judgement be imposed, but compassion be available. For these reasons and these reasons alone, it is my decision that Mr Abdelbaset Ali Mohamed Al-Megrahi, convicted in 2001 for the Lockerbie Bombing, now terminally ill with prostate cancer, be released on compassionate grounds and be allowed to return to Libya to die.

Megrahi died in May 2012.

Wednesday 16 December 2009
STV News

He abducted, drugged and murdered three young women, showing not a shred of remorse for his victims or their families. But Peter Tobin has finally been revealed for what he is, a sexually motivated serial killer. A jury found him guilty of murdering 18-year-old Dinah McNicol in 1991. He's already serving life sentences for taking the lives of Vicky Hamilton and Angelika Kluk.

Tonight, the police have issued photographs of jewellery they believe could be trophies from other victims.

David Cowan, Chief Reporter, STV News

Every night during Peter Tobin's trial for the murder of Angelika Kluk, our cameras were able to film him being escorted to a prison van parked outside the High Court in Edinburgh. The vans were too big to fit into the garage at the back of the building, and we stockpiled footage of the daily ritual.

Tobin was clearly concerned about his image. With one eye on the TV crews, he would chat amiably to his guards about what was for tea in the jail that night, looking like the harmless old victim of a terrible misunderstanding.

The mask dropped with an almighty clang after he was convicted. As he was frog-marched away to start his first life sentence, Tobin kicked a crouching photographer in the throat. For the first time we saw Mr Hyde, his face contorted with rage.

I looked into Tobin's background for STV's coverage at the end of the trial. He was a convicted sex offender on the run from the police, working under a false name at a Glasgow church, when he subjected Angelika to a hideous death. One church volunteer said to me with complete sincerity, 'How often do you meet evil? I don't know. But I know I met it the night I met Peter Tobin.'

In the months that followed the true extent of that evil emerged. Two more victims, murdered years before, buried in a back garden in the south of England.

It was impossible not to become involved emotionally. I got to know the families of the two girls later discovered in England and realised the unique hell suffered by the relatives of missing people. After years of tortuous uncertainty, it was almost a relief when they were told the bodies had been found, because at last they knew where they were, at last they had them back.

Some weeks after the Angelika Kluk verdict, Tobin was brought back to court to face the music for going on the run. Given his life sentence, it was academic, but I went along for the sake of completeness and a chance conversation opened up a new chapter. I was told the police were going to search Tobin's former home in Bathgate, having realised he was living there in 1991, when a teenager called Vicky Hamilton went missing in the town. The police confirmed their plans and we broke the story that night. Their search uncovered a knife hidden in the attic, bearing traces of Vicky's DNA. Tobin was charged with abduction.

Soon afterwards another police force started searching another house, 400 miles away in Kent. Tobin had moved to Margate from Bathgate a few weeks after Vicky went missing. The police were looking for Dinah McNicol, an 18-year-old who'd vanished later that summer as she made her way home from a music festival. They found a body in the back garden.

I phoned a contact. I told them I didn't expect them to say whether it was Vicky, but would it be a waste of STV's money if I flew down south? I was told it wouldn't be.

Later that day, outside 50 Irvine Drive, I saw two big guys who looked like forwards from the Scotland 1st XV. They were Lothian and Borders Police. We didn't talk at the time but Detective Chief Inspector Keith Anderson later told me they were astonished Vicky was there. They had evidence suggesting a link to Dinah, but not Vicky.

I struggled to find words for my report that night. It was incredible and horrible. Vicky had disappeared in West Lothian years before, but she was here. A Scottish schoolgirl whose face we all knew, buried in a rundown council estate in a fading seaside town at the other end of Britain.

The police continued searching for Dinah. I heard her father on the radio and realised he had a Scottish accent. Ian McNicol told me off for addressing him as Mr McNicol. He was an old jazz musician from Glasgow whose travels had led to retirement in a sleepy village in the Essex countryside.

I went to see him and we were halfway through the interview when the doorbell rang. A young reporter from the local ITV station told us the police had found more human remains. Ian agreed to continue. In a gesture I'll never forget, he raised his hand with his fingers crossed and said, 'If that's what they have said, please be Dinah... and get us out of this... misery.'

It was snowing when Vicky went missing in Bathgate, and it was snowing 16 years later when her family arrived at the High Court in Dundee to watch an unperturbed Tobin receive his second life sentence. I'd interviewed Lindsay and Lee Brown, Vicky's younger brother and sister the night before, and watched as Lindsay read out a gut-wrenching statement to Britain's media.

We had a second interview to ourselves. Detective Superintendent Davy Swindle had led the investigation into Angelika Kluk's carefully concealed murder, and had realised it was unlikely to be the first time Tobin had killed. He launched Operation Anagram, a nationwide scoping exercise which tried to unearth every scrap of information about Tobin's entire life. A team led by Detective Sergeant Graham MacKellar linked Tobin to Bathgate, which led in turn to Margate.

Tobin was tried for Dinah McNicol's murder at Chelmsford Crown Court. In a preliminary hearing I had to stand up in the press box and dissuade the English judge from banning us from reporting the proceedings. They were worried the coverage might muddy the waters if Tobin appealed against the verdict from Dundee. I was baffled and told the judge there was unlikely to be anything he could appeal about. From the dock, Tobin fixed me with a baleful glare. I looked away first.

Peter Tobin died in prison in 2022 aged 76. No relatives or next of kin claimed his remains.

2010

Monday 1 February 2010
STV News

Sir Alex Ferguson enjoyed a roll and sausage today as he returned to his roots in Govan. The Manchester United manager, fresh from a victory over title rivals Arsenal, was back home to lend support to local charities and tonight will celebrate the centenary of his old school.

DIARY: Sir Alex Ferguson was touring some projects in Govan and I was sent to the first one – a drug rehabilitation centre of which he's the patron. Got quite a lot of colour as he spoke to people in the place and I got as close as I was going to get to a one-to-one. I've always found him reasonably friendly and approachable, although I'm never harrying him with football questions.

Friday 12 February 2010
STV News

David Cameron has asked the Scots to back him to become Prime Minister during his latest trip north of the Border. The Conservative leader insists it is a straight choice between him and Gordon Brown. He told the Scottish Conservative conference in Perth that in a tight election, Scottish votes cannot be written off.

DIARY: Went to the Journalists' Charity lunch at the Thistle Hotel today, where the main speaker was the Conservative leader David Cameron. He could possibly be Prime Minister in little over two months. He is impressive – very fast on his feet, very comfortable, very slick. His main political point was essentially that whoever comes to power will have 'no money' because of the financial crisis of the last 18 months, and also that he wanted to work closely with the Scottish Parliament. He maybe didn't have quite the air of authority that Tony Blair had, but that may come. With Cameron the question is always is there substance behind the gloss?

Thursday 25 March 2010
STV News

An alliance of three newspaper groups has been named as the preferred bidder to produce publicly funded Scottish news programmes on STV. The Scottish News Consortium says it's planning 'the biggest shake-up of news in Scotland for decades.' The newspapers defeated a rival bid from three broadcasters, including STV itself.

The Labour Government had initiated a process to make public money available for the funding of news on Channel Three.

DIARY: We've lost out on the public funding. An absolutely gobsmacking decision that can only be explained as being political, with members of the selection panel in thrall to the newspapers. How can you award a TV news pilot to a consortium that could not even provide a video in its bid? Inexplicable.

It makes for a very uncertain future. They must decide who of the STV News staff they want to keep. After a year they can change conditions and they have a ruthless reputation for doing that. Everyone in the newsroom shattered. *Reporting Scotland* headline tonight was me with my opening line, 'I'm John MacKay. This is the STV News at Six... but for how much longer?' Sore one.

Thursday 15 April 2010
STV News

All flights in and out of the UK remain grounded tonight as a gigantic ash cloud engulfs much of Northern Europe and the British Isles. That ash from an erupting volcano in Iceland, carries a deadly safety risk for every passenger jet. It has caused travel chaos with no flights in or out of the country since 11.00am this morning.

DIARY: The prevailing winds are pushing this cloud across northern Europe at about 20,000 feet and the silicon particles in it can seriously damage jet engines, so flights have been grounded. Never heard the likes before.

GENERAL ELECTION 2010

Thursday 15 April 2010 *(cont)*
STV News

Another milestone in television and political history tonight as the leaders of the three main UK parties go head-to-head in the first ever Prime Ministerial debate. But as Gordon Brown, David Cameron and Nick Clegg prepare to battle it out on this channel, Alex Salmond, who's been excluded from the televised event, says none of it will apply to Scotland.

DIARY: The SNP have rightly made a fuss about not being involved and up to half the issues discussed were irrelevant to Scottish viewers because they come under the power of the Scottish Parliament. Clegg did well, Gordon Brown better than expected and David Cameron not so well. Clegg was personable and did simple things like speaking directly to camera. I don't know who advises politicians, but they get it wrong so often.

This was the debate that produced the 'I agree with Nick' catchphrase, repeated by both Cameron and Brown.

Tuesday 20 April 2010
Scotland Debates

Welcome to *Scotland Debates* live from the National Piping Centre in Glasgow and broadcasting to the whole of Scotland. Everything you hear tonight will have a direct relevance to Scotland. Over the next hour, four of Scotland's leading Westminster politicians will be facing questions from an audience of voters.

JIM MURPHY, Labour: I know that people are angry as we go into this election campaign. I think there has been the perfect storm of the recession, there's been the expenses scandal, there's been the bankers taking enormous immoral bonuses, and I think all of that has come together and created this perfect storm that has scunnered so many people across Scotland.

ANGUS ROBERTSON, SNP: We've got huge economic problems that we have to deal with, we've got a Westminster system which is broken – there's a break in trust between the public and politicians – and we have to try and fix that because I fear an ever-growing number of people are totally scunnered.

ALISTAIR CARMICHAEL, Liberal Democrat: I've been a political activist man and boy since I was 14, that's 30 years of political activism, and I have to say I have never known an election which I found as genuinely exciting and inspiring as I find this one.

DAVID MUNDELL, Conservative: This is one of those once-in-a-generation elections where there is a real chance to change the Government. I think if we're honest the last couple of General Elections, the outcome was a foregone conclusion. This time your vote... really will count.

The dominant issue was the economy and measures to tackle Britain's budget deficit. The other issues the audience focused on were the ongoing wars in Iraq and Afghanistan and the timetable for withdrawal, restoring public trust after the expenses scandals and the possibility of a hung Parliament.

Tuesday 4 May 2010

DIARY: Had a 20-minute conversation with the First Minister Alex Salmond this evening. He was in the newsroom to do a down-the-line interview with Channel Four and afterwards started talking and seemed in no great hurry. At one point he referred to his absence from the leaders' debates as 'fucking disgraceful'.

Thursday 6 May 2010

DIARY: Election Day in one of the most interesting elections for years. The exit polls indicate a hung Parliament, which is pretty much what has been predicted by previous polls.

Friday 7 May 2010
STV News – from Westminster with Andrea Brymer

It's 7 May 2010. A day that will go down in history as one of the most dramatic days in modern British politics. The people of the United Kingdom have exercised their democratic right and the result is a constitutional conundrum.

Tonight, we don't know for sure who will lead our country in this most difficult of times. Throughout the day, the party leaders have stated their positions in public. Behind the scenes here at Westminster, the activity may be even more frenetic as the parties fight for power.

This is the national picture. The Conservatives have 306 seats – short of that magic number of 326. Labour have 258. The Liberal Democrats are on 57 and others 28.

And this is how the picture looks in Scotland. The seats remain the same as the last election, but Labour increased their percentage share for the first time since 1997. In terms of seats, the Conservatives continue to hold just one in Scotland, Labour have 41, the Liberal Democrats are still on 11 and the SNP held their six, far short of the 20 they had predicted.

DIARY: A long, eventful and uncertain day. Apart from writing the intros and keeping across the day's developments – it wasn't especially stressful. Neither was there any real sense of atmosphere around Parliament, apart from College Green with all the media platforms.

Monday 10 May 2010

DIARY: Back down to London this morning in what proved to be an eventful day. Met Clair *(Clair Stevens – producer)* and we spent much of the day getting a feel for what was happening – which in terms of what could be seen – wasn't much. We walked between Whitehall and Westminster, but it was just busy with tourists. Only really on College Green was there any real buzz and that's because it was the media base with TV platforms everywhere.

STV News – from Westminster – never transmitted

Good evening from Westminster which today has seen the most dramatic events since the resignation of Margaret Thatcher. In the last hour the Prime Minister Gordon Brown has said he will resign as leader of the Labour Party. The move is designed to encourage Liberal Democrats to form a coalition with Labour. It follows a day when it seemed that talks between the Lib Dems and the majority Conservative Party had been progressing well.

DIARY CONT: Drama at 5.00pm when, without any sign of an agreement between the Tories and Lib Dems, Gordon Brown – who's still Prime Minister – appeared on the steps of Downing Street to say that he would stay on to help facilitate a Lab/Lib Dem coalition, then step down later in the year. That's put the cat among the pigeons and things might take an unexpected turn.

I was standing in position ready to go when at 5.55pm we were told ITN were taking the full hour. Disappointing. We had a cracking programme ready to go, even with the late drama.

Tuesday 11 May 2010
STV News

Tonight, Britain stands on the brink of a new Government. A deal seems imminent between the Conservatives and the Liberal Democrats that will put David Cameron into Downing Street. Late overtures from Labour came to nothing and tonight Gordon Brown is preparing to resign as Prime Minister.

DIARY: Tonight, Gordon Brown resigned as PM in a statement outside Number Ten. He then left with his wife and two sons, an image that shows a human side to the man, but which to his credit he didn't try to exploit.

He was an impressive Chancellor at first, but he and Blair threw away what they could have achieved when first elected. Blair over Iraq and Brown because of his belief that he had some sort of right to become Prime Minister. I think history will reflect on him as a thwarted man who did much to undermine Tony Blair and who came to power when it was too late for him.

Wednesday 12 May 2010
STV News

It's been a day when political enemies became allies to form a new government. A handshake at the door of Number Ten showing the unity of the coalition at the very top of British politics. Prime Minister David Cameron and his deputy Nick Clegg promised a government built on freedom, fairness and responsibility.

DIARY: Strange to see today's news conference with Cameron and Clegg standing side by side. They came across well, but I can see these images coming back to haunt Clegg. Maybe I'm wrong and the 'new politics', as they've called it, might work. They seem to have made a good start, but a lot of commentators give it 18 months maximum.

The Conservative–Liberal Democrat Coalition lasted the full five years of the UK Parliament, but the Liberal Democrats suffered heavily in subsequent local elections and were reduced to a rump party in the 2015 General Election, from 57 seats to only eight.

Tuesday 8 June 2010
STV News

Plans to use public money to subsidise regional news, including this programme on STV, have been scrapped by the coalition Government. The Culture Secretary Jeremy Hunt today axed a series of pilots set up by the previous Labour Government.

DIARY: The IFNC that has been hanging over us at work since that perverse decision in March has definitely been binned.

Tuesday 8 June *(cont)*
STV News

A woman has been jailed for three years for dipping a baby's dummy in methadone to stop him crying. The ten-week-old boy almost died after the incident in Edinburgh. Another woman has been jailed for ten months for failing to tell medics what had happened.

DIARY: A junkie mum jailed for dipping her ten-week-old son's dummy in methadone was a real pride in Scotland moment.

POPE BENEDICT'S VISIT TO SCOTLAND

Thursday 16 September 2010
STV News – live from Bellahouston Park with Andrea Brymer

Hello and welcome to this special edition of the STV News – broadcast across the nation – as Pope Benedict the 16th celebrates mass with the faithful here in Bellahouston Park on the southside of Glasgow. Twenty-eight years ago his charismatic predecessor John Paul the Second made history with the first ever Papal visit to Scotland. Three hundred thousand came here from far and wide. Now, as his successor follows in his footsteps on Scottish soil, the crowds may be smaller, but the welcome is every bit as enthusiastic. The 83-year-old Pontiff undertakes this journey, however, against a radically different backdrop from the historic and joyous visit in '82. Dissent, controversy and falling congregations cast their shadow. But this first state visit to the UK remains, as First Minister Alex Salmond says, an important and inspiring day for Scotland as the world watches.

POPE BENEDICT XVI: It is with some emotions that I address you not far from the spot where my beloved predecessor Pope John Paul the Second celebrated mass nearly 30 years ago with you and was welcomed by the largest crowd ever gathered in Scottish history. Much has happened in Scotland and in the Church in this country since that historic visit. I note with great satisfaction how Pope John Paul's call to you to walk hand in hand with your fellow Christians has led to greater trust and friendship with the members of the Church of Scotland, the Scottish Episcopal Church and others. Let me encourage you to continue to pray and work with them in building a brighter future for Scotland based upon our common Christian heritage.

This was one of the first occasions that I and several of my colleagues used Twitter to report what was happening. It was basic observations about the crowds arriving and such, but it was about the first time we did it seriously. I noted at the time that I was 'taken with Twitter which, amid the dross and nonsense, can be extremely informative'. It didn't last.

Monday 20 September 2010
STV News

A maximum break. It's what all snooker fans want to see. And yet in Glasgow today, the paying audience were nearly denied it because a top snooker player – Ronnie O'Sullivan – didn't think it was worth the £4,000 he would have won. All this on the day that world snooker chiefs launched an integrity unit to stamp out match fixing and urged players to go back to playing for the love of the game.

DIARY: That's what's wrong with so much sport – money not glory.

Tuesday 28 September 2010
STV News

The new Labour leader, Ed Miliband, says he will drive David Cameron from office after one term. In his first leader's speech at the party conference, Mr Miliband said he represented a new generation which would change Labour and the country. He accepted that Labour had made mistakes in power and must address voters from a position of humility.

DIARY: Producing and presenting today. An obvious lead was the first speech to the Labour conference by the new leader, Ed Miliband. I think Labour have made a big mistake. This guy will not appeal to the electorate.

THE BIG FREEZE

Monday 6 December 2010
STV News

Chaos has continued across Scotland today with renewed falls of snow and – now – icy temperatures. Many drivers have spent hours trapped in their cars as the roads seized up in gridlock. Journeys that would normally take no more than 20 minutes have become a four-hour endurance. Airports have been closed again and passengers left stranded.

Tuesday 7 December 2010
STV News Special – live on the STV balcony in -14C with weatherman Sean Batty

Scotland in the winter. A picturesque winterscape from the air. On the ground some have described it as a winter apocalypse.

Weather fronts from Siberia and the Arctic have dumped inches of snow and sank temperatures to near record lows.

Communities have been isolated.

Schools have been closed.

And the country ground to a halt. Hundreds trapped in their cars for ten hours and more.

Children forced to sleep in their schools, cut off from their families.

Scotland is back in the grip of the Big Freeze, shivering in record-breaking cold weather. The Central Belt is going through the perfect storm. Just yesterday, three hours of heavy snowfall – right in the middle of rush hour resulting in quite horrendous problems for thousands of drivers.

The real drama happened overnight. Hundreds of drivers were stranded in their cars – in Lanarkshire, Stirlingshire and West Lothian, stuck in the middle of motorway misery – many having taken hours to move less than a mile.

That's it from your news team at STV on this bitterly cold December night. A night that follows a day of turmoil for thousands of people in a long week of disruption, gridlock and standstill. In the warmth of your home this evening, you could perhaps be forgiven for dreaming of a Christmas that's not quite so white. Goodnight, keep warm and stay safe.

Tuesday 17 December 2010
STV News

Two young women waiting to cross a road in Glasgow city centre have been killed after a 4-by-4 lost control and mounted the pavement. Another man was hit just seconds before. Other motorists stopped to help the injured, as emergency services rushed to the scene.

I was tweeted pictures from the scene, nothing graphic, but enough to alert me to the fact that this was a serious incident. We would never use Twitter as a confirmed source, but it did get us onto the story far more quickly than we might have otherwise.

TOMMY SHERIDAN'S CONVICTION

Thursday 23 December 2010
STV News – Live from the High Court in Glasgow with Bernard Ponsonby

Good evening from inside the High Court in Glasgow where, for the last three months, Tommy Sheridan has been defending himself against charges of perjury. But tonight he has lost and been found guilty of lying. The former Socialist MSP now faces up to six years behind bars. In this special edition of the STV News at Six – the first time a news programme has been fully broadcast from inside a court in Scotland – we bring you the full story of the firebrand's fall.

DIARY: It brings to an end a soap opera that's been going on for more than four years now. I always liked Tommy Sheridan's presence in Scottish politics. He was a very charismatic figure. If we start trying people for perjury in every trial, then the courts will be chock full. But we won't. This is one of the few. This particular trial has lasted three months and it kept us going at quiet periods. We got an indication that he was going to be convicted when the jury returned to ask whether part of one charge could be deleted. We did the entire programme from inside the High Court – a broadcast first.

Tommy Sheridan was released from jail in 2012.

2011

Tuesday 1 February 2011

DIARY: Group of schoolkids touring at lunchtime and they came into the studio. I gave them a quick talk – no point in making it too long – and then asked them if they had any questions. Wee girl at the front throws her hand up enthusiastically. 'Yes,' says I. 'Who are you?' she asks.

Thursday 3 March 2011
STV News

A top-level summit will be held to review the ugly scenes at last night's Old Firm game. Neil Lennon and Ally McCoist squared up at the final whistle of a Scottish Cup tie which saw three red cards, 13 bookings and 34 arrests inside the ground. The actions were condemned by the First Minister as repugnant. The SFA Chief Executive said he was saddened and deeply embarrassed.

DIARY: All about last night's explosive Old Firm game and the usual uproar. First Minister calling it a disgrace and there's a summit to discuss the problem. All old hat as far as I'm concerned. However, my inclination to leave it as something that occasionally happens at Old Firm games is tempered by reports of the domestic chaos that ensues and first-hand accounts I've heard of A&E being a battleground.

Monday 18 April 2011

DIARY: The big issue for us on an otherwise quiet day was the continued news blackout on three bombs (one at least was viable) sent to Celtic's QC Paul McBride, manager Neil Lennon and a Celtic-supporting former MSP Trish Godman. Howard *(Howard Simpson, News Editor)* was called to a police briefing along with all the other Scottish editors. The police seem to be very touchy about this and fear copycats.

Tuesday 3 May 2011
STV News

The SNP are on course for a landslide victory in Thursday's Scottish election. An exclusive poll for STV News shows a surge in support for the Nationalists – with a major slump in backing for Scottish Labour. It comes as all four main party leaders prepare for tonight's crucial final televised debate on this channel.

SCOTTISH ELECTION 2011
Thursday 5 May 2011
STV News

The long Scottish election campaign is over. The TV debates are done and dusted, the pledges and promises published. Now the battle of the ballot boxes has begun. Polling stations opened at seven this morning and close in just four hours' time. The final 24 hours saw party leaders criss-cross the country fighting for every vote. Activists in towns and cities across the nation are now focusing on getting their supporters to the polls.

DIARY: It's been a remarkable turnaround because polls over the last 12 months have suggested a Labour win. I think, though, that the SNP leadership team – Salmond, Sturgeon and Swinney has impressed people.

Friday 6 May 2011
STV News – Live from Holyrood with Andrea Brymer

Good evening live from Holyrood – the heart of Scottish democracy. The people of Scotland have voted for a once-in-a-generation transformation to Scottish politics. Tonight, Alex Salmond is returned as First Minister and the SNP has a majority of seats. And this Parliament will deliver a referendum on independence. Labour has seen its traditional power base in the Central Belt destroyed. The party leader Iain Gray will resign in the autumn. Many of its big names have lost their seats. The Liberal Democrats vote collapsed. The Conservatives are not the king-makers they hoped to be, and none of the small parties, including the Greens, could break through.

Tonight, with the last of the votes counted this is the shape of the new Scottish Parliament. The SNP hit 69 seats. Labour on 37. The Conservatives have 15. The Lib Dems have five and the Greens have two. The one Independent is Margo MacDonald.

ALEX SALMOND, First Minister: We're not fixed on the past in all its bright colour. Our eyes are on the future and the dreams that can be realised. I'll govern for all of the ambitions of Scotland and all the people who imagine that we can live in a better land. This party, the Scottish party, the National Party carries your hope. And we shall carry it carefully and make the nation proud.

JM: We're joined now by the Deputy Leader of the SNP, Nicola Sturgeon. Congratulations on a momentous vote. You couldn't possibly in your wildest dreams have seen that coming.

NICOLA STURGEON, Deputy First Minister: I think it's fair to say it was beyond our expectations. We had been quietly confident over the past few days of winning the election... I remember the days, as I'm sure do many of your viewers, when people said we'd never have a Scottish Parliament or we'd never have an SNP Government. Now these same people say we'll never have independence. It's right that the issue of independence is decided in a referendum. When that referendum comes the SNP will campaign vigorously for a Yes vote and I'm confident that we will win the day on that.

IAIN GRAY, Scottish Labour Leader: We have to address some fundamental questions about the structures and organisation of the Labour Party in Scotland, what went wrong and where we go from here. I want to start that process off, but in the autumn I will stand down and it will be for the Labour Party to decide how we go forward from there.

Vox Pops

Labour must be reeling in shock.

I'm not surprised. Not with what's been happening currently and everybody being out of jobs.

They've really got us into the mess that we're in.

Anything you ask them to do or whatever, not interested.

They're just not for the people now, they're out for themselves.

If you put a monkey in a Labour suit they would get in here and that used to be the case, but unfortunately, it's come back to bite them.

JM: The people of Scotland have delivered a Parliament which overwhelmed all expectations. Bernard, put this result into context for us?

BERNARD PONSONBY, Political Editor: The word historical is the most over used word on election night, but last night it was absolutely apt. Historical because it is the first time any party has won a majority under a voting system almost designed to prevent it. Historical because there is a majority for an Independence Referendum and that turns the nature of the constitutional debate on its head. Historical because the SNP victory came in the north, the south, the east and the west and they can legitimately claim tonight to be a national party representing all communities and classes.

JM: Your overall assessment?

BP: The political map of Scotland has been redrawn, but more than that the mould of Scottish politics has been recast and it suggests that the SNP are a natural party of Government. Labour's dominance is at an end and for them some far reaching soul-searching as generational loyalty seems to be a thing of the past. With this victory comes a new chapter in Scotland's evolution. The campaign for independence starts right here.

DIARY: No one saw this coming, no one. It means there will be a referendum on independence within the five-year term of this Parliament. Labour have lost their power base in the Central Belt with some of their senior people losing their seats. The Lib Dems have been crushed – a direct consequence of their involvement in the coalition at Westminster. The polls had predicted an SNP win, but nothing on this scale. This is a sea change – a once-in-a-generation transformation. I don't believe it means Scotland is marching towards independence, rather they recognised that the SNP have governed well these past four years and that Labour are a complacent shambles. Still, you never know what the debate might bring. Into work where I wrote most of the scripts for the evening special before 10.00am. It was that clear. I headed through to Edinburgh with Bernard – who'd been up all night. The programme with Andrea went very smoothly.

Monday 9 May 2011
STV News

The resignation of Annabel Goldie as leader of the Scottish Conservatives came on the day new MSPs started to arrive at Parliament to familiarise themselves with their new home for the next five years. It begins a new political era with SNP holding power with a majority government.

Tuesday 21 June 2011
STV News

Glasgow's new £74 million Transport Museum has opened to the public and, despite the rain, hundreds of people turned up to witness the building receive a Clyde-style ship launch. Described by the architect as a 'sophisticated shed', The Riverside Museum is expected to become one of the city's biggest attractions.

Thursday 23 June 2011
STV News

The First Minister Alex Salmond is backing calls for a public inquiry into Edinburgh's trams, as council officials published a long-awaited report into the troubled project. The report recommends the councillors press ahead with a tram line from the city centre to the airport at cost of more than £770 million. As STV News revealed last night, officials say that cancelling the project would cost up to £740 million.

Tuesday 16 August 2011
STV News

Hollywood stars Brad Pitt and Angelina Jolie arrived in Glasgow today, but it wasn't by private jet or helicopter, instead the couple chartered a train. The arrival of the actors and their family prompted great excitement amongst commuters and their fans, many of whom are on a mission to meet Brad while he's here filming his latest movie.

DIARY: Big excitement with Hollywood star Brad Pitt in Glasgow to film his movie *World War Z* – Glasgow is playing Philadelphia. He arrived in a specially chartered train, but hid from his fans. An arse thing to do.

Monday 5 September 2011

DIARY: A 13-year-old dies after a weekend incident. Sixteen-year-old in custody. Two wasted lives right there.

A new STV current affairs programme was first mooted in the late summer of 2011. Scotland was crying out for it, especially in the wake of the Scottish election and the anticipated referendum to come. The BBC's *Newsnight Scotland* was a compromise right from its inception and never recovered from that, being widely dismissed as 'Newsnicht'.

The former *Sky News* correspondent Rona Dougall was the surprise choice as my co-presenter over other, more obvious candidates after an impressive audition. The intimate set, with its black and red sofas and colour scheme of burnt orange, reassured me that the programme would be a success. With a small, enthusiastic production team behind us we went on air on 24 October 2011 and it was a success from the very beginning, critically, anecdotally and in the size of our audience.

Howard Simpson, Editor, STV News & Scotland Tonight

I always thought that Scotland had waited too long for a programme about current affairs that wasn't either too anoraky, too insular or too aggressive. The brief for *Scotland Tonight* was for a programme that felt at ease with politics, but also took other walks of public life just as seriously. Sports, cinema, art, business and most importantly world affairs. I think that as long as programmes in Scotland feel they have to be just Scottish first and foremost then we are not being ambitious enough. We just had to think in terms of what the most interesting stories are from the day no matter where they are. On any given *Scotland Tonight* we could be doing the Greek financial crisis, the business problems at Rangers and an examination of the Scottish film industry. This eclectic mix kept the audience fresh. They knew they were not just going to get a strict diet from Holyrood.

The feel of the show was as important as the subject matter. We were on at 10.30pm at night, so the audience need to want to watch the programme as opposed to the news, which can become habitual. We picked presenters who relate to the viewers, not agitators, perpetually probing and interrupting. We wanted to keep the programme as modern as possible, social media is at its core, being able to hold a conversation with our viewers. We also endeavoured to get as many fresh voices on as possible, and new ways to report on the stories that matter. *Scotland Tonight* changed the way current affairs is broadcast in Scotland.

Thursday 8 September 2011
STV News

The Justice Secretary says single police and fire forces will save Scotland billions over years. Kenny MacAskill made the prediction as he revealed more details of the emergency services shake-up. However, concern was expressed that millions of pounds are to be slashed from the fire service budget as the eight regional divisions merge to cut costs.

Police Scotland came into being in 2013, ending the eight regional forces – Strathclyde, Lothian & Borders, Central, Grampian, Northern, Tayside, Fife, Dumfries & Galloway.

Monday 24 October 2011
Scotland Tonight

This is *Scotland Tonight*. The US Billionaire Donald Trump divides opinion. A would-be President. One of the richest men in the world. Trump Tower in New York City tells you that this is a man who doesn't do 'small'. And yet it's to Scotland he came with a big idea – the greatest golf course in the world. But it's been plagued by endless planning rows and protests, yet it's him who is objecting now. He doesn't like plans for an offshore wind farm near his luxury resort.

DONALD TRUMP: When you look at these towers they are ugly and they're very, very depressing to be looking at and, frankly, it's a bad thing for Scotland. Y'know, one of the things that I went to Scotland – the big one was that my mother was born in Scotland, as you know, and she was something very special. She was a great person and loved Scotland. And part of the beauty of Scotland is its incredible heritage and its shoreline and its beauty, it's just the beauty of the environment. And when you put up these big, ugly windmills, y'know, if you put them in certain areas it's perhaps not so bad, but Cape Cod in Massachusetts they vetoed it. Many other places throughout the United States and other places in the world where they have a beautiful area, like shoreline and coastline and really good areas, they don't allow 'em to go up... From the standpoint of Scotland, you have one of the greatest coastlines anywhere in the world and to put these really atrocious looking structures up in the water, I think will be really detrimental to Scotland.

The first programme came close to falling around us. Our opening item was a set-piece interview with Donald Trump, who was in a wrangle with the Scottish Government over a luxury golf resort he was building in the North East. A satellite link would be prohibitively expensive, so with the sort of imagination that has characterised the programme, we arranged for a US crew to film him as he answered my questions which he was hearing down a regular phone line through an earpiece. Meanwhile, my side of the interview was recorded in the studio. We would get the American footage sent back and marry the two together. The interview went well and he was as colourful and controversial as we'd expected. The American crew duly sent the material to us, but inevitably it got lost somewhere in the ether. With little more than an hour to go, it looked like we had no programme on our launch night. Fortunately, we tracked it down and it was edited together at the last moment. The success of Scotland Tonight might have been very different if we'd got off to a bad start.

Donald Trump's golf course opened in 2012. The wind farm opened in 2018.

Tuesday 25 October 2011

DIARY: *Scotland Tonight* got great ratings for last night, a 10 per cent share peaking at 13 per cent. That's about double what we were expecting. The feedback continues to be good. Rona's debut tonight and I stayed on to give her some support. It went well.

The feedback included my Faither's view that, 'It's no' bad. You're fair losing your hair.' This was prompted by a favoured shot of the programme directors which showed the guest over my shoulder, but also the back of my head and emphasised my expanding bald patch. I called it the 'bastard shot'.

Tuesday 29 November 2011
STV News

Hundreds of thousands of cleaners, teachers, nurses and civil servants took to the streets today, angered by cuts to their pensions. Schools, hospitals, transport and the courts were all affected in this national walk out involving millions across the UK. A defiant David Cameron described the strike as a damp squib. Our Chief Reporter David Cowan followed the biggest mass action in a generation.

DAVID COWAN, STV Chief Reporter: The strike caused division amongst politicians north and south of the border. In Scotland the SNP crossed picket lines at the Parliament while Labour boycotted a debate on the pension reforms. At Westminster Ed Miliband was branded irresponsible, left-wing and weak by the Prime Minister who was in turn accused by the Labour Leader of revelling in the strike action.

Wednesday 30 November 2011

DIARY: The champion Scottish cyclist Graeme Obree was a *Scotland Tonight* guest in a discussion about suicide – he's attempted it twice himself. He talked about the state of mind that takes you to 'kicking away the chair'. One of the most powerful interviews I've ever done and that was down to his candour and the experience he'd endured. Scotland has a high level of suicide and it is deeply disturbing that people can be that desperate and yet those closest to them don't know.

Scotland Tonight

GRAEME OBREE, Former World Cycling Champion: I feel obliged because people like Gary Speed (*the Welsh football manager who died by suicide*) are not here to say how much I wish I hadn't done that. I was the guy who kicked the chair away with two kids and a wife who I dearly loved. People in the family of those who've committed suicide, they struggle to understand the reasons and there's a lot of resentment, there's a lot of anger, there's a lot of feeling that the person didn't love them enough. There's all these resentments and feelings left over. I feel they need to hear it from somebody who's actually done that and survived and lived to tell it.

JM: That phrase you used there, you kicked the chair away. What took you to that position? What was your mindset?

GO: One was a feeling of isolation. I felt, even in company, I felt there was a bell jar around me, I wasn't part of the world, I was observing it, I was no part of this world whatsoever, wasn't connected.

JM: Even with a wife and two children?

GO: Even with that I felt totally disconnected and purposeless. You could have given me a million pounds and I'd have gone, that's great, but pointless. People can't understand that. Can I give you an analogy, just to nail it for people, ordinary people who just can't understand this? Supposing you went to a party and you really, really didn't want to be at that party. You thought, oh I really want to go home now, I'm tired, I really hate this company, but you keep it happy, smiley and chatty, you're clock watching, you're thinking it's going to be over soon. Imagine you woke up and every day was like that and it takes ten times the energy to deal with each person, just happy, smiley. And life went on like that. And you ultimately go, I want to go to sleep now, but there is no sleep. So, it seems like the only option is actually just not to be here anymore. And also, that state of mind is proper mentally ill and it changes your perspective of reality. I actually believed that I was a terrible person, my kids would be so much better off I wasn't here, I'm a terrible person. And it wasn't that I didn't love them... The main thing I want to say is that if somebody has left you through suicide, it's not because they didn't love you.

Sunday 4 December 2011
STV News

After five years of negotiations, two pandas finally arrived in Scotland from China this afternoon. Sunshine and Sweetie flew into Edinburgh Airport with dignitaries talking up the significance of the day. But a large crowd who gathered to see them outside the zoo were left disappointed as they were not able to get a glimpse of the bears.

Tian Tian and Yang Guang were described as a gift from China, although it was more of a loan with a significant bill for their upkeep. The hope was that they would mate, but

they never did. They were still a big commercial success for Edinburgh Zoo, though. The pandas returned to China in 2023.

HURRICANE BAWBAG
Thursday 8 December 2011
STV News

Don't drive. Keep the kids at home. Stay off the streets. The stark warnings across the country tonight as the nation is put on red alert. Throughout the day storms battered roads, railways, hospitals and schools with gusts reaching 85 miles an hour. Thousands were forced to take the day off or headed home early. A picture of widespread damage is emerging. So far – fortunately – there have been no fatalities.

DIARY: Weather red alert with winds of up to 85 mph hitting urban areas. 165mph on top of the Cairngorms, close to 175mph record. It was certainly bad, but perhaps not to the extent that had been feared. It has very quickly become known as Hurricane Bawbag – a term which was trending worldwide on Twitter.

Wednesday 14 December 2011
STV News

Within the last hour MSPs have approved tough new laws aimed at eradicating football-related bigotry and hate crime on the internet. However, all of the opposition parties voted against the SNP's proposals during a debate which was passionate and, at times, bad tempered.

DIARY: It's being called the 'Bigotry Bill' because of its focus on the football. The SNP Government used its majority to push it through, which seems to be lacking in detail.

The controversial act was repealed in 2018. The Scottish Labour MSP James Kelly, who proposed the repeal said, 'the Football Act did nothing to tackle sectarianism because it was such cheap law.'

2012

Monday 9 January 2012
Scotland Tonight

A referendum on Scottish independence is coming. But as yet it's unclear when it will happen and what, and how many, questions will be asked. Claiming that uncertainty is damaging the economy, the UK Government is now ramping up the pressure on the SNP administration to hold an early poll with a clear cut yes or no option for voters.

DIARY: Constitutionally any referendum has to be approved by Westminster – most see this as a technicality. The point is that the debate has started for real and the unionists are taking the fight to the SNP, who have been making the running until now. *Scotland Tonight* was lively with four parties represented. It was a problem at times to keep order.

Tuesday 10 January 2012
Scotland Tonight

Autumn 2014. That's the date the SNP Government wants to hold a referendum on Scottish independence. Tonight's disclosure from Alex Salmond came just after Scottish Secretary Michael Moore had told MPs that, as things stand, a Holyrood organised vote would be unlawful. UK ministers have indicated they're prepared to devolve authority, but only if certain conditions are met.

DIARY: The Scottish Independence issue kicked off big style today. The Scottish Secretary Michael Moore stood up in the Commons and confirmed what had been revealed yesterday ie that the Scottish Parliament has no legal right to hold such a referendum. Westminster will hand over that power, but with conditions attached. That much was expected, but then First Minister Alex Salmond – live on our news at 6.00pm – announced that the referendum will be in the autumn of 2014. Up until now he's only ever said it would be in the second half of the Parliament. So, Holyrood and Westminster squaring up to each other. At first look it is a political masterstroke by Salmond, regaining the initiative straight away, but it is also a bit disrespectful to the Scottish people. Why wait when he clearly knew all along? Of course, 2014 is the 700th anniversary of Bannockburn and the year of the Commonwealth Games. National fervour will be high. It's the nature of politics I suppose.

Monday 16 January 2012
Scotland Tonight

Yes or No to full blown independence. That's the simple choice the Westminster Government wants voters to have in the referendum on our constitutional future. But a string of recent surveys has shown that a third option is the one which most Scots want. Under Devo Max our MSPs at Holyrood would get far greater powers, but Scotland would remain in the UK. Tonight, a YouGov poll showed 39 per cent public backing for a separate Scottish state, with 61 against. But, when the option of greater powers within the UK was offered, 58 per cent backed 'devo max' with 42 against.

DIARY: A good *Scotland Tonight*. First discussion on 'What is Devo Max?' and the answer is no one really knows, although polls show it to be the favoured option to the status quo or full independence. Second chat was about the risks of social media for people in the public eye as another MP resigns over something inappropriate (Tom Harris Labour MP over a spoof video of Alex Salmond as Hitler in *Downfall*. I think it's a nonsense he had to resign). That worked well. Best of the lot was an enthusiastic professor from Glasgow University talking about the use of apostrophes (Waterstone's dropping it from their name). His name was Jeremy Smith and he was excellent. The entire crew adored him. Good programme.

Tuesday 17 January 2012
Scotland Tonight

Ed Miliband is leading Labour to electoral disaster. The stark assessment today from the boss of Unite, the UK's biggest union and Labour's biggest donor. Len McCluskey made the comments following the party's decision to accept coalition cuts and a public sector pay freeze. Mr Miliband dismissed the attack, insisting his position was both 'right' and 'responsible'. But today's public battle has fuelled speculation that his days as Labour Leader are numbered.

DIARY: During an interview with one contributor in London a monitor on the screen behind him flashed up images of a sex scene with bouncing breasts prominent. Nothing I could say because he knew nothing of it and it would have thrown him. It was only brief, but I'm sure we haven't heard the last of it.

Thursday 19 January 2012

DIARY: The bouncing boobs on *Scotland Tonight* made the front page of *The Sun* as an 'exclusive' today – exclusive 36 hours after it appeared on live TV. *Daily Record* lifted it, on *Daily Mail* website, P3 of *London Evening Standard* and has even been picked up by foreign media outlets – Russia, Belgium, Vietnam. It's all good publicity, but ridiculous given that it was a two-second flash.

RANGERS GO INTO ADMINISTRATION
Monday 13 February 2012
STV News

Rangers Football Club have applied to go into administration. The SPL Champions lodged notice at the Court of Session this lunchtime. And tonight the Ibrox club stated the tax bill they owe could be substantially more than the £50 million that has been widely reported. That is, of course, £50 million the club cannot pay. Within ten days administrators will move in to run Rangers who will be deducted ten league points.

DIARY: All went crazy this afternoon when announced that Rangers had applied to go into administration. We'd just come to the end of the *Scotland Tonight* production meeting and had a detailed discussion on what we were going to do, but that all had to get ripped up. Filled the news and tonight's programme. Gloomy day for Rangers.

Mike Farrell, STV online sports reporter

'Oh aye, they filed something this afternoon.' I nearly fell out my chair and dropped the phone when the clerk at the Court of Session confirmed what we'd been expecting for weeks – Rangers Football Club were going into administration. That call on the afternoon of 13 February 2012, was the culmination of a fortnight of daily 'check calls' with the petitions department.

After putting the receiver down, I stood up and shouted something to the newsroom about Rangers going into administration, despite barely believing what I'd been told. The place went haywire and I recollect spending the rest of the day writing and checking out other lines, often with senior members of the news team looking over my shoulder.

It soon transpired that Craig Whyte had not just taken us by surprise by signalling his intention to appoint Duff and Phelps – he hadn't told any of his staff. He managed to beat officers of HM Revenue and Customs to the doors of Parliament House by a matter of hours. The tax authority was seeking to declare The Rangers Football Club PLC insolvent. It turned out that Rangers hadn't paid millions in National Insurance and PAYE in Whyte's nine months in charge.

But, as ever is the case with this story, it was not as straightforward as laying the blame at the door of one party – in this instance an asset stripper who convinced many he was a 'Motherwell-born billionaire' despite having no discernible wealth. The meltdown had its beginnings in the two decades Sir David Murray ran the club using a seemingly limitless credit line with Scottish banks and a ruse to avoid paying tax on the inflated salaries of players and directors (the Big Tax Case).

As a journalist, it emphasised to me the importance of the written word. Talk around finances, plans and ambitions – especially in football – is cheap. This was demonstrated through the Murray years, where mega casinos and getting Ronaldo to switch the Galacticos for Govan were reported as stories.

What often mattered in covering this has been the 'paper trail'. It was not what 'off the record steer' a PR man had given me – it was what was put down in black and white. It involved seemingly endless hours trawling through company documents, poring over court cases and attempting to map out an increasingly complex cast of players. But it also involved a lot of 'old fashioned' journalism, such as doorstepping those involved.

Tuesday 14 February 2012
STV News

Rangers Football Club are tonight in administration. And question marks over the Club's fixture with Kilmarnock on Saturday as Strathclyde Police threatened not to commit resources to the match unless they received guarantees about payment from the administrator.

DIARY: Basically, it gives them time to try to reach a deal with creditors. If they fail to do so, it means the club goes bust. Given the main credit seems to be the Tax Office and they have been playing hard ball, there could be every chance of this happening. It's that serious. A black, black day for the club, probably the worst ever after the Ibrox Disaster.

Also, last night I made a reference to 'the situation we're in now' and, of course, rather than being seen as the generic reference it was, plenty have been claiming it showed my loyalties. There really is no point in arguing.

Wednesday 18 April 2012
STV News

STV cameras were in court today to film the sentencing of a killer to life in prison. It was a legal first that made Scottish courts the focus of UK-wide attention. The killer, David

Gilroy, was sentenced to life after a jury convicted him of the murder of his former lover Suzanne Pilley. Our cameras showed the judge ordering that Gilroy should serve at least 18 years and urging him to reveal where he had hidden her body.

DIARY: It is a first and, hopefully, will lead to more TV in the courts. Justice should be seen to be done.

The filming in courtrooms hasn't progressed much further. Like so much that seems antiquated in the legal system, there seems little justification in seeing a judge making their address, but not the convicted person to whom they are directed.

DEATH OF THE LOCKERBIE BOMBER
Sunday 20 May 2012
STV News

The Lockerbie Bomber, Abdelbaset Al-Megrahi has died in Libya. His family said that he passed away around 11.00am this morning UK time. Megrahi was convicted of the worst-ever terrorist atrocity on UK soil. 270 people died when Pan Am Flight 103 was blown out of the skies over Lockerbie in 1988. Nearly three years ago, he was controversially released from a Scottish jail on compassionate grounds because he had terminal cancer.

DIARY: The obituary, pre-prepared since his release – has been sitting at the bottom of our running order for years now. Had always planned for a big programme, but in the end just did a bulletin.

I always thought the release of the Lockerbie Bomber was a misstep by the SNP administration. I suspect that they were unconvinced of Megrahi's guilt and didn't want him dying in a Scottish jail if that was later proved.

IMRAN KHAN
Sunday 20 May 2012 *(cont)*

DIARY: Interviewed Imran Khan this evening at the Marriott Hotel. Surprised by lack of security, given the record of political assassinations in Pakistan. He was a bit cold at first, ignoring my preambles, but warmed up as the interview progressed. Interesting on Western misconceptions about Pakistan.

He was in Scotland to raise funds and encourage the Scottish Pakistani community to get involved in the country's election.

Monday 21 May 2012
Scotland Tonight

Pakistan. 'Dangerously divided'. On the brink of becoming a failed state. That's the view of some. But Imran Khan wants to be his country's next Prime Minister. The cricketing legend has been campaigning in Scotland after a change in the law gave overseas Pakistanis a vote in upcoming elections. Khan has pledged to cut military ties with the United States, end corruption and bring more democracy to Pakistan. And he told *Scotland Tonight* the view from the West is not just wrong, but damaging.

IMRAN KHAN: Pakistan is stuck in this war on terror. We had nothing to do with it. We ended up becoming a frontline state and that has devastated the country. 40,000 people have died, the economy has lost about $70 billion, about three million people internally displaced because of this war, and there's no end to it... If I was an American, I would be very concerned about the impact of drone attacks. Number one – it violates all humanitarian laws. Here's America and the US, telling the world about human rights. No humanitarian law allows suspects to be eliminated, their relatives, their friends – anyone in the neighbourhood could be eliminated through these bombs, through drones. So that in itself creates a lot of hatred against the US – it creates anti-Americanism.

Imran Khan served as Prime Minister for Pakistan from 2018 to 2022 and is currently in jail facing charges he denies.

Friday 25 May 2012
STV News

It is the campaign determined to capture the hearts and minds of the Scottish people. The battle for an Independent Scotland is underway. Alex Salmond set the party a target of enlisting the support of a million Scots for a declaration of Scottish Independence. The nationalists say their campaign will be the biggest community effort in Scottish history.

DIARY: A rather uninspiring affair. It should have been in Stirling with music and all. Instead, a rather flat event at an Edinburgh cinema.

THE OLYMPIC TORCH
Friday 8 June 2012
STV News

The Olympic Torch for London 2012 has arrived in Scotland to an enormous welcome. Huge crowds have greeted the flame as it begins a tour around the country. It arrived in Glasgow this evening, where thousands are at a party organised to celebrate the occasion.

I was chosen to be an Olympic Torchbearer, presumably because of my TV profile. I did feel rather unworthy in comparison to many of the other torchbearers, but it was a great honour and if you're asked to carry the Olympic Flame you're not going to say no.

DIARY: The meeting point for the first torchbearers was a hotel in Stranraer for processing and briefings. When we left the hotel just before 6.00am the crowds on the street were astonishing, later estimated at 2–3,000. An incredible turnout and replicated at all the stops north to Glasgow. A real sense of community engagement with children, especially, prominent. I'm not sure I've seen anything like it.

It's all very choreographed and the exchange or 'kiss' of the flame was all pretty much done by the supervising runners. Then off on my run. I made a point of proffering the torch and flame to the onlookers because that was what was important. I took it to the edge of the town, so the crowds thinned out considerably. Had to say something to camera as soon as I finished. I thought in advance what would be appropriate and I think I pitched it right, emphasising the pride and privilege I felt. The torch convoy was already off to the next stop – the flame having been transferred from my torch to a lantern. When I came back into work one of the cameramen had collected my torch for me and left it on my desk. In my absence loads of colleagues took the opportunity to have their photos taken with it – not all of them as respectful as they might have done – baseball and golf poses for example! Many more from the building came to me asking if they could pose with it too. Genuinely amazed by the reaction to it – shows what it means.

Later to George Square for a big event. Again, astonishing crowds. We were doing a live on top of a bus. Leaving the Square, I was stopped by scores of people wanting their photo taken with the Torch. Amazing day.

RANGERS GO INTO LIQUIDATION
Tuesday 12 June 2012
STV News

Rangers face liquidation after HMRC rejects plans for a Company Voluntary Arrangement. The decision means a new company will be created as part of Charles Green's takeover. He says he is hugely disappointed and claims that ultimately creditors will get less money than they would have through a CVA.

DIARY: The tax authorities, HMRC, have rejected a debt deal with the new owner Charles Green because they don't believe it's in the best interests of the taxpayer. So now that's it. Interesting question is whether the SPL clubs will allow them to stay in the SPL or will they have to drop down the leagues? Many clubs' supporters believe Rangers should be forced down, but the club owners realise the financial implications of that. They'll vote by the end of the month. It's sad that a Scottish institution should be brought to its knees like this. And the HMRC have not performed well. If this is their policy, why wait until now to say it?

Scotland Tonight Special

This was the day of reckoning. The day the

old Rangers died and the new Rangers was born, fighting to stay alive.

Vox Pops of Shareholders

It's like being at a funeral with no coffin there.

Quite emotional. (*voice breaking*) Disappointing.

I'm sick. I haven't slept for three months.

Words fail me. It's shattering.

ARCHIE MACPHERSON, football commentator: This is almost historically overwhelming. This is a turning point in the Scottish game as a whole, not just for Rangers.

JM: In football terms, this would be a classic. It's got all the ingredients; dramatic high stakes, passion, players who are loved and loathed, a match that ebbs and flows and now seems to be going into extra time. Rangers are fighting for their very existence. After more than 100 years they have a new name – THE Rangers Football Club. And it has a new Chief Executive, Charles Green. Its most successful manager Walter Smith has also dramatically emerged to front a bid to buy the club from Green. But either way, it'll be a new Rangers, a newco. For many fans it'll never be the same.

For 140 years Rangers entertained and allowed a vast diaspora of followers to dream. They are more than just a club and always will be. Some of their traditions have alienated those who do not follow them. Not all the tears being shed are done in sorrow. This is a chapter in which a once great club has been brought to its knees. Other indignities lie ahead. But tonight those who might consider themselves Rangers men are refusing to lie down. The passion for the red, white and blue will transcend and endure what is, after all, a corporate kill off. Rangers will be reborn to fight another day. For the moment, though, purgatory is their state.

This was the closing section of a piece I recorded on Rangers' history. Several Rangers fans said it expressed exactly how they felt. The irony was that it was based upon a script written by my Celtic-supporting colleague Bernard Ponsonby.

DOLLY PARTON
Wednesday 20 June 2012

DIARY: Interviewed Dolly Parton via satellite from Nashville. It was one of a series she was doing, one after the other. Have to admire her professionalism. It was something like 5.00am over there, but she was very warm, while sticking to the corporate line and the country gal shtick. Good one to do.

STV News

And finally – The Dolly Parton song '9 to 5' has become a dance floor and karaoke favourite. It comes from the '80s movie of the same name about three women getting their own back on their chauvinist boss. Now the stage show is coming to Scotland in November. Dolly has written the music for it and spoke to STV News from Nashville about Scotland, her music and the show.

JM: Some of the girls were asking how would you deal with a '9 to 5' type boss?

DOLLY PARTON: (*laughs*) You just got to stand up for what you believe and who you are, and if it means you lose that job go find another one, but don't let anybody mistreat you.

JM: When we told people that we were going to be interviewing you here in Scotland, there was great enthusiasm, there was a great deal of love for Dolly Parton. Why should that be, do you think?

DP: Well, I think people relate to me. I think they feel themselves in me because I'm just a country girl and, like I say, the folks that came over all those many years ago, brought all those wonderful stories and songs, and that feeling that I have is just in my DNA to write these kind of songs, and I think we're just the same people, and I think they feel me, I feel them and I really think we just feel like relatives, because we really are.

JM: Well, Scotland will always love you, Dolly Parton. Thanks for joining us.

DP: Thank you. Appreciate you.

My pay off to the interview looks cheesy in print, but it worked well in the moment. She has that effect on you. When we were establishing the communications with Nashville I could see and hear her playing with my name, 'John MacKaaaay', probably because the pronunciation was so different from the name written before her. I thought maybe I was witnessing the beginning of a new Dolly composition. I wasn't, but I wait in hope.

Monday 25 June 2012
STV News

We're better together, that was the message today as the campaign to save the Union got underway. Former Chancellor Alistair Darling is leading the movement and said that the vote on independence would be the most important decision Scots will make in 300 years. He warned that voting for independence would be an irrevocable move.

ALISTAIR DARLING, Leader, Better Together: Chairing this campaign is one of the most important things I have ever done in politics. The decision we make is the most important we will make in our lifetime. If you're going to separate, you're on your own. There's no way back from that. I think that the debate has only just started, because it was necessary to ensure that we constructed a sensible campaign of people united in their view that Scotland should remain within the United Kingdom.

DIARY: Formal launch of the No campaign in the Independence Referendum. It was a bit better than the Yes campaign's misfire launch.

Friday 13 July 2012
STV News

Rangers have been told they'll have to play in the SFL's Third Division this season. Members rejected calls for the crisis hit club to start in the First Division by a massive majority vote. Tonight, the newco's Chief Executive says he accepts the decision.

DIARY: That is where most Rangers fans want them to go – take the punishment and start again. However, there is a lot of resentment around and most Rangers fans also believe that going into Division Three will force other SPL clubs to go bust. Scottish football has long needed a rebalancing.

ANDY MURRAY WINS THE US OPEN
Tuesday 11 September 2012
STV News

Many doubted whether he would ever do it. Last night Andy Murray proved them wrong and – at his fifth attempt – won his first Grand Slam trophy. He beat the World Number 2, Novak Djokovic at the US Open in New York. It's another historic achievement to add to Britain's summer of sport.

DIARY: Andy Murray did it! As we have constantly been reminded, he's the first British male to win a major tennis honour in 76 years. He was two sets up, but lost the third and fourth set and I would have assumed at that point he would have lost. To his great credit, and it's where he's improved, he had the mental strength to come back and win the fifth. At STV we have archive of him as a 12-year-old. Everyone very pleased.

OLYMPIC HOMECOMING PARADE
Friday 14 September 2012
STV News – live from George Square

Good evening, live from Glasgow's George Square on a night where the true Olympic spirit lives on. Around me here, and along the victory parade tens of thousands have been cheering the remarkable sportsmen and women who have given us a summer to remember. This is their chance to say thank you to those who have supported them. This is also our chance to thank them for the legacy they leave – a legacy to build upon – as we look ahead to the Commonwealth Games in this city in just two years' time.

JM: You're on the STV *News at Six* live. What's it been like for you today?

SIR CHRIS HOY, six-time Olympic gold medallist: It's hard to express how I'm feeling, how the whole team are feeling just now. This is way beyond what we were expecting. Very emotional, overwhelming really. What a reception, not just here, but the whole route from the start to the end was full. Amazing. Amazing... It's a strange feeling now. It's going to come to an end eventually, but these celebrations and these parades are just way beyond what you expect. And it's our chance to thank the public for their support. Incredible.

JM: And we can build on this for the Commonwealth Games in 2014?

CH: Absolutely. You see the energy and the enthusiasm, the positivity. And it's only two years to go now and everyone is going to be behind it. It's a great time to be a sports person or to be looking to get into sport.

DIARY: A great programme tonight on the welcome home to Scotland's Olympic and Paralympic athletes. I anchored it live from George Square where some 17,000 were packed in. It couldn't have gone better for us in terms of timing, just as we came on air Sir Chris Hoy was still on the stage, so I ad-libbed into that. We then got Sir Chris onto our platform along with Kathleen Grainger – gold medal rower – and Neil Fachie – gold/silver Paralympic cyclist. By that point I was flying solo because I couldn't hear the gallery for the noise. I knew we had a report to go to, but I was concerned about losing the guests if I went into it, so I brought them on live which gave a sense of immediacy. I went with my gut on that and it seemed to work. I was impressed by the Olympians. Nice people, thrilled by the reaction. Sir Chris Hoy – our greatest Olympian – is a genuine guy. Also, good to see what a boost the Paralympians got.

Tuesday 25 September 2012
STV News

In what could prove to be one of the most important speeches by a party leader since Devolution, Scottish Labour Leader Johann Lamont has warned that a whole range of benefits from free tuition fees, prescriptions, bus passes and free personal care may have to be axed as the age of austerity bites. She has asked a party committee to provide policy options for her ahead of the next election when Labour could be ready to put some unpalatable choices before the voters.

Scotland Tonight

JM: The Scottish Labour Leader is with us now. Johann Lamont, why did you make that speech?

JOHANN LAMONT, Scottish Labour Leader: Increasingly, I was conscious there was a gap between what we were being told in the chamber on a Thursday by the First Minister – everything is wonderful – and the people talking to me across the communities of Scotland. The woman who is the school secretary telling me how difficult it was in the school managing budgets; the care worker who told me she now goes in for a 15-minute visit to an elderly person, is told 'talk and go', nothing to do with personal support and care; the young teacher worried about whether they are going to actually have a permanent job; and I am concerned we are in a place now where with the SNP and the Scottish Government we have this claim that everything is fine, but the reality on the ground is very different. We need to have a debate about it... I want the debate. I don't have all the answers, but I know there are some very hard questions we have to address.

JM: You cannot force the SNP to take part in this debate though, should this not have been a discussion your party had behind closed doors?

JL: Well, you could do that, but I have to say we lost badly in the last election just over a year ago and I think it would be unacceptable for people in this country to think that somehow we're going to go back off into a room, come out with solutions and present them to people. The first thing we have to do is recognise that there is a problem.

JM: But the SNP say it is affordable. They say they can pay for it.

JL: The reality is on the ground there are consequences to these policies. I am not saying that all of these policies are bad, but if at the same time the consequence, for example, of council tax freeze is a care worker is more stretched and more pressured in their work and the care they are delivering is less adequate then we have got a problem. I want to bring that out into the open.

DIARY: It's quite a stance for a Labour figure to take, but an honest one. My interview with her was not hounding – that's not my style – but firm. I think Johann Lamont is a decent, honest woman, but as someone said, leaders lead, they don't open up for debate. They set the path.

Monday 1 October 2012
Scotland Tonight Interview with Deputy First Minister Nicola Sturgeon

JM: Johann Lamont was saying last week that we can't have universal free benefit, it is not affordable. Can it be afforded?

NS: It is afforded because the Scottish Government, within the constraints, with the resources that we have now, we put forward balanced budgets. Politics is all about choices and we have made the choice to prioritise growth, but to protect household budgets.

JM: Can that continue with an ageing population and all that comes with it?

NS: What we have to remember is that many of these things are preventative spend as well. If we invest in helping older people stay in their own homes, to live independently for as long as possible, then we will reduce the expenditure in the long term on hospital admissions for example. So, these things are all about preventing much costlier interventions. I think that was the mistake Johann Lamont made last week, as well as threatening many of the benefits lots of people in Scotland really, really value, we are, notwithstanding these difficult economic times, a wealthy country. We have got massive natural resources, and it makes my blood boil that we have got so many kids living in poverty when we are an energy rich country. We can change that if we have the powers of independence.

JM: Last week's First Minister's Questions was interesting with yourself, Johann Lamont and Ruth Davidson. A lot of people said that women would bring a different tone to Scottish politics. First Minster's Questions was described as a stairheid rammy.

NS: (*laughs*) I have to confess, you probably would say that.

JM: Why is that the case?

NS: Well, I am not sure you can expect the women who are in the Scottish Parliament now to single-handedly change the tone of our politics. We still have a very adversarial system, although I would say that although people see FMQs, a lot of what the Scottish Parliament does, our committee system for example, is not adversarial. It is consensus building and people across the political spectrum working together. I think I would like to see more women involved in politics. Scotland does a lot better than many other countries, but we can still do better. I would like to see lots of younger women get involved and that is why I am so encouraged by Women for Independence and what they bring to the debate.

JM: You were a younger woman who got involved.

NS: I still am!

JM: Of course you are, I beg your pardon. What sacrifices did you have to make in terms of who you were to compete in this very male dominated environment?

NS: I think looking back on it, as a young woman I took myself far too seriously. Because I thought I had to be ultra serious in order to convince people that I was as good as male counterparts. One of the things I hope I have learned as I have got older is to take myself less seriously to concentrate on doing the best job I can do. But there are other things in life and I think it is always good to be reminded of that.

JM: And still young, Nicola Sturgeon. Thank you.

DIARY: Always hugely impressive, but a warmer side coming through after being very stern for many years. Interview was fine, but only got as much out of it as she was prepared to give.

KEVIN BRIDGES
Saturday 10 November 2012

DIARY: Interview with Kevin Bridges the comedian in Glasgow. I think he's superb. Just a funny, funny guy. A great half hour interview which ranged over many things. It'll make a cracking piece for a *Scotland Tonight*. Relaxed chat with him as the cameras were set up. Really enjoyed the time with him.

Scotland Tonight

JM: Kevin Bridges, thanks for joining us on *Scotland Tonight*.

KEVIN BRIDGES: It's a pleasure John, I've been a big fan for years.

JM: Really?

KB: Aye.

I know this initial exchange is superfluous, but I had to leave it in.

JM: It's been a great year for you. You're on tour, of course, but nominated for two BAFTAS and record sell out of the SECC.

KB: You don't really realise it's been a great year until it's finished. When you go on tour you sort of go in a wee bubble. I've been on tour since the end of May and 8 December is the last night, so after that then you look back and go wow, the amount of people I've played to! It is quite humbling, the amount of people coming out, the queue outside for the DVD, to look at them standing in the rain and that, it's a wee bit... it's just me.

JM: Take us right back to the 17-year-old who thought he might want to be a stand-up comedian. What made you think that?

KB: I had just left school, I was 16 and I had the idea, I think we were in one of my pal's houses, he had a house party or something and I left at five in the morning, you know that way where you're just walking home, thinking, 'I'm going to be somebody'. I went in, I think half-five, six o'clock in the morning, got my computer up, just e-mailed The Stand, just saying, 'I would like to give stand-up comedy a wee go and here's some jokes,' and they got back to me. I'd totally forgot about it, I woke up the next day, never even remembered sending the e-mail, and they said, 'We'll book you in for a five-minute spot in Glasgow.' So, I thought I just need to walk on, it's just talking to people. All my pals think I'm quite funny, I just need to try and convey that as naturally as possible, just turning a group of strangers into a group of your pals. I never had an opening line, I had some ideas about being 17. My USP, my unique selling point, is going to be that I'm the youngest guy on the bill. I showed up, and they said, 'There's a 17-year-old on, underager, under no circumstances anybody sell him alcohol, we'll be facing disciplinary action.' All the staff had this wee memo through from the head office in Edinburgh. So, I read that, and I walked on stage and said, 'I'm only 17 and I just got sold a pint, so get it up you.' It's not the greatest gag you're ever going to hear, but I think the audience, they erupted. It was my dad that was there, he was quite emotional just going, 'Where did that come from?' He just thought I was just a waster at school because he would go to parents' night and the teachers would say 'Kevin's funny, but...' It was always 'but', 'Kevin's funny but...' So, I think my dad was almost proud that I had put it to something more creative.

JM: Kevin Bridges, it's been a pleasure.

KB: John, thanks a lot mate. Good man. Cheers.

Like Billy Connolly before him, some have claimed that there are people on every street in Glasgow who are as funny as Kevin Bridges. During our conversation Kevin acknowledged that may be so, but they should do what he did and take it onto stage. I think he does himself a disservice. There are few who can do what he does. I saw him have

a crowd of 10,000 in the SECC in constant laughter. Few of the bar room funny men could do that. His humour takes me back to my youth. His resurrection of the exclamation 'Yaldy!' is just one of many delights for me.

OSCAR PISTORIUS
Monday 12 November 2012
Scotland Tonight

Olympian and Paralympian Oscar Pistorius says it will be a dream come true to make his Commonwealth Games debut in Glasgow. The South African sprinter, who is known as the blade runner, spoke of his excitement at 2014 as he received an honorary degree from the city's Strathclyde University. I spoke to him as he visited the university's National Centre for Prosthetics and Orthotics.

JM: Oscar Pistorius, thanks for joining us on *Scotland Tonight*. You're here at Strathclyde University earning an honorary degree for the work that you've done in prosthetics here – what developments are you seeing?

OP: If you look at the way the Paralympic movement has enabled people to see Paralympians and people living with disabilities in a new light, I think that's fantastic, but being here at this centre, a lot of the innovation that's at the forefront of what people are going to be using in the coming years is getting used here, getting trained here, and it's fantastic to see that. The students are very excited and very passionate about what they do, and at the end of the day it rubs off on the users and on the patients here.

DIARY: He lost his legs below the knee almost at birth because his lower legs didn't have a fibula. He runs on blades, giving him the name Blade Runner. He was very pleasant and open and the kids were in awe of him. As usual, the flunkies start trying to cut the interview early. Anyway, a good piece for tonight and an inspirational guy.

Two months after this interview Pistorius shot and killed his girlfriend Reeva Steenkamp at his home in South Africa. His trial for murder drew worldwide attention. Pistorius said he had mistaken Reeva for an intruder. He was found guilty of culpable homicide and jailed. He was released on parole in 2024.

ANDY MURRAY
Tuesday 13 November 2012
Scotland Tonight

2012 has been the greatest year of Andy Murray's tennis career, with an Olympic gold on home soil and a Grand Slam triumph at the US Open. Today, the World Number Three was in Edinburgh with his mother Judy as part of an initiative designed to get the younger generation to develop the skills required for sport.

JMK: Andy, welcome to *Scotland Tonight*, it has been a fantastic year for you.

ANDY MURRAY: It has been the best year I have had on the tour in my career by a pretty long way.

JMK: What do you reflect on most, the Olympics?

AM: Yes, it's very different the Olympics and the US Open. The Wimbledon final as well was probably one of the toughest moments I'd had in my career, but then followed by the Olympics, which was the biggest high in my career a few weeks later on the same court. So, I had lots of ups and downs this year, but I would say the Olympics as a whole, just because of the magnitude of the event and how well it went, how successful the British athletes were, to be part of that was great.

JMK: You've said that sometimes when you had lost a match, it was difficult, it took days for you to manage to get yourself going and for all this training to be worthwhile. And now you realise why pushing yourself was worthwhile, but before you ever got to that stage, what was it that kept you going?

AM: I'm not sure. It used to take me a long time when I had lost big matches and Grand Slam finals, it took me sometimes months before I felt right again on the court. But after Wimbledon this year, it wasn't like that, it only took me a few days and I felt something change, I don't know if it was in that match in particular, but I got over that loss much quicker than I had in previous big matches and then I practised unbelievably in the build-up to the Olympics and then played one of my best tournaments ever there. So, I don't know exactly what changed around that time, but something did, and I went on to have the best few months of my career.

JMK: And Judy, you have always believed that your boys would go to the very top, not just be good, but go to the very top. You have always had that faith, why?

JUDY MURRAY: You don't ever know that they are going to. I think with them really from, probably when they were both 14 or 15, they never really wavered from the fact that they wanted to be tennis players and I think as a parent you just try to encourage them as much as you can and try and create the right opportunities for them at the right time, it's up to them to go off and do it and to work hard and to maximise their potential and they have certainly done that.

JMK: So, we are looking towards next year. How do you push on, Andy?

AM: After the US Open a lot of people had said to me, 'Do you think it will be difficult to motivate yourself now?' because it is something I was waiting for for so long. It has been the last, really, five years of my life I have been trying to win a Grand Slam, so to finally do it was great. But actually, the few days afterwards, it made me realise that all the hard work and stuff was worth it. So, I'm going to go away and train really hard in December, go away to Miami for a three and a half, four weeks training block and get myself in the best shape possible for the Australian Open.

JMK: And Judy, when Andy won the US Masters, we had a discussion on *Scotland Tonight* about how we get more young children involved and there was a lot of concern about tennis perhaps being an elitist sport. We're in Craiglockhart in the capital, it's the only indoor centre and is still quite costly. Is there still a problem getting it open to everyone?

JM: Yes, I think we need more public courts. We lost a lot of public courts over the last 20 years. A tennis court takes up a big space, so we have lost it to housing, supermarkets, sometimes even to other sports because there wasn't much of a demand for tennis then. But now you are realising what you don't have because so many kids want to play, so resurrecting local public courts and school courts, I think is absolutely crucial so that more people can play and we certainly need more indoor facilities because our weather is rubbish. But they need to be affordable as well as being accessible and they are quite expensive, sadly.

Andy Murray went on to win Wimbledon the following season, the first British male to do so in more than 70 years.

DIARY: Murray is sometimes seen as grumpy, but I found him to be perfectly affable. He was happy to have his photo taken and I was struck by how lean he was – I could feel his ribs. If I hadn't known better I'd think the fellow needed a good feed.

Tuesday 11 December 2012

DIARY: Interview with Charles Green. He was distrusted at first because nobody knew him or what he was about, but he's won over most Rangers fans by playing to the gallery to please the Bears – fighting the SFA and SPL and more. The interview covered as much as I could in the time allowed. Celtic fans thought I gave him an easy ride, most others thought I got as much out of it as I could. He stayed on in the green room and enjoys holding court. It's entertaining listening to him and he has big plans for Rangers. However, all the stuff he's been saying about the international leagues and owning their own broadcasting rights has been said before by David Murray and it didn't happen.

2013

Thursday 10 January 2013
Scotland Tonight

Alistair Darling has this week taken his fight to save the Union on the road, on a self-styled 'listening tour of Scotland'. The leader of the 'Better Together' campaign joined me in the *Scotland Tonight* studio.

DIARY: First time I've interviewed Alistair Darling – the former Chancellor – now leader of the Better Together campaign in the studio. I found him to be much warmer than his reputation would suggest. The interview was extended, ended up being nearly 12 minutes. I let him make his case, but I also challenged him – uncertainty remaining within the UK and sharing a platform with David Cameron and Nick Clegg. I don't see the point in shouting matches.

Monday 14 January 2013

DIARY: Latest polling showing support for independence stalled at 28 points – 20 behind those who'd vote No, with almost one in four undecided. It is a big ask, but the Yes campaign remain positive. They have no option.

Tuesday 29 January 2013
Scotland Tonight

One thing both sides in the independence debate agree on is that next year's referendum will be the biggest political decision Scotland has faced for more than 300 years. The pro-unionists enjoy a strong lead in the opinion polls, but Yes campaigners insist the battle is there to be won. We're now joined by the First Minister Alex Salmond.

ALEX SALMOND, First Minister: We have the next 18 months to convince the people. Scotland will listen to arguments, and if we can win the argument we can win the referendum.

JM: Can an independent Scotland appeal to business and be socially just? So, attracting businessmen, but appealing to those who want a more socially just society?

AS: Yes, I'm not saying it will appeal to every businessman or every member of the community. There's plenty of Scottish business people who believe in a more socially just country, and plenty of research says that most successful countries are just. One of the reasons Scotland will prosper is it will be a just nation. One or two people are not for the community, but many, many in business have an acute sense of community responsibility. I think there is nothing incompatible with having an economically successful and a socially just Scotland. People vote for independence for a range of reasons, but above all, the vote for it as they believe the people who live in a country are the best placed to take decisions affecting the country. It's not Alex Salmond's version of independence, it's not necessarily the business person or trade unionist's version. Independence will develop as the people of Scotland decide, they will vote for the party they want to govern them.

DIARY: We had a production meeting and structured the interview – social justice/economy/Europe/NATO/polls. I went into the interview well prepared. It was a straightforward interview in the sense that I asked him considered questions and he, in fairness, answered them straight. He didn't waffle. I wonder if I should be a bit more aggressive, but these interviews are increasingly dull and nothing is learned. I'm sure there will be criticism that it's not challenging enough, but there is also praise that I let people answer. Salmond himself was quite relaxed and not full of the bombast that sometimes overtakes him.

Wednesday 30 January 2013
STV News

Should Scotland be an independent country? That's the question you will have to answer in next year's referendum. Today the Scottish Government accepted changes to the question they wanted asked, as all sides united behind the recommendations of the Electoral Commission. But there could be trouble ahead over a commission proposal that the UK and Scottish Governments should agree now what process would be followed in the event of a Yes vote.

DIARY: The Electoral Commission recommended the referendum question be changed from 'Do you agree Scotland should be an independent country?' – which was considered to be leading – to 'Should Scotland be an independent country?'

Tuesday 5 February 2013
STV News

The Scottish and UK Governments are at loggerheads tonight over claims from the SNP that Scotland could be independent by March of 2016 following a Yes vote next year. The timetable has been described as ludicrous with the Scottish Secretary insisting the nationalists are using the issue as a distraction from key debates surrounding the attempt to break with the Union.

DIARY: The Scottish Government issued a 'road map' outlining their plans for Scotland becoming independent should there be a 'Yes' vote in the referendum. Basically, they're saying the process would be all but complete by March 2016. That does seem rather optimistic and they've come under fire for it. However, at least they're setting out what they expect to happen post-referendum. The No campaign haven't and I don't think they will.

JOHN C REILLY

Monday 11 February 2013
Scotland Tonight

He's an acclaimed Hollywood actor known for his roles in films such as *Chicago*, *Gangs of New York* and the latest Disney 3D animation, *Wreck-it Ralph*. John C Reilly is also an accomplished musician with a passion for country and roots music. Tomorrow night the 'John Reilly and Friends' band is playing a special concert in Glasgow.

JM: You're known as an Irish-American, but you've actually got Scottish roots as well.

JOHN C REILLY: Yeah, I do... A few years ago our family did a genealogy and, yeah, there's a pretty strong Scottish contingent there. John, I have to say, I'm a little disappointed that we're not going to talk about the Pope or Scottish Independence *(Scottish Independence and the resignation of Pope Benedict were the other subjects on the programme).*

JM: Let me hear your opinions, then?

JR: I'm in favour of both! First of all, my father's retirement was one of the happiest days of his life, and second of all, I'm an American, so freeing yourself from England worked out quite well for America, so I'm in favour of it...

JM: Has that whole Scottish, Irish background, is that what influences the music that you play?

JR: Yeah absolutely. If you look at roots music, and we do play traditional roots music, like Appalachian, kinda old folk music and old country standards, and everything all the way down to the roots of the tree of song in America. And if you go far enough into those roots you end up discovering Irish and Scottish and English music that came over on the ships. And it somehow feels full circle that we're back here doing this music...

DIARY: He's been in loads of movies and is one of those guys whose name isn't so well known, but whose face is very familiar. He was clearly very tired and, in fact, the music concert he was promoting with his band had sold out, so he could have pulled out. To his credit he didn't. Very personable and no entourage. I liked him and it would have been good to have had a beer with him.

Monday 25 February 2013
STV News – live from St Mary's Cathedral in Edinburgh

The Catholic Church in Scotland is in turmoil tonight. The Pope has told the leader of Scotland's Catholics to step down with immediate effect following allegations by three priests and a former priest of 'inappropriate behaviour'. The Vatican will investigate the claims.

DIARY: Coming just ahead of his departure to vote in the conclave for the new Pope, it was dynamite. We did an STV News Special live from St Mary's Cathedral in Edinburgh. Sad day for the Catholic Church and for Cardinal O'Brien, who has the reputation of being a decent man. However, he is outspoken on gay rights issues and the implication is that there was a deep hypocrisy in that.

What is the way forward for the Catholic Church? One guest on *Scotland Tonight*, Michael McMahon MSP, put it best – the RC Church should focus on the issue in which it excels – charity, support for the poor etc.

Monday 4 March 2013

DIARY: Invited to lunch with some senior execs from the Royal Bank of Scotland (RBS) which is one of the biggest bogey banks from the 2008 crisis. It's owned 87 per cent by the taxpayer, but they have awful PR – not the guys who do it, but what they have to deal with. Talked about turning the bank around, but what they cannot or will not change is the huge bonus culture (which applies to banking globally) and they will never have public understanding until they do.

Thursday 21 March 2013
STV News

18 September 2014 – the date Scotland will decide its future. The Scottish Government has kept the nation guessing, but today they revealed the date of the Independence Referendum. Alex Salmond made the revelation to the Scottish Parliament this afternoon.

DEATH OF MARGARET THATCHER
Monday 8 April 2013
STV News

Baroness Thatcher has died at the age of 87. The former Conservative leader passed away following a stroke. She was the first female Prime Minister. The first to win three General Elections in modern times. And one of the longest serving occupants of 10 Downing Street. In Scotland she'll be remembered most for the introduction of the Poll Tax, the closure of Ravenscraig and the death of the mining industry. But she's also recognised tonight by friends and enemies alike as a towering political figure.

Scotland Tonight

Baroness Thatcher... was an extraordinary politician whose policies changed the face of Scotland. To her supporters she was a great Prime Minister who saved the country from economic collapse. For others she was a deeply divisive figure who pursued an agenda which decimated industries and destroyed communities.

LORD MICHAEL FORSYTH, Former Scottish Secretary: I will remember her as a very kindly, caring lady who was a great friend to me and my family... She was a giant... Not even the hardest line Socialist would argue that it was possible to keep going with mines or steel mills that were no longer competitive and it was important to create new jobs. Now, that does not in any way diminish the pain and suffering that was caused by that change. What made Margaret Thatcher unique is that she was a politician who was prepared to do the right thing and take the opprobrium in the interests of the country. Sadly, today I think we have too many politicians in all political parties who are too worried about what next day's press is going to say about them.

LORD GEORGE FOULKES, Labour: The changes would have come, but they could have come more slowly and more carefully and with more consideration for the people, not as ruthlessly as Thatcher did it... She was actually quite a kind person on a one-to-one basis and this was a dilemma because she was very ruthless and vindictive politically, but kind personally.

JOAN MCALPINE, SNP: It's all very well saying there needed to be structural reform on the economy, but if we behaved like the Europeans and supported some of our industries, like our shipyards, we'd still have a better manufacturing base than we had after the Thatcher years.

DIARY: She was a huge public figure in my lifetime and remains a divisive figure even now. What is not in doubt is her status as a political giant. A conviction politician who provided strong leadership. Interesting to see the reaction in different areas. The London media were rather uncritical. Hundreds gathered in George Square to celebrate, which I think was distasteful.

Tuesday 16 April 2013

DIARY: A real error at lunchtime. We reported on a Scot named Chris McKenzie who'd been injured in the Boston Marathon Bombing. We even had a photo. Turns out he didn't exist. The photo was indeed of a Chris McKenzie, but just a face that came up in a Google search. STV, the BBC and other organisations all believed an asshole on Twitter who seemed to find it funny. Contemptible. Nonetheless, we fell below our own standards.

Wednesday 8 May 2013
STV News – live from Manchester with Raman Bhardwaj

Good evening, live from Old Trafford – on the day Sir Alex Ferguson announces he is retiring from the beautiful game, ending the most successful managerial career in British football history. In all Sir Alex won 49 trophies, including here at Man United – 13 Premier League titles and major success in Europe. Today's news draws to a close one of Scotland's greatest success stories.

FIRST INDEPENDENCE DEBATE
Thursday 16 May 2013
Scotland Tonight

On 18 September next year the Scottish people will be asked to make the biggest political decision in more than 300 years. The Independence Referendum campaign will be fought on various fronts. Tonight, in the first of a series of live debates, we spotlight the key battleground of economics. Joining us are two of Scotland's most senior politicians.

From the Scottish Government, we have Deputy First Minister Nicola Sturgeon; from the UK Government, the Secretary of State for Scotland Michael Moore. They'll be crossing swords in debate and will also get the opportunity to cross-examine each other.

The format of the debate was agreed by both sides beforehand. They'd make a statement, I would question them both separately, then they would cross-examine each other for a set period of time each. I could not intervene other than to alert them to how long they had left. It was intriguing seeing them react under a different pressure from what they are used to. Nicola Sturgeon was an obvious winner. Michael Moore allowed her to dominate his cross-examination. She would reply to his questions with another question, which he would then try to answer. He was too gentlemanly and never really got going against her.

Monday 20 May 2013
STV News

It's an issue which has caused deep division in the Church of Scotland – whether to allow gay people to be ordained as ministers. The Kirk's General Assembly has been debating the controversial issue all afternoon and is due to take a historic vote on the matter shortly.

The vote permitted the ordination of gay ministers, but only if a congregation actively elect to do so.

ANDY MURRAY WINS WIMBLEDON
Sunday 7 July 2013
STV News

Andy Murray has made sporting history, after becoming the first British man to take the Wimbledon singles title in 77 years. The Scot defeated world number one Novak Djokovic in straight sets.

DIARY: For the most part, he played superbly. He turned round difficult positions he would have lost previously. Up there as possibly the greatest ever Scottish sporting achievement.

Monday 8 July 2013
STV News – live from Dunblane

This is the STV *News at Six*, live from the hometown of Scotland's sporting hero Andy Murray. Dunblane is where it all began. Where a boy with a racquet, talent and a dream started on the road to becoming a legend. Conquering Centre Court assures the 26-year-old his place amongst the greatest Sportsmen. And what achievements along the way – glory at the Olympics when he won gold, Grand Slam victory at the US Open and now this very modest young Scot is the first British man to take the Wimbledon men's singles title in 77 years.

DIARY: A scorcher of a day. I was standing on the courts where Murray played as a kid. The Dunblane Tennis Club was very accommodating. Especially during the evening programme, Annette *(Annette Wiseman – make-up)* was having to dab my brow between each link. I could feel the heat of the sun through my shoes. The official temperatures were in the high 20s, but our car thermometers were showing it to be 30C plus.

SECOND INDEPENDENCE DEBATE
Thursday 5 September 2013
Scotland Tonight

Tonight, in the second of our series of live referendum debates, we spotlight the key battleground of welfare and pensions. To debate what sort of benefits system we'd have in an independent Scotland, we're joined by two of Scotland's most senior politicians. From the Scottish Government making the case for independence, is Deputy First Minister Nicola Sturgeon; and from the Scottish Labour Party making the case for staying in the Union, we have Deputy Leader Anas Sarwar.

DIARY: It ended up being quite controversial because of the tactics used by Sarwar. He badgered and nipped at Sturgeon constantly and she rose to it once or twice. I chaired it for the first part and had to take control a few times. However, in the second part they cross-examine each other and I step back. That's when it became a shouting match at times. I wanted to step in, but couldn't. 'Politics in the raw' and 'a stairheid rammy' were some of the observations. Sarwar's tactic was clearly to get under Sturgeon's skin. We were trending on Twitter across the UK and there has been a lot of reaction, not all of it favourable. I'm unconvinced that it added much to the debate, but it's maybe a sign of the way it's turning.

Monday 16 September 2013
DIARY: An announcement that Billy Connolly has shown initial signs of Parkinson's Disease and has been treated for prostate cancer. We learned that the Independent MSP Margo MacDonald, who knows Connolly and is also suffering from Parkinson's, was at a hotel across the river. So, it was a quick dash to get over and set up a two-camera shoot. My interview was off the cuff, but it wasn't a hard one, just getting her to talk about her own experience. She's a big figure in Scottish politics and has a feisty reputation. I always find her to be good fun and quite flirtatious.

MARGO MACDONALD: When I was diagnosed with Parkinson's *(in 1995)* it was like a bolt out of the blue. I didn't really know what Parkinson's was. I came out of the doctors in a bit of a dwam, went to the hairdressers, had a good drink and had a good bubble with my hairdresser. And after that I decided, well I've got Parkinson's, I can't see it, I can't feel it, I'll just get on with it. As you can see, I've got a bit of a shake, but that's only because I'm talking to you *(laughs).*'

ONE YEAR UNTIL THE INDEPENDENCE REFERENDUM
Wednesday 18 September 2013
STV News – live from Holyrood

18 September 2014. Decision time for Scotland. A year from today we, the voters, will choose the future of our country. Remain within the Union or opt for independence? It's the biggest decision the nation has had to make in hundreds of years. In this special edition of STV News we mark 365 days to the poll.

DIARY: An STV poll showed Yes 31 per cent No 59 per cent, which is consistent with the trends. The Yes campaign is laying much store on persuading the undecided and soft No vote. It's a big ask.

Presenting the news from outside Holyrood. We had a camera position marked off with some cones and a very basic set up. We had the First Minister on live. He announced himself as 'Hi, I'm John MacKay!' He's losing weight. He needed to. He actually nicked my water. I told him he was welcome, but I'd already drunk from it. He didn't bother, doing the old childhood thing of wiping it with his sleeve.

JAMES McAVOY & IRVINE WELSH
Tuesday 24 September 2013

DIARY: Interviewing film star James McAvoy this afternoon along with controversial author Irvine Welsh about the film *Filth*. Excellent interview covering the film, the Scottish film scene and independence. I found McAvoy to be pleasant and grounded and his presence caused quite a stir in the building. Given the darkness of Irvine Welsh's writing, he was surprisingly light and personable. It was a good 'get'.

IRVINE WELSH, Author: I am obsessed with failure. I think that failure's really interesting because success only comes in one kind of form. If you're successful you think 'this is great', but it doesn't really teach anything, but failure comes in all different types of form, so you learn so much from failure. I am fascinated by the way when things are going against us we make our own decisions to compound it or we inevitably make our own decision to compound that. If you're sometimes compelled to keep acting it's just time to stop and let things take their course.

JMK: You had Scottish talent, a Scottish director and a Scottish supporting cast, but a lot of this had to be filmed elsewhere. It comes back to this question we hear a lot, the need for a Scottish film studio.

JAMES McAVOY, Actor: We don't have a proper studio in Scotland and that is a real shame, not just a shame because of job creation, but because culturally we don't have the facility to tell stories about ourselves on a regular, frequent and prolific basis, which we need. It's important for our own cultural confidence and identity and it would be useful. It's not even something you can talk about in business terms, is it economically unfeasible, will we make money back? It's got to be subsidised, it's a service, it's not just an industry, we serve the ego and the collective identity of the culture you represent and we just don't have that. The tangibles of it can't be measured, but they're immense. Huge for your self confidence as a nation.

Monday 7 October 2013
STV News

The Scottish Secretary Michael Moore has been sacked. The Berwickshire MP has been replaced by chief whip Alistair Carmichael. Liberal Democrat leader Nick Clegg said he wanted to 'draw on different experience' in the run up to the Independence Referendum.

Many commentators believed that one of the factors which contributed to Michael Moore's dismissal was his performance in the STV debate against Nicola Sturgeon.

DIARY: Michael Moore was a polite, not unwarm individual whom I always liked. His replacement is the more combative Alistair Carmichael, whom I met during a debate at the last General Election and took to right away. I think we'll see more scrapping.

He was clearly uncomfortable about why Michael Moore had been chopped.

Monday 11 November 2013
STV News

Finally, it has become a Glasgow tradition – the placing of a traffic cone on top of the Duke of Wellington Statue in the city centre. But it could be coming to an end. The city council is considering raising the height of the monument to discourage pranksters from climbing it.

DIARY: The council is misjudging people's views on it – so misjudging that you have to think there is an ulterior motive. Twitter campaigns, Facebook campaigns and by tonight they'd already backed down. We carried it on *Scotland Tonight* and maybe not as light-hearted as I'd have liked, but the guy opposed made some good points – essentially, it's a war memorial.

JACK VETTRIANO
Tuesday 19 November 2013
Scotland Tonight

He's a painter whose work has long divided opinion in the art world. But Jack Vettriano continues to enjoy widespread acclaim among the public. The first major retrospective of his work in Glasgow is on course to break records, with thousands of people coming through the doors at the Kelvingrove Art Gallery.

JACK VETTRIANO, artist: I said when it opened that if I had come into this exhibition on my own, I would have cried. I had several men with me and I thought, 'Big boys don't cry,' but it was absolutely astonishing. To see some of the earlier work; what I think worried me most was some of the early work, you could see it was limited, I was limited in my technical ability, so I did… I was doing the best I could. I thought, 'What will the public think of this?' Then I thought to myself, what is a retrospective if it's not a 20-year development of someone's career?

SCOTTISH GOVERNMENT WHITE PAPER
Tuesday 26 November 2013
STV News

The Scottish Government has unveiled its White Paper on independence. The 670-page document reveals the priorities the SNP say they will negotiate for Scotland if the nation votes Yes in next year's referendum. Proposals for childcare, economy, defence, currency and pensions are all covered. Critics argue the document is no more than a wish list and cannot be delivered.

DIARY: In recent months we've been told that certain questions will be answered 'in the White Paper'. The launch was a fairly low razzmatazz event at the Glasgow Science Centre, but widespread interest from the UK networks and abroad. First Minister Alex Salmond and Deputy FM made the presentation. The initial impression is of a weighty document, some 670 pages, which doesn't reveal much that is new. I did the lunchtime programme from outside the Science Centre. That was straightforward. This afternoon I went through to Edinburgh, twice dozing off as I read the White Paper. No reflection on the book, which is actually very easy to read.

Wednesday 27 November 2013

DIARY: We had another *Scotland Tonight* debate this evening with the Deputy First Minister Nicola Sturgeon up against the Scottish Secretary Alistair Carmichael. Many believe the poor performance of his predecessor Michael Moore in the first debate contributed to his sacking. Carmichael – who has a reputation as bruiser – was no better. Sturgeon verbally floored him. I don't know if he was conscious of holding back because of Anas Sarwar's performance in the last one, but he never got going. Rona hosted.

This debate became famous for the line, 'Help me, Rona'. In fact, Alistair Carmichael didn't say that. He turned to Rona and asked, 'Are we going to stop this?'

Thursday 28 November 2013

DIARY: Tried a new concept on *Scotland Tonight* which seems to have been well received. The regular programme with Rona ran as usual on air, meanwhile I was hosting a 'Google hangout', which was five guests with me in the studio and five more joining us from various locations via Skype, including actor Brian Cox – in Switzerland. We ran for half an hour just online, but when the regular transmission ended, we then went on air on STV for another half hour. We've received much praise for being innovative, but more than that people enjoyed that the Google chat wasn't of political point scoring, rather one of thoughtful discussion. I enjoyed doing it. There is no question the technology could be better quality, but it was good to try it.

It didn't happen again.

CLUTHA TRAGEDY

Friday 29 November 2013

DIARY: I got a text from *(my son)* saying 'See a helicopter has crashed into the Clutha Bar in Glasgow?' I actually asked him for the punchline. Tragically, not a joke. A police helicopter came down and crashed through the roof of the pub which was packed with people enjoying a live band. Initially, it looked as if there might be no fatalities, but soon there were reports that people had been killed.

Saturday 30 November 2013
STV News – live from next to The Clutha

The Clutha vault helicopter crash has been described as a 'Black Day for Scotland' by the First Minister. Three people from inside the helicopter and five from inside the pub are dead. In the city's hospitals 14 others lie seriously injured. The Queen and the Prime Minister have sent their condolences to the bereaved families and tonight emergency services continue their painstaking operation to find those beneath the rubble.

DIARY: It is so randomly sad. You go out for a beer on a Friday night and you die because a helicopter crashes through the roof. We did a live programme at lunchtime which went well. The wreckage of the pub was behind us beyond the police control. It is still so hard to believe. Back down again this evening and the full scale of the tragedy was now clear. Eight people, including three in the helicopter, had been killed. As I went on air, there was quite a crowd of people on the other side of the camera. I had no autocue, so was remembering the script. I was aware of a woman waiting with her husband listening intently. When I went on air saying, 'Eight people have died,' she threw her hand to her face in horror. It's rare to see the instant impact of the news you are delivering. I hope she didn't know anyone.

Monday 2 December 2013

DIARY: The helicopter wreckage was finally moved from the Clutha Pub today, revealing one more body. That's the death total now nine. It also allowed for the removal of all the bodies still there. There was a terribly sombre scene when the bodies were taken away and the emergency services lined up and saluted.

DEATH OF NELSON MANDELA
Friday 6 December 2013
STV News

This is an STV News Special, live from Nelson Mandela Place. There can be few places anywhere that the name Nelson Mandela isn't known. And not a single politician who could command the same respect in their homeland or on the world stage. In the end he died peacefully at home with his nearest and dearest. Throughout last night and today, politicians, personalities and the public have been paying their respects to the man who inspired a generation. First Minister Alex Salmond described Mandela as a 'towering statesman.' Former Prime Minister Gordon Brown said he was 'the greatest leader of our generation.'

DIARY: There was a celebration of Mandela's life with maybe about 300 people there. I'm pleased that we did it, but I'm not so convinced that we should have done it to the exclusion of all other news.

ANCHORMAN CAST
Wednesday 11 December 2013

DIARY: To Claridges for the interviews with the *Anchorman 2* cast. The journalists are gathered in a room and then called for a designated five minutes. It's just a conveyor belt and not something I would want to do all the time. Anyway, my plan was to ask the actors for advice to take home to the STV News team. First, I was with Paul Rudd and Steve Carrell and they played along really well. Will Ferrell – the Anchorman Ron Burgundy – did too. I'd brought props (ties and false moustaches) and, although he wouldn't put them on, he was willing to react. Director Adam McKay and I discussed our shared surname. Will Ferrell was asking me about independence – 'You guys will lose all your money, right?'

Paul Rudd who plays ace reporter Brian Fantana advised our reporters to douse themselves with the strongest cologne they could find, get a chest toupee, grow a moustache and wear polyester pants (trousers – at least I hope he meant trousers). Steve Carrell who plays Brick Tamland the weatherman, said roving reporters should go commando 'to capture the essence'

Scotland Tonight

He's a man who was put on this earth to read the news and have salon quality hair. The legendary Anchorman Ron Burgundy comes from a time when everyone believed what they saw on TV. In short, Ron Burgundy is kind of a big deal. He and his news team have assembled for the latest chapter in the *Anchorman* saga. I've been privileged to meet the man who knows him best.

JM: I'm a news anchor in Scotland. We all look up to the doyen that is Ron Burgundy. You know him better than anyone. How could he advise me?

WILL FERRELL, (Ron Burgundy): From Ron's perspective the first thing I see is that you don't have a moustache. Ron would be appalled. Yeah, you gotta grow some facial hair. Are you wearing cologne?

JM: I'm not. Should I be?

WF: It should be enough cologne that it makes my eyes water from ten feet.

JM: Ron was put on the earth to read the news and have salon quality hair. I can do the first bit, not so much the second. How do I achieve that?

WF: (*laughs*) Your hair is very short, yeah, yeah. You just have to use a lot of conditioner. It's also just DNA and fortunately Ron was given the gift of beautiful hair.

JM: He also wears suits that make Sinatra look like a hobo. These are ties I've worn in the past...

WF: (*laughing*) That's an amazing selection. Are those really from your...?

JM: They're from my illustrious career. Would Ron wear any of these?

WF: Probably that one, the loudest. (*An especially garish tie*)

JM: We've got a lot of big issues in Scotland, independence and such. Ron very much takes the line of give people what they want, so is that the line we should follow?

WF: It's a big question, right, for Scotland? Whether to go it alone? I think try it for a week. Then if you guys don't like it, come right back.

2014

Monday 6 January 2014
Scotland Tonight

The Year of Decision has arrived, and between now and polling day the two referendum campaigns will be doing everything they can to win the hearts and minds of Scotland's four million voters.

DIARY: This is likely to be the most significant year of my professional life. *Scotland Tonight* kicked off as we are likely to go on – with the referendum. A pre-recorded interview with Deputy First Minister Nicola Sturgeon and the same with Scottish Secretary Alistair Carmichael. Marking interviews, really.

Thursday 16 January 2014
STV News

A major search is ongoing tonight to find a little boy who disappeared from his home after being put to bed. Three-year-old Mikaeel Kular's mother reported her son missing when she woke this morning. She last saw Mikaeel at 9.00pm last night. Police helicopters are in the sky over Edinburgh. Detectives are on foot and horseback. Locals are helping as gardens, coastlines and homes are searched.

DIARY: Sounds like an abduction to me. I can't see that a three-year-old would get up, dressed and out of the flat without being seen or heard.

Mikaeel's mother pleaded guilty to culpable homicide after his body was found in Fife and was sentenced to 11 years in jail.

Monday 20 January 2014

DIARY: There was a study by some academic which claimed both BBC and STV are biased against the Yes campaign. Usual lack of insight or understanding of the media they claim to analyse.

WILLIAM McILVANNEY
Monday 3 February 2014
Scotland Tonight (broadcast Wednesday 5 February 2014)

He's credited with inspiring a generation of Scottish crime writers, now the author William McIlvanney is enjoying a new wave of interest in his work after the publisher Canongate reprinted his back catalogue.

JM: You have always been held in very high regard by, particularly, Scottish crime writers. They have looked up to you very much. How has that made you feel?

WILLIAM McILVANNEY: That has been another revelation for me because it was not till republication and I was appearing at readings along with some of these writers and they were just so generous towards me. I hadn't realised I was credited with, you know, establishing a genre in Scotland. It was an amazing feeling. I don't know if it is true, but it is nice! I've convinced myself I believe it anyway!

JM: You did write about crime in Scotland, and a detective novel set in Scotland, a particularly gritty detective novel. It seems to be the first of that genre in Scotland. Why did you write that? What inspired you to write that?

WM: Well, I had written a book called *Docherty*, which was about the first quarter of the 20th century, and I had kind of contemporary starvation. I had gone back and talked to ex-miners and read about that era, and I was desperate to write about something contemporary. And maybe it sounds a bit like Joan of Arc, but I heard a voice and it was a man's voice, quite abrasive, and I made a lot of notes of some of the things he was saying. And I thought 'He is quite a… He obviously has to be in hard places,' so I thought, 'He has to be a detective'. And so, I came to write a detective novel through the character of Laidlaw. I did not decide I will write a detective novel and this guy Laidlaw will be in it. I created the idea to write this book and I thought it's got to be a detective novel. So, I stumbled into writing a detective novel. It wasn't any deliberate long-term plan.

JM: What is the process for you, what is the writing process?

WM: It is, I suppose, first of all, making endless notes because I want the confidence. I want to believe, to be able to believe, there is a genuine book in there. And then it is writing longhand. I write with a biro pen and a piece of paper. I am not, you know, the most technologically advanced performer you ever saw and I suppose that makes it long as well, that makes the time long. But I don't mind that. If the words don't come from the head, down the arm, onto the page, I'm not quite convinced that I'm getting it right.

JM: And is it something you try to avoid? Do you have to force yourself to do it, or is it a pleasure for you?

WM: It's both. Sometimes, as Hemingway said, when you get the juice up, you really want to go. And other times I find it quite a painful process. So, you just have to go through it. You have great moments, moments of euphoria when you think, 'This is really working.' And moments of self-doubt, and you just have to have the nerve to go through all of that to get to where you want to go.

DIARY: Out to the southside home of acclaimed author William McIlvanney for a pre-recorded interview. A very pleasant, warm guy. I enjoyed hearing him talk about the writing process, 'Do you have these doubts?' And, of course, I do.

Tuesday 4 February 2014
Scotland Tonight

The first gay and lesbian weddings in Scotland could take place this autumn after MSPs tonight passed the Same Sex Marriage Bill by 105 votes to 18. The Health Secretary Alex Neil hailed the decision as an historic moment for equality. But religious groups, who had strongly opposed the change, said it had been steamrollered through by parliamentarians who had completely ignored public opinion.

DIARY: We had an excellent audience last night – an 11 per cent share peaking at 13 per cent (200,000). For a current affairs programme that is excellent. I do enjoy it. The only downside is the childish and incessant cybernats online who flood our feed. Sifting genuine comment from the clichés can be a challenge.

Wednesday 5 February 2014

DIARY: I hosted an event with Bernard Ponsonby on the art of the political interview. I don't consider myself in Bernard's class, so it was interesting to hear what he had to say. He confirmed what I've always felt, that preparation is the absolute key.

BBC Scotland have announced a new political programme at 10.30pm Monday–Thursday fronted by Sarah Smith, daughter of former Labour Leader John Smith. It's about time, but also a flagrant abuse of position. However, we have nothing to be concerned about. We have well established ourselves.

BARRY HUMPHRIES

Tuesday 11 February 2014
Scotland Tonight

He's an entertainment legend who's been making audiences laugh around the world for more than five decades. Barry Humphries is now taking a final bow with a farewell tour. The man behind the iconic Australian suburban housewife Dame Edna Everage is saying 'goodbye possums' with an all-singing, all-dancing spectacular. Tonight, he was at the King's Theatre in Glasgow. Before he went on stage, he spoke to *Scotland Tonight*.

DIARY: Interviewing the Australian comic entertainer and satirist Barry Humphries, better known as Dame Edna Everage. I had interviewed one of his other alter egos, Sir Les Patterson, some 15 years ago – perhaps 'was a straight man for' might be more accurate than interviewed. I found him to be charming and a very interesting interviewee. He's 80 next week and it's remarkable how sharp he is. His description of political correctness as the modern Puritanism was perfect.

JM: You've been doing Dame Edna since the '50s. That's a long, long time.

BARRY HUMPHRIES: Edna has been in my repertoire, in my life, really.

JM: You're going to miss her, surely?

BH: It's very hard to explain. Edna has a life really of her own. I don't have much to do with it. In the old days, when I first thought I'd invented Edna, it was like having created a puppet. And when I'd done a little show with this puppet Edna, I'd put the puppet in a box, close the lid and forget about it. Next time I came back, however, I'd open the box and the puppet would be wearing funny glasses. The puppet would say things that I would never dare to say to my audience. And I realised that I had invented something rather, to use Edna's favourite word, 'spooky'. Something which did have its own separate life, and so if I have to improvise on the stage I can improvise very easily, because it's as though Edna exists and is a sort of ventriloquist, telling me what to say. It's not a thing I ever analyse. I leave it sometimes to academics, and you know, John, academics do write about me now. That's a sign really of being more or less dead.

JM: You also do satire very well, even now, and a lot of people would think satire comes from a youthful anger, perhaps. How do you sustain that? Where does that anger come from?

BH: I did have a little anger in my youth, which is only proper. I don't approve of a youth who is not angry. But I was brought up in a middle-class background in Melbourne, Australia, and Melbourne was a city in a very remote part of southeast Asia, trying to be English. And it almost succeeded. I felt frustrated living there. It was too cosy, too comfortable, too self-satisfied, for a priggish little know-all like me. And so, I began to sort of take the mickey out of Melbourne. I invented characters which somehow to me described the boredom of Melbourne, but people laughed. I couldn't win. They didn't go away hurting, they went away laughing.

JM: Is political correctness damaging do you think?

BH: Political correctness is another form of Puritanism, which I dislike intensely.

JM: You came to the United Kingdom, you were based in London, you worked with a lot of the satirists of the time, Peter Cook and such.

BH: Yes, I did.

JM: How does now, 2014, compare to that era of the 1960s? The world has clearly changed, but has it really?

BH: Well, the satire, so-called satire movement of the '60s, the stars of which were people like Peter Cook, Dudley Moore, Spike Milligan, even David Frost, all of those people were wonderfully bright, interesting men. Significantly, mostly men. And I worked with all of them. It was a very interesting period, the '60s in Britain, because it was just coming alive after the war. So, we were still licking our wounds in the '50s. By the '60s we were wearing coloured clothing again, as I'm pleased to see you are. It was a very funny time.

Wednesday 12 February 2014
STV News

The Scottish and UK Governments are at loggerheads tonight over the creation of a sterling currency area in the event of a Yes vote. The Chancellor George Osborne is expected to rule out such a plan when he speaks in Edinburgh tomorrow. A move that has been branded by ministers here as mere bluff.

DIARY: It throws into jeopardy the SNP's plans for a sterling zone. They say he is bluffing and I'm inclined to think they are right, but I can see it causing doubt. And, of course, the media is being manipulated. Leak it beforehand and then the actual speech and you get two prominent days of coverage. And we can't not cover it.

Thursday 13 February 2014
STV News

In one of the most significant days in the Independence Referendum debate, the three main unionist parties have said they would veto Scottish Government ambitions for a currency union in the event of a Yes vote. The day started with the Chancellor saying he had received advice from Treasury officials that a currency union wouldn't work. Labour and the Lib Dems quickly followed with similar statements as the Scottish Government said the parties were trying to bully voters into the No camp.

DIARY: The Chancellor of the Exchequer, George Osborne, made a speech in Edinburgh in which he said an independent Scotland would not be able to share the pound with the UK. The SNP accuse him of bluff and bluster, but it has certainly shaken them. They've been saying all along it would be fine. It's a difficult issue for them. However, Osborne did no sit-down interviews, took three questions and he was off. Why they think that coming north, making pronouncements and then running off again without explaining themselves is going to be persuasive to the Scottish electorate is beyond me.

RICHARD DREYFUSS
Saturday 22 February 2014

DIARY: An interview with Oscar-winning actor Richard Dreyfuss, who's in Glasgow for the Film Festival. We had ten minutes with him at the Malmaison Hotel.

JM: Okay if we get a quick snapshot?

RICHARD DREYFUSS: A lot of actors are quite short. Dustin Hoffman isn't that tall, y'know. *(Pause...)*

JM: Er... no a quick snapshot. A photo.

RD: Oh.

Monday 24 February 2014
STV News

The Prime Minister has declared he would not seek to block Scottish membership of the European Union in the event of a Yes vote. Speaking as he and his Westminster Cabinet met in Aberdeen, David Cameron also told STV News that he would be delighted to take part in a referendum programme where he would answer questions from undecided voters. But with the Scottish Cabinet meeting in the very same city, the two Governments went into battle over oil and gas.

DIARY: The UK Cabinet was meeting in Aberdeen, only the second time it's come to Scotland in 90 years. Meanwhile, the Scottish Cabinet was meeting in Portlethen, some seven miles away. The UK Cabinet met in the Shell HQ, the Scottish Cabinet in a village hall. It was the usual posturing and game playing. Unlike the Chancellor, the Prime Minister at least did some interviews, as did the First Minister.

Tuesday 25 February 2014
Scotland Tonight

Welcome to the fourth in our series of *Scotland Tonight* referendum debates. Tonight, we have with us the two most senior women in Scottish politics. Returning to the fray from the SNP Scottish Government is the architect of the Independence White Paper, Deputy First Minister Nicola Sturgeon. And making the case for staying in the Union, we have the Scottish Labour Leader Johann Lamont. They'll be crossing swords in debate and will also get the opportunity to cross-examine each other.

DIARY: We had expectations that it might give a different tone to the debate, but it didn't. The cross-examination was another rabble with the two talking over each other constantly. Nobody will have learned anything from it and many will have been put off. I was doing the analysis with Bernard Ponsonby and Colin Mackay and as we came off air Bernard said we would be slaughtered for that and we were on the social networks. Neither of the politicians was happy either. Johann Lamont had left by the time I came out of the studio, but Nicola

Sturgeon was saying that both sides know they can't back down in that format.

Tuesday 4 March 2014

DIARY: Alex Salmond was making a speech in London on independence. He is well regarded in the UK – one of the few Scottish-based politicians they'll know. So, we went on that in *Scotland Tonight*, plus day two of our poll which shows the SNP are still way ahead in popularity for the Holyrood elections in 2016. Incredible for a mid-term government.

Tuesday 18 March 2014
Scotland Tonight

What happens if there's a No vote in September's Independence Referendum? It's a question each of the pro-union parties is under pressure to answer. Today, Scottish Labour set out its stall, proposing a package of measures which would give MSPs greater control over income tax and some welfare spending.

DIARY: Scottish Labour announced their increased powers for Devolution in the event of a 'No' vote in the referendum. No sweeping ideas, rather tinkering. It's a compromise imposed, no doubt, by the Westminster MPs. If there is a 'Yes' vote they'll need to look at themselves.

Monday 24 March 2014
Scotland Tonight

The momentum is now with the Yes campaign. That was the message from the SNP after the latest ICM opinion poll revealed a significant swing in favour of independence. The survey put support for independence at 39 per cent, just seven points behind support for the Union. How concerned should Better Together be by the findings? Is the No side beginning to look like a campaign in trouble? We're now joined by two senior pro-Union figures who have called for a more positive strategy to connect with voters. At Westminster is the former leader of the Liberal Democrats Charles Kennedy.

And in Dundee is the former Labour First Minister Henry McLeish.

DIARY: Interviewing former Lib Dem Leader Charles Kennedy on *Scotland Tonight*. It was a down-the-line interview, but I've always been impressed by him. He's always seemed straight and believable.

Tuesday 1 April 2014
STV News

A major inquiry is underway after a wall at a secondary school in Edinburgh collapsed and killed a 12-year-old girl. Keane Wallis-Bennet, who was in first year at Liberton High, died at the scene despite the efforts of the emergency services. Friends have been arriving to lay floral tributes since the tragedy this morning. The campus will remain closed for the rest of the week.

Thursday 3 April 2014
STV News

Commonwealth Games organisers say Glasgow's Red Road flats will be demolished live as part of the opening ceremony to be broadcast around the world. The decision to blow them up as part of the celebrations has delighted some and dismayed others.

GRANT RUSSELL, Sports News Correspondent: The buildings were once a solution to Glasgow's housing problems. There is a reason for all this, say Games organisers. The regeneration of Glasgow through the Commonwealth Games has transformed parts of the city. By bringing down Red Road, the message they want to put across to the world is that their impact will ensure that regeneration continues.

DIARY: The main story was the quite bizarre decision by Glasgow City Council to feature the live explosive demolition of the Red Road flats as part of the Opening Ceremony of the Commonwealth Games. They say it's 'bold', but most people think it's daft. I'd be surprised if they go ahead with it and it could be fraught with risk if they do.

They didn't. The demolition was cancelled for safety reasons. The flats were pulled down the following year.

Friday 4 April 2014
STV News

'The brightest light in the Scottish political firmament has gone out.' With those words Jim Sillars led the tributes as he announced his wife Margo MacDonald died peacefully today at their Edinburgh home. She was 70 years old and had been suffering from Parkinson's Disease for some time. The political world was quick to react, with affectionate recollections of the most popular politician of her generation. The First Minister said she made politics exciting and human.

DIARY: She was a major political figure in Scotland for the last 40 years, spectacularly winning a by-election in Govan in 1973. From then on, she was always a familiar face, very highly regarded for her forthright views and commonsense approach. I had the pleasure of interviewing her a few times and always found her fun. A big loss to Scottish politics, especially for independence, which she campaigned for all her political life. Many, many tributes today, all of them sincere.

Tuesday 8 April 2014
STV News

The former Secretary General of NATO has claimed Scottish independence could have a 'cataclysmic' impact on the world. Speaking in Washington, Lord Robertson claimed the loudest cheer in the event of a Yes vote would come from the enemies of the West. However, the Deputy First Minister said she was shocked by the former Defence Secretary's language and branded his comments insulting and offensive.

DIARY: It's certainly the most controversial anti-Indy speech there has been and the language does seem excessive. His basic point was that an independent Scotland weakens the UK, which weakens Western security. Did a pre-recorded interview with him. He was complaining about being kept waiting in the green room in Washington for 20 minutes (*we were told he was still travelling in his car*).

Tuesday 22 April 2014
STV News

Gordon Brown has said an independent Scotland's first annual pension bill would be 'three times the income from oil'. In a speech for the pro-unionist Better Together campaign in Glasgow, the former Prime Minister said pensions would be more secure and cheaper to administer if Scotland remains part of the UK. The SNP accused him of being 'economically illiterate' and said pensions are more affordable here than in the rest of the UK.

Scotland Tonight

Gordon Brown has made his first foray into the cross-party Better Together campaign, outlining his vision of Scotland's future within the UK. Tonight's speech from the former Labour Prime Minister came in the wake of a weekend opinion poll suggesting that Yes Scotland now needs a swing of just over 2 per cent to secure independence.

Monday 28 April 2014
STV News

The First Minister has called Scotland a 'lynchpin of the European Union' as he made the case for independence in the heart of Europe. Speaking in Bruges he said Scotland had a key role to play in the EU, citing vast natural resources and human talent. However, his speech was somewhat overshadowed by comments he made in an interview about Russian President Vladimir Putin's leadership.

Mr Salmond said that while he didn't approve of Russian actions he admired certain aspects of President Putin, in particular that he had restored Russian pride.

Tuesday 29 April 2014
Scotland Tonight

What does it mean to be Scottish? It's a question that has taken on added significance in 2014. A special conference being held tomorrow at Edinburgh University is to explore the different aspects of Scottish identity and how it's been shaped by various forces. The latest Census found 62 per cent of us defined ourselves as 'Scottish only'. Eighteen per cent said they were British and Scottish. Eight per cent said they were just British.

PROFESSOR TOM DEVINE: Essentially, I will take the puzzle of why Scotland survived the Union. In the late 18th century some of Scotland's greatest intellectuals thought it would be assumed by England's assimilation. And I want to know why that did not occur. Because Scotland was such an ancient nation. It had, if you like, a collective sentiment and awareness of nationhood at all levels of society, which proved resilient. Some of our great institutions, the Church of Scotland, education,

Scottish private law. Because identity is a collective sentiment it can change over time in relation to circumstances. If the Union had not occurred, Scottish identity today would be different. The Union helped to shape Scottish identity. The other thing I would say is there are such things as the markers of your identity – sport, values.

These can change remarkably over time. This has happened in Scotland. In the mid-19th century many Scots regarded Wallace as a unionist. This hybrid identity we have of Scottishness and Britishness has swung consistently over time. During World War II and afterwards Britishness was on the ascendance. Now, Scottishness is overwhelmingly on the ascendant.

DIARY: Eminent historian Tom Devine was the lead guest, but a good support panel. His basic point was that national identity is fluid and the 'Scottishness' we have now would be unrecognisable to those from the 18th century.

In a later interview in 2016 on the release of his book Independence or Union, Professor Devine expanded on this, saying that there was little celebration to mark the Union in 1707 and recalling Donald Dewar's observation that if the 1980s could be removed from Scottish history there would probably not have been a Scottish Parliament.

Wednesday 30 April 2014
STV News

Parents affected by the Mortonhall baby ashes scandal have been left horrified by a report which revealed their children's remains may have been mixed in with those of adults. That was just one of the grim findings of the official investigation which says families have now been left with a 'lifetime of uncertainty' over what happened to their babies.

DIARY: The baby ashes scandal. Stillborn or premature babies who were cremated without their parents' knowledge. It now seems their ashes may have been mixed with those of adults who were cremated first thing in the morning. The pain of the parents is clear. More to do with the standards of the time *(started in 1967)* than any badness.

Friday 9 May 2014

DIARY: An unfortunate mispronunciation on the news this evening, saying 'webshite' rather than 'website' caused a huge reaction on social networks. My name – @RealMacKaysTV – was trending on Twitter. As I noted on Facebook, 'You read crafted intros and hold chaotic programmes together and nobody notices. You say "webshite" instead of "website"? Meltdown!' I apologised and moved on, but knowing all the time that I daren't smile.

Tuesday 13 May 2014

DIARY: *Scotland Tonight*'s subjects – Scottish cultural 'miserablism' and a review of the end of the football season. The cybernats were on their high horse about a poll that wasn't being released at Westminster.

GEORGE IS SCOTLAND'S CHAMPION WHISTLER

1986 · One of my early headlines.

1988 · Pan Am flight 103. For those who died on the ground – beneath a flight scheduled to last hours – in an area surrounded by miles of farmland – mere seconds and feet determined their fate.
STV

1991 · BBC Radio Scotland
This was news as it was happening, or as close as it could be for the time.
JM

1994 · First time presenting *Scotland Today*. I was told to wear a better shirt and tie the next time.
STV

1999 · With co-presenter Shereen Nanjiani.
STV

1995 · VJ Day, Joe Henry. These Old Boys — surely all gone now — remain among the most memorable interviewees I have ever met.
STV

```
13/03/96 10:52 pmk ?:?? 136-.. HHH
.. HHH
PAH5784 6 MRC 8192 MERCURY WIRE
1 SHOOTING
CENTRAL SCOTLAND NEWS AGENCY
Copy from TIM BUGLER, CENTRAL SCOTLAND NEWS AGENCY, 10
Viewfield Place, Stirling, FK8 1NQ. Tel: 01786 462423 (office)
or 01786 824140 (home). Pager -- dial 0345 333 111 and quote
0235 821. Date: 13.3.96
tim bugler/central/shooting/flash..1
REPORTS are coming in of a shooting at Dunblane Primary School,
Perthshire. The Scottish Ambulance Service said 12 CHILDREN ARE BELIEVED
DEAD, and eight or nine injured.
     Police have been called in from throughout the area, and
all five doctors from Dunblane Surgery are reported to have
been called to the school.
ends....
MMMM
```

(handwritten: "time printed")

1996 · We drove up to Dunblane with that PA copy and not convinced it was correct. How could it be?

1997 · 'The settled will of the Scottish people is there for all to see.' Donald Dewar.
STV

1998 · The World Cup on tour. I don't believe it was the genuine article, whatever they say.
STV

1999 · Donald Dewar's first TV interview as First Minister. 'Scotland's Parliament is no longer a political pamphlet, a campaign trail, a waving flag. It is here. It is real.'
STV

1999 · Alex Salmond – 'We're joined by the leader of the SNP and now the leader of the official opposition in the new parliament.'
STV

2000 · Madonna's Wedding — It went against every professional instinct, talking with little knowledge of the subject and, worse, no confirmation.
It was great fun.
STV

2000 · 'In a hundred years when the history of this time in Scotland is written, Donald Dewar's name will stand out.'
STV

2003 · Seville with Jane Lewis – A bottle came out of the darkness and hit me on the back of the head. I just buckled and went down.
STV

2007 · Scottish Parliament with Andrea Brymer. Within the last half hour, at the last count of the last region to declare, the SNP secured victory.
STV

2007 · The Blair era is over. The Brown era has begun.
STV

2008 · Barlinnie Special — The prisoners started shouting and hammering the doors when I made reference to 'murderers and rapists' among them.
STV

2011 · Our eyes are on the future and the dreams that can be realised.
STV

2011 · *Scotland Tonight* launched with Rona Dougall.
STV

2012 · Kevin Bridges — Just a funny, funny guy. His resurrection of the exclamation 'Yaldy' is just one of many delights for me.
JM

2012 · Andy Murray — He was so lean. If I hadn't known better I'd have thought he needed a good feed.
JM

2012 · Olympic Homecoming – Sir Chris Hoy 6x Gold Medallist.
JM

2013 · The Clutha Tragedy – I was aware of a woman waiting with her husband listening intently. When I went on air saying, 'Eight people have died,' (later confirmed as ten) she threw her hand to her face in horror. It's rare to see the instant impact of the news you are delivering. I hope she didn't know anyone.
STV

2014 · Alistair Darling – You can get the change you want with a stronger, more secure Scottish Parliament by staying in the UK.
JM

2014 · Alex Salmond's last interview before the referendum – We know we want to be a more equal and just society, so vote for that future, vote Yes tomorrow.
JM

2014 · Independence Referendum – As Big Ben chimed and I delivered that line to the nation about two capitals waiting, the hairs stood on the back of my neck.
STV

2015 · General Election – Nicola Sturgeon. She'd been up all night and was saying she wasn't sure she could remember her own name.
JM

2016 · Brexit from Downing Street – We were all expecting that we would be entering a period of relative political calm, but not now.
JM

2017 · Kenny Dalglish – I'll always be Scottish, I'll always be a Glaswegian. This is our home in Liverpool… But we'll never ever forget our roots.
JM

2020 · Billy Connolly – I was always nervous because you can't lie properly in your hometown. Every other town you can lie about your background and invent stuff and experiences that you supposedly had. But you can't do it in Glasgow.
JM

2021 · COP26 with Kelly-Ann Woodland – No question it's a world event… different languages and races rushing about. I did get a sense of busy being busy – to what end?
STV

2022 · The Palace of Holyroodhouse, The Royal Mile, St Giles have borne witness to great events. The very stones are steeped in centuries of history. And today has been another day for the ages.
JM

2024 · Humza Yousaf, First Minister – This was an almost identical list of subjects covered in an interview with the former First Minister Nicola Sturgeon eight years previously in January 2016. The only change was that the UK had by now left the European Union

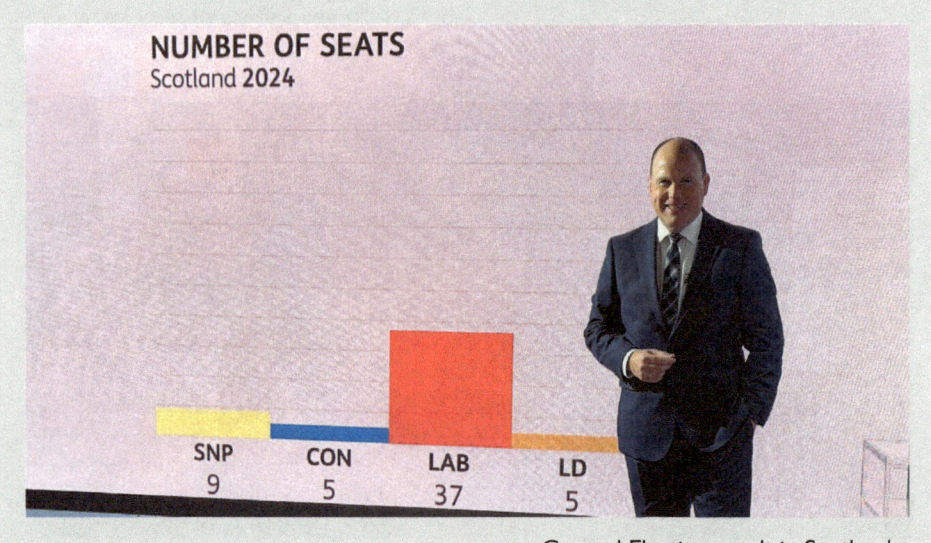

2024 · General Election result in Scotland - Labour are back in power in the United Kingdom. Sir Keir Starmer is our new Prime Minister. The Conservatives have collapsed. The SNP dominance has ended. It has been a memorable election, one of those that will be a reference point in the future – the '24 Election.

They swamped the *Scotland Tonight* feed with their herd mentality. It ruins what social networks can be.

Wednesday 14 May 2014
STV News

The Chancellor George Osborne has told MPs there would be no deal to allow an independent Scotland to share a currency with the rest of the UK. Giving evidence to the Commons Scottish Affairs Select Committee, he said the only way for Scotland to keep the pound was to vote No. But the SNP said he's putting himself on the wrong side of economics and the Scottish people.

DIARY: The SNP says it's bluff and bluster, but it is one of the clearest statements of the entire campaign. I think it's a weakness for the SNP. Even if there is a shared currency, then you are ceding significant control of your economic policy.

Thursday 15 May 2014
STV News

The Prime Minister has told STV that the unionist parties should work together to agree new powers for Holyrood in the event of a No vote for independence. David Cameron, in an interview for *Scotland Tonight*, said it would be good 'if the parties could talk to each other about their proposals and put them into place'. It came on the day the First Minister accused the No campaign of being in disarray

JM: Prime Minister, you're the Prime Minister of the austerity agenda, the bedroom tax, the zero hours contract. You are the embodiment, are you not, of why so many people in Scotland think a yes vote is necessary?

DAVID CAMERON, Prime Minister: Obviously, I don't agree with that. We're not voting about the Government, we're not voting about policies. This vote, this referendum is about Scotland's future. Does Scotland want to stay in the United Kingdom? Or does Scotland want to separate itself irreversibly from the United Kingdom? That is the question on the ballot paper. Of course, I would argue that we're making good economic progress. We've seen another fall in unemployment in Scotland, the economy is growing and strengthening and we're seeing lots of problems being addressed, but that's not the question in the referendum. The referendum is to stay in the United Kingdom with all the advantages that it has all our family of nations or go separately irreversibly in another direction.

JM: You have a dilemma, don't you? The fact is that polls here show that the better you perform in the polls moving towards the General Election next year the greater the chance of a Yes vote in Scotland.

DC: People in Scotland know there are separate questions. This is the most important decision Scotland has had to take for 300 years which is, do we stay as part of the United Kingdom, a successful family of nations or do we forever separate ourselves from it? That is a separate question to who is elected to the UK Parliament.

JM: But however you're saying there are two questions the fact is that's what people take from it. They are less likely to vote no if there isn't a Conservative Government at Westminster.

DC: I'm just telling you there are two separate questions, I'm making two separate arguments, one alongside Labour, Liberal Democrats and people who have no political affiliation at all that we should keep our family of nations together. Think of the things we've achieved in the past, whether establishing the NHS or defeating Hitler, think of the things we can do in the future as a family of nations, that is a separate question from the outcome of the British General Election in 2015.

DIARY: He answered as smoothly as you might expect, but was wobbly on the timetable for new powers – initially suggesting it'd be in the first Queen's Speech of a new Parliament, but then backing away – and on the *(refusal to release details of the)* poll in which there was evidence of steel – 'We just don't.' I found him to be quite personable. When we were setting up I asked him about kids he'd met in Maryhill, he complimented the set, laughed at my usual line about the Bond villain chair, urged us to cover the forthcoming European elections. Then he and his entourage were away, and it was some entourage – MI5, Police Scotland and his advisers and staff. The security staff wanted to know about exits, his staff were all questions – so, he's sitting there and he'll be mic-ed up? Who does that? All of it being sent back by Blackberry.

When the Prime Minister was in make-up he was briefed by his people about the interview. They described me as a 'straight anchor' and mentioned my Twitter handle @RealMacKaysTV. Evidently, they'd checked it, which made my heart sink. Unfortunately, my most recent tweets had been some online nonsense involving photos of my big feet jammed into a pair of stilettos.

Tuesday 27 May 2014
DIARY: The BBC launched their much-vaunted new show tonight, *Scotland 2014*, and we wiped the floor with them. They have tried to copy every idea we introduced on *Scotland Tonight* and even come on at the same time. At our *Scotland Tonight* meeting I heard what they were doing on their first night and knew then that they had got it wrong. They should have had a big splash and didn't. We had Deputy First Minister Nicola Sturgeon and Scottish Labour Leader Johann Lamont. They were head-to-head in one of our debates before on *Scotland Tonight* and that became a rabble. This one was far more considered – they both knew it had to be better – and there was favourable feedback.

This was utterly shameless by BBC Scotland. They saw how successful Scotland Tonight was and recognised that their own offering was inadequate. Had they truly wanted to use their public funding to provide a service for the licence fee paying audience, they could have put on a new, original programme at 11.00pm. What they did instead was attempt to challenge Scotland Tonight with a cloned version of the same programme at the same time. It rarely came close to matching Scotland Tonight's audience and was eventually cancelled.

Wednesday 28 May 2014
DIARY: We got one of our best audience shares for *Scotland Tonight*. The BBC took a pasting. Half of our audience and poor production decisions. Much satisfaction, but we can't be complacent. They will sharpen up their act. They'll have to.

Friday 30 May 2014
STV News

It's been almost 60 years since a passenger tram last ran through the streets of Edinburgh. It's been more than decade since plans were first mooted to bring them back. Now, after months of testing they are finally ready to roll and early tomorrow morning the first tram will leave the depot at Gogarburn and make the short trip to the nearby Gyle Centre to pick up its first customers. Edinburgh's trams have become one of the most controversial transport projects in recent years. Years of delays, soaring costs, legal disputes and cuts to the route. One person involved in the project described it as 'hell on wheels'.

Monday 2 June 2014
DIARY: The STV News relaunch tonight and it went very well. The new set reflects that a lot of money has been spent on it. It's very blue, big and shiny and I think it's the best set I've worked on.

Tuesday 3 June 2014
STV News

In the clearest signal yet that Labour, the Conservatives and Liberal Democrats could agree a common package of new powers for Holyrood, the former Prime Minister Gordon Brown has told a 'United with Labour' event a deal could be done and legislation passed 'earlier than people think'. It is part of his message to the party's core support who may fear a No vote to independence will mean an end to any further devolution of power to Edinburgh. However, the Chair of Yes Scotland, the former Labour MP Dennis Canavan says Labour values can only be realised through independence.

DOUGIE MACLEAN – 'CALEDONIA'
Scotland Tonight

JM: You're best known for 'Caledonia'. Do you get a wee bit annoyed at times that maybe your other music is being overshadowed by it?

DOUGIE MACLEAN, singer: No, I'm very proud of 'Caledonia'. I wrote the song when I was in my early 20s when I was genuinely homesick on a beach in France. And I've watched it over the years in all its incarnations and all the places where it goes. It's now become a kind of part of common culture, y'know, people use it. They play it at weddings and funerals and parties and very rarely songs do that, make that leap over to where people use it in their everyday lives.

JM: What about 'Caledonia' being an anthem, a new Scottish anthem, particularly with the Commonwealth Games coming up?

DM: I think with songs like that, people will choose their own songs and if people want a song to sing, if it happens to be 'Caledonia' that would be great. But it's the people who'll make that decision. People talk about it, but in the end, I'm a folk singer and that's what I do in my life, I play to people and I know that the people will make their own choice and I'm happy either way.

Dougie played us off air with a beautiful rendition of 'Caledonia'. It remains a Scotland Tonight highlight.

Monday 9 June 2014
STV News – live from Holyrood

In 100 days it's make your mind up time as we go to the polls to answer the question 'Should Scotland be an independent country?'. Today sees the campaigns for and against the Union crank up a gear. Over the next three months both Yes Scotland and Better Together know they must do all they can to win undecided voters to their cause. They recognise getting the message across in the media and on the doorsteps is crucial.

DIARY: Interviewed the leader of Better Together Alistair Darling in a hall in Maryhill where he'd been speaking. Pushed him on the lack of agreement on what extra powers will be delivered in the event of a 'No' vote. That's their weak point. Through to Edinburgh to present the 6.00pm from Holyrood. Two live interviews, Nicola Sturgeon and Ruth Davidson *(Scottish Conservative leader)*. Immediately after I had to do a down-the-line interview with Alex Salmond – he was in Aberdeen. There was a time lag and if you try to interject it all becomes very messy. So, it probably appeared I gave him an easier ride. Later accused of being biased by unionists. It's one side or the other.

Wednesday 11 June 2014

DIARY: STV News won an RTS Scotland award for our coverage of the Clutha Tragedy last year. I do think we deserved it because it was a cracking programme. There is a slight discomfort in winning an award for our coverage of a tragedy, but that is the nature of the business we are in and we are at our best during the big stories.

Monday 16 June 2014

DIARY: *Scotland Tonight* went on incursions in Iraq and pledges from the union parties on more powers for Holyrood and the Scottish Government's proposals for a Scottish Constitution. Nobody could really get fired up – the World Cup providing much distraction.

Tuesday 24 June 2014
STV News

It's one of the most iconic moments in Scottish history. On 24 June 1314, Robert the Bruce's army inflicted a devastating defeat on the English forces at the Battle of Bannockburn. Today, to mark the event's 700th anniversary, children from different parts of the UK went to the scene to lay a wreath to commemorate the thousands who fought and died.

Scotland Tonight

Now, before Robert the Bruce, there was William Wallace. The name of the legendary Scottish warrior is, of course, known far beyond his homeland in large part due to a certain Hollywood movie. Mel Gibson's *Braveheart* was a massive box office hit on its release, with a cultural impact that continues to be felt to this day. This evening in Edinburgh stars from the picture gathered for a gala screening celebrating 20 years since production began.

JIMMY WALES – Wikipedia

Wednesday 25 June 2014
Scotland Tonight

For many of us, Wikipedia has become a key source of information. Since it was formed more than a decade ago, the on-line encyclopaedia has grown to become one of the top five most visited websites. And its founder Jimmy Wales is now one of the world's most successful internet entrepreneurs.

JM: You founded Wikipedia. In layman's terms, how did that happen?

JIMMY WALES, Wikipedia Founder: Sure. I had the idea. I was watching the growth of open-source software, free software, seeing programmers coming together to collaborate, to build all the great software that runs the internet. And I thought that kind of collaboration could extend beyond software into all kinds of cultural works, so I launched a project called Newpedia, which was the predecessor, which was a failure. It was a very top-down, very academic system. There was a seven-stage review process to get anything published and as that began to fail, we stumbled across the idea of wiki,

meaning a website that anyone can edit. And I decided to give that a shot and see if we can get the work done better that way and we got more work done in two weeks than we had done in almost two years.

JM: So, it wasn't having to be peer-reviewed, it came from the bottom up?

JW: Yeah.

JM: And wiki is not a name you came up with, then?

JW: Wiki is the idea of the software. From '95 until 2001 when I launched Wikipedia, wikis were really a small underground phenomenon. People were experimenting with the idea of open editing and things like that, and then we took it and obviously made it very popular.

JM: You are a man who had a past in trading, you were a trader... You're maybe not typically somebody who would be seen as taking such an altruistic view. How did that come about?

JW: Well, I am just a person who gets up every day and does the most interesting thing I can think of to do. As a kid I was always quite fanatical about my encyclopaedias and I read the encyclopaedias all the time, so it was a natural fit. I thought that would be really great if there was a site where you could just look anything up and there would be a detailed encyclopaedia entry about it. Because of the dot-com crash that happened there was no possibility of raising money. There was no obvious business model but because of that, things that we did as a community, we did in a different way than we probably would have. If I had had millions of dollars in venture capital backing me, you know, you see some problem on the site and you'd think we have to hire more moderators, we have to hire more editors, and controls. We didn't have the option of doing that, we didn't have any money to do that. So, we had to devise ways of having democratic control within the community, of having open dialogues and debates and what kind of consensus rules do we need to get things done. So, a lot of that innovation was born out of the fact that we had no choice, we had no money.

JM: Some would, maybe, put you alongside Sir Tim Berners-Lee, who set up the web and has made nothing from it. You have this phenomenon and you really have made nothing from it. Is that a regret for you at all?

JW: No, no. Not at all. I have the most interesting life, and I make plenty of money. My for-profit company Wikia, which has advertising-supported wikis is now the number 19 website in the world, so doing incredibly well. And I always say that there are loads of people who earn a lot more money than me whose lives are incredibly boring compared to mine, so I'm pretty content as I am.

DIARY *(Tuesday 24 June 2014)*: He was receiving an honorary doctorate. Wasn't sure about him at first. 'Is it okay if I call you Jimmy?' 'That's my name.' Then he was checking his phone as I outlined what we were doing. However, once we got going he was fine… A wide-ranging interview. An unremarkable-looking man, but he's created a phenomenon.

Scotland Tonight

It's created nearly half a million new homeowners in Scotland since 1980. But the right-to-buy scheme for council tenants was abolished this afternoon by an overwhelming majority in the Scottish Parliament. Whilst in England they're making it easier for people to buy their council homes, here the Scottish Government says the move will protect 15,000 social houses.

Tuesday 1 July 2014

DIARY: Interview with Allan Wells, the 100-metre Olympic gold medallist from the Moscow Olympics. He's a genuine childhood hero of mine. I still remember his victory vividly. He was very pleasant and we had a good interview.

COMMONWEALTH GAMES
Wednesday 23 July 2014
STV News

Glasgow has been transformed into a sun-drenched festival city. After years in the planning, the Commonwealth Games of 2014 have arrived. The Queen will formally open the historic event at Celtic Park. It begins at 14 minutes past eight or 2014 – with the official ceremony at 9.00pm. As the clock counts down, our reporters are live across the city as Glasgow prepares to party.

DIARY: Glasgow is buzzing and I got a sense of that even just at Pacific Quay with the events that are going on. The weather is helping.

Tuesday 29 July 2014
STV News

Good evening from the heart of the Commonwealth Games. It has been a record-breaking day for Team Scotland in Glasgow. The nation's athletes have eclipsed their previous best in the competition, with the 34th medal of the Games coming in the gymnastics at the Hydro this afternoon. And there is promise of yet more medals to come for the host nation.

Thursday 31 July 2014

DIARY: Every evening of the Commonwealth Games I've stood on the balcony doing the programme. Astonishing the number of people walking along the Clyde and across the Squinty Bridge. The city is throbbing. Just being in the city you get a real sense of something happening. We're picking up medals too.

Sunday 3 August 2014
STV News

The sporting action at the Commonwealth Games in Glasgow came to an end today. Scotland picked up another silver medal in the badminton, bringing the medal tally to 53.

STEVEN BROWN, reporter: Before the transformation of Hampden for tonight's closing ceremony, the curtain fell on the athletics last night in the national stadium. As expected, one man stole the show. Jamaica's Usain Bolt, along with his teammates, eased to victory in the 4 x 100 metres relay. After the race the Olympic sprint champion showed, if anyone was in doubt, that he had enjoyed these Games.

There had been reports that the fastest man in the world had not been enjoying the Games, claims he dismissed.

Monday 4 August 2014

DIARY: *Scotland Tonight* was previewing tomorrow's big debate. The leaders of both campaigns – or chief execs – Blair McDougall and Blair Jenkins seem to get on very well and there is no personal animosity between them, unlike the politicians.

FIRST REFERENDUM DEBATE
Tuesday 5 August 2014

DIARY: Today was all about the first referendum debate between Alex Salmond and Alistair Darling. No question this was event television. TV crews from various parts and worldwide interest. Just as we were going on air – in the final ten-second countdown – autocue disappeared – apparently all my cameras died – and I was thinking I'd have to busk it – and they reappeared on three secs. Close, very close. In the cross-examination section Alex Salmond did not perform well – daft questions on alien invasion and driving on the right side of the road – and Alistair Darling focused effectively on the lack of a Plan B on currency. The Yes camp were very down after it and our reaction and snap polls said Darling won. Maybe not by as much as many were declaring, but a definite win.

Thursday 7 August 2014
STV News

'It's our pound and we are keeping it'. The defiant words of the First Minister Alex Salmond today when he came under sustained attack at Holyrood to reveal a Plan B, if he can't negotiate a post-referendum currency union. Opposition Leaders used *Question Time* to berate the Scottish Government's lack of contingency on the issue. It's six weeks today until Scotland goes to the polls

DIARY: The First Minister under continued pressure for his perceived failings in the debate. The whole question over Scotland's currency should we not get agreement on the pound is the big issue.

Wednesday 13 August 2014
STV News

The Chief Counting Officer for the Scottish Independence Referendum has told STV News that the final result should be known at breakfast time on 19 September. Mary Pitcaithly revealed the ambition as more than four million polling cards were printed ready for distribution in the coming days.

Friday 15 August 2014
STV News – live from George Square

People make Glasgow. Tonight 5,000 are here in George Square to celebrate the biggest sporting and cultural event the city has ever hosted. In terms of sporting success, the 2014 Games were the most successful ever. But the winners, too, were the people of Glasgow and Scotland. Tonight, we all join in the victory party.

DIARY: The programme came live from George Square for the Commonwealth Athlete's Parade. Among our guests was Charlie 'I'm buzzing like a jar of wasps' Flynn – a boxing gold. A great character and one of the personalities of the Games. The crowd adored him. He's just very natural. Good luck to him.

JM: (*amid loud cheers*) This is one popular man, let me tell you. What did it feel like today coming along in the procession?

CHARLIE FLYNN, Commonwealth gold medal winner: It was like Hydro number 2.

(*He'd won his boxing gold at the Hydro*) Back again. A blast from the past, man. Just like when I won the gold the public are embracing me and I love them for it. (*Huge cheers*)

JM: What have you done since you won your medal? Have you been able to get back to your normal life?

CF: What have I no' been doin', man? I've been everywhere. (*Cheers of Charlie! Charlie!*)

JM: Has the postman been delivering? (*He had been a part-time postman before the Games and famously quipped after his medal win, 'The Postman delivers.'*)

CF: I've no' been delivering, I've been chilling. I've been delivering interviews.

JM: And what now, back to training?

CF: Aye, I started back a couple of days ago, trying to get back into a routine, man, let the dust settle and look at the long-term boxing plan and get focused again.

JM: And what about this newfound fame you've got?

CF: Ah, it's madness, man. I'm like a son of Glasgow, I go in and they're all cheering and everybody loves you. I honestly would love to thank the public for their help and support because I wouldn't be here without them.

Monday 18 August 2014
STV News

The referendum battle has intensified with a month to go before we make one of the most important decisions in our country's history. The First Minister launched a 'declaration of opportunity' in Arbroath evoking that town's famous place in Scottish constitutional history. Better Together focused on the drive to win over undecided voters with a massive logistical exercise ahead to contact every voter.

DIARY: A month until the referendum and polls at the weekend showed Yes gaining again. This could be very tight.

Tuesday 19 August 2014
Scotland Tonight

The Scottish Government has put the future of the NHS at the heart of its referendum campaign, with the Health Secretary Alex Neil claiming today that only a Yes vote can protect our health service in Scotland from cuts and privatisation. The opposition pro-Union MSPs hit back accusing the SNP ministers of peddling lies and scare stories.

DIARY: The SNP are trying to get the NHS on the agenda because of the hit they've taken on the currency. Health is devolved and any choices on spending are those of the Scottish Parliament. It's a fairly transparent tactic, but could just connect with women voters especially.

When the Labour spokesperson, Neil Findlay, arrived in the studio before we went on air he joined in a discussion I was having with the crew about pies and bridies. He ventured that when he was a builder his favourite was a Scotch pie in a Greggs roll because they were the perfect size for each other. He was thoroughly engaging, just like his counterpart, the SNP's Stewart Maxwell, who has been good chat previously in the hospitality room after programmes. It's no coincidence that both men have had experience of life beyond the political bubble. Contrast that with a group of students we had in previously supporting some guests. They were earnest and eager, but competed with each other in political clichés. It was clear that they were headed for the politics pathway with no diversions. I don't know that it is good for them or for politics.

Wednesday 20 August 2014
STV News

A leading figure in the oil and gas industry has claimed the Scottish Government's North Sea estimates are up to 60 per cent too high. Sir Iain Wood has warned the country will begin to feel the effects of depleting reserves in just 15 years' time. The tycoon said an independent Scotland's economy would suffer with significant increases in energy bills. However, the Scottish Government insists the future of the industry is brighter than he predicts.

DIARY: There's no denying that is a blow for the Yes campaign, no matter how they're trying to play it down. It is qualified by him saying that there are further discoveries, but still.

Monday 25 August 2014
Scotland Tonight

The currency, oil and gas and the NHS were among the key issues as Alistair Darling and Alex Salmond crossed swords for the second time in the referendum campaign. For an hour and a half, the First Minister and Better Together leader put forward their cases, cross-examined each other and took questions from the audience in the BBC debate.

DIARY: Second major debate between Alex Salmond and Alistair Darling. Salmond had it all to lose after being widely considered to have lost the last time. Much like the last time, the reaction of one being a runaway winner was rather overplayed. Salmond was much better, but Darling wasn't terrible. The Yes campaign will get a big bounce from it.

Tuesday 26 August 2014
STV News

Alex Salmond says his performance in the debate will give the Yes campaign a boost. However, both sides believe the referendum battle will be won or lost on the doorsteps not on television. A snap poll declared the First Minister the winner last night and the odds of a Yes vote have been shortened by the bookies. Better Together say Yes Scotland still need to answer big questions before the nation decides.

Wednesday 27 August 2014
STV News

The Electoral Commission says there's been an unprecedented surge in people registering to vote in the referendum, but as many as half a million Scots could still be denying themselves the chance to have their say – and they're running out of time. The deadline to register is midnight, next Tuesday.

DIARY: It's all referendum now. A big push on to make sure people are registered to vote. I am getting an ever increasing sense that this is becoming closer and closer.

Friday 29 August 2014
STV News

The Prime Minister has told STV News he'll attempt to forge a cross-party consensus on more devolution should he win the next election. Continuing his visit in Scotland, he gave his clearest signal yet that he'd seek a joint approach with Labour and the Liberal Democrats to give Holyrood more powers in the event of a No vote in the referendum.

DIARY: This is the lull before the storm. The next two weeks might be quiet, but then it'll kick off. Much being made of Jim Murphy MP being 'egged' on his tour of 100 towns in 100 days. Some people saying it is trivial and maybe it is, but I still think it brings the debate into disrepute. This is supposed to be a civilised campaign and that shouting and barracking puts people off. It may be politics in the raw, but it is unpleasant.

Monday 1 September 2014

DIARY: A poll released tonight showing the Yes vote has gained another four points, putting it at No 53 per cent Yes 47 per cent. That's an eight-point shift in a month by an organisation – YouGov – that hasn't typically had Yes high. That result is also within the margin of error. It's all getting very close and no question the momentum is with the Yes campaign. A lot of people are saying 'There is something in the air.' Mind you, after the first debate a month ago the Yes campaign was quite flat, so things can change quickly.

Tuesday 2 September 2014
STV News

A new poll has suggested the Yes campaign need just a 3 per cent swing to win the referendum. Better Together have said the poll highlights that Scots who want to stay in the Union must vote, while the Yes campaign say the momentum is now with them.

DIARY: The second STV debate – the third televised one overall – was this evening. We went with a different format – three from the Yes and No camps and not the head-to-heads that have been more typical. As a result, it was less confrontational and STV received widespread praise because people felt they heard reasoned discussion.

Sunday 7 September 2014
STV News

There's been confusion on the referendum campaign trail today. The leader of Better Together was forced to clarify comments made by the Chancellor. Following a TV appearance by George Osborne, there has been speculation a new statement on more powers for Holyrood would be revealed next week. However, the No campaign say all that will actually be announced is a timetable for when previously proposed powers could come into force if there's a No vote. It came as one poll put the Yes campaign in the lead for the first time.

The *Sunday Times* poll put Yes on 51 per cent and No on 49 per cent.

DIARY: I wonder if it's come just too early for the Yes campaign and people who are swithering will be panicked by the fact it could be a reality.

Monday 8 September 2014
STV News

Shares in Scottish companies have fallen sharply after a poll suggested the 'Yes' campaign was in the lead in the referendum. The pound has also dropped to a ten-month low against the dollar. Better Together claims the City's jitters have been caused by the uncertainty over the economy – Yes Scotland says the Chancellor George Osborne is to blame. Labour have launched a charm offensive across the country. Some of the party's big hitters were out trying to firm up their vote following the Yes campaign's poll lead. However, Yes drafted in celebrities and claimed they now have the momentum.

DIARY: The weekend polls – and another today – showing how close the camps are has put Better Together into a panic. Now offering more powers, only they aren't more powers, just a timeline for the ones already promised. And they're falling back on Gordon Brown to stem the flow of Labour supporters to Yes. I don't think he's the ace they perceive him to be.

Tuesday 9 September 2014
STV News

David Cameron and Ed Miliband have cancelled their weekly clash in the House of Commons tomorrow to campaign in Scotland for a 'No' vote. In a joint statement with Nick Clegg, the leaders of the three main Westminster parties said they wanted to be north of the border, listening and talking to voters. Alex Salmond has predicted their visit will backfire – and provide a massive boost for the Yes campaign.

DIARY: Is that really an advantage to Better Together? I'm not so sure. One vignette that summed up their travails was an attempt to raise the saltire over Downing Street – as they tried to raise it, it fell down!

Wednesday 10 September 2014
STV News

The Conservatives, Labour and the Liberal Democrats united in Scotland for the United Kingdom. The party leaders made impassioned pleas to voters to stick with the Union. But as far as Alex Salmond is concerned, David Cameron, Ed Miliband and Nick Clegg were here just to save their jobs.

DIARY: The Prime Minister David Cameron, the leader of the Opposition Ed Miliband and Lib Dem leader Nick Clegg were all campaigning in Scotland today. The No campaign given a severe jolt by recent opinion polls, although one tonight has No 53 per cent Yes 47 per cent. The No campaign also had warnings coming from major institutions about financial companies moving HQs, not as much oil etc. Quite the barrage.

Thursday 11 September 2014
STV News

A number of High Street businesses say their costs and prices could go up if the nation votes for independence. Their intervention in the debate comes as historic Scottish banking institutions laid out contingency plans to move their head offices south of the border. The First Minister said none of the moves will have any impact on jobs or the operations of the banks. He said it was about moving 'brass plaques'.

DIARY: The polls swinging back towards No, but still too close to call. However, the supermarket Asda has said prices will rise in an independent Scotland, likewise John Lewis. Now, despite other stores (eg Tesco) saying otherwise, I think that could have an impact. Banks talking about moving is one thing, but Asda is another. No question we are seeing the full might of the British establishment being brought to bear. It could work, too.

Friday 12 September 2014
STV News

Alex Salmond says the Yes campaign are within touching distance of a win, as the polls remain on a knife edge. The First Minister took to the skies today in a tour of cities across the country to galvanise grassroots campaigners for one last push to polling day. Better Together have again been raising the issue of economic uncertainty on the campaign trail. They've claimed the price of a weekly shop would increase with independence. It comes as Ed Miliband traverses the country and some famous sporting faces lent their names to the No camp.

Monday 15 September 2014
STV News – live from Holyrood

Good evening from Holyrood at the beginning of this momentous week in Scottish politics. We go into the final days of the campaign with both sides claiming they are heading for victory. The polls are narrower than they have ever been and can't give any side a clear lead. By the week's end we will know our nation's destiny. Both sides have been campaigning relentlessly in these final few days, trying to win over the undecided voters. Today, Alex Salmond repeated his claims that Westminster was behind what he called a 'scaremongering' campaign over what would happen to business in Scotland if there's a Yes vote.

The Scottish Secretary has called on Alex Salmond to 'call off the dogs' and stop intimidation from Yes supporters on the campaign trail. Alistair Carmichael said this behaviour 'came from the top' and was directed only at those who support the Union. The First Minister said both sides 'had a few idiots', but people are energised and empowered by the campaign.

The Prime Minister issued a warning that Thursday's referendum is a 'once and for all' decision as he made a last-ditch trip north to urge voters to save the Union. Speaking in Aberdeen, The Prime Minister warned that if Scots vote for independence it would result in a 'painful divorce'.

DIARY: Through to Edinburgh for the *Six O'Clock* which will be the pattern for this week. Usually, I'm just standing on the grass in front of Holyrood without even a pergola for protection. This time a big media village has been built, with gantry positions. There is some clambering up narrow stairs, but we are in an elevated position which will give a good view of the Parliament. Not tonight, though. It was shrouded in mist. A cold, foggy day in Edinburgh.

Tuesday 16 September 2014
STV News – live from Holyrood

There's now less than 48 hours to go until the polls open and the nation decides its future. But there's been no let up in the fight for every single last vote with more claims, counter-claims and impassioned pleas to the electorate. Today saw Yes campaigners dismiss a Westminster pledge of more powers for Scotland as a 'desperate offer of nothing'. The leaders of the three main parties promised 'extensive new powers' for the Scottish Parliament if the country votes to stay in the Union. But the move was described by opponents as a panic measure with no real detail.

DIARY: In a lovely, sunbathed Edinburgh – much different from the mist of last night. Main line today was a 'Vow' from the three Westminster leaders of more powers for Scotland. Their constant problem with that has been their inability to detail what these powers are. And MPs in England are, understandably, getting aggrieved. Would these powers even get through? Accusations about the Yes campaign getting overly aggressive. Ed Miliband had to abandon a walkabout in Edinburgh because of the jostling. It has been an aspect of the Yes campaign that has been unpleasant. And it doesn't win votes.

Wednesday 17 September 2014
STV News – live from Holyrood

Good evening from the Scottish Parliament in Edinburgh on the LAST day of campaigning over the Independence Referendum for Scotland.

And on the eve of this historic vote, a new poll for STV tonight reveals the Yes and No camps are neck and neck. The Ipsos Mori survey puts the pro-independence camp on 49 per cent and Better Together on 51 per cent.

JM: Our political editor Bernard Ponsonby joins me now. Bernard will Better Together be satisfied with their campaign this evening?

BP: Everybody at this stage of a campaign says that it has been wonderful and will deliver victory. At the end of the day, this was a tactically more difficult campaign to fight because it was always going to have to raise the issues of risk and uncertainty and in doing so was going to stand accused of being negative. But there is no doubt that around the issue of currency, in particular, it has been successful in putting the Yes side on the back foot. Whether in the end they perhaps overplayed the currency card is more difficult to tell. It is interesting that yesterday and again today Gordon Brown saying to voters, if you are unsure, uncertain, you must not gamble with the future, you should vote no. So even right to the end, the issue of unquantifiable risk is one that the No side are raising in the hope that it carries them to victory tomorrow.

JM: Alistair Darling, we've heard what the polls are saying tonight. It is that close. Have you done enough?

ALISTAIR DARLING, Better Together: Well, I always said it would go down to the line and what it means is that tomorrow when we go to the polls every one of us can tip the balance one way or another. And I do think there is a clear choice now. We can have a stronger Scottish Parliament with more powers so that we can safeguard our health service and education and at the same time we can have the opportunities that come from being part of something bigger because so many jobs in Scotland depend upon there being no border between Scotland and England. The choice between that and, frankly, taking a leap into the unknown where there are so many unanswered questions, so many doubts about currency, who'll pay pensions? And what I say to people is if you don't know, then you should vote No because otherwise you are taking a real risk, not for yourselves, but for generations to come as well.

JM: Are you glad it's nearly all over?

AD: Well, y'know, I think two-and-a-half years is a long, long time to be discussing our constitution. It's an important matter, passions are running high on both sides, but this is the time we've got to decide. But it's such a big decision, it's bigger than anything that any of us have ever taken before, it's important that we get it right.

JM: If you had one message to give to the many who are still undecided, still not sure how to vote, what would it be tonight to persuade them?

AD: You can get the change you want with a stronger, more secure Scottish Parliament by staying in the UK. You can get the security, the better job opportunities which we desperately need in years to come. The alternative is to take a leap into the unknown. And if you don't know the answers to these questions, if you're taking a big decision of buying a house or deciding to marry someone or to live with somebody, you'd be asking hard questions before you took that leap. We're being asked by Alex Salmond to, y'know, tear down the foundations on which our country is built and he's got nothing to offer in the place. That's not good enough for me and I guess it's not good enough for most people living in Scotland.

JM – Our political reporter Carole Erskine is in Perth ahead of a Yes campaign rally there this evening... Carole, sum up what you have made of their campaign.

CAROLE ERSKINE, Political Reporter: This campaign has been a grassroots movement, people of all ages across Scotland becoming engaged in politics and spreading the Yes message. We've seen the traditional door knocking and phone canvassing along with concerts, town hall debates and the creation of many groups for independence – English Scots for Yes, Carers for Yes and Women for Independence just to name a few. They have been pushing forward what could be seen as a positive message, a message for change. Many people have done this off their own back, some moving back from living abroad to become involved. It has really galvanised the spirit of those who want a Yes vote, the feeling that they didn't want to wake up on 19 September and wish they had done more. No one can fault their enthusiasm but what we don't know is if that will be enough for the majority of the country to go for independence.

JM: We're now joined by the First Minister Alex Salmond, the leader of the Yes campaign. You've heard tonight's poll, it could not be closer.

ALEX SALMOND, First Minister: Yeah, and it's very encouraging because obviously right through this campaign it's the Yes side who've been gaining ground as we've convinced more and more of our fellow citizens that a Yes vote is best for Scotland's future, to create a more prosperous economy, but also to create a more just society.

JM: The polls open tomorrow. Are you relieved it's nearly all over?

AS: No, I'm enjoying myself wonderfully. I've met so many people and I've learned so much on the campaign. There's been so many points of fun as well as very serious points. But people are really interested, they're taking their responsibilities so seriously. They're taking this great opportunity and they're studying it and they're part of it and it's part of an enlivening process, the like of which I've never seen in Scotland. Perhaps there are few parallels in the whole of Western Europe. That's why it's so much a privilege to be part of this great campaign, this people up campaign, this campaign which is empowering Scotland and why it's a privilege to present that vision of a Yes vote, that prosperous economy and that just society.

JM: A number of undecided voters tonight going into the poll tomorrow still undecided. What's your final, clear message to them this evening?

AS: Vote for the future. I think we've managed to illustrate to people how so many things are secure in Scotland. We saw today 45,000 new jobs in Scotland. I think that symbolises that political and economic confidence go together. So, as we've satisfied immediate concerns, this is about voting for what's to come in Scotland, what the future is going to be. So, my advice, and it's advice offered to people who are still making up their mind, is we know this country can be a successful country. We know we want to be a more equal and just society, so vote for that future, vote Yes tomorrow.

JM: There are then, just hours to go until Scotland goes to the polls. By any measure this has been an unprecedented political campaign fought from city street corners to Highland mountain tops. Our political editor Bernard Ponsonby has been there every step of the way. Bernard, your final thoughts?

BERNARD PONSONBY, Political Editor: John, I would simply say that I have seen nothing like this before. I don't think that anything I've covered before would come anywhere near the kind of excitement that has been generated in Scotland in recent times. There is a sense in which commentators covering events like this get gripped by hyperbole, the word historic is bandied about so often it almost becomes the stuff of cliche. But the decision that this nation will take tomorrow is so profound, so profound on so many different levels that the word historic almost seems inadequate. But be in no doubt about one thing; the politics of this country will never be the same again. The narrative has changed in recent days. The only question tomorrow is what is the end game of that particular narrative? Yes, it's been exciting, yes, it's been bad tempered at times, but overshadowing all of that, and both campaigns and personalities is one single reality – you, John, me, everybody in Scotland tomorrow is master of their own destiny. A civic duty by Scots tomorrow will make history. And change a country.

JM: That is where have to leave it tonight. The campaigns are almost run. Tomorrow you will decide. From Holyrood... a very good evening.

DIARY: So, the campaigning is over and now it's up to the people of Scotland to decide. I spoke to leaders of both campaigns live on air tonight. I thought Alistair Darling seemed fresher, maybe slightly more upbeat. The First Minister Alex Salmond said he was fine, but I had the slightest sense of flatness and fatigue. No surprise given the pressure he's been under this past while. Alistair Darling has been part of a far wider political team.

They both repeated much the same lines as they have throughout the campaign and I didn't challenge them on that. The idea was that these would be the final summings-up for their campaigns. It was Alex Salmond's final interview of the campaign and, I believe, Alistair Darling's too.

Tonight's polls all favour No marginally, but with narrowing gaps. All you hear is 'too close to call'. I did get a couple of Yes people saying to me that even if it's a No vote things will change. I wonder if they're getting ready for defeat in their own minds. But if you are on the ground it's the Yes campaign that dominates, sometimes boorishly. I wonder if that'll count against them.

A big day tomorrow. The sense of nervous excitement is palpable everywhere.

SCOTTISH INDEPENDENCE REFERENDUM

Thursday 18 September 2014
STV News

Good evening. Live from the Scottish Parliament in Edinburgh. On an historic day for Scotland voting is well under way to determine whether the country should leave or remain part of the United Kingdom. More than three years after the Scottish National Party secured a landslide victory at Holyrood, the long-awaited referendum on independence is finally taking place. Polling stations the length and breadth of the country opened at 7.00am and people have until 10.00pm tonight to cast their vote, with the result expected to be known by breakfast time tomorrow. The question facing voters is a simple one: Should Scotland be an independent country?

DIARY: The rules of elections/referendums mean that there is not much that can be reported other than the fact of it and people turning up at the polls. The turnout is expected to be very high.

STV News at Ten – live from Edinburgh

A defining moment in our history. Welcome to a special edition of the STV *News at Ten* live from the capital of Scotland. We have all been asked 'Should Scotland be an independent country?' We the people have given our answer. With the vote on a knife edge, far too close to call, the eyes of the world are upon us. From every corner of the country, on every street in every village, in towns and cities people have been out en masse to make their vote count. Two political, passionate and at times polarising campaigns fought right down to the wire.

The chimes of Big Ben

As Big Ben marks 10.00pm on 18th September 2014, two capitals await. Will the Union remain intact, a shared democracy between Westminster and Holyrood, or will complete sovereignty be restored to Scotland?

The bongs of Big Ben

The referendum is now over. The polls are now closed. Scotland is ready to count our votes and declare whether or not we are indeed to become an independent country.

I consider this to have been the pinnacle of my career. As Big Ben chimed and I delivered that line to the nation about two capitals waiting, the hairs stood on the back of my neck. It was a moment of history for our nation and no one could know for sure what the next hours would bring and what it would mean for our future.

DIARY: I was staying in Edinburgh to do a special STV *News at Ten* from the Edinburgh roof. It was very ambitious because the technical capacity of Edinburgh's gallery is not the same as Glasgow's. We had rehearsed the opening link to tie in with the bongs of Big Ben to mark the closing of the polls and it seemed to work very well. A train back to Glasgow, where George Square was full of Yes voters. A quick stop at STV where the results programme was on air. It already seemed that No had won.

INDEPENDENCE REFERENDUM RESULT

Friday 19 September 2014

Scotland This Morning – with Andrea Brymer

Hello and welcome to this special breakfast show marking the most momentous political day in our history for 300 years. Last night millions of people answered the question 'Should Scotland be an independent country?' The result? A victory for the No campaign.

MARY PITCAITHLY, Returning Officer: It is clear that the majority of the people voting have voted No to the referendum question.

For First Minister Alex Salmond a devastating night. A conclusive victory for the No campaign.

ALEX SALMOND, First Minister: There is going to be a majority for the No campaign. And it's important to say that our referendum was an agreed and consented process and Scotland has by majority decided not, at this stage, to become an independent country. I accept that verdict of the people and I call on all of Scotland to follow suit in accepting the democratic verdict of the people of Scotland.

As dawn breaks across the land, celebrations from the victors in the battle for hearts and minds.

ALISTAIR DARLING, Better Together: The people of Scotland have spoken. We have chosen unity over division, positive change rather than needless separation. Today is a momentous result for Scotland and also for the United Kingdom as a whole.

DAVID CAMERON, Prime Minister: The people of Scotland have spoken and it is a clear result. They have kept our country of four nations together and like millions of other people I am delighted... The three pro-union parties have made commitments, clear commitments on further powers for the Scottish Parliament. We will ensure that those commitments are honoured in full... Just as the people of Scotland will have more power over their affairs, so it follows that the people of England, Wales and Northern Ireland must have a bigger say over theirs… I have long believed that a crucial part missing from this national discussion is England. We have heard the voice of Scotland – and now the millions of voices of England must also be heard. The question of English votes for English laws – the so-called West Lothian question – requires a decisive answer. So, just as Scotland will vote separately in the Scottish Parliament on their issues of tax, spending and welfare so too England, as well as Wales and Northern Ireland, should be able to vote on these issues and all this must take place in tandem with, and at the same pace as, the settlement for Scotland.

BERNARD PONSONBY, Political Editor: I think that is perhaps the most significant contribution ever made by a British Prime Minister in terms of constitutional change throughout the totality of the nations of the United Kingdom.

DIARY: Not much time afterwards before I was heading through to Edinburgh again to present lunchtime. A general air of flatness everywhere, I felt.

ALEX SALMOND RESIGNS

STV News – Live from Holyrood

It's been a monumental and emotional day for Scotland and for Scottish politics. Tonight, Alex Salmond announced his resignation. The shock statement came after the nation voted No to independence by 55 to 45 per cent. The First Minister said his time may be over, but he said for Scotland the dream will never die. In a dramatic news conference in the capital, he added the country could still remain a real winner, but it's time for someone else to lead that battle.

JM: I'm joined now by our political editor Bernard Ponsonby. Bernard, why has he gone?

BERNARD PONSONBY, Political Editor: For the reason he gave. There are fresh battles ahead and the Government and SNP need a fresh perspective. In his statement he said that if mistakes were made in the campaign, he accepted responsibility for them as he led the campaign. Remember there are two priorities; prosecute the case for more powers and ensure the SNP win again in 2016. Realistically, I don't think he ever intended to go all the way to 2020 so this makes perfect sense.

The Prime Minister was quick to respond to the No vote this morning. Speaking outside Number 10 David Cameron claimed more powers for Holyrood would be delivered. The unionist parties' last-minute plea to give extra powers for the Scottish Parliament was a key feature of the closing stages of the referendum debate with Gordon Brown in particular promising a speedy process. However, that timing could be in doubt tonight and there may be more devolution for England, Wales and Northern Ireland.

That ends our referendum coverage here in the capital city. It's official. The nation has spoken. The 300-year-old Union remains. The break-up of Britain does not begin. Instead, a new settlement is promised, a new chapter in Scotland's story begins. The question now, for tomorrow and the next day is will Westminster deliver?

DIARY: Alex Salmond announced his resignation. That threw all the programme plans in the air. We acquitted ourselves well – Bernard's fine bio (delivered to camera without notes) – lives with John Swinney and Johann Lamont and off cleanly. A very good programme and a momentous day. This won't happen again and if it does, not with the same resonance. Some trouble caused by Loyalists in George Square, unfortunately.

Monday 22 September 2014
Scotland Tonight

As the debate intensifies over English votes on English issues, the SNP is claiming that the vow made by the main Westminster leaders to strengthen Holyrood is unravelling. They say UK ministers have signalled a threat to Scottish funding through the omission of any reference to the Barnett Formula in the parliamentary motion published today.

DIARY: Back to work for the post-referendum period and the question, what are we going to talk about now? In actual fact, there was plenty, principally on the powers being offered by Westminster – still don't know precisely what they are – and where now for the Yes campaigners?

Tuesday 23 September 2014
STV News

Alex Salmond has said more powers must be delivered to Scotland as promised. The First Minister said Holyrood would hold the Westminster leaders to their vow. However, Labour Leader Johann Lamont gave her personal commitment that increased powers over welfare and tax would be delivered. The exchanges came as Lord Smith who has been tasked with getting the parties to agree on what should be offered to Scotland met with leaders at Holyrood.

Wednesday 24 September 2014
STV News

Nicola Sturgeon has launched her bid to succeed Alex Salmond as the new Leader of the SNP. If elected at the party's conference in November she is likely to become First Minister. Today, the current Deputy First Minister told STV News that she will not rule out backing another Independence Referendum if she judges it necessary.

Thursday 25 September 2014
STV News

One of the world's great sporting events, the Ryder Cup, has opened at Gleneagles. Just one week after the Scottish Independence Referendum, the eyes of the world are once again on Scotland, as Europe and the United States battle it out for the biggest prize in team golf. Forty-five thousand fans will watch the drama unfold each day along with millions more around the world.

Monday 29 September 2014
STV News

The Prime Minister has told STV News he is confident that agreement can be reached with the other unionist parties to give Scotland the new powers promised in the referendum. But he also said that new powers for the rest of the UK must proceed on a similar timetable. He also said he was happy that the issue of independence has been settled for a generation.

Tuesday 30 September 2014
STV News

Gordon Brown has launched a strong attack on David Cameron over his handling of more powers for the Scottish Parliament. The former Labour Prime Minister has called on Mr Cameron to 'pull back' on his pledge to back English votes for English laws, saying it was never discussed before the referendum. Mr Brown is urging Scots to sign a petition demanding the Prime Minister implement his referendum vow on new powers.

DIARY: This is the same Gordon Brown who brokered 'The Vow' among the Westminster leaders for more powers and who is being given much credit for securing a No vote, now asking people to sign a petition. This 'extra powers' issue is going to drag on.

Monday 20 October 2014
STV News

Shops across Scotland have started charging for carrier bags. Whether you're at the supermarket or just a local takeaway you'll have to pay the five pence levy. It's been brought in by the Scottish Government to try to reduce litter and applies to all bags, whether they're plastic, paper or biodegradable.

Scotland Tonight

Scotland may have voted No in the Independence Referendum, but the momentum in Scottish politics appears to lie firmly with the SNP, whose membership has more than trebled since the big vote. For Scottish Labour, it's a very different picture with two of its former First Ministers warning that the party has lost its way and alienated many of its traditional supporters.

Tuesday 21 October 2014
STV News

The first party talks on more powers for Scotland have taken place in Edinburgh. The initial meeting was described as constructive by Lord Smith who has been tasked with brokering an agreement on increased devolution. However, experts have questioned the commission's tight timetable.

Wednesday 22 October 2014

DIARY: The first meeting of the Smith Commission to decide on new powers for Scotland. This will become a long running political row. On the one hand the nationalists who say we were promised more, on the other, the unionist parties who'll say there was a decisive No vote.

JOHANN LAMONT'S RESIGNATION
Monday 27 October 2014
Scotland Tonight

Scottish Labour has been left reeling by the explosive departure of leader Johann Lamont, who accused the UK party of treating Scotland like 'a branch office' and described some Labour MPs as 'dinosaurs'. As yet no politician has put themselves forward to succeed her, but there is growing speculation that the MP Jim Murphy is poised to stand.

DIARY: Labour's preparation for a new leader and the fallout from Johann Lamont's resignation – Scottish Labour treated as a branch office and too many dinosaurs... Perhaps a new leader could invigorate them, but none of the recent ones have – or (*it could*) just come nothing. Fascinating.

Thursday 30 October 2014

DIARY: An STV poll today for the General Election next year shows Labour in meltdown with only four seats, down from 41. The SNP dominate with more than 50 seats. I can't see it playing out like that, but a major shock for Labour.

Friday 14 November 2014
STV News

Thirty-seven years after the World's End murders, two teenage girls have finally received justice with the conviction of a man who's been called Scotland's secret serial killer. Angus Sinclair, already serving two life sentences for murder and sex crimes, has been found guilty of raping and strangling Christine Eadie and Helen Scott in 1977.

DIARY: The killer Angus Sinclair is already in jail for other murders, is suspected of more and had spent time in jail as a youth for killing a young girl. Why was he ever released? The usual question we hear so often. He's being called Scotland's 'silent serial killer' because he got away with it for so long. Jury out this afternoon because of six weeks of evidence. Much debate over whether they'd be back today or not. I'd no doubt they would be – it's the weekend, there's a big game tonight *(Scotland v Ireland in a Euros Qualifier)* and his defence wasn't credible. They came back just after 5.00pm.

Tuesday 18 November 2014
STV News

Scotland will become an independent country. With those words delegates cheered the First Minister Alex Salmond as he bowed out of the party leadership at the SNP annual conference in Perth. Mr Salmond warned the Westminster parties that they will pay a heavy price if they renege on promises made during the referendum on more powers for the Scottish Parliament.

Scotland Tonight

Alex Salmond resigned today as First Minister, describing his

seven-and-a-half-year tenure as the privilege of his life. In a speech paving the way for Nicola Sturgeon's promotion, he told Holyrood he was sure that 'more change and better days lie ahead for Scotland'.
DIARY: Little doubt he's been a success and leaves on a high, despite actually losing a referendum. We can't forget that when he came to power in 2007 not much was expected. He has transformed his party and while there are domestic issues, his governments have been stable.

Wednesday 19 November 2014
STV News – live from Holyrood

Nicola Sturgeon is the new First Minister of Scotland. She was elected by MSPs this afternoon during a session of Parliament when opposition leaders joined her in marking what is a significant day for women in politics. The SNP leader pledges to be a First Minister for all of Scotland.

JM: The First Minister joins us now from her official residence, Bute House. Congratulations on becoming First Minister.

NICOLA STURGEON, First Minister: Thank you. It is a great honour. I am excited about this, but I am under no illusion this is a big responsibility. I will do this job to the best of my ability. I was anxious to stress in Parliament and will do so again now. I am First Minister for all of Scotland, so if you are SNP or not, voted yes or no, my job is to represent and serve you and I will do that to the best of my ability.

JM: And the first female First Minister?

NS: That is, I think, a symbolic moment. I very much hope my election as First Minister will send a strong message to women and girls all over the country, it doesn't matter your background, gender, if you're good enough or work hard enough you should be able to fulfil your potential and reach your dreams. That is a message that means a lot to me. I have an eight-year-old niece and I want by the time she is a woman for the things that are holding women back now to be in the past. So, it is a proud moment and symbolic. I want to extend opportunity to all women that will be more than the simple example of my holding this office.

JM: What will your priorities be?

NS: I have begun setting out those priorities. I have been a member of Alex Salmond's Government for seven years. I am proud of the achievements of this Government and I want to build on them. I am absolutely clear we must do more to tackle the inequalities that afflict Scotland, too many children live in poverty. I have set out clear plans to extend the living wage to more people, not just in the public sector but in the private sector, extend childcare to give our children the best start in life. I understand very well you can't achieve social justice without a vibrant growing economy, so being on the side of business and promoting their interests at home and around the globe will be a key task of mine as First Minister and one that I relish.

JM: Briefly, will we see another referendum while you are First Minister?

NS: That is down to the people. I won't pretend other than that I support independence and I will seek to continue to persuade people that Scotland should be an independent country, but the decision is not mine to take. I can't impose a referendum on Scotland, no more than I can impose independence on Scotland. We will only have another referendum when people vote for that in a manifesto. It will be the will of the people, not the will of this or any other First Minister that determines that.

JM: Nicola Sturgeon, First Minister, thank you for joining us.

NS: Thank you.

DIARY: I think she is very capable and will be very effective. Not only is she talented, but, as she says, she has served a seven-year apprenticeship as deputy, so she knows what to expect.

Tuesday 25 November 2014

DIARY: *Scotland Tonight* was the three

candidates for the Scottish Labour leadership. Jim Murphy is the clear favourite. Neil Findlay has an 'old' Labour position which is the clearest. Sarah Boyack was much improved from the nervous individual I interviewed when she declared her candidacy.

Thursday 27 November 2014
STV News

The Better Together parties say they have delivered on their referendum vow. Today Lord Smith revealed a deal has been struck which will allow the biggest transfer of powers since the establishment of Holyrood, though the Scottish Parliament budget will stay the same size regardless. The SNP and Greens say the vast majority of tax and welfare powers will remain reserved, branding it not so much home rule, as continued Westminster rule.

DIARY: The headlines are income tax is to be devolved with some welfare. Of course, nothing is clear cut, so it's not really all income tax and it isn't anything like all welfare. It's all way too complex for most people to bother with. The nationalists say it doesn't deliver what was promised, the unionists say it does.

Monday 1 December 2014

DIARY: Gordon Brown – former Chancellor and Prime Minister – announced he's standing down as an MP at May's election. I wanted him to be the political giant people thought he could be *(because of his Scottish background)*. His sense of entitlement damaged what could have been a transformational Blair/Brown leadership and he's had as many failures, if not more, than successes. History might be kinder to him, but I doubt it.

Friday 5 December 2014
STV News

Scotland has a new, lower drink-drive limit. As of today, the maximum is 50 milligrams of alcohol in every 100 millilitres of blood. Police and the Scottish Government say the only way to ensure you are safe to drive is not to drink at all. Campaigners believe the lower limit will reduce the number of deaths and casualties on Scotland's roads.

Monday 15 December 2014
STV News

The new Scottish Labour Leader has announced plans to rewrite the party's constitution to say that it will run its own affairs in Scotland. Jim Murphy says he will ask members to agree to a new 'clause four' at the party's conference in March. In his first major speech after being elected on Saturday, he said the move would represent the 're-founding and the rebirth' of the party.

Scotland Tonight

JM: Jim Murphy, thanks for joining us. Congratulations. What do you stand for?

JIM MURPHY, Scottish Labour Leader: I stand for making Scotland the fairest nation on Earth. It's not good enough that there are too many people trapped by poverty, who find it so hard to escape the circumstances of their parents and grandparents, who were born into council estates or council schemes and don't have the chance to get the best school education, to get the chance to go to the greatest universities. I'm not going to use a lot of facts and figures, but there are only 220 pupils in our country to get good enough school results to get a chance to go to our greatest universities. 220 in our entire country each year. That is something I am determined to change. I am really comfortable about people being successful and I think it's something people should celebrate... But saying that we have these problems is not talking the country down, it's the sense of creating Scotland, not just as the fairest nation in the UK, but with hard work and determination, the fairest nation in the world. It can be done.

Tuesday 16 December 2014
STV News

Scotland's first same sex marriages have taken place as the country's new Equality Laws come into effect. First to tie the knot were a couple at the British Consulate in Australia, who took advantage of the change and time difference to convert their civil partnership on the stroke of midnight. In Dundee Mrs and Mrs Banks made their vows and made history.

KAREN GREENSHIELDS, Reporter: The new laws come into force on the same day it was revealed that there's a greater acceptance of gay marriage as never before, with 68 per cent of people saying they approve, compared to 41 per cent in 2002.

MARIE BANKS: It's pretty special. It's more than just a conversion, it's a culmination, it's a completion. It's the end of a journey, really, and the start of a new one.

GEORGE SQUARE TRAGEDY

Monday 22 December 2014
STV News – live from George Square in Glasgow

Six people are dead tonight in a tragedy in the heart of Glasgow, amid the Christmas lights and shoppers. A council bin lorry left a trail of devastation after appearing to go out of control and ploughing into people on the street. Several others have been injured.

Karen Greenshields, STV Reporter

I was off duty when I happened upon the scene, but within ten minutes I was reporting 'live.' As my shaken husband stood by my side, holding our carrier bags of Christmas shopping, I described to our news anchor in a hastily arranged live phone interview exactly what I was seeing around me.

Over the years I have become used to covering breaking news stories, but on that day as I stood in the middle of a city centre street in chaos, I was utterly unprepared. I had neither notepad, nor pen and my mobile phone was almost out of charge. (I was en route to the repair shop to have its smashed screen repaired.) Nevertheless, I reckoned that I had to be one of the first reporters on the scene and I wanted our viewers to know exactly what was happening.

I encountered two problems almost immediately. Firstly, I couldn't understand why my fingers were trembling so much (I later put this down to shock). It took at least six attempts to dial the newsroom number from my keypad. Secondly, I felt suddenly ashamed that whilst hundreds of onlookers stood in shocked silence, I had slipped very quickly into 'reporter mode'. As I approached bystanders to ask what they had seen, I felt unusually self-conscious without a camera crew by my side.

I solved the practical problems by borrowing a pen from a passing print reporter. She also gave me an old receipt and I quickly made notes for the imminent interview with studio. Again, I found it difficult to write with a steady hand as I noted the positions of the three bodies I could see just yards from me.

With 45 seconds to go before the live phone interview, it dawned on me – no camera no pictures – I quickly imagined myself as a radio reporter, but as I spoke I realised just how much TV reporters rely on the camera to convey the finer details. I struggled to find the best adjectives. As I talked, I walked in a 360-degree circle as I would have done with a camera to capture the totality of the scene. Old habits die hard.

In interviews for the two later bulletins, I felt more composed than usual. In live situations, a watching crowd can sometimes be daunting and that night our location was thronging with TV crews and onlookers. However, it was almost a relief, therapeutic even, to give my eyewitness account. I was using first person, not third. I instinctively changed my tone. I was recounting an awful event which had affected me and my husband. It didn't feel right to employ my normal detached, dispassionate tone.

Whilst I wish that I had never had to tell the story, I hope that personally and professionally, I struck the right balance.

At about 1.30pm I had finished updating a voiceover for STV's Hogmanay review of the year with details of late developments at Rangers. The producer Brendan O'Hara made comment that he hoped nothing else would happen and the programme would now be complete. I made reference to not being so sure, there was often a tragic news story just before Christmas. It was a throwaway comment. Within an hour, two colleagues phoned the STV newsdesk saying something serious had happened in George Square. At first there was talk of at least one dead and then more. Clearly, this was a major breaking story and we mobilised our news team. We then heard that six people were dead, but there was no official confirmation of this despite at least one media outlet tweeting it. The rumours piled on top of each other – the victims included a family of four with two young children, a baby had been killed in its pram, one of the victims was pregnant. By the time we went on air at six the facts had been established. Six dead. It seemed unbearably cruel on the city of Glasgow. Just like a year ago, people looking forward to Christmas dying in a completely random accident.

very sad. And yet in streets nearby people were laughing and joking. What else are they going to do?

Tuesday 23 December 2014
STV News – live from Royal Exchange Square

(*final lines*) This is where yesterday's tragic events began to unfold. The scene now here in the heart of the city is one of serenity. The light canopy provides a soft shroud for the flowers. For the candles. And for the people paying silent tribute.

DIARY: There was a strange serenity to the floral tributes at Royal Exchange Square from where we did the programme this evening. Stark contrast to yesterday afternoon when the horror began. The names of the dead were released today – regular folk going about their business. And there is a particular tragedy at Christmas when families are looking to come together. So

2015

Friday 9 January 2015
STV News

It was expected, but when it came it was with a vengeance. The hurricane-force storm which slammed into Scotland last night packed 100-mile-an-hour winds, brought down power lines and caused travel chaos, with disruption to road, rail and ferry services. Tens of thousands of people are still without electricity this evening and even as the clean-up gets underway a second storm is bearing down on the country.

Friday 22 January 2015
STV News

The battle for hearts and minds on television took another twist today as broadcasters offered to host a General Election debate programme which would include the leaders of all main parties running for Westminster. It means Nicola Sturgeon would go head-to-head with David Cameron, Ed Miliband and Nick Clegg. The leaders of the Greens, Plaid Cymru and UKIP would also be included in the seven-way line up.

Tuesday 27 January 2015
STV News

With 100 days to the UK General Election, David Cameron and Ed Miliband need to battle it out for every single vote. Polls suggest neither Labour nor the Conservatives will win a majority of seats. The SNP hope to hold the balance of power, but they've ruled out any deal with the Tories and Labour aren't keen on a coalition with them.

DIARY: Everyone saying it's too close to call. From a Scottish perspective what is so fascinating is that the SNP should be the third largest party in terms of seats. They could hold the balance of power. However, they've ruled out a coalition with the Tories and today Labour ruled out a coalition with them. The SNP's red line on Trident is not acceptable to them. One of our analysts tonight said it wouldn't be in the SNP's best interests either. As the Lib Dems found out, sharing power at Westminster contaminates you. So, we might have a coalition of others, or a minority government. Again, our analyst – the excellent Steve Richards – said the example of the Labour Government in 1974 was that six months was about as long as you could last. It's going to get very intense. Of course, the polls take one figure and spread it across the country, individuals and local issues in each constituency might disprove them. Nobody seems to expect the SNP will get the 50 seats some polls suggest – 25 seems to be the expectation of most. Still a huge leap forward for them.

SPANDAU BALLET

Monday 2 February 2015
Scotland Tonight

At their height, Spandau Ballet were one of the super groups of the 1980s, selling more than 25 million records. They're now returning to the stage for their first tour in five years.

MARTIN KEMP, Spandau Ballet: To understand the clothes from the '80s, you have to be there because it was, everything was larger than life, from the shoulder pads to the hairspray to the money people were earning. So, it was an incredible decade and it produced some great bands and it produced some great songs.

JM: You had your first hit in 1980 and you first disbanded in 1989, so you spanned the Thatcher era. And a lot of people have spoken about how it was spawned by Thatcherism. Is that something you'd recognise, Tony?

TONY HADLEY, Spandau Ballet: Our outlook on life was spawned by our parents, because we were, in a sense, the post-war generation. That our parents felt that you can do anything you wanted in life. You could aspire to this, that and everything else and the class system was slowly being watered down. So, as ordinary working-class kids you can go to grammar schools. I've got cousins who are scientists and stuff like that, so I think it was instilled, that sense of opportunity, was instilled in us by our parents. And also coming out of the punk era, where it was all kind of destroy, darkness, and everything else, never meant to last. Out of that came this kind of amazing sort of movement, this New Romantic.

JM: London is often seen in the UK as being the centre of fashion. And you took that style and took it beyond London. You came to Scotland. Did you find that the audiences here were matching you for what was coming out of London? Were they slightly behind the curve?

MK: Well, they were pretty much matching what was going on in London in terms of fashion. In terms of enthusiasm they were crazier than the London crowd, because the London crowd were being sort of very cool and stuff. But they were into it and in Scotland, I find the audiences up here, they've paid for their night out and they're going to have a good night. But there were pockets of New Romantics coming up everywhere.

DIARY: It was more reflective of the times and the influences, rather than the usual pop stuff. They were both bright guys and very informed on politics in Scotland, which we chatted about afterwards at their instigation. Their presence in the building caused much excitement.

Wednesday 4 February 2015
STV News

It's the most detailed General Election survey ever undertaken in Scotland. Sixteen thousand people were asked their views and it's a grim outlook for the Labour Leader Jim Murphy. The prediction – rock solid Scottish strongholds stormed, wipeout at Westminster, a landslide victory for the SNP. Potential high-profile casualties include the Labour campaign supremo Douglas Alexander and the Shadow Scottish Secretary Margaret Curran. Lord Ashcroft's study looked at more than a quarter of the Scottish constituencies, many of those in Glasgow, and found the SNP to be ahead in 15 of the 16 seats.

DIARY: The recent polls have all pointed towards an SNP dominance of the coming election, but that has been attributing one figure across the country. The Conservative peer Lord Ashcroft has done 16 individual constituencies and they have said the same thing. Labour is facing meltdown and such is the detail of the polling that you can point to individual MPs who look like they're out. In Glasgow they may have only one MP. That is remarkable.

ALAN RICKMAN

Monday 23 February 2015
Scotland Tonight

Some of his movies, including *Die Hard* and *Harry Potter*, have been watched by millions, but Alan Rickman rarely sits down for interviews, preferring to let a host of characters do the talking for him. Now, he's playing Louis XIV in a project that sees him act and direct. The film had its Scottish premiere at the Glasgow Film Festival on Saturday.

JM: It is a very varied career you've had, but in particular a lot of our audience will know you as Snape from *Harry Potter*. Is it, maybe resent is a strong word, but do you regret sometimes a role like that, however good it is, overshadows the other work that you have done?

ALAN RICKMAN: I am not so sure that is even true. People have pieces of work in mind, other people's that they like. It is not the only thing I hear about. Most of the time I spent my life just wandering around being me, not being some amalgam of characters I've played at all.

JM: It has been said, I don't know whether this is accurate or not, Snape was, some of the appearance of Snape, was inspired by Sharleen Spiteri from the Scottish group Texas... You have been in a video with Texas just recently and you had done one previously. How did that come about?

AR: Yes, Snape has nothing to do with Sharleen.

JM: Glad we cleared that up.

AR: She would be appalled. She spends far more on her haircut. Eh... how it came about? I did two. One was 'In Demand'. She just rang up and said will you dance a tango with me in a petrol station? Oh, alright. And then it has been the 25th anniversary of Texas, so she gets what she wants. She ran up and said, 'Will you come and do this duet?' Fortunately, I wouldn't dare sing with her. Speaking.

DIARY *(interview on Saturday 21 February 2015)*: Not the warmest of individuals. 'I believe it's your birthday.' 'Oh yes, it is.' 'Happy Birthday.' 'And we will leave it there.' He wasn't uncooperative, but there was a stupid no photograph imposition by his PR. It's a feckin TV interview, so what nonsense is that? He was doing the interview as a duty. These 'celebrity' interviews are often like that.

Tuesday 24 February 2015
STV News

The oil and gas industry has reported its worst annual performance for 40 years. The industry is warning of heavy job losses and a steep drop in investment in the North Sea unless there are urgent tax breaks to combat the low oil price and rising costs.

Thursday 5 March 2015
STV News

The latest crop of constituency polls from Tory peer Lord Ashcroft have sent fresh waves through Scottish politics today. They suggest Labour will lose Gordon Brown's seat to the SNP as well as that currently held by Alistair Darling. The former Lib Dem Leader Charles Kennedy would also be ousted by the SNP who are neck and neck with David Mundell in the only Tory-held seat in Scotland.

Friday 6 March 2015
STV News

Dave King has taken control at Rangers after a landslide victory at the club's general meeting. John Gilligan and Douglas Park have been appointed to salvage the Ibrox side after the ousting of the current board. Paul Murray will act as chairman while King seeks approval to be appointed as a director.

GRANT RUSSELL, Sports News Correspondent: It was building up to this day. Rangers fans are hopeful of a new dawn for their club after all the uncertainty in recent years. Gone are the old regime who the fans desperately wanted out. In come a group of businessmen who the fans hope can turn their club around and put it back on a sound footing – both on and off the pitch.

DIARY: The Rangers board has been cleared out at an EGM today and Dave King and his team are in. I don't know how good they will be, but there seems little doubt they have the club's best interests at heart, unlike the self-serving chancers who have trotted through in recent times. Perhaps this is the beginning there should have been three years ago.

Thursday 19 March 2015
STV News

The Scottish Government is to revise its own figures for oil and gas production. It comes after the UK Office for Budget Responsibility downgraded its projections for oil receipts, wiping billions of pounds off expected revenues in the next five years. Labour said this meant the SNP's plans for full fiscal autonomy would mean 'devastating' cuts.

Monday 23 March 2015
STV News

Ed Miliband has dismissed claims the SNP could hold power over a minority Labour Government. In a speech in Glasgow today, the Labour Leader said Alex Salmond's claims were nothing more than 'bluff and bluster' and he again ruled out a coalition with the SNP. Though he repeatedly failed to rule out a looser arrangement with the nationalists.

Friday 27 March 2015
STV News

New research on why voters cast their vote the way they did in the Independence Referendum suggests The Vow on more powers by the unionist parties made little difference to the final result. Alex Salmond has suggested the move was pivotal, but a survey of 4,000 voters by the Centre for Constitutional Change suggests people voted No because many believed the country would have been worse off.

Monday 30 March 2015
Scotland Tonight

The political parties have been out on the streets on the first official day of the General Election campaign. Between now and 7 May they'll be battling to win your vote in what the polls are predicting will be one of the tightest races in decades.

Tuesday 7 April 2015
STV News

The leaders of Scotland's four main political parties are to go head-to-head on STV tonight. It's the first time they will have clashed on TV during the General Election. They'll face a grilling from a 200-strong audience in Edinburgh.

DIARY: There were no great revelations. Jim Murphy of Scottish Labour needed a big win – or to land a significant blow at least – and that didn't happen. Nicola Sturgeon had most to lose after her success in last week's UK leaders' debate, but wasn't really pushed on the detail of some SNP policy. Ruth Davidson of the Scottish Conservatives will have come across well – feistier than she's normally seen to be – and with a clearly different argument from the others. The Lib Dems Willie Rennie is clearly a decent man, but was rather sidelined. No major winners or losers.

Thursday 16 April 2015
STV News

Heartfelt tributes have been paid to Irish student Karen Buckley, after her body was found on a farm just outside Glasgow. Officers spoke of the family's pain and grief as people in her home community around Cork say they remembered her as a beautiful, hard-working girl who wouldn't hurt a fly. A 21-year-old man is due to appear in court tomorrow in connection with her death.

Karen had been missing for three days after a night out in Glasgow's west end. At the High Court in Glasgow Alexander Pacteau admitted murdering Karen in his car. He hid her body in his Glasgow flat and then bought caustic soda. Karen's body was later found in a barrel with the chemicals at a farm near Milngavie. He was sentenced to a minimum of 23 years in prison.

Monday 20 April 2015
STV News

The SNP have launched their manifesto with a pledge to make Scotland stronger at Westminster. But in a pitch to voters down south too, Nicola Sturgeon said she'd use any influence the party have after 7 May to bring about positive change for people across the UK. The manifesto commits the party to full fiscal responsibility, but does not lay out the cost of the policy to Scotland.

DIARY: Short notice of a down-the-line interview with the First Minister on the SNP manifesto, which was launched today. They're saying slow the cuts and spend our way out of the deficit and debt. It seems counter-intuitive, but they say it'll work. The opposition say it doesn't add up. The interview was on the manifesto – the only party not talking about cuts, no mention of independence and full fiscal autonomy now called full financial responsibility and not so imminent. Seems to have been an effective manifesto launch with London-based journalists impressed by her 45-minute Q&A session afterwards. They say they don't get that from other leaders. As we sound checked I asked her the best question she'd been asked all day, which rather stumped her. By default that's got to be the winner!

Tuesday 21 April 2015
STV News

The Scottish Government has announced it is dropping controversial plans to abolish the need for corroboration. The centuries-old rule means evidence in criminal trials has to come from two sources. The proposal had been met with fierce opposition from the legal profession who claimed it could lead to miscarriages of justice.

THE PROCLAIMERS

Monday 27 April 2015
Scotland Tonight

In more than 30 years of performing The Proclaimers have written some of Scotland's best loved songs, as well as having their music adapted for the stage and film. Today, they released their tenth album, 'Let's Hear It For The Dogs', and will head back out on tour next month.

JM: Take me through the writing process, how does that work for you both?

CHARLIE REID: There's a couple of songs here on this record that I got from people saying phrases to me. And I just went straight away. There's a song called 'What School?' And somebody said to me, somebody from the west of Scotland, and they said to me – about living in England – they said, cos it's not that whole thing about what school did you go to? Or what religion are you? And I went, oh, thanks very much and I'll use that. And I kind of just – that was built from the phrase, then I worked around it and I got the tune at the same time. There's a couple others that were quite like that. Generally, nine out of ten, with me, I get a tune and I'll get basically the whole tune and I won't know what the song is about until I get the first couple of lines. So, the first couple of lines, they're the kind of trigger for me.

JM: And where does the tune come from?

CHARLIE REID: I don't know where they come from. You sit at the piano and... When I'm writing – I try and write every single day – even for just a couple of hours. Push yourself a bit, but not too much. Most times I don't get anything. Sometimes I'll get something that works and then build it from there. You know, just playing about. And that's it.

CRAIG REID: Usually, it's tune first. Usually, with the both of us it's the tune first. A chord sequence or melody and then a lyrical idea. And it's the same with me. If you get a good first line you know you'll finish the song. And then it does, in a way, kind of suggest a subject. Rather than going, I'm gonna write a song about the referendum. Just let it come.

DIARY: Great guys who produce some fine music. I've always liked them. Very down to earth and dismayed by Hibs' defeat in the Scottish Cup semi-final and whether they or Rangers will make the play-offs. Wide-ranging chat from their music to politics to football.

Tuesday 28 April 2015
Scotland Tonight

All the opinion polls point to an SNP tide sweeping across Scotland at next Thursday's General Election. It's an extraordinary time for the party and its leader Nicola Sturgeon. Tonight, she's with us live for the latest in our series of election interviews conducted by STV's political editor Bernard Ponsonby.

DIARY: Bernard pushed her on a couple of areas of vulnerability – one of which is emerging more obviously – the possibility of the SNP being a 'Feeble 50', ie a large tranche of MPs, but no real influence. That's a given if the Conservatives win. But if Ed Miliband wins, the SNP will back him by default. They will have to. So, what happens if he proposes something of which the

SNP don't approve? Nicola Sturgeon says that her experience of minority government in Scotland is that sometimes, when you couldn't get your policy through you had to go back and change it. But what if Miliband challenges the SNP to vote against him? She contends that a vote against wouldn't necessarily bring a government down, but it could lead to instability.

Wednesday 29 April 2015
STV News

With just eight days until the country votes, the SNP surge appears to be reaching tsunami proportions. Our exclusive poll shows a seemingly unstoppable tidal wave that could engulf Scottish Labour. The once mighty People's Party faces total wipeout. A landslide victory is forecast, with Nicola Sturgeon's SNP capturing every single seat in the country and returning 59 MPs to Westminster.

DIARY: It's a good headline, but I don't think anyone really believes it. Most will predict the SNP getting 40 plus seats, which is still an almighty achievement. Jim Murphy was interrogated by Bernard on *Scotland Tonight* and is too experienced for it to be the slaughter some expected. However, he didn't put across any message that is going to transform the result over the next week.

Monday 4 May 2015
STV News

A man has died and a police officer has been injured in Kirkcaldy. Thirty-one-year-old Sheku Bayoh died and a female officer was hurt during the incident in Hayfield Road yesterday. The case has been referred to the Police Investigations and Review Commissioner.

Wednesday 6 May 2015
DIARY: The last day of campaigning before the polls open. No one is expecting a majority government, so will it be the same coalition as the last time, a minority government or Labour with the SNP backing? My gut is that the Conservatives will perform better than predicted. I think a lot of English voters about to cast their vote will be fearful of a Labour-SNP alliance, however informal.

GENERAL ELECTION 2015
Friday 8 May 2015
STV News – live from Westminster

A disunited kingdom.

Scotland rewrites political history as the Conservatives return to Downing Street with a majority.

Under the might of the Sturgeon Surge, the people return an army of 56 MPs to Westminster.

It was a disaster for Labour. A wounded Ed Miliband quits as leader.

So, the question tonight – where does this leave Scotland in the Union?

Good evening and welcome to Westminster. An incredible result. There has been nothing like it before. Ever. The least predictable General Election in living memory has returned a majority Conservative Government under Prime Minister David Cameron. Alongside an historic, seismic shift in Scottish politics under the leadership of Nicola Sturgeon.

The Conservatives defied the polls and won 331 seats. It was bruising night for the Labour Party, they returned 232 MPs. The SNP won a landslide in Scotland with Nicola Sturgeon's party seizing 56 out of the 59 seats. The Liberal Democrats have been left with just eight MPs. The Greens hold on to one. UKIP also has one MP, leaving 21 MPs from other parties.

DAVID CAMERON, Prime Minister in Downing Street: In this Parliament I will stay true to my word and implement as fast as I can the Devolution that all parties agreed for Wales, Scotland and Northern Ireland. Governing with respect means recognising that the different nations of our United Kingdom have their own governments as well as the United Kingdom government... In Scotland our plans are to create the strongest devolved government anywhere in the world.

ED MILIBAND, Labour Leader: Britain needs a Labour Party that can rebuild after this defeat so we can have a government that stands up for working people again. And now it's time for someone else to take forward the leadership of this party. So, I'm tendering my resignation.

NICK CLEGG, Lib Dem Leader: Clearly the results have been immeasurably more crushing and unkind than I could ever have feared. For that, of course, I must take responsibility and therefore I announce that I will be resigning as leader of the Liberal Democrats.

JM: Bernard, this result was a tale of two elections, really, and a tale of two results that have collided spectacularly. What does it mean for the Scottish dimension at Westminster?

BERNARD PONSONBY, Political Editor: In a sense, John, it's also a clash of two mandates. David Cameron has a mandate to pursue deficit reduction, including £13 billion worth of unspecified welfare cuts and he also has a mandate to deliver more powers for Holyrood through the Smith Commission proposals. But Nicola Sturgeon has a mandate to say no to austerity and she has a mandate to pursue further powers for Holyrood. Now, this inevitably is going to lead to a clash. In a sense there can only be one winner – 56 SNP MPs simply cannot trump a Conservative majority at Westminster. But here's where the politics comes in. Does David Cameron look at this and say I have to be slightly more flexible given that there is now a different Scottish dimension? Well, today he said, yes there will be more powers for Holyrood, but he said that was more or less it. And if that is more or less it, that will mean conflict. That conflict and how it plays out could determine the political terrain in Scotland in the coming months.

Vox Pops

I voted SNP rather than Conservative, which I'd normally vote, because I want a voice in Westminster. I don't want independence, I just want a voice in Westminster.

Labour's time in Scotland pretty much is over.

Scotland is a people and we wanted to make that heard at Westminster.

I've came all my life, a working-class family, and your heart and your feelings is Labour, that somehow you're maybe betraying what you believe in. But no, I think that I genuinely believe that the SNP is the way forward for the next generations.

It's a wee bit worrying. I think we're probably going to go to a referendum a bit sooner than most people want.

The people are disillusioned with Labour, with them joining the unionists, and they've swung to the SNP for it.

JIM MURPHY, Scottish Labour Leader: There is a responsibility in good times and in bad times as a leader. And our judgement, and our view and our determination is rebuild from here.

JM: The First Minister Nicola Sturgeon is with me now. Congratulations on a remarkable success in Scotland.

NICOLA STURGEON, First Minister: Thank you very much indeed. It was a result, I think, of historic proportions. The tectonic plates of Scottish politics shifted yesterday and the Scottish people put their trust in the SNP to stand up for Scotland at Westminster and make Scotland's voice heard and that's exactly what we intend to do.

JM: How are you going to be able to do that, though, given that 56 MPs at Westminster, but you're up against a Conservative majority?

NS: The fact that we're up against a Conservative majority is something I didn't want and unfortunately that's because Labour weren't strong enough to beat the Conservatives in England. But the fact that is the scenario we face makes it all the more important there is that big team of SNP MPs to stand up for Scotland and to protect Scotland's interests and make our voice heard. The second point I'd make is this, the Government cannot ignore what happened in Scotland yesterday and it can't be business as usual. There has to be a recognition that people in Scotland in significant numbers voted for an end to austerity, voted for stronger investment in our public services and voted for a more empowered Scottish Parliament. So, these issues that we put at the heart of the election campaign, our MPs will now seek to put at the heart of the House of Commons.

JM: But, nonetheless, it is a majority Conservative Government, which nobody expected, on an austerity agenda. They can ignore you, it could be the Feeble 56.

NS: But they can't ignore Scotland and if they do it would be completely unacceptable. Scotland didn't just vote in small numbers for a different party yesterday. Some of the swings we saw across Scotland yesterday were unprecedented in Westminster political history. Scotland decisively voted against austerity and for an alternative approach. I briefly spoke to the Prime Minister this afternoon and made it clear that it cannot be business as usual, the democratic will of the Scottish people as expressed in that election yesterday has to be recognised. So, our MPs and me as First Minister will be working hard to make sure that those issues that were so dominant during the election campaign are just as dominant down here in Westminster.

JM: You said throughout the campaign this was not about the referendum, but you now have a position that you have a Conservative majority, a very large tranche of SNP MPs. Does it make a second Independence Referendum more likely?

NS: No, I don't think it does one way or the other. I said during the election that this election wasn't about independence and it wasn't a vote for a second referendum. I said very explicitly, very directly to voters across Scotland if you vote for the SNP I will not take your vote as an endorsement of independence. I'm not going to turn my back on that, I'm going to stick to my word. If there's ever another referendum in Scotland on independence, that will only come about if people vote for that in a Scottish Parliament election. Yesterday's election was a vote to make Scotland's voice heard and the 56 SNP MPs that will be shortly coming to this place behind us here are here to make Scotland's voice heard and that's exactly what they intend to do.

JM: The General Election of 2015 might be considered as two elections. In Scotland the predicted SNP landslide. Across the UK the unexpected Conservative majority. Tonight, the SNP have a powerful grip on Scotland. Here at Westminster David Cameron and the Conservatives hold power in the UK. The next big question – what happens now?

DIARY: The Conservatives have won a majority with 331 seats, which almost no one saw coming. The SNP won 56 – all but three of the seats in Scotland. That had been predicted, but the SNP leadership, like the rest of us, were unconvinced it'd be on that scale and played it down. Labour have been destroyed in Scotland – only one MP – and they have only themselves to blame. I don't think this is a protest vote, I think the SNP have replaced Labour as the party of the Left. The Lib Dems have been reduced to a rump – punishment for being part of the coalition and not getting anything of their key principles passed in return. Labour failed in England, too, quite aside from their Scottish collapse. I don't think people ever saw Ed Miliband as being Prime Minister right from the moment he was chosen leader.

It made for straightforward programmes with a clear narrative. I interviewed Nicola Sturgeon on the *Six O'Clock News*. The important point was on whether it brings a second referendum closer. She said this election was not about independence, and she wouldn't make it so. She'd been up all night and was saying she wasn't sure she could remember her own name. Also, a chat with John Swinney on Abingdon Green. He said that on the day after the referendum he'd wondered what would become of his party. He has no such doubts now.

Monday 11 May 2015
STV News – live from Westminster

Good evening from Westminster. After a landslide victory in Scotland, 56 SNP MPs are here promising Scotland's voice will be heard like never before. As the majority Conservatives had their photocall with the Prime Minister next to Big Ben, the SNP stood together with the First Minister at Westminster – a large saltire flying nearby. The party says being the third largest in the Commons will open up unparalleled opportunities to make their case and be a principled opposition.

DIARY: There was the usual media crush as Nicola Sturgeon stood in front of them all. This is an image that will be shown again and again in years to come. It was a remarkable sight. Earlier, David Cameron had posed with the new Tory MPs, Big Ben in the background. That was very grand compared to the rather squeezed area for the SNP photocall at St Stephen's Entrance. I wonder if it'll be a metaphor for this Parliament.

During the photocall there was a vivid demonstration of the tensions between established and new media. The BBC cameraman transmitting live pictures of the event had his picture spoiled by another guy holding up his iPhone. When the cameraman asked him to drop his phone lower the response was, 'Periscoping mate. I'm periscoping.' He was broadcasting pictures using an app from his phone.

'How many followers you got?' queried the increasingly irate cameraman.

'Couple of hundred,' the periscoper claimed.

'Well, these pictures will be seen by millions and you're ruining them.'

The periscoper carried on regardless.

Friday 15 May 2015
STV News

David Cameron has said he will consider any proposals for further devolved powers for Scotland following talks with the First Minister. The two met today for the first time following last week's General Election. Nicola Sturgeon told STV News she will now put forward priority powers to be handed to Holyrood as soon as possible, along with arguing for full fiscal autonomy.

RONNIE BROWNE OF THE CORRIES
Tuesday 19 May 2015
Scotland Tonight

RONNIE BROWNE: What we used to do at the end of a tour is say, right I'll see you before the next tour. We'd get together two or three weeks before. What have you got, what have I got? You'd never do a concert tour with 24 new songs. You use some of the old ones you've done, some of the ones that are standard which you know are going to do well, and introduce, maybe, three or four in each half. And these three or four in each half we had learned individually. We came together and sat down and said, right, you do this and I'll do that. And it was as simple as that, John, honestly, because we had nothing written down, we had no complicated arrangements, we didn't read or write music. And we just sat there and I would listen to what Roy was doing and bring in a harmony – I was a natural harmony singer. I learned to do basic guitar, basic chords, and I got to a standard that suited Roy, that if he would accept it, then I was good enough. Rub my brass neck and go on stage. And it allowed him to expand on what he was doing, because he was the musician. So, that's how we got the songs, just, right d'you like this and d'you like that? Sometimes, you'd say *(pulls face showing dislike)* and then when the two of us got together and tried to sing it, it didnae gel, so forget it.

DIARY: I'd been looking forward to it. I saw them in concert a few times. My knowledge of Scottish folk music and through that Scottish history came mainly from The Corries. He is a larger-than-life character. Astonishing that he'd never sung in public before and only started playing the guitar later in his career.

Tuesday 2 June 2015
STV News

Politicians from all parties have united in paying tribute to the former Liberal Democrat leader Charles Kennedy, who died suddenly in his home in the Highlands yesterday. Just 23 when he was first elected, he was an MP for 32 years. To his friends he embodied decency. Among his opponents he commanded respect. And to his constituents, he was Charlie – one of them.

DIARY: He was respected across politics because, as many have said, he would disagree respectfully and without rancour. That's rare. I was always struck by how reasonable and human he was. It says much that so many people, like me, who didn't really know him were deeply saddened by the news.

Wednesday 10 June 2015
STV News

Scotland is facing a housing crisis unless a substantial number of new homes are built. That's the warning from an expert commission which says 150,000 families are on social housing waiting lists. The Scottish Government says it has invested heavily, but there are concerns that there isn't anywhere near enough to tackle the problem.

DIARY: Given that I'd made the observation about it being a running problem for decades, I suggested digging out previous reports with the same message. It worked rather well.

Thursday 11 June 2015
STV News

The SNP is demanding that the UK Government gives full tax-and-spend powers to the Scottish Parliament. The party is tabling an amendment to a bill going through Westminster which seeks to give Holyrood the right to full fiscal autonomy. The UK will oppose the move, but some Conservative backbenchers are backing an amendment of their own saying Scotland should have all the powers it wants and as quickly as possible.

Monday 15 June 2015
STV News

The outgoing Scottish Labour Leader, Jim Murphy, says there will be a second Independence Referendum and the Conservatives will give the SNP the excuse they need to bring it about. In a farewell speech given to the London-based think tank, The Policy Exchange, he said David Cameron was putting party above country by appealing to English nationalists in his drive to make sure English MPs can vote on English laws. He also urged the Labour Party not to forget the lessons of Tony Blair's three election victories.

Thursday 9 July 2015
STV News

An independent investigation has been launched into why police failed to act on a report of a serious road accident which left a man dead and a woman badly injured. It happened near Stirling on Sunday, but it took until yesterday morning for the wreckage to be discovered – with the couple still in it.

The car in which 25-year-old Lamara Bell and 28-year-old John Yuill went off the M9 near Stirling on 5 July 2015. A local farmer reported seeing a car off the road to police, but the call was never logged. They lay in the car for three days. When police finally arrived after being alerted by a second witness, John was pronounced dead at the scene. Lamara died four days later in hospital. An inquiry concluded in 2024 that Lamara might have survived if she had been discovered sooner. It blamed an 'organisational failure' in police call handling procedures.

Tuesday 14 July 2015
Scotland Tonight

The UK Government has pushed back a vote on fox hunting in England and Wales after the SNP announced they would vote against the reforms. The nationalists said their decision to vote on the measure was in protest at the handling of the English votes for English laws. The Prime Minister has described the SNP's position as entirely opportunistic.

DIARY: Significant because the SNP has used that as an example of when they wouldn't interfere with English votes. Nicola Sturgeon could not have been clearer. Then they changed their minds to send a message to the PM over the English votes for English laws debate and lack of movement for new powers in Scotland. Certainly, they have won a victory without even having to vote, but I think it is short-sighted. There could not be a clearer example of the SNP going back on their word. Their supporters will be happy and political buffs will admire the politics. However, it will give many people more reason to distrust party politics.

Friday 7 August 2015
STV News

Scotland's top law officer is considering a report into the death of a man in police custody in Fife. The Lord Advocate has received an interim report into the death of Sheku Bayoh from the Police Investigations and Review Commissioner.

Monday 17 August 2015
STV News

She has one of the toughest jobs in Scottish politics. Following her landslide victory as Scottish Labour Leader, Kezia Dugdale is now set on tackling a series of problems confronting her demoralised party.

DIARY: She comes across well and people respond to her warmth, but some criticise her for not saying anything of substance in her answers. That may be a lack of assurance from inexperience. If she can bring more of herself through, she may do well. It's a thankless task, but they have to start rebuilding somewhere. It might not be made any easier depending on the outcome of the UK leadership contest.

CATHOLIC CHURCH APOLOGY
Tuesday 18 August 2015
STV News

'We say sorry. We ask forgiveness.' Those were the words of Scotland's most senior Catholic today as he apologised to survivors of abuse within the church. The statement was made after a two-year inquiry into the church's handling of abuse allegations. It has recommended a series of changes, but victims say the church's reputation is in tatters.

Thursday 20 August 2015
STV News

The driver of the bin lorry which killed six people in Glasgow last December said he had passed out 'like a light switch', without any warning. Harry Clarke described his memory of the incident, but declined to answer hundreds of questions over his medical history, having been told by the sheriff he could choose not to. Relatives of the victims left the court in tears during a highly charged day at Glasgow Sheriff Court.

DIARY: The driver of the bin lorry tragedy, Harry Clarke, appeared at the FAI. At first he refused to answer questions, but spoke more later. Danger of a witch-hunt against him, but the fact is six people died because he was driving a truck that he shouldn't have been because of a medical history about which he lied.

Thursday 20 August 2015 *(cont)*
STV News

Scotland's population has reached a record high, and we're living for longer. New figures from the National Records of Scotland show life expectancy has improved, but it remains lower than the UK as a whole. The number of births has also increased, and more people are coming to Scotland than are leaving.

The estimated population was 5,347,600.

Monday 24 August 2015
Scotland Tonight

The leadership of Scottish Labour is seen by some as the poisoned chalice of British politics. But Kezia Dugdale has boldly taken up the challenge of reviving the once-dominant force left devastated by the all-conquering SNP.

KEZIA DUGDALE, Scottish Labour Leader: I'm going to focus on Labour values first and foremost, tell people why I'm Labour, what I believe in, what that means in 2015 and then explain to people how I'm going to go about making that real for them with the detailed policies they want to see. So, first and foremost, I'm going to talk about education, about closing the gap between the richest and poorest kids in society. Making sure that every Scot can realise their potential and use the power of government to do that.

DIARY: She has warmth, but during our interview there was straight question about whether she agreed with her new deputy, Alex Rowley, that there should be a referendum on Trident. A straight question which didn't bring a straight answer. That doesn't serve her well. She did talk about political co-operation and it'll be interesting to see if that is something she can develop. She has a long haul ahead, but she has time on her side because nobody is expecting much from Labour in next year's Scottish elections.

Tuesday 25 August 2015
Scotland Tonight

There were 613 drug-related deaths in Scotland last year, the highest figure ever recorded and an increase of 72 per cent over the past decade. The minister responsible for the country's drugs policy has admitted that some users have been failed by the system.

A recurrent issue throughout this book.

Tuesday 1 September 2015
STV News

The Scottish Government is launching a new system of national testing for primary school children. It is one of eight bills to go before MSPs ahead of next year's Scottish Parliament elections. The First Minister Nicola Sturgeon says closing the attainment gap is her single most important objective.

DIARY: I had to do an interview with the First Minister down-the-line from Edinburgh at 5:05pm. Rather amusing watching her telling our new Holyrood Editor Colin Mackay how to cable her up. I didn't really feel prepared enough and, although it was just a marking interview, she batted it all away too easily.

Sunday 6 September 2015
STV News

Passenger services have begun on the longest domestic railway to be built in Britain for 100 years. Following two days of special trains along the Borders Railway, the line is now open to the public.

JEREMY CORBYN IS NEW LABOUR LEADER
Saturday 12 September 2015
STV News

Jeremy Corbyn has won a landslide victory in the Labour leadership contest. The Islington North MP won on the first ballot, polling over a quarter of a million votes, that's almost 60 per cent of all votes cast. In his speech he pledged to deliver a new kind of politics and said he would work with the Scottish party to kick start Labour's fortunes.

DIARY: The general view is that it's a catastrophic error which will keep Labour out of power for a long time, much as the Foot years of the early '80s did. I can see that. However, maybe I'm missing something. Maybe there is a groundswell from the left that is the beginning of a sea change. I just don't think so.

Sunday 13 September 2015
STV News

The SNP manifesto for the 2016 Holyrood election will set out a timetable and circumstances in which the party would push for a second Independence Referendum. The First Minister Nicola Sturgeon outlined the pledge in the week which sees the anniversary of last year's poll. Opposition Leaders have accused her of putting party above national interest.

Monday 21 September 2015

DIARY: A mid-afternoon pre-record with Kezia Dugdale who indicated over the weekend that were there to be a second referendum Labour MPs would be free to campaign for vote Yes. She confirmed that and says her leadership is very much about democratising the party, listening to the membership. On one side you can see the appeal of that – not least the populism – but it can lead to accusations of a lack of leadership.

KEZIA DUGDALE, Scottish Labour Leader: I don't see another referendum for a very long time. We were told it was a once-in-a-lifetime, once-in-a-generation opportunity and we were also told that the First Minister would respect that outcome. So, I hope that we don't see another referendum for a long time indeed. So, what I'm setting out is that if you support Yes or No in the referendum last year, but you share Labour Party's values there is a place for you in the Labour Party. That applies to our MSPs just as much as it would to our Labour Party members, but it's very much an argument of the past now. The referendum was last year.

Tuesday 29 September 2015

DIARY: Today was all about the Alex Ferguson interview that didn't happen. We were to interview him at Glasgow Caley Uni at 9.20am. He was announcing a £500,000 donation to the university, but he also has a book out. When I arrived James Cheyne *(producer)* and Iain McCall *(cameraman)* had the room ready, but there was already a problem. Ferguson's assistant was rude to the guys, sticking his head into the room and without saying who he was announcing, 'Well, that's not going to be behind Sir Alex and that's not going to be behind Sir Alex.' *(referring to the* Scotland Tonight *screens)* There was clearly a problem. I told him – as I would normally – that we'd be discussing the book and donation. He said no, only the donation... I said we can't just do a ten-minute interview on a donation and if they were insistent on that the interview wouldn't happen. There was a stand-off – with Alex Ferguson in the room next to us *(he may have been dealing with other business)* for longer than the interview would have lasted, and embarrassed university PR people shuttling between us. Finally, I saw through the glass door in our room Alex Ferguson walking away.

Thursday 8 October 2015
STV News

A woman has been jailed for three years for threatening and attempting to extort money from a mother and daughter who later died in an apparent double suicide. The family deceived by Linsey Cotton described the 33-year-old as an evil individual. A sheriff told Cotton that she was responsible for an 'extraordinary, complex web of deceit and lies.'

SHARON FREW, STV reporter: The 33-year-old used 15 different mobile phones and four computers to convince her victims that she was more than a dozen fictitious people. The sheriff highlighted extracts from some of the threats that Cotton made to Nicola McDonough and her mother – both women said to be petrified after being told by Cotton that they were facing prison for breaching confidentiality agreements... Three days after receiving these threats, Margaret, a foster carer and Nicola, who studied social work, were found dying at a hotel in Greenock. It's believed they took their own lives. Linsey Cotton was not prosecuted for the women's deaths.

Thursday 8 October 2015 *(cont)*

DIARY: Yet again Scotland fail to qualify for a major tournament – that's getting on for 20 years. Our big issue used to be that we couldn't qualify for later stages. Now we can't even qualify for the tournaments even when, as in this case, it had been expanded... There is something fundamentally wrong at the root of Scottish football and there has been for the last 20 years and more.

Scotland drew 2–2 with Poland, Robert Lewandowski equalising with the last kick of the game. It ended our hopes of reaching Euro 2016.

Tuesday 20 October 2015
STV News

They knew it was coming but tonight the loss of 270 jobs at Tata's steelworks in Lanarkshire will be no less of a blow for staff and the local community. Unions say the announcement effectively marks the end of Scotland's steel industry.

DIARY: Confirmation of the closure of Tata Steel – the former Dalzell Steelworks in Motherwell. A bit of a throwback to the days of reporting on industrial decline. There's not much industry to decline now. It seems daft to me that we run down our manufacturing industry, partly because of European rules that insist on competition within Europe, but also the inability to set tariffs against extremely cheap – and subsidised – imports.

SCOTLAND BILL DISCUSSED AT WESTMINSTER

Monday 9 November 2015
STV News

Legislation which will transfer more powers to the Scottish Parliament will complete its passage through the House of Commons tonight. MPs will vote on the Scotland Bill, which was drawn up after The Vow made by the three unionist parties before the referendum and the subsequent review carried out by the Smith Commission. The UK Government says it will fulfil all the promises made to the people of Scotland. The SNP says it doesn't go far enough.

HARRY SMITH, Westminster Correspondent: It has been the subject of many, many hours of discussion and negotiation. It runs to many thousands of words. The amendments now being debated run to 76 pages. The Government says it is the Vow delivered. It will make Holyrood the most powerful devolved Parliament in the world. It will give Edinburgh the power to set tax rates and bands and control over large areas of welfare. Many of the changes have been pushed through by the Labour Party. Many more are being proposed by the SNP who say it does not transfer all the powers recommended by the Smith Commission. In the next few hours there will be votes on the whole list of amendments. And finally, a vote on the bill itself. Once that's completed, it will then pass to the House of Lords where it is not expected to encounter much opposition. It will then have to be voted through the Scottish Parliament before it receives the Royal Assent.

Thursday 12 November 2015
STV News

Threatening gusts of up to 90 miles per hour are set to batter parts of Scotland as Storm Abigail hits the country. All schools are closed in the Western Isles tomorrow and some ferry crossings have been cancelled. Other parts of the country are being warned to be prepared for disruption.

Storm Abigail was the first to be given an official name in an attempt to raise public awareness.

Wednesday 18 November 2015
STV News

David Cameron today brushed aside an SNP demand that any move to extend British military action into Syria must first get UN authorisation. Speaking during Prime Minister's Questions, he said that while a UN Security Council resolution was welcome, he believed it wasn't necessary and he would not 'outsource to Russian veto any decisions about British security'.

DIARY: Focus of the news was the PM trying to get Commons support for the bombing of ISIS in Syria. We already do in Iraq and the point is that it's therefore not illogical to pursue them in Syria as well. There's been some debate about this in work. I'm of the view that the invasion of Iraq in 2003 proved disastrous because there was no end plan. What do you replace Saddam with? Well, the same issue applies here, I think. Others think it's a simple matter of self-defence because we're at war. When the bombers come over, then we're at war.

Wednesday 2 December 2015
STV News

MPs are debating a motion seeking to extend UK airstrikes against ISIS targets in Syria. The Prime Minister made a passionate case for a change in Government policy, but he had to endure sustained criticism for branding opponents as 'terrorist sympathisers.'

DIARY: Incredible to hear so many MPs in the debate demand that the Prime Minister apologise for a silly remark last night suggesting those opposed to bombing were 'terrorist sympathisers'. It was clear from his first reply that wasn't going to happen… Instead of using the valuable time to ask about the detail of the PM's proposals, too many of them wasted the opportunity demanding apologies. Condemn it by all means in their speeches, but focus on the crucial points, not the side issues.

Thursday 3 December 2015
STV News

RAF Tornado jets have carried out their first air strikes against the self-styled Islamic state in Syria. Four Tornados from RAF Akrotiri in Cyprus took part in the operation soon after MPs voted last night. The Ministry of Defence described the strikes against oil production sites as successful. But the Prime Minister David Cameron said the campaign would take time.

RUNRIG
Thursday 3 December 2015 *(cont)*
Scotland Tonight

The band Runrig has been around now for 43 years and has legions of fans both here in Scotland and the world over. In January they're set to release their last studio album called 'The Story'. Much of 2016 will be spent touring the UK, culminating in gigs at Edinburgh Castle. Two of the original band members, Rory and Calum Macdonald remain with the band and lifelong fan John met them earlier.

RORY MACDONALD, Runrig: As we were writing the songs there was a sense that there was a winding up and putting to bed a lot of things and it felt like an album that is resolving a lot in our careers. At the end of it, we thought, 'No, it feels natural'. This is the last one and it felt good.

JM: What would you like to think that Runrig's legacy would be?

CALUM MACDONALD, Runrig: Gosh, a few good songs. That would do me.

RM: Touched people, I would hope.

JM: And Loch Lomond played at the end of many Scottish weddings.

CM: That old carry on.

JM: You must go to weddings yourself and on it comes.

RM: When that happens, I make for the…

CM: And so do I!

RM: It's not cool to dance to your own song.

SHARLEEN SPITERI
Thursday 17 December 2015
STV News

The Scottish band Texas are celebrating 25 years in the music industry. They play the Hydro tonight as their tour to mark a quarter of a century comes to an end.

SHARLEEN SPITERI, Texas: It's been absolutely fantastic. We went out on the road with the 25th anniversary. Eighteen months later we're still here...

JM: You came from Scotland and that's a key part to you. Had you come from anywhere else, do you think you would have made it? Was it key that you are Scottish?

SS: I think growing up in Glasgow, I think that's a big part of who we are as a band. I guess maybe the fight and the struggle at the beginning, because you are an outsider, was always something that was good. We were always, kind of like, at the back of the queue. They were like, oh yeah, that Scottish band, oh yeah, them. And I guess it's that thing where you just dig your heels in hard and you stick to your guns. And people always say we're very direct *(laughs)*. And that's a big part of growing up in Glasgow. We don't mince our words. We say what we want, that's how we want it to work and we say it politely. And if that can work, then fantastic. And if it doesn't, we'll see you later.

JM: You've been forced onto a non-wheat diet, which for a Scot must be particularly difficult. You were saying you're missing your after-concert meal.

SS: To come home to my mum and dad's and not be able to peel open that lovely wax paper of a Mother's Pride and put an outsider in the toaster is breaking my heart. Please, please can everyone on the plant – Tunnock's, Mother's Pride – please, please just make gluten-free ones. I would cut off my right arm to have, honestly, a roll and potato scone right now. I would absolutely love it.

JM: 25 years on, if it doesn't work out in the future, you could maybe...

SS: I could go back to the hairdressing. Of course, I was that good *(laughs)*. You know what, I still get dragged in. Whenever I come back home, my mum's like, did you bring your scissors? Like, seriously mum? That's basically the way it goes in our house. And I don't even get a roll and potato scone at the end of it anymore. It's rubbish.

2016

Monday 25 January 2016
STV News

In a hundred days from now the campaigning will have ended in the 2016 Scottish Parliament election. If the opinion polls are to be believed, the SNP is on course for an even bigger landslide win than they achieved in 2011.

DIARY: Nicola Sturgeon interview. We had points I had to hit – Education, Health, Council Tax freeze, Indyref in the event of a UK vote to leave the EU. She calmly batted it all back at me. I didn't feel it had been a very challenging interview, but the production team thought I got as much as I could from it. She is a class act and there is no doubt she will be First Minister through the next Parliament.

Tuesday 26 January 2016
Scotland Tonight

It's not often you see a GP surgery as quiet as this – but for the next half hour we've got out-of-hours access to somewhere many of us spend, or are likely to spend, a lot of time. We all know Scotland has an ageing population and with that comes more health problems and more pressure on our NHS. Today though, the people who work in these rooms, the GPs themselves, are telling us that we, the patients, are being served by under-resourced and understaffed practices. They also say the Scottish Government is treating what they do as dispensable.

DIARY: Focused on a *Scotland Tonight* special on the 'GP crisis' which I was anchoring from a GP surgery in King's Park... Basically, GPs saying they are at breaking point – underfunded and understaffed. Scottish Government view is that they value GPs, but that primary care needs to change with patients not necessarily having to see a doctor, but another health professional.

Tuesday 16 February 2016
STV News

The Prime Minister has continued today with another round of frenetic meetings ahead of Thursday's EU summit. He hopes to get agreement on a new relationship between the UK and the European Union on issues such as curbs to migrant benefits. It comes as the First Minister says she will use the referendum campaign to focus on the wider case for the UK remaining in the EU.

BERNARD PONSONBY, Political Editor: I think what we are seeing at the moment is different countries and institutions putting their cards on the table. Last night it was the French anxious that whatever David Cameron negotiates it shouldn't disadvantage France. Central European leaders saying any reform to migrant benefits should be for new claimants... If David Cameron doesn't emerge with something credible at the end of this week, it will increase the chances of a Brexit and that will have consequences for all 28 states.

WORK STARTS ON TWO NEW FERRIES

Tuesday 16 February 2016 *(cont)*
STV News

Work has started on two ferries to be used on the Clyde and Hebrides network. Scotland's Transport Minister Derek Mackay took part in a steel-cutting ceremony at the Ferguson shipyard in Port Glasgow earlier. The £97 million contract was signed in October last year, securing around 150 existing jobs.

DEREK MACKAY, Transport Minister: The people of the west coast will see two new ferries, which will be much more resilient and more reliable than the ferries there currently just by virtue of the way they have been constructed, their carrying ability and back-up at the machinery and various other equipment onboard. That should make ships more resilient and more reliable, particularly in heavier weather.

The contracts for the construction of the new ferries were signed on 16 October 2015. This was to become an enduring fiasco for the Scottish Government.

Saturday 20 February 2016
STV News

The Prime Minister has set the date for the In/Out referendum on the UK's membership of the European Union. Voters will go to the polls on Thursday 23 June. David Cameron is warning that leaving the EU would hit security and the economy. But five of his Cabinet colleagues have already signed up for the leave campaign.

Monday 22 February 2016
STV News

In a heated debate on Europe in the Commons, the Prime Minister has told the SNP that 'as far as Scotland is concerned, it is one UK vote'. The SNP had warned that a No vote in the EU Referendum could lead to a second Independence Referendum. But David Cameron rejected the suggestion that the EU Referendum had a separate constitutional dimension for Scotland. To Downing Street now. Bernard what did you make of the Prime Minister's response to Angus Robertson on the Scottish dimension to the EU Referendum?

BERNARD PONSONBY, Political Editor: Well, the reply was short and to the point, this is a UK vote and that is where it starts and that is where it ends. That won't do for the SNP of course who say it would be intolerable for Scotland to be taken out of the EU on the back of non-Scottish votes. In a sense David Cameron can't say anything other than that, he has enough on his plate without playing a game of constitutional theoreticals.

DIARY: Today was all about the European Referendum. Much happened over the weekend – the PM's 'deal', the announcement of a day for the referendum and then Boris Johnson declaring for out.

Tuesday 23 February 2016
STV News

The Scottish and UK Governments have agreed a deal on a fiscal framework to fund the Scotland Bill. It's taken almost a year of talks, but in the last hour the First Minister Nicola Sturgeon has announced an agreement in principle has been made.

RICHARD GERE
Sunday 28 February 2016

RICHARD GERE, Actor: My brother went to the University of Edinburgh. I took a long trip… I was making a movie called *Yanks* a long time ago and I had a week off and I ended up driving all over Scotland, which was an incredible experience. So beautiful. Great people.

DIARY: He said the day before he'd asked his driver to take him to Loch Lomond. He had wandered along the pier at Luss unrecognised wearing a coat and hat. There would have been a stampede among a certain generation of women had they known it was him.

My wife was a fan of Richard Gere when she was younger. I got my photo taken with him and there they were – fantasy and reality side by side.

Thursday 3 March 2016

DIARY: I had to go to the new Glasgow Children's Hospital to present a cheque for more than £100,000 from the STV Appeal. I won't deny that I was a bit reluctant because of the whole cynicism about 'charridee'. However, when I met some of the kids who are seriously ill, I was very moved. One wee girl, Latitia – who was maybe ten or so – was showing me her 'bravery beads' for all the things she has had to go through – operations, lumbar punctures, hair loss – and it was just – I really can't find the words for it. If these places get more money just by someone off the telly posing for a photo, then do it.

20th ANNIVERSARY OF THE DUNBLANE SHOOTINGS
Tuesday 8 March 2016
Scotland Tonight

This Sunday marks the 20th anniversary of the tragedy in Dunblane. On the morning of 13 March 1996 Thomas Hamilton walked into Dunblane Primary School armed with four handguns. He shot and killed 16 young children and their teacher. We were joined by the mother of five-year-old Mhairi McBeath who was killed on that day.

ISABEL WHITE, mother of Dunblane victim Mhairi McBeath: She was a normal five-year-old. I think she was quite bright… She had a slightly quirky personality. But she was five, you know, her personality was very unformed and that's a difficult question because… Five years is not a long time to get to know your child. There was so much of the becoming, there is so much of the developing that I didn't get to see… I don't have to (*deal with Thomas Hamilton*). I don't have to because he killed himself. I think because he died it's taken a burden off me. I don't know if that makes sense. I don't need to forgive him. I don't need to wonder if I should forgive him. I don't need to process the reality of Thomas Hamilton at all because he's dead, because he's deceased. And that in a sense, I suppose, has been quite helpful. I never wanted this incident to define me. I realised pretty early on that if I had any chance of giving my younger daughter Catherine a normal life then that was really what I should focus on and she was my first priority, but a close priority on the heels of that was me and I wanted to do the things that I enjoyed. I wanted to get back into teaching. I wanted to have my career back and I wanted to have a life. I think having a good quality of life was only possible by leaving Dunblane.

DIARY: She was very strong and told me when she arrived that she didn't want a 'soppy' interview about how did you cope? She had things to say and said them very clearly with no hint of emotion… I began by asking her what Mhairi was like and she said that at the age of five her personality was still not fully formed. It was very sad, but not the tone of the interview. She did not want to be defined by Dunblane, she said.

One of the most memorable interviews I have ever conducted on *Scotland Tonight.*

Tuesday 15 March 2016
STV News

Some have described it as the worst humanitarian crisis since the Second World War, but for one group of Scottish doctors scenes of hope were found in the Calais Jungle. STV News travelled with the medical volunteers to one of Europe's largest refugee camps as they delivered medical aid, clothing and tents. They say they want to provide hope to the thousands of people living here while reminding people back home of their ongoing plight.

Thursday 24 March 2016
STV News

The Longannet Power Station in Fife has been disconnected from the national grid, ending 46 years of providing electricity to over two million homes in Scotland. The operators, Scottish Power, have closed the station four years earlier than planned, ending a century of coal-fired electricity production north of the border.

Friday 1 April 2016
STV News

He's the schoolboy killer who shocked Scotland. A 16-year-old who stabbed fellow pupil Bailey Gwynne to death at Cults Academy in Aberdeen has been detained for nine years. Sentencing the teenager, the judge Lady Stacey described him as naïve and immature. She said the tragic outcome could have been avoided if he had not taken a weapon to school.

Tuesday 5 April 2016
STV News

With a month until the vote, campaigning is stepping up a gear in the Holyrood election battle. The Conservatives are promising a new fund to tackle potholes, Labour claim scrapping the Council Tax could save average householders more than £100. The SNP is raising questions about Tory plans for graduate charges and the Lib Dems still have questions to answer about investment links with China.

Monday 18 April 2016
STV News

The European Referendum campaign took off in earnest today with the Chancellor claiming the UK would be 'permanently poorer' outside the EU. And a claim that Brexit would cost families £4,300 per year have been rubbished by Leave campaigners, who accuse the UK Government of scaremongering.

DIARY: Of course, the figures will be argued over, but so very interesting to see the same arguments, often the same language, being used as during the Scottish Independence Referendum, 'Leap in the dark' etc. Ironic that some of those who support staying in and those who want to leave are using the opposite arguments of what they used during Indyref.

SCOTTISH ELECTION 2016
Friday 6 May 2016
STV News – live from Holyrood

Nicola Sturgeon returns as Scotland's First Minister – saying she will lead a minority government after securing a 'clear and unequivocal mandate' in the elections. It was a brutal night for Scottish Labour, their worst election defeat in more than 100 years, battered into third place by a resurgent Conservative Party. And a good night for the Greens who overtake the Liberal Democrats. This is how the new Parliament looks. The SNP return 63 MSPs – 59 first-past-the-post and four list. The Conservatives took 31 – seven constituency and 24 on the list vote. Labour are on 24 – they won just three constituencies and picked up 21 on the list vote. The Greens have six MSPs all from the list. Which pushed the Liberal Democrats into fifth place with five MSPs. So, after an Independence Referendum, a Westminster election and now a Holyrood election the political map is redrawn. The plates have shifted. The Conservatives, for so long an irrelevance, are now the opposition in Scotland. The Greens have become a party of influence. The former parties of power, Labour and the Lib Dems, are facing the harsh reality of being on the margins. And above them all sit the SNP beginning an historic third term in Government. The people of Scotland have made their voices heard.

DIARY: The SNP won the election as expected, but came two seats short of a majority, despite an increase in the popular vote... An historic (although the Parliament has only been in existence since 1999) third term for the SNP, but the significant story was the return of the Conservatives and the collapse of Labour.

Nicola Sturgeon talked about 'persuading' people about independence and not being divisive. A lot of people suggesting there will be no 'IndyRef2' in this Parliament. That's rather definite – the Greens are pro-independence – but it's more the lack of declaration from the First Minister that makes me think it won't happen. Through to Holyrood for a Scotland-wide programme. Not the buzz I've seen on previous elections. Ruth Davidson, the Scottish Conservative leader came and, although naturally buoyant, said she was so tired I could ask her for anything, even her bank PIN and she'd probably answer. Nicola Sturgeon didn't come – choosing to make a statement from Bute House earlier. I wonder if she'd have done it if they'd had a majority. A sense of a mood for compromise, both talking about the possibility of that, in education especially.

Tuesday 14 June 2016
STV News

The Labour Leader Jeremy Corbyn has launched his strongest bid yet to rally support for Britain remaining in the European Union after a series of polls suggests the Leave campaign is establishing a firm lead. He challenged Leave supporters to admit the devastating effect Brexit would have on public services such as the NHS. Those campaigning to take Britain out of the EU say the money saved could be spent on a better health service.

Tuesday 14 June 2016 *(cont)*

DIARY: A pre-record with a delightful six-year-old called Caitlin McFadden who had quadriplegic cerebral palsy among many other conditions. Her mother, Pauline, and the pop star Clare Grogan were in to talk about how the Nordorff Robbins charity uses music to help such children. When her mother mentioned the word 'dance' Caitlin slipped off her knee with a big smile and began stepping about in glee (with her mother's support). It was a lovely moment.

Thursday 16 June
STV News

Labour MP Jo Cox has died in hospital after an horrific attack at lunchtime today in her West Yorkshire constituency. The 41-year-old mother of two young children was left in a pool of blood after her killer shot and knifed her in the street. Police have arrested a 52-year-old man. Campaigning in the EU Referendum has been suspended as politicians offer messages of support to her family.

DIARY: A 41-year-old woman has had her life cut short in a terrible way, leaving two young children without a mother. On that level alone it is tragic, quite aside from the broader picture of an MP murdered doing her job.

Jo Cox's killer was a Scottish-born far-right extremist.

BREXIT VOTE

Thursday 23 June 2016
STV News

In just under four hours' time, the polling stations will close, the counting will start and sometime tomorrow morning an historic decision by the people of the United Kingdom will be announced. Leaders from both sides of the debate on the UK's future in Europe have been casting their votes. In Scotland almost four million people are registered to have their say.

DIARY: The polls are very close, but I think it'll be a comfortable win for remaining. Tonight's polls suggest a narrow Remain.

Friday 24 June 2016
STV News – live from Downing Street

The UK electorate has given instruction to the British Government. Leave Europe. The consequences are laid bare. A crisis at the heart of the UK Government – as David Cameron resigns as Prime Minister. 51.9 per cent – almost 17-and-a-half million UK voters chose Leave – among them over a million Scots. But when we look at the detail of how Scotland voted, the picture was very different – 62 per cent of voters chose to remain within the EU. The First Minister of Scotland Nicola Sturgeon responded, saying being dragged out of the EU is a significant and material change. Another referendum for independence is 'highly likely'.

BERNARD PONSONBY, Political Editor at Bute House: We have a United Kingdom in name but the question tonight for me is whether it can last under the competing demands of different nationalisms. In some respects, the vote in England is the most obvious manifestation of English nationalism that I have seen in my lifetime. That message 'take back control' resonated and it resonated with voters in England across social classes, but particularly in working-class communities. Take back control. In a sense it is what Nicola Sturgeon is saying too. Take control out of the hands of Westminster to help maintain Scotland's place in the EU and if that involved another referendum on independence, she will plan for one. And in Northern Ireland, Irish nationalists demanding a border poll looking at the possibility of a United Ireland. Whatever we can say of these competing nationalisms, it looks increasingly the case that they can't all co-exist in one United Kingdom. I simply don't know where Scotland and the UK and Europe are headed tonight. What's more, I suspect neither do our political leaders.

JM in Downing Street: The financial markets saw billions of pounds wiped off the value of shares in the UK and around the world. The pound dropped to its lowest level in more than 30 years as news of the result sank in... 24 hours ago it seemed that after four major votes in 18 months, Scotland was facing a period of relative political calm. The polls said so and the bookies said so. Today, we learn the UK is leaving the EU, the Prime Minister is to resign and a second Independence Referendum is highly likely. After a day of high drama, live from Downing Street. Goodnight.

DIARY: There is a lot of dismay and anger and not a little fear about what the future holds. We were all expecting that we would be entering a period of relative political calm, but not now. The upheaval and wearying uncertainty continues. In Downing Street we were in the strangely serene setting of the seat of UK power in the midst of a significant crisis. There were other crews there, but very little sound. There is a real divide in the UK and Scotland having voted to Remain emphasises that. We need calm in the period to come.

Monday 27 June 2016
STV News – live from Downing Street

The fallout from Brexit gathers pace – the shocks of the political earthquake still being felt all around. David Cameron made it clear it was the job of the next Prime Minister to launch formal exit proceedings. Earlier, the Chancellor attempted to calm the markets – as the pound hit a 31-year low. Meanwhile, Labour are in deep, deep crisis.

DIARY: A very pressurised broadcast. We established comms from Downing Street with only four minutes to on-air. No autocue and network teams next to us. Had to get everything right first time.

100th ANNIVERSARY OF THE SOMME
Friday 1 July 2016
STV News

A Scottish service to mark the 100th anniversary of the Battle of the Somme has heard an appeal for acts of remembrance to continue for years to come. The organisers of the event in Northern France said the lessons from the First World War are still relevant today – and the men and women who died should not be forgotten.

DIARY: There were a group of lads walking around the city in First World War uniform and it was a striking reminder. They were giving out cards with details of the Fallen.

CHILCOT INQUIRY
Wednesday 6 July 2016
STV News

The long-awaited report into the Iraq War has been published. Sir John Chilcot didn't pull his punches – the UK Government oversold the intelligence and undermined the United Nations. And he came as close as he could to hinting the war might have been illegal. The Former Prime Minister Tony Blair said today he was sorry for the loss of life, acted in good faith and was exonerated on the charge he misled Parliament.

DIARY: It took longer to produce the report than the war lasted. Damning. Said the UK had gone to war before all possible peaceful options had been exhausted and that there had been failures in intelligence and planning. Tony Blair, who was Prime Minister at the time and whose political legacy has been ruined by it, said he regretted the errors, but under the same circumstances he would have taken the same action… I don't accept that Blair is a war criminal. He was wrong in a big way, but I've often wondered why a politician who was usually so sure-footed could have got it so wrong and I have to conclude it's because he thought he was doing the right thing.

ANDY MURRAY'S SECOND WIMBLEDON WIN
Sunday 10 July 2016
STV News

Andy Murray has won his second Wimbledon title. The Scot beat Milos Raonic in straight sets on Centre Court. The tennis ace produced a sensational display to defeat the Canadian 6–4, 7–6 (7–3), 7–6 (7–2) in two hours and 48 minutes in front of a packed Centre Court crowd. It's Murray's third Grand Slam title.

DIARY: I think this makes him Scotland's greatest sportsman of all time.

THERESA MAY WINS CONSERVATIVE LEADERSHIP
Monday 11 July 2016
STV News

David Cameron has announced that Theresa May will be appointed the next Prime Minister on Wednesday. The campaign to succeed Mr Cameron was thrown into confusion this morning, when the only other candidate – the Energy Minister Andrea Leadsom – pulled out of the race after a weekend of embarrassing headlines that exposed her inexperience in politics. Theresa May, who today launched what she expected to be a two-month campaign, will now walk into Number 10 in two days' time.

DIARY: The challenger for the Tory leadership, Andrea Leadsom, has withdrawn citing the abuse had been too much (I think she knew she couldn't win), so Theresa May will be the new Prime Minister. Theresa May was the only realistic choice and might offer stability in unsettling times.

THERESA MAY BECOMES PRIME MINISTER
Wednesday 13 July 2016
STV News

THERESA MAY, Prime Minister: The full title of my party is the Conservative and Unionist Party and that word unionist is very important to me. It means we believe in the Union, the precious, precious bond between England, Scotland, Wales and Northern Ireland. But it means something else that is just as important. It means we believe in a union not just between nations of the United Kingdom, but between our citizens, every one of us, whoever we are and wherever we're from… We will make Britain a country that works, not for the privileged few, but for every one of us. That will be the mission of the Government I lead.

DIARY: It has been an astonishing period in politics. I don't know much about her, but she's been at the Home Office for six years and is regarded as a steady operator. That's what we need just now. Good luck to her.

OIL RIG RUNS AGROUND ON WESTERN ISLES
Monday 8 August 2016
STV News

It was a summer storm that left its mark. Marine accident investigators and salvage experts have begun assessing how to recover a drilling rig which ran aground after being blown ashore on the Western Isles. The rig, which has more than 200 tonnes of diesel on board, was under tow west of Lewis when it was hit by severe storms.

DIARY: The images of the rig from the shore with the cemetery and Dalmore Beach in the foreground are very dramatic. It's not often a story affects me personally, but this one definitely has *(my family is from the area)*… Thank goodness it wasn't an oil tanker. That beach I love so well would have been ruined.

Tuesday 9 August 2016
STV News

A Muslim taxi driver who murdered a Glasgow shopkeeper for claiming he was a prophet has been jailed for a minimum of 27 years. The judge told Tanveer Ahmed the killing of Asad Shah had been a barbaric, chilling 'execution'. As he was led away Ahmed raised a clenched fist and shouted praise of the Prophet Mohammed.

DAVID COWAN, Chief Reporter: This is Tanveer Ahmed confronting Asad Shah in his shop in Glasgow. Armed with a knife the taxi driver had travelled from Bradford to challenge the newsagent for claiming he was a prophet. Within minutes he had stabbed, kicked, punched and stamped Mr Shah to death. Today, his defence lawyer told the High Court Ahmed hadn't come north with the intention of killing Mr Shah – but the judge said it had been, in effect, a religiously motivated execution. Ahmed was jailed for life and ordered to serve 27 years before he can apply for parole. The judge accepted that the murder had not been an attack on Glasgow's Ahmadiyya community, of which Mr Shah was a member. But the community doesn't feel that way. They praised the authorities for bringing Ahmed to justice – but they fear copycat attacks – and asked for vigilance against extremism.

MARK MILLAR
Monday 5 September 2016
Scotland Tonight

The comic book writer and movie producer Mark Millar turned his passion into a highly successful career and now he's giving aspiring writers and artists the chance to follow suit.

JM: You're a big international success and yet you still live in Scotland. Why and how do you manage it?

MARK MILLAR: I actually really like it here. I'm starting to take it personally because so many of my friends say to me, when are you going to move away? People are like, why are you still here? But, actually, I really like it here, it's really nice. I think it's a good place to live, it's got a good balance of everything. I'll give you a perfect example. The *Civil War* premiere a few months ago. A pretty glamorous do. You've got Robert Downey Jr and all these guys who are in the film, all at it. It's a big, splashy event in LA. And I couldn't go because it was my brother's birthday party in Coatbridge. And, like, I says to my brother, d'you mind if I skip your party, I've got an invite to this thing in LA? And he's like, oh, thanks very much. But I think if you lived in LA your life would just be that. Whereas, if you live here you are reminded that you're an actual human being. And at one time, this career won't exist. So, you have to keep your feet on the ground a wee bit. And the patter is better here.

Wednesday 7 September 2016
STV News

The fallout from Brexit has dominated politics at Westminster and the Scottish Parliament today and inevitably sets the two Governments on a collision course.

Bernard, Theresa May wants a common approach to Brexit, but the two Governments are at loggerheads well before Brexit talks start?

BERNARD PONSONBY, Political Editor at Westminster: Theresa May's position today is that she will not give a running commentary on possible scenarios because to do that would involve revealing her negotiating hand even before talks start. Now, I fully expect in the fullness of time both Governments will be at war with one another over Brexit, but I did not think the brisk exchanges would be quite so bad quite so early.

DIARY: Theresa May in her first Prime Minister's Questions. Jeremy Corbyn asked nothing of note, so it was down to the SNP's Angus Robertson to ask about Brexit. We went with the line that Westminster and Holyrood are heading for a showdown on this. The fact is, though, that other than calling a second referendum – which they are clearly reluctant to do – the SNP have no serious leverage.

Wednesday 28 September 2016
STV News

Jeremy Corbyn put his party on alert for a snap General Election as he renewed his appeal for unity at the close of Labour's annual conference. He said there was every chance Theresa May will decide to 'cut and run'.

DIARY: He comfortably won a second leadership election at the weekend, so Labour have to accept he is their leader… I think Labour will be in the electoral wilderness for the next nine years minimum – this Parliament and the next – unless they get rid of him. For such a habitual opposer to his own party to call for unity is hypocrisy.

Friday 7 October 2016

DIARY: (*hosting COSLA conference at Crieff Hydro*) The main issue throughout has been the restricted budget handed down by the Scottish Government and its interference in some of the choices that councils have to make about their spending. I got questioners to say their name, area and party. It was so telling that not one SNP councillor asked a question. Not one. That might be admirable party discipline, but it's bad for democracy.

DONALD TRUMP WINS US PRESIDENTIAL ELECTION
Wednesday 9 November 2016
STV News

It is one of the most dramatic electoral upsets America, or anywhere, has ever seen. The repercussions are being felt globally. Here, the Prime Minister insisted she will preserve the enduring and special relationship between the two countries. Scotland's First Minister, who previously was highly critical of Mr Trump's campaign, said the result of the election should be respected, and that Scotland values its relationship with the US. The next leader of the Free World is a half-Scottish billionaire whose mother came from the Isle of Lewis. A property magnate who's never held public office will oversee the world's biggest military, the world's biggest economy, the world's biggest arsenal of nuclear weapons. 2016 has delivered another political earthquake – but what will it mean for his mother's old country? To date, Donald Trump's main contribution to life in Scotland has been owning two golf courses and falling out with the Scottish Government and its then First Minister over a windfarm.

DIARY: In a year of political upsets this must be the biggest... It's like all these seismic events – there's a rush of adrenalin as you wonder what's going to happen now. I don't think he'll be as bad as many fear, nor do I think he'll be as transformative as his supporters doubtless anticipate. Hillary Clinton didn't face the public until nine hours after her shock defeat. She was very dignified, but she's finished. Some think the US wasn't ready for a woman – or is it that Hillary Clinton was not that woman?

Tuesday 15 November 2016
STV News

If a couple have a row in their home there is a chance one of them will be led away in handcuffs. That was the judgement today of the General Secretary of the Scottish Police Federation, Calum Steele. He was giving evidence to a Holyrood Committee discussing domestic abuse cases as part of an inquiry into the prosecution system. And a former Advocate Depute told MSPs that cases were presented in court that had no realistic prospect of conviction. Tonight, the Crown Office insisted prosecutions only take place if there is evidence of criminality.

2017

FIRST MINISTER RULES OUT INDEPENDENCE REFERENDUM IN 2017

Monday 9 January 2017
STV News

The First Minister is ruling out an Independence Referendum in 2017. Nicola Sturgeon is urging the Prime Minister to negotiate a soft Brexit deal keeping the UK in the European single market. But she is warning that if the UK Government pursues a hard Brexit then another Independence Referendum remains highly likely.

NICOLA STURGEON, First Minister: There is not going to be an Independence Referendum in 2017. I don't think there is anybody that thinks that is the case, but an Independence Referendum has to be on the table to make sure that Scotland does not end up in the position of being driven off a hard Brexit cliff edge by a UK Government that said in 2014 that voting No was the only way to stay in the EU and now wants to steamroller Scotland's voice and opinion. I will not let that happen.

COLIN MACKAY, Holyrood Editor: A lot of people thought it a bit obvious there would be no second Independence Referendum this year, but this is the first time the First Minister has categorically ruled it out. And it's important to get that confirmation. I think there will be a lot of people on both sides of the debate breathing a sigh of relief tonight. The First Minister is not taking it off the table, but she is not going to rush into it. She wants to see what happens with Brexit and she'll be hoping for a bit of movement in public support.

THERESA MAY INDICATES A HARD BREXIT

Tuesday 17 January 2017
STV News

The Prime Minister Theresa May has given her clearest indication yet of how her

Government sees Britain's future outside the European Union. In a long-awaited speech in London, she said the UK would no longer remain within the single market, or the customs union. And she warned her European partners against taking measures to 'punish' Britain for its vote to leave. The First Minister Nicola Sturgeon said Scotland can't be forced down a hard Brexit path that will damage jobs and living standards.

DIARY: A complete break, no halfway house. She's really signposted that from the start, 'Brexit means Brexit'.

INAUGURATION OF PRESIDENT TRUMP
Friday 20 January 2017
STV News

Within the past hour Donald Trump has become the 45th President of the United States of America. Scotland's First Minister has wished the Trump administration well in dealing with 'great global challenges'. As Mr Trump made his inaugural speech in Washington DC, campaigners gathered in Glasgow and Edinburgh as part of worldwide protests, urging the new President to abandon what they say are his politics of hate.

DIARY: There is widespread concern about what sort of President he will be… I heard one woman weeping, 'He's not my President.' Well, he is and there's no hiding from that… His first speech – a campaign speech on the state America was in and the America-first rhetoric – was clear and unambiguous, but very unstatesmanlike and lacked class. It didn't augur well.

Tuesday 24 January 2017
STV News

One court. Eleven judges. Two Governments defeated. Theresa May will be forced to seek the approval of both Houses of Parliament before her Government can trigger Article 50 – beginning the formal process to leave the European Union. The Prime Minister has promised to bring forward a bill within days. And no comfort for Nicola Sturgeon as the judges unanimously agreed there is no legal reason to consult the Scottish Parliament before proceeding. But the First Minister pledged a vote regardless of the Supreme Court decision.

BERNARD PONSONBY, Political Editor: The judges were unanimous that there is no legal obligation on Westminster to consult the devolved administrations on what is a reserved matter. Now, when the Lord Advocate on behalf of the Scottish Government addressed the Supreme Court, he explicitly said that he was not arguing that the Scottish Parliament should have a veto on the process merely that it should be consulted. That consultation process is a Convention, a rule of political behaviour. It does not give rise to a legal right and from that point of view that is a significant statement on the legal status of legislative consent. This Parliament is a creature of a Westminster act of Parliament and today's judgement underlines when it comes to parliamentary sovereignty it is Westminster that ultimately can call the shots.

Thursday 26 January 2017
STV News

People who used their mobile phones to record the attempted murder of a police officer have been described as 'disgraceful and disgusting' by a High Court judge. Lady Rae was told that no one came to PC Kevin Taylor's aid when he was stabbed in a Glasgow street. Instead, some onlookers used their phones to take pictures. The furious judge jailed the man who carried out the attack for 12 years.

Thursday 26 January 2017 *(cont)*
STV News

An alarming new report says the health of Scottish children is among the worst in Europe. Experts say the gap between the rich and poor is jeopardising the health of the youngest generation. They're now calling for urgent action to tackle the issues of obesity and child poverty for the sake of the nation as a whole.

DIARY: One operator of a foodbank claimed people were bringing food back because they were too poor to be able to afford the energy to cook it.

Monday 30 January 2017

DIARY: A pre-record with Ford Kiernan and Greg Hemphill from *Still Game*... They let off a 'fart spray' afterwards which was really pungent. I had my suspicions, but you can't accuse people. The technicians were involved and I felt a bit of a mug assuring the guys it was a burnt tube on a monitor. They were straight-faced. Later learned it was them.

Monday 30 January 2017 *(cont)*
Scotland Tonight

Downing Street is insisting Donald Trump's planned UK state visit will go ahead despite his controversial travel ban targeting nationals from seven Muslim-majority countries. An anti-Trump petition has attracted more than one and a half million signatures, and tonight thousands of people took to British streets in opposition to the US President.

DIARY: This is what he said he was going to do and the Americans voted for it. Demonstrations here. The issue is whether he should be accorded a state visit as planned. Of course, he should. We've had state visits with plenty of other unpleasant leaders who weren't democratically elected and who weren't allies.

DAVID TENNANT
Monday 23 February 2017
Scotland Tonight

He's one of Scotland's most versatile and popular actors, best known for his starring roles in *Broadchurch* and *Doctor Who*. David Tennant's latest film project sees him take on the role of the famed Scottish psychiatrist RD Laing.

JM: You're an actor with a great body of work, particularly some of these dark characters you're talking about. You are a son of the manse. Do you have to shed a lot to do these dark characters?

DAVID TENNANT: I don't know, there's something liberating about it in a way. I'm right in the middle of rehearsing a play at the moment. I'm going to play Don Juan, who is something of a lothario, something of a cynic. Not a man with a lot of moral fibre. There's something rather liberating about that. You get to live onstage for two hours guilt free. I'm very happy for the upbringing I had being the son of a manse. But the Scottish Presbyterian puritanical hairshirt means that one is often propelled forward through life by guilt. So, it's quite nice to not have to worry about that for a while.

JM: You've had this stellar career, but you were rejected for *Taggart* 26 times.

DT: I think it grows, this anecdote. I don't think it was 26 times. But it was certainly quite a few.

JM: How did you deal with that?

DT: I traipsed up to Scottish Television time and again, never got anywhere. I stopped being disappointed and started just chalking them up to experience. To be honest, part of an actor's life is getting rejected for things. You get rejected for many, many more jobs than you actually get. But with *Taggart*, I did think, 'Some people have done, like, three different murders. Some people have been killed eight times. I couldn't get a foot in the door.

DIARY *(interview on Sunday 26 February)*: He was very pleasant and it was an easy interview. He had declined to be interviewed by me once before – with great courtesy and good reason *(an overenthusiastic PR had made promises without confirming David could do it)* – and remembered that. Nice fellow.

Thursday 2 March 2017
STV News

Tributes have been paid to Tommy

Gemmell, one of the Lisbon Lions who won the European Cup in 1967 with Celtic. The 73-year-old passed away this morning after a long illness. Gemmell scored one of the goals in the famous final 50 years ago, as the Glasgow side became the first British team to win the trophy.

GRANT RUSSELL, Sports News Reporter: He even scored in a second European final in 1970. He is revered by the Celtic faithful not just for his place in a legendary team. There is real appreciation, too, that a great could also be so humble. Gemmell the man as well as the footballer is mourned tonight. As one posting on a fans' forum put it today what a player, what a lion, what a loss.

DIARY: Remarkably, spent much of his later life as an insurance salesman. Such a contrast to today when young boys who don't even make it into the first team can be set up for life.

Monday 9 March 2017
STV News

A poll for STV News has found half of Scots would back independence if a referendum was held tomorrow. The rise in support for a Yes vote comes as the Prime Minister prepares to trigger Britain's exit from the European Union later this month. The First Minister Nicola Sturgeon has said autumn 2018 would be a 'common sense' date for any second Independence Referendum to be held.

DIARY: Lead today was an exclusive STV poll showing support/opposition to independence at 50/50. I've made my observation before about polls – as a group that can be an indicator – but they're so discredited that to focus on one is pointless. Producers disagree, so that's that.

Monday 13 March 2017
STV News

The First Minister has called for a second Independence Referendum within the next two years. Nicola Sturgeon says the Prime Minster has rejected any compromise on Brexit, leaving her no choice, but to give people another vote. Theresa May has yet to say whether she will grant Holyrood permission to organise the poll.

DIARY: The First Minister Nicola Sturgeon called for a second Independence Referendum this morning, saying that they have a mandate for it. Their manifesto spoke of 'material change' and they say Brexit is that and that Theresa May is not representing or negotiating with Scotland in any meaningful way. It's not a surprise, but I wonder if she has made an error. I don't think there is any enthusiasm for yet another referendum and the economic case is weaker. Also, the SNP's reputation for competence is beginning to fray with issues on health and education.

THERESA MAY SAYS, 'NOW IS NOT THE TIME' FOR SECOND INDEPENDENCE REFERENDUM

Thursday 16 March 2017
STV News

A constitutional stand-off between Westminster and Holyrood is inevitable after the Prime Minister rejected calls for a second Independence Referendum insisting, 'now is not the time'. This afternoon the Scottish Secretary confirmed the UK Government will refuse to even discuss a second poll saying the test of a 'legal, fair and decisive' referendum had not been met.

THERESA MAY, Prime Minister: I am responding to the proposal that's been put forward by the First Minister, I say now is not the time. And the reason I say that is because all our energies should be being put into the negotiations with the European Union to make sure that we get the right deal. The right deal for people across the whole of the United Kingdom, the right deal for Scotland and the whole of the UK.

JM: Where does this leave Nicola Sturgeon?

COLIN MACKAY, Holyrood Editor: Today I would say it has left her angry, but angry and up for a fight. Downing Street may have hoped this would make the Scottish Government step back and take next week's Section 30 Order vote off the table. That is NOT going to happen. There is a Holyrood majority for another referendum. Nicola Sturgeon will win that next week, then seek negotiations with the Prime Minister about that second referendum. The Scottish Secretary is ruling out negotiations on the Section 30 Order transferring the powers to hold another referendum from Westminster to Holyrood. Something's going to have to give.

Wednesday 22 March 2017
STV News

Westminster is on lockdown after a suspected terror attack where a knifeman ploughed a car into pedestrians before stabbing a policeman outside the Houses of Parliament. Four people have died and a number of people have suffered 'catastrophic' injuries in the incident where a number of people were mowed down on Westminster Bridge by the attacker. The Scottish Parliament has been suspended following the attack, on the day MSPs were preparing to vote on whether to press for a second Independence Referendum.

DIARY: Today was one of those earn-your-corn days. The original plan was for Andrea Brymer and me to present a news special from Holyrood to mark the expected passing of the Scottish Government's proposal for a second Independence Referendum. As I travelled to Edinburgh on the train, I got an alert of a policeman being attacked at Westminster and a separate incident involving a car. It was clear that the story was going to develop... Then the rain began to pour down in Edinburgh. When we got into position it was clear to me that the conditions would make it chaotic – not to mention the danger of electrical equipment. I told Glasgow it was foolish. The director Laura *(Trimble)* suggested I could maybe do it from inside the Parliament, but with no autocue. This was with 20 minutes to go. Had to go through the Parliament's airport-style security, collect my pass and get into position, record hellos, work out what we were doing and then deliver on air... It's good to show your worth at times.

Monday 27 March 2017
STV News

The Prime Minister is refusing to say whether she will respect tomorrow's vote in the Scottish Parliament – repeating her warning that now is not the time for a second Independence Referendum. Theresa May met the First Minister in Glasgow just 48 hours before she starts the process for 'Article 50' EU exit talks.

COLIN MACKAY, Holyrood Editor: The two leaders met in the Crowne Plaza hotel just across the river there – curiously less than a mile away from the Scottish Government's own offices here in Glasgow. The Prime Minister wanted to meet on neutral territory, making the First Minister come to her. Maybe that was a bit of a power play, but it had no effect on Nicola Sturgeon. She said she wasn't really much further forward after meeting Theresa May for almost an hour. But she said the meeting was cordial and that the PM was confident of getting the Brexit deal and trade deal within the next two years after Article 50 is triggered by the PM tomorrow.

DIARY: Managed poorly by Downing Street. No filmed footage of them meeting, only stills. What's the point? And then terse, two-minute interviews with broadcasters. Again, what's the point? Time and again Westminster gets Scotland wrong.

SCOTTISH PARLIAMENT VOTE ON SECOND INDEPENDENCE REFERENDUM
Tuesday 28 March 2017
STV News – live from Holyrood with co-presenter Andrea Brymer

Within the last hour, the Scottish Parliament has given its backing to the First Minister's demand for a second Independence Referendum. The debate resumed this afternoon after being postponed last week as a mark of respect following the Westminster terror attack. MSPs from the Scottish Greens have backed the Government – the vote, 69 to 59 in favour of the motion. The decision puts Holyrood on a collision course with the UK Government and comes just a day before Prime Minister Theresa May triggers Article 50 to begin the Brexit process.

BERNARD PONSONBY, Political Editor: It is the will of the Scottish Parliament so it is not insignificant, but of course, it cannot be enforced in constitutional terms since the authority to hold a second poll is a reserved matter for the Westminster Parliament and in strict legal terms there is little that Holyrood can do to force the UK Government into a change of heart. By far the most significant thing that the First Minister said today was a pledge to come back to the Holyrood chamber after the Easter recess and outline how the Government intends to take forward the will of Parliament. I have to say that the options to get the UK Government to change its mind would appear to be political rather than constitutional and tonight it is not at all clear what the Scottish Government will propose. What is clear is that they will not take a rebuff lying down.

DIARY: No weather issues this time – and we had a gazebo – but it was very cold. The bigger issue was the protesters – not the best example of our independent Scotland…There were security guards there and the police came to ensure order. The BBC was the focus of much of their ire. The SNP officials were clearly embarrassed and Deputy First Minister John Swinney gestured to them to be quiet.

PRIME MINISTER TRIGGERS ARTICLE 50 TO WITHDRAW FROM EU
Wednesday 29 March 2017
STV News – live from Westminster

The Prime Minister has formally triggered the process that will end with the United Kingdom leaving the European Union. Theresa May says there's no turning back as she embarks on the road to redefining this country's relationship with Europe. But the fallout from that decision increases tensions between Holyrood and Westminster, putting the 300-year-old Union at risk.

BERNARD PONSONBY, Political Editor: We have two leaders – Nicola Sturgeon and Theresa May – playing a game of political poker and the stakes are high… A momentous day here. A profound one for the Westminster Parliament, but one with far reaching consequences for all of the constituent nations of the UK.

THERESA MAY CALLS SNAP ELECTION FOR 8TH JUNE
Tuesday 18 April 2017
STV News

In a surprise announcement, Theresa May has called for a snap General Election on 8 June. MPs will vote on it tomorrow, but Labour has already welcomed the move. Despite repeatedly claiming that she was against the idea of an early vote, the Prime Minister said opposition parties were jeopardising her Government's preparations for Brexit. Nicola Sturgeon said the announcement was one of the most extraordinary u-turns in recent political history.

HARRY SMITH, Westminster Correspondent in Downing Street: Theresa May has a reputation for running a tight ship, for micro-managing and for keeping her own counsel. She certainly did that today. Downing Street is used by Prime Ministers for only the most important announcements. Right up to the end she kept everyone guessing what this one would be.

THERESA MAY, Prime Minister: The country is coming together, but Westminster is not. In recent weeks Labour have threatened to vote against the final agreement we reach with the European Union. The Liberal Democrats have said they want to grind the business of government to a standstill. The Scottish National Party say they will vote against the legislation that formally repeals Britain's membership of the European Union. And unelected members of the

House of Lords have vowed to fight us every step of the way. Our opponents believe because the Government's majority is small that our resolve will weaken and that they can force us to change course. They are wrong. They underestimate our determination to get the job done.

COLIN MACKAY, Holyrood Editor: The announcement took all the parties' leaders by surprise today, all that is except Ruth Davidson who got an early morning warning call from the Prime Minister. This week we had expected to hear the First Minister's plans to put pressure on the Prime Minister to allow IndyRef2 – now the General Election might prove to be a bit of a referendum on the referendum.

DIARY: She has repeatedly said there would be no early election and she has built a reputation for sticking to her word, so this has come as a surprise. Perhaps it shouldn't be – the Conservatives way ahead in the polls, Labour under Jeremy Corbyn and it will give her a larger majority and less in hock to her more right-wing backbenchers. Different situation in Scotland where it'll be more about IndyRef2.

Monday 24 April 2017

DIARY: An interview with the First Minister Nicola Sturgeon for our new *Scotland Tonight* set-piece launch. She was fine and we exchanged some small talk, something she never used to be comfortable with. Interview was on General Election issues... I did get somewhere with pressing on how effective a 'Voice for Scotland' did the SNP MPs provide? Can say plenty, but what do they actually change? Quite noticeable on social media how there is so much criticism of the nationalist position in contrast to before the referendum when it was almost all cybernats.

Tuesday 25 April 2017
STV News

Holyrood has seen a furious debate about the cap on child tax credits and what's been dubbed the 'rape clause'. The First Minister accused the Conservatives of ignoring humanity. The Scottish Tory Leader was heckled as she said the Scottish Parliament could reinstate support for bigger families.

Tuesday 2 May 2017
Scotland Tonight

JM: Did you actually come into politics, Ruth Davidson, to support policies like forcing women who have been the victims of rape to declare that to civil servants to get much-needed benefits?

RUTH DAVIDSON, Scottish Conservative leader: No, no, I don't accept the way in which you are asking that question. This is about the restriction of child tax credits to the first two children.

JM: That's the effect of it, is it not?

RD: What I'm saying, and I think this is quite important, is that where you have restrictions like that, I think it's absolutely right that in the worst possible circumstances people aren't drawn into that. That there are exceptions in these exceptional and very difficult cases. When you're talking about declaring or anything else. Now, I absolutely accept that if there's better ways of doing it then we should always look at that. But the system that's in place doesn't require some of the things that people have been saying it does.

DIARY: She is a good performer. Her weakness is on the so-called 'Rape Clause' – caps on child benefit – with which she is clearly uncomfortable and her original opposition to leaving the EU. Pushed her on them and her discomfort was clear, but no real new lines.

MANCHESTER ARENA BOMBING
Tuesday 23 May 2017
STV News – live from Manchester

Two teenage girls from Barra remain unaccounted for this evening after a suicide bombing here in Manchester. They travelled to the city to attend a pop concert – just like the 22 people killed and 60 others injured in the explosion at the end of the show. A fun night out turned to terror as thousands made their escape. Fifteen-year-old Laura MacIntyre and 14-year-old Eilidh MacLeod have not been seen since the outrage. The Prime Minister condemned the appalling, sickening cowardice of those behind the attack. ISIS have claimed responsibility for the atrocity.

Tragically, Eilidh died in the bombing. Laura suffered serious injuries.

Wednesday 24 May 2017
STV News – live from Manchester

With the terrorist threat level here in Manchester, across Scotland and the UK at critical, the hunt intensifies for accomplices of the suicide bomber who killed 22 people and left dozens injured. Soldiers on the streets of London, three more arrests and an off-duty police officer confirmed among the dead. In Libya, Salman Abedi's younger brother has been detained over suspected links to the so-called Islamic State.

DIARY: Wandered about trying to get a sense of the mood… These stories follow the same pattern. And all the talk of 'community coming to terms with' doesn't really apply in cities – if anywhere. Away from the media intensity people are generally just getting on with their lives.

Saturday 3 June 2017
STV News

Thousands of people have marched through the streets of Glasgow demanding a second Independence Referendum. But on the last weekend before the General Election, opposition leaders have been all over Scotland calling on the SNP to drop plans for another vote.

Wednesday 7 June 2017
STV News

The Scottish Labour Leader Kezia Dugdale is denying she told the First Minister she would not oppose a second Independence Referendum following the Brexit vote. The row erupted on STV's *Leaders' Debate* last night and today at First Minister's Questions Nicola Sturgeon says she stands by it 100 per cent. But Ms Dugdale says it is a 'categoric lie'.

NICOLA STURGEON, First Minister: You and I spoke the day after the EU Referendum and you told me then you thought the change occasioned by Brexit meant that you thought Labour should stop opposing a referendum. Now you've changed your mind, but why should everyone else in Scotland be denied the choice?

KEZIA DUGDALE, Scottish Labour Leader: It's a categoric lie from the First Minister and I actually think it diminishes her office. I've never been anything but clear that I stand firmly opposed to independence and a second Independence Referendum because of the damage it would do to Scotland's economy.

BERNARD PONSONBY, Political Editor: It's put Labour on the backfoot. Kezia Dugdale failed to categorically kill this on last night's broadcast, she attempted to do so on social media after the event and today in Parliament she earned a rebuke from the Presiding Officer when she clashed with the First Minister again… I suspect it is one of those 'bubble stories'. It excites people in the political village, I am not sure how it plays out there.

GENERAL ELECTION 2017
Wednesday 7 June 2017
STV News

JM: Harry, what are the final messages the UK party leaders are stressing?

HARRY SMITH, Westminster Correspondent: Given how little time they have, they are all trying to get back to what they see as their core messages. Remember, this election was called because Theresa May wanted voters to decide who was the best person to negotiate Britain's future in Europe. We have actually heard very little of Brexit or the economy. Today she tried to put that right.

THERESA MAY, Prime Minister: Who do you trust to actually have the strong and stable leadership that is going to deliver the best deal for Britain in Europe? Because Brexit matters. Brexit is the basis of everything else. We need to get that Brexit deal right.

HS: What has thrown the Conservative campaign off balance is the issue of security with the two terror attacks in Manchester and London. Theresa May said last night that she would be prepared to change Britain's commitment to the European Human Right Courts in order to protect citizens against terror attacks. That has drawn a strong response from the opposition leaders.

JEREMY CORBYN, Labour Leader: The way you deal with a threat to democracy is not by reducing democracy it's by dealing with the threat. That means properly funding our police and security services. She's the one who took 20 thousand off the street, we'll put ten thousand back on the street straight away.

HS: Both Labour and the Lib Dems also tried today to emphasise their core messages – more police for England and Wales. More money for education and the health service. The SNP wound up their campaign by emphasising they are the only ones who can stand up to the Conservatives and provide a strong voice for Scotland.

BERNARD PONSONBY, Political Editor: Worth reminding ourselves that when the votes were counted here two years ago the SNP swept the board in Glasgow as they almost swept the whole of Scotland. They won 56 out of the 59 seats on a 50 per cent share of the vote. It was a record high for a party at a General Election and for that reason it is unlikely to be matched. In reality, most of the seats in Scotland are safe and tomorrow night we will really be keeping an eye on about 20 key battlegrounds.

Friday 9 June 2017
STV News – live from Westminster

Tonight – Humiliation, but no resignation. Disaster for Theresa May and the Tories as the voters return a hung Parliament. But she will form a minority Government.

And a bruising night for Nicola Sturgeon. She still leads the largest party in Scotland, but huge swings slash majorities and cost the SNP 21 seats at Westminster.

Labour may be back in Scotland with seven MPs. But it was lucky 13 for Ruth Davidson's resurgent Scottish Conservatives.

Battered and bruised, but defiant. Theresa May is tonight trying to soldier on in Government with the support of Northern Ireland's Democratic Unionist Party after her gamble of calling a snap election to boost her Brexit hand backfired. In a night of incredible political upset, far from increasing her majority, Mrs May lost the majority she had. Scotland helped soften her woes a little with the resurgent Scottish Tories winning 13 seats. While some outlying polls had pointed to the possibility of the Conservatives losing their majority, none had predicted the slump in support for the SNP. With the loss of 21 seats and hundreds of thousands of votes, Nicola Sturgeon says she is taking stock of IndyRef2. Jeremy Corbyn confounded his many critics with Labour's performance and the party enjoyed a modest Scottish revival.

THERESA MAY, Prime Minister: What the country needs more than ever is certainty. And having secured the largest number of votes and the greatest number of seats in the General Election, it is clear that only the Conservative and Unionist Party has the legitimacy and ability to provide that certainty by commanding a majority in the House of Commons. This will allow us to come together as a country and channel our energies towards a successful Brexit deal that works for everyone in this country. Let's get to work.

JEREMY CORBYN, Labour Leader: Incredible result for the Labour Party because people voted for hope. Young people and old people all came together yesterday, very high turnout, huge increase in the Labour vote. And they did it because they want to see things done differently and they want hope in their lives. We put on more than three million votes yesterday.

NICOLA STURGEON, SNP leader: We will reflect on these results. We will listen to voters. And we will consider very carefully the best way forward for Scotland. A way forward that is in the interest of all Scotland.

ALEX SALMOND, former First Minister who lost his Westminster seat: In the midst of your glee, you've not seen the last of my bonnets and me.

The Conservatives are the biggest party with 318 seats. Jeremy Corbyn's Labour are up 29 seats taking their total to 261. The SNP remain the third largest party in the UK on 35 seats. And in Scotland, they remain the biggest party. But the biggest victory was for the Scottish Conservatives, now with 13 seats. Labour and the Lib Dems have also made gains with seven and four seats respectively.

COLIN MACKAY, Holyrood Editor at Bute House: Speaking to senior people in the party they say it needs to refocus and get on with the day job delivering on education, health and jobs – just what the opposition were saying throughout the campaign. They are particularly keen to move on from talk of a referendum as soon as possible in case there is another election later this year. Ruth Davidson says another referendum is dead. The message from Nicola Sturgeon seems to be that it's not so much dead as resting.

JM at Westminster: Our Political Editor Bernard Ponsonby is in Stirling tonight – a seat where the SNP lost out to the Conservatives. Bernard, can the First Minister really press ahead with demands for a second referendum?

BERNARD PONSONBY, Political Editor in Stirling: There was an explicit acknowledgement today that this issue was a key factor in the election not least because all of the unionist parties made it an issue. The SNP line on this election is fine as far as it goes. Yes, this was their second most impressive performance in a UK election. Yes, they won the election and, yes, they have more seats than their opponents put together. Nicola Sturgeon, however, knows that momentum is everything in politics and in two years their share of the vote has gone from 50 per cent in 2015, to 46 per cent last year and now to 37 per cent. It simply isn't the backdrop to proceed with any hope that a referendum could be won. Remember the vote for unionist parties yesterday was 63 per cent.

DIARY: Theresa May has announced she is staying on as PM, but she's a dead woman walking in political terms. She'll be gone in months. Every possibility of another election too. It leaves the UK rudderless at a crucial time… A remarkable result and the stability that people have been seeking for a long time now seems a long way off.

Tuesday 13 June 2017
STV News

A financial adviser who ripped off homeowners in a large-scale property fraud has been jailed for 11 years after the longest criminal trial in UK legal history. Edwin McLaren orchestrated the £1.6 million scam by deceiving people into signing over their properties. His wife was jailed for 30 months after being found guilty of mortgage fraud and money laundering.

Tuesday 27 June 2017
STV News

The First Minister says she will reset the timetable for a second Independence Referendum. But Nicola Sturgeon has told STV she still thinks it is likely to be held in this Holyrood term, which runs to 2021. In a statement to MSPs she said she had listened to voters in the General Election who were not ready for another vote, but her opponents said nothing had changed.

NICOLA STURGEON, First Minister: I want to reassure people that our proposal is not for a referendum now or before there is sufficient clarity about the options, but rather to give them a choice at the end of the Brexit process when that clarity has emerged. I am therefore confirming today that having listened and reflected, the Scottish Government will reset the plan.

RUTH DAVIDSON, Scottish Conservative leader: She appears to be in denial about her mistakes over this last year and as a result is leaking credibility and confidence in her leadership by the hour.

KEZIA DUGDALE, Scottish Labour Leader: The threat of an unwanted second Independence Referendum is dead. And this didn't happen because Nicola Sturgeon wanted it to. The people of Scotland have taken that decision for her.

COLIN MACKAY, Holyrood Editor: The SNP's allies in the Yes campaign, the Scottish Socialists described today's statement as a climbdown and the Greens were disappointed. The First Minister hasn't kicked her referendum plans into the long grass, in fact they are barely in the medium grass, but they are a bit further away than before the election.

OPENING OF QUEENSFERRY CROSSING

Tuesday 29 August 2017
STV News

After the biggest construction project in Scotland in a generation, the Queensferry Crossing is now just hours away from opening to general traffic. The Scottish Government is spending £1.35 billion on the replacement for the old Forth Road Bridge. The first cars and lorries will start crossing in the early hours of tomorrow morning.

DAVID COWAN, Chief Reporter: Ten years after the design work began, six years after the builders moved in, the Queensferry Crossing takes its first traffic. The convoy headed north at a stately ten mph. When it's fully operational, this will be a 70 mph motorway.

Vox Pops

It's a world beater.

It is the world's longest three tower cable-stay and yeah, world-class engineering.

Done much smaller bridges than this before but to do this bridge, being Scottish, it's fantastic to have been a part of it, it really is.

GEORGE ROSIE, writer: The steel deck sections come from China, the steel cable boxes come from China, the steel cables come from Switzerland, the steel caissons come from Poland, the steel sheeting for the coffer dams come from Spain. The only steel major component that comes from Britain is the box girders for the south viaduct. It's being said that when the tenders went out for the deck sections, which is a big job, not one British company bid for the job. And this situation will lead to British companies doing less and less and relying more and more on other people. I think the question we've got to ask ourselves is, could we have done this bridge for ourselves? And the way things stand the answers might be no, we couldn't.

KEZIA DUGDALE RESIGNS AS SCOTTISH LABOUR LEADER

Tuesday 29 August 2017
STV News (cont)

Tonight – Kezia quits. As the Labour Leader announces her shock resignation, the party searches for its fifth Scottish leader in six years.

Kezia Dugdale has told STV News she had given all that she could in the last two years as Scottish Labour Leader and feels she is leaving the party in a better state than she inherited it. She announced her resignation in a message to Labour MSPs last night.

KEZIA DUGDALE, former Scottish Labour Leader: I took the summer to reflect on the General Election result. I've taken the view that the Scottish Labour Party's made a lot of progress under my leadership, but for it to take even greater progress there needs to be someone new at the helm.

Kezia Dugdale is Scottish Labour's eighth leader since Devolution. Donald Dewar helped deliver Devolution and was probably the last leader to really be loved by his party. After his death came Henry McLeish, followed by Jack McConnell who was the last Labour Leader to win a Holyrood election in 2003. But in 2007 he was the first to lose to the SNP, followed briefly by Wendy Alexander then Iain Gray who lost to a majority SNP Government. Johann Lamont led the party through the Independence Referendum, but quit in a huge row to be replaced by Jim Murphy. He quit after Labour were almost wiped out at the 2015 Westminster election. Kezia Dugdale took over in 2015 and tried to steady the ship but led the party to some of its worst election results, despite taking six more seats at this year's General Election.

JM: She says she jumped and wasn't pushed, so what are the political dynamics at play in the forthcoming leadership contest?

BERNARD PONSONBY, Political Editor: Quite a simple one, really: will the new leader march in sync with Jeremy Corbyn or will they not? For supporters of Mr Corbyn who have been frustrated with Kezia Dugdale, it is frankly time to 'wee or get off the pot'. That means a candidate from their perspective who shares Mr Corbyn's Socialism and who will lead from the Left.

DIARY: She's a decent woman Kezia Dugdale, but I don't think she was cut out for leadership. Probably too nice.

Wednesday 4 October 2017
STV News

It was billed as the speech which would reassert her authority, but today the Prime Minister's keynote address to her party conference was marred by a prankster presenting her with a P45, a coughing fit and a backdrop which began to fall apart as she spoke.

It was very uncomfortable watching it live. People were cringing for her on a human level.

Thursday 2 November 2017
Scotland Tonight

Plans are underway that would see gender recognition laws in Scotland radically reformed. Launched today by the Equalities Minister, the consultation proposes that people will be able to legally change gender from 16 years old without having to provide medical evidence, and allow people to register as non-binary – identifying as neither male or female.

JM: What does non-binary mean?

OCEANA: It means a lot of different things to a lot of different people, but essentially it's identifying as something other than male or female. There are lots of different non-binary identities and I think you would probably get a different answer from every single non-binary person you went to. But essentially, it's an ability to identify as something other than male or female. Whilst these terms fit for lots of people, for some of us they just don't.

JM: But you can understand, perhaps, why the public might have a problem with this. There's a big debate, even within the wider LGBTQ community, about this. And if that's there, can you understand why, maybe, the public has a problem with it?

VIC: I think that it's completely understandable that people might not know a lot about non-binary issues, or struggle to understand them, because I think that one of the first things we're taught, even from when we're little, basically, is that you have people in the world and people are either men or women. And it's quite a big deal to say that's not really the case and there's a bunch of us who don't feel like that's the case for us. We don't expect people to be experts, but what we want is the same thing that everyone wants. We want people to use language that includes us and is respectful of who we are. And we want to be able to have documents that reflect who we are, and don't make us feel like we aren't seen.

JM: We are talking – and I think the official statistics say 0.4 per cent of the population. It is a very small number and it's a big change to accommodate that. Some might say the accommodation should come from you.

VIC: I think the first thing to say is we definitely don't know how many non-binary people there are... I agree with you, it's probably a really small number of us. But it's also important to say that we're very much not calling for the whole world to become gender neutral. We are very happy for the approach to be taken that there is a mixture of facilities, some of which are separate, some of which are gender neutral, but all of which make sure that all people who use spaces have the option to go to the place that makes them feel comfortable.

DIARY: This 'non-binary' issue is especially controversial, even in the LGBTQ community. Feminists, especially, have an issue with men – biological men – identifying as women. I found little sympathy for them among gay colleagues.

Tuesday 10 November 2017
STV News

Alex Salmond's decision to launch his own weekly TV talk show on RT, a Russian state-controlled broadcaster, has been criticised by the First Minister. Nicola Sturgeon said had she been asked in advance she would have told her predecessor to take the show elsewhere. She said her party will not shy away from criticising the Russian Government when necessary.

KENNY DALGLISH

Wednesday 15 November 2017
Scotland Tonight

Kenny Dalglish's achievements, as a Scotland international, a club player and as a winning manager are well documented. It's not often that the man himself, though, lays bare his soul and talks about some of the trials and tribulations he's faced along the way. Aged 66 and with a new film about his life hitting the big screen, John MacKay travelled down to Liverpool for a chat with the footballing legend.

JM: The film goes back to your roots in Glasgow and we see you where you were brought up with your sister. Obviously, you talk about a very, very happy upbringing. In footballing terms, you tell the story about when Sean Fallon came to sign you for Celtic, that you actually confirmed that story about taking down Rangers posters. Do you remember that clearly?

KENNY DALGLISH: Yeah, we moved to Ibrox by that time and we were sitting having our tea, and my dad was coming home from work as usual, and mostly people that were working came home, had their tea and then went and had a sleep on the couch. My dad was having a kip on the couch and the doorbell went and it was Sean. We invited him in and I thought there were a couple of Rangers pictures up there and it might be as well Sean never saw them. By the way, Sean would not have bothered, he wouldn't have bothered. He wasn't signing a picture, he was there to sign me and ask me to come to Celtic and train, and my dad said, 'It's the best place for you to go.'

JM: And what did Jock Stein tell you, what did you learn from him?

KD: He used to take a great deal of time coaching the kids because obviously the Lions were flying. They won everything except the lottery, I think. So, they were flying and, by the way, they were really humble and welcoming, and we used to train pre-season and everybody trained together and there was no arrogance, no big headedness. They welcomed you in and they were never hard on you if you made a mistake. They encouraged you. So, that was hugely helpful. So, between them, the Lions and Big Jock, we'd a good chance at having a go at being a footballer, didn't we?

JM: You tell a lovely story, I think it was your debut for Celtic, and you were asked if you were nervous?

KD: That was Bobby Murdoch asked me that. That was my league debut and Bobby had been injured and had been away at a health farm and came back up for the game against Raith Rovers. And I was getting ready and he said, 'Are you nervous?' And I went, 'No, not really.' He says, 'You're trying to put your left boot on your right foot.' I don't know if I was or not, I just went, 'OK Bobby.' But anyway, I think I went out with them on the right feet.

JM: You've spent probably more than half your life now in England. Your family is in England. What does Scotland still mean to you?

KD: I'm very, very proud to be Scottish. I'm a proud Glaswegian. A lot of people say I've lost my accent. It did used to be stronger than this, but I think I've still got it. For me, I'll always be Scottish, I'll always be a Glaswegian. But this is our home in Liverpool. Marina's the same. She's been down here longer than both of us lived in Scotland. She's proud to be a Glaswegian and proud to be Scottish. But this is where the kids have been brought up and invariably you live where your children have been brought up, although they fly the nest as well and set up their own life. So, we're here and we're very content here. But we'll never ever forget our roots.

DIARY: One of the few people to whom the description 'legend' applies. He was very Glaswegian – down to earth, very modest and with the range of facial expressions for which he's renowned and mimicked.

Saturday 18 November 2017
STV News

Richard Leonard is the new Leader of the Scottish Labour Party. He defeated Anas Sarwar by 3,000 votes and quickly declared he hopes to be the next First Minister.

BERNARD PONSONBY, Political Editor: He won by 3,000 votes across an electorate comprising members, registered supporters and affiliated supporters. He won 52 per cent to 48 per cent among individual members and was turbo charged to victory by the votes of trade unionists beating Anas Sarwar 77 per cent to 23 per cent in the vote among affiliated supporters.

Monday 20 November 2017
STV News

Kezia Dugdale was not given permission from the Labour Party to take part in *I'm A Celebrity Get Me Out Of Here*. The party's new leader Richard Leonard says she spoke to him about taking three weeks off to raise money for charity, but not about going into the jungle. The former leader has come in for severe criticism from her colleagues who will meet tomorrow to consider suspending her from the parliamentary group.

Scotland Tonight

JM: It has overshadowed the early days of your leadership.

RICHARD LEONARD, Scottish Labour Leader: I am disappointed and I would like to be sitting here talking about the policies on which I was elected, the platform on which Scottish Labour Party members have now given me a mandate. So, it is a distraction and it is one that the media are particularly interested in looking at for reasons I completely understand. But when I was out yesterday afternoon in Rutherglen, and the local council by-election, who was in and out of the jungle was not the question that people were putting to us.

JM: You are the seventh Scottish Labour Leader in ten years. Labour are now in third place in Scotland. What are you going to do that's any different? What are you going to be able to do to transform that other leaders have said they would do and haven't done?

RL: I was elected with a mandate on a radical platform of extending public ownership, of ending austerity, the thing we've just been speaking about, and of redistributing not just wealth but power from the few to the many. And it is about how that looks in the Scottish context.

DIARY: Calls for her suspension, sacking etc. I don't have a strong opinion, but more people will know who Kezia Dugdale is after this in Scotland than will know their new leader Richard Leonard. Politics needs different approaches to engage.

2018

Tuesday 13 February 2018
STV News

The Scottish and UK Governments are being urged to intervene over the future of the Bifab fabrication yards in Fife and the Western Isles. Management today issued around 260 redundancy notices to core workers as work dries up. The yards now face possible closure.

DIARY: Job losses threatened at fabrication yards dealing in renewables. I asked the question on *Scotland Tonight* – why has Scotland missed the boat on constructing infrastructure for wind power? Denmark and Germany well ahead. Sounds like Government inconsistency and incompetence.

BEAST FROM THE EAST
Wednesday 28 February 2018
STV News

The Siberian blast dubbed the Beast from the East has slammed into Scotland with a vengeance. Much of the Central Belt is on red alert for serious disruption and even risk to life. Blizzards and plunging temperatures brought standstill with every form of transport hit hard. Hundreds of schools shut down. Workers across Scotland stayed home or left early. We have comprehensive coverage from around the country.

KAYE NICOLSON, Reporter, at Transport Control Centre, South Queensferry:

The screens behind me show some treacherous conditions across Scotland's trunk roads. Just outside this building are the three bridges over the Forth – traffic on the Queensferry Crossing is light as drivers heed the warnings, the Forth Road Bridge is closed because of high winds and no trains are travelling over the Forth Bridge. Scotrail has cancelled all train services, while there are no flights from Glasgow Airport.

Thursday 1 March 2018
STV News

As Scotland remains in the grip of its worst snowstorm in years, the First Minister has criticised hauliers after several trucks jack-knifed blocking the M80 motorway during the weather red alert. Hundreds of motorists were stuck enduring freezing temperatures. Stranded, hungry and desperate. The authorities had repeatedly told drivers to stay off the roads.

CHRIS CLEMENTS, Reporter on M80: The M80 is just behind me and it's now opened in both directions. A handful of vehicles remain stranded just north of the Castlecary viaduct, but traffic is moving slowly but surely. Last night was another story. This stretch was gridlocked. Myself and the crew ended up stuck in that tailback for a few hours before we managed to make our way into Cumbernauld. That was a ghost town, with cars abandoned left and right. Back on the motorway, unable to go forward, unable to go back, motorists had to sit tight and wait for rescue.

JM: The public transport network has been virtually paralysed across Central Scotland. It was hoped that cancelled trains and buses would begin to run again. But continued bad weather means disruption remains.

EWAN PETRIE, Reporter at Glasgow Central Station: This is Scotland's biggest and busiest railway station but just take a look at it this evening. Normally at this time the concourse would be packed with commuters making their way home from work. But tonight, there are just a few people here looking to find a way home. And it's been like this for most of the day. There are currently just two services running from here, one to Kilmarnock and the other to Ayr. All other services, including the west coast main line route, have been cancelled all day. It's a similar story at Queen Street – services have been running between Glasgow and Edinburgh every half hour from lunchtime today, but are due to finish around 7.00pm.

Vox Pops

I've had to cancel two flights and one train trip, so far.

I'm trying to get to Inverness and have been since yesterday afternoon.

It's just tiring now. At first it was a bit of fun, it was exciting, but now it's just boring. Fed up.

JM: Communities all across Scotland have been pulling together. Sharon Frew has been out in Fife and the Lothians seeing how they're coping with winter at its worst.

SHARON FREW, Reporter: Popping out for supplies in Newtongrange involved quite a trek for many... For this mother of two making it to her front gate through deep snow is easy compared to last night's journey. She walked for three hours to get home from work – nine miles in snow after all buses from Edinburgh were cancelled.

SAMANTHA ADDERLEY: I just kept on walking... There was moments of icy eyelashes and my phone was dead. I've got two little girls to get home to, so I don't think there was any other option, so that's why I took it. I just thought, I'll just walk. I'll get there eventually and just plod on.

Vox Pop

The shelves are half empty, there's virtually nothing left. There's no bread, milk, anything like that. Everybody is out trying to help neighbours and stick together.

JM: When times are tough that's when community spirit is often at its best. From delivering food to those stuck in their cars overnight, to driving nurses into work – just some of the incredible acts of kindness shown by everyday people since the snowstorm swept in.

KELLY-ANN WOODLAND, reporter: From the volunteer crew at the RNLI delivering prescriptions to the elderly in Anstruther. To locals digging out fire engines in Skelmorlie... Among the heroes of the night – Barry Currie who raced out, with his friend, armed with food and drinks for stranded motorists on the M80 at Cumbernauld.

BARRY CURRIE: We had flasks with Bovril, cans of Irn Bru, biscuits.

KAW: Getting around in the snow was no problem for Ross MacKinnon. So, when he heard hospital staff were stuggling to get into work, he took to social media to offer lifts in his company's 4x4.

ROSS MACKINNON: The type of people that we're dealing with in health care and nursing, y'know, these are lassies that work in the premature care ward and they're so passionate about what they do. I mean, I was hearing stories about girls walking for three hours to get to their work through the blizzard... That's Glasgow, innit? That's what happens in Glasgow when there's any sort of adversity. People just come together. I love that.

MICHAEL SHEEN
Monday 19 March 2018
Scotland Tonight

He's one of Britain's most acclaimed actors, but in recent years Michael Sheen has begun to focus more and more on matters beyond the stage and screen. A drive for social justice has seen him embrace a number of causes. Today, he is in Glasgow targeting the household debt crisis with the launch of a campaign aimed at providing more affordable alternatives to high interest credit providers.

JM: Is there a concern there may be a backlash? You sometimes see it with other significant and famous figures in political activism, Bono or George Clooney, for example. There is a reaction to that, rich people telling us what to do. Is that a risk?

MICHAEL SHEEN: That is fair enough. I think you have to be measured by what you do and what you achieve. I have made conscious decisions to change my life and the circumstances of my life and the focus of my life. Ultimately, you have to be judged by what you do, not what you say, so I totally understand why people are suspicious of that kind of stuff... It is fair enough. But hopefully, when the day of judgement comes, I can stand there and be judged on what I did rather than what I said.

JM: You have portrayed some quite challenging figures. Sir David Frost, Kenneth Williams, Brian Clough and Tony Blair, of course. What drew you to these characters? Was it something about the challenge of it?

MS: I was offered the job.

JM: There goes that question!

MS: It always tends to come down to that. I can dress it up and make it fancy, but ultimately, thankfully, Peter Morgan, who wrote many of those things you just named, asked me to do it... But they are great parts and they were great scripts and it was a real honour to be able to do them.

DIARY: Unlike some celebrities, for whom it seems like it's virtue signalling, he clearly believes what he's saying and is prepared to work for it. Nice warm guy... I didn't call him Martin Sheen *(another famous actor)*, so that was good.

Monday 26 March 2018
STV News

The lawyer representing a former Catalan Government minister being threatened with extradition from Scotland to Spain says she will hand herself in to police later this week. An international arrest warrant has been issued for Clara Ponsati who works as a researcher at St Andrews University. The First Minister says the Spanish Government's action is deeply regrettable.

DIARY: Legally, there is little the Scottish Government can do, but the nationalists are going crazy. The law is the law and the Catalan ministers all knew what they were getting into. That said, it seems ill-judged by the Spanish Government to jail them.

The Catalan Government had unilaterally held an Independence Referendum, which the Spanish declared as illegal.

Monday 16 April 2018

DIARY: A planned discussion between three MPs became problematic when it looked like all three would have to pull out because of a late vote at Westminster. Then one of them could make it, then another, then all three again. Just before going on air one of them was instructed by his whips not to leave Westminster, so back to two again.

Thursday 26 April 2018
STV News

The Scottish Conservative Party Leader Ruth Davidson has announced that she is pregnant and due to give birth in the autumn. She and her partner Jen Wilson say they are excited and daunted by the prospect of parenthood. Her Deputy, Jackson Carlaw, will take over interim charge of the party for a few months when she's on maternity leave.

DIARY: The Scottish Conservative leader, Ruth Davidson, announces her pregnancy – an unmarried lesbian. It is another sign of how much the world has changed in that regard.

ARCHIE MACPHERSON
Monday 30 April 2018
Scotland Tonight

The football World Cup starts in six weeks – and yet again it will take place without Scotland. As every Scottish fan knows, two decades have passed since the national team last qualified for a major tournament. Before that, World Cup qualification was almost routine. The golden age between 1974 and 1998 has now been chronicled in a new book from the doyen of football commentators, Archie Macpherson, who commentated on every one of the Scottish games.

JM: So, Archie, was this truly a golden age, a golden era for Scottish football?

ARCHIE MACPHERSON, Sports Broadcaster: If you consider the howls of anguish we've been hearing every time we failed to get to a World Cup since '98, the answer is quite simply yes. We achieved it, we got there. Yes, there was frustration, disappointment, sometimes howls of despair, but we were there. And we now regret, we look back, not just with nostalgia, but with pain. And I'm trying to penetrate this thicket of disappointment and get through to people and show them what it was like to be there. And I was fortunate maybe to be, uniquely, at all 18 games as a commentator, so I was in the trenches, as it were. And I want to convince people that there's not one person I talk to, player, official, or supporter, who regrets being there, who would want this to be eradicated from their memories.

DIARY: It's my era of football and Archie was the voice of that. Didn't need any notes. Could have talked all day to him about that.

Friday 4 May 2018
STV News

Steven Gerrard is the new Rangers manager. He has signed a four-year contract and takes up his new role next month. Gerrard says it was a no-brainer to accept the job after he was approached and he will relish the challenge.

DIARY: It's up there – although not quite – with Souness in 1986. I say not quite because of the fact that it has happened before and Souness was epoch-changing. It's great box office and brings a spotlight onto Scottish football. It's a huge risk – despite Gerrard's superb career at Liverpool. That doesn't always transfer to being a good manager.

Wednesday 13 June 2018
STV News

The entire SNP group at Westminster walked out of the Commons today after their leader was ordered out of the chamber for refusing to accept a ruling from the Speaker. The MPs were complaining that not enough time had been allowed to debate how powers would be returned from Brussels to Holyrood after Brexit. The SNP say it amounts to a power grab by Whitehall. The UK Government says they are indulging in gesture politics.

GLASGOW SCHOOL OF ART SECOND FIRE
Saturday 16 June 2018
STV News – live from Glasgow city centre

There is a sense of shock and devastation here in the centre of Glasgow, and across Scotland tonight, following the dramatic scenes of the past few hours. A massive fire has ripped through the world-famous Glasgow School of Art – for the second time in four years. This is what it looks like now – the historic Mackintosh Building reduced to little more than a smouldering shell. So ferocious was this blaze, that once it took hold, it quickly spread to the O2 ABC venue next door. As you can see, that too has suffered extensive damage. The fire broke out just after 11.00pm last night. Local pubs and nightclubs, which were packed with Friday night crowds, had to be evacuated, as more than 120 firefighters battled the flames.

DONALD TRUMP IN SCOTLAND
Saturday 14 July 2018
STV News

The US President has been heckled by demonstrators while playing a round of golf at his Turnberry resort. Donald Trump is in Scotland with his wife ahead of a summit with the Russian President in Finland on Monday. A small group of campaigners shouted at him from the beach as he went past. Police today confirmed they're investigating a breach of the air exclusion zone, after a paraglider flew near the hotel last night.

DIARY: A lot of protests about President Donald Trump's visit to Scotland and thousands took part, mostly in Edinburgh… Donald Trump lives in an alternative reality – or so it appears – but he was elected and still has huge support in the US. We should take advantage of that – our First Minister included – but we don't.

RUNRIG'S LAST CONCERT
Thursday 16 August 2018
Scotland Tonight

It's the last dance for Runrig. Thousands of fans from across the world will gather in Stirling over the weekend for sell out concerts as the band take to the stage for the final time. From their island background they took their music to an international audience, giving a modern voice to traditional Gaelic culture. But now, they say the band has come to a natural end.

RORY MACDONALD, Runrig: We're going to feel very sad not to be doing this anymore, that's for sure, because when you go on stage and play there's nothing like it, it's just a wonderful feeling and it always has been that way with us. But having said that, the decision we took is one that I believe we've all taken for the right reasons. It doesn't feel like it's something that's been taken away from us by an external source. We've decided, we've controlled the agenda. So, we're at peace with that... We didn't want to carry on and then start to get the sense we were going down a bit and that can be a bit sad. So, to go out when we feel we're at a peak – I think that we feel that – is a positive thing to do.

CALUM MACDONALD, Runrig: What we've always done from day one is produce music. And whatever we've done and whatever influence is through the medium of music, the song... The band have been perceived and commentated on in positive and negative ways through the years. And I think there's a lot of commentators that haven't quite grasped maybe the essence of the band. Because we were trying to make a noise in rock music, that didn't happen for artists from the West Highlands and from Gaelic backgrounds. So, there was a disconnect in the way that we were and are perceived. For some.

DIARY: These guys have been the greatest artistic influence on my life. It's a privilege of the job to interview people you admire.

POLICE INVESTIGATE ALEX SALMOND
Friday 24 August 2018
STV News

Police Scotland have confirmed enquiries are at an early stage concerning allegations that the former First Minister Alex Salmond sexually harassed two women. Today Mr Salmond launched a strong attack on a Scottish Government probe into the allegations, vowing to take them to court to show he had no opportunity to adequately defend himself against his accusers.

BERNARD PONSONBY, Political Editor: Alex Salmond stands accused of inappropriate sexual conduct towards two women in December 2013. In January the Scottish Government received two complaints in relation to Mr Salmond's conduct. The Permanent Secretary – Scotland's top civil servant – Leslie Evans – launched a probe. The former First Minister was informed of these complaints in March. The results of the probe were given to Alex Salmond on Wednesday. Yesterday, lawyers for Mr Salmond sought to prevent the Government from making the probe public by raising an action at the Court of Session. He alleges the Government probe is illegal, claiming in effect it breaches the rules of natural justice. Today, the First Minister defended the Permanent Secretary and the integrity of the harassment procedures. Mr Salmond claims the Scottish Government have referred the matter to the police. After a long period of refusing to confirm anything, Police Scotland said this afternoon they were carrying out an assessment of information, adding enquiries were at an early stage. Opposition politicians say alleged inappropriate conduct should be investigated. The news has stunned the body politic and SNP colleagues in particular. It's worth stressing, Alex Salmond stands accused, nothing has been proved against him. This, though, is another story of a public figure embroiled in serious allegations where respecting the rights of the aggrieved and the presumption of innocence seems a difficult balancing act for the scales of justice.

Tuesday 28 August 2018

DIARY: BBC hiring our staff in numbers. What an indictment of existing BBC staff that they're choosing people from STV for the plumb jobs.

BBC Scotland hired several STV News staff in advance of the launch of their new channel. Almost all of the prominent roles in their news programmes were filled by these former STV News colleagues. It seemed to be insulting that they didn't consider their existing staff up to it. The audiences for its news programmes, *The Nine* and *The Seven*, were negligible from the start. *The Nine* was taken off air in 2024.

KELLY-ANN WOODLAND BECOMES CO-PRESENTER

Thursday 30 August 2018

DIARY: It was announced to the newsroom that Kelly-Ann would be my co-anchor. A spontaneous round of applause. Kelly-Ann deserves it. Very popular because she has a great attitude and works hard.

Thursday 6 September 2018

DIARY: Kelly-Ann and me doing interviews. She let it be known that she watched me when she was at school, so I'm sure that'll be a line.

Kelly-Ann became my co-anchor on Monday 10 September 2018. Since then the STV News at Six, along with our colleagues at STV North, has outperformed the BBC *Six O'Clock News* and *Reporting Scotland* almost continuously.

This was different from the co-anchoring I had done earlier in my career. Kelly-Ann was in the studio in Edinburgh, so quite aside from the technical challenges, we didn't have the visual cues that are such an important part of an on-screen relationship. We knew each other well, though, so we managed to establish that important rapport quickly.

From this date on most of the STV News scripts would have been read by both Kelly-Ann and me.

CLOSURE OF MICHELIN TYRE FACTORY

Monday 5 November 2018
STV News

Breaking news as we come on air first, and tyre giant Michelin is to close its Dundee factory by 2020. The 850 staff have been summoned to a meeting tomorrow morning.

DIARY: Long time since we've had a closure on that scale. A huge blow for Dundee.

Tuesday 6 November 2018
STV News

Scottish Government ministers are to attempt to persuade tyre giants Michelin to change the decision to axe their Dundee plant. It was confirmed today almost 850 jobs are to go, with the firm facing falling demand for its products and increasing competition from the Far East. The French company's local manager has apologised to the workforce for the manner in which they heard the news, after the announcement was revealed through the media last night.

CENTENARY OF FIRST WORLD WAR ARMISTICE

Sunday 11 November 2018
STV NEWS

It's 100 years since the guns fell silent on the Western Front and the First World War was over. Thousands of people around Scotland joined together to mark the centenary of the armistice with remembrance events up and down the length and breadth of the country.

EVANNA HOLLAND, reporter: It will take seven hours for the names of the war dead of Scotland to run over the face of Holyrood tonight, a poignant reminder of the human cost of World War One.

They shall grow not old, as we that are left grow old.

Age shall not weary them, nor the years condemn.

At the going down of the sun and in the morning

We will remember them.

THERESA MAY'S BREXIT DEAL
Tuesday 13 November 2018
STV News

Just over an hour ago, it was announced a Brexit deal has been reached by negotiators in Brussels and will be the focus of a crunch Cabinet meeting tomorrow. A UK Government source confirmed there had been an agreement at a technical level, but Theresa May will need to win the support of her Cabinet. There has been no official confirmation from either Downing Street or Brussels.

Wednesday 14 November 2018
STV News

There is a fevered atmosphere in Westminster tonight as the Prime Minister fights to win support for an agreement with the European Union on Brexit. Theresa May has been locked in Downing Street with Cabinet colleagues all afternoon, with no sign yet of a conclusion to discussions. Tomorrow, the Commons will get the opportunity to debate the draft agreement although, as yet, the text of the documents are yet to be published. It is looking increasingly unlikely that there is a Commons majority for Theresa May, with Scottish Conservatives tonight seeking clarification on what it will mean for the Scottish Fishing Industry.

Thursday 15 November 2018
STV News

In an astonishing day at Westminster, the collective ministerial line on the Brexit deal fell apart. The Prime Minister endured a torrid time in the Commons defending her draft agreement. Two Cabinet members resigned and more are rumoured to be on the brink as Conservative MPs moved to oust her. And as we come on air, Theresa May has launched a fightback at a hastily arranged news conference in Downing Street where she defended her position.

THERESA MAY, Prime Minister: I believe with every fibre of my being that the course I have set out is the right one for our country and all our people. From the very beginning I have known what I wanted to deliver for the British people to honour their vote in the referendum.

Monday 10 December 2018
STV News

Tomorrow night's key Commons vote on Theresa May's Brexit deal with the European Union has been deferred. After a chaotic day at Westminster, the Prime Minister conceded that the vote would be lost, telling MPs she would now seek assurances from other EU leaders on the issue of the Northern Ireland backstop. The decision brought criticism from across the chamber and from the Speaker, John Bercow. Mrs May would not say when the vote would be re-scheduled, but it could now be in the New Year.

BERNARD PONSONBY, Political Editor: I think you would have to go back to Black Wednesday during John Major's Premiership to witness a more shambolic day in the life of a British Prime Minister. For days ministers told us this vote would go ahead. This morning Cabinet Minister after Cabinet Minister insisted it would go ahead, including the Scottish Secretary David Mundell. When journalists started to speculate it would not go ahead, Downing Street continued to insist that it would. Then we were told it would not, much to the anger of many of the 164 MPs who have already spoken in the debate and the annoyance of Mr Speaker. This is a shambles, no other word for it.

Tuesday 11 December 2018
STV News

The Prime Minister started a diplomatic charm offensive today as she tried desperately to get EU leaders to agree to clarifications on the Brexit deal that will get rebellious Conservative MPs on side. It comes as rumours sweep Westminster that there could be close to 48 Tory MPs ready to force a confidence vote in her leadership.

Wednesday 12 December 2018

DIARY: The Conservatives held a vote of no confidence in Theresa May. The indications early on were that she would win, but by how much? The result at 9.00pm showed she'd won by 200 votes to 117. A win, but not a resounding one. I don't know that she'll last much into the New Year, with a new vote on her Brexit deal due towards the end of January.

THERESA MAY, Prime Minister: This has been a long and challenging day, but at the end of it I'm pleased to have received the backing of my colleagues in tonight's ballot. Whilst I am grateful for that support, a significant number of colleagues did cast a vote against me and I've listened to what they said following this ballot. We now need to get on with the job of delivering Brexit for the British people and building a better future for this country that delivers on the vote that people gave. That brings back control of our money, our borders and our laws. That protects jobs, security and the Union. That brings the country back together, rather than entrenching division.

2019

Tuesday 8 January 2019
STV News

Alex Salmond has won his court case against the Scottish Government, who admitted acting unlawfully. The First Minister says it makes no difference to the allegations of sexual misconduct, which Mr Salmond denies. The Scottish Government appointed a civil servant to investigate the allegations who had prior involvement in the case. Mr Salmond says the Government's top civil servant should quit.

Tuesday 15 January 2019
Scotland Tonight

In the end, it wasn't even close. Tonight, the House of Commons overwhelmingly rejected Theresa May's draft deal for taking the UK out of the European Union. MPs voted it down by a majority of 230 – the biggest defeat ever suffered by a British Government. A vote of no confidence in Theresa May's administration will now be held tomorrow evening.

DIARY: It is a mark of our times that that record-breaking defeat – which any other time would surely have led to the collapse of the Government and resignation of the Prime Minister – really just means she will have to try another approach.

Wednesday 16 January 2019
Scotland Tonight

Theresa May has retained her grip on power after her minority Government saw off a Commons no confidence vote by a majority of 19. Tonight's vote came in the wake of yesterday's massive defeat of her Brexit deal. But this time around the Tory rebels and the DUP coalesced behind her in opposition to Jeremy Corbyn's attempt to spark a General Election.

DIARY: Theresa May called for party leaders to consult on how to move forward and

Corbyn refused. The only admirable thing about May is her resilience, but we need better than that and Corbyn is utterly incapable of providing it. And everything trundles on.

Thursday 17 January 2019
STV News

The mother, who successfully underwent a double hand transplant, says she is 'absolutely elated' and has vowed to the donor's family to 'do something wonderful' after her life-changing surgery. Corinne Hutton has been speaking for the first time, since her operation, of her growing confidence after being able to move her new fingers. Surgeons are delighted with the 48-year-old's progress.

SHARON FREW, Chief Reporter: The mother of one had almost given up hope of this transplant after dozens of false alarms over the last five years. Corrine's hands and feet were amputated when she developed acute sepsis. The 25 blood transfusions she was given then to save her life meant finding a suitable match was difficult. Then last Monday, she got the call a donor had been found.

CORINNE HUTTON, hand transplant patient: I am able to move all my fingers. I have to be held back a bit in case I do too much. That has given me a lot of confidence that I can go on and make them do more than is expected of me. I know I am determined. I will push it hard.

ALEX SALMOND ARRESTED AND CHARGED

Thursday 24 January 2019
STV News

Scotland's former First Minister Alex Salmond has appeared in court facing 14 charges including two of attempted rape. Speaking after a short court appearance he said he rejects any allegations of criminality. Mr Salmond was charged yesterday. Police Scotland launched the investigation into the former First Minister after Scotland's senior civil servant passed on the findings of an internal investigation last year.

Thursday 21 February 2019
STV News

A 16-year-old has been convicted of the abduction, the rape and the murder of Alesha MacPhail. The jury returned after only three hours with their verdict. Alesha was killed after being taken from her grandparents' home in Rothesay last July. The trial was so grim that the jurors have been offered counselling to deal with what they saw in court. A forensic pathologist said the injuries Alesha sustained were the worst he'd ever seen. The judge said it was one of the most wicked, evil crimes the court had ever heard.

Friday 22 January 2019
STV News

The schoolboy who became a killer can be identified as Aaron Campbell after a judge removed his right to anonymity. The 16-year-old lived just minutes away from the Rothesay flat where he abducted, raped and murdered Alesha MacPhail. Legal restrictions on naming him were lifted due to the severity of his crimes after an application from STV and other media organisations.

DIARY: What's striking about recent cases is that you can now see the killer and the poor victims in videos online. Previously, all you'd have would be grainy, blurred photos. It makes them more real somehow and it's their normality that shocks.

Monday 25 February 2019

DIARY: The new 'Nine' news programme launched on the BBC Scotland channel after much hoopla. Not that impressive. Looks good, but being an hour, it is very flabby.

Tuesday 26 February 2019
STV News

Neil Lennon will make a sensational return to Celtic after Brendan Rodgers quit the club for Leicester City today. The timing of Rodger's departure has dismayed many Celtic fans with the club aiming to win a historic treble of domestic trophies. Lennon, a former captain and manager at the club is expected to be named as interim manager until the end of the season.

Monday 4 March 2019
Scotland Tonight

Dame Emma Thompson and a number of SNP MPs have joined other influential women from across the UK in signing an open letter in support of transgender women in Scotland. Concerns have been raised about women's spaces such as changing rooms being accessed by men who identify as women, but haven't undergone any physical changes. But the letter takes aim at what it says is a rise in 'ill-informed articles and commentary' where writers insinuate that transwomen are not women. And it goes on to state that the right of transpeople to access gender specific services is an already settled legal matter.

A particular feature of the transgender debate has been the refusal of pro-trans organisations to debate with anyone who holds an opposing view. That stance cannot be allowed to prevent the issue from being explored, but it makes it harder.

Monday 11 March 2019
STV News

A serial killer branded 'the most dangerous man to have walked the streets of Scotland in our lifetimes' has died in prison, aged 73. Angus Sinclair was convicted of taking the lives of four women and linked to the deaths of several more. It's understood he suffered a series of strokes. He was serving a 37-year sentence for the murders of Helen Scott and Christine Eadie – the teenagers disappeared from Edinburgh's World's End pub in 1977. Sinclair was finally brought to justice almost four decades later.

Scotland Tonight

We assessed the crimes of Angus Sinclair with the former Deputy Chief Constable Tom Wood, who led the 2004 police investigation into the World's End murders.

DEPUTY CHIEF CONSTABLE TOM WOOD: Angus Sinclair was probably one of the most dangerous men to disgrace the face of Scotland in the last 100 years. He spent 47 years in prison and he was only at liberty for 12 years as an adult, and yet in that time he was convicted of murdering four women, he raped and abused another ten children and we suspect that he murdered another three women. So, by any measure, he rates amongst the most dangerous men who we've ever had the misfortune to have in Scotland.

JM: In your role investigating him, you did meet him. What sort of man was he?

TW: When we met him in 2004, he was a small, thin, grey-haired man that you would have passed in the street and never taken a second look at. When you meet these people and you know what their backgrounds are, you expect somehow to be meeting somebody extraordinary, you expect somehow to be able to tell from their demeanour or their appearance what kind of person they are. It's not true. Angus Sinclair was a nonentity.

JM: What was it like working on that investigation, the murder of two young women?

TW: I was one of hundreds of officers who worked on that for nearly 40 years. And it's important to say that. It was a generational investigation. There were hundreds of... People talk about the great detective theory, let me tell you that that's a myth. There was no great detective, there were dozens of great detectives and officers who worked on the World's End. And it became a way of life. It was our duty and responsibility here in Lothian and Borders to solve these murders. And we are very fortunate in that one of our scenes of crime officers who was at the scene of the deposition of the two girls here in Edinburgh was an incredible man, who was very fastidious about the way he lifted, secured and retained the evidence. And years later, over 30 years later, when forensic science has moved on, we were able to take benefit from that and that is what, eventually, convicted Angus Sinclair.

DIARY: He was saying that DNA and forensic advances mean that serial killers are much less likely now. They'll be apprehended sooner.

PRIME MINISTER THERESA MAY LOSES SECOND 'MEANINGFUL' VOTE ON BREXIT DEAL

Tuesday 12 March 2019
STV News

The Brexit crisis convulsing British politics deepened further tonight with the Prime Minister massively defeated on a meaningful vote for the second time. The Commons rejected her revised Brexit deal by a majority of 149. Afterwards, Theresa May confirmed that MPs will now get to vote on whether the UK should leave the EU without a deal. If that is rejected, there will then be a vote on delaying the whole Brexit process.

Wednesday 20 March 2019
STV News

And we can report that 40 Scots words have been added to the Oxford English Dictionary, including coorie and coupon. Weegies have been left black-affronted as a whole host of Scottish words including bawbag and bampot were added to the Oxford English Dictionary. So now if some tube tries to say your patter is bowfin' then you can tell them to shut their geggie as the slang words are now official. More than 40 Scots words including; rooked, bidie-in, bigsie, black-affronted, bowfing, coorie, coupon, roaster and grass have been added to the dictionary for its March 2019 update.

KELLY-ANN: Does that mean it's okay for me to call you a bawbag?

DIARY: The word 'bawbag' has been added to the *Oxford English Dictionary*, so I wrote a wee skit for Kelly-Ann and me to use at the end of the programme, basically her calling me a 'bawbag.' It's gone viral, which was always likely. Of course, there has been one complaint.

Friday 29 March 2019
STV News

The Prime Minister has suffered a third defeat on her Brexit plans on the day the UK was supposed to be leaving the European Union. MPs rejected Theresa May's withdrawal agreement by a majority of 58. It means the UK Government has two weeks to ask for a longer extension, or else leave the EU with no deal. Opposition parties have called on Mrs May to resign and hold a General Election.

DIARY: This is the day we were scheduled to leave the EU and we haven't. Big crowds in Westminster... The whole shambles runs on.

Monday 1 April 2019
Scotland Tonight

We are now into extra time in the Brexit process and there is still no sign of a resolution to the crisis. Tonight, the Commons tried but failed to break the deadlock with indicative votes on four alternatives to the Prime Minister's Deal. An amendment from Ken Clarke called for the UK to be in a permanent Customs Union with the EU. It just failed to win a simple majority. The Nick Boles amendment, Common Market 2.0, was for an even softer Brexit with the UK remaining in the single market with the continuation of freedom of movement. That attracted even less support. The amendment from two Labour MPs demanding that any Brexit deal be put to a referendum got the most support but not enough to pass. The final amendment was from the SNP's Joanna Cherry and called for scrapping Brexit altogether to prevent a No-Deal departure. That proved to be the least popular choice.

EU LEADERS AGREE TO DELAY BREXIT

Thursday 11 April 2019
STV News

The Prime Minister has been defending another delay to Brexit. The European Union has agreed to a new deadline – 31 October – Halloween. Jeremy Corbyn said it was another milestone in the Government's 'chaotic handling' of our departure. The SNP are urging Theresa May to use the extra time to hold another EU Referendum.

KATHRYN SAMSON, Westminster Correspondent: Many Conservative Brexiteers are furious about this extension and one of them, Bill Cash, stood up in Parliament today and called for her to quit. But the Prime Minister is sticking to her guns. Still trying to get a deal with Labour. Still hoping to try and get something over the line in there as quickly as possible to try and avoid using the full length of this extension and to try and avoid the UK having to take part in European Parliament elections at the end of May. After months of late votes and bitter battles, she urged MPs to take the Easter break to reflect on how to break the deadlock.

Friday 3 May 2019
STV News

Thousands turned out to honour the former Celtic captain and manager Billy McNeill as his funeral took place this morning in Glasgow city centre. The requiem mass was relayed to Celtic Park where supporters gathered to remember a giant of the Scottish game and a legend of their club. There were emotional scenes as Billy McNeill's family joined fans to mark the life of a man described by a football rival today as a 'superstar and a super human being'.

THERESA MAY ANNOUNCES RESIGNATION

Friday 24 May 2019
STV News

Tonight – Struggling to hold back the tears. After weeks of speculation Theresa May will stand down as leader of the Conservative Party.

She says she's done all she can. Serving as Prime Minister has been 'the honour of her life'. Theresa May struggled to fight back tears today as she called time on her premiership. She'll stand down as Conservative leader in two weeks. The party is expected to choose a new leader – and so Prime Minister – by the end of July.

THERESA MAY, Prime Minister: I feel as certain today as I did three years ago that in a democracy if you give people a choice you have a duty to implement what they decide. I have done my best to do that. I negotiated the terms of our exit and a new relationship with our closest neighbours that protects jobs, our security and the Union. I have done everything I can to convince MPs to back that deal. Sadly, I have not been able to do so. I tried three times… It is now clear to me that it is in the best interests of the country for a new Prime Minister to lead that effort. So, I am today announcing that I will resign… I will shortly leave the job that it has been the honour of my life to hold. The second female Prime Minister, but certainly not the last. I do so with no ill will, but with enormous and enduring gratitude to have had the opportunity to serve the country I love.

DIARY: It's been a long time coming, but has seemed inevitable over the last few days. She almost broke down at the end of her statement and you had to feel for her. I do think she was dutiful, but she is unquestionably the worst Prime Minister of my lifetime… She seemed incapable of persuading people to support her and wouldn't change.

Tuesday 28 May 2019
Scotland Tonight

The European Parliament Election was a disaster for Labour right across Britain. In Scotland, the result was particularly dire, with the party plunging to fifth place on just 9 per cent of the vote. It has prompted much internal soul-searching, and today the pressure on the Scottish Labour Leader Richard Leonard increased with the resignations of two members of his Shadow Cabinet. First to go was Leonard's left-wing ally, Neil Findlay, who quit his job as constitution spokesperson, citing divisions within Scottish Labour and a 'toxic culture of leaks and briefings'.

Wednesday 29 May 2019
STV News

The Scottish Government is proposing new legislation which could make provisions for another Independence Referendum next year. The First Minister says it would be a democratic outrage if Westminster blocks a second vote. But opponents say it is a distraction and stunt, piling further chaos on top of Brexit.

COLIN MACKAY, Political Editor: This legislation should be passed by the end of this year – the First Minister says that clears the way for IndyRef2 in the second half of next year… She says it is democratically unacceptable for the UK Government to continue to withhold a Section 30 Order transferring the powers, but that isn't cutting much ice with them. And she would never do it without the powers – no wildcat referendum.

DIARY: Nobody really believes she wants to hold it then – polls still not in her favour – but she needs to appease the fundamentals in her support. The Brexit outcome could be a decisive factor.

DANNY MACASKILL
Monday 1 July 2019
Scotland Tonight

Widely seen as the best stunt cyclist in the world, Danny MacAskill shot to fame in 2009 when he put a five-minute film onto YouTube. Since then, his extreme cycling videos have racked up more than 350 million views worldwide. Next month he'll be taking his tricks to the Edinburgh Fringe with an hour-long show featuring three other star riders.

JM: You say a few injuries, how many bones have you actually broken?

DANNY MACASKILL, stunt cyclist: A lot, I think over 30 if you count all the little bones in the hands and feet and things. It's been a few over the years, but that's part and parcel of any sport, whether it's athletics, tennis, or some of the more extreme stuff on the bicycle, like downhill or trials. I'd say you've got to have a wee crash here and there to progress. So, it's just a bit of wear and tear… I grew up on the Isle of Skye, so there wasn't much else to do at night times when my friends weren't about. So, I'd just go out and practice my skids and wheelies and I've been doing the same thing for the last 20 years. And you might see me sometimes out at night riding around Buchanan Galleries or out in the streets of Glasgow just practising some of my skills.

Tuesday 9 July 2019
Scotland Tonight

In July 1969 the world watched in wonder and awe as Neil Armstrong and then Buzz Aldrin became the first humans to set foot on the surface of the moon. Fifty years on from the Apollo 11 mission, we reflected on the moment in history and its legacy with the NASA historian Brian Odom.

DIARY: Talked about landing on the moon again in the next ten years with a view to making a habitable base on it. That's exciting.

Tuesday 16 July 2019
STV News

The highest ever number of drug-related deaths has been recorded in Scotland. The annual figure has doubled in the last ten years, to more than 1,000. You're more likely to die of drugs in Scotland than in any other European country. There were 1,187 drugs related deaths in Scotland in 2018. That's an increase of 27 per cent in a single year. The Greater Glasgow and Clyde Health Board area saw the most deaths – 394 people. But Dundee City has the highest death rate, per head of the population.

DIARY: The usual wails over what to do about it. I've been hearing it for over 30 years and it's the same failed arguments. It needs radical action and one of them should be supervised drug-taking rooms.

BORIS JOHNSON WINS CONSERVATIVE LEADERSHIP CONTEST

Tuesday 23 July 2019
STV News

Tonight – Johnson's in. Conservatives elect Boris Johnson as their new leader. Tomorrow he'll become Prime Minister.

Boris Johnson has won the race to become leader of the Conservative Party, comfortably defeating Jeremy Hunt in a poll of party members. It means that tomorrow he will become the Prime Minister. In his victory speech, Mr Johnson promised he would 'deliver Brexit, unite the country and defeat Jeremy Corbyn'. The First Minister Nicola Sturgeon says she has 'profound concerns' about his suitability and warned him not to force through a No-Deal Brexit.

BORIS JOHNSON, Conservative leader: We are going to unite this amazing country and we're going to take it forward. I thank you all very much for the incredible honour that you have just done me. I will work flat out from now on with my team that I will build, I hope, in the next few days to repay your confidence. But in the meantime, the campaign is over and the work begins.

KATHRYN SAMSON, Westminster Correspondent: No huge surprise to see Boris Johnson win. Sixty-six per cent of Tory members who voted chose him over Jeremy Hunt… Of course, it is one thing for Boris Johnson to win over Tory members. It's going to be quite another to win over the country and unite his party. He said tonight he would 'love bomb' MPs who didn't vote for him. A slightly surreal end to a day where it felt like the heat here was going to everyone's heads.

DIARY: I may be wrong and I hope I am, but I see a shambles ahead.

BORIS JOHNSON BECOMES PRIME MINISTER

Wednesday 24 July 2019
STV News

Tonight – May's moved out and Johnson's moving in. He says he's a Prime Minister of the whole United Kingdom and will unite the UK.

He has a mammoth 'to do' list. Top is leaving the EU – he says 'no ifs no buts' – and he's giving himself 99 days to do it. But Brexit's impact on Scottish politics may only grow if the UK is forced into a No-Deal outcome. As Prime Minister Boris Johnson gets down to business, it makes for an eventful first 100 days in office.

BORIS JOHNSON, Prime Minister: I am standing before you today to tell you, the British people, that those critics are wrong. The doubters, the doomsters, the gloomsters – they are going to get it wrong again. The people who bet against Britain are going to lose their shirts because we are going to restore trust in our democracy and we are going to fulfil the repeated promises of Parliament to the people and come out of the EU on 31 October. No ifs or buts. And we will do a new deal, a better deal that will maximise the opportunities of Brexit while allowing us to develop a new and exciting partnership with the rest of Europe based on free trade and mutual support... And I will tell you something else about my job. It is to be Prime Minister of the whole United Kingdom and that means uniting our country, answering at last the plea of the forgotten people and the left behind towns by physically and literally renewing the ties that bind us together. So that with safer streets and better education and fantastic new road and rail infrastructure and full fibre broadband we level up across Britain with higher wages, and a higher living wage, and higher productivity. We close the opportunity gap giving millions of young people the chance to own their own homes and giving businesses the confidence to invest across the UK because it is time we unleashed the productive power not just of London and the south-east, but of every corner of England, Scotland, Wales and Northern Ireland – the awesome foursome that are incarnated in that red white and blue flag...

COLIN MACKAY, Political Editor: The job he has long coveted is his. Now he has to deliver. He has to deliver on his one big pledge – leave the EU by 31 October. I think there was a bit of an olive branch today from the European Parliament's Brexit Steering Group offering talks on the political declaration to make the Irish backstop unnecessary. But remember, yesterday I said he had to be ready to fight on two fronts. Today, he talked about being forced to leave without a deal, already shifting blame on to the EU. And his speech sounded like he was launching an election campaign. Politics is stuck on Brexit. Boris Johnson says he will work flat out to give it the leadership to get things moving.

DIARY: Some say he'll be the last Prime Minister of a United Kingdom. That's very possible. We can only wait and see.

BORIS JOHNSON ANNOUNCES THE PROROGUING OF PARLIAMENT
Wednesday 28 August 2019
STV News

Tonight – Ruth Davidson set to quit. The Scottish Conservative leader's decision comes as the UK Government announces an unexpected suspension of Parliament.

In further developments. The Prime Minister's man Jacob Rees-Mogg is sent to Scotland – to get the Queen to agree to delaying the return of Parliament.

Ruth Davidson is set to quit as Scottish Tory Leader. It comes after Boris Johnson today began the process of suspending Parliament at Westminster – making a No-Deal Brexit far more likely. Ms Davidson has been leading the party at Holyrood since 2011. Since Boris Johnson became Prime Minister, she's increasingly found herself at odds with his leadership and hardline Brexit support.

Tuesday 3 September 2019
STV News

The Prime Minister is preparing for a major Brexit showdown. Boris Johnson faces revolt in the Commons as opposition MPs and some Tory rebels try to seize control of Parliament to prevent the UK leaving the EU without a deal. If he loses the vote later tonight, the Prime Minister says he'll call for a snap General Election. But his task got even tougher this afternoon as his Government lost its majority, with a former minister crossing the floor to join the Lib Dems.

KATHRYN SAMSON, Westminster Correspondent: Back to work with a bang for MPs today – chaos outside – chaos inside, with the Prime Minister in the chamber trying to fight off this attempt to take control of the order paper and force a delay to Brexit until 31st January... There are maybe around 20 Tory MPs planning to vote against Boris Johnson – if they do they face being sacked from the party... But tonight's vote really will come down to trust. Boris Johnson insists he is trying to get a deal, but so many MPs on all sides simply don't believe him.

Tuesday 3 September 2019 *(cont)*
STV News

The First Minister is demanding the power to hold a second Independence Referendum next year. Outlining her Programme for Government, Nicola Sturgeon said she would put opposition to Brexit and Scotland's right to choose independence at the heart of the next election campaign. On day-to-day issues she promised plans to lift children out of poverty, but her main focus was on tackling climate change and cutting carbon emissions.

COLIN MACKAY, Political Editor: Nicola Sturgeon... thinks a General Election is coming and that a good result for the SNP could boost her demands for a Section 30 Order. Her opponents accuse her of exploiting the Brexit chaos for independence – have they only just noticed?

Monday 9 September 2019
Scotland Tonight

Just a week after MPs returned from their summer recess, they are now being sent away until 14th October. Boris Johnson's decision to suspend Parliament for five weeks has been widely condemned, not least by the Speaker John Bercow, who announced today that he will resign on the Brexit deadline day of Halloween. This final day of the current session has also seen the Queen approve the bill to block a No-Deal Brexit and MPs are poised once again to reject Government calls for a snap Election.

DIARY: There is a feeling of complete chaos.

MARTINA NAVRATILOVA

Tuesday 10 September 2019
Scotland Tonight

One of the greatest female tennis players of all time, Martina Navratilova, has also been a long-standing advocate for equality and human rights. Today she took part in a diversity summit at Gleneagles Hotel...

MARTINA NAVRATILOVA, tennis champion: We've come a long way. But we still have a long way to go. We still don't get equal prize money or equal endorsements. Tennis is about the only one that has equal prize money at the majors. Women golfers don't make as much as men golfers. In fact, men senior golfers make more than professional women. That's because positions of power, the people that have the purse, the power of the purse, are mostly men. They are much more willing to give it to men. But slowly and slowly it's changing because we have more women in positions of power. And also, the men that have children, have daughters. They want them to participate. They want them to be getting equal prize money, equal opportunities. It's all changing very slowly. But I think in about 100 years we'll have total quality. No, I'm kidding. Hopefully it will happen a lot sooner.

JM: In reference to sport, obviously equality is ongoing in sport. That struggle. But there are added complications. I'm thinking particularly in terms of transgender athletes. How do we adapt to that, how do we change for that?

MN: Well, it's difficult because you want to be as inclusive as possible, but you still want to have a fair situation, level playing field as much as that is possible. So, by including transgender women in women's and girls' sports, now the women and girls that are playing, are, like, wait a minute, I'm looking at someone who's much stronger, much bigger than I am. How is that fair? We have different levels of transgenderism inclusivity in sport. Some sports have rules about testosterone levels etc and transitioning and taking hormone therapy. And some only self-ID. Obviously, it's got its challenges because just self-ID cannot be the only thing that makes a difference, that says whether you play as a female or a male. So, it's about being fair in sports. Sports is about biology. I just want to make sure the girls and women that compete have a fair chance and they are not getting pushed out by somebody that's much stronger and bigger because of transgender. It's a tricky situation. I want to be as inclusive as possible, but it's all about fairness at this point.

DIARY: She holds her line on transgender women who were previously men competing in sport not being fair. It's been a polarising debate this year. Originally supposed to go up to Gleneagles to interview her, but PR types saying we'd only get three questions, so pointless. In the end I got 6 minutes 30 seconds from her.

Wednesday 11 September 2019

DIARY: Really good news day with any of four potential leads.

NEW EDINBURGH CHILDREN'S HOSPITAL DELAYED
STV News

It'll be at least another year until children are being treated at Edinburgh's new children's hospital. The latest delay is to ensure problems with the brand new building's ventilation system can be sorted. The Health Secretary says it will add an extra £16 million to the already over-budget bill. Jeane Freeman is rejecting opposition calls for a public inquiry and says human error at the tendering stage of the project was to blame. And a report today has identified multiple occasions when critical errors should have been identified during construction.

COURT OF SESSION RULES PROROGUING OF PARLIAMENT ILLEGAL
STV News

There are calls tonight for the UK Parliament to be re-called after three senior Scottish judges at the Court of Session ruled that Boris Johnson's proroguing of Parliament is unlawful. Scotland's most senior judge Lord Carloway held that the real reason for suspending Parliament was to stymie parliamentary accountability, not to facilitate a Queen's Speech as the Government claims. Downing Street say they are disappointed by the ruling. The UK Government has appealed to the Supreme Court who will now hear the legal issues in the case next Tuesday.

MAN CHARGED IN 40-YEAR-OLD RENEE MacRAE MURDER
STV News

A man has appeared in court charged with the murder of Inverness woman Renee MacRae and her son Andrew 43 years ago. 77-year-old William MacDowell, whose address was given as Penrith, also faces two charges of attempting to pervert the course of justice. The court appearance follows a forensic search of Leanach Quarry, near Inverness, as part of a cold case review by Police Scotland.

NICOLA MCALLEY, Highland Reporter: Renee MacRae and her three-year-old son Andrew were last seen in November 1976. Renee had confided to her best friend she was to visit her lover, but her car was found on fire in a layby off the A9. Neither she nor Andrew were ever seen again. Police believe they were murdered. There have been numerous searches for the mother and son over the years.

REPUBLICAN MARCHES IN GLASGOW BANNED THIS WEEKEND
STV News

A number of public parades due to take place in Glasgow this weekend have been banned by the city council.

EWAN PETRIE, Political Correspondent: There were five marches planned to take place in Glasgow this Saturday and Sunday... The decision to ban all five is in light of submissions made by a senior officer. And it comes in the wake of sectarian violence in the city over the past two weekends. The police warned that there would be a high likelihood of violence from counter-protests and crucially they expect the public to be at risk. Organisers had argued that to impose a blanket ban was a dangerous road for the council to go down.

Tuesday 24 September 2019
STV News

Tonight – A humiliated but defiant Prime Minister. What now for Boris Johnson after a court rules he misled the Queen into suspending Parliament?

The highest court in the land has ruled the Prime Minister's suspension of Parliament is unlawful. In its unanimous judgement, the Supreme Court ruled that the Commons was prevented from carrying out its duties, without reasonable justification. Speaker John Bercow is calling for the resumption of Parliament tomorrow. And the PM is flying back to the UK from New York amid calls for his resignation. Once again, Brexit is in disarray.

Wednesday 25 September 2019
STV News

Cowardly MPs. A dead Parliament. A zombie Prime Minister. There were angry exchanges in the Commons as MPs resumed business following the unlawful decision to suspend it. One MP said they were horrified by the language being used. Another branded a Government minister a disgrace. While the insults were being traded, the Prime Minister returned from New York to face MPs after the Supreme Court ruled that his proroguing of Parliament had been wrong.

Tuesday 22 October 2019
Scotland Tonight

MPs tonight gave their approval in principle to the Prime Minister's Withdrawal Agreement Bill. But just minutes later, they voted down the bill's three-day timetable for debate. In so doing, they wrecked Boris Johnson's 'do or die' pledge to deliver Brexit by 31 October. Following the events in the Commons, the European Council President Donald Tusk tonight signalled that EU leaders will agree to give the UK a Brexit extension up until the end of January.

DIARY: We – the collective media – have failed in explaining the Brexit process, mostly because we don't know ourselves. All these parliamentary procedures and tactics that seem to take us all by surprise. We haven't been helped by the shambles of a Parliament, but no analyst/specialist/expert has nailed it. Most people don't understand what is happening because we haven't explained it. We haven't explained it because we don't know.

Tuesday 29 October 2019
Scotland Tonight

The Prime Minister tonight finally secured Commons backing for the early General Election he has craved. Voters are set to go to the polls on 12 December. With the stakes so high, this pre-Christmas campaign promises to be one of the hardest fought political battles we've ever seen.

Wednesday 30 October 2019
STV News

The inquiry into the Clutha helicopter crash has found that the pilot 'took a chance' and ignored low fuel warnings. The sheriff concluded the tragedy happened because Captain David Traill ignored the five warnings he received during the flight. Ten people died when the police helicopter crashed into the roof of the busy Glasgow pub six years ago. Relatives of those who lost loved ones that night have expressed anger at the inquiry's findings as they feel they've been left with many unanswered questions.

SHARON FREW, Chief Reporter: The sheriff said there is no suggestion that Captain David Traill deliberately caused the helicopter to crash, and the evidence showed he had 'made a valiant attempt to land after both engines flamed out'.

Thursday 7 November 2019
STV News

Boris Johnson says he sees no reason ever to allow a second referendum on independence. The Prime Minister was speaking on his first election campaign visit to Scotland. The First Minister said he should have used the visit to a distillery in Elgin to apologise for the chaos caused by Brexit.

DIARY: The usual – visit a distillery, get photo taken, maybe answer a couple of questions and then gone. No meeting the electorate, nothing. It is all rather cynical and we, the media, play our part in it.

Tuesday 12 November 2019
STV News

Why did he die? Were the circumstances covered up? To what extent was race a factor? These are the questions the family of Sheku Bayoh have about his death. And today they were told there will be a public inquiry to answer them. The 32-year-old lost his life after being restrained by police in Kirkcaldy in 2015. Yesterday, the Crown said none of the officers involved will be prosecuted.

Monday 18 November 2019
STV News

Urgent action is needed in Scotland to safeguard cancer services and help more people survive. That's the findings of a Scottish Parliament cross-party group which says staff shortages are leading to increased waiting times for diagnosis. Charities say the findings are deeply concerning, as diagnosing early can make all the difference. Cancer patients we've spoken to tell us that longer waits add to their fears.

DIARY: It's not a cash issue, the vacancies just cannot be filled. Health journalist Pennie Taylor talked about AI (artificial intelligence) actually being more accurate than humans at assessing scans, but vested interests won't let it happen. Got cancer survival down to two in four and aiming for three in four by 2035.

Thursday 21 November 2019
STV News

Tonight – Alex Salmond in court. He's accused of committing 14 sexual offences against ten women – including attempted rape – while serving as Scotland's First Minister.

The former First Minister Alex Salmond will stand trial in the spring accused of a string of sexual assaults against ten women. In a court hearing today he pled not guilty to the charges. The most serious allegation is that he attempted to rape a woman at his official residence just months before the Independence Referendum in 2014. He insists he is innocent.

PETER HOWSON
Friday 9 December 2019
Scotland Tonight

It perhaps says something about the human condition that more than 70 official British War Artists since the start of the First World War have created thousands of images of conflict. Over the course of a century they've recorded the horror on and off the battlefield. Amongst their number is artist Peter Howson, who portrayed the conflicts in Bosnia and Kosovo. Now, as the 25th anniversary of the Srebrenica massacre approaches, he has unveiled new work at the St Mungo Museum in Glasgow.

JM: You said a very interesting thing, that the mediaeval church got it right with an emphasis on image rather than words. What did you mean by that?

PETER HOWSON, Artist: I think that images can't be misconstrued, whereas words can be. And I think that has caused a lot of trouble. And people have fought wars over words, but never over paintings. Drawings, sculpture, it's something that can appeal to everyone.

JM: Another point you made that was intriguing was you said that we embraced death in the past, but we don't do that now.

PH: In times gone by, which probably were a lot harder than they are today, people probably welcomed it more and accepted it more. And life was harder. But faith was what they had, and they had a faith that when they died, if they'd had a hard life they'd go hopefully up to heaven. You know, in this modern world, this cynical world, people don't believe that anymore, and they laugh at it. But I think it's wrong to laugh at these people, people from the past, and think that we're somehow cleverer than they are. Because we're not, we haven't changed... They don't become more civilised and better. In fact, if anything, the wars we fight these days are more brutal than they were before.

DIARY: He spoke candidly about how painting helps him escape his mental problems and how, despite thinking how better we are now, man's base instinct is the same as ever it was.

GENERAL ELECTION 2019

Friday 13 December 2019

STV News – live from Westminster

After a night of drama and upset, the result of the 2019 General Election is clear. A dominant party. A Labour collapse. And a clear message on the constitution. Except – these statements are true in different ways for Scotland and the United Kingdom. And it gives rise to the prospect of a constitutional crisis. Boris Johnson won a landslide victory, giving him the mandate to get Brexit done. And quickly. But in Scotland, the SNP landslide allows Nicola Sturgeon to make a similar case for a second Independence Referendum. Some might think that the shroud of scaffolding around the Palace of Westminster could be a metaphor for the United Kingdom.

Here is how Scotland voted. The SNP won 48 seats. The Conservatives took six. The Liberal Democrats won four seats, and Labour's tally was reduced to one.

GORDON CHREE, Senior Reporter: All he wanted for Christmas was a working majority in Parliament. But tonight, Boris Johnson has much more than that. A landslide victory giving him a firm grip on the keys to Number Ten... Across the UK the Conservative win was built on turning many traditional Labour seats blue. The message of 'get Brexit done' clearly struck a chord in constituencies who had voted to leave the European Union. But there's a clear contrast between the picture south of the border and here in Scotland which is once again a sea of yellow... The tale of two nations is likely to be the dominant theme of Scottish political discourse in the foreseeable future. The First Minister sees the result as a clear mandate for another referendum on independence – and says she will next week publish the case for the power to hold one to be transferred to Holyrood. For Labour, shaped so much in the image of its leader Jeremy Corbyn, this election was disastrous. All but wiped out in Scotland, it also saw many of its former heartlands in the English midlands and north fall to the Tories. Losing more than 50 seats, it was the party's worst result since 1935 and it's now contemplating a future with someone else at the helm. Jo Swinson went into this election declaring herself as a candidate for Prime Minister. But for the second time in four years she lost her seat in East Dunbartonshire – the defeat ending her leadership of the Liberal Democrats... This was the third UK General Election in a little over four years. The result will leave many Scottish voters asking if for them it will be the last.

BORIS JOHNSON, Prime Minister: If you ask yourselves what is this new Government going to do, what is he going to do with his extraordinary majority, I will tell you that is what we are going to do. We are going to unite and level up. Unite and level up. Bringing together the whole of this incredible United Kingdom – England, Scotland, Wales, Northern Ireland together taking us forward unleashing the potential of the whole country delivering opportunity across the entire nation and since I know that after five weeks, frankly, of electioneering, this country deserves a break from wrangling, a break from politics, and a permanent break from talking about Brexit.

NICOLA STURGEON, First Minister: This is not about asking Boris Johnson, or any other Westminster politician, for permission. It is, instead, an assertion of the democratic right of the people of Scotland to determine our own future.

JEREMY CORBYN, Labour Leader: I was elected to lead the party and I think the responsible thing to do is not to walk away from the whole thing and I won't do that. I will stay here until there has been somebody elected to succeed me and then I will step down at that point.

JM: So, the Brexit election is over. And Brexit has won. Jeremy Corbyn's Labour has been roundly defeated. The Conservatives now look set to rule until 2024. But Scotland voted overwhelmingly for MPs who want to stay in Europe and also want Scottish independence. It's a Kingdom divided along clear lines. What happens now?

Monday 16 December 2019
STV News

Tonight – Arriving in Westminster for the first time the newly elected team of 47 SNP MPs – and a call for the Prime Minister to respect democracy and allow a second referendum.

The Leader of the SNP at Westminster has called on the Prime Minister to respect democracy and the Scottish people following last week's election. Ian Blackford says the vote has reaffirmed the case for a second Independence Referendum. He was speaking as the party's 47 MPs gathered in Westminster for the first time following Thursday's poll. He also claimed the SNP would be the effective opposition to Boris Johnson.

DIARY: Nicola Sturgeon talking about having a mandate for a second Independence Referendum. Boris Johnson saying no. That will be the repeated arguments until at least the 2021 Scottish elections.

2020

Thursday 9 January 2020
Scotland Tonight

Tonight, the NHS. Most of us cannot remember a time when it wasn't there for us. From birth all through our lives, the NHS is there when we need it. But it's under strain. Tonight, we have frontline stories. Not from politicians. Not from experts. But from a nurse. A doctor. A midwife. And a surgeon. Their answers may surprise you. It's not just about money. We need to look to ourselves. The people who use the National Health Service. About how we use it and what we should expect. How do we heal the NHS?

ANDREA WILLOX, Nurse: I would say the most difficult aspect right now is volume. We are coming into queues of ambulances out the front door, queues through the door for triage. I think a lot of it comes back to public education and responsibility. Not coming to A&E with a cold that you've had for two days, even worse phoning an ambulance which we see on a daily basis. If the public were more aware of why they should and shouldn't be in A&E. Not coming with non-emergency complaints. We're inundated daily with 75 per cent of our patients not being emergency patients.

DR SANDESH GULHANE, GP: We are losing about £200 million a year in the NHS with missed appointments. One in five appointments throughout GPs are going unfilled. So, actually seeing people is by far the best thing for me. I only have ten minutes to really deal with what could be one very complex thing and three little things. I simply don't have time to do everything I want to do, to really look after my patient and care for them holistically. Right now, I'm having to firefight and I don't want to firefight. I want to make them better in total. Make their health better.

LEAH HAZARD, Midwife: If somebody asked me what I'd most like to change about the NHS I think the obvious trite answer would be money. We all want more money and more funding no matter which sector or the service we're coming from. But what would also be really helpful would be if the general public were able to have a more nuanced understanding of how best to use the service more efficiently. It's really helpful if, for example, women and their families know which issues need to be seen acutely by my department and which issues maybe are for a GP or a community midwife or a chemist. And if we all work together as a team to use the service efficiently, we can provide the right services to the right people who need it the most at the right time.

NIGEL JAMIESON, Surgeon: I think at the end of the day, even though I'm a surgeon, the most important thing for health care is going to be primary prevention, as it's called. Increased activity levels, doing anything we can to reduce diabetes and obesity because they impact very much on my job as a surgeon. Many diagnoses of cancer are secondary to smoking, not all of them, but many of them. And smoking cessation, including exercising activities, would be the most important aspect of improving health care going forward.

UK FORMALLY LEAVES THE EU
Friday 31 January 2020
STV News

It's been four years in the making, but like it or loathe it, Brexit Day is with us. In just five hours the UK will leave the European Union. An historic moment which will be marked by candlelight vigils and celebrations. It's been a move which has divided Britain, and tonight it looks like that division could widen still further. The First Minister has announced what she says will be the next steps towards Independence for Scotland.

JM: How significant is this in historical terms?

BERNARD PONSONBY, Special Correspondent in George Square: It's huge. Post-war, signing up to Europe was the recalibration of Britain's role in the world following the decline of Empire. 2016 binned that. Politicians now have to decide what post-Brexit relationships look like. But you know, the UK looks like an uneasy relationship of competing nationalisms with quite distinct debates taking place in Scotland, England and Northern Ireland. Brexit has unleashed a process that we can't quite predict how it will end. One union is at an end, we know that. Closer to home the question is whether the current union will survive all of the turbulence.

DIARY: On social media there has been a lot of bemoaning and there have been some demos and celebrations, but I do get the sense that the general public weren't that interested. Brexit has become an incessant bore to them.

Monday 17 February 2020
STV News

Nicola Sturgeon's ministerial team is now the first-ever Cabinet in the UK with more women than men. The change came today, as Scotland's new Finance Secretary was appointed. Kate Forbes is 29 and the first woman to hold the post. She's been promoted in a mini reshuffle following the sudden resignation of Derek Mackay. Kate Forbes's performance when she stepped in at short notice to deliver the budget earlier this month was widely praised at Holyrood. But the role won't be without major challenges.

Thursday 20 February 2020
Scotland Tonight

On *Scotland Tonight* we are talking about identity and the legal right to define who you are. Man or woman. Some people from within the trans community welcome the proposed reform of the Gender Recognition Act – a set of proposals allowing you to change your sex legally. It strips away the need for medical assessments and is based solely on self-identity. Seems simple? Well, not quite. Not everyone agrees. In fact, the debate has become extremely heated and even toxic at times. Some fear change could compromise women's rights and female only spaces and have a detrimental effect on young people exploring who they are.

JM: Is it transphobic to want to keep male-bodied people out of women's spaces, do you think?

SHIRLEY-ANNE SOMERVILLE, Cabinet Secretary: I recognise that there are genuine concerns out there. This is a debate that has created a lot of misunderstandings, sometimes. But a lot of genuine questions and concerns out there. And I think it's my responsibility, it's the Government's responsibility to try and talk about the facts about what is… what the bill does propose, what it does not propose, and what we are absolutely determined to take into account as we go forward. And the most important thing as I move forward is around maintaining and actually extending protection of women as part of this process, as well as the trans community.

JM: Do you believe that biological sex is less important than gender identification?

SAS: I don't think it's a matter of priorities. I absolutely appreciate that women's rights are exceptionally important. They have been long fought for and long campaigned on. And there is absolutely nothing I would do as a member of this Government to jeopardise any of that. So, that's why I really do make sure that I listen to the concerns that are out there on this issue. Because we are not just wanting to protect what we have as women, but we want to make sure our rights are extended… I mean, this debate absolutely has generated a lot of heat. There are areas where there is strong opposition. Either because the Government is not going far enough or the Government's going too far. What I would ask anyone involved in this debate is to try and make sure that we are carrying on this debate in a respectful fashion, where people are recognising that there are different opinions on this and work forward to see if there's a way of developing a solution to this. As I say, we need a process in Scotland. We are required to have a process in Scotland about gender recognition. What I am trying to achieve is a way where I think we are taking away the medicalisation of the current process and the burden it was creating, and the impact that was having on mental health and wellbeing within the trans community. And we need to find a way of being able to do that, but absolutely along that way, be able to reassure women in particular that there is no threat whatsoever to their rights as part of that process.

Sunday 23 February 2020

DIARY: More cases of the coronavirus in the UK, none yet in Scotland. This is a potential pandemic that has begun in China and has been running for a month or so. Still small numbers infected and much fewer dying, but much cause for concern among health workers and governments. No real sense of concern among the public.

FIRST COVID CASE IN SCOTLAND
Monday 2 March 2020
STV News

Tonight – coronavirus in Scotland. Measures in place to contain the outbreak as the country's first victim is treated in hospital.

We've been told for weeks it was only a matter of time. Since the coronavirus was first confirmed in Wuhan in China in January, the spread has been relentless. While Scotland remained virus free, it continued to edge ever closer. Through Europe, and into England, Wales and Northern Ireland. And in the last 24 hours it arrived – the first case of Covid-19 in Scotland. A patient in Tayside tested positive and is being treated in hospital. So, what do we know? Well, we know that they contracted the virus after returning from northern Italy. What we don't know is who they are, or where they're from. We do know that they self-isolated, and that steps are being taken to track down anyone they have been in contact with. We know they are in hospital, but we're not even sure which hospital they are in. And we're expecting it to spread further still. Today, Scotland's Chief Medical Officer said between 50 and 80 per cent of the population could catch the virus. And up to 250,000 will need hospital treatment during the course of the outbreak.

DIARY: I still don't get any sense of over-anxiety, though.

Wednesday 4 March 2020
STV News

Three people in Scotland have now tested positive for coronavirus. The two new cases of Covid-19 are in Ayrshire and in Grampian and come on top of one person already identified in Tayside. But those three people with positive results here are a small number. More than 1,000 people have now been tested. One of the new patients recently returned from northern Italy, where the outbreak is acute. The other has had contact with someone who has already identified as having the virus, but authorities stress that it is not the person in Tayside.

DIARY: Two more cases of coronavirus, bringing the total to three. Still being contained, but the assumption is it'll get worse. Some shops selling out of hand gel and such. People talking about it, but no real sense of panic, other than people questioning whether to travel.

Tuesday 10 March 2020
Scotland Tonight

The streets of Italy were left near deserted today with its population put under an unprecedented lockdown in the battle against coronavirus. The Government has ordered its people to stay at home and avoid all non-essential travel until April. The country is home to the world's most severe outbreak outside of China.

DIARY: A lot of major events are being cancelled.

BILLY CONNOLLY
Thursday 12 March 2020
Scotland Tonight

Shipyard welder, folk singer, stand-up comedian, actor and artist – on his return to his native Glasgow for a showing of his drawings, we talk to the much-loved Sir Billy Connolly about his remarkable life.

BILLY CONNOLLY: It's the same as when I was performing in Glasgow. I was always nervous because you can't lie properly in your hometown. Every other town you can lie about your background and invent stuff and experiences that you supposedly had. But you can't do it in Glasgow, 'cause you'll get... *(blows raspberry)*... in the middle of it. And the art is the same. You can't lie, they'll find you out. And, so, you live in fear of being found to be an imposter... All I wanted was to be interesting. I didn't want to be Willie the Welder, although that's a noble thing to be. For myself, I wanted to wander the world, to see things, to do things, to meet people, to expand my experiences. And I did it... I was never going to stay in the shipyards. I saw myself as windswept and interesting, wandering the world.

DIARY: One on the wish list. He had a few interviews before me and kept passing me by. He apologised to me, saying, 'I keep passing this man.' I told him I was happy to wait and we bumped elbows because of the coronavirus. A highlight of my career.

FIRST CORONAVIRUS DEATH IN SCOTLAND
Friday 13 March 2020
STV News

Tonight, the first coronavirus death in Scotland. A patient, who was being treated by Lothian Health Board, has died. We're told the person had been diagnosed as positive for Covid-19 and was older and had underlying health conditions. The announcement came from Scotland's Chief Medical Officer, who sent her sympathies to friends and family, this afternoon. The number of cases in Scotland has now risen by 25 to 85. In the Glasgow and Clyde area, numbers have doubled in the last 24 hours to 21. In Lothian, there are 20. Cases of infection are creeping up elsewhere. The

Western Isles is one of the few places in the UK which are coronavirus free.

Sport was also thrown into the spotlight today with an announcement from the Scottish Football Association. This morning, the SFA announced there would be no professional or grassroots football for the foreseeable future. No Motherwell versus Aberdeen tonight, and no Old Firm match at the weekend. Europa League and Champions League Games have also been postponed. And this afternoon, rugby followed suit – Scotland v Wales in the Six Nations also postponed. Huge disappointment for fans, but could this spell disaster for clubs?

DIARY: A senior health official told me that something like 80 per cent could get it, 50 per cent have symptoms, 14 per cent need treatment, 7 per cent hospitalised. It was something like that. Concern for the impact on vulnerable groups and the change in the way we live. And the serious economic impact – already panic buying of toilet rolls, paracetamol and pasta. There has been nothing like this in my lifetime and it is very disturbing. And it's going to last for weeks, probably months.

Monday 16 March 2020

DIARY: The coronavirus crisis stepped up again today. The PM announces all over-70s should remain at home for 12 weeks. Social gatherings and going to pubs.

STV News

'These measures will change life for all of us as we know it for a substantial period of time.' A frank warning from the First Minister in the past hour on the severity of the coronavirus outbreak and the impact the big changes we must make to the way we live our lives will have. Nicola Sturgeon says EVERYONE – if they can – should avoid social contact, work from home and avoid travel, but that we can and will get through this. 171 people in Scotland now have coronavirus, that's 18 more cases than yesterday.

DIARY: Speaking to medics on *Scotland Tonight*, the issue is that there will be people who will die who don't need to because the NHS is overwhelmed.

Tuesday 17 March 2020
STV News

A second Scot with coronavirus has died. There are now almost 2,000 people infected across the UK – almost 200 in Scotland. Both Governments are again stepping up to deal with the crisis. In the past hour, the UK Government has announced mortgage holidays for people struggling to pay the bills – and tax cuts and huge sums of cash to help businesses small and large – as the economy grinds to a halt. The Scottish Health Secretary says our NHS is on an 'emergency footing'. Officials stress that the daily confirmed figures are likely to underestimate the true extent of Covid-19 in Scotland due to a change in the approach to testing.

ALEX SALMOND TRIAL
Tuesday 17 March 2020 *(cont)*
STV News

Alex Salmond has told the High Court some of the allegations against him are 'deliberately fabricated' or exaggerated. The former First Minister was giving evidence at his trial over multiple charges of sexual assault, which he denies.

GORDON CHREE, Senior Reporter: The former First Minister was asked if he'd ever been conscious of a problem with female members of staff. He said, 'In general, no'. Mr Salmond said, 'From where I stand now I wish I'd been more careful with people's personal space, but events are being reinterpreted and exaggerated out of all proportion.' He later said, 'Some, not all, are deliberate fabrications for a political purpose. Some are exaggerated.' The former First Minister accepted he had issued an apology to a woman Ms F after an incident in Bute House. But asked about the allegation he had sexually assaulted her with intent to rape, he said, 'I've never attempted to have non-consensual sexual relations with anyone in my entire life.'

DIARY: Had anyone said a month ago that such an event would be halfway down the programme, they'd have been scoffed at.

Friday 20 March 2020

DIARY: Coronavirus numbers rising, but no further deaths in Scotland. The Prime Minister this evening told pubs, cinemas and restaurants to close. The Chancellor Rishi Sunak has announced a huge support for those facing job losses – 80 per cent of wages up to £2,500.

STV News

It is less than three weeks since the first case of coronavirus was identified in Scotland. Since that first infection was confirmed, it has spread rapidly infecting 322 Scots and claiming the lives of six of them. Schools are closed, thousands of jobs lost, the future uncertain.

Monday 23 March 2020
Scotland Tonight

Amid concerns that the UK hadn't been moving fast enough in its response to the coronavirus, the Prime Minister tonight made a statement to the nation, signalling that we're now following other countries into an effective lockdown. In a move endorsed by the First Minister, Mr Johnson said that people must now stay at home to stop the spread of the disease.

BORIS JOHNSON, Prime Minister: From this evening I must give the British people a very simple instruction. You must stay at home. Because the critical thing we must do *(is)* to stop the disease spreading between households. That is why people will only be allowed to leave their home for the following, very limited purposes: shopping for basic necessities as infrequently as possible, one form of exercise a day, for example a run, walk or cycle along, or with members of your household; any medical need, to provide care or to help a vulnerable person; and travelling to and from work, but only where this is absolutely necessary and cannot be done from home. That's all – these are the only reasons you should leave your home… No Prime Minister wants to enact measures like this. I know the damage that this disruption is doing and will do to people's lives, to their businesses and to their jobs. Each and every one of us is now obliged to join together. To halt the spread of this disease. To protect our NHS and to save many, many thousands of lives. And I know that as they have in the past so many times. The people of this country will rise to that challenge. And we will come through it stronger than ever. We will beat the coronavirus and we will beat it together. And, therefore, I urge you at this moment of national emergency to stay at home, protect our NHS and save lives.

DIARY: Several have been calling for this sooner, but you have to wonder how long the general populace will thole it. I think we'll have a mental health crisis soon.

Monday 23 March 2020 *(cont)*
STV News

Alex Salmond has been cleared of all charges in his sex assault trial… The verdict came late this afternoon and the former First Minister has walked out of court a free man. He's been cleared of all 13 charges against him. Nine women came to court with allegations of sexual and indecent assault. Over the last fortnight they gave details of these claims. But this afternoon the jury delivered verdicts of not guilty on 12 charges and one not proven. As he left court, Mr Salmond claimed evidence that was not able to be heard in court will now 'see the light of day'.

Tuesday 24 March 2020
STV News

Today was the first day of Scotland being in lockdown. The first day of living with new restrictions as we are told to stay at home in a bid to curb the spread of the coronavirus.

There were two more deaths, bringing the total to 16. And there are now 584 confirmed cases of Covid-19 here, an increase of 85. The number of intensive care beds is to be quadrupled to prepare our health service for what is expected to become a worsening situation.

SHARON FREW, Chief Reporter: We woke up to a new reality – our everyday lives now restricted like never before. Those venturing out have been told they must only do so if it is essential – not just for today, tomorrow, but for days to come. The prospect of three weeks of measures is creating great anxiety for those already in self-isolation… Public gatherings of more than two people have been banned. There will be no weddings or baptisms. Funerals will be allowed. Even when following this guidance, people should minimise the amount of time spent out of their homes and should keep two metres away from anyone they do not live with… The retailers allowed to stay open include supermarkets and other food shops, pharmacies and petrol stations.

DIARY: One of the words of the moment is Zoom – an app that allows video conferencing. We had a *Scotland Tonight* meeting using it. Almost all TV interviews now are being done using video calls and there's much interest in seeing inside people's homes.

Sunday 29 March 2020

DIARY: Talk of the lockdown lasting until June. I don't believe that. Some restrictions maybe, but people will not accept this for so long. Quite aside from the restrictions and economic damage, I think you'll start seeing other problems emerge – suicides, alcoholism, which could be every bit as devastating as the virus.

Wednesday 1 April 2020
STV News

Another steep increase in the number of people across Scotland infected with coronavirus. The Scottish Government is abandoning flagship policies it had hoped to introduce this year. Instead, as construction continues on the temporary hospital at the SEC in Glasgow, and moves to boost beds across the NHS take place, tonight, emergency legislation is still being debated at Holyrood to keep the country running, as the outbreak worsens. 2,310 people have now tested positive for coronavirus – that's an increase of 317 cases since yesterday. Seventy-six people have died from the disease. There are now 147 patients being treated in intensive care units, that's up from 51 a week ago.

DIARY: The big issue just now seems to be the lack of testing, especially of NHS staff in the frontline. It does seem a remarkable oversight. Many are self-isolating, but a test would show if they were okay to work.

Friday 3 April 2020
STV News

Last night Scotland turned out on their doorsteps to thank the NHS and other key workers. People lined their streets to the sound of bagpipes, applause and the banging of pots and pans in a show of support. Landmarks across the country also lit up in blue to say thank you to those who are keeping us safe.

DIARY: People quite tense about keeping distance. Some even wearing masks. The deaths are now in their hundreds in the UK and tens in Scotland. Disagreement in messages – suggestion from the UK Government that the peak might be reached next weekend. Scottish Government saying no evidence of that… At first, younger people thought it won't matter if they get it, but hearing more and more cases of young people succumbing.

Monday 6 April 2020
STV News

A new face is fronting Scotland's NHS tonight – after Catherine Calderwood's embarrassing departure. Dr Gregor Smith's appointment should help get the Government's message back on track. His predecessor as Chief

Medical Officer breached her own warning to stay indoors, by twice visiting her holiday home in Fife. Tonight, there's concern about deaths in care homes and the ongoing safety for people living and working in the care sector. There are now 3,961 confirmed cases of coronavirus in Scotland. 222 people have died.

PRIME MINISTER IN INTENSIVE CARE
STV News – Late bulletin

The First Minister and the leader of the Scottish Conservatives are among those sending their best wishes to Boris Johnson, after the Prime Minister was admitted to intensive care with 'worsening' coronavirus symptoms.

DIARY: He'd first gone into hospital last night. It was reported to be a 'precautionary measure', but it's been clear for the last few days he's not been recovering. I think it's been a real jolt to everyone.

Sunday 12 April 2020
STV News

A further 24 people with coronavirus have died in Scotland, bringing the total to 566. There has been a slight fall in the number of people in hospital from Covid-19, but the Health Secretary says it's 'too early' to read anything into that. The news comes as the Prime Minister has been released from hospital, having spent seven days in hospital with coronavirus.

Tuesday 14 April 2020
STV News

The controversy surrounding the Scottish Professional Football League board's recommendation to end the current season has taken a fresh twist. Partick Thistle say they have received legal advice which states Dundee's retracted vote 'must stand'. Dundee had originally voted against the resolution before withdrawing their 'no' vote.

RAMAN BHARDWAJ, Sports Presenter: The decision on whether to call the football season – so in essence the current league standings across all four divisions would be final – rests on one vote – that of Dundee Football Club. Clubs were asked to submit their votes last Friday. Dundee did cast a 'no' vote. But the league said this didn't register with them until AFTER the club contacted them to not consider the vote. If Dundee were to change their vote to 'yes', Partick Thistle who play in the Championship, along with Hearts in the Premiership and Stranraer in League One would be relegated. Thistle have been critical of the governing body. The Glasgow club have called into question the vote and also the voting process.

Dundee changed their vote to 'yes' the following week.

Monday 27 April 2020
STV News

We're all still urged to stick to the lockdown to save lives, but there is also new advice if you leave the house. The Scottish Government now recommends wearing a face covering in 'limited circumstances' when you are in a place where it is difficult to keep two metres apart from other people. More than 10,000 people have now tested positive for Covid-19 in Scotland, 200 more than yesterday. There have been 70 more deaths. The death toll is now more than 2,000.

Wednesday 29 April 2020
STV News

Tonight – the frontline of the crisis. More than half of coronavirus deaths in Scotland are now happening in care homes. It's like nothing they've ever had to endure before. Staff at care homes say the coronavirus pandemic is taking its toll on their emotional wellbeing as they try to keep residents safe and keep their spirits up. In the last week more than half of the deaths from Covid-19 in Scotland have been in care homes.

EWAN PETRIE, STV Political Correspondent: To make a news programme we rely on people telling us their stories every day. Often that involves sitting in their living room or kitchen, rearranging furniture to make room for the camera equipment, and having a chat over a cup of coffee.

Covid changed that.

Suddenly it was no longer safe for us to enter people's homes. In the early days of the pandemic, like everyone else, we were feeling our way through the new restrictions, working out what was possible within the guidelines.

Understandably many people became very wary of allowing us even near their home. Many interviews moved online. However, we also need pictures around an interview to explain the story, and that simply wasn't possible with Zoom.

To get round that we began asking people to film themselves on their phone watching TV, typing at a keyboard or making a cup of tea, and send it to us. We even made a short tutorial video we could pass on to them giving an idea of what we were looking for.

It was a makeshift solution which had mixed results. Where possible we tried to keep as many face-to-face interviews as we could. That meant using gardens or even speaking to people through open windows with microphones on extended poles to keep our distance.

The whole choreography around interviews changed. Reporters could no longer travel with camera crews. We would arrive separately, ring the doorbell, then often have to go through a side gate or down a lane to the back garden. We did interviews on patios, in playparks, on the street outside workplaces.

To keep our distance from each other the camera operator would set up a microphone on a stand, step away and get the interviewee to step in. The camera would be further than normal from our guest, leaving us, at times, having to shout over traffic noise. The reporter would also be further from the camera than normal.

On the rare occasion a personal microphone was used on a collar or lapel, it would have to be wiped down before use, left on a table for the interviewee to collect, then instructions given for how to put it on. Then the whole process would happen in reverse once the interview was over.

This setup was in place all through the Scottish Parliament election campaign in 2021. Photocalls were carefully planned to be outdoors, in wide open spaces, often in parks – not ideal when you have a fear of dogs like Nicola Sturgeon. Gone were the crowds following politicians to heckle or cheer, gone were the handshakes with voters, the kissing of babies. Broadcast interviews were pooled between organisations to reduce contact.

We are back to filming in people's homes. But the memory of those restrictions still lingers every time we set foot inside.

Sunday 10 May 2020
STV News

The First Minister has confirmed an easing of the lockdown exercise guidelines. From tomorrow, the once-a-day limit will be removed. However, Nicola Sturgeon has stressed the situation remains 'fragile' and has asked the UK Government not to advertise its new 'stay alert' campaign in Scotland.

DIARY: Splits emerging in the unified approach to tackling coronavirus. The Prime Minister tonight addressed the nation talking about a gradual easing of restrictions and a new slogan about 'Stay Alert'. Not so in Scotland. Here the message is still stay at home, with the only easing being that you can now go out to exercise more than once a day. It has caused confusion. Nicola Sturgeon is always getting in first to announce what the UK Government is about to announce, but today was different. The mixed messages will cause confusion and be a charter for chancers.

Friday 29 May 2020
STV News

In blazing sunshine, across Scotland, families are being reunited. With the rules now allowing outdoor meetings between households – albeit maintaining social distance – lockdown has officially eased. The police say engaging with the public will be the priority, but they will take enforcement action if people push things too far.

Tuesday 9 June 2020
STV News

Transmission of Covid-19 within the community in Scotland may have taken place in February, earlier than confirmed. The Interim Chief Medical Officer Dr Gregor Smith has said genetic studies reveal it was likely the virus existed before the first cases emerged in March – that's weeks before the lockdown. After two days of no reported deaths, a further seven people have died from the disease. The total number of deaths now stands at 3,971. Fourteen more people have tested positive.

COLIN MACKAY, Political Editor: Scientists reckon there were around 112 separate introductions of the virus to the country in those early days of it and these led to the widespread transmission around the country with the R number thought to have been between four and six.

The R number was the number of people an infected person would go on to infect.

Thursday 18 June 2020
STV News

Scotland is making 'clear and substantial' progress in suppressing coronavirus and can begin moving to the next phase of easing lockdown restrictions. Here are the main changes: from tomorrow you'll be able to meet people from up to two households outdoors. People living alone will be able to form an 'extended household' without social distancing. Face coverings will be required on public transport from Monday. And shops, zoos and playgrounds will re-open on 29 June. But if you're keen to go to the pub or a restaurant you'll need to wait a bit longer. There's no date yet for beer gardens to start welcoming customers.

DIARY: Nicola Sturgeon... says she has to be cautious and I see that, but there are many who say she's being too cautious and the economy will suffer for it.

Friday 26 June 2020
STV News – Kelly-Ann live from Glasgow city centre

You join us in the heart of Scotland's biggest city – Glasgow city centre – where armed police have locked down part of this usually busy street, after a stabbing attack which left one dead and six in hospital, including a police officer. The incident happened within a hotel which has been offering temporary accommodation during the pandemic. The main suspect was confronted and shot dead by police.

Thursday 9 July 2020
STV News

Scotland is taking another step back to normality. But we're being warned the easing of lockdown measures are some of the highest risk changes being made so far. From tomorrow, we'll be able to meet people from two other households indoors and even stay overnight. And, among other things, dates have been confirmed for a return to places of worship, cinemas and hairdressers.

Tuesday 4 August 2020
STV News

Thousands of school pupils across the country will have received their exam results this morning, despite them being cancelled – for the first time – because of the coronavirus pandemic. Grades this year are based on teacher estimates and are moderated by the Scottish Qualifications Authority.

Tuesday 11 August 2020
STV News

'I am sorry. We did not get it right.' The words of the Education Secretary John Swinney as he announced a Scottish

Government u-turn on the exam results. 75,000 students, whose results were downgraded, will now be sent new exam certificates with the grades estimated by their teachers. The opposition say the episode has been a shambles and are calling for Mr Swinney to resign.

This came after protests that pupils from poorer backgrounds were hit hardest by the moderation of the SQA.

ABERDEEN TRAIN CRASH
Wednesday 12 August 2020
STV News – Andrea Brymer live from near Stonehaven

Behind me – a mile or so away in that hillside – the 6.38am train from Aberdeen to Glasgow came off the line this morning in horrendous weather. Three people died at the scene. Six others are being treated in hospital for minor injuries. The driver is thought to have been among those killed. We're near Stonehaven – just three miles from the coast. A huge emergency response from multiple emergency services has been going on all day in this patch of Aberdeenshire countryside.

Thursday 3 September 2020
STV News

Selfish and irresponsible. There's been an angry reaction to more than 300 people attending a house party at a hired venue in Midlothian. Police have said the partygoers showed a blatant disregard for restrictions imposed to help save lives and prevent the spread of coronavirus. The event was one of 300 house parties police had to attend over the weekend with some people arrested or fined. The police say further investigations are being carried out with a view to what other charges may be brought. It comes as 101 new cases of Covid-19 have been reported.

Wednesday 9 September 2020
STV News

As the First Minister hinted today that more lockdown restrictions may be coming our way, one Scottish Government adviser has warned of the possibility of civic unrest.

The Prime Minister has announced that the numbers of people allowed to gather in England will be significantly reduced and Nicola Sturgeon said she was looking at changes here.

EWAN PETRIE, Political Correspondent: The steep rise in Covid cases is pushing Scotland to the cliff edge of more restrictions. The average daily number has trebled in the past three weeks. Reversing any easing of lockdown will heighten existing frustration. In England the Prime Minister has announced gatherings of more than six people will be illegal from Monday. Here eight people from three families can still gather indoors, and 15 from five families outside.

DIARY: Some differences, though, from back at the beginning of the pandemic. Far more testing, so more cases will crop up, fewer – much fewer – going to hospital and very few deaths.

Thursday 10 September 2020
STV News

There will be no relaxation of coronavirus restrictions in Scotland. In fact, they are set to get tougher. The First Minister tightened the lockdown rules today about how many people can meet. And changes have been put on hold as the number of Covid cases increases once more – 161 in the last 24 hours. From Monday, with some exceptions, no more than six people from two households can meet up both indoors and out. Face coverings will become mandatory going into and moving around bars and restaurants. And long-hoped-for plans to reopen theatres, live music venues and indoor soft play areas could be delayed for at least three weeks amid the warning that the country is in a 'precarious position'.

Friday 2 October 2020
STV News

The First Minister is calling on Margaret Ferrier to resign as an MP for breaking the Covid rules. She travelled from London to Glasgow by train after testing positive for coronavirus. The SNP have already suspended her from the party. Nicola Sturgeon said she had no power to force her to quit Parliament, but said she hoped she would do the right thing. The First Minister said she did so with a heavy heart because Margaret Ferrier was a friend and colleague. But her actions were dangerous and indefensible.

COLIN MACKAY, Political Editor: There's more pressure on Margaret Ferrier to quit than I have ever seen before. When details of this emerged on the programme last night it wasn't clear just how much she had broken the rules, but the more you hear the more stupid this looks. I think most people have been left incredulous. Margaret Ferrier told her party at Westminster she was going home because a member of her family was sick, but it was her who tested positive for coronavirus. The First Minister described her mistakes as monumental and incomprehensible. Usually, political allies rally round in a crisis, but not on this one.

Wednesday 7 October 2020
STV News

As the number of new Covid infections tops 1,000, the First Minister has announced new restrictions. Without them, Ms Sturgeon says, by the end of this month the virus will be rampaging to the same extent as it was in the spring. The changes are not the same everywhere. Basically, the country has been split into two based on health board areas. The Central Belt's hospitality sector is facing the complete closure of pubs and restaurants. The restrictions in the north and south of the country are less severe.

DIARY: A lot of anger – especially from the hospitality industry – doomsday warnings. More and more people questioning the effectiveness of these measures. We've had the housing restrictions in Glasgow and Renfrewshire for several weeks now, but the figures are going up.

Friday 9 October 2020
STV News

Scotland's two-tier restrictions on the hospitality industry have come into force in the past few minutes. For pubs and restaurants in the Central Belt it's a complete closure for more than two weeks. Those in the rest of the country face curbs on when and where they can serve alcohol. Cafes have more leeway – prompting questions over what is the difference between a cafe and a restaurant? For any who are having to close as a result of coronavirus rules in the coming months, the Chancellor has announced the furlough scheme will continue.

DIARY: A lot of discussion about what constitutes a cafe – which can stay open – and a restaurant – which can't. Somewhere that serves light meals and snacks, apparently. You can see why restaurants are raging. Government view is that hospitality is the second worst spreader, after home visits.

Monday 2 November 2020
STV News

Could we be heading for another national lockdown? On the day a new five-level Covid-19 restriction system came into force, the First Minister said she couldn't rule out far stricter measures across the board and a move to level four for the whole of Scotland. The decision hinges on whether an extension to the furlough scheme is extended beyond England. The issue was discussed at a COBRA meeting this morning. Today 951 new positive coronavirus cases were reported. There were no deaths, but the daily test positivity rate is 9.6 per cent, up from 7 per cent yesterday.

ANNOUNCEMENT OF VACCINE
Monday 9 November 2020
STV News

It won't make a difference today or tomorrow, but tonight the prospect of a route out of the coronavirus pandemic is looking a bit clearer. A vaccine being developed in Germany has been found to prevent more than 90 per cent of people from contracting Covid.

GORDON CHREE, Senior Reporter: In the last eight months since the first case of coronavirus was confirmed in Scotland our everyday lives have often been gloomy – but now some optimism that fog could soon be lifting. The vaccine being developed by Pfizer could get emergency approval for use by the end of the month.

Thursday 12 November 2020
STV News – late bulletin

Scotland are through to Euro 2020 after beating Serbia in a thrilling 5–4 penalty shoot-out win in the play-off final tonight. It'll be Scotland's first major tournament since 1998.

RAMAN BHARDWAJ, Sports Presenter: After 22 years of heartache and pain this is the magical David Marshall moment that sent the nation into delirium. A game which Scotland dominated for 90 minutes, then were up against it in extra time, came down to spot kicks. And for once there was no glorious failure. Euro 2020 here we come.

Wednesday 25 November 2020
STV News

If you were in any doubt about the true economic impact of Covid, it was set out in stark detail this afternoon by the Chancellor. He spoke of 'lasting damage' and the worst recession in nearly 300 years. Unemployment is predicted to soar next year and we can expect the highest level of borrowing in peacetime history.

Monday 30 November 2020
STV News

The public inquiry into the death of a man who was restrained by police officers will have to scrutinise around 50,000 documents before it hears from witnesses. Sheku Bayoh's family believe race played a part in his death in Kirkcaldy in 2015 and criticised the subsequent investigation. The judge leading this independent inquiry pledged it will be thorough and fearless.

Tuesday 1 December 2020
STV News

Another day, another retail giant facing collapse. Less than 24 hours after Arcadia called in the administrators, Debenhams is to shut its doors for good. JD Sports has pulled out of rescue talks for the troubled department store because it houses many Arcadia brands, like Topshop and Miss Selfridge, within its branches. Between the two businesses 25,000 jobs now hang in the balance, on top of the thousands already lost on the High Street during the pandemic. Unions are now in talks on how to save jobs. But analysts warn it's the end of the High Street as we know it.

Tuesday 8 December 2020
STV News

It's the day we've been waiting for since the start of the coronavirus pandemic. Vaccinations against Covid-19 have been taking place, marking the start of the biggest vaccination programme in history. Health care workers at hospitals around the country have been the first in Scotland to get the jab. We're told it's too soon to say when the process will be completed for all of us, but within weeks tens of thousands of people will have had their first dose.

GORDON CHREE, Senior Reporter: Andrew's a nurse at the Western General Hospital in Edinburgh – and the first person to be seen being vaccinated in Scotland for Covid. He'll get a second dose in a few weeks' time and shortly after that should be protected from getting ill from the virus. Next week care home workers and residents will begin to be vaccinated. The programme will work through people aged over 80 as well as NHS and social care staff. Then it's those aged 75 and older, before the over-70s and people considered clinically extremely vulnerable. Over-65s are next and then people with underlying health conditions and working down through the remaining age groups.

Saturday 19 December 2020
STV News

Christmas is being cut back to just one day and Scotland's borders are being closed – to prevent the spread of a new strain of coronavirus. From Boxing Day almost all of Scotland will go into level four restrictions, and a strict travel ban will be in place between Scotland and the rest of the UK. The First Minister says she has rarely felt more worried than she has today.

DIARY: I recognise the First Minister's dilemma and I don't see her as playing politics this time, but is the balance right? The excess deaths from Covid against the other mental and health issues and devastation of large parts of the economy. They'll say it comes down to people's lives, but the fear is we start losing lives in other ways.

AGREEMENT ON BREXIT DEAL
Thursday 24 December 2020
STV News

It's been a waiting game all day, but finally 'the deal' is done. The UK and EU have agreed a trade deal on Brexit, some four-and-a-half years on from the UK's vote to leave the European Union. The Prime Minister Boris Johnson says the deal will benefit every part of the United Kingdom. The majority of Scots did not vote to leave and the First Minister says, 'No deal will never make up for what Brexit takes away from us.'

KATHRYN SAMSON, Westminster Correspondent: Four-and-half-years on a trade deal has been done. It's worth over £660 billion. It will come as a relief to many Scottish businesses and to Boris Johnson who has got this over the line at the last minute. The hold-up was over fishing. We now know there will be a five-and-a-half-year transition period... But of course there's a unique flavour to this in Scotland. Nicola Sturgeon tweeting her line that Brexit is happening against Scotland's will with a 62 per cent remain vote in Scotland... The Prime Minister spoke today about the need to finally put Brexit behind us. With a Holyrood election coming next year, perhaps that's optimistic.

Tuesday 29 December 2020
STV News

There's a warning people throughout the country could be living under the new strict lockdown rules for the next two months. Professor Linda Bauld says the restrictions are necessary to control the virus, but that the vaccine roll-out should mean things could look brighter in the spring. It comes after a further seven coronavirus deaths since Christmas and as the number of cases continues to rise. Nearly 1,900 new cases of Covid were confirmed today. The First Minister is urging people to stay at home for Hogmanay.

LOUISE SCOTT, reporter: Today recorded the highest daily number of coronavirus cases since the beginning of the pandemic at 1,895, but this could be due to a lag from Christmas. Meanwhile, cases in Scottish hospitals continue to rise as those on the frontline warn there are serious concerns.

2021

Monday 4 January 2021
STV News

Tonight – Stay at home. Schools will remain shut till the start of February as further restrictions are placed on meeting outdoors and workplaces.

A new Scottish lockdown. The First Minister has announced a return to restrictions similar to those in March after a continued steep rise in Covid cases. From midnight – it will be the law to stay at home unless for essential purposes and anyone who can work from home must do so. There is also new guidance for those shielding. If you can work from your house, you shouldn't go into work. Outdoor gatherings are now restricted to two people from two households. From Friday places of worship are to close. Twenty people can attend a funeral and five people can attend a wedding. And schools and nurseries will be closed until 1 February… Today's announcement comes as a new vaccine was rolled out across the country.

EWAN PETRIE, Political Correspondent: It's another step on the road out of this pandemic. 82-year-old James Shaw is among the first in Scotland to receive the Oxford AstraZeneca vaccine along with his wife. It's hoped everyone over the age of 50 as well as the most vulnerable will have their first dose by May. As the spread of the virus accelerates, the race to vaccinate becomes even more critical to ease pressure on an NHS approaching its limits. While the vaccine does offer hope for the future, the Scottish Government is taking action now to try to slow the spread. Schools will be closed until at least the start of February with learning moving online. A decision on reopening will be reviewed every fortnight. Opposition parties highlighted concerns over the impact on young people. Unions want employers to furlough anyone who can't work because of childcare commitments. For parents it means at least another month of home learning. These measures take us close to the lockdown of spring last year. 2020 may be behind us. For now, the new year looks just as dark before any light appears in the coming months.

DIARY: How has it come to this? Yes, the virus has been challenging, but there have been so many Government missteps along the way. Not the least has been the failure of efficient and adequate testing. Still, at least we have the prospect of mass vaccination before too long.

Monday 25 January 2021
STV News

The ties that bind the UK appear increasingly under strain amid Brexit and the pandemic. With 20 polls in a row putting support for Scottish independence in the ascendancy, the SNP have drawn up a new plan to secure a second referendum. But Boris Johnson remains opposed to granting a Section 30 Order to authorise such a vote. This means the battle could end up being fought in the courts. The former Prime Minister Gordon Brown also believes that now is not the time for an IndyRef2. But he is warning that if the UK doesn't reform itself, it will be at risk of becoming a 'failed state'.

DIARY: *Scotland Tonight* looked at the open civil war in the SNP – who sacked prominent and popular Westminster frontbencher Joanna Cherry. The party is divided on the timing of independence and pushing for gender recognition.

Thursday 11 February 2021
STV News

As much of Scotland continues to shiver under a blanket of snow, the lowest temperature in the UK for more than 25 years has been recorded in Braemar. The Aberdeenshire village notched up 23 degrees below freezing.

Monday 22 February 2021
STV News

After almost a year, and endless days of reporting lockdowns, hospital admissions and deaths – tonight there are some glimmers of hope. First, a study on the impact of Covid vaccines in Scotland has found what's been described as a 'spectacular' result in keeping people out of hospital. And second – the roadmap out of lockdown will be sketched out tomorrow with some signs the second half of the year could look a lot more normal.

Tuesday 23 February 2021
STV News

Unlocking at last… but the keywords are caution and patience. It's hoped by the end of April the full country will move back to level three with the reopening of the likes of gyms and hairdressers and additional retail. But the journey will be slow and reviewed every three weeks. Phase one is already underway with the partial return of schools and plans for care home visits early in March. From the middle of March, the remainder of primary school pupils will return to the classroom, and more senior pupils part-time. Non-contact sports for 12-to-17-year-olds will return and four people from two households can meet outside. From 5 April, stay at home is lifted. Everyone will be able to go back to school. Places of worship will be reopened with restricted numbers. Click and collect for non-essential retail will restart. And six people from two households can mix. We'll be back to level three and the gradual reopening of the economy and easing of social restrictions. All of course, provided the vaccine continues to roll out and infection rates are under control.

DIARY: Following on from Boris Johnson's statement yesterday on the road map out of the pandemic for England, Nicola Sturgeon did hers today. Much more cautious and patient – no promise that life will resume pretty much by mid-June. I get the caution and I understand the need to be data led, but it left people really flat.

Friday 26 February 2021
STV News

Tonight – Salmond Strikes Back. The former First Minister slams Nicola Sturgeon, Scotland's prosecutors and civil service leaders.

Alex Salmond has told a Holyrood Committee that Nicola Sturgeon has broken the ministerial code and he called for resignations – from Scotland's top civil servant, Scotland's top prosecutor and the Chief Executive of the SNP. He says Scotland's leadership has failed. The committee is investigating how complaints of sexual misconduct allegations by Mr Salmond were dealt with by the Scottish Government. For more than five hours this afternoon we saw just how the relationship between the former First Minister and his successor has crumbled.

DIARY: Much heralded and much delayed. I think he damaged the First Minister's reputation, but whether it's enough to bring her down seems unlikely.

Wednesday 3 March 2021
STV News

Nicola Sturgeon has dismissed claims of a plot against Alex Salmond as 'absurd' and insists she had no reason to want to 'get him'. The First Minister was speaking at her long-awaited appearance before the inquiry into her Government's handling of harassment complaints against her predecessor. She also apologised to the women who made the complaints.

DIARY: She is covering up. There was too much she couldn't remember. That said, there is nothing that will force her resignation.

Sunday 7 March 2021
STV News

Thousands of Rangers fans have gathered in Glasgow's George Square and at Ibrox to celebrate the side winning the Scottish

Premiership. That's despite warnings from the First Minister and the police to stay at home. Steven Gerrard's side were crowned champions this afternoon after Celtic were held to a goalless draw at Dundee United.

DIARY: Rangers fans gathered in numbers at Ibrox and George Square in flagrant defiance of lockdown. Chorus of disapproval, but many of these voices had no issue with demonstrations last summer. Ah, but that's different, they say.

Tuesday 9 March 2021
STV News

It's the interview everyone has been talking about. Harry and Meghan's tell-almost-all interview broadcast on STV last night has supposedly rocked the royal family. The couple spoke about racism, mental health and the media. Campaigners here hope it will open up an honest conversation about these issues.

More than a million Scots tuned in to watch the interview on STV.

Monday 22 March 2021
STV News

The First Minister Nicola Sturgeon has been cleared of breaking the ministerial code by an independent inquiry. The investigation by the lawyer James Hamilton had been examining whether she had misled Parliament over meetings with her predecessor, Alex Salmond. Mr Hamilton said he believed she had not breached any of the provisions of the code. Nicola Sturgeon has welcomed the findings.

DIARY: There had been no leaks or hints from this inquiry, so nobody was quite sure what it would deliver. It was widely acknowledged that this was the crucial one because there was no political partisanship involved and if he had found against her she'd have been under pressure to resign. I think general surprise that he has given her such a broad clearance and found it possible she could have forgotten meetings.

Tuesday 23 March 2021
STV News

It's a year since the first national lockdown to protect us from coronavirus began. Since then, more than 200,000 people in Scotland have tested positive for Covid. Many more will have had it. Nearly 10,000 deaths linked to the virus have been recorded. And the impact on wider physical and mental health has been significant. Today has been declared a national day of reflection – a time to remember those who've died and support those who've been bereaved.

Tuesday 23 March 2021 *(cont)*
STV News

The First Minister has been accused of misleading a Scottish Parliament Committee looking into the Government's handling of harassment complaints. A report by MSPs says she gave an inaccurate account of a meeting with her predecessor Alex Salmond. However, the four SNP committee members said they did not agree with the finding. This afternoon she survived a vote of no confidence at Holyrood brought by the Scottish Conservatives.

DIARY: It split down party lines. The irony of the SNP accusing other parties of partisanship when their own four MSPs voted together.

This parliamentary inquiry was different from the independent inquiry of James Hamilton.

Friday 26 March 2021
STV News

Alex Salmond has announced his attempt to return to frontline politics with the creation of a new pro-independence party. The former First Minister is among the candidates standing for the Alba Party in the Holyrood election. He claims the aim is to build what he calls a supermajority for independence. Other parties are questioning his suitability for office following his own admission of inappropriate behaviour towards women.

DEATH OF THE DUKE OF EDINBURGH
Friday 9 April 2021

The Duke of Edinburgh, Prince Philip, died at Windsor Castle this morning. He was 99. Throughout his life he had deep and long-standing ties to Scotland – from his patronage of the Duke of Edinburgh's Award to his commitments to countless charities and organisations. He was a frequent visitor to Royal Deeside where he and the Queen called Balmoral Castle their home. Tonight, flags are flying at half-mast, but the public outpouring of grief is muted. Of course, his death comes in the midst of a global pandemic and will impact on how the nation marks his passing.

Thursday 22 April 2021

DIARY: On the drive home I passed or avoided three different traffic jams. Whatever is being said, the lockdown has well and truly ended.

Monday 26 April 2021

STV News – live on location from a Glasgow bar and Edinburgh's Princes Street

Tonight – Welcome back! Scotland unlocks. Shops, restaurants and pubs reopen as restrictions ease.

JM: Good evening from Glasgow's Clydeside where many are enjoying the first steps of restrictions being eased and a taste of freedom. More than a year since the first lockdown began, Scotland's road back to normal life has taken a major step forward. For a start, pubs like this one are now open outdoors as we move to level three of the coronavirus restrictions.

KAW: Here on Edinburgh's Princes Street, of course, the shops have reopened – there were queues outside stores across the country from early this morning. Gyms, beauticians and museums and galleries are also back in business.

DIARY: The *Six* involved live dual presentation – me in an outdoor bar – Cranside Kitchen – across the river from STV. Kelly-Ann was in Princes Street… No question it was a risk being live in a bar, but the patrons were no problem. Plenty of selfie photos afterwards. If I don't pick up Covid after that, I must be fine. As cameraman Ian McCall said, strange to be in a crowd again.

SCOTTISH ELECTION 2021
Friday 7 May 2021
STV News – live from Holyrood

Tonight – The SNP are on track for a historic fourth term in office. Counting won't be over until the weekend. And Nicola Sturgeon doesn't yet know if she'll have a majority here at Holyrood.

Good evening from the Scottish Parliament in Edinburgh. Scotland has voted, counting continues and Nicola Sturgeon is set to stay on as First Minister. The SNP will be the biggest party, but it's not yet clear if they'll have a majority in Holyrood. Results are still coming in – with more counting tomorrow.

But, first tonight, let's take a look at the results so far. The SNP have secured 27 seats. The Liberal Democrats have three. The Conservatives have one seat. And no seats confirmed yet for Labour or the Greens.

EWAN PETRIE, Political Correspondent: By the time Nicola Sturgeon arrived at her count already it seemed clear the SNP were on course to emerge as the largest party. The question remains whether they will secure an overall majority. There was no surprise as the SNP leader fended off a challenge from Scottish Labour Leader Anas Sarwar to hold on to her Glasgow Southside seat. Covid has extended the wait for these results. With no overnight count – instead the first ballot boxes were opened at 9.00am this morning. 48 of the 73 constituencies are due to be declared by the end of today, with the final result not expected until later tomorrow. To get a majority the SNP need a strong performance on the constituency vote. After a campaign like no other, this is a count with a difference

– Covid restrictions are in place to protect staff. But despite the pandemic turnout has been higher across the country.

DIARY: There was no overnight count – because of Covid restrictions – so the counts began this morning and will span two days. Instead of going on air at 6.00pm with the complete story, we had an abbreviated news in the midst of a full election programme.

Saturday 8 May 2021
STV News – live from Holyrood

Good evening from Edinburgh. Nicola Sturgeon is First Minister – and her party will stay on for an historic fourth term in Government, following a second day of counting in the Holyrood election. But the SNP seem unlikely to have an overall majority.

EWAN PETRIE, Political Correspondent: Nicola Sturgeon described her party's victory as extraordinary and historic, adding another Independence Referendum is a matter of fundamental democratic principle. On the regional lists – in Central Scotland Labour and the Conservatives won three each, while the Greens picked up one. In the Highlands Labour were down to one seat, along with the SNP and Greens while the Conservatives picked up four. A pro-independence majority raises the question of a formal coalition. The Prime Minister described another referendum as irresponsible and reckless, signalling the upcoming clash between Holyrood and Westminster over the constitution.

DIARY: Probably the strangest ever election because of the pandemic. And the result was essentially the same.

Thursday 13 May 2021
STV News

Hundreds of protesters are blocking a street in Glasgow, stopping immigration officers from removing two people. Officers were called to Kenmure Street in Pollokshields just before 10.00am this morning. Protesters have filled the road, chanting, calling for the men to be released. The First Minister said she was 'deeply concerned' at the scenes.

Saturday 15 May 2021
STV News

Police say they've made a number of arrests as thousands of Rangers fans gather outside Ibrox and in George Square to celebrate the side lifting the Scottish Premiership title and ending the league season undefeated. Supporters were warned against celebrating in large crowds with Covid restrictions still in place and concerns over recent outbreaks in the Glasgow area.

DIARY: Inevitably, it descended into violence, drunkenness and vandalism that constantly shames Rangers and other clubs.

Monday 17 May 2021
STV News

It has been an intense period for policing in Glasgow. Saturday saw Police Scotland having to deal with thousands of Rangers fans defying lockdown rules and marching through the city. Several officers were injured. Two days earlier, in a very different context, public health concerns were also high when officers were called to attend a protest in Pollokshields aimed at disrupting a Home Office immigration raid. There was also a pro-Palestinian rally held yesterday in George Square.

DIARY: *Scotland Tonight* led with an interview with ACC Gary Ritchie of Police Scotland on the issues of dealing with the Covid-busting gatherings of last week and the weekend. I am amazed at how many people – including colleagues – thought it was okay to ignore Covid restrictions to protest, but not to celebrate. It really is a case of it's okay as long as I agree with it. The principle is clear. Do not gather. If one group is seen to do it, then where's your argument to deny others just because you don't like them?

SCOTLAND'S FIRST GAME IN AN INTERNATIONAL TOURNAMENT IN 23 YEARS

Monday 14 June 2021
STV News

Scotland have lost their opening game in the Euros, beaten 2–0 by the Czech Republic. After all the optimism and hype it was an all too familiar story for Scotland in international competition. Almost 10,000 fans were in Hampden for the game, the biggest organised crowd gathering in Scotland since the start of the pandemic.

Friday 18 June 2021

DIARY: Well, well, well – Scotland got a creditable 0–0 draw with England at Wembley in the Euros. They even had a couple of chances to win and would have deserved to. Bitter experience tells me it's the hope that is so crushing. But it's too easy to be cynical – let's hope and believe. We were given cause for that tonight.

Tuesday 22 June 2021

DIARY: Scotland failed to qualify from their group in the Euros, going down 3–1 to Croatia at Hampden. Outclassed and errors made. I was more optimistic because we do have more quality players than for a long time, but still glaring weaknesses in defence and attack… I never fully bought into the hype, but I can understand people's desperation for success. It's been so long.

Our *Six O'Clock* tonight was a shambles. Kelly-Ann and I in a garden overlooking Hampden. Everything ready, openers recorded and set to go. As soon as we went on air the generator in the satellite truck failed, so almost the entire programme came from Sophie as back-up in the studio.

This led to a desperately uncomfortable moment at the end of the programme when Sports Presenter, Ronnie Charters, reintroduced Kelly-Ann and me who appeared at his side as if we were a separated couple forced to attend.

Friday 30 July 2021
STV News

As the pandemic brought Scotland to a halt in the past 18 months, one industry continued uninterrupted: the trade in illegal drugs. And the toll is devastating. Drug-related deaths in Scotland have hit record levels for the seventh year in a row with 1,339 people dying in 2020. It is the largest number of drug-related deaths since records began in 1996 and – once again – is the highest rate in Europe. Glasgow had the highest number of deaths, with Ayrshire and Tayside following close behind. 93 per cent of overdoses were caused by taking multiple drugs and there is a continued rise in fatalities involving pills known as street benzos.

DIARY: It's a national disgrace… It's been the same old story since I started – inconsistency, lack of follow through and vested interest. There have been careers made out of the drugs problem.

Friday 20 August 2021
STV News

A new chapter in the story of Scotland's Parliament. The Greens are joining the SNP in governing the country. It's being called a power-sharing deal and not a coalition. It also means there's a majority in favour of Scottish independence now governing Scotland. And, just months away from the COP-26 global climate conference in Glasgow, it gives the Greens two ministerial posts and commitments on environmental policies. The Scottish Conservative leader Douglas Ross says it's a 'nationalist coalition of chaos.'

Monday 23 August 2021
Scotland Tonight

An historic step forward for Green politics. That's how the party has hailed its draft power-sharing agreement with the SNP. The deal, which is still to be ratified by Green grassroots members, will see two of their MSPs become junior ministers in Nicola

Sturgeon's Government. But they're not calling it a coalition as the party has opt-outs from supporting the administration in a range of policy areas which they can't agree on.

JM: What does Scotland get out of this partnership?

PATRICK HARVIE, co-leader Scottish Greens: I think the most important thing that Scotland gets and should expect from all political parties is that we get some maturity and some constructive attitude to our politics. If you remember the last six months or so before the election, it was just so ugly and toxic, the atmosphere. And political parties were forgetting how to find common ground. I think it's really important that you can deal with your differences constructively, respect those differences, but also work together on the common ground. So, on areas from investing in railways, doubling the onshore wind capacity in Scotland, a national environment bill to start protecting species which have been in decline for so long, dealing with rights for people in the private rented sector who are all too often getting exploited at the moment... The opportunity here is not just to sit in the chamber in the Scottish Parliament and say we are right, everybody else is wrong. The opportunity is to actually make a difference. What we'll see here is a shift away from that rhetoric about maximum economic extraction and a shift towards things like sustainable transport, reducing people's energy bills, making sure that we are able to heat our homes without paying through the nose for energy that's going out through windows and doors and roofs and walls. All of that phenomenally important stuff about actually meeting the climate targets that have been missed for the last three years.

JM: There are several opt-outs – on aviation policy, economic policy, NATO membership. That's opportunistic, is it not? You're part of the Government, but not really part of the Government.

PH: No, I think this is the only honest way really for political parties that do have big differences to work together, is to say you can have those differences, you can try to work through them constructively, and you can work together on the common ground at the same time.

Friday 10 September 2021
STV News

When you make an emergency call it's usually because something serious has happened and you need urgent help. But as pressures mount on the NHS, patients are being forced to wait. Today, the head of the Scottish Ambulance Service apologised for delays in getting to patients. In some cases, people have had to wait hours for paramedics to reach them. In others they've faced significant hold ups once they reach hospital.

Monday 13 September 2021
Scotland Tonight

Democracy must and will prevail. That was the First Minister's message today on Scotland's constitutional future as she renewed her demand for the UK Government to drop its opposition to another referendum. In her speech to the SNP's virtual conference, Nicola Sturgeon also hit out at the damage she claims is being done by Brexit.

Tuesday 21 September 2021
STV News

Scotland's hospitals have recorded their worst-ever Accident and Emergency waiting times. 71.5 per cent of patients were dealt with within four hours which is well below the 95 per cent target. At the Queen Elizabeth University Hospital in Glasgow, Scotland's flagship hospital, fewer than half of patients were treated within that time. Now, firefighters will step in to help the struggling ambulance service, after reports of extremely long waits in emergency situations. The service is receiving an extra £20 million from the Scottish Government.

Wednesday 22 September 2021
STV News

The Lord Advocate says people caught in possession of Class A drugs could receive a police warning rather than being charged and ending up with a criminal conviction. In her first parliamentary statement, Dorothy Bain said it would help more drug users get treatment and support. Some drug addiction campaigners are welcoming the move, but the Conservatives say it amounts to the decriminalisation of the most dangerous drugs on Scotland's streets.

Friday 24 September 2021
STV News

'Don't panic buy.' That's the message to commuters after a small number of petrol stations in England closed after running out of fuel because deliveries haven't arrived. There have been queues at some petrol stations in Scotland and across the UK. BP, Esso and Tesco garages have been worst affected by shortages caused by a lack of HGV drivers to operate fuel tankers. The haulage industry is calling for changes to make it easier to hire drivers from abroad to help ease the pressure.

DIARY: There is also panic buying of fuel, I saw queues in Port Glasgow, not because of shortages of the actual fuel, but of drivers to deliver it. Brexit and Covid the main explanation. Shortage of HGV drivers is leading to some empty shelves and warnings over Christmas supplies.

Thursday 21 October 2021
STV News

A 61-year-old man from Carluke has died after saving his two grandsons from being swept out to sea off the Greek island of Crete. Rescuers have described how they tried in vain to reach him after he managed to get the boys to safety.

DIARY: It seems unusual to lead with a story that would have been a standard lead in the *Scotland Today* days.

COP 26
Friday 29 October 2021
STV News

World leaders, scientists, campaigners, diplomats, journalists. All converging in Scotland this weekend with one task in hand: saving the world. The aim: to cut emissions and limit climate change. Everyone agrees action is needed. But today the First Minister warned success can't be taken for granted. Tens of thousands of people are already here in Glasgow collecting accreditation and getting crucial Covid tests. They need all of that to get into the United Nations Blue Zone which is laid out behind us here. You may have known it as the SEC. It's no longer Scottish territory it's now UN territory.

Sunday 31 October 2021
STV News

The last, best chance to limit rising global temperatures. That was the message from the COP26 President Alok Sharma as the United Nations Climate Conference formally began in Glasgow today. World leaders will begin discussions tomorrow on how emissions can be reduced. Meanwhile, campaigners and activists have descended on Scotland to make their voices heard.

DIARY: A miserable day in Glasgow – no fun for arriving visitors. Still not looking hugely busy, but a lot of international people now here. Different levels of TV coverage – some with a craft cameraman, some self-shooting and, as is now standard, people with a lighting rig and stand for their iPhone.

Monday 1 November 2021
STV News – live from STV balcony across the river from the COP26 conference

'Glasgow must kick off a decade of ambition and innovation to preserve our shared future.' The words of President Joe Biden as he addressed the COP26 climate conference across the River Clyde from us here. His were among many dramatic words delivered today. The UK Prime Minister warned the world stood at 'one minute to midnight' facing catastrophe if it failed to act. As he opened the conference, Boris Johnston said the 'anger' of the world's population will be 'uncontainable' if the leaders didn't 'get real' over the next two weeks. Their mission is clear. To deliver on agreements that will help reduce carbon emissions and rising temperatures. World leaders from across the globe are in Scotland to try to make that happen. So far, there haven't been the demonstrations that were expected, but the climate campaigner Greta Thunberg says she expects nothing from the politicians – and that it is the youth of today who will change the world.

BERNARD PONSONBY, Special Correspondent: They have been delivered in impatient tones and come with dire warnings. If ending the climate crisis was measured by the toughness of political rhetoric, there wouldn't be one. The President of Seychelles put it like this – the time to act is yesterday. The proof of the pudding is whether the final agreement matches the rhetoric. Whether the speeches of all of these world leaders are a turning point in history or the point when the war was lost. The protests have been muted today. They will gather apace in the coming days. And you know protest matters. Great changes in the world whether it be an end to child labour, the exploitation of workers, the oppression of whole races don't happen because of the benevolence of rulers. They happen because people agitate for change and there will be a lot of agitation in the coming days.

JM: What are the prospects of a game changing deal?

BP: Stating the obvious, anything's possible. But given the muted tones of the G20 meeting in Rome yesterday, the scepticism of the Russian foreign minister over the timetable for cutting emissions and the lack of any unambiguous commitments from China, you have to say the sense is that by conference end it will probably amount to progress, but probably not enough. The geopolitical politics of climate is a story of trying to catch up. But over there, they all know there's a point when they can't. Hence the now or never tones.

DIARY: Yes, world leaders are here, but, apart from President Biden's motorcade racing along the M8 from Edinburgh, there wasn't much sign of them. The anticipated protests were rather low-key, if at all. As someone observed, this is something that's happening to Glasgow, rather than in Glasgow. I spent a while in the Blue Zone, which is United Nations territory. It was like airport security. The queues this morning were taking up to two hours. The conference campus envelopes the Hydro, the Armadillo and the SEC and then it was a maze of temporary white tunnels through to the other venues. No question it's a world event... different languages and races rushing about. I did get a sense of busy being busy – to what end?

Then some nonsense involving the young climate campaigner, Greta Thunberg, who was to hold a rally on waste ground next to STV. There was some back and forth as to when she was arriving. Ended up running – with cameraman in tow – to get her coming out of a vehicle. Immediately, her young protectors surrounded her, shouting at me to go away and how rude I was. Meanwhile, I'm calling to her – 'A message for Scotland, Greta?' It was a silly pantomime.

Wednesday 3 November 2021
STV News

Today has seen the first significant disturbances of the COP26 climate conference. Hundreds of climate activists staged several protests in Glasgow city centre. There were scuffles and two arrests after police officers were sprayed with paint. Protesters accused the police of being aggressive. The protests came on the day the conference discussed the finances of climate change. The Chancellor Rishi Sunak said that it wasn't just governments who should fund the global fight against climate change. The private sector needed to step up too.

DIARY: Most protests have been staged photo opportunities. All rather dull. I feel the campaigners are every bit a part of the show as the politicians and it's so much posturing.

Saturday 6 November 2021
STV News

Tens of thousands of protesters have marched through Glasgow city centre as part of a day of 'Global Action' against climate change. It's the biggest demonstration during the COP26 summit so far. Other protests led to multiple arrests.

Monday 8 November 2021
STV News

It was hard to stay away from COP26 in Glasgow, said the former President Barack Obama. He told the climate conference that he was no longer required to attend summits, but he had to come. His attendance inside the Blue Zone caused probably the biggest excitement of the entire event so far. And his message was clear. Time is running out to deal with the climate crisis. Mr Obama said meaningful progress had been made in Glasgow. But he warned that collectively and individually we are still falling short. He said that whether more is done or not comes down to each and every one of us. And he had a message for protesters, too. Listen more, he said, to those reluctant to take action.

DIARY: Did seem rather confused about where he was, referencing both the 'emerald isles' and Shakespeare. He brought some excitement to the place.

Friday 12 November 2021
STV News

The deadline has passed. More than 120 world leaders, almost 200 delegations, a smattering of celebs and two weeks of talks. And tonight – still the world waits for agreement on a plan to cut climate change. The aim was to come up with a deal which would limit global warming to 1.5 degrees Celsius by the end of the century. But still no sight of that. Protesters have been in force outside the venue all day.

Saturday 13 November 2021
STV News

After another full day of talks delegates have finally agreed a deal at COP26 in Glasgow. The final decisions have been hailed by some as showing real progress in the bid to tackle the climate crisis. But protesters believe the conference has been a failure.

LAURA PIPER, Climate Correspondent: For Extinction Rebellion... these past two weeks have come to nothing.

CATHY ALLEN, Extinction Rebellion: We wanted to represent the tragedy for all mankind that these annual events, these annual attempts to solve the climate crisis come to nothing so, yet again, COP26 is a pathetic failure.

LP: Inside the venue the clean-up was already underway this morning. Even as negotiators continued to battle through to get a final deal swept over the line. The general feeling among climate campaigners has been mixed. There's been progress on nature protection and methane reduction, but a lack of meaningful action on fossil fuels and on funding for people most vulnerable to the climate crisis. Many have said that while COP26 is not an overall failure, it's not a complete success either. Out of COP has come new alliances like China and the US. Relationships that will be needed in the battle ahead. Campaigners in Scotland though say lessons can be learned from COP. The world's eyes were on Glasgow for a deal that would drive forward change. Now they must look to the next COP to see if it will deliver what Glasgow did not.

Monday 29 November 2021
STV News

'Potentially the most challenging development in the course of the pandemic' – that's how the First Minister's describing the discovery of a new variant of Covid in Scotland. Omicron was first identified in Southern Africa, but today six cases were linked to the strain here. There is concern vaccines may be less effective and the virus could spread more quickly. Nicola Sturgeon, alongside her Welsh counterpart, is calling on the UK Government to hold a four-nation emergency COBRA meeting and bring in stricter rules for people arriving from abroad. But their requests have been rejected by Boris Johnson.

Monday 6 December 2021
STV News

Scotland's Deputy First Minister insists people can be trusted not to cheat the Covid testing system. From tonight, negative lateral flow results will be accepted for admission to venues which previously required vaccine passports. But lateral flow tests rely on the individuals honestly reporting their results. The change comes as officials continue to closely monitor cases of the Omicron variant – cases are up and there's particular attention on outbreaks in the Highlands and Renfrewshire.

Tuesday 7 December 2021
STV News

The SNP's Westminster leader Ian Blackford is calling on the Prime Minister to resign immediately if new allegations about a party at Downing Street last Christmas are found to be true. Leaked footage, obtained by ITV News, suggests a party was held at Number 10 during lockdown last December when gatherings were illegal. The clip shows Boris Johnson's then spokesperson Allegra Stratton joke about a gathering at which there was no social distancing. The UK Government denies the event took place at all, but the SNP say the evidence suggests otherwise.

Friday 10 December 2021
STV News

We are facing a tsunami of infections. The words of the First Minister as she announced changes to self-isolation rules. It's predicted there will be a doubling of Covid cases every two days – and that the Omicron variant will become dominant within days. The situation is being monitored hourly – and further restrictions may be announced in the days to come. So where are we and what has changed? Well, overnight cases rose sharply to more than 5,000 – almost doubling in the past 24 hours. Confirmed cases of the Omicron variant have risen 'exponentially' from nine cases ten days ago, to 110 yesterday. There are now more than 1,000 possible and probable cases – and modelling shows that figure could rise to as high as 25,000 a day in the worst case scenario. So, from tomorrow, if you test positive for Covid, all household contacts will have to self-isolate for ten days. Any contact outside your household will need to isolate until tested negative. We're also being advised to cancel our Christmas parties.

DIARY: This is not like back at the beginning of the pandemic, but I can see restrictions ramping up. The question, though, is to what extent they'll be obeyed, especially with the ongoing row about a party in Downing Street last year. The advice now that household contacts of a positive case must self-isolate for ten days, even if they are negative themselves, will not be adhered to.

Tuesday 14 December 2021
STV News

We've been here before – the race to slow the virus, which threatens to spiral out of control. As you just heard, the First Minister has laid out the battle plan to tackle the Omicron variant. Christmas celebrations can go ahead without limit, but in the days before and after you should meet with no more than three households indoors. There will be new work from home legislation and supermarkets and the like will need to introduce social distancing measures. We're being asked to test before meeting people, and make sure we've had our vaccines and boosters.

Thursday 23 December 2021
STV News

Three health boards are seeking military assistance as Scotland records 6,215 new Covid cases in the past 24 hours. Of those 674 have been identified as Omicron – the biggest rise since the variant arrived north of the border. Nightclubs are the latest casualty and will be forced to close from Monday unless they can operate with social distancing and table service. It follows a study which shows, though, the highly infectious, Omicron could be less severe than feared. Waste water sampling for Covid in Scotland has shown an increase of 135 per cent in the past week.

DIARY: Sturgeon doing more things without evidence. It looks more and more that it's political to show how different we are from England... Many are beginning to resent it. She can control public events, but on a personal level people will increasingly ignore her.

2022

Monday 10 January 2022

DIARY: *First Minister interview* – Focused on four areas – Covid and the different restrictions between us and England, education and exams, IndyRef2 and the Gender Recognition Reform... You know these interviews will always be more scrutinised than any other and you'll get the usual abuse regardless. It was a down-the-line interview using our satellite truck. Politicians of her calibre are never going to reveal anything unless they want to, so you can only ask the questions you think people want asked, don't let them waffle too much and let the audience decide.

Tuesday 11 January 2022
STV News

Accusations that Downing Street hosted a 'bring your own booze' drinks party during the first lockdown are 'indefensible'. That's according to former Scottish Conservative leader Ruth Davidson, after claims the Prime Minister attended the event. One hundred people were invited to the gathering on 20 May 2020 – a time when rules in England stated people should only meet one other person outside. The Met Police say they are in contact with the Cabinet Office over the reports.

DIARY: This latest Boris Johnson row is a major one. Clear evidence of a drinks party outside Downing Street in May 2020 during lockdown. When people were not permitted to be with dying loved ones. A lot of tearful people today speaking about their anger at the pain of being ignored by the very Government that imposed the limitations. Johnson has got away with a lot, but this one is hitting home. He was avoiding cameras today.

Wednesday 12 January 2022
STV News

The calls for Boris Johnson to resign are mounting. First Labour, then the SNP, and then this afternoon even the Scottish Conservative leader said the Prime Minister must go. Mr Johnson apologised today for attending a 'bring your own booze' gathering in the garden of No 10 during the first lockdown. The Prime Minister admitted he was there, but told angry MPs he thought it was a work event rather than a party. The Labour Leader Sir Keir Starmer called him 'a man without shame' and said the explanation was 'offensive to the British public'. The SNP's Westminster leader described it as 'an open and shut case.'

BORIS JOHNSON, Prime Minister: I want to apologise. I know that millions across this country have made extraordinary sacrifices over the last 18 months. I know the anguish that they have been through. Unable to mourn their relatives. Unable to live their lives as they want or to do the things they love. And I know the rage they feel with me and with the Government I lead, when they think that in Downing Street itself the rules are not being properly followed by the people who make the rules... When I went into that garden just after 6.00pm on 20 May 2020 to thank groups of staff before going back into my office 25 minutes later to continue working, I believed implicitly that this was a work event.

Thursday 13 January 2022
STV News

Bitter infighting has erupted within the Conservatives over the Downing Street party row. There is a particular split between the Scottish Tories and their colleagues in London. At Holyrood MSPs are furious that senior Conservative Jacob Rees-Mogg dismissed the leader of the Scottish party as a 'lightweight figure'. It all flared up after Douglas Ross publicly called for the Prime Minister to resign after Boris Johnson admitted being at a Downing Street garden party during lockdown.

DIARY: What a gift for the SNP, what contempt for Scotland.

Friday 14 January 2022
STV News

It was one of the defining images of lockdown last year – the Queen sat alone at the funeral of her husband Prince Phillip. However, it has emerged that hours earlier Downing Street staff held two parties at Number 10 in breach of Covid regulations.

Downing Street has apologised to Buckingham Palace after the gatherings were reported in the *Daily Telegraph* newspaper. The Prime Minister was not at either party, but the revelations have amplified calls for him to quit.

Friday 14 January 2022 *(cont)*
STV News

There's cautious optimism tonight that better times may not be too far off as Scotland moves through the current wave of coronavirus. The Health Secretary says the outbreak appears to be slowing. And one of the country's top virologists has told us, 'It will not go on for much longer.' In the short term, though, some businesses are continuing to pay the price.

Thursday 20 January 2022

DIARY: At the end of the programme in the '...and finally', we featured a wonderful old woman having a fuss made on her 101st birthday because she'd marked her 100th on her own. Great character. Ended with her talking enthusiastically about watching *Scotland Today* every evening and loving it so much. When she was then asked about 'John MacKay', she said, 'Who's that?' Very funny and caused much hilarity in the newsroom.

Monday 24 January 2022
STV News

Today the final barriers to near-normality were lifted. From 5.00am this morning, Covid rules put in place during festive season to limit the spread of Omicron ended. Nightclubs can reopen. Pubs and restaurants can remove table service. And there are no limits on indoor events. The number of Covid cases are down. The number of people in hospital is down. The number of patients in ICU is down. And there have been no new deaths. The First Minister said restrictions were 'worth it' and Scotland had turned a corner with the virus.

RUSSIA INVADES UKRAINE
Thursday 24 February 2022
STV News

Ukraine says 40 people are dead and several dozen injured after Russia's invasion of the country overnight. Across much of the world, there's been condemnation of the continued escalation of military action. Boris Johnson is promising the toughest sanctions on Russia. Here, the Scottish Parliament united in condemnation of Russian President Putin. And among the 4,000 Ukrainians living in Scotland there's now real fear for the safety of their loved ones and the future of their country.

Monday 21 March 2022
STV News

A new record on the day almost all remaining legal Covid restrictions, brought in to prevent the spread of infection, were lifted. Scotland has more people in hospital with coronavirus than at any time since the pandemic began. Doctors say the immense pressure is likely to continue for several weeks.

DIARY: As someone said today, you'd rather get Covid now than flu. We are pretty much at the stage of living with it.

Tuesday 29 March 2022
Scotland Tonight

The heat is on Nicola Sturgeon's Government over the Ferguson Marine shipyard ferries fiasco. The whole saga centres on the construction of two massively delayed and over-budget vessels which were ordered by ministers in 2015. SNP politicians are coming under heavy scrutiny and are accused of having cut corners and wasted taxpayers' money. The shipyard became state-owned in 2019 and the Cabinet Minister now answering questions on the project is the Finance and Economy Secretary Kate Forbes.

JM: £240 million of public money wasted. Who is taking responsibility for that? Because we've gone from you not knowing, to Derek Mackay to Keith Brown to collective responsibility. I even heard John Swinney's name thrown in today. It's a blurring merry-go-round. Who is to blame?

KATE FORBES, Economy Secretary: Ministers do take collective responsibility. But you will have heard last week the First Minister takes responsibility. She is the head of Government.

JM: What does that mean?

KF: Ministers do operate within collective responsibility. It is no secret who was Transport Minister at the time. The Transport Minister signs off on procurements like this. Derek Mackay was in that role at the time.

JM: So, it was Derek Mackay that signed it and not Keith Brown?

KF: In terms of individual ministers who proceeded in October 2015 that was Derek Mackay. But ultimately, the Scottish Government goes by collective responsibility. And the First Minister as the head of Government takes responsibility.

JM: What does that mean? I accept that you are making that point but what does that mean? What does collective responsibility mean? What are the consequences of that?

KF: Collective responsibility means that I'm answering your questions seven years after the decision was made as a member of Government, despite not being elected at the time. That's what collective responsibility means.

JM: Is that all though? OK, thank you for doing that. Is that all it is? £240 million of public money? Is that all the responsibility? Is that all the consequence?

KF: No, and I go back to where I started. Which is the cost overruns, the delays to these ferries and the impact on island communities is not acceptable. We understand that...

JM: If these boats aren't ready when we're told they will be, next year 2023, will you take responsibility? Will you resign? We're hearing a lot of collective responsibility but we're not hearing who's to blame and what the consequences of that are? We've not heard that. We're hearing learning lessons. We're hearing the buck stops with the First Minister, but what does all that mean?

KF: I think that is so critical. Because you have a First Minister of the Government who stood up in the chamber of the Scottish Government last week and said that the buck did stop with her, that she was responsible.

JM: But those are words. What does that mean?

KF: Ultimately it means we accept responsibility for a situation that is entirely unacceptable. That we have learned lessons that Audit Scotland already referred to and we're implementing those lessons in procurement going forward. This is not the first review into the ferries. We also had a Scottish Parliament inquiry last year. All of this is well documented and the material has been in the public domain now for two years. So, the recommendation from the Audit Scotland report we agree with. We are making progress in implementing them and ensuring that ultimately these vessels are completed for the sake of island communities.

Tuesday 12 April 2022
STV News

He said there were no parties, he denied being at any parties, then he claimed it was a work event. He said he wasn't lying. Now, after months of investigations, it's been proven not only were there parties, he was at them and he's broken lockdown rules. The Prime Minister, his wife Carrie Johnson and the Chancellor Rishi Sunak will all be fined for breaking lockdown rules. Tonight, there are already repeated calls for Boris Johnson's resignation. But the Scottish Conservatives leader Douglas Ross has told STV News now is not the time to remove a Prime Minister.

RANGERS IN EUROPA LEAGUE FINAL
Wednesday 18 May 2022
STV News – live from Seville

Good evening from Spain. And from the Auditorio Rocio Juardo in Seville. Eight thousand Rangers fans are heading here tonight. They'll be rooting for their team alongside a minimum of 9,500, lucky enough to be inside the stadium and tens of thousands more – all over this city – packed into every bar and restaurant they can find. For the fans, it's been a journey like no other. For the players, a chance to make history and end a European adventure that started in August of last year in a way that few could have dreamed of. But now they're daring to dream.

SHEELAGH MCLAREN, Sports Reporter: This is the night Rangers fans have been waiting for. Seville has been taken over by the Ibrox side's supporters and they're going to savour every moment. It's estimated around 100,000 Rangers fans will be in and around Seville today, but tickets are like gold dust – and some are changing hands for thousands of pounds. These fans have come from every direction to be here and in just a few hours they hope to see their heroes lift the Europa League trophy.

Rangers lost 5–4 on penalties after the match ended 1–1.

Scotland Tonight

RONA DOUGALL: John, a step too far for Rangers tonight?

JM: Rangers were here on merit. They beat a lot of good teams to get here. And even here in the final they performed very well. It went up to a penalty shoot-out, it could not have been closer. I think disappointment is maybe the overall feeling here. Thousands of Rangers fans came here to Seville and there seemed to be a real confidence the team might be able to succeed tonight. They came very, very close. Disappointment, certainly. A step too far? No, I don't think so.

DIARY: *(I flew over on a fans' charter flight with chief reporter Sharon Frew)* ... although I was getting a lot of banter from the fans on board it, it was good natured and didn't go overboard... When we went on air the noise from the fans was loud. I could hear nothing, but the director Keith's cues and the PA's timings. Could barely hear any of the lives and reports. It really was like going into a black hole and hoping for the best... The flight back was, naturally, much quieter than the outward bound. A sense of deep disappointment because Rangers could have won... Quite unsettling when one guy seemed to take a fit standing next to us. Turned out to be heat stroke. There were two cases on the plane *(after a day of 35-degree heat)*. Home to Glasgow less than 24 hours after we'd left. A remarkable day.

Monday 30 May 2022
Scotland Tonight

Filling in the once-in-a-decade Census is a legal requirement for all households. But this year's survey of the Scottish population has been met by a strikingly low response rate from the public, leading critics to brand its operation 'a shambles'. Tomorrow is the last chance for people to submit their forms. and there are now deepening concerns over the credibility and worth of the exercise. Officials set a target for 94 per cent of the forms to be completed. But the current Scotland-wide returns rate stands at just 86.6 per cent. The SNP Cabinet Secretary responsible for the Census, Angus Robertson, declined our request to interview him on tonight's programme. And we were also told that no one from the National Records of Scotland was prepared to appear.

DIARY: The Scottish Government decoupled from the rest of the UK – usual talk about Covid etc – but really just to be different. Result is that England and Wales had a 97 per cent return, Scotland on 86.6 per cent, which critics say renders it worthless.

THE QUEEN'S PLATINUM JUBILEE CELEBRATIONS
Thursday 2 June 2022

DIARY: The Queen made an appearance on the balcony with 'working Royals', meaning no appearance for Harry and Meghan or the disgraced Andrew. The full pomp is quite a thing to watch and more people are into it than the social media ranters would like to think.

Tuesday 28 June 2022
STV News

The First Minister has laid out her plans for an Independence Referendum. The date is set for 19 October next year. Now her task is to prove that it will be a legal poll. Nicola Sturgeon wants the Supreme Court to rule on the legality of the referendum. And this afternoon, the Lord Advocate – the Scottish Government's chief legal officer – referred the matter there. Whatever the result, the First Minister says the people of Scotland will have a say.

NICOLA STURGEON, First Minister: The path I've laid out today is about bringing clarity and certainty to this debate. Above all it is about ensuring Scotland has a say on independence. I want this to lead to a lawful referendum and for that to take place on 19 October 2023. That is what we are preparing for. If the law says that is not possible the General Election will be a de facto referendum. Either way the people of Scotland will have their say.

COLIN MACKAY, Political Editor: This could prove the biggest political move Nicola Sturgeon has made as First Minister. It was always expected to end up in the Supreme Court, so what the First Minister is doing today is pre-empting that. Instead of legislating for a referendum then seeing if it is legal, the First Minister wants to test the legality of her referendum plans first. This is less about painting your face blue and crying freedom, this is more about crying process – less Braveheart, more bold thinking. This is a big gamble.

DIARY: All quite dramatic and clear. However, I suspect this is her last hurrah. The Supreme Court is unlikely to allow such a referendum and would the SNP get the majority they require in any General Election? I think she wants to present that she did everything she could to deliver independence and it was Westminster that prevented it.

BORIS JOHNSON RESIGNS
Thursday 7 July 2022
STV News – live from Westminster

The rollercoaster career of a Prime Minister who has – at times – appeared to defy political gravity – is coming to a crashing halt. Boris Johnson has finally relented to extreme pressure from within his party to quit. But he says he'll stay on until he has a successor, which might not be until the autumn. A growing number of Tory MPs are calling on him to leave No 10 now.

BORIS JOHNSON, Prime Minister: It is clearly now the will of the parliamentary Conservative Party that there should be a new leader of that party and, therefore, a new Prime Minister. And I've agreed with Sir Graham Brady, the chairman of our backbench MPs, that the process of choosing that new leader should begin now. And the timetable will be announced next week and I have today appointed a Cabinet to serve, as I will, until a new leader is in place. And I want you to know how sad I am to be giving up the best job in the world. But them's the breaks.

NICOLA STURGEON, First Minister: I'm not sure that anybody could look at Boris Johnson and conclude that he is capable of genuinely behaving as a caretaker Prime Minister. He will want to do things, and in the process of that, undoubtedly cause even more chaos than he has already. So, the interests of people in all parts of the UK surely must be to bring this farce to an end and to bring it to an end without any further delay.

SIR KEIR STARMER, Labour Leader: It is obvious he is unfit to be Prime Minister. That's been blindingly obvious for a very, very long time. And if they don't get rid of him, then Labour will step up in the national interest and bring a vote of no confidence because we can't go on with this Prime Minister clinging on for months and months to come.

BERNARD PONSONBY, Special Correspondent: The Prime Minister is mostly the chief architect of his own downfall, not that you would know it from the statement he gave. There were few admissions of any shortcomings on his behalf. Instead, he concentrated on what he regarded as his achievements in office. His supporters watched on and cheered him but there were many more in the party who would have greeted the statement with relief. Over 50 ministers have resigned in recent days, paralysing Government. So, he had no choice, but to signal he will go.

Tuesday 19 July 2022
STV News

Scotland has had its hottest-ever day amid a day of record temperatures across the UK. While many people have been making the most of the weather, the excessive heat has caused disruption to railways and brought warnings about health, water supplies and the risk of wildfires. It is still roasting hot across much of the country. One of the hottest parts, right now, is in the Borders. Temperatures there have been over 30 degrees. And it's where the Scottish temperature record has been broken.

The record temperature was 34.8C (94.6F) in Charterhall in the Borders.

Monday 8 August 2022
STV News

It's been a bumper haul of medals at the Commonwealth Games. Team Scotland has recorded its most successful Commonwealth Games outside of Glasgow, with 51 medals – 13 of them gold. It's the highest tally for a Games away from home, with eight medals being won yesterday and another two today. Team Scotland bosses admit it's beyond all expectation and hope it can inspire athletes of the future.

Monday 15 August 2022
STV News

Scotland is the first country in the world to protect the right to free period products. As of today, councils and education providers are legally required to make sanitary products available without charge. Since 2017, around £27 million has been spent to provide access in public settings.

Wednesday 17 August 2022
STV News

The cost of living is on everyone's mind – and it's getting worse. Inflation has now hit double digits to 10.1 per cent, the highest rate in 40 years. And it's set to rise even more. As schools go back, making money go further is at the forefront of parents' minds. Ahead of winter, further big rises are also due on energy bills. It all means the gap between the richest and poorest is the largest it's been since the financial crash. And the hospitality sector says it's in a circle of crisis due to rising costs and changing consumer habits.

Thursday 18 August 2023
STV News

The summer of discontent is spreading. In Edinburgh cleansing workers walked out this morning, bins aren't being emptied. Workers at other councils will join that action next week. Scotland's rail network also ground to a halt as signallers took strike action again. Care workers, teachers, nurses, contractors at Grangemouth, even coffin makers are planning action in the weeks and months ahead.

Tuesday 23 August 2022
STV News

The dispute involving refuse collectors escalates tomorrow as staff from another 13 council areas join the walk out over pay. We're now on the sixth day of the strike in Edinburgh where the piles of rubbish on the streets get ever bigger.

Friday 26 August 2022
STV News

Energy prices will nearly double in October. They'll rise by 80 per cent, pushing hundreds of thousands of people into fuel poverty. Average bills will be more than £3,500. We're headed for a winter of discontent. The toughest of times since the 1970s: rampant inflation, soaring energy costs and strikes as people seek pay rises to meet the cost of living. Long-term plans to help everyone aren't going to make any progress until the new Conservative leader becomes Prime Minister in a couple of weeks' time.

LIZ TRUSS BECOMES PRIME MINISTER

Monday 5 September 2022
STV News

After weeks of campaigning, the waiting is over. Liz Truss has beaten the former Chancellor Rishi Sunak in the race to become the next Prime Minister. Picking up around 57 per cent of the votes, she pledged that she 'would deliver'. The Foreign Secretary will now travel to Scotland, where she'll meet the Queen and be asked to form a government and become Prime Minister. She'll take over officially tomorrow, and with the cost-of-living crisis on everyone's mind, her pledge will be put to the test immediately.

LIZ TRUSS, Conservative Leader: I will deliver on the energy crisis dealing with people's bills, but also dealing with the long-term issues we have on energy supply. We will deliver, we will deliver and we will deliver.

NICOLA STURGEON, First Minister: I will do my very best, despite our big political differences, to build a constructive working relationship with her. I've sought to do that with her three predecessors as Prime Minister. But she must act now, not in the next few weeks, but literally in the coming hours and days to freeze energy prices for people and for businesses, to deliver more cash support to people who are already finding it impossible to pay their bills.

SIR KEIR STARMER, Labour Leader: We've heard far more from the latest Prime Minister about cuts to corporation tax over the summer than we have about the cost-of-living crisis – the single most important thing that's bearing down on so many millions of households. And that shows not only that she's out of touch, but she's not on the side of working people.

Outside the primary school in Paisley where she was once a pupil parents gave us their reaction to a Prime Minister taking the reins at such a crucial time.

Vox Pops

I just hope with this cost of living and everything, that she tries to balance it out with the cost of everything going up.

We can only hope for the best. I don't think there's been any real actions put forward in regard to the cost-of-living crisis from any of the Government, and what they could help people.

DIARY: It will need strong, clear decisions – not stuck in ideology – to get through the cost-of-living/inflation crises we're having. I have my doubts she's up to it.

Tuesday 6 September 2022
STV News

The transfer of power is complete. In Royal Deeside today, Liz Truss was asked by the Queen to form a government.

Tonight, the new Prime Minister returned to Downing Street to deliver her first speech – in between bursts of torrential rain – which seemed fitting, given the economic storm the country is facing.

EWAN PETRIE, Political Correspondent: In a break with tradition, the outgoing Prime Minister travelled to Balmoral rather than Buckingham Palace for his farewell audience with the Queen. The tranquil surroundings the setting to bring to an end one of the more turbulent terms in office. Shortly after he departed Liz Truss arrived. Her meeting with the monarch in the castle's drawing room completed the transfer of power. Back in Downing Street the weather threatened to postpone plans for her first address as Prime Minister. It cleared up just in time for her arrival. And with the podium back in place, Liz Truss continued the weather theme.

LIZ TRUSS, Prime Minister: As Prime Minister, I will pursue three early priorities. Firstly, I will get Britain working again. I have a bold plan to grow the economy through tax cuts and reform. I will cut taxes to reward hard work and boost business-led growth and investment. I will drive reform in my mission to get the United Kingdom working, building, and growing. We will get spades in the ground to make sure people are not facing unaffordable energy bills and we will also make sure, that we are building hospitals, schools, roads, and broadband. Secondly, I will deal hands-on with the energy crisis caused by Putin's war. I will take action this week to deal with energy bills and to secure our future energy supply. Thirdly, I will make sure that people can get doctors' appointments and the NHS services they need. We will put our health service on a firm footing. By delivering on the economy, on energy, and on the NHS, we will put our nation on the path to long-term success. We shouldn't be daunted by the challenges we face. As strong as the storm may be, I know that the British people are stronger. Our country was built by people who get things done. We have huge reserves of talent, of energy, and determination. I am confident that together we can ride out the storm. We can rebuild our economy. And we can become the modern brilliant Britain that I know we can be. This is our vital mission to ensure opportunity and prosperity for all people and future generations. I am determined to deliver. Thank you.

DIARY: Unusually, because of the Queen's frailty, she had to go to Balmoral to be appointed, which delayed proceedings. Then torrid downpours in London delayed her speech. Some see it as an omen.

DEATH OF QUEEN ELIZABETH
Thursday 8 September 2022
STV News – lunchtime bulletin

The Queen is under medical supervision at Balmoral with doctors concerned for her health. In a statement, Buckingham Palace has confirmed the monarch remains comfortable.

EWAN PETRIE, Political Correspondent: It was during the Prime Minister's statement on energy costs this morning that news began to filter through about the Queen's health. Word quickly spread across the front benches and the concern was clear. A short time later – 12.30pm – we got the statement from Buckingham Palace. It was a short statement that read simply, 'Following further evaluation this morning, the Queen's doctors are concerned for Her Majesty's health and have recommended she remain under medical supervision. The Queen remains comfortable and at Balmoral.' Now, it is highly unusual for the Palace to release an update on the Queen's health like this. We had been told about mobility issues which had caused her to pull out of events such as the Braemar gathering last weekend.

There was no STV *News at Six*. ITN provided rolling news coverage through the afternoon as we waited for an announcement. The death of the Queen was finally announced at 6.28pm.

DIARY: Throughout my life – and those of most in the country – she has been a constant through rapid change. The girl who wasn't born to the throne, but will go down as a great monarch – the longest serving. And service or duty is what is always ascribed to her. Yes, it was a life of privilege, but there can be no denying her commitment and dedication to her role. Crowned before TVs were popular, before the transformative 1960s, the space age, the computer age, the digital age, she was a constant, some would say, a reassuring presence. And now she's gone.

Friday 9 September 2022
STV News – live from Balmoral and Edinburgh

Our new King has spoken. A short time ago King Charles the Third made his first address to the nation. He spoke of his profound sorrow and the debt he owed his mother – and promised to give lifelong service, as she did. He spoke from Buckingham Palace, from where the Queen recorded countless addresses to the country.

KING CHARLES III: I speak to you today with feelings of profound sorrow. Throughout her life, Her Majesty the Queen – my beloved mother – was an inspiration and example to me and to all my family, and we owe her the most heartfelt debt any family can owe to their mother; for her love, affection, guidance, understanding and example. Queen Elizabeth's was a life well lived; a promise with destiny kept and she is mourned most deeply in her passing. That promise of lifelong service I renew to you all today. Alongside the personal grief that all my family are feeling, we also share with so many of you in the United Kingdom, in all the countries where the Queen was head of state, in the Commonwealth and across the world, a deep sense of gratitude for the more than 70 years in which my mother, as Queen, served the people of so many nations... In our sorrow, let us remember and draw strength from the light of her example. On behalf of all my family, I can only offer the most sincere and heartfelt thanks for your condolences and support. They mean more to me than I can ever possibly express. And to my darling mama, as you begin your last great journey to join my dear late papa, I want simply to say this: thank you.

EWAN PETRIE, Political Correspondent: For the new King there was little time for private mourning. He left Balmoral to fly back to London, less than 24 hours after the death of his mother. At Buckingham Palace he spoke to the crowds gathered outside and spent time reading messages of support. One of his first duties was a meeting with the Prime Minister ahead of his address to the country. At Edinburgh Castle a traditional salute – 96 rounds fired – one for every year of the Queen's life. Crowds continued to lay flowers at the gates of Balmoral throughout the day. At midday church bells tolled in celebration of the Queen's life. Books of condolence have also opened. At Holyrood the Presiding Officer left her own tribute. And at Westminster MPs stood to observe a minute's silence before the Prime Minister led tributes in the Commons. Crowds also gathered at Holyrood Palace, the Queen's official residence here. A period of national mourning is underway. It will last until the end of the day of the Queen's state funeral.

JM: It is literally the end of an era. The change from the Elizabethan era to the new one of King Charles. And Scotland will be at the heart of that transformation. The late Queen will be brought from Balmoral to here at Holyrood and then taken to St Giles Cathedral where she will lie in state. The new King will return north for these events. What we will be seeing over the next few days most of us will never have seen before because of the length of the Queen's reign. These are historic days.

Sunday 11 September 2022

The Queen's coffin was transported from Balmoral to Edinburgh with the entire journey being covered live.

DIARY: Plenty of people lining the roads. There was something unifying about it – such a simple thing.

On live coverage... The waffling that was going on to fill the time. Commentators spouting utter bollocks about the Queen and the crowds. I'm not knocking them. It's difficult to do and there is a lot of time to fill. I'm questioning why the producers didn't just allow silence at times. It's the way rolling news is done and it's often too much. Striking images of the hearse going down a packed Royal Mile and the coffin being taken into Holyrood Palace.

Monday 12 September 2022
STV News – live from Holyrood Palace

Tonight, the Queen lies in rest in the Scottish capital. The Crown of Scotland has been placed on her coffin. It is a day of history. The King and the Queen Consort have returned to Scotland. In a few moments he will hear the condolences from the Scottish Parliament – the people's representatives in Scotland. This afternoon the late Queen was removed from the Palace of Holyroodhouse and taken the short distance up the Royal Mile to St Giles Cathedral. There she will lie through the night until tomorrow afternoon. Crowds have been gathering all day to file past.

These have been a remarkable few days since the death of the Queen last Thursday. And Scotland has been at the heart of it. Traditions and rituals we never knew were part of our country. We may not have seen it before. But this place has. The Palace of Holyroodhouse, The Royal Mile, St Giles have borne witness to great events. The very stones are steeped in centuries of history. And today has been another day for the ages.

Tuesday 13 September 2022
STV News – live from Edinburgh

The end of an era. In the last 20 minutes, Queen Elizabeth has left Scotland for the very last time. Tens of thousands have filed through St Giles Cathedral to pay their respects as she lay in rest. That procession of people continued even throughout the night. Her coffin is now heading to Westminster in London where she will lie in state for four days. It's been a genuinely historic few days for Scotland.

So, Scotland has said its last farewell to the Queen. She was a monarch who was open about her love for this country and its people. It is said this is where she wanted to end her days. Well, she got her wish and Her Majesty's coffin has left Scotland. Now the pageantry moves to London. But these recent days will live long in the memory. When will we see their like again?

Monday 19 September 2022
STV News – live from Edinburgh and Balmoral

The eyes of the world have been on the Queen's funeral today. It's estimated around four billion people watched the service, which was attended by representatives from more than 100 countries. Here in Scotland, a crowd gathered at Holyrood Park, not far from where we're standing, to join together to watch the service, and pay their respects. Up and down the country, people watched. It marks the end of a period of national mourning which began with the monarch's death in Balmoral.

SHARON FREW, Chief Reporter: To the sound of pipe and drums of Scottish and Irish Regiments the slow funeral procession began. A final farewell to a head of state, but also a mother, grandmother and great-grandmother. The wreath on top of the Queen's coffin contained a handwritten card from the King. The message read, 'In loving and devoted memory'. Hundreds of members of the Armed Forces in Scotland played a role in this procession as the monarch made the journey through the streets of London – the city of her birth. They solemnly marched to Westminster Abbey, the setting for so many significant events throughout the seven decades of her reign. Before a congregation that included world leaders past and present.

ARCHBISHOP OF CANTERBURY: Her late Majesty famously declared on a 21st birthday broadcast that her whole life would be dedicated to serving the nation and Commonwealth. Rarely has such a promise been so well kept.

SF: The Moderator of the General Assembly of the Church of Scotland, who was at Balmoral the weekend before the Queen died, read a prayer. The two minutes of reflection was also observed by hundreds watching the service in Edinburgh's Holyrood Park, just yards from the Queen's official Scottish residence. This last journey that began hundreds of miles away in Balmoral ended at Windsor. Her beloved corgis were among those awaiting her arrival. The grandeur and the scale of the state funeral shrank in size to a more intimate service inside St George's Chapel. As the service drew to a close – the crown, spectre and orb were removed from the Queen's coffin and placed on the altar. A symbolic end to the second Elizabethan age.

JM: So, the queues have dispersed. The processions have ended and the drumbeats are silent. It's been a remarkable period when history played out before us. Tonight, the royal family will take part in a private service at Windsor. Tomorrow we return to normal. Albeit, a normal with a new King. And a normal with challenges facing the nation. But these are days most of us have never experienced before. At Balmoral. Here in Edinburgh. And in London. And they are days that will not be forgotten.

KWASI KWARTENG'S MINI-BUDGET
Friday 23 September 2022
STV News

It was pitched as a 'mini-budget', but today the Chancellor announced a huge package of tax cutting measures. Kwasi Kwarteng's plans bring benefits for big companies and for the wealthy – the cap on bankers' bonuses will be scrapped. But Scots on lower incomes will also pay a bit less because of a decision to reverse a hike in National Insurance payments.

KWASI KWARTENG, Chancellor of the Exchequer: We promised a new approach for a new era to release potential. Our growth plan has delivered all those promises and more.

Tuesday 27 September 2022
STV News

Tonight – the economy in crisis. Counting the cost of the plummeting pound.

Businesses and borrowers are among the losers.

The UK Government is sticking to its plans for tax cuts despite the pound plunging to record lows against the dollar. The former Chancellor Nadhim Zahawi insists the markets will recover when they see economic growth being delivered. However, the Scottish Government says it will not be drawn into a race to the bottom by replicating what it calls reckless tax cuts.

Financial advisers have been inundated with calls from clients after some banks and building societies withdrew a number of mortgage deals from the market. It comes after the Government's mini-budget on Friday prompted concerns for the impact on inflation. Halifax, Virgin Money and Skipton Building Society are among those taking action.

Thursday 29 September 2022
STV News

One of Scotland's longest running murder cases – that of Renee MacRae and her son Andrew – has ended with the conviction of her lover more than 45 years later. Renee and toddler Andrew disappeared in 1976. Today, William MacDowell, who was the child's father, was found guilty of the killings. The judge described the premeditated murders as 'an execution'. MacDowell, who is 80, will die in jail after being given a life sentence. The police have urged him to disclose what he did with his victims' bodies.

Monday 3 October 2022
STV News

With the ink barely dry on his mini-budget the Chancellor made a huge u-turn today – ditching plans to scrap the top rate of income tax in the rest of the UK. Yesterday, the Prime Minister had insisted the policy would not be abandoned. The Scottish Conservatives leader Douglas Ross says that's the right thing to do – despite calling on Nicola Sturgeon to replicate tax cuts for the rich just a few days ago.

DIARY: The PM was still defending it yesterday. It is humiliating for them and has led to claims of this being the worst start to a premiership ever. The Chancellor now has the name 'Kwasi-Kame' *(kamikaze)* which I find funny.

Saturday 8 October 2022
STV News

One of Scotland's most notorious serial killers Peter Tobin has died. He was 76 and had been serving three life sentences at Edinburgh Prison for raping and murdering women. He was linked to several more murders, so his death leaves a number of families with unanswered questions.

Friday 14 October 2022
STV News

In the space of a few hours the Prime Minister sacked her Chancellor and ditched one of her key economic policies. In a day of turmoil, Liz Truss reversed planned cuts to corporation tax. The Prime Minister admitted parts of her mini-budget went further and faster than the markets had expected. But she insisted she was staying on at Number 10.

LIZ TRUSS RESIGNS
Thursday 20 October 2022
STV News

Liz Truss is resigning as Prime Minister – she'll be gone in a week. After a chaotic 44 days in office, she'll go down in history as the shortest-serving PM ever. She'll remain at Number 10 while the Conservatives choose her replacement next Friday. It follows the resignation of the Home Secretary yesterday and chaotic scenes in the Commons last night when it was alleged Tory MPs were bullied into supporting the Government in a vote.

LIZ TRUSS, Prime Minister: I cannot deliver the mandate on which I was elected by the Conservative Party. I have therefore spoken to

His Majesty the King to notify him that I am resigning as leader of the Conservative Party.

SIR KEIR STARMER, Labour Leader: We cannot have another experiment at the top of the Tory party. There is an alternative, and that is a stable Labour Government. And the public are entitled to have their say. And that is why there should be a General Election.

NICOLA STURGEON, First Minister: There must be a General Election. It is a democratic necessity. The idea that the Tories can unite behind a Prime Minister now, any Prime Minister, let alone one that is in the public interest, I think is for the birds.

COLIN MACKAY, Political Editor: Truss is leaving Downing Street, but trust left long ago. She has only been Prime Minister for about six weeks. She spent longer campaigning to be Prime Minister than she has spent in the job. At just her third PMQs yesterday – she did more leadership hustings than PMQs, but yesterday she said, I am a fighter not a quitter. Today she has quit and that pretty much sums up her short period as Prime Minister – u-turn after u-turn. She wasn't up to the job and couldn't do the job. And this is not just humiliating for Liz Truss. Just six weeks ago Conservative Party members picked her to be Prime Minister. They won't even get a say in the next one. For the last few weeks politics has seemed a bit like a reality TV show with journalists waiting for Liz Truss to be evicted from Number 10. But the true reality of her leadership has been soaring mortgage rates for millions, uncertainty over energy bills and the threat of cuts to services and support for the poorest – because of the bad decisions of her Government.

DIARY: She had to go. On a human level it's hard not to feel sorry for her humiliation, but this is the game she played and it was her own doing.

RISHI SUNAK BECOMES PRIME MINISTER
Monday 24 October 2022
STV News

Rishi Sunak will become the next Prime Minister of the United Kingdom. The third Prime Minister this year. He was picked by Conservative MPs after the final contender, Penny Mordaunt, dropped out of the leadership race at the last minute. He has already told them there will be no early General Election. In his first speech as Conservative leader, Mr Sunak warned of the 'profound economic challenge' faced by the nation. He said his priority was to bring the country together.

At 42, Rishi Sunak is the youngest Prime Minister in 200 years and the first British Asian to hold the office.

Tuesday 25 October 2022
STV News

Rishi Sunak has walked through the door of Number 10 Downing Street today with a promise to fix some of the mistakes made by his predecessor, Liz Truss. And he vowed to deliver the manifesto that won the Conservatives their election victory in 2019. But in his first speech as Prime Minister, he warned of a 'profound economic crisis' and said tough decisions would need to be taken in the coming days. The biggest problem for the new Prime Minister will be tackling the cost-of-living crisis. Soaring food and fuel prices, combined with the economic instability brought about by the former Prime Minister Liz Truss's mini-budget just a few weeks ago, means the new leader doesn't have his challenges to seek. He's yet to outline his fiscal plans to plug a £40 billion black hole in the country's finances.

RISHI SUNAK, Prime Minister: It is only right to explain why I am standing here as your new Prime Minister. Right now, our country is facing a profound economic crisis. The aftermath of Covid still lingers. Putin's war in Ukraine has destabilised energy markets and supply chains the world over. I want to pay tribute to my predecessor Liz Truss. She was not wrong to want to improve growth in this country, it is a noble aim. And I admired her restlessness to create change. But some mistakes were made. Not borne of ill will or bad intentions. Quite the opposite, in fact. But mistakes, nonetheless. And I have been elected as leader of my party, and your Prime Minister, in part, to fix them. And that work begins immediately. I will place economic stability and confidence at the heart of this Government's agenda. This will mean difficult decisions to come... The mandate my party earned in 2019 is not the sole property of any one individual, it is a mandate that belongs to and unites all of us.

Thursday 27 October 2022
STV News

Divisive legislation to make it quicker for transgender people to have their gender recognised, as well as lowering the age to 16, has passed its first hurdle at Holyrood. But the debate didn't come without its casualties. The Community Safety Minister Ash Regan resigned from the Scottish Government just before the debate began, saying she couldn't support it. Campaigners from both sides also made their voices heard outside the Parliament.

Friday 4 November 2022
STV News

The First Minister has rejected a suggestion that awarding of a ferry contract to the Ferguson Marine shipyard was a case of jobs for the boys. The two vessels are currently five years overdue and could end up being three times the original budget. Giving evidence to MSPs at Holyrood, Nicola Sturgeon said she regrets the impact the delays are having on islanders. They have told STV News they feel ignored and let down.

DIARY: This is a running sore for her and her Government. It's all very well saying she takes responsibility, but as we've asked throughout, what does that mean?

Friday 11 November 2022
STV News

It began with the arrest of a man in a Glasgow Covid ward. Interpol said he was Nicholas Rossi, who faked his death to evade rape charges in the United States. He said he was Arthur Knight – a victim of mistaken identity – an orphan from Ireland. Over the last 11 months there have been multiple court appearances, hospital re-admissions, further arrests, and continual denials. Today, a sheriff rejected his evidence as implausible and fanciful after hearing his tattoos and fingerprints matched those of the man wanted in Utah. It's a story which has gripped both sides of the Atlantic.

DIARY: This farce has played out for most of the year. The guy is so obviously a liar. Why it took the court so long is beyond me, due process or not.

UK SUPREME COURT RULES AGAINST INDEPENDENCE REFERENDUM
Wednesday 23 November 2022
STV News

Where now for Scottish independence? Five judges at the highest court in the UK – the Supreme Court – have ruled the Scottish Parliament does not have the power to hold another Independence Referendum. The First Minister says it is disappointing and raises profound questions about the future of the UK. She plans to use the next General Election as a de facto referendum. Tonight, thousands of people across Scotland have taken to the streets in pro-independence rallies.

LORD REED, President of the Supreme Court: The purpose of the proposed bill is to hold a lawful referendum on the question of whether Scotland should become an independent country. That is on ending the Union and ending the sovereignty of the United Kingdom Parliament in relation to Scotland... The court unanimously concludes that the proposed bill does relate to reserved matters... The Scottish Parliament does not have the power to legislate for a referendum on Scottish independence.

NICOLA STURGEON, First Minister: While I am, obviously, very disappointed by it, I do respect and accept the judgement of the court... The fact is the SNP is not abandoning the referendum route. Westminster is blocking it... The next national election scheduled for Scotland is, of course, the UK General Election, making that both the first and most obvious opportunity to seek what I described back in June as a de facto referendum. This is no longer just about whether or not Scotland becomes independent, vital though that decision is. It is now more fundamental. It is now about whether or not we even have the basic democratic right to decide our own future.

DIARY: It pushes a second Independence Referendum into the long grass... Sturgeon has seen how this will play out and it gives her a way out.

Thursday 22 December 2022
STV News – late bulletin

MSPs have voted to reform trans rights, moving Scotland to a self-identification system for people who want to change gender. But there was a record rebellion among SNP MSPs and the Conservatives say it's bad legislation which attacks women's rights.

COLIN MACKAY, Political Editor: A clear result, but this has been one of the most divisive debates I have ever seen in the Scottish Parliament. On one side the campaign to improve trans rights, to make it easier and quicker to legally change gender. And on the other, women fearing that this is an attack on their rights, particularly for women-only spaces. After years of campaigning and days of debating the final points were made in Parliament this afternoon. Most SNP and Labour MSPs, all Green and Lib Dems and a few Conservatives backed the bill, but some voted against their own party lines. But the deep divisions remained. Inside and outside Parliament. The Gender Recognition Reform Bill is passed – but this debate is far from over and could yet end up in court.

2023

Friday 6 January 2023
STV News

Scotland is facing a triple threat of Covid, flu and strep-A this winter, as the number of people with flu in hospital is the highest it's been in seven years. Medics say it is putting more pressure on an NHS already stretched to near-breaking point, in primary and emergency care. It comes as new figures show one in 25 people currently have Covid in Scotland – the highest number since last summer.

Monday 16 January 2023
STV News

And breaking news this evening. The UK Government is blocking the Scottish Gender Reform bill. The announcement came in a statement a short time ago. At a news conference earlier today, the First Minister said it would be an 'outrage' if the UK Government moved to block reforms passed at Holyrood to help people change their gender more easily.

DIARY: The Scottish Government forced this through – creating open opposition within their own ranks for the first time. I have wondered why Nicola Sturgeon has chosen this fight, knowing growing public opposition to it.

Tuesday 17 January 2023
STV News

The First Minister has blasted the UK Government's plans to block Holyrood's Gender Recognition Reform Bill as an 'outrageous and an outright attack' on the Scottish Parliament. For the first time in the history of Devolution, a Section 35 Order is being used to stop the bill, which aims to make it easier for transpeople to change their legal gender, from being approved by the King. The Scottish Secretary Alister Jack told the Commons the decision was not taken lightly, but the legislation would interfere with UK equalities law and threaten women's rights. The move is described by pro-trans campaigners as 'devastating' and 'playing party politics with trans people's lives'.

Tuesday 24 January 2023
STV News

A transgender woman has been found guilty of raping two women when she was a man. Isla Bryson, from Clydebank, committed the crimes in Clydebank and Drumchapel before she transitioned to female. The High Court in Glasgow heard Bryson met both her victims online, with prosecutors saying she 'preyed' on vulnerable women.

Wednesday 25 January 2023
STV News

There's mounting debate about how the Scottish justice system deals with criminals who self-identify as women. This rapist carried out two attacks while known as Adam Graham, but made the decision to transition while awaiting trial and is now known as Isla Bryson. Bryson is now in Cornton Vale women's prison. And its former governor has told STV News 'everyone should be shocked'. The Scottish Prison Service insists a full risk assessment is being carried out.

Monday 30 January 2023
STV News

The First Minister has insisted transwomen do not have an automatic right to go to women's jails. It comes as a review is launched into a rapist who was initially sent to a female prison, after committing crimes as a man and then identifying as a woman. The case of the prisoner now using the name Isla Bryson has been politically controversial. Then it emerged another violent criminal who now identifies as Tiffany Scott had a move to a women's prison blocked too. Tonight, a trans campaigner has said the debate around this is rooted in 'moral panic'.

NICOLA STURGEON RESIGNS AS FIRST MINISTER
Wednesday 15 February 2023
STV News – live from Holyrood

Tonight – The end of the Sturgeon era. After eight years, Scotland's longest serving First Minister – and the first women in the role – announces she's stepping down.

NICOLA STURGEON, First Minister: In my head and in my heart, I know that the time is now. That it is right for me, for my party and for the country.

After eight years in the top job, this morning, just after 11.00am, Nicola Sturgeon announced her resignation as Scotland's First Minister. Ms Sturgeon says it's not a reaction to short-term pressures of difficulty in Government. She says she's been wrestling with the decision for weeks and is going before she stays too long in the job. She'll remain in the role, while a new leader is chosen. The timetable for that is still to be decided.

COLIN MACKAY, Political Editor: This really been a bombshell today. Just three weeks ago Nicola Sturgeon said she had plenty in her tank, but today her tank is empty. Taking her press conference at face value she is knackered. She is the longest serving First Minister. She has won eight elections in eight years, that's an incredible record. She won the last Scottish election in 2021 to some degree on the back of her popularity with many voters on her handling of the Covid pandemic. But today she said she couldn't see herself leading the SNP into next year's General Election. That's an election she has said she wanted to make a de facto referendum on independence.

JM: So where does this leave the Scottish Government?

CM: It leaves them in a bit of a mess frankly. They have big policy problems, particularly on gender, which saw the SNP's biggest revolt. But there are other problems with the National Care Service and a deposit return scheme for re-using bottles and cans. The SNP is also in a real guddle over independence. Nicola Sturgeon had pinned her hopes on a Scottish Parliament referendum this October – the Supreme Court ruled that out so there is no clear way forward for independence supporters.

DIARY: It strikes me that's she's being honest about having had enough, but that's because she knows there will be no new referendum in the foreseeable future... Sturgeon will be remembered for winning elections and her presence during Covid, but ultimately she promised a lot and delivered little.

Friday 17 March 2023
STV News

Genes that cause ovarian and breast cancer in women are ten times more likely to be found in those with an ancestral link to the island of Westray in Orkney than those in the rest of Scotland. Scientists at Edinburgh and Aberdeen universities have been looking at the prevalence of the cancer-causing gene BRCA1. Funding has been provided so that those in Westray can test for the gene. It's hoped that cancers will detected and treated early as a result.

Tuesday 21 March 2023

DIARY: We ran a *Taggart* piece just before the sport, so I suggested to Raman that straight off the back of it we turn to each other and say in sync, 'there's been a murrrder!' – the classic *Taggart* catchphrase. It worked well and we had a good chortle together. Only then did we realise it hadn't gone out in the east – they were on their opt-outs, so nobody would have seen it. They would have come back to us saying, 'there's been a murrrrder' and wondered what the hell we were on about.

Fortunately, the Edinburgh opt had ended on a weather promo. Had it been a story about somebody missing or having been arrested we could have been in deep trouble.

Wednesday 22 March 2023
STV News

Nicola Sturgeon has issued a 'sincere, heartfelt and unreserved' apology to all those affected by historic forced adoption. In one of her final acts as First Minister, Ms Sturgeon condemned a practice she said was relatively common until the 1970s. Thousands of women were 'forced or coerced' into adoption by charities, churches and health professionals. Campaigners hope this will be the start of healing for both mothers and adoptees.

NICOLA STURGEON'S FINAL ADDRESS TO THE SCOTTISH PARLIAMENT
Thursday 23 March 2023
STV News

In her final First Minister's Questions, Nicola Sturgeon has thanked the people of Scotland for giving her the privilege of her life. She said her eight years in office had been challenging and exhausting, but a profound honour. Opposition leaders challenged her record in Government over higher than ever A&E waiting times, drugs deaths and ferry delays. But the First Minister defended her handling of the Covid crisis, her education record and introducing the Scottish Child Payment and said she was confident her successor would build on that.

NICOLA STURGEON, First Minister: No matter what I do in future, nothing will come close to the experience of the past 3,046 days. Being First Minister of the country I love has been a profound honour. I have led Scotland through good times, but also through the toughest period of our recent history... Covid shaped all of us. I know it changed me and, in many ways, defined my time as First Minister. Above all it reinforced in me an abiding admiration for the people of this country, who made such painful sacrifices to keep each other safe. In the toughest of times, our country showed the best of itself with love, care and solidarity. That will live with me forever... And it is now to the people of Scotland – all of you, whether you voted for me or not – that I reserve my final words from this seat. Thank you so much for placing your trust in me. Words will never convey the gratitude and awe I hold in my heart for the opportunity I have had to serve as your First Minister. It truly has been the privilege of my lifetime. And with those words, Presiding Office, I draw it to a close.

HUMZA YOUSAF BECOMES NEW FIRST MINISTER

Monday 27 March 2023
STV News – live from Holyrood

Humza Yousaf is the new Leader of the SNP and is set to become Scotland's first ethnic minority First Minister. And the youngest. The 37-year-old is the first Muslim to lead a major UK party and will be the sixth First Minister of Scotland. He won the leadership race by a narrow majority – just over 2,000 votes ahead of nearest rival Kate Forbes. 50,000 SNP members cast their votes, a turnout of 70 per cent. Now MSPs will have their say – and we should have a new First Minister by tomorrow afternoon.

Tuesday 28 March 2023
STV News – live from Holyrood

A defining moment – Scotland's New First Minister. The youngest, and the first from an ethnic minority background. Humza Yousaf pledged to argue tirelessly for independence, after being voted into the top job by MSPs this afternoon. Just hours earlier, Nicola Sturgeon resigned her reign, with a letter to the King, and quit Bute House for the last time. Tonight, he's appointing his Cabinet, but Kate Forbes won't be a part of his top team. Tomorrow, the formalities will conclude with a swearing in at the Court of Session, then the business of government will begin.

HUMZA YOUSAF, First Minister: It is a proud day for me and my family. I hope it is also a proud day for Scotland as it speaks to our values as a country as I stand here as the first ever Muslim to lead a Western democratic nation… The years after 9/11 were not easy for Muslims growing up here in Scotland or, indeed, across the UK. I've lost count of how many times my identity, my loyalty to Scotland – the only country I have ever and will ever call home – has been questioned over the years. There was a time not all that long ago when I felt that I simply did not belong here in Scotland. To go from there to now leading the Government as Scotland's sixth First Minister, I hope sends a strong message to every single person out there who feels that they don't belong. No matter what anyone says, no matter who you are, whether Scotland has been your home for a day or for ten generations, no matter your ethnicity, no matter your gender, no matter your religion, no matter your sexual orientation, your transgender identity or disability, this is your home… This Parliament has just given me the opportunity to help steer this nation's course as we make the next stage of that journey together. Doing that will be the honour and the privilege of my life. I will strive every single minute of every day to be worthy of it. I look forward to working with each and every one of you as I do so in the best interests of our nation.

Wednesday 5 April 2023
STV News

It's little more than a week since Nicola Sturgeon stepped down as First Minister. She'd spoken about getting some time away from the spotlight. Instead – early this morning – the police were at the front door of the home she shares with her husband – former SNP Chief Executive Peter Murrell. Officers erected a forensic tent on their front lawn. Mr Murrell was arrested and questioned by detectives who are looking into the SNP's finances.

SHARON FREW, Chief Reporter: When the former First Minister lives on your street, you become accustomed to seeing a security presence or a hive of media activity, but until now, there has been nothing on this scale. Neighbours say they believe they saw

Nicola Sturgeon leaving her home around 20 minutes before police arrived at around 8.30am this morning. Later it was confirmed her husband, Peter Murrell is being questioned by detectives. The blue tent over the entrance to the couple's home shielded from view the search inside the house and garage. Officers could be seen taking photographs in the back garden. At the same time, in Edinburgh at SNP headquarters, police were executing a search warrant... 18 months ago formal inquiries into the SNP's finances began after questions were asked about £600,000 of donations given for use in independence campaigning.

DIARY: The image of the day was a police cordon, vans and an evidence tent at the former First Minister's home. That is a humiliation on any level.

Tuesday 2 May 2023
Scotland Tonight

Joanna Cherry says she has been cancelled for holding gender critical views. This comes after Edinburgh's Stand comedy club called off an event she was due to appear at because a number of its staff were unwilling to work at the gig. The SNP MP has been outspoken against the Scottish Government's Gender Recognition Reform Bill, which was passed by MSPs last year. Some who disagree with her claim her views are transphobic.

JOANNA CHERRY MP: I think it is completely unreasonable. They invited me to do this event in full knowledge that I am someone who as part of my political career has been outspoken in support of women's rights and lesbian rights. So, they knew that before they engaged me to do this event and it does seem rather unreasonable that staff can have an event cancelled because they do not agree with my views on lesbian and women's rights.

JM: But don't they have a right to do that?

JC: Well no, they don't actually. I have a right not to be discriminated against on the basis of my philosophical beliefs or indeed my sexuality. If they were cancelling me because I was a Catholic then I think people would universally accept that that was unacceptable. They are cancelling the event because the staff don't like my views as a lesbian and a feminist and I think that is, as well as being unlawful, it is unacceptable and it is really not in the spirit of the Edinburgh Festival Fringe.

JM: We asked The Stand Comedy Club if anyone was available to join us. They did not respond.

The show was reinstated and went ahead without incident.

KING CHARLES III CROWNED
Saturday 6 May 2023
STV News

King Charles and the Queen Consort have been crowned at Westminster Abbey. Millions of people from around the world watched the British monarchy's first coronation in 70 years. And in Scotland events were held across the country to mark the occasion.

Vox Pops in Scotland

Did not expect to feel the emotion, for sure.

As that crown was put on the King, it was just amazing.

Long time since I saw the first one and now to see it again.

Extremely emotional but absolutely wonderful.

We just love the royal family. Happy that Charles is having his day.

Monday 15 May 2023
STV News

The world's first self-driving bus service got underway in Edinburgh today with hundreds of passengers crossing the Firth of Forth in vehicles that can drive themselves. Fitted with sensors, the buses will be able to sense nearby traffic and potential hazards, but they won't be without staff.

Tuesday 16 May 2023
STV News

The cost of the second ferry being built at the Ferguson Marine shipyard has increased so much it would be cheaper to build a brand new vessel. However, the Scottish Government says work on the unnamed Hull 802 will continue because a new ferry would not be ready until 2027. The final bill for the two vessels under construction in Port Glasgow is three times the original budget. Opposition parties say the whole process has been a scandal.

EWAN PETRIE, Political Correspondent: We heard the words shambles and scandal being used there, not for the first time it has to be said in relation to this project. Time and again the Scottish Government has had to shovel in millions of pounds of taxpayers' money to keep this process going. Now, in purely financial terms, it would be better off scrapping Hull 802 and starting the whole process again. No detail today on exactly how much cheaper that would be. But there is no way ministers were going to let that happen. It would mean no second vessel until 2027. And they say it would put the future of the yard in doubt, threatening hundreds of jobs. So really, they were left with no option and there was acceptance of that around the chamber today. But opposition parties say this is a humiliation – and it's still not over yet.

Wednesday 17 May 2023
STV News

Glasgow is the rodent capital of Scotland. That's the finding from research which suggests, as the country emerged from the pandemic, the city's population of rats thrived. Last year the city's council dealt with more than 10,000 rodent infestations. That's up 31 per cent from 2020. By comparison, Edinburgh City Council were called out just over 15,000 times. Fife also saw a big jump in rodents being reported in the years since Covid, but on a smaller scale. Fewer pet control visits were carried out during lockdown and those on the front line say the problem is getting worse.

Wednesday 31 May 2023
STV News

Fire crews are still battling a wildfire in the Highlands which is so big it can be seen from space. The blaze has been raging since last week, just to the west of Loch Ness. It is devastating vast areas of a nature reserve.

Wednesday 7 June 2023
STV News

The Scottish Government's deposit return scheme is being delayed until at least October 2025, around the same time as a UK-wide roll-out. Lorna Slater, the minister responsible, is blaming the UK Government for insisting glass be excluded. But opposition MSPs say the proposals were 'disastrous' from the start and accuse the SNP and Greens of picking another constitutional fight. The scheme aims to increase recycling and reduce waste by adding a surcharge onto bottles and cans, but some drinks producers say the idea was 'defunct from the start.'

NICOLA STURGEON ARRESTED
Saturday 11 June 2023
STV News

The former First Minister, Nicola Sturgeon has been arrested in the police investigation into SNP's finances and funding. Police Scotland said after being questioned by detectives she's been released without charge. Ms Sturgeon is the third senior SNP figure to be taken into custody.

SHARON FREW, Chief Reporter: The home of Nicola Sturgeon and Peter Murrell is once again the focus of media attention following this latest development in Operation Branchform. Four months after her resignation, the former First Minister was taken into police custody. Confirmation of her arrest came shortly before 2.30pm this afternoon. The timing may have come as a surprise, but many had been speculating for weeks she was next in line to be questioned by detectives. An SNP spokesperson said,

'Nicola has consistently said she would co-operate with the investigation if asked and continues to do so.'

Wednesday 5 July 2023
STV News – live from Holyrood Palace

On a day of pomp, pageantry and procession. King Charles and Queen Camilla have been presented with the Scottish crown jewels. The event is intended to be a moment for Scots to mark the coronation which took place in London in May. A so-called 'People's Procession' made its way down the Royal Mile from Edinburgh Castle to St Giles' Cathedral for the church service, a Red Arrows flypast and a 21-gun salute. Some have questioned why all this is even taking place in a cost-of-living crisis. Most of the money is coming from the Scottish Government.

DIARY: At one point I was stuck among the masses trying to cross the Royal Mile, while passage was made for the dignitaries leaving St Giles' Cathedral. I don't think I've ever seen the class division in this country so apparent. I was really struck by it.

Sunday 16 July 2023
STV News

More than 50 pilot whales have died after a major rescue operation in the Western Isles. Around 55 mammals washed onto the beach on the Isle of Lewis around 7.00am this morning. Marine rescue teams have worked through the day to try to save the animals, but vets deemed it was too late to refloat the whales that survived.

Tuesday 1 August 2023
STV News

A by-election will be held in Rutherglen and Hamilton West after enough voters signed a petition backing a vote. The current MP Margaret Ferrier was suspended from the House of Commons for breaking Covid rules. The former SNP MP has sat as an independent since being removed from the party. This will be the first recall by-election in Scotland.

EWAN PETRIE, Political Correspondent: She was suspended from the House of Commons for 30 days after travelling by train between London and Glasgow despite testing positive for Covid. That triggered the petition giving voters here the chance to demand a by-election. It needed 10 per cent of the electorate to sign it. That would be just over 8,100 people. In the end that threshold was easily reached. And that means this constituency will go to the polls later this year.

Wednesday 2 August 2023
STV News

A court has ruled a fugitive, who faked his own death to avoid prosecution, can be extradited to the United States. The sheriff branded Nicholas Rossi 'as dishonest and deceitful, as he is evasive and manipulative'. The 35-year-old, who claims he is the victim of mistaken identity, is wanted by authorities in Utah in connection with rape allegations. The final decision on his extradition now rests with Scottish Government ministers.

DIARY: As he has done before – and it seems to be happening more and more elsewhere – he wasn't forced to be in the dock to face the verdict. Ridiculous.

Tuesday 15 August 2023

DIARY: I came across the UK Labour Leader Sir Keir Starmer and the Scottish Leader Anas Sarwar. They were filming a political broadcast and campaigning for the forthcoming Rutherglen by-election. Chatted to them for a few minutes. Starmer – potentially the next Prime Minister – perfectly pleasant, but lacks the charisma that's maybe required. Sarwar saying, 'You can feel things changing'... Interesting vignette.

Wednesday 23 August 2023
STV News

A pioneering Scottish surgeon is at the forefront of the UK's first ever womb transplant.

Professor Richard Smith, from Glasgow, and his team carried out the procedure in Oxford on a 34-year-old woman, who was receiving her sister's womb. Professor Smith said it had been an emotional day. It's also a medical milestone and it's giving hope to thousands of women across the country.

LAURA ALDERMAN, Reporter: Experts are calling what happened in this operating theatre in Oxford six months ago, the dawn of a new era. A 34-year-old woman, born without a womb, received a transplant from her sister, who had already completed her family, giving another woman the chance to do the same. The Scottish surgeon who led the organ retrieval team said it was an emotional day.

PROFESSOR RICHARD SMITH: Probably the most stressful week of my surgical career. But also, unbelievably positive in the outcome. For the donor and the recipient. Just over the moon, really over the moon. We were all there for the patient. We wanted her to end up with a successful uterus transplant.

LA: And, hopefully, a baby.

RS: Yes absolutely.

The woman, who wishes to remain anonymous, is now hoping to use her own embryos, frozen before the surgery, to have a family. And there's good reason to be hopeful – whilst this is a UK first, 100 womb transplants have taken place worldwide – with 50 babies being born as a result. More than 15,000 women in the UK who were born either without a womb or have had a hysterectomy could now benefit from this pioneering surgery.

Friday 1 September 2023
STV News

Botched and left with a bill of over £20,000 worth of corrective surgery. One woman has told STV News about her harrowing experience undergoing cosmetic procedures in Turkey which led to her spending a month in hospital in Scotland. As part of our series of special reports, Claire – whose identity we are protecting – wants to warn others about what help they can get if their surgery abroad goes wrong. The NHS says they will only treat life threatening wounds and infections – not botched bodies.

Cosmetic surgery in Turkey has been increasing in popularity. Busy flights return carrying passengers with new hair and 'Turkey teeth', among other enhancements.

Wednesday 27 September 2023
STV News

Tonight – a landmark moment in the battle against Scotland's drugs deaths crisis. The UK's first drugs consumption room will open in Glasgow.

It's been a long-fought campaign, but the introduction of a drugs consumption room has finally been given the go-ahead in Glasgow. The facility in the city's East End will allow drug users to take illegal substances under medical supervision, without the risk of criminal prosecution. Campaigners say it could be life-changing in Scotland's battle against the crisis of drug deaths, which saw more than 1,000 people die in the last year.

SHARON FREW, *Chief Reporter:* It is a chilly October morning in 2020. The man in front of me has just injected cocaine. It is a world away from an official photocall for the opening of a drugs service. There is no shiny new clinic smelling of fresh paint or a Government minister shaking hands with staff. This man, hours out of prison and desperate for a hit, was not hidden away down a dark alley either. He was sitting in a tent on a pavement in Glasgow's East End. We were reporting on one of Scotland's first unsanctioned 'safe spaces' where people could take their own drugs under supervision.

Inspired by international campaigners, an activist, who himself was in recovery, decided to challenge the law. He later switched to a converted ambulance and ran his service for nine months. The illegal action and media coverage appeared to provide the momentum needed for a long-awaited pilot of an official facility. Ironically, four years on, the sanctioned service, to be run by Glasgow's Health and Social Care Partnership, will open just a stone's throw away from the pitch of its 'pop up predecessor'.

Before changes were made to release quarterly statistics, each summer had a grim date in the calendar. The publication of Scotland's drug-related death toll prompts inevitable annual outrage, with a slew of headlines demanding better leadership, services and funding. To those grieving, sympathies are expressed and promises made. In the past the media spotlight shone bright for a day or two and then moved on. Scrutiny now is intense. 'Lived experience' has become a buzz phrase for politicians and health officials, who talk of the value of listening to these voices. But a frequent cry from drugs groups is where is the emergency response?

In our reporting, we always strive to tell the real stories behind the statistics. Stigma and shame in the past often stopped people from giving TV interviews or showing their face on camera. Slowly that has changed. Many tell me they feel unable to stay silent when the numbers continue to rise. People in the grip of addiction describe a familiar pattern of shattered lives and a broken system. Those with the job of picking up the pieces share their despair at budget cuts and funding frustrations.

The scale of the crisis has allowed us to access services previously off limits to cameras. Crisis centres, detox units and rehabilitation centres opened their doors to show the reality and challenges for both staff and residents.

Millions of pounds have been ploughed into tackling what is a complex and ever-shifting crisis. Some on the frontline describe the current situation as 'same old, same old, but different.' To them, progress is not happening on a large enough scale or with enough urgency. Scotland's crisis is fuelled by poly drug use and there is a new threat from increasingly toxic and synthetic street pills.

Having reported on this subject over the decades, it is easy to be pessimistic but, in the chaos, there are stories of hope. Voices of recovery that inspire and show others what can be possible. When you ask them what worked? The reply is often that they found access to the right help at the right time.

Wednesday 27 September 2023 *(cont)*
STV News

It has split political opinion and sparked protests in the debate over the future of oil and gas drilling in the North Sea. And today, the controversial Rosebank oil field, off the coast of Shetland, was given the go-ahead. The firm behind the development says it will help energy security and provide an economic boost. But climate activists have warned the field which could produce more than 300 million barrels of oil, is reckless.

Friday 6 October 2023
STV News – live from Cambuslang

Good evening from Cambuslang, in the very heart of this constituency which has been at the centre of a political storm. After last night's resounding by-election victory for Labour – a 20.4 per cent swing from the SNP – this area now has a new Labour MP. For the SNP, a difficult time ahead, particularly for its leader Humza Yousaf. Could this result signal an end to his party's dominance of elections in Scotland? So, let's remind ourselves of the results. A clear victory for Labour. The party won a 58.6 per cent share of the vote, up from 34.5. The SNP in contrast has dropped to 27.6 per cent from 44.2.

COLIN MACKAY, Political Editor: This was a spectacular victory for Labour – and a nightmare for the SNP and it signals a big change in Scottish politics… Last night's result won't be completely replicated across Scotland in next year's election, but if it was Labour could end up with 42 seats. Since the SNP's 2015 landslide they have dominated Scottish politics – last time in 2019 they won 48 seats. Next year, again if similar results play out, they could be left with just six. That would be like going back in time before the Independence Referendum. They need a big rethink. It is really difficult to persuade voters to come out and vote for independence when you can't tell them how you would deliver it, so they really need to work that out. It's also hard to persuade voters to focus on a constitutional crisis when they are trying to navigate their way through a cost-of-living crisis.

Tuesday 10 October 2023
STV News

The First Minister Humza Yousaf is calling for an immediate ceasefire and humanitarian corridor between Israel and the Gaza strip, to help Scots stuck in the conflict. It comes as his mother and father-in-law spent what he described as a 'terrifying' night in the war-torn area. Meanwhile, the Jewish community are coming to terms with the death of Bernard Cowan from East Renfrewshire who was killed in the war. Those supporting Scottish families in Israel say they're growing more concerned for their welfare as the fighting continues.

Tuesday 17 October 2023
STV News

Scotland are through to Euro 2024. The Scotland squad and the Tartan Army are celebrating and already making plans to head to Germany for next year's tournament. Head coach Steve Clarke joked he isn't sure Germany is ready for five million Scots to turn up, but we'll certainly take a 'big crowd'. We're through, thanks to a Spanish victory over Norway last night. Our previous five wins from six group games enough to cement a place with two games remaining. It marks a continuing revival in Scotland's international football performance.

Monday 23 October 2023
STV News

The First Minister has pledged financial support for the residents of Brechin, following the catastrophic flooding during Storm Babet. On a visit to the Angus town Humza Yousaf said there would be a 'long road to recovery', but the local authority would receive the funding it required. His visit came ahead of news that a third person in Scotland lost their life in the storm. A 56-year-old man and a 57-year-old woman were pronounced dead in separate incidents in Angus.

Tuesday 31 October 2023
Scotland Tonight

The Former Prime Minister Boris Johnson's character and fitness for office during the pandemic was trashed today at the UK Covid Inquiry. The bulk of the evidence came from Dominic Cummings, a highly controversial figure who was once Mr Johnson's chief adviser. He painted a picture of a chaotically run, dysfunctional government with many people out of their depth.

Wednesday 1 November 2023
STV News

The revelations about the conduct – and chaos – in Downing Street – during the pandemic – continued today. A former senior UK Government official claims Covid rules were broken on a daily basis at Number 10. Helen MacNamara was the Deputy Cabinet Secretary during the pandemic. She told the UK Covid Inquiry Boris Johnson failed to tackle a toxic culture at the heart of his Government.

DIARY: Unprecedented times, of course, but the lack of capability in the political leadership was shocking.

Monday 6 November 2023
Scotland Tonight

Riot police were deployed in the Niddrie area of Edinburgh on what the force has described as a night of 'unprecedented levels of violence'. Police estimate that around 50 people were responsible for directing fireworks, petrol bombs and other projectiles at buildings, vehicles and offices. Bonfire Night incidents also occurred in other places, including Dundee and Glasgow.

DIARY: Inevitable calls for fireworks to be banned from public sale. Now, I've thought why should the ned minority spoil it for everyone else, but as a guest explained, we're not talking about the Roman Candles and Catherine Wheels of my youth, but monster fireworks with names like Armageddon. So maybe it is time.

Wednesday 15 November 2023
STV News

The Prime Minister has promised to introduce emergency legislation to prevent his asylum policy facing further legal challenge. It follows a ruling from the UK's highest court that his plans to send asylum seekers to Rwanda are unlawful. Rishi Sunak says the European Court of Human Rights should not be allowed to block flights.

Thursday 16 November 2023
STV News

The Health Secretary is admitting an £11,000 bill on his parliamentary iPad was caused by his teenage sons watching football. Michael Matheson ran up the roaming charges on a family holiday in Morocco over New Year. The cost was initially paid by the Scottish Parliament, but Mr Matheson paid the money back last week when he found out what had happened. However, opposition leaders say he has misled Parliament and should be sacked.

Wednesday 22 November 2023
STV News – live from Grangemouth

Good evening, live from Grangemouth oil refinery. On the day where hundreds of workers here were given the news their jobs are at risk. Scotland's only oil refinery is to cease operations in 18 months' time. Owners Petroineos say this is in response to market pressures and the transition to net zero. This plant has been a huge employer in the area for almost 100 years. Tonight though, around 500 of those workers are now contemplating their future.

COURTNEY CAMERON, Reporter: It's one of the biggest employers in Scotland. Generations of families have worked at the site now owned by Petroineos since it was built in the 1920s. Yesterday, employees at the oil refinery received an e-mail from bosses, informing them it could cease operations as early as 2025. Petroineos says it's facing a future of unsustainable losses and it's planning to turn the refinery into a fuels import and distribution terminal. But what this means for the hundreds of people that work there is unclear. Grangemouth is the only crude oil refinery in Scotland and currently supplies 80 per cent of the country's fuel.

Thursday 30 November 2023
STV News

Tributes have been paid to the former Chancellor Alistair Darling, a huge figure in Scottish and UK politics who died today aged 70. Admired across the political divide, he spent almost three decades as an MP and 13 years in Government under Tony Blair and Gordon Brown. While Chancellor he steered the UK through the financial crash of 2008 and returned to the spotlight to lead the Better Together campaign.

Friday 8 December 2023
STV News

Scotland's highest civil court has ruled that the UK Government's blocking of controversial gender reforms is lawful. The Scottish Government mounted the legal challenge after Westminster tried to prevent the Scottish Gender Recognition Reform Bill from receiving Royal Assent. The UK Government has welcomed today's ruling, while the First Minister says it shows Devolution is 'fundamentally flawed'.

LAURA ALDERMAN, Political Reporter: This is a crushing blow to the Scottish Government and to trans rights groups who campaigned relentlessly and for years for these reforms. But given the lengthy legal battles already that have entangled both Governments in the courts and the cost of that – pressing ahead with another appeal, which could eventually go all the way to the Supreme Court in London – it's unclear just how much appetite there is for that amongst the wider public. they are not even sure if they can, so it will sit in limbo waiting to see what happens at the General Election. This has been one of the most divisive pieces of legislation in the Scottish Parliament, in fact other than the Brexit Referendum and the Independence Referendum, I'm hard placed to think of a more divisive issue in Scottish politics in recent years. It could come back, but realistically it probably won't.

Tuesday 19 December 2023
STV News

Higher earners in Scotland will pay more in tax from next year. The Deputy First Minister Shona Robison said those with the 'broadest shoulders' should pay more. As she set out the Scottish Government's tax and spending plans, she announced a 1 per cent increase to the highest rate. It means the better paid will be paying thousands more in tax than those in England. However, Ms Robison told the Scottish Parliament 51 per cent of taxpayers in Scotland will still pay less than if they were in the rest of the UK. She also announced spending increases in welfare and the NHS.

Wednesday 20 December 2023
STV News

The Scottish Government is abandoning its legal challenge against Westminster's veto of gender reforms. The Social Justice Secretary has confirmed ministers will not appeal a ruling by the Court of Session that the UK Government's block is legal. The legislation to make it easier for people to change their legally recognised sex received cross-party support when it was passed last year.

COLIN MACKAY, Political Editor: Last Christmas MSPs were sitting late into the night to get this legislation through reforming Gender Recognition, but it's still not law and looks like it never will be. The UK Government will not let it go ahead, the Scottish Government won't withdraw it,

2024

Monday 15 January 2024
STV News

'Closure isn't the right word, but justice certainly is.' The words of a mother who has waited almost three decades to see her daughter's killers jailed. Caroline Glachan was 14 when she was murdered by what a judge has described as extreme violence. Two of her killers who brutally attacked the teenager and left her to drown in the River Leven have been given life sentences. Robert O'Brien will spend at least 22 years behind bars, Andrew Kelly a minimum of 18 years.

DIARY: Mother Margaret McKeich came into *ScotNight* for interview. Really powerful. Knew what she wanted to say and was very open and honest. One of those interviews you remember.

UK COVID INQUIRY IN SCOTLAND
Friday 19 January 2024
STV News

Nicola Sturgeon deleted all of her WhatsApp messages from the pandemic. That's what the UK Covid-19 inquiry in Edinburgh heard today. The former First Minister had previously refused to say if she'd kept the communications and stated that Scottish Government decisions were not made using the messaging platform. The inquiry also revealed that the National Clinical Director, Jason Leitch, referred to deleting WhatsApp messages as a 'pre-bed ritual'. The inquiry saw messages from Nicola Sturgeon's former Chief of Staff describing the UK Government's emergency COBRA meetings as a 'shambles', adding that Boris Johnson ignored their calls for reassurance.

Thursday 25 January 2024
STV News

They were far from being friends or political allies, but the rift between Scotland's First Minister and the UK Prime Minister during the pandemic was laid bare at the Covid Inquiry today. In a series of expletive WhatsApp messages between Nicola Sturgeon and her Chief of Staff, Liz Lloyd, the then First Minister called Boris Johnson a clown. This afternoon, the current First Minister was accused of breaking the bond of trust with the public over deleted WhatsApp messages. Humza Yousaf apologised and launched an inquiry into how informal messaging is handled in government.

DIARY: Great for a headline and, of course, the production gallery had fun with a caption over me saying 'F***ing Clown'. Of more concern is apparent evidence that Sturgeon wanted to keep decision making close – a characteristic of this Government – and suggestions of fights being picked with Westminster for political rather than practical reasons.

Monday 29 January 2024
STV News

A city-wide ban on drivers parking on pavements in Edinburgh has come into full effect today. Those caught breaking the rules can be fined up to £100. It's hoped the move will make streets safer and more accessible for pedestrians, particularly those with mobility issues or impaired vision.

This nationwide law was passed in December 2023. Edinburgh City Council has, so far, been the only local authority to announce its implementation. Parts of the West End and Southside of Glasgow would become impassable if it was enforced.

Wednesday 31 January 2024
STV News

Tonight – emotion from Nicola Sturgeon at the Covid Inquiry. The former First Minister denies decisions were taken for political reasons – and says a large part of her wishes she hadn't been in charge when the pandemic struck.

LAURA ALDERMAN, Political Reporter: She

was at the helm throughout the pandemic, at the heart of decision making – and at this stage of the Covid-19 Inquiry's hearings – the key witness. Facing a gruelling full day of questioning, Nicola Sturgeon promised to answer directly and openly. But the issue of her missing WhatsApp messages dominated the start. During her evidence the former First Minister often made reference to the magnitude of decisions and the frenetic pace at which they were being made in the early stages of the pandemic. She added she often felt overwhelmed, but would carry the impact of her decisions forever.

Friday 2 February 2024

DIARY: A work presentation on AI – Artificial Intelligence. Being compared to the steps forward made by first the personal computer, then the internet and the smartphone. I have seen all the sea changes over my career and every one of them has resulted in the loss of good jobs. I'm absolutely not resisting it – it'll happen anyway and that's what progress is – but we shouldn't be blind to the realities. It won't make much difference to the rest of my career, but I'd be concerned for younger colleagues.

Friday 2 February 2024 *(cont)*
STV News

Draft copies of the Island Connectivity Plan have been published by Transport Scotland for public consultation. The twin documents outline overall aims as the Ferries Plan is replaced. They mention the possibility of fixed links, favoured in the Outer Hebrides, Mull and Shetland.

The ideas include bridges and tunnels linking the islands. Examples already exist in the Faroes.

VAL McDERMID

Monday 5 February 2024
Scotland Tonight

One of the most celebrated names in crime writing, Val McDermid, has now sold around 20 million books worldwide. Her new paperback release, *Past Lying*, is the seventh in her series of novels featuring Karen Pirie, brought to life… in the drama series broadcast on STV.

VAL McDERMID: Most books take me between three and four months to write, but mostly they've been kicking around in my head for a long time before I'm ready to start writing them. The most important thing is to get the voice right. But with a series like Karen Pirie – this is the seventh book in the series – I've got an idea of what the voice of the book is going to be… It's hard to explain the way it works, but I start working on something and I start thinking about the problems that lie ahead and figuring out how to negotiate my way out of them and, really, just how to tell the story.

JM: And do you sit down and write or do you plot it all out?

VM: I don't plot it all out. I started off in my career plotting it all out very carefully because I felt that plotting was the weakest tool of my toolbox, really. So, I spent a lot of time planning ahead and I'd write on file cards, a file card for each scene or each chapter. And if it was a multi-viewpoints story I'd have different file cards for the different viewpoints. It looked a bit like a Fair Isle jumper by the end of it. It worked for me for about a dozen books or so and then it just stopped working. I think it was probably because I felt a bit more confidence in my narrative skills by that stage. I'd worked through the 'I can't plot, I don't know how to do this!' and so that's what I do now. I always have a sense of the arc of the story, I know who's done what to whom and, probably, most of the why.

JM: And it just flows from there?

VM: And I know two or three key turning points along the way. And then I just aim for them.

JM: And you have discipline? We keep on hearing about writer discipline. Are you disciplined?

VM: I don't know if I would say disciplined.

I start off quite slowly. Usually, the first month I'm lucky if I get 50 pages down. I'm feeling my way in, getting to know the characters, who's story is this, why am I telling this story? And then it speeds up and then as the deadline approaches, it gets much faster. Towards the last couple of months, I'm probably working seven days a week, more or less.

Thursday 8 February 2024
STV News

Michael Matheson has quit as Health Secretary, but is staying on as the Falkirk SNP MSP. He says he did not want a row over how he racked up £11,000 in iPad roaming charges to become a 'distraction'. Matheson admitted lying last year saying the tablet was only used for work, but later said his children were watching football on it, and then agreed to foot the bill. Critics of the First Minister Humza Yousaf say he should have sacked Mr Matheson when the scandal emerged in November.

DIARY: As ever, it was the attempted cover-up rather than the original mistake which has done for him.

Tuesday 13 February 2024
An election year interview with Scottish Labour Leader Anas Sarwar – Scotland Tonight

JM: If the polls are correct, you're going to get a lot of former SNP supporters moving to you. Under what circumstances would a Labour Government offer a second Independence Referendum that might be reassuring to these people if they come to Labour?

ANAS SARWAR, Scottish Labour Leader: It's Nicola Sturgeon that previously said that they have to build the settled will for independence. Humza Yousaf then in the leadership election, and since, has talked about building a settled will here in Scotland. There is no settled will. They previously talked about 60 per cent support for independence.

JM: So, is that what you'd be looking for?

AS: I'm making a different appeal... I am saying directly to people I don't support independence. I didn't support a referendum. But my goodness, do I recognise why you want to run a million miles away from this rotten Tory Government.

JM: So, a Labour Government might allow a second Independence Referendum?

AS: No, not at all. We have to demonstrate that through good government we can make the UK Government work in the interests of people here in Scotland.

JM: And how will you do that?

AS: I think people will want to give an incoming UK Labour Government that chance to deliver that change... We may ultimately disagree on the final destination for Scotland. But on this part of the journey we all agree we need change. So, let's work together, deliver that change and allow us to demonstrate we can have a government across the UK and here in Scotland that can work in the interests of everybody across our country and, therefore, demonstrate that politics can work, rather than having to go down that route being suggested by the SNP.

DIARY: In fairness to him I found his answers to be essentially honest, accepting divisions, but saying it was part of a process of taking the country beyond 'getting rid of the Tories'. There wasn't too much obfuscation or diversion. He was impressive.

Tuesday 20 February 2024
An election year interview with First Minister and SNP Leader, Humza Yousaf – Scotland Tonight

JM: The Government record: waiting times, education, drugs deaths, housing crisis, the ferries fiasco. It's not great, is it?

HUMZA YOUSAF, First Minister: Our record is a really good record, hence why, of course, we've been re-elected again and again and again...

JM: So, you're saying your government record is good. In all these things your record is good?

HY: Of course, our record is good. It's why we keep getting re-elected. Are there challenges? I don't doubt that for a minute, but I'll stand on our record very proudly to say that we've delivered for the people of this country.

This was an almost identical list of subjects covered in an interview with the former First Minister Nicola Sturgeon eight years previously in January 2016. The only change was that the UK had by now left the European Union.

Monday 8 April 2024
Scotland Tonight

Our new hate crime law criminalises threatening or abusive behaviour which is intended to stir up hatred on the grounds of a range of characteristics, including age, disability and transgender identity. Ministers say it is needed to protect vulnerable minorities, but the first week of its implementation has raised a lot of concerns about how the policy will be policed and its potential impact on freedom of speech. And police officers, themselves, have been said to be struggling to cope with the volume of hate crime complaints.

DAVID THREADGOLD, Scottish Police Federation: The contact that I have had has been that some people are not making complaints to the police under this legislation because they feel that they are victims of crime. They are doing so to make a political point or their own personal point. Or simply, in one case, to protest against the current Government. No one is saying that if you feel that you are the victim of a hate crime that you should not contact the police. It's absolutely a given. But there are clearly many thousands of people across Scotland who are making some sort of point by complaining and using this legislation to do so.

ANGELA CONSTANCE, Justice Secretary: I think this is why, whether it is as the Scottish Government or indeed Police Scotland, we anticipated an elevated amount of interest as the bill was implemented. We will continue to monitor the situation very closely, but it is important for me to stick to the facts that this legislation is about protecting people at risk of hate crime. But also embedded within the act in numerous ways, in numerous lines of legislation, is that protection for freedom of expression.

More than 7,000 hate crimes were reported in the first week. Police assessed only 250 to be actual crimes. The complaints quickly dropped into the hundreds.

Wednesday 18 April 2024
STV News

The Scottish Government was leading the world in tackling the climate crisis, but tonight it has scrapped its flagship target of reducing greenhouse gas emissions by 75 per cent by 2030 after accepting that is now 'out of reach'. The move has been branded the worst environmental decision in Holyrood's history. And climate campaigners say the announcement is 'bitterly disappointing'. Even though the targets are legally binding, they have been missed for eight out of 12 years. But the Scottish Government insists the target to reach net zero by 2045 – five years earlier than the UK – remains.

Monday 22 April 2024
Scotland Tonight

In the summer of 2021, the Scottish Greens signed an historic power-sharing agreement with the SNP. It saw their two co-leaders become ministers in Government, where they've stayed ever since. But the future of that deal is now in the balance amid internal unrest. The anger felt by Green members seems to relate to three areas – the ditching of Scotland's 2030 climate target to cut emissions by 75 per cent; the Government's pushing through of a council tax freeze; and NHS Scotland's decision to pause the prescribing of puberty blockers.

Thursday 25 April 2024
STV News – live from Bute House

This morning Humza Yousaf ended the SNP's power-sharing deal with the Scottish Greens. An emergency Cabinet meeting followed before confirmation the SNP was returning to leading a minority government. The Greens have reacted furiously, accusing Mr Yousaf of political cowardice. Meanwhile, the Conservatives have lodged a motion of no confidence in the First Minister, a vote that Humza Yousaf could struggle to survive.

COLIN MACKAY, Political Editor: This is the biggest gamble of Humza Yousaf's political life, and it could ultimately cost him his job as First Minister. Forty-eight hours ago he was committed to the Bute House Agreement with the Greens. Today he has dumped them. He says it shows the strength of his leadership. His opponents, now including the Greens, say it shows his weakness.

HUMZA YOUSAF RESIGNS AS FIRST MINISTER
Monday 29 April 2024
STV News – live from Scottish Parliament

Humza Yousaf has resigned as Scotland's First Minister. After more than a year in the role, his demise came as he faced a vote of no confidence after terminating the power-sharing agreement with the Greens. As the search begins for a successor, there are calls for a Scottish election.

COLIN MACKAY, Political Editor: It's been clear he's been facing the sack with these confidence votes looming. So today, he jumped before being pushed. He might have been saved by Alba, but he said he was 'not willing to trade his values to retain power'. He said again today he was right to end the Bute House Agreement with the Greens, but he knows he mishandled the break-up spectacularly. Do you remember that famous clip of him falling off his scooter in Parliament? This was the political version of that and left him flat on his face again.

JOHN SWINNEY BECOMES SNP LEADER FOR A SECOND TIME
Monday 6 May 2024
STV News

John Swinney has been confirmed as the next Leader of the SNP and is on course to be elected as the next First Minister. He ran unchallenged for the position and is expected to be sworn in later this week. In his acceptance speech this afternoon, Mr Swinney claimed he was the leader to restore harmony and will begin a new chapter within the party. But opposition MSPs say he represents more of the same.

JOHN SWINNEY, SNP leader: The fact that I'm the only candidate demonstrates that the Scottish National Party is coming back together again now... Today, is the beginning of a new chapter in our party's history, a chapter that will be about coming together, uniting and dedicating ourselves to the service of Scotland.

DOUGLAS ROSS, Scottish Conservative leader: John Swinney served in Alex Salmond's cabinet, in Nicola Sturgeon's Cabinet and was one of Humza Yousaf's strongest supporters from the backbenches. So, I'm not sure this continuity candidate is the person to change things.

ANAS SARWAR, Scottish Labour Leader: The idea that this is somehow change, I think, is frankly laughable. This is continuity, more of the same, about managing his political party, not running the country and delivering for Scotland.

Tuesday 7 May 2024
STV News

John Swinney has been elected the new First Minister of Scotland, the third in little over a year and the seventh in the history of the Scottish Parliament. He replaces Humza Yousaf, who formally stepped down this morning. Mr Swinney said it was an extraordinary privilege to fill the role after 25 years in the Parliament. John Swinney said he offered himself as the First Minister to everyone in Scotland. And he said that, as a minority government, he would need to work with other parties to make things happen. And he acknowledged the Parliament is intensely polarised.

JOHN SWINNEY, First Minister: To the people of Scotland I would say simply this, I offer myself to be the First Minister for everyone in Scotland. I am here to serve you. I will give everything I have to build the best future for our country.

COLIN MACKAY, Political Editor: At the end of his speech today, he went round the chamber shaking all the hands of the opposition leaders. A clear indication of how he hopes to do business... But there were harsh words from the opposition leaders too. Alex Cole-Hamilton talked about the great enmity across the chamber. Anas Sarwar described John Swinney as the worst-ever Education Secretary of Devolution. And Douglas Ross said what Scotland needs is a national leader, not a nationalist leader. So, although there were smiles and handshakes today, those handshakes weren't about doing deals. I think John Swinney, leading a minority government, is going to find those deals very, very difficult to come by.

Wednesday 15 May 2024
STV News

Scotland is in a nationwide housing emergency. The declaration from the Scottish Parliament comes after five local authorities – including Glasgow and Edinburgh – had already declared housing emergencies in recent months. The Scottish Government has cut almost £200 million from the housing budget. Labour piled pressure on the issue and in the past 125 minutes MSPs backed their motion at Holyrood. Campaigners say the crisis in housing took decades to get into, with a lack of council and social properties being built. They fear it could take decades to put things right.

Wednesday 15 May 2024 *(cont)*
STV News

It's been revealed that the UK Government is planning for the first new nuclear power plant in Scotland in nearly 40 years, in spite of opposition from the Scottish Government.

PARIS GOURTSOYANNIS, Westminster Correspondent: The SNP opposes new nuclear power and planning laws are devolved, so there's effectively been a ban on any new reactors in Scotland. But at a Westminster committee, the Scottish Secretary Alister Jack said plans are already being made for one of a new generation of what are called small modular reactors to be built in Scotland... Under the UK Government's Great British Nuclear programme, existing atomic energy sites will be prioritised for these small reactors. That includes decommissioned sites like Hunterston and Dounreay. They're supposed to be quicker and cheaper to build, and provide clean, consistent power when the wind doesn't blow. The plans have Labour's backing, but the SNP says this announcement undermines Scottish democracy and Scotland doesn't need nuclear power. It needs more support for renewables.

INFECTED BLOOD INQUIRY REPORT
Tuesday 20 May 2024
STV News

Thousands of people have had their lives destroyed after receiving infected blood in a treatment disaster that has been described as 'no accident'. The Infected Blood Inquiry's final report documents a 'catalogue of failures' which had 'catastrophic' consequences for patients and their families. Around 3,000 people in Scotland were infected with HIV and Hepatitis C from 1970 to 1991 through contaminated NHS blood products. Sir Brian Langstaff's report accuses successive governments and the NHS of repeatedly failing patients and trying to cover up what happened. The Prime Minister has issued an apology and said, 'It's a day of shame.'

SHARON FREW, chief reporter: They applauded as the final report was made public. For five years campaigners have travelled from Scotland to attend the inquiry. One said today felt different, 'like a pilgrimage to the truth.'

BRUCE NORVAL, contaminated blood victim: Stuff we were called, conspiracy theorists, they were saying that we were besmirching medics' reputation. We were vindicated today. The problem with that vindication is that it's 41 years too late.

SIR BRIAN LANGSTAFF, Infected Blood Inquiry Chair: There was no accident. People put their trust in doctors and the Government to keep them safe. And that trust was betrayed.

Tuesday 21 May 2024
STV News

For the first time, fewer than half of Scots are religious. The latest Census results were published today and 51 per cent of us don't identify with any faith group. The biggest, the Church of Scotland, has declined from more than 30 per cent of the population a decade ago to around 20 per cent now.

Wednesday 22 May 2024
STV News

The Prime Minister has just fired the starting gun for a summer General Election. Within the last hour, Rishi Sunak surprised the country with an announcement that the UK will go to the polls on 4 July. Mr Sunak said he was ready to fight for every vote and, indeed, polling experts say he may well have to.

PARIS GOURTSOYANNIS, Westminster Correspondent: Today, it was decision time for Rishi Sunak, and he faced an impossible choice. Launch an election campaign in the worst conditions any sitting government has faced in living memory. Or wait, potentially, for things to only get worse. Westminster was consumed by rumour throughout the day, as ministerial visits were cancelled and the Cabinet was summoned to Downing Street. Within the past hour, under drenching rain and the sound of protest echoing, the Prime Minister said he was the man to take tough decisions. He'd done it on Covid and on the economy. His decision today – face the people now.

RISHI SUNAK, Prime Minister: The decision now is how and who do you trust to turn that foundation into a secure future for you, your family and our country. Now is the moment for Britain to choose its future, to decide whether we want to build on the progress we have made or risk going back to square one with no plan and no certainty. Earlier today, I spoke with His Majesty the King to request the dissolution of Parliament. The King has granted this request and we will have a General Election on 4 July.

SIR KEIR STARMER, Labour Leader: A moment the country needs and has been waiting for. And where, by the force of our democracy, power returns to you. A chance to change for the better your future, your community, your country.

Friday 7 June 2024
STV News

It's a night like no other. Here in Edinburgh, it's absolutely mobbed with more than 200,000 Taylor Swift fans descending on the city. The global superstar is already here. Right now, you can probably hear the support act. This is a huge night for Edinburgh.

And in Glasgow we're braced for the big send-off for the Scotland team, as they take to the pitch for the last time before they head for Germany and, hopefully, European glory.

SCOTLAND IN EURO 2024
Saturday 15 June 2024
STV News

Scotland's opening game of Euro 2024 ended in misery for the Tartan Army after a 5–1 thrashing by Germany. But for those in Munich's official fan zone things were made even worse, with the event branded a 'shambles'. Scotland fans waited for food and drink in hours-long queues at Olympiapark. And while officials warned on social media overcrowding would cause the fan zone to close, one supporter told STV News the event was poorly planned and chaotic.

Monday 24 June 2024
STV News

The Tartan Army have done Scotland proud. But, yet again, Scotland have failed to get through to the group stages of an international tournament. Scotland lost 1–0 to Hungary last night with a disappointing performance in a game we had to win. We have been here so often. The hope, the expectation and the Scottish fans earning goodwill wherever they've been. The disappointment is acute this time. Scotland had a real chance to qualify for the knock-out stages of an international tournament for the first time in 12 attempts. But they failed to do so.

DIARY: Another failure by Scotland to progress beyond the group stages of a tournament. Needed a win against Hungary tonight to give us a chance. Scotland were dour and over-safe. We didn't have a shot on target and yet looked promising to start with… Usual story – Tartan Army do us proud, the team are stultifying.

Tuesday 2 July 2024
STV News

Andy Murray says he's extremely disappointed after withdrawing from the singles at Wimbledon, but he will compete in the doubles with his brother Jamie. The former world number one had hoped to recover from back surgery in time for his first-round match, which was scheduled for today, but has failed in his bid to be fit.

GENERAL ELECTION 2024
Wednesday 3 July 2024
STV News

After six weeks party leaders are racing around the country in the final hours of campaigning. The leader of the Conservatives in Scotland, Douglas Ross, says that if the polls are accurate his party is heading for defeat. That would see the Labour Leader Keir Starmer heading into No 10 on Friday morning. Sir Keir came to Scotland this afternoon pledging a Labour Government would have Scotland at its heart. With polls suggesting the SNP vote could be down, John Swinney says it's a knife edge race between the SNP and Labour. Meanwhile, the Lib Dems say they're focusing on getting their vote out.

SIR KEIR STARMER, Labour Leader: The SNP say the most important election for, I don't know how long, and they say what? Send a message. Who wants Scotland to send a message? I want Scotland to send a government.

JOHN SWINNEY, SNP leader & First Minister: People in Scotland have got a choice between a Labour Party that will just do what it's told by Keir Starmer and will implement spending cuts where the Tories have just completed doing spending cuts, or an SNP that will always put forward the interests of Scotland, will make sure that we campaign and resist austerity in our public finances and we can have a future that's made in Scotland for Scotland.

DIARY: Rishi Sunak has done as much as he could as Prime Minister, but his legacy from Boris Johnson and the disaster of Liz Truss was too much to overcome. The Conservatives are long past the end of this political cycle.

Friday 5 July 2024
STV News Election Special

The UK is a different place today. And so is Scotland. For the first time in 14 years there is a Labour Government in the UK.

The Conservatives and SNP have been the big losers. The new Prime Minister Keir Starmer says the work of change will begin immediately. Conservative rule has not just been defeated, it has been trampled. Attacked from all sides by Labour, the Lib Dems and their defectors, Reform. The outgoing Prime Minister Rishi Sunak told the nation he was sorry.

In Scotland it is all change too. The SNP have endured a night of huge losses. From being dominant in the UK elections, winning almost all Scottish seats less than ten years ago – the third largest party at Westminster, indeed – they are now a rump party of only nine MPs.

This is what the political map of Scotland looked like yesterday. That sea of SNP yellow has turned red. And here is the detail behind that change. This was the landscape in Scotland in 2019 – the SNP the biggest party with 48 MPs, the Conservatives had six, the Lib Dems on four and Labour just a single MP. But how all that has changed. Now Labour has 37 MPs, a disastrous night for the SNP, who now have only nine. The Scottish Conservatives have performed better than their UK counterparts, retaining five seats. While the Lib Dems have gained one, returning five. *(The Inverness, Skye and West Ross-shire constituency went to a second recount on Saturday 6 July and gave the Lib Dems six seats.)*

The huge Labour landslide across the UK means they have nearly doubled their seats to 412. The Conservatives have collapsed to just 121. The Lib Dems have made big gains, they're up to 71, while the SNP have nine.

SIR KEIR STARMER, Prime Minister: I have just returned from Buckingham Palace where I accepted an invitation from His Majesty the King to form the next Government of this great nation… With respect and humility I invite you all to join this government of service in the mission of national renewal. Our work is urgent and we begin it today.

RISHI SUNAK, former Prime Minister: To the country I would like to say first and foremost I am sorry. I have given this job my all, but you have sent a clear signal that the Government of the United Kingdom must change and yours is the only judgement that matters. I have heard your anger, your disappointment and I take responsibility for this loss.

JOHN SWINNEY, SNP leader and First Minister: I have to accept that we failed to convince people of the urgency of independence in this election campaign. And, therefore, we need to take the time to consider and to reflect on how we deliver our commitment to independence, which remains absolute.

COLIN MACKAY, Political Editor: I think a lot of STV voters stayed at home, they weren't motivated. Nicola Sturgeon says independence was on page one line one of the manifesto, but then pretty much ignored. She had wanted this to be a de facto referendum on independence. If John Swinney had gone along with that it might have been the only thing that could have made this worse. There will be criticism, but I don't think his leadership is under any threat. He recognises the SNP got gubbed, lost public trust and has to refocus on delivery. If he doesn't he is facing defeat from a resurgent Labour in the 2026 Scottish election. But it's not going to be plain sailing for Labour. The Prime Minister Keir Starmer has a huge majority, almost two-thirds of the seats at Westminster, but he only got a third of the vote. When Tony Blair won his landslide in 1997 he had 45 per cent. When Jeremy Corbyn lost in 2017 he had 40 per cent. That suggests to me there is no great love for Keir Starmer, so it's all about delivery for him too. People need to see Labour make a difference to their lives and soon. Otherwise, the great political pendulum could swing away from Labour the next time.

JM: Labour are back in power in the United Kingdom. Sir Keir Starmer is our new Prime Minister. The Conservatives have collapsed. The SNP dominance has ended. It has been a memorable election, one of those that will be a reference point in the future – the '24 Election.

THE DEATH OF ALEX SALMOND
Sunday 13th October 2024
STV News

'A formidable politician, an amazing orator, an outstanding intellect.' Alex Salmond's family have been leading tributes to the former First Minister who died yesterday at the age of 69. It's understood he suffered a heart attack while attending an international conference in North Macedonia.

ALEX SALMOND, last recorded speech: Respect for legitimate , democratic aspirations leads to good outcomes. Disrespecting it one way or another, and often surprisingly, can lead to bad outcomes for everyone.

JOHN SWINNEY, First Minister: I think Alex Salmond transformed the prospects for the Scottish National Party, taking us from being a party on the fringes of politics to being a party of government. And he then took the country incredibly close to independence and we now have generations of people in Scotland who are committed to Scottish independence in a way that wasn't the case when I was in my formative years politically Scotland.

NICOLA STURGEON, former First Minister: Obviously, I cannot pretend that the events of the past few years which led to the breakdown of our relationship did not happen, and it would not be right for me to try. However, it remains the fact that for many years Alex was an incredibly significant figure in my life. He was my mentor, and for more than a decade we formed one of the most successful partnerships in UK politics.

SIR KEIR STARMER, Prime Minister: For more than thirty years, Alex Salmond was a monumental figure of Scottish and UK politics. He leaves behind a lasting legacy.

15 years later, as First Minister and leading a majority SNP Government, I was questioning him in his last interview the night before the independence referendum, a vote that polls suggested was on a knife edge. It was Alex Salmond who made that happen.

DIARY: Salmond and Dewar stand above all other Scottish-based politicians as having made a difference. I interviewed him after the first Scottish Parliament election in 1999 and pressed him then on the SNP again not making the breakthrough in the central belt.

Endnote

Scotland has been transformed since this reporter first pulled on his trench coat in the mid-1980s. This book has charted that change.

We know where we've been. We know where we are. The question is always where are we going?

The past can help inform us about the future. The wheel always turns, patterns repeated.

I have interviewed many informed people, heard from experts and academics, politicians and commentators. No one has called it right every time.

We may have our ideas about where we are headed as a nation and society, but none of us knows.

That's what makes what lies ahead so fascinating. Just like what's gone before.

Some other books published by **LUATH PRESS**

The Road Dance

John MacKay

ISBN: 978-1-910022-97-9 PBK £8.99

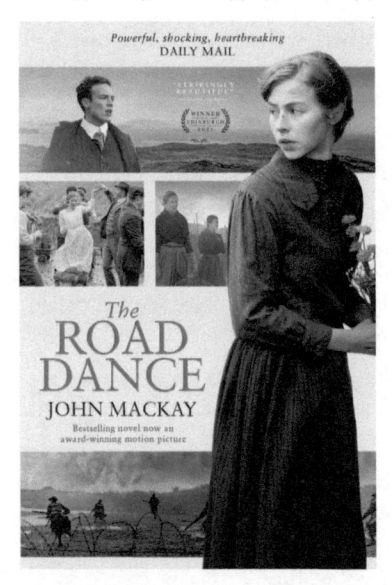

Life in the Scottish Hebrides can be harsh – the edge of the world some call it. For the beautiful Kirsty Macleod, the love of Murdo and their dreams of America promise an escape from the scrape of the land, the repression of the Church and the inevitablility of the path their lives would take. But as the Great War looms Murdo is conscripted. The villagers hold a grand Road Dance to send their young men off to battle. As the dancers swirl and sup, the wheels of tragedy are set in motion.

Powerful, shocking, heartbreaking. SCOTTISH DAILY MAIL

Captures time, place and atmosphere superbly. MEG HENDERSON

A gripping plot that subtly twists and turns, vivid characterisation, and a real sense of time and tradition, this is an absorbing, powerful first novel. THE SCOTS MAGAZINE

Heartland

John MacKay

ISBN: 978-1-910021-90-3 PBK £7.99

A man tries to build for his future by reconnecting with his past, leaving behind the ruins of the life he has lived. Iain Martin hopes that by returning to his Hebridean roots and embarking on a quest to reconstruct the ancient family home, he might find new purpose. But then he uncovers a secret from the past.

A broody, atmospheric little gem set in the Hebrides. THE HERALD

A powerful Hebridean novel. THE SCOTS MAGAZINE

Last of the Line

John MacKay

ISBN: 978-1-910021-91-0 PBK £7.99

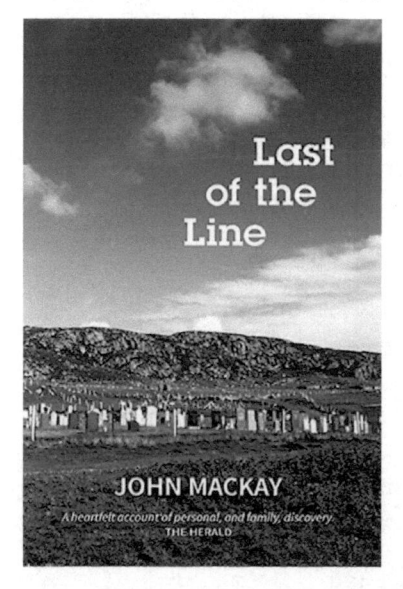

When Cal MacCarl gets a phone call to his bachelor flat in Glasgow asking him to come to the bedside of his Aunt Mary, dying miles away on the Isle of Lewis, he embarks on a journey of discovery. With both his parents dead, his Aunt Mary is his only remaining blood link. When she goes he will be the last of the family line and he couldn't care less. In the days between his aunt's death and funeral, he is drawn into the role of genealogy detective.

A strong modern story of personal conflict. NORTHWORDS NOW

Where MacKay differs from most other Hebridean-based novels is in his obvious research into the geography, and meticulous background into island traditions and cultures. THE STORNOWAY GAZETTE

The Hebridean scenes are powerful. THE SUNDAY HERALD

Home

John MacKay

ISBN: 978-1910022-40-5 PBK £9.99

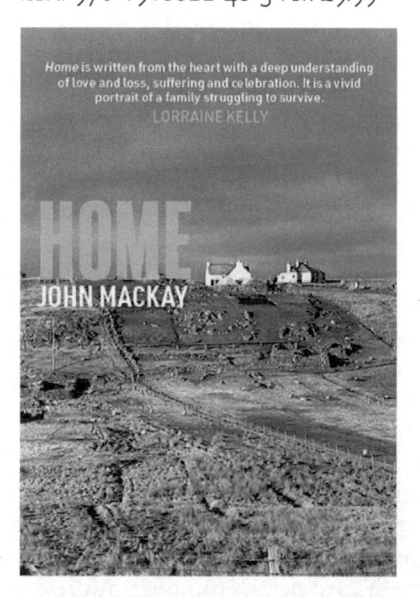

The sweeping saga of one family through a momentous century. Different people, divergent lives and distinctive stories. Bound together by the place they called home. But one of them was missing, lost to the world. An unknown grandchild, born to a son who'd gone off to war and never came back. As the years pass through wars and emigration, social transformation and generational change, the search continues. And the questions remain the same: Who is he? Where is he? Will he ever come home?

Home *has been written from the heart with a deep understanding of love and loss, suffering and celebration. It paints a vivid portrait of a family who have to cope with so much and somehow manage to survive. I read it in one sitting and I'm already looking forward to John's next book.* LORRAINE KELLY

Home *is an epic tale – a magnificent Hebridean opus.* CALUM MACDONALD, RUNRIG

Details of these and other books published by Luath Press can be found at:
www.luath.co.uk

Luath Press Limited

committed to publishing well written books worth reading

LUATH PRESS takes its name from Robert Burns, whose little collie Luath (*Gael.*, swift or nimble) tripped up Jean Armour at a wedding and gave him the chance to speak to the woman who was to be his wife and the abiding love of his life. Burns called one of the 'Twa Dogs' Luath after Cuchullin's hunting dog in Ossian's *Fingal*. Luath Press was established in 1981 in the heart of Burns country, and is now based a few steps up the road from Burns' first lodgings on Edinburgh's Royal Mile. Luath offers you distinctive writing with a hint of unexpected pleasures.

Most bookshops in the UK, the US, Canada, Australia, New Zealand and parts of Europe, either carry our books in stock or can order them for you. To order direct from us, please send a £sterling cheque, postal order, international money order or your credit card details (number, address of cardholder and expiry date) to us at the address below. Please add post and packing as follows: UK – £1.00 per delivery address; overseas surface mail – £2.50 per delivery address; overseas airmail – £3.50 for the first book to each delivery address, plus £1.00 for each additional book by airmail to the same address. If your order is a gift, we will happily enclose your card or message at no extra charge.

Luath Press Limited
543/2 Castlehill
The Royal Mile
Edinburgh EH1 2ND
Scotland
Telephone: 0131 225 4326 (24 hours)
Email: sales@luath.co.uk
Website: www.luath.co.uk